Phyllis Chesler, PhD
Esther Rothblum, PhD
Ellen Cole, PhD
Editors

Feminist Foremothers in Women's Studies, Psychology, and Mental Health

Pre-publication
REVIEWS,
COMMENTARIES,
EVALUATIONS . . .

"**F** eminist Foremothers in Women's Studies, Psychology, and Mental Health is a welcome addition to the women's history literature. The multidisciplinary focus will interest scholars in a variety of fields. Each chapter is a mini-autobiography or biography in which the women's major contributions are highlighted and the way they found feminism is described. Some chapters go well beyond biography and belong on course syllabi; for example, Louise Armstrong presents her work in the context of the backlash against the incest survivor's movement, which she describes insightfully and concisely.

The autobiographies are particularly interesting to read. Each woman's unique personality comes through. After reading the book I felt that I had made new friends and learned more about old ones. This is a fascinating and empowering book; I highly recommend it to feminist foremothers, daughters, and granddaughters."

Joan C. Chrisler, PhD
Associate Professor of Psychology
Connecticut College

More pre-publication
REVIEWS, COMMENTARIES, EVALUATIONS . . .

"**F**eminist Foremothers in Women's Studies, Psychology, and Mental Health is a remarkable, moving and inspiring collection of 48 personal stories. These women were asked to write about what led up to their achievements, what their accomplishments were, and how their lives were consequently changed. While the women were given the choice of being interviewed by a graduate student, most chose to write their own stories.

Some authors are well-known, for example, Gloria Steinem, Andrea Dworkin and Shere Hite. Some are academics, among them Nancy Chodorow, Carol Gilligan and Bonnie Strickland. There are feminist artist activists such as Judy Chicago and Nancy Azara and women who have taken and led others in spiritual journeys.

The range and depth of political experience and personal risk is astonishing–the accomplishments of these foremothers are truly worthy of pride and emulation. Reading about these revolutionary achievements makes the emergence of the anti-feminist backlash seem inevitable."

Susan Contratto, EdD
*Co-Director, Interdisciplinary Program in Feminist Practice,
University of Michigan*

"**R**eading this book is a little like panning for gold. All it takes is finding one's first nugget to ignite and maintain the process. "Feminist Foremothers" rewards readers with a plethora of nuggets. I found myself unwilling to skip even a single contribution. Many are written by women I know quite well, about whom I learned more. Others are by women I know only slightly, or only through their writings and speeches, on whom I have new perspectives after reading their contributions to the book.

Each reader will wade to the edge of the stream holding her or his sieve and pan, to enjoy the flow of the personal writings as well as the gold sands and pebbles that shine most brightly."

Jeanne Adleman, MA
*Independent Consultant
in Feminist Therapy
and Co-editor of RACISM
IN THE LIVES OF WOMEN:
Testimony, Theory and Guides
to Antiracist Practice*

The Haworth Press, Inc.

Feminist Foremothers in Women's Studies, Psychology, and Mental Health

Feminist Foremothers in Women's Studies, Psychology, and Mental Health

Phyllis Chesler, PhD
Esther D. Rothblum, PhD
Ellen Cole, PhD
Editors

The Haworth Press, Inc.
New York • London

Feminist Foremothers in Women's Studies, Psychology and Mental Health has also been published as *Women & Therapy,* Volume 17, Numbers 1/2 3/4 1995.

The Haworth Press, Inc., 10 Alice Street, Binghamton, NY 13904-1580, USA

The sculpture on the book cover is SHELL GODDESS by artist Nancy Azara, one of the authors of this book. The sculpture is in the collection of Myra Wheeler, Lookout Mountain, Georgia. The cover photograph was taken by Christopher Burke, Quesada/Burke NY.

Library of Congress Cataloging-in-Publication Data

Feminist foremothers in women's studies, psychology, and mental health / Phyllis Chesler, Esther D. Rothblum, Ellen Cole, editors.
     p. cm.
     "Has also been published as Women & therapy, volume 17, numbers 1/2-3/4, 1995"–T.p. verso.
     Includes bibliographical references.
     ISBN 1-56024-767-3 (alk. paper).–ISBN 1-56023-078-9 (alk. paper)
     1. Feminists–United States–History. 2. Women's studies–United States–History. 3. Feminist psychology–United States–History. 4. Feminist therapy–United States–History. I. Chesler, Phyllis. II. Rothblum, Esther D. III. Cole, Ellen.
HQ1410.F47 1995
305.42'0973–dc20
                                              95-41897
                                                CIP

This volume is dedicated to our dear colleague, Dr. Naomi Weisstein, who has been with us from the beginning and whose spirit lives in us still. Naomi has been bedridden with CFIDS since 1980.

INDEXING & ABSTRACTING

Contributions to this publication are selectively indexed or abstracted in print, electronic, online, or CD-ROM version(s) of the reference tools and information services listed below. This list is current as of the copyright date of this publication. See the end of this section for additional notes.

- *Abstracts of Research in Pastoral Care & Counseling*, Loyola College, 7135 Minstrel Way, Suite 101, Columbia, MD 21045

- *Academic Abstracts/CD-ROM*, EBSCO Publishing, P.O. Box 2250, Peabody, MA 01960-7250

- *Academic Index (on-line)*, Information Access Company, 362 Lakeside Drive, Foster City, CA 94404

- *Alternative Press Index*, Alternative Press Center, Inc., P.O. Box 33109, Baltimore, MD 21218-0401

- *Current Contents: Clinical Medicine/Life Sciences (CC: CM/LS) (weekly Table of Contents Service), and Social Science Citation Index. Articles also searchable through Social SciSearch, ISI's online database and in ISI's Research Alert current awareness service*, Institute for Scientific Information, 3501 Market Street, Philadelphia, PA 19104-3302 (USA)

- *Digest of Neurology and Psychiatry*, The Institute of Living, 400 Washington Street, Hartford, CT 06106

- *Expanded Academic Index*, Information Access Company, 362 Lakeside Drive, Forest City, CA 94404

- *Family Violence & Sexual Assault Bulletin*, Family Violence & Sexual Assault Institute, 1310 Clinic Drive, Tyler, TX 75701

- *Feminist Periodicals: A Current Listing of Contents*, Women's Studies Librarian-at-Large, 728 State Street, 430 Memorial Library, Madison, WI 53706

- *Higher Education Abstracts*, Claremont Graduate School, 740 North College Avenue, Claremont, CA 91711

- *Index to Periodical Articles Related to Law*, University of Texas, 727 East 26th Street, Austin, TX 78705

- *INTERNET ACCESS (& additional networks) Bulletin Board for Libraries ("BUBL"), coverage of information resources on INTERNET, JANET, and other networks.*
    - JANET X,29: UK,AC,BATH,BUBL or00006012101300
    - TELNET: BUBL,BATH,AC,UK or 138.38.32.45 login 'bubl'
    - GOPHER: BUBL,BATH,AC,UK (138.32.32.45). port 7070
    - NISSWAIS telnetniss,ac,uk (for the NISS gateway).
    The Andersonian Library, Curran Building, 101 St. James Road, Glasgow G4 ONS, Scotland

(continued)

- *Inventory of Marriage and Family Literature (online and hard copy)*, Peters Technology Transfer, 306 East Baltimore Parkway, 2nd Floor, Media, PA 19063

- *Mental Health Abstracts (online through DIALOG)*, IFI/Plenum Data Company, 3202 Kirkwood Highway, Wilmington, DE 19808

- *PASCAL International Bibliography T205: Sciences de l'information Documentation*, INIST/CNRS-Service Gestion des Documents Primaires, 2, allee du Parc de Brabois, F-54514 Vandoeuvre-les-Nancy, Cedex, France

- *Periodical Abstracts, Research I* (general & basic reference indexing & abstracting data-base from University Microfilms International (UMI), 300 North Zeeb Road, P.O. Box 1346, Ann Arbor, MI 48106-1346), UMI Data Courier, P.O. Box 32770, Louisville, KY 40232-2770

- *Periodical Abstracts, Research II* (broad coverage indexing & abstracting data-base from University Microfilms International (UMI), 300 North Zeeb Road, P.O. Box 1346, Ann Arbor, MI 48106-1346), UMI Data Courier, P.O. Box 32770, Louisville, KY 40232-2770

- *PILOTS Database, The*, National Center for Post-Traumatic Stress Disorders (116 D), VA Medical Center, White River Junction, VT 05009

- *Psychological Abstracts (PsycINFO)*, American Psychological Association, P.O. Box 91600, Washington, DC 20090-1600

- *Sage Family Studies Abstracts (SFSA)*, Sage Publications, Inc., 2455 Teller Road, Newbury Park, CA 91320

- *Social Work Abstracts*, National Association of Social Workers, 750 First Street NW, 8th Floor, Washington, DC 20002

- *Studies on Women Abstracts*, Carfax Publishing Company, P.O. Box 25, Abingdon, Oxfordshire OX14 3UE, United Kingdom

- *Violence and Abuse Abstracts: A Review of Current Literature on Interpersonal Violence (VAA)*, Sage Publications, Inc., 2455 Teller Road, Newbury Park, CA 91320

- *Women Studies Abstracts*, Rush Publishing Company, P.O. Box 1, Rush, NY 14543

- *Women's Studies Index (indexed comprehensively)*, G. K. Hall & Co., 866 Third Avenue, New York, NY 10022

(continued)

SPECIAL BIBLIOGRAPHIC NOTES

related to special journal issues (separates)
and indexing/abstracting

☐ indexing/abstracting services in this list will also cover material in any "separate" that is co-published simultaneously with Haworth's special thematic journal issue or DocuSerial. Indexing/abstracting usually covers material at the article/chapter level.

☐ monographic co-editions are intended for either non-subscribers or libraries which intend to purchase a second copy for their circulating collections.

☐ monographic co-editions are reported to all jobbers/wholesalers/approval plans. The source journal is listed as the "series" to assist the prevention of duplicate purchasing in the same manner utilized for books-in-series.

☐ to facilitate user/access services all indexing/abstracting services are encouraged to utilize the co-indexing entry note indicated at the bottom of the first page of each article/chapter/contribution.

☐ this is intended to assist a library user of any reference tool (whether print, electronic, online, or CD-ROM) to locate the monographic version if the library has purchased this version but not a subscription to the source journal.

☐ individual articles/chapters in any Haworth publication are also available through the Haworth Document Delivery Services (HDDS).

Feminist Foremothers
in Women's Studies, Psychology,
and Mental Health

CONTENTS

ABOUT THE EDITORS

Phyllis Chesler, PhD, is the author of seven books including *Women and Madness* (1972), *About Men* (1978), *Mothers on Trial: The Battle for Children and Custody* (1986) and most recently, *Patriarchy: Notes of an Expert Witness* (1994). She has published articles in both popular and academic journals, including law journals. Dr. Chesler has been working on a book about the nation's so-called first female serial killer. She has been suffering from Chronic Fatigue Immune Dysfunction Syndrome for four years. Dr. Chesler has testified as an expert witness in a wide variety of cases. She is a co-founder of the Association for Women in Psychology, The National Women's Health Network, and the Editor-at-Large for *On The Issues* magazine.

Esther D. Rothblum, PhD, is Professor in the Department of Psychology at the University of Vermont. She was the recipient of a Kellogg Fellowship that involved travel to Africa to study women's mental health. Her research and writing have focused on women's mental health, lesbian issues, and women in the Antarctic. She has co-edited thirteen books on women's mental health, lesbian psychology, and diversity.

Ellen Cole, PhD, is a psychologist and sex therapist and Professor of Psychology at Alaska-Pacific University in Anchorage. A prolific writer, Dr. Cole has written and edited a variety of books, articles, and book chapters about women's health, including the long-term effects of sibling incest and sex at menopause. From 1985-1995, she co-edited the journal *Women & Therapy* and currently co-edits, with Esther Rothblum, the Haworth book program "Innovations in Feminist Studies." A current interest for Dr. Cole is "ecopsychology," a collaboration between psychologists and ecologists to reestablish connections between human beings and the nonhuman natural world.

Foreword

I have met brave women who are exploring
the outer edge of human possibility,
with no history to guide them, and
with a courage to make themselves vulnerable
that I find moving beyond words.

–Gloria Steinem

There are many accounts of what is often called "the first wave"
of the feminist movement in U.S. history, beginning with the abolition movement of the 1830s when women found they were not
allowed to function as political equals with male abolitionists. With
the passage of the Nineteenth Amendment in 1920, giving women
the right to vote, feminism "virtually collapsed from exhaustion"
(Hole & Levine, 1971), but the names and deeds of women such as
Lucretia Mott, Elizabeth Cady Stanton, Susan B. Anthony, and
Sojourner Truth remained synonymous with women's courage.
These are the politically oriented foremothers who paved the way
for those of us who awakened in the 1960s and 1970s to the realization that something was terribly wrong.

The collection you are about to read is by and about this more
recent wave of foremothers, in particular those women who have
created the fields of feminist therapy, feminist psychology, and
women's mental health as they exist today. We have included artists
as well, and other women who, while not identifying as mental
health professionals, have contributed significantly and lastingly to
how we, as women, behave, think, and feel.

[Haworth co-indexing entry note]: "Foreword." Chesler, Phyllis, Esther D. Rothblum, and Ellen
Cole. Co-published simultaneously in *Women & Therapy* (The Haworth Press, Inc.) Vol. 17, No. 1/2,
1995, pp. xxiii-xxvi; and: *Feminist Foremothers in Women's Studies, Psychology, and Mental Health*
(ed: Phyllis Chesler, Esther D. Rothblum, and Ellen Cole) The Haworth Press, Inc., 1995, pp. xv-xviii;
and: *Feminist Foremothers in Women's Studies, Psychology, and Mental Health* (ed: Phyllis Chesler,
Esther D. Rothblum, and Ellen Cole) Harrington Park Press, an imprint of The Haworth Press, Inc.,
1995, pp. xv-xviii. Single or multiple copies of this article are available from The Haworth Document
Delivery Service [1-800-342-9678, 9:00 a.m. - 5:00 p.m. (EST)].

xv

Originally, Ellen Cole and Esther Rothblum conceived of the idea of asking feminist psychology's foremothers to write about their lives and their accomplishments. It occurred to us that we work in a field whose founders are not only still living but continuing to make vital contributions to women's mental health. Early on we asked Phyllis Chesler to join us as co-editor because, of all the women who originated and continue to contribute to the development of the psychology of women as a discipline and a political commitment, it is Phyllis Chesler who stands out as the woman who in so many instances said it first, thought about it first, wrote about it first, first dared to think into the future and stand up for her truth. It is not surprising, then, that so many of the authors in this collection note that it was Phyllis who first inspired them to do their work. Of course Ellen and Esther were delighted and honored when Phyllis agreed to collaborate on the editorship of this volume.

Although we tried to choose our authors wisely, there are many women who might have been part of this collection who are not. Missing are those who were invited to contribute but could not; the dozens we thought about inviting too late; and of course the thousands of women who have been foremothers to other women. Despite our best efforts at networking, only 13% of our contributors are women of color.

Interestingly, many of the women we invited, despite their hard work and spectacular achievements, were astounded to be considered a foremother. Many said they did not feel "qualified" to be a feminist foremother. Luckily, we knew better.

We asked the authors to write about what led up to their achievements, what their accomplishments were, and how their lives were consequently changed. We assured them that this was no time to be modest and that each of them had an interesting and important story to tell. Because we wanted to include more rather than fewer women, we asked each author to limit her article to about ten pages, which we recognized was very little space to describe a life! Finally, we gave each author the choice of writing her own article or being interviewed by a feminist graduate student or a feminist colleague who would then assume second authorship.

Some authors shared with us their dilemma about self-disclosure, wanting to be honest and fearing the consequences. One foremother, a woman of color, declined to participate after writing a terrific article, because she was concerned about who might read it. So some stories cannot be told–yet.

One second author used spellcheck and was informed by her computer that "foremother" is not a word. The computer suggested "forefather" as an alternative! If any reader still doubts the power of language and wonders if the patriarchy is still in place today, this may change your mind.

As we read and re-read the articles we received, many themes seemed to coalesce as central to these foremothers' lives. It seems important to note some of these themes here, both so they may serve as a map through the variety of stories that follow, and so we may be inspired and encouraged to take our own risks, our own journeys to "the outer edge of human possibility."

Many women see in hindsight how prior projects and ideas and even dreams were the forerunners of their most important work. Many note the importance of sisterhood, other women, the loneliness and isolation when they don't exist, and particularly the validation they received from grassroots feminists in contrast to disbelief from professionals. These are women who had few mentors, who had to forge their own way, "hit the ground running." Although these women have been and continue to be looked up to as foremothers, they realize how much better off their male counterparts are and how little recognition they've been given from society-at-large. Some foremothers write about the feeling of being different, not meshing with the culture of the time, challenging the system as an outsider, not an insider.

One foremother described the early years of feminism as a time when "misogyny was in the very air we breathed." These were the days when women's groups and consciousness-raising (C-R) groups provided impetus to get started, validation for one's work.

Significantly, some foremothers noted how being a member of an oppressed group, African Americans and lesbians, for instance, influenced every part of their lives. Because these are the foremothers of feminist psychology and feminist therapy, many acknowledge childhood circumstances in influencing their later work. They describe the stages of development of becoming a feminist, from unawareness to activism and action.

Many foremothers write about the power of naming and language, and in fact it is to a great extent these very women who have created the feminist language we now have. Themes of pessimism and optimism weave in and out of the articles that follow: some women focus on the painful barriers to success, fame, and social change; others on the surprise they experience at how well they and we have done.

Throughout these pages runs a sense of excitement and vibrancy: of lives lived well, of being there during the early years of our movement, of making sacrifices, of taking risks and living to see enormous changes result. Throughout these pages, too, just under the surface, sounds a call not to take these changes for granted: to recognize that feminists, rather than arguing over picayune issues or splitting politically correct hairs, are battling for the very soul of the world.

To each of the feminist foremothers represented in the following pages we owe a great debt. Because there is no way to measure impact, and because women's work is often collaborative and interdependent, we have chosen to present these foremothers in feminist psychology and feminist therapy in alphabetical order. We begin with Phyllis Chesler because it is with Phyllis Chesler that it began.

Phyllis Chesler
Esther D. Rothblum
Ellen Cole

REFERENCE

Hole, Judith and Levine, Ellen (1971). *Rebirth of feminism.* NY: Quadrangle.

A Leader of Women

Phyllis Chesler Interviewed by Ellen Cole

One's first book takes one's whole life to write. Maybe I was born to write *Women and Madness*. I think I would have written it no matter when I'd been born—but without a radical feminist movement *moving* in the world, you would never have heard of it, no one would have cared about it, other feminists couldn't have inspired it, blessed it, passed it round, from hand to hand.

I–and my generation of feminists–hit the ground running. We were part of an extraordinary moment in history. I am extremely privileged. Women tell me that my work has saved and changed their lives. *Women and Madness* has been cited literally thousands of times in hundreds of academic journals, and in the popular media, it's been translated into many European languages. I have trav-

Dr. Phyllis Chesler is the author of seven books including *Women and Madness* (1972), *About Men* (1978), *Mothers on Trial: The Battle for Children and Custody* (1986) and most recently, *Patriarchy: Notes of an Expert Witness* (1994). She has published articles in both popular and academic journals, including law journals. Dr. Chesler has been working on a book about the nation's so-called first female serial killer. She has been suffering from Chronic Fatigue Immune Dysfunction Syndrome for 4 years. Dr. Chesler has testified as an expert witness in a wide variety of cases. She is a co-founder of the Association for Women in Psychology, The National Women's Health Network, and the Editor-at-Large for *On The Issues* magazine.

Correspondence may be addressed to Phyllis Chesler at 732A Carroll Street, New York, NY 11215.

[Haworth co-indexing entry note]: "A Leader of Women." Cole, Ellen. Co-published simultaneously in *Women & Therapy* (The Haworth Press, Inc.) Vol. 17, No. 1/2, 1995, pp. 1-23; and: *Feminist Foremothers in Women's Studies, Psychology, and Mental Health* (ed: Phyllis Chesler, Esther D. Rothblum, and Ellen Cole) The Haworth Press, Inc., 1995, pp. 1-23; and: *Feminist Foremothers in Women's Studies, Psychology, and Mental Health* (ed: Phyllis Chesler, Esther D. Rothblum, and Ellen Cole) Harrington Park Press, an imprint of The Haworth Press, Inc., 1995, pp. 1-23. Single or multiple copies of this article are available from The Haworth Document Delivery Service [1-800-342-9678, 9:00 a.m. - 5:00 p.m. (EST)].

eled all over the world to lecture, and to meet with other feminists. This is no small thing; this is a miraculous, and wonderful thing.

I don't know what kind of life I would have lived had there been no modern feminist movement. A lesser life, I'm sure, and a more miserable one. When I was a child, I'd met no woman who'd graduated from college or who'd had a "career," other than that of teacher, nurse or secretary. In high school, college, and graduate school, I had only a handful of women teachers. I had no female (or male) mentors or role models. Women were not my intellectual comrades–only books were.

Then in 1967, life gained its fourth dimension, the world was suddenly bursting with brave, bold, beautiful, adventurous creatures–and most of them were women. And feminists. How interesting!

In 1969, I was 29 years old. I was a brand-new PhD, a psycho-therapist-in-training, an Assistant Professor and a researcher. And I knew almost nothing about how to help another woman save her own life.

Most of what we take for granted today was not even whispered about thirty years ago. For example, none of my graduate school teachers in the 1960s ever mentioned that women (or men) were oppressed or that people suffer when they're victimized, and then blamed for their own misery. None of my clinical supervisors (or analysts) ever suggested that I use my own experience as a woman in order to understand women and mental health. In fact, no one ever taught me to administer a test for mental health–only for mental illness.

No matter. I was studying what women "really wanted" when they entered psychotherapy; I planned to present my findings at the 1970 annual convention of The American Psychological Association (APA) in Miami. I went to the convention and decided not to deliver my prepared paper. Instead, on behalf of the newly founded Association for Women in Psychology (AWP), I asked APA members for one million dollars "in reparations" on behalf of women who had never been helped, but who had, in fact, been further abused by the mental health professions: punitively labelled, overly tranquilized, sexually seduced while in treatment, hospitalized against their will, given shock therapy, lobotomized, and deeply disliked as too "aggressive," "promiscuous," "depressed," "ugly," "old," "disgusting" or "incurable." "Maybe AWP could set up an alternative to a mental hospital with the money," I said, "or a shelter for runaway wives."

The audience laughed at me. Loudly. Nervously. Some of my two thousand colleagues made jokes about my "penis envy." Some looked embarrassed, others relieved. Obviously, I was "crazy."

I started writing *Women and Madness* on the plane back to New York. I immersed myself in the psychoanalytic literature, located biographies and autobiographies of women who'd been psychiatrically diagnosed or hospitalized; read novels and poems about sad, mad, bad women; devoured mythology and anthropology, especially about Goddesses, matriarchies and Amazons. I began analyzing the "mental illness" statistics and relevant psychological and psychiatric studies. I also began interviewing the experts: women patients.

The ideas in *Women and Madness* announced, anticipated, many of the next steps in feminist theory and practice, including many of the themes I'd subsequently explore. For example, *Women and Madness* may have been the first feminist work (in this era), to talk about incest and rape, about female role models, female heroism, in both military and spiritual terms, and about warrior and mother goddesses. (They're role models–which was precisely the subject of my Ph.D. dissertation "The Maternal Influence in Learning by Observation in Cats and Kittens." And I published it in *Science* magazine, in 1969.) The unconscious always moves in rather obvious ways.

In the 1972 Introduction to *Women and Madness,* I retell the myth of Demeter, a mother goddess, and her daughter, Persephone; their losing each other is what happens to most mothers and daughters in patriarchy. However, their remaining together means that Persephone merely repeats a maternal destiny, and rarely develops beyond her relationship to her mother. Years later, I now see I was also writing about a custody battle! between a mother, Demeter, and a father, Hades, the king of the underworld.

In a sense, although I worked very, very hard to research and write *Women and Madness,* it's almost as if I'd *channelled* the book. How else did I know what I obviously "knew," and yet had never read or heard about before? However, I was inspired, empowered, by an outpouring of feminist pamphlets, books, articles, conferences, and by meetings with extraordinary women: Ti-Grace Atkinson, Pauline Bart, Rita Mae Brown, Joann Evans Gardner, Vivian Gornick, Barbara Joans, Flo Kennedy, Jill Johnston, Leigh Marlowe, Kate Millett, Robin Morgan, Marge Piercy, Martha Shelley, Alix Kate Shulman, Kate Stimpson, Gloria Steinem, Elaine Stocker, Naomi Weisstein–to name only a few.

Women and Madness was published in October, 1972. Over the years, it would sell more than two million copies and be translated into many European languages and ultimately into Japanese and Hebrew. For awhile, I was deluged by media requests and interviewed everywhere on every conceivable subject. I received at least 10,000 letters. (I have answered them by continuing to write and act.) Women told me that I'd "saved their lives"; Would I be their therapist? If not, would I recommend one? Could I get them *out* of a mental hospital or into a *better* one? Would I testify for them in court, supervise their doctoral dissertations, conduct a workshop at their clinic, lecture at their universities? Would I be willing to talk to their husbands, mothers, children?

Although a lot has changed–after all, here we are; in reality, very little has changed. Today, women psychiatrists at the National Institute of Mental Health and Naval officers are ordered into psychiatric treatment when they allege sex-discrimination or harassment; mothers who allege that their children are being incestuously abused usually lose custody and gain psychiatric diagnoses such as Munchausen's Syndrome By Proxy or Borderline Personality.

Women with heart disease and other medical ailments often go undiagnosed and untreated, while impatient physicians, male and female, tranquilize and psychiatrically diagnose their symptoms away. Disabled women, myself included: women with Multiple Sclerosis, Lyme Disease, Chronic Fatigue Immune Dysfunction Syndrome, Lupus, etc., are routinely forced into psychiatric exams. Catch-22: If they pass, they lose their disability coverage; if they fail, they win a useless, inaccurate psychiatric diagnosis.

Women in need of treatment: incest and rape survivors, and battered women, for example, can rarely find quality, affordable treatment. The same is true for women alcoholics and drug addicts, and for those who truly suffer from mental illness.

After nearly 30 years of struggle, I and most other radical feminists still have no *institutional* power. What we know, dies with us. Without institutional power, we can't pass our knowledge on to the next generations.

My greatest sorrow is that I have, so far, been prevented from continuously teaching the next generations in a hands-on way; and that my work, like so many radical feminist works, has, over and over again, been "disappeared" in my own lifetime.

For example, three of my six books are currently out-of-print: *Women, Money and Power* (1976), *With Child: A Diary of Motherhood* (1979) and *Sacred Bond: The Legacy of Baby M* (1987). [Currently in print: *Women and Madness* (1972), *About Men* (1978), and *Mothers on Trial: The Battle for Children and Custody* (1986).]

At first, I never even noticed when one of my books went out of print, I was too busy writing new books, embarking on new campaigns. Only gradually, did I begin to understand that I'd have to campaign, over and over again, to keep each book in print–or it would die.

Ah, even as I write this, I think: women are *dying* just because they're women, and I'm talking about books going out of print! How dare I complain? I'm not dead, homeless, or in jail; I'm literate, educated, I do not have to earn my living on my back or in the fields, I'm living in America, not in a war zone . . . but I *am* living in a war zone.

What I'm about to describe has happened to every *radical* feminist lucky enough to have had a university position. And to me, too.

In 1969-70, at Richmond College, now the College of Staten Island, The City University of New York (CUNY), I taught one of the first "accredited" Womens' Studies courses and co-founded one of the first Womens' Studies Programs in the country. (If I were a man, perhaps I'd have been rewarded for doing something as innovative and enduring as this.)

By 1970-71, I had also convinced my mainly male colleagues to hire 6-7 women for 9-10 available positions; Drs. Maxine Bernstein, Dorothy Riddle, Nancy Russo and Sandra Tangri were among them. I also helped set up a student-run feminist OB/GYN clinic, a child care center, and a rape crisis center on campus. For good measure, I also persuaded the school to allow women to study self-defense for credit. Early on, I was also associated with the womens' class action lawsuit against CUNY.

I loved teaching, I loved my students. I lectured with passion and devotion. I "hung out" with my students, invited them over for coffee, just as if they were at Oxford or Cambridge, and not at a working class public institution. (I was often *accused* of holding extra classes off-campus, and threatened with exposure and expulsion for doing so.)

By 1971, my colleagues, the administration, and some well-briefed students, were constantly bringing me up on "charges" at my own campus: I was anti-male, I used "sexually explicit" language, I forced my students to read feminist works, I didn't "love" my students (the way a Good Mother should)—how could I? I was too busy publishing! And lecturing, off-campus, and on the airwaves.

Some say: "publish or perish." I published—in academic journals and in the mainstream media, and I was still forced to battle for tenure: hard; for the right to keep my tenured position: constantly; and for each and every promotion thereafter.

I'll never forget the questions my Staten Island colleagues asked when I'd formally appeal my non-promotions. Some colleagues who sat in judgement, both male and female, had rarely published anything; and in my view, those who had, had published either mediocre, minor, imitative, or fiercely patriarchal works. But I was not there to judge them. Their comments, upon turning down my various appeals of non-promotion, included: "But you're only publishing things about women! That doesn't count"; or "You're publishing too much"; or "Your reading lists have the wrong books on them"; or: "You're not sitting on any committees"; etc.

It took 22 years of constant battle for me to finally be promoted to Full Professor. Each promotion was due to the President overriding his own faculty's vote.

Defeats are all relative. I'm a tenured professor, right? However, despite numerous formal applications, I was never allowed to teach graduate students at my own university. No explanation given, none required. (I am in good company: over the years, many overqualified women and men have also been prevented from teaching at the CUNY Graduate Center.)

CUNY and most other universities around the country treated me and every other radical feminist badly because we were women and because everything we believed in, and did, threatened everything they believed in and did.

There I was–there *we* were–beginning to put a strong feminist agenda into place on *their campuses,* there I was–there *we* were– founding and attending womens' caucuses within the professions, coordinating Speakouts, taking part in televised demonstrations, being quoted in the newspapers, presenting papers at academic conferences. At my college, I was a symbol of this ferment and the powers-that-be hated it, and acted accordingly.

In 1972, when *Women and Madness* received a front page New York Times Book Review, not a single person at my university *in a position of power* over me ever said "Congratulations." Not one. The same profound silence greeted my second front page New York Times Book Review, in 1988, of my sixth book, *Sacred Bond: The Legacy of Baby M.* (To be fair though, once, in the mid-1970s, a male colleague on my campus received a national book award. I called to congratulate him; he said I was the only one who had.)

Friends: The patriarchal academic world is not set up to appreciate/nourish creativity, only to crush it.

Ultimately, women at CUNY won our lawsuit, a judge agreed that CUNY discriminated against women, but the lawsuit took nearly fifteen years, the remedies were token, and, despite the usual hard-won exceptions, structurally things have changed very little, both for me and for other women at CUNY. Despite the existence of a woman Chancellor and a woman Graduate Center President, women employees at every level, and students, are still underpaid, overworked, sexually harassed, and punished for being associated with what is mocked as the "politically correct" line.

Creative excellence and achievement is only one reason I, and many of my Second Wave peers, have never received a serious, permanent teaching offer from a university. In my case, there's another reason: my/our utter seriousness about activism.

I took what those European intellectuals said seriously: that it's important to put your body where your ideas are. Some 1960s leftists briefly agreed–and have, ever since, mainly occupied Armchairs in the Academy. I tried to keep my body-on-the-barricade. I kept publishing, but, like so many other feminists, I didn't leave it at that. I also left my desk to create and maintain a visible opposition, rally in solidarity, raise funds for worthy causes, sign petitions, testify in courtrooms. Like other feminists and radicals, I faced hostility, contempt, even danger, in the service of my ideals.

I've *paid* to do things that never helped my "career," only hurt it. I've done things that have netted me death threats and FBI investigations, not prizes. (I've never received a single, honorary degree or any national or international prizes–not even from the two organizations I co-founded: The Association for Women in Psychology and the National Women's Health Network.) But, that's no surprise. Being a feminist pioneer means that one can rarely benefit, personally, from one's own accomplishments; with luck, sometimes other women can.

For example, I have written letters of recommendation that have gotten others admitted as students or hired as faculty at universities that would never hire me, or anyone like me.

In 1972, I was summoned to both Radcliffe and Harvard. I spoke at a Radcliffe Conference on Women and Mental Health, and at Harvard's Graduate Program in Community Psychiatry. (If I were a man, this might mean I was being looked over for a teaching appointment.) Within a week of my lecture, four women physicians had quit their residencies in Psychiatry. They wrote to say that my lecture had changed their lives. Needless to say, Harvard never wanted me, and neither did Radcliffe. To be fair, they didn't want to lose any more students and weren't about to change the curriculum I'd critiqued. Harvard only approved its first Women's Studies curriculum nearly 20 years after we had one in place at Richmond/CUNY.

No matter that Radcliffe's President in the early 1970s was a woman, and a feminist, too; no matter that she called upon me for advice once or twice; no matter that I once asked her point-blank, if she knew of an academic perch worthy of my talents. As I understood it then, and understand it now, most women, especially Jews and women of color, have a very hard time getting hired or getting tenure at Harvard. Someone explained it to me this way: the WASPS at Harvard are not happy about having to live with their pushy Jewish men; they don't want any pushy Jewish sisters there, too. I applaud Derrick Bell, who left/was forced out when he refused to continue teaching at Harvard unless Harvard started hiring and tenuring qualified women of color.

On the other hand, the very visibly Jewish male President of CUNY's Grad School all through the 1970s made a point of telling me how much he admired my work; nevertheless, he claimed he was 'helpless' to facilitate my teaching at the Graduate School.

I've often been asked what *I* consider my major contribution to be. That's a scary question. Maybe it's too soon to tell. My books and articles, surely. Giving speeches that saved womens' lives or sanity, and contributed to feminist awakening, among women and men. Co-founding the Association for Women in Psychology (AWP) in 1969-70, and the National Womens' Health Network in the early 1970s, was also a contribution.

I've made some important contributions to feminist theory and consciousness. However, many of these contributions have not yet entered the feminist "canon/discourse." For example, only the incomparable Dale Spender has written an essay about *Women and Madness* in which she viewed it as a work of feminist *theory*, not just as a critique of institutional psychiatry. She did so in *For The Record: The Making and Meaning of Feminist Knowledge*, which was published in England, in 1985, 13 years after *Women and Madness* first appeared.

More than 22 years elapsed before even a *feminist* academic journal, the wonderful, and relatively recent, *Feminism and Psychology*, also based in England, published a Retrospective of *Women and Madness*. Yes, *Women and Madness* is cited everywhere, but most of my subsequent work has never been reviewed (or even debated) in feminist academic journals. My work on female (and male) psychology, and especially on motherhood—subjects I address in each of my books, has never been seen as a whole, or studied as such. Not in *Signs*, not in *Ms.*, not in the patriarchal press.

Feminist work, if it's bold enough, large enough, pioneering enough, not strictly academic, not strictly mainstream, just has a way of slipping through our collective fingers and down into living deaths.

For about 10 years, feminists like myself were very much in demand on campus, on television, in publishing, on legislative panels–but mainly as "dancing dog" sensations. The pioneer whistle-blowers didn't get to inherit the ships of state and industry, the jobs went to ever-younger white men–and, in token numbers, to anti-feminist women, and then to those feminists who were more interested in their own non-activist careers than in risky, revolutionary struggle (no crime, by the way, but a shame, nonetheless).

Some of my theoretical contributions that are waiting to be discovered: *Women, Money, and Power* was first published in 1976. It's been out of print for awhile. In the first chapter, I theorize/describe how sexual abuse in early childhood shames a girl into self-destructive naivete, obedience, "femininity." I talk about how sexual abuse (or "sexualizing") a girl in childhood operates, when it's coupled with a failure to develop a strong body-self, and group-self, through team bonding in sports. I discuss what this does to female psychology.

In an 11-page chapter entitled "I'd Rather Be Dead than Ugly: The Psycho-economics of Female Beauty," I describe the entire beauty myth that Naomi Wolf wrote about so well many years later (I doubt she'd ever read *Women, Money and Power,* by the way). But what I did with the "beauty myth" information was to tie it to the need for sovereign space and a feminist government. Safe space. The right to defend yourself if you're attacked–one of the themes I'm now writing about.

Then there's *About Men,* first published in 1978. The first section is a meditation on some of the themes in Genesis in the Old Testament. Its point of gravity, its sensibility, its voice, is primarily poetic, prophetic, psychoanalytic. (This is also true for *With Child: A Diary of Motherhood.)* I don't think either book has been taught in Literature or Women's Studies programs, I don't think that psychoanalysts use it, I don't think that Robert Bly or Men's Studies/Queers Studies professors are familiar with either book.

About Men asks: what *do* men really want? How have fathers failed, been absent, distant or cruel to their sons? Why do men obey male tyrants, cruel fathers, missing fathers? If men really mean to kill each other, why do they kill women instead? Especially since they're so dependent upon women (as Masters are always dependent on slaves and servants). I took the concept of womb-envy very seriously. I looked at friendships among men, at "brotherhood." I wrote about matricide here for the first time, beginning with the murder of God as a Woman.

Is it really so important that I don't have 20 years of serious graduate students behind me already? Yes, it is. It is very important. How can I bring others along if my achievements are used to disempower me—and us all?

Today, many women—including feminists in their twenties and early thirties, including graduate students, don't know my work. They do not know my work. Many students today do not know radical feminist theory, they have no models for organizing legislative, educational, grassroots, or media campaigns. They are not interested in high-risk rescue missions. Mainly, they haven't had a chance—at least, not in school, and not in virtual patriarchal reality, to see feminists do these things, over and over again. Like breathing. That's a terrible loss. For me—and for them.

We have few feminist-run or controlled mental health centers, graduate or medical schools.

Now, I would like to write about my academic career in terms of what it means to be sexually harassed instead of being mentored.

Like most women, I've been sexually harassed by my professors, employers, boyfriends and husbands—and by utter strangers on street corners, too. Like others of my generation, I was bred to accept and enjoy it, above all, to keep quiet about it, forget it, and to blame myself if something about these peculiar arrangements bothered me. For years, in isolation, I did so, until movement in the late sixties allowed me to analyze my fate in feminist terms.

Like most women, I've always had to fend off "unwanted advances." One pays a price for doing so. As every woman knows, Hell hath no fury like a man spurned. Two examples, among thousands: In the late 1960s, after dinner, the head of a department at a prestigious medical school tried to rape me. I was a graduate student and we'd met, at his suggestion (I'm guilty, I confess, I went, I ate), to discuss how he could assist me in getting my research funded. In the decidedly non-amorous scuffle that ensued, I broke his ribs, and although I helped him to a nearby hospital (only women actually do things like this), this professor never did mentor my research.

In the early 1970s, another professor arrived to rate my college's curriculum for a national review board. I admit it, I did it again, I accepted his invitation to a dinner party with Very Famous (white male) Intellectuals and their wives. My equally ambitious heterosexual male counterparts also accepted dinner invitations without having to face sexual harassment at the hands of their heterosexual mentors. However, I had the audacity not to be impressed by the company this professor kept, and to reject his every subsequent social and sexual advance. He retaliated. He arranged for a scathing review of *Women and Madness* to be published in Partisan Review. He got a woman to write it–a woman who, years later, apologized to me about it.

These two professors did not see me as their heir, as a future member of their team; nor were they overcome with love for me. They treated me as they did because I was a woman. It was nothing personal. This is what makes it poignant, utterly heartbreaking–the inexorable lead-weight impersonality of prejudice.

These professors were not unusual. Back then (not now, Heaven forbid, not now), most men viewed women as pussy: wife-pussy, girlfriend-pussy, whore-pussy. This harassment and lack of mentoring didn't stop me–here I am–but it certainly didn't help me. And, over a lifetime, it mounts up, it mounts up.

Sexual harassment and rape was so common, so pervasive, so accepted, that it was virtually invisible. The shame, the stench, stuck to the victim or to the whistle-blower, the victimizer never experienced the consequences of his actions, he was never named, and when he was, all ranks closed to protect him and to destroy his accuser. In the 1950s and 1960s, the Great Men (and Token Women) of the Academy neither named nor studied sexual violence; ultimately, their contribution would be to characterize the 1970s grass-roots feminist claims as exaggerated and unscientific, as proof of man-hating, unworthy of further discussion. Or funding.

In 1978, Lin Farley published the first full-length book on the subject: *Sexual Shakedown: The Sexual Harassment of Women on the Job.* Women launched lawsuits, and feminist media published their first stories on the subject. However, in my view, despite some noteworthy exceptions, the most-often-quoted (white) feminists still had a hard time acknowledging their own powerlessness, their own complicity, in the face of male sexual violence, both on and off the job. Or in their own backyards.

In 1979-1980, I was hired by the United Nations to coordinate an international feminist conference that I'd "pitched" to them. Shortly after I signed my employment contract, my employer, Dr. Davidson Nicol, Under-Secretary-General of the United Nations and the Executive Director of the UN Institute for Training and Research (UNITAR), raped me. Yes (there I go again), I'd had dinner a few times with him, too, to discuss my proposal, but that didn't mean I wanted to fuck him/have an affair/be raped.

I absolutely refused to quit. UNITAR was paying me a great deal of money to do something I passionately wanted to do; I was a single mother, and I needed the money desperately. ("Famous" women still have to work, fame doesn't equal wealth; this can't be said too often.) I wanted to shepherd this first-of-it's-kind conference, and my idea, into being. I'd be damned if I'd let a rapist force me off the field of battle, interfere with my feminist dreams.

No, I didn't "cry rape," at least, not out loud. I immediately told some trusted friends and my UN assistants what Nicol had done—and why I was staying on anyway. My friends were outraged, and compassionate. Neither they nor I could "do" anything about it. As a diplomat from Sierra Leone, and a UN official, Nicol had immunity—and I had a conference to create.

After Nicol raped me, I made sure I was never alone with him again. Of course, Nicol kept harassing me, but I paid one of my female assistants out of my own pocket to accompany me at all times. I evaded Nicol's every advance. He retaliated, packed my steering committee with every anti-feminist, anti-western, anti-white, anti-American, anti-Jewish, anti-Zionist, UN female employee he could find, and there were many to choose from. I endured. My conference endured, too.

What was happening to me was not unique. In the mid-1970s, I was having dinner with an Australian-born diplomat, when, suddenly, she began to weep. She told me she'd been raped by an Iranian diplomat in Teheran. She had been hired by the Shah's sister, Princess Ashraf, as one of her chief advisors on a Women's

Institute: "I had no money, I couldn't get them to give me a salary check, I was actually starving. And then, this. I was so ashamed!" At the time this woman was the highest ranking international feminist civil servant, at least whom I knew. "They've raped our Foreign Minister," I said, "and we have no army to avenge you!"

What was unique, at least to me, was the way in which my own feminist comrades behaved when I tried to confront my rapist. In July, 1980, in Oslo, Norway, Nicol, who was intoxicated most of the time, began sexually harassing women at the conference, myself included. "Phyllis, come be with me. You've made me wait long enough. You've got your conference. I need you. I want you. I will have you."

I called a midnight meeting, revealed that Nicol had just sexually harassed three women at the conference, and me, and that he'd sexually harassed me before, in New York, where he'd raped me, too. I cried "rape" as soon as I could, when I thought I'd be heard, get some kind of justice. "Maybe I was wrong not to quit right away," I admitted. "This conference has my blood all over it. I'm ready to confront him. Are you? A private confrontation is the only justice I'll ever get. Nicol has diplomatic immunity. I don't think I'll get anywhere trying to sue him through the UN, or through the D.A.'s office in New York, or in his home country, where he tells me he's a prince of his tribe." At least ten women were listening intently.

One Nicol-harassed feminist said she couldn't afford to jeopardize her connection to the UN. "Anyway, that's how men are. I guess I feel flattered that men still find me attractive, even at my age." Another of Nicol's victims was terrified, but willing to confront him. "This has brought back memories of my rape when I was 4 years old. I don't know if I have the strength to do this. I'll try though," she bravely said. "I'm ready, let's go," said the third, and youngest woman Nicol had harassed.

A Portuguese diplomat was at the meeting, counting her rosary beads rather frantically. "I always knew something like this could happen."

"The man's disgusting," said a black woman from South Africa. "Let's go talk to him."

"Okay," said a black woman from Zambia. "But it's so upsetting."

Two of the white radical (and lesbian) feminists whom I'd invited, took the following approach: With passion, and in tears, A. begged me/us not to confront Nicol. "If (white) feminists were to accuse a black man of rape, it would expose our movement as a racist movement." White feminists *were* racists; A.'s concern was, perhaps, with public exposure. The black African women were ready to confront Nicol. (Nicol, by the way, blocked my every move to subsidize and/or invite more than one African-American woman to Oslo; he wanted white blondes, he paid for them, and he got them.)

B., the second white feminist, and an internationally well-known feminist, too, was equally persuasive; she smoothly managed to delay our confronting Nicol. "Let's handle this back in New York, let's not destroy this conference, the rape happened on American soil, maybe Phyllis can pursue it better there."

Back in New York, to my amazement, B. ended up collaborating with Nicol. B. wrote the Foreword to the conference proceedings in my place, the UN published it as a book in 1983, without a single line from me. Yes, I had been asked to write the Foreword; I said I would. Nicol wrote, and called, several times, to say that the book was, "once more, a little delayed, no hurry with that Foreword of yours." My feminist "sister," B., also went on to solicit many of the women I'd found, and invited to Oslo, as contributors to her own international feminist (!) anthology.

When I first saw B.'s foreword, I said I'd sue, both B., Nicol, and the UN. Ironically, B. had been sued in the early 1970s by another feminist, allegedly for plagiarism; too late, B. had asked me to intercede on her behalf. This time, in pain, in rage, I was confronting my formerly beloved comrade. I did not understand why she'd done this and I wanted to. I proposed a feminist court, a Bet Din (a religious court), a war crimes tribunal.

It was not hard to line up some leading feminists to participate in this feminist Bet Din, but once we got together no one wanted to Take Sides, i.e., to take a stand on the issues. Most wanted to keep their political friendships with both B. and me intact—without getting into the "messy stuff."

At the meeting, B. was sullen, silent, made no eye contact with me; from time to time, she said things like: "I don't remember a lot about that year"; "You're the one who stopped talking to me"; "I wrote the Foreword because Nicol told me you'd refused to do it."

"But why didn't you just call me and ask if this was true?" I asked, to which B. said: "Well, I thought you weren't talking to me."

C., one of the women I'd invited, said that B. had been systematically "disappearing" her and every other North American feminist's contribution to global feminism, shutting them out of the information loop. C. wondered whether B. "had also been competing with Phyllis's plans for an international anthology, but isn't there room for more than one such anthology anyway?"

I wanted feminist justice, not public scandal or lawsuits. Behind closed doors, I wanted B. to acknowledge that she'd behaved the way women in incestuous families do; I wanted to know why. We'd been friendly, loving, towards each other. What went wrong? What didn't I understand? Mainly, I wanted B. and our closest feminist comrades to confront Nicol with me. "That rapist should not go to his grave thinking he could divide the likes of us," I said.

My sisters–and ideologically, they were and still are my sisters– finally agreed to do this, but they never did, and now Nicol is dead. He died, late in 1994, 15 years after he raped me, and I can publish his name, but we can never confront him, alive, together. This failure of nerve, B.'s craven feminist collaboration with a rapist, stands; it's part of the historical record.

Sadly, these same well-known white feminists finally "got it" (at least they publicly said they did) when Anita Hill accused and exposed Clarence Thomas–but that took place eleven years after Nicol raped me.

B. and I never spoke again and from time to time I miss her still. I have no idea what B. ever told our many mutual friends after our Bet Din, or what she now thinks. I only know that, for fifteen years I waited for feminists–whom I still cherish–to make good on their promise to confront my rapist with me.

"This can't have happened to you!" is the response I often get, when I share any of this information. My point: being a feminist doesn't change or "protect" a woman from the female condition. If it's something that happens to women, it happens to feminists, too. If it happens to any woman, anywhere, then it can happen to any woman anywhere.

For example, my friend, D., who's also a feminist, turned out to be a severely battered wife. All through the 1980s, her second husband had been breaking her bones, and her spirit. She didn't try to escape. She didn't "tell." One day, unexpectedly, she asked me to testify for her in court as her expert witness, and she told me everything, more than I could bear to hear, all the grisly, sickening details. How it haunted me, shamed me, that our ideology could not "protect" her–and us–from patriarchal violence.

Perhaps the white feminists who either collaborated with or failed to confront my rapist with me, as I'd asked them to do, as they finally promised to do, were as horrified, as disheartened, as frightened, by our collective vulnerability, as I later was by D.'s Tales of a Battered Wife. How could this happen to one of us! (Ah, did we think our ideology functioned like Wonder Woman's magic bracelets?)

But, as I always say, "If the Patriarchs don't get you, the Feminists will."

Over the years, I and everyone else, have observed feminists "trash" any feminist who does something–and, at the same time, refuse to confront those heterosexual and lesbian feminists who verbally abuse, bad-mouth, even physically batter other women, or who exploit, and have sex with their patients, students, employees, junior colleagues, groupies. Anselma dell'Olio wrote about "trashing" in 1971 and I quoted her in *Women and Madness* in 1972; Jo Freeman/Joreen also started writing about this early on. However, naming it didn't stop it from happening.

I have seen feminists shamelessly submit themselves to, even create cults around, feminists who have money, access to the media, or who are mentally ill. Yes, mentally ill. Co-dependent madness, slave-habits, who knows, but you can't fashion movement, only stars, out of such craven behavior.

I have observed feminists ostracize the woman who dares cry "foul," as they themselves do double-entry moral bookkeeping, and refuse to expose, even privately, those feminists who have seething behind-the-scenes contempt for other women, who prefer men, deeply.

Well, I'm biased, I'm a feminist who always does something; and I cry "foul" a lot, too. Over the years, as you can imagine, this has gotten me into a great deal of trouble.

Feminists are as misogynistic as everyone else. Sisterhood is an ideal, it's not yet a reality.

Once, long ago, another well-known white feminist demanded that I not write my book on *Woman's Inhumanity to Woman*, because "some of her best friends were women." "Are you going to name names?" she asked. "Name names? I might as well publish the phone book, annually," I said. Not naming names didn't get us anywhere, did it? Maybe naming names, as a way of demanding some accountability, is as good a way to begin as any other.

I struggled over whether to "name names" here and decided to name my rapist, but not his collaborators, the kapos, those who couldn't deny themselves the slightest career or friendship opportunities—not even for the sake of their own principles. Their names are legion, they're feminists and they're anti-feminists too. Every woman's got her own list.

It's treacherous, though, when a woman publicly preaches one thing, and then, hypocritically, unconsciously, behaves the same way her so-called opponents do. If you say you're a feminist, try to practice what you preach, but since that's hard to do, when you fail, why not say so, name it, acknowledge it, apologize profoundly, try again. B.'s crime was not merely the collaboration, or her opportunism; it was her refusal to make ammends politically, her refusal to name what she did, her "amnesia," her 15-year silence. This is what women do to women in patriarchy all the time.

Some say there are many conflicting "truths." But what happened to me and to every other woman who's ever been sexually harassed and raped was not Rashomon; there are no alternative, competing realities here.

How we, as a movement, relate to the truth of male sexual violence toward women matters. As feminists we must learn how not to lie: to ourselves, to each other. As a movement, we must reckon with the ways in which women, feminists included, collude with patriarchy. But girls: the bullshit and the cover-ups have got to go.

The conclusion I draw from these facts is not that "doing feminism" is too hard, or hopeless. My conclusion is that no feminist should think that what's happened to her is unique, that if only she'd done something differently she'd have been spared, that Somewhere, Over The Rainbow, there are cannier, cleverer, luckier, feminists who can do no wrong and can cope with anything.

Sure, we Second Wave feminists had more "fun" in the late 1960s and early 1970s. We were young and felt invincible. We had no idea that this struggle would take all we had; it's a lifetime struggle, and it's much harder than anyone thought. Holding one's own against patriarchy, just holding one's own, is not easy. Resisting it–building a resistance movement–takes all we have. And more.

What keeps me going? Feminist honor-in-action inspires me, mothers me, into doing my best. I get real maternal, I'm at my best, when I can join, support, encourage, witness, feminist thoughts and deeds that are courageous, radical, talented, risky, generous.

No, we haven't "lost"; feminism is not "on the run." The party's over, the velvet gloves are off, on both sides; we're in the trenches now, fighting for the soul of the world, for its ruling consciousness. I think we're putting up a hell of a struggle. May we endure, may we live to battle another day, may we acquit ourselves with honor.

SELECTED BIBLIOGRAPHY

1994

Patriarchy: Notes of an Expert Witness. Monroe, ME: Common Courage Press, 1994.
Introduction to *Women of the Asylum: Voices From Behind the Walls,* 1840-1945. J.L. Geller, and M. Harris (eds.), New York, NY: Doubleday, 1994.
"The Dead Man Is Not On Trial." *On The Issues,* Winter 1994.
"Sister, Fear Has No Place Here." *On The Issues,* Fall 1994.
"When They Call You Crazy." *On The Issues,* Summer 1994.
"A Wolf in Feminist Clothing." *On The Issues,* Spring 1994.
"Heroism Is Our Only Alternative." *Feminism & Psychology,* Vol. 4, No. 2, May 1994.

1993

"Marcia Rimland's Deadly Embrace." *On The Issues,* Winter 1993.
"Sexual Violence Against Women and a Woman's Right to Self-Defense: The Case of Aileen Carol Wuornos." *Criminal Practice Law Report,* October 1993, Vol. 1, No. 9.
"A Woman's Right to Self-Defense: The Case of Aileen Carol Wuornos." *St. John's University Law Review,* Fall-Winter 1993.

"An Update on Aileen Wuornos." *On The Issues*, Summer 1993.

1992

Sacred Bond: The Legacy of Baby M. Tokyo, JAPAN: Heibon-Sha, 1992.
"Custody Determinations: Gender Bias in the Courts." Barbara Katz Rothman (ed.), *Encyclopedia of Childbearing. Critical Perspectives*, Phoenix: Oryx Press, 1992.
"The Men's Auxiliary: Protecting the Rule of the Fathers." *Women Respond to the Men's Movement.* Kay Leigh Hagan (ed.), San Francisco: Harper San Francisco, 1992.
"Women and Illness." *On The Issues*, Winter 1992.
"The Shellshocked Woman." A review of Dr. Judith Herman's book *Trauma and Recovery. The New York Times Book Review*, August 23, 1992.
"When A 'Bad' Woman Kills: The Trials of Aileen Wuornos." *On The Issues*, Summer 1992.
"A Double Standard for Murder?" *The New York Times* OP-ED, January 9, 1992.

1991

Mothers on Trial: The Battle for Children and Custody. New York, NY: Harcourt Brace Jovanovich, New Introduction, 1991.
A review of Andrea Dworkin's book *Mercy. On The Issues*, Winter 1991.
A review of Letty Cottin Pogrebin's book *Deborah, Golda, and Me: Being Feminist and Jewish in America. On The Issues*, Winter 1991.
"Mothers On Trial: The Custodial Vulnerability of Women." *Feminism and Psychology*, Vol. 1, No. 3, 1991.
"Mothers on Trial." *Ms Magazine*, May/June 1991.
"Women and Custody." *New York Daily News*, March 3, 1991.
"Mothers On the Run in Sweden." *On the Issues*, Spring 1991.

1990

Sacred Bond: The Legacy of Baby M. London, ENGLAND: Virago Press, 1990.
About Men. New York, NY: Harcourt Brace Jovanovich, 1990.
"Mothers on Trial: Custody and the 'Baby M' Case." *The Sexual Liberals and the Attack on Feminism*, Dorchen Leitholdt and Janice G. Raymond (eds.), Pergamon Press, April 1990.
"Twenty Years Since *Women and Madness*." *Journal of Mind and Behavior*, Special Issue: Challenging the Therapeutic State: Critical Perspectives on Psychiatry and the Mental Health System, Vol. II, Nos. 3 & 4, Summer/Autumn 1990.
"Mother-Hatred and Mother-Blaming: What Electra Did to Clytemnestra. Motherhood: A Feminist Perspective." *Women & Therapy*, Vol. 10, Nos. 1/2, Summer 1990.
"Women at the Wall in Jerusalem. A Lawsuit on Behalf of Women's Right to Pray." *On The Issues*, Summer 1990.

1989

Women and Madness. New York, NY: Harcourt Brace Jovanovich, New Introduction, 1989.

Sacred Bond: The Legacy of Baby M. New York, NY: Vintage/Random House, 1989.

"Strong Mothers, Weak Wives. The Search for Gender Equality." *Canadian Journal of Women and The Law,* Vol. 3, No 1, Summer 1989.

"Re-examining Freud." *Psychology Today,* September 1989.

"And the Walls Came Tumbling Down." *On The Issues,* Vol. XI, Spring 1989.

1988

Sacred Bond: The Legacy of Baby M. New York, NY: Times Books/Random House, 1988.

"Sacred Bond: The Legacy of Baby M." *Ms Magazine,* May 1988.

1987

Mothers on Trial: The Battle for Children and Custody. Seattle: The Seal Press, Paperback, 1987.

Women and Madness. Tel Aviv, ISRAEL: Zmora, Bitan, 1987.

1986

Mothers on Trial: The Battle for Children and Custody. New York, NY: McGraw-Hill, 1986.

"How Fares Motherhood in the Age of Divorce." *Newsday,* May 11, 1986.

"Beneath the Surface: The Truth about Divorce, Custody and Support." *Ms Magazine,* February 1986.

1985

"Anorexia Becomes Electra: Women, Eating and Identity." *New York Times Book Review,* July 21, 1985.

1983

Women and Madness. Tokyo, JAPAN: Yukka-San, 1983.

About Men. Malmo, Sweden: Raben and Sjogren, 1983.

With Child: A Diary of Motherhood. Paris, FRANCE: Des Femmes, 1983.

1982

With Child: A Diary of Motherhood. Malmo, SWEDEN: Raben and Sjogren, 1982.

About Men. Paris, FRANCE: Des Femmes, 1982.

1981

With Child: A Diary of Motherhood. New York, NY: Berkeley Paperback, 1981.
With Child: A Diary of Motherhood. Amsterdam, HOLLAND: Uitgeverij De Arbeiderspers, 1981.

1980

About Men. Copenhagen, DENMARK: Gyldendahl, 1980.
About Men. New York, NY: Bantam Paperback, 1980.
With Child: A Diary of Motherhood. Hamburg, GERMANY: Rowohlt, 1980.
"With Child. A Diary of Motherhood." *American Baby*, May 1980.
"Motherhood Journal." *Ms Magazine*, January 1980.

1979

With Child: A Diary of Motherhood. New York, NY: Lippincott & Crowell, 1979.
About Men. Hamburg, GERMANY: Rowohlt, 1979.
About Men. Amsterdam, HOLLAND: Uitgeverij De Arbeiderspers, 1979.
"Celebration of Life." *Redbook*, February 1979.

1978

About Men. New York, NY: Simon and Schuster, 1978.
About Men. London, ENGLAND: The Women's Press, 1978.
"Sons and Fathers." *New York Times*, April 13, 1978.
"A Psychologist Takes on Male Mythology." *Ms Magazine*, April 1978.
"Men: Why Male Friendship Is a Myth." *Mademoiselle*, February 1978.

1977

Women, Money and Power. New York, NY: Bantam Paperback, 1977.
Women and Madness. Torino, ITALY: Einaudi, 1977.

1976

Women, Money and Power. New York, NY: William Morrow & Company, 1976.

1975

Women and Madness. Paris, FRANCE: Edition Payot, 1975.

1974

Women and Madness. London, ENGLAND: Penguin Books, 1974.
Women and Madness. Hamburg, GERMANY: Rowohlt, 1974.
Women and Madness. Amsterdam, HOLLAND: Uitgeverij De Arbeiderspers, 1974.

1973

Women and Madness. New York, NY: Avon Paperback, 1973.

"Sex Role Stereotyping and Adjustment." *Psychology of Adjustment*, James F. Adams (ed.), Holbrook Press, 1973.

"Women as Psychotherapeutic Patients." *Women's Studies: An Interdisciplinary Journal*, Spring, 1973.

"Psychological Differentiation and the Response of Opiate Addicts to Pharmacological Treatment." Stanley Feldstein, Phyllis Chesler and Max Fink. *British Journal of Addiction*, Vol. 68, 1973.

"A Word about Mental Health and Women." *Mental Hygiene*, Summer 1973.

1972

Women and Madness. New York, NY: Doubleday and Company, 1972.

"The Amazon Legacy: An Interpretive Essay." *Wonder Woman*, New York, NY: Holt, Rinehart and Winston, Inc., 1972.

"Women and Mental Illness." *Women: Resources for a Changing World*, The Radcliffe Institute, Radcliffe College, October 1972.

"Images–From Sanity's View." *Ms Magazine*, December 1972.

"Are We a Threat to Each Other?" *Ms Magazine*, October 1972.

"Women and Madness." *Ms Magazine*, July 1972.

"The Sensuous Psychiatrists." *New York Magazine*, June 1972.

1971

"Patient and Patriarch: Women in the Psychotherapeutic Relationship" in *Women in Sexist Society: Studies in Power and Powerlessness*. Vivian Gornick and Barbara K. Moran (eds.), San Francisco: Basic Books, June 1971.

"Women as Psychotherapeutic Patients." *Journal of Marriage and the Family*, October 1971.

"Women and Psychotherapy." *The Radical Therapist*, September 1970. Reprinted in *The International Socialist Review*, November 1970: *The Radical Therapist Collective Anthology*, Jerome Agel (ed.), Ballantine Books, September 1971.

"Men Drive Women Crazy." *Psychology Today*, July 1971.

1969

"Playing Instant Joy in the Lonely Crowd." *The Village Voice*, December 25, 1969.

"Maternal Influence in Learning by Observation in Kittens." *Science*, November 1969 v. 166; 901-903.

"Memoirs of Afghanistan." *Mademoiselle*, June, 1969.

1968

"Observation Learning in Cats." E.R. John, P. Chesler, I. Victor, P. Bartlett, *Science*, v. 159, 1489-90, 1968.

Incest:
A Journey to Hullabaloo

Louise Armstrong

We have heard a lot, in recent years, about what incest causes (disorders like depression, drug-addiction, dissociation . . .). I suppose you could say that, in me, it caused feminism.

That may be a shade facile, but still–you could not have found an *unlikelier* candidate to pin *radical feminist politico* on in all of early 1970s New York City. An advertising copywriter, no less, and *married,* and with twin sons. Sure, I was also publishing books, but they were humorous little things that explained a few puzzling phenomena–like Freud,[1] economics, micro and macro,[2] and international relations.[3]

Surely there was nothing *feminist* in trying to follow and explain the logic of common belief systems. Or was there?

Perhaps once you make the discovery of the power of junk system-language to construct a reality everybody *believes,* once you

Louise Armstrong's work has focused on incest and issues of violence against women and children, and the role assigned psychiatry/psychology as society's clean-up crew on these issues, since the mid-1970s. Her most recent book is *Rocking the Cradle of Sexual Politics, What Happened When Women Said Incest* (Addison-Wesley, 1994).

Correspondence may be addressed to Louise Armstrong, c/o Addison-Wesley, 170 Fifth Avenue, New York, NY 10010.

[Haworth co-indexing entry note]: "Incest: A Journey to Hullabaloo." Armstrong, Louise. Co-published simultaneously in *Women & Therapy* (The Haworth Press, Inc.) Vol. 17, No. 1/2, 1995, pp. 25-31; and: *Feminist Foremothers in Women's Studies, Psychology, and Mental Health* (ed: Phyllis Chesler, Esther D. Rothblum, and Ellen Cole) The Haworth Press, Inc., 1995, pp. 25-31; and: *Feminist Foremothers in Women's Studies, Psychology, and Mental Health* (ed: Phyllis Chesler, Esther D. Rothblum, and Ellen Cole) Harrington Park Press, an imprint of The Haworth Press, Inc., 1995, pp. 25-31. Single or multiple copies of this article are available from The Haworth Document Delivery Service [1-800-342-9678, 9:00 a.m. - 5:00 p.m. (EST)].

intuit that power systems run on group faith in them–you've taken a step toward intuiting the power of *naming.* And perhaps once you've begun to question thought systems that are taken for givens, once you've begun to analyze their relationship to your experience of reality–you can no longer draw the intellectual capital you need in the currency available at the Automated Belief Machines.

But if, in me, incest caused feminism, it did not do so in a vacuum.

In the 1970s, feminist literature boldly addressed the need for social change–as distinct from later emphasis on social and economic access. It was a vibrant force, both in the market and in the marketplace of ideas. Women were speaking out forcefully on rape as a male crime of violence against women. Wife-battering, too– now widely referred to as "spousal assault"–was analyzed as an issue of male prerogative, male right.

It was in this climate that I began thinking about what had happened to me–and wondering why no one was talking about that. (I did not know, then, that a few radical feminists like Florence Rush already had.) It was in this climate that I absorbed the concept: The personal is political. The idea formed to offer a forum within which women would explore our common experience, and see what we could identify as the commonalities of our experience–that would help us identify what it was that had happened to us that had meaning beyond the individual.

I was certain there *were* other women out there. The publishers were less so ("Incest is certainly a *sensational* subject, but since it's so rare, who would the readers be?"). But I did get a book contract.[4] I advertised, mainly in the then-abundant feminist press. And letters poured in from women, and they phoned, and we met, and we talked, and we corresponded.

And what emerged was a sharing that was truly elegant: a collective journey of discovery.

And what we discovered was brilliantly simple, and utterly inescapable: different though our individual stories may have been, our fathers had all done this to us not in spite of the fact that they knew it was wrong, but because they believed it was *their right,* or at least justifiable. What we discovered was that incest was among the male violences against women and children long-permitted through history–sometimes tacitly, sometimes explicitly. And that abuse of the child was often intended as violence against the wife (our mothers)–that, in a crazy way, we'd been caught in the cradle of sexual politics.

To know this was to know that children's issues were inextricably linked to women's issues–that both belonged under the umbrella of feminism.

This was epiphany. This was the "click."

One thing more I learned: that because I was calling for social change, for social censure of male behaviors that had historically been routine and uncensured–I was not only a feminist. I was a radical feminist.

And what *was* the mainstream view of the widespread paternal rape of children (which it had taken feminists to expose)? It was as a mental health problem. Virtually from the moment we spoke out, mental health professionals had been society's appointed social sanitation engineers. It was to newfound "experts" among their ranks that the powers-that-be turned to defuse the "discovery" of the rampant patriarchal tyranny, the sexual slavery, that is incest.

They said it should be "decriminalized." They said it was no more than a "symptom of family dysfunction." "Family dysfunction," it quickly turned out, was code. And what it was code for was: *She* made me do it, my wife. (This was change of a kind: it *had* been, She made me do it, my daughter.) And so they unveiled, for our oohing and ahing–the real culprit, the "incest *mother*." And I began speaking and writing about this turn of events, the medicalization of child-rape and of all crimes in the home.

And even as I wrote, paternal child rape was being tied into a noose to hang those the new experts identified as the real culprits: the mothers who "failed to protect." Those who "knew or *should have known*." And I watched as mental health ideology, mental health language coalesced into a great shield covering the entire issue, impermeable by reality. I watched as, in 1984, social work sentimentality promised salvation for Amelia in the ABC made-for-TV movie, "Something About Amelia"–and the actor-daddy said he was ashamed of himself, and the actress-mother looked as though, after a suitable period of *family* "treatment" (during which she acknowledged she *had* made him do it), she might welcome poor-ashamed-of-himself daddy back into the marital bed.

This even as (as I watched) more and more kids in real life were being yanked from mothers who not only did not know she'd made him do it, but didn't even know until just this minute he *was* doing it. Even as more and more mothers were being charged with "failure to protect."

Hot damn, I said then, What next (I said then)? They'll arrest the women? Sure enough, next thing–they were arresting the mothers who, the minute they did find out, rose up and acted to protect the children; mothers who were having none of this "family treatment"–mothers who then, alas, discovered they were not now cooperating, not now fulfilling their role of "incest mother" as recently scripted. And so now–with psychiatrists and psychologists eager to certify these mothers as vindictive–the women were now "diagnosed" as hysterical. These women were found to be *in contempt* for refusing to turn their child over to a rapist. And so I included this new assault by mental health medical personnel in what I wrote.[5]

Was I contributing to feminist mental health with this assault on the mental health scions? I thought so. (I think so still.) Because by now it was clear to me that what they sought was dominion over this now visibly sizable and potentially profitable issue. And it seemed clear to those scions (as it was to me) that for mental health ideology to win, feminist analysis had to lose.

And so I spoke about this, wrote about this. And what is funny is–I still thought we could win. Even as I watched, and the celebration of treatment was joined by the celebration of "prevention" and more experts arose selling programs to teach children about the sanctity of their "bathing suit area" (as though little kids, thus armed, could stop daddies)–I still thought we could make ourselves heard.

And even as I thought that, things got worse. Under glossy theories about children's "best interests" (being the right to a loving father), more and more kids were court-ordered to live with their rapists–removed from the mother who attempted rescue, though in the eyes of the experts she was attempting to impede the child's best interests.

More and more kids were, alternatively, subjected to "social rescue"–the opportunity to experience foster care. And here, too, the mental health professionals were busy. Their dire warnings about what incest *caused* placed more and more kids who spoke up under mental health surveillance, at risk of psychiatric institutionalization. And so I (what else?) spoke and wrote about this.[6]

But mental health ideology had already triumphed. And one sign of that triumph was that these issues—the issues of what happened to child-victims of incest in this brave new world following feminists' breaking the silence—were not perceived as being feminist. By now the issue of children had been segregated from the issue of adult survivors, swallowed by child welfare experts, dominated by that set of mental health professionals specializing in "incested" children.

Because by now (I am speaking of the late 1980s, early 1990s here) all that was recognizably feminist had been obliterated from the entire issue of incest, as more and more adult survivors were swallowed into the great Recovery Movement Maw; as we were inundated with evangelical calls to Healing; as women were everywhere importuned to Gain Empowerment—by turning their power over to psychological experts. Instead of (as we had hoped) feminist analysis prevailing on the issue of incest, the recovery movement had hijacked the issue and silenced feminist analysis.

By now, incest had long since been declared "gender neutral." Victims were genderless; offenders were genderless. Indeed, they were almost spectral. Those few who were spotlighted had long-since learned to recite the exculpatory mantra: not only had their wives made them do it, but their mothers had made them rapists by letting their fathers "do it" to them when they were children.

The entire focus was on what incest *caused*—all those disorders, all those diseases. No one, any longer, spoke of the societally, the historically, sanctioned right of males to sexually violate their children. No one spoke of the grotesque abuse of power, of the sense of male entitlement, that caused incest.

It is common, now, to speak of the *backlash* on the issue of incest. It is most often referred to in connection with the newest manufactured "syndrome," False Memory Syndrome (the one that followed False Accusation Syndrome, and Parental Alienation Syndrome.) No one points out that the rise of the mental health ideology—beginning at the very moment when we first spoke out—was itself backlash.

"Decriminalization" was backlash. "Family dysfunction" was

backlash. The "cycle of violence" is backlash: it feeds the idea that incest is a public health problem, not a problem of male predation. (Worse, it acts as a prediction of doom, telling children that it is their destiny to become that which they so fiercely hate–molesters.) The recovery movement with its primary focus on incest as the victim's pathology is backlash: it individualizes–makes the problem medical; it infantilizes women, and makes of their suffering medical curiosity. It sells community in frailty, not in feminism. The sequestering of the children-now issue, the issue of protective mothers, from the adult survivor issue is backlash: it fractures the picture, is divisive. It leads to status quo, not social change.

And it is all cozily capitalism-compatible.

What is my major contribution to the field of feminist mental health? (Smile.) Simply to, one way and another, keep trying to remind women that the therapeutic *ideology*–which turns women into patients and inmates–has always been antithetical to feminism: that when this ideology wins, feminism loses. All of which I now, again, say.[7]

Since the instruction sheet for this paper says most emphatically that *this is no time to be modest*, I will offer what the September 1, 1994 Kirkus review says of my recent informal history of the issue of incest: "An important, incendiary, unapologetic history written in hopes of rekindling the possibility of radical change–nothing less than a redistribution of gender power."

Such language.

And in 1994, no less.

Shocking.

As for me, personally? How did my life change personally? (Older and wiser, girls; older and wiser.) I've come a ways, certainly–from product campaigns to social change campaigns. (I'd certainly have made more money the old way.) On a more serious plane, the personal remains, for me, profoundly tied to the political.

Optimism is a struggle (far more than it once was). Pessimism is unbearable. To stand on neither side of an ever-tensing polarity is to feel excluded, to feel–well, yes: alone. The energy and passion that informed our early protests are now dismissed as unstylish. The clarity, the naming, is labeled simplistic. The humor that leavened the early stages of the journey is now taken for sacrilege.

Do I believe there will come a time soon when women will, on this issue, once again listen to their own voices, follow their own moral compass toward their own defined goals–independent of "experts"? I need to believe that if I continue to hope for change.

For all the talk of *listening to the children*, in a very important sense the children continue unheard. Their voices come to us through interpreters. Do I believe we will ever start really listening to the kids themselves? Again, I need to believe that if I continue to hope for change.

And of course I *do* quite profoundly hope for change.

I've been down all the fascinating highways and byways that radiate out from this issue so far.

It's been one hell of a trip.

For all the curlicues, filigree, and baroquery, however–and for all the syndromes, disorders, and experts–I remain as convinced as ever that we were not incorrect the first time out in identifying incest as the cradle of sexual politics.

We gave it a push.

The bough is still holding.

The cradle's still rocking.

And I'll be watching (and most likely writing and speaking about) whatever it is that happens next.

NOTES

1. *A Child's Guide to Freud* (Simon & Schuster, 1963) illustrated by Whitney Darrow.

2. *How to Turn Lemons into Money, A Child's Guide to Economics* (Harcourt Brace Jovanovich, 1975); *How to Turn Up into Down into Up, A Child's Guide to Inflation, Depression, and Economic Recovery* (HBJ, 1978).

3. *How to Turn War into Peace, A Child's Guide to Conflict Resolution* (HBJ, 1979).

4. *Kiss Daddy Goodnight* (Hawthorn, 1978; Pocket Books, 1979; 1987).

5. *The Home Front, Notes from the Family War Zone* (McGraw-Hill, 1983).

6. *Solomon Says, A Speakout on Foster Care* (Pocket Books, 1979); *And They Call It Help, The Psychiatric Policing of America's Children* (Addison-Wesley, 1993).

7. *Rocking the Cradle of Sexual Politics, What Happened When Women Said Incest* (Addison-Wesley, 1994).

Working with the Light:
Women of Vision

Nancy Azara
Roxanne M. Green

" . . . like amnesiacs
in a ward on fire, we must
find words
or burn. "

—Olga Broumas "Artemis"

In a true metaphor of feminist collaboration, sculptor Nancy Azara offers her spirit of art, therapy, and women's healing as testimony to the evolution of feminist culture. Like a blues

Nancy Azara is a sculptor whose work–carved, painted, and gold leafed wood–is about female energy and power. She teaches workshops on art and the unconscious both nationally and in Europe. Her sculpture and collages are shown at museums and galleries around the country and she is represented in New York City by the E. M. Donahue Gallery.

Roxanne Green is a PhD student studying Comparative Cultures and Literary Studies at the University of Arizona in Tucson, AZ. She is a licensed addiction counselor and feminist psychotherapist whose main interest is studying feminist theory and literature. She is pursuing a writing and teaching career.

Correspondence may be addressed to Nancy Azara, 91 Franklin Street, New York, NY 10013.

[Haworth co-indexing entry note]: "Working with the Light: Women of Vision." Azara, Nancy, and Roxanne M. Green. Co-published simultaneously in *Women & Therapy* (The Haworth Press, Inc.) Vol. 17, No. 1/2, 1995, pp. 33-42; and: *Feminist Foremothers in Women's Studies, Psychology, and Mental Health* (ed: Phyllis Chesler, Esther D. Rothblum, and Ellen Cole) The Haworth Press, Inc., 1995, pp. 33-42; and: *Feminist Foremothers in Women's Studies, Psychology, and Mental Health* (ed: Phyllis Chesler, Esther D. Rothblum, and Ellen Cole) Harrington Park Press, an imprint of The Haworth Press, Inc., 1995, pp. 33-42. Single or multiple copies of this article are available from The Haworth Document Delivery Service [1-800-342-9678, 9:00 a.m. - 5:00 p.m. (EST)].

chord that reaches way down deep to hook a dangling piece of heart, she fosters a complicated aching in a world of colors and textures. In her work, art, relationship, and therapy merge to evoke in women the unacknowledged in their lives, to make them visible and to give them reflection. The more our own experience is kept invisible from others, the more it becomes inaccessible to ourselves. The essence of women's art, therapy, and feminism is the migration across the boundaries of patriarchy and the transmigration with each other. This enables a journey home by literally making these experiences visible through women's art work, passing along our foremothers' culture. This is an invitation to enter the bloodhut and join the other women in the initiation of Azara's sculpture and her artmaking through a filter of feminist psychological theory centered in affiliation, engagement, and connection to others. Women's journeys to art lie in living in the tension of opposites–the beautiful, the brutal–that defines them and speaks to our existential guilt and the tension of creating our lives.

WORKING WITH THE LIGHT

A feminist therapist and writer once described my work as a critique of a masculine-oriented culture–a culture that values separatism, conquest, and dominance at the expense of a focus on the expansiveness of the unconscious self and of a spiritual reference. My art reflects the struggle of women. I want to broaden the idea of political struggle to offer it also as a journey within. This migration parallels concepts of shamanism and a very personal journey to find the unacknowledged truths. Delving into the self brings up the struggle that is there and in that struggle and discovery is meaning about ourselves and others. When women work this way, they stop being so foreign to each other and to themselves because they take the designs from their journey and make these healing designs visible to themselves and each other. They become a communal gift.

One of the reasons I am an artist is because art is a visual language, a graphic manifestation of the way I think and feel. Unfortunately, we learn very little culturally about using visual information to describe our lives. By developing a visual sense, a visual form, and a visual presence, and/or by also being an onlooker or a viewer of a work that has a visual presence, we enter a more spacious, broader dimension than words can offer. Realizing this visual dimension as a possibility for wisdom, as well as an expression of experience, is why I began to make art. The more I do so, the more interested I become in looking at the unconscious, my unconscious, and at the unconscious of others, that deeper place inside of us.

Women have had little opportunity to describe this place verbally or visually. In the late 1960s and the early 1970s, I began to describe the experience of women by describing myself. I wanted to excavate these parts of myself, to give them presence, and to testify to those who wished to know–to show them what I had found–and to acknowledge that someone was listening. My art work and my teaching are an expression of feminism. My work provides evidence of the politics and spirituality of my everyday life and the form of my, our, own experience as women.

My sculpture is made of wood carved from trees. The carved wood is often assembled, several pieces put together to make the whole. It is painted and it is gold leafed. I find the wood that I use on the streets of New York City, the beaches of the Dominican Republic, the shores of Northern Minnesota, and other places.

Some of the wood that comes from the streets of New York is battered and unattractive, but when I begin to carve into it, the wood's beauty is revealed. Using raw material from different places allows the trees to offer different meanings to my work. In this way, my art is about discovering and reclaiming both the spirit of the tree and my own spirit.

Trees have been traditionally used as a metaphor for the human self, frequently for women. When I carve the tree I engage with the history of the life within it. I listen to it, so that the tree participates with me in the experience of becoming a sculpture. I am carving an object that was once animate and has that presence embodied within. When I carve into it, I release the quality that is treasured there. I speak with it. The carving resuscitates the life that's been held in stasis.

There is a symbolic connection for me in this respect as well as an intention of collaboration that I bring to the tree. Tree and human have a long connection to each other. There are many sacred trees in the world's religions. The tree becoming sculpture represents a way for me to parallel and illustrate our history as women. It echoes a memory of what went before and as I carve it, it changes into a newer, stronger, more timely, more relevant presence. By working with the sculpture, carving and listening to the trees, I can find the voice within, the infinite female self.

Many cultures believe that the tree speaks when we commune with it. It is an inner voice like the voice we seek in therapy. Through this dialogue we begin a migration to the heavens and an immigration to our own meanings. The tree represents the essential part in a shamanic sense, connected to the spine of the human. The roots of the tree are the base of the spine. As the tree climbs with its energy reaching up to its leaves, its energy, our energy, connects us to the heavens. It is believed that in this climb toward the heavens we are transformed in our relationships with the earth, with other women, and with ourselves.

The sculpture I make tries to create this climb. In the process of working on it, it becomes animate for me. I believe that this is what happens with really good art–it has a life of its own. In like manner, women engaging in therapy develop a life of their own, separate from the cultural dictates that denied and restricted them. I see their evolution in its own way, as the birth of an art form, the makings of their inner paintings and sculptures.

Part of what I'm doing as an artist and healer is trying to understand that place in us that is both beautiful and brutal–that place we consistently have to live with–two parts of the many parts of ourselves. I believe we have to make some kind of peace with this tension in order to live our lives, to follow our vision.

I paint and color the wood, often with handmade paint and gold leaf. It dresses and clothes the wood, so to speak, so that the actual forms begin to develop the presence of garments. In the sculpture, gold leaf represents the spirit light one finds deep inside, the life force. I try to bring this beauty–this life force–into the open. The stronger the presence of radiant gold appears, the more I work with the sculpture and the clearer this life force becomes. Gold leaf symbolizes sunlight, without which none of us can experience life. Its glow gives a wake-up call to a voice from our distant past. It is similar to finding our own symbols in therapy or in relationships with others. We use this new knowledge as our spine or our skeleton, and we flesh it out with each new piece of insight or sensory experience or memory.

I also introduce spirals into my sculpture. They speak of the journey to the center of the psyche, a step toward wisdom. I created a sculpture called "Double Yoke," a yoke shaped piece of wood literally sliced in two and re-formed. When it is viewed you get the feeling of a former split which is now joined together, a merging, an invitation to come in and look at the spiral's journey. The yoke is split in two now and pointed upwards so it speaks about the confines of a yoke as just the memory and history of its bondage.

The Sculpture "Fertile Goddess" is made with ripe forms that I use frequently. They're nubile contours, little seed pods that seem to be growing out of the space that holds them. The "Fertile Goddess" talks about mature womanhood, about desire strongly stated and about dual exchange of passion.

The piece called "Tender Goddess" invites you to visit a deep center with a symbolic heart of tender red branches at its core. It talks to the heart of the young sapling in all of us. It cautions us to be careful with our hearts, to treat them gently, with empathy and nurturing for ourselves. "Tender Goddess" is about compassion for ourselves, bringing tenderness to our hearts.

I think women are more receptive to my work now, especially to the ideas of women's issues, than they were five or six years ago. Many women have learned that there are other ways to define ourselves than by the confusion and pain we've experienced. If we sort out the confusion, we can move through it to the other side, where there is the beautiful and enigmatic balance of life and death. This is what I wanted to portray in the piece "Goddess Wall," a free-standing 12-foot sculpture about grappling with a psychic confusion and coming into the bright light found in the darkness.

Moving through pain and confusion requires that we discriminate between what benefits us and what interferes with our freedom to create. Once we do this, we no longer feel as if we're drowning in it. In that "wrestling with the angels," we also see the light as being extraordinary and exquisite, offering us an opportunity to work with those two facets, pain and light, back and forth. Life is pain and suffering as well as joy and beauty. This is inescapable. There is always frustration. We have to live with the knowledge of this tension, but we don't have to drown in it. My art came more from pain and confusion when I was younger. Now it comes from a kaleidoscope of the brutal as well as the extraordinary excitement and joy of the beautiful.

Women are also more responsive to my art work, perhaps because they intuitively sense the quality of initiation I envision when I create. I am reminded of the elders who sat with the young Native American girls during the menstruation rituals in order to soothe them and explain to them the honor they were experiencing. These young girls needed someone to translate their confusion and the new changes in their lives. Women recently are more curious, more willing to have a dialogue with my work. I believe the more we become self aware and self confident, the more we can see and understand, the more we can work to change the world. That's real political change. That is the core of my teaching.

I feel that my workshops have evolved from the wisdom that I developed from making art. As I keep working, as I keep making art, the process is so healing–listening to the trees, listening to yourself during the process when you make art–because it's just you and the silence. It's you and your inner voice. This silence gave me an awareness that has led me to not only express it in the actual practical material work that is the made art but then to take this understanding and translate it into the experience of sharing it with others in a classroom situation.

WOMEN OF VISION

In 1979 I founded a feminist art school called the New York Feminist Art Institute/Women's Center for Learning (NYFAI) with five other women. I taught a workshop called "Visual Diaries, Consciousness-Raising, Art Making." We chose a topic in the standard consciousness-raising manner and went around the room, with each woman speaking about her own experience. What made this gathering different from other consciousness-raising groups was that all the women drew in a book as other women were talking. By the end of the evening everyone in the room had a visual diary, a visual record, of what was being said.

I developed this method because I originally started doing this for myself in my visual diary during my own consciousness-raising group in the early '70s. I initially wanted to figure out if I could visually describe what was being said during those meetings. It was an unsuccessful endeavor in that sense because what I was able to describe was something other than the words spoken. Something else came onto the page–the emotional import, the feelings, the kind of emotional dialogue that was happening for the evening–a whole new presence beyond words. While I was doing this for myself I began to see new things about myself revealed in the diaries and to find my own original forms as an artist which I had ignored because they didn't adhere to the formulas for art making I had learned in art school.

While teaching the class, I started to work with this concept of removing the formulas for making art as well as living life. The point of the process was to find one's own inner language and to discover one's own inner experience through participating in the consciousness-raising group. Facilitating this kind of a workshop showed me how important changing and shifting things in women was. However, it wasn't reaching the depths it could because women weren't able to guide themselves deeper into their unconscious where the more powerful changes originate.

I began to devise new workshops based in part on the Eastern philosophies, such as Hinduism and Tibetan Buddhism, that I had been studying. These workshops used guided meditation to take women deep into their unconscious to find their inner forms and their inner language. In describing these forms in drawing, painting, and sculpting, the participants were able to confront and dialogue with the enemies in their head as well as identify their friends. Workshops such as "Art Making as an Act of Healing," "Visual Diaries/Inner Journeying," "Images of the Spirit Wheel," and "Building Spirit Houses: A Sculpture Workshop" step beyond the kind of experience of the consciousness-raising in the initial classes. Out of these new workshops came more definitive, deeper shifts in women's lives. (Most of the classes were taken by women even though a few men have attended the workshops. Everyone is welcome, from the curious about art making to and including the professional artist.)

Two things resulted from these workshops: First, the parts of ourselves hidden in the recesses of our minds surfaced and became accessible. They were undeveloped, unformed, fragmented experiences. Sometimes what was discovered held anger, sometimes fear, sometimes joy. Frequently they were from traumas long since vanished from consciousness. By realizing and recognizing them, by getting them out in the open, by drawing and painting them, a new awareness came into being.

Second, women found their own creative language in the painting and sculptures. The formulas learned in art school by women trained as artists were devised by men. Underneath were the deeper visions they wanted to express in their art. Many of the women who came to these workshops had stopped being artists because they couldn't find anything to say after their formal training. They were lost because they had been pressured in art school to work so much from the structure that they lost where they were with themselves and were not able to express their inner visions. They were no longer excited about making art. But the workshops offered these women a new sense of creative thought by excavating the old, forgotten blockages which had prevented them from achieving.

Teaching has given me new insights, new excitement about how other people interpret the meditations. I design these journeys into the inner self, these guided meditations. All sixteen women in the room will create different images, pictures, and experiences from the same meditation. I gain so much from listening to them about their lives. I feel invited to grow and develop. In turn, I invite women to express themselves through the workshops. "Building Spirit Houses: A Sculpture Workshop" is for people who want to create sculptures that emanate from their inner spirits, offering visible homes as sacred structures and sanctuaries of wisdom. Drawing from the writings of Christian mystics such as Theresa of Avila, Hildegard of Bingen, and Julian of Norwich as well as being inspired by Tibetan Buddhists, Chogyam Trungpa and Soygal Rinpoche and the Native American healer Hyemeyohsts Storm, I devise and shape stories from ancient myths and my own psyche to serve as guided meditations.

If I were to work with you in the "Building Spirit Houses: A Sculpture Workshop," I would begin by asking you to close your eyes for a moment, listen to the cadence of your own heart, the sound of yourself. Imagine yourself in a circle of trusted women beneath a thatched canopy of trees. Follow your breath as it traces your blood's path throughout your body. Slowly, release your body's aches with each breath and imagine my voice speaking gently in the soothing, promising rhythm of the storyteller. Come look at this journey and I'll shift something in you. Commit yourself to looking inside, to opening your inner eye, and you can share this journey and interpret the journey for yourself, for your own wisdom. You can paint, draw, and build it.

In the first several sessions of this workshop, I will guide you to the path of a sacred mountain and you will make an entrance through the mountain to your interior selves. You will search for a Spirit House with many rooms inside, housing different parts of your emotions and intellect. Later I will ask you to walk into the basement of your house and retrieve many unresolved parts of your psyche from the darkness. In this journey you will look at the structure of your house, how it is built, what its door is made of, the construction of the stairway to the basement and so forth. Then you will draw, paint, and construct an actual replica of what you see and feel.

In the middle of the workshop you will be asked to find seven major rooms: one room represents your will to live, another holds your decision making, another your love. Again, after guided meditation I will invite you to visually describe the different rooms you find by adding to your art work. On the fifth day, having been through the different rooms, the walls, the windows, etc., you will come to a place that is the central axis for your house, representing your goals for the future held deep within you. You look for a means of implementing the changes you find and then build this information into your house. At the end of the week each of you will have created your own house sculpture influenced by my story and by others in the group but nonetheless an amazingly unique art work.

In this method, women work at their own pace, using their imagination as a window to the unconscious. The guided meditation, with its flowering of the imagination, catches the unconscious as it is—initially unaware. After a while, as women learn that this kind of exploration is safe and healing and valuable (it usually takes about two days for this to happen), they relax and their imagination and their unconscious begin to work together, bringing forth major gifts of wisdom and understanding for their personal use.

What would I say to women today? Everyone can draw, just as everyone can learn to speak or write. Everyone can express themselves. If you ask a three year old to draw and give them crayons or paints, they will have no trouble. Approach your own adventure in the same manner. Express yourself. Look inside of you–it's all there. Everything you need, everything you want, has its seed inside you. Allow yourself to listen.

REFERENCE

Broumas, Olga (1977). *Beginning with o*. London: Yale University Press.

Working on Gender
as a Gender-Nonconformist

Sandra Lipsitz Bem

In October of 1993, I was asked to give a lecture on the connection between my life and my work for a conference on Women and Scholarship at Elmira College. Having just finished reading my book entitled *The Lenses of Gender,* one of the coordinators for the conference, Kathleen Gayle, spontaneously came up with exactly the right title for my lecture and thereby helped me to crystallize one of the things about my approach to gender that makes it feel, if not unique, then at least distinctively mine. Because, as I hope you will see after reading this adaptation of my lecture, no superficially plausible identity categories could have possibly worked instead of the category she came up with. I do not work on gender as a woman, or as a lesbian, or as a Jew, or as a psychologist, or even as a garden-variety feminist. No, the sensibility that I bring to my

Sandra Bem, PhD, is Professor of Psychology and Women's Studies at Cornell University. From 1978-1985, she was also Director of the Women's Studies Program. For the past three years, she has been one of Cornell's two senior sexual harassment counselors–which means that she was in charge of "prosecuting" the case that led to the resignation of a tenured professor–and she has also been actively involved in the institutionalization of Cornell's Lesbian, Gay, and Bisexual Studies Program.

Correspondence may be addressed to Sandra Bem, PhD, Department of Psychology, Uris Hall, Cornell University, Ithaca, NY 14853.

[Haworth co-indexing entry note]: "Working on Gender as a Gender-Nonconformist." Bem, Sandra Lipsitz. Co-published simultaneously in *Women & Therapy* (The Haworth Press, Inc.) Vol. 17, No. 1/2, 1995, pp. 43-53; and: *Feminist Foremothers in Women's Studies, Psychology, and Mental Health* (ed: Phyllis Chesler, Esther D. Rothblum, and Ellen Cole) The Haworth Press, Inc., 1995, pp. 43-53; and: *Feminist Foremothers in Women's Studies, Psychology, and Mental Health* (ed: Phyllis Chesler, Esther D. Rothblum, and Ellen Cole) Harrington Park Press, an imprint of The Haworth Press, Inc., 1995, pp. 43-53. Single or multiple copies of this article are available from The Haworth Document Delivery Service [1-800-342-9678, 9:00 a.m. - 5:00 p.m. (EST)].

43

work on gender is that of the gender nonconformist, the outsider, the misfit, who can see the culture's socially and historically constructed categories because they have always been so alien to my sense of self.

Let me begin to clarify what it means that I work on gender as a gender nonconformist by quoting extensively from my preface to *The Lenses of Gender*. In essence, what I said there was that although I had lived monogamously with a man I loved for twenty-eight years, I was not then and never had been "a heterosexual." But neither had I ever been either a "lesbian" or a "bisexual." Rather, I wrote:

> What I am–and have been for as long as I can remember–is someone whose sexuality and gender have never seemed to mesh with the available cultural categories, and *that* . . . is what has most profoundly informed not only my feminist politics but also the theoretical analysis of this book.
>
> When I say that my sexuality does not mesh with the available cultural categories, I mean that the sex-of-partner dimension implicit in the three categories of heterosexual, homosexual, and bisexual seems irrelevant to my own particular pattern of erotic attractions and sexual experiences. Although some of the (very few) individuals to whom I have been attracted during my forty-seven years have been men and some have been women, what those individuals have in common has nothing to do with either their biological sex or mine–from which I conclude, not that I am attracted to both sexes, but that my sexuality is organized around dimensions other than sex.
>
> Similarly, when I say that my gender does not mesh with the available cultural categories, I mean that since earliest childhood, my own particular blend of temperament and behavior has not only seemed to fall outside the categories of male and female, masculine and feminine; indeed, being female has never seemed a salient feature of my self-concept. Like being human, it is a fact, but a taken-for-granted background fact rather than a nucleus around which I have constructed my identity. (Being a feminist, on the other hand, is such a nucleus.)
>
> Living in a heterosexual marriage and rearing two children

have also contributed to my feminist politics by prompting me to theorize about, and experiment with, both egalitarian relationships and gender-liberated child-rearing. But it is still my subjective sense of being outside the categories of my culture that has most profoundly contributed to my feminist politics, because it has enabled me to see how cultural categories construct and constrain social reality by providing the historically specific conceptual framework through which we perceive our social world.

My ability to understand and to articulate this insight in the domain of gender and sexuality has evolved dramatically over the past twenty years. In the early 1970s, I focused almost exclusively on the concept of androgyny (from the Greek terms *andro*, meaning male, and *gyne*, meaning female) because that concept seemed to challenge the traditional categories of masculine and feminine as nothing before had ever done. By the late 1970s and early 1980s, however, I had begun to see that the concept of androgyny inevitably focuses so much more attention on the individual's being both masculine and feminine than on the culture's having created the concepts of masculinity and femininity in the first place that it can legitimately be said to reproduce precisely the gender polarization that it seeks to undercut. Accordingly, I moved on to the concept of gender schematicity because it enabled me to argue even more forcefully that masculinity and femininity are merely the constructions of a cultural schema–or lens–that polarizes gender.

Finally, in this book, I theorize the concept of the gender-polarizing lens more completely than I did before, and I expand the underlying insight into a comprehensive analysis of how a society's gender lenses systemically perpetuate not only the oppression of women but the oppression of sexual minorities as well. Specifically, I now believe there are actually *three* gender lenses embedded in the culture: gender polarization, androcentrism, and biological essentialism.

These three gender lenses provide the foundation for a theory of how biology, culture, and the individual psyche all interact in historical context to systemically reproduce male power. . . . [They also enable me] to write the book that, as a younger feminist struggling to make sense of the oppression of women and of sexual minorities, I would have most wanted to have read.

There are two implicit subtexts in both this preface and my book that have been with me since I first began working on gender in 1966 and that derive directly from my working on gender as a gender nonconformist.

Subtext #1: The central political passion in both my life and my work has never been to challenge the subordination or marginalization of women per se–which I sometimes describe as feminism's first moral imperative. Instead, my central passion has always been to challenge the longstanding cultural belief in some kind of a natural link or match between the sex of one's body and the character of one's psyche and one's sexuality.

This commitment to what I think of as feminism's second moral imperative clearly derives from my lifelong sense of being outside the culture's sex and gender categories. And where it takes me, both intellectually and politically, is to a vision of feminism and feminist scholarship that struggles to embrace both of these moral imperatives at the same time. That's why *The Lenses of Gender* theorizes–and argues for the dismantling of–both androcentrism and gender polarization. And that's also why it makes no conceptual separation between its analysis of sexism and its analysis of heterosexism. Instead, the cultural requirement that one be exclusively heterosexual is treated as but a special case (albeit the most culturally institutionalized and emotionally loaded case) of the more general requirement that one must not violate the culture's androcentric, gender-polarizing, and biologically-essentialist definition of a *real* woman or man.

Subtext #2: There are historically-constructed cultural lenses embedded in the social institutions and cultural discourses of society which insidiously make their way into our individual psyches and thereby lead us to become unwitting collaborators in the social reproduction of the existing power structure. These cultural lenses must be exposed, resisted, and subverted–and new social and ideological forms must be constructed in their place–if the reproduction of rich, white, Christian, male, heterosexual power is ever to be disrupted. Put somewhat differently, the culture's whole organization of gender and sexuality is a historical construction that aids and abets the social reproduction of male power. The feminist challenge must thus be not only to fight the marginalization of women per se, but to undermine the alleged solidity, universality, and naturalness of the existing categories of sex, gender, and sexual orientation.

Enough about *The Lenses of Gender* and its implicit subtexts. Let me now shift into the past and trace what working on gender as a gender non-conformist looked like during the twenty-five or so years before I wrote my book. I'll begin with the part of my work that is conventionally called my "scholarship," and then I'll move on to the part that is conventionally called my "parenting" or "child-rearing." This divide is pretty artificial in my case, however, because I also write about my child-rearing and thereby make it a part of my scholarship.

My work on gender began in 1967 with an article entitled "Training the woman to know her place: The power of an unconscious ideology," that I wrote with my ex-husband, Daryl Bem. This article was written at a time when the term "sexism" hadn't even been invented yet. Nevertheless, by introducing the concept of an egalitarian marriage and by further arguing that the internalization of gender stereotypes is what is responsible for both gender difference and gender inequality, this article not only challenged the naturalness of both gender difference and gender inequality; it also challenged the very notion of a natural link between sex and behavior.

After having argued for several years *without data* that traditional gender roles were not only unequal but that they restricted both women and men alike to only half their humanity, I finally decided in 1970 to organize my own empirical research around this idea. More specifically, I decided to try to gather data in support of my feminist conviction that, contrary to both conventional wisdom and the claims of the mental health establishment, people who are conventionally gendered (i.e., masculine men and feminine women) are actually less well off in certain ways than people who are not conventionally gendered. Thus began my research on the virtues of androgyny, which not only introduced the concept of androgyny into the psychological literature but also had as its two subtexts both (a) that society's gender lenses make their way into our psyches and thereby constrain us and (b) that there is no natural link between sex and psyche.

By 1974 or so, the focus of my empirical work had shifted from the virtues of being androgynous to the underlying psychological processes constraining people who are not androgynous. The hypothesis here was as follows: Conventionally gendered people have what we might think of as internal "antennae" tuned to cultural definitions of gender appropriateness. In other words, they have internalized the culture's gender prescriptions and thus nonconsciously use those prescriptions to shape their perceptions of themselves and the social world. To test this hypothesis, I did a whole series of studies on what I called "gender schematicity." This research not only demonstrated empirically that conventionally gendered people do indeed have a greater readiness than androgynous people to encode information in terms of gender. Even more importantly, by demonstrating this, it also suggested that there is nothing natural or obligatory about human beings encoding information in this way.

By the 1980s, I was finally able to begin to ground all this theorizing about gender in a cultural context. In 1981, for example, I suggested explicitly in a *Psychological Review* article that conventionally gendered people come to be gender-schematic–that is, they come to process information in terms of gender rather than in terms of some other dimension that might be just as appropriate–because they have lived in a society since birth that is filled with implicit cultural metamessages telling them in 1001 ways that sex is–and ought to be–critically important in every domain of social life. And in 1983, I went even further, writing in an article for *Signs* about how one might raise what I called "gender-aschematic" children even while living in a "gender-schematic" society.

All this work predating *The Lenses of Gender* reflects my working on gender as a gender-nonconformist because it disrupts the longstanding cultural belief in some kind of a natural link between sex and psyche. Rather than this link being natural, the work suggests, it is instead a historical construction, a product of what I would have then called cultural and individual "gender schematicity." There are two things this early work does not do, however. In contrast to *The Lenses of Gender*, it does not theorize male/female inequality per se and it also says strikingly little about sexuality.

Sexuality figured more prominently in the theorizing that I did in the context of my feminist child-rearing where, once again, my overarching goal was very clearly to challenge the cultural illusion that there is some kind of a natural link between the sex of one's body and the character of either one's psyche or one's sexuality. This experiment in feminist child-rearing began in the mid-1970s, with the birth of my daughter Emily in 1974 and my son Jeremy in 1976. In part, I began experimenting with feminist child-rearing for the same reason I had earlier begun experimenting with egalitarian marriage–it was the only way I could imagine living. But in part, I was also using my home as a laboratory of sorts in order to demonstrate to my own satisfaction that Kohlberg was wrong. In other words, even young children *can* be gender-liberated if they are inoculated against the culture at an early enough age. And how are they to be inoculated? I always describe my attempt to inoculate my own children as having two phases.

During the first phase, my goal was to enable my children to learn about male/female differences and the body without simultaneously learning any cultural stereotypes about males and females or any cultural stigmas about the body. Put somewhat differently, my goal was to retard their gender education while simultaneously advancing their sex education.

To retard their gender education, I did everything I could for as long as I could to eliminate any and all correlations between a person's sex and other aspects of life. In our everyday life in the home, for example, my ex-husband and I took turns cooking, driving the car, bathing the baby, and so on and forth, so that our own parental example would not teach a correlation between sex and behavior. I monitored, doctored, and even censored the books my children had access to, putting off-limits even some feminist children's books until my children had gotten older. After all, to a child who doesn't yet know that boys aren't supposed to have dolls, even a book that argues boys should have dolls is teaching a gender stereotype. And I also made sure that from a very early age, my children knew that some people had partners who were their own sex and other people had partners who were the other sex. This was very easy for me to do because there are so many gay people in my family.

To advance my children's sex education, I *taught the body*, as it were, as early as I could. That is, I provided a clear and unambiguous bodily definition of what sex is: A boy, I said again and again, is someone with a penis and testicles; a girl is someone with a vagina, clitoris, and uterus; and, most important of all, whether you're a boy or a girl, a man or a woman, doesn't need to matter–or shouldn't anyway–until and unless you want to make a baby. Consistent with this premise, I also refused to provide a simple answer when my children asked me in the supermarket, for example, whether someone was a boy or a girl, a man or a lady. Instead, I said (quietly so as not to draw attention to myself) that I couldn't really tell without seeing under the person's clothes.

Both the liberation that can come from having a narrow bodily definition of sex and the imprisonment that can come from not having such a definition are strikingly illustrated by the now-famous story of what happened to my son, Jeremy, when he naively decided to wear barrettes to nursery school. Several times that day, another little boy insisted that Jeremy must be a girl because "only girls wear barrettes." After repeatedly insisting that "wearing barrettes doesn't matter; being a boy means having a penis and testicles," Jeremy finally pulled down his pants to make his point more convincingly. The other boy was not impressed. He simply said, "Everybody has a penis; only girls wear barrettes."

But I didn't try to "teach the body" only to provide a stereotype-free definition of male and female. I also tried to teach the body as a stigma-free foundation for sexuality. Thus, there was much nudity in our home on the part of both children and adults alike. And many bodily functions were also performed by the adults in the children's presence. In everyday language, this included such things as peeing, pooping, and even putting tampons in and taking them out. Making women's bleeding visible to my children at the earliest possible age was important, as I saw it, because just as I wanted them to know about the difference between males and females and also about the existence of gay people *before* they learned any related cultural stereotypes or stigmas, so too I wanted them to learn about menstruation before they learned any cultural notions of women's being polluted or women's blood being "yucky."

Retarding children's gender education and advancing their sex education can clearly delay their being exposed to the cultural belief that there is a natural link between what sex one is and what kind of psyche and sexuality one is supposed to have. But how to keep this cultural belief from being internalized when the child is finally exposed to the culture's ideology? This question brings me to the second phase of my inoculation process.

During this second phase, my overarching goal was to turn my children into junior cultural critics or "deconstructionists," to teach them to approach most messages that are presented to them on television or in books with the assumption that the message was created, whether now or in the past, by a particular human being with a particular set of beliefs. The stance to take toward such messages is thus not to assume that it is either true or relevant to their lives, but to assume instead that it can tell them something about the beliefs, attitudes, and biases of its creator.

Perhaps the most obvious example of my trying to teach this stance to my children occurred when I read to Emily from her first book of fairy tales. "These stories," I said, "were written a long long long long long time ago by people who had some very peculiar ideas about boys and girls. The stories are wonderfully exciting, but the people who wrote them thought that girls are the kinds of people who always get into trouble and need to be saved by boys, who are naturally brave and wise. So that's what happens in story after story, and that's why it never happens that a boy gets into trouble and needs to be saved by the bravery and wisdom of a girl." Emily loved the stories, just as I thought she would, but after each one, she giggled with glee about how I had been right. "There's another one, mom," she would say. "Aren't the people who made up these stories silly?"

I tried to provide other, more specific, subversive lenses for my children as well—including the lens of sexism, which I hoped could replace the more traditional lens of natural sexual difference. But what I particularly want to emphasize here is that, as my children got older, I also continued to "teach the body" with my own brand of sex education that I hoped could subvert what Gayle Rubin has called the "sex negativity" of U.S. culture. Among other things, I thus emphasized that sex should not be categorized as one of the triumvirate of vices along with alcohol and drugs, which is the way that it seems to be categorized in health classes in the public schools. Instead, I said that it should be categorized as one of the many developmental tasks–along with such things as crawling, walking, talking, reading, writing, and so on–that need to be mastered on the way to maturity.

In my theorizing both "at work" and "at home," the same underlying themes thus emerge: Lenses embedded in both our cultural discourses and our social institutions construct a prison of gender for each of us individually by getting into our psyches and thereby leading us to construct personalities, identities, and sexualities that are consistent with those lenses. For feminists in general, the challenge is thus to expose and subvert those lenses at both the cultural level and the individual level. And for me in particular, the single most important lens to expose and subvert is what I now call the lens of gender polarization, i.e., the superimposing of a male/female dichotomy on every aspect of human experience from modes of dress and social roles to ways of expressing emotion and experiencing sexual desire.

Where all of this would have led by itself, I do not know. But in the late 1980s, during a sabbatical year at Harvard, I decided to finally try to figure out whether or not I had "a book in my head." If so, I knew that it would be a "big picture" book and I also knew that it would finally integrate my longstanding interest in gender, which I had been writing about for years, with my longstanding interest in sex and sexual orientation, which up until that time I had primarily dealt with in my child-rearing.

I didn't know exactly how I was going to do all this, however, so I read voraciously for the full year on anything and everything that seemed even vaguely interesting to me. And of all the things I read, perhaps the most significant was Catherine MacKinnon's essay on "Difference and Dominance," because it enabled me to see that our social world is indeed an invisible affirmative program for men.

And with this realization, I was not only able to build a theory that tried to explain how both sexism and heterosexism are reproduced in generation after generation. I was also able to get a grasp on something like the "whole" of what I had been teaching and theorizing both at work and at home for twenty-some years. And I loved that.

REFERENCES

Bem, S. L. (1981) Gender schema theory: A cognitive account of sex typing. *Psychological Review, 88*, 369-371.

Bem, S. L. (1983) Gender schema theory and its implications for child development: Raising gender-aschematic children in a gender-schematic society. *Signs: Journal of women in culture and society, 8*, 598-616.

Bem, S. L. (1993) *The lenses of gender: Transforming the debate on sexual inequality*. New Haven: Yale University Press.

Bem, S. L., & Bem, D. J. (1970) Training the woman to know her place: The power of a nonconscious ideology. In D. J. Bem, *Beliefs, attitudes, and human affairs*. Belmont, CA: Brooks Cole.

MacKinnon, C. A. (1987) Difference and dominance: On sex discrimination (1984). In C. A. MacKinnon (ed.), *Feminism unmodified: Discourses on life and law*. Cambridge, MA: Harvard University Press.

Rubin, G. S. (1993) Thinking sex: Notes for a radical theory of the politics of sexuality. In H. Abelove, M. A. Barale, & D. M. Halperin (eds.), *The lesbian and gay studies reader*. NY: Routledge.

By My Sisters Reborn

Teresa Bernardez

I was named after Santa Teresa de Avila, the saint reformer of the church. Whether names and what they represent have an influence on the bearer, I leave up to others to decide. However, growing up as a girl Catholic, I fervently wanted to be a saint. I read the books of saints' lives and I climbed to high places to read them as if altitude would get me sooner to my goal.

My mother was of profound influence in my life. Deeply religious, thoughtful about life, willful and just, she won my admiration during my childhood. She had an extraordinary sense of the injustice done to women but she didn't fight her conditions nor defy the social order. She did defy the conventional way of raising a girl. I was

Teresa Bernardez, MD, is faculty and Supervising Psychoanalyst, Michigan Psychoanalytic Council and former Professor of Psychiatry, College of Human Medicine at Michigan State University. She had previously been staff Psychiatrist at the Menninger Clinic, a member of the Training and Supervising Faculty, Menninger School of Psychiatry, Faculty and Clinical Associate of the Tavistock Clinic, London, and a Fellow of the Bunting Institute, Harvard University. Her research and clinical practice have focused on women's issues: cultural prohibitions governing the behavior of women and men, gender-based countertransference and social issues that are relevant in the treatment of women and minorities.

In gratitude and tenderness to my mother Dolores and my sister Aurora, September 1994.

Correspondence may be addressed to Teresa Bernardez, MD, 835 Westlawn, E. Lansing, MI 48823.

[Haworth co-indexing entry note]: "By My Sisters Reborn." Bernardez, Teresa. Co-published simultaneously in *Women & Therapy* (The Haworth Press, Inc.) Vol. 17, No. 1/2, 1995, pp. 55-70; and: *Feminist Foremothers in Women's Studies, Psychology, and Mental Health* (ed: Phyllis Chesler, Esther D. Rothblum, and Ellen Cole) The Haworth Press, Inc., 1995, pp. 55-70; and: *Feminist Foremothers in Women's Studies, Psychology, and Mental Health* (ed: Phyllis Chesler, Esther D. Rothblum, and Ellen Cole) Harrington Park Press, an imprint of The Haworth Press, Inc., 1995, pp. 55-70. Single or multiple copies of this article are available from The Haworth Document Delivery Service [1-800-342-9678, 9:00 a.m. - 5:00 p.m. (EST)].

allowed to run around in the streets until late and I was dressed in comfortable clothes that didn't inhibit exploration and physical activity. I was curious and adventurous as a girl and neither of my parents (both of whom grew up in the country, in Spain) put obstacles to my satisfaction. Being the last born after 5 children of my father and 2 of my mother and father, I grew up free of most parental expectations in a remarkable household with interesting adults of both sexes to learn from. Although my father was kind and very generous and he had true respect for my mother, he was hot-tempered and was used to being in command. He had raised himself in a new country and no one had placed restraints on him. From him and from my siblings, I got an inspiring, open and unrestricted way of looking at my life and its possibilities. Anything was possible. From my mother I got a deep sense of the spiritual, transcendent and magical meaning of life but with the burdens of responsibility and awareness.

My childhood was unencumbered by tragic events except for the common sorrows of childhood. I was by all accounts, "well adjusted," a sweet girl, and an excellent student. I began writing at age 8 after an illness, and all thought then that I might become a novelist. But no one heard from me that my wildest ambition was to be a saint and that the first moments of rapture that I experienced were connected with my proximity to God. I admired Jesus but the Virgin Mary left me indifferent. I was to model myself after him, this model revolutionary. His self sacrifice did not make any sense to me and I can say now that the idealization of his crucifixion, the church's exclusion of women and the distrust of the body played equal parts in my later abandonment of the church and the final renunciation of my aspiration to be a saint.

Early on I was aware of my mother's deep dissatisfaction of which I constantly tried to make sense. Was my father responsible for it? Was it her inability to be a religious person as she envisioned it? Slowly, with pieces of her current biography, I began to put it together: she had wanted to have time to read and reflect, she would have gone to the University. My love for my mother made me very aware of her desires. I wanted to give her the whole world, I wanted her to be happy and laugh, I knew she was extraordinary. Why wasn't she leading the country? My father was an original, but my mother had depth in her intelligence. My mother reflected on the meaning of life; my father lived it. My mother worried about the future; my father made of the present the only reality. My mother saw the injustice in the world as enormous and odious: she was always aware of how much else there was to do. My father gave of himself whenever he was confronted with a situation of inequity or fixed it right away, sometimes grandiosely, but his sleep was undisturbed by the state of the world. There were no obstacles for my father; he was an innocent who had immense luck because people saw him without guile and they loved to give to him to fulfill his optimistic expectations of the world. That combination and contradiction was to have a powerful effect on me because as I envisioned it as a child, I wanted to transform my mother's life as she deserved, and my father offered the way.

My religious education did not have only negative influences: I grew accustomed to examine my conscience, to reflect on my behavior, to be aware of others, to do what was just, to ponder the mysteries of life and love and to seek grace. The pomp and ceremony of the church were impressive. I was intoxicated with virtue and incense, in this very carnal and sensorial religion. I questioned the wisdom of accepting one's fate because there was a better world beyond but Jesus had been quite interested in modifying this one and I, too, inclined myself in that direction.

The shock came with adolescence: with sex in the picture and with the sudden realization that I had been reared to comply after all with the designs of my society for my gender, a most unlikely, obnoxious and defiant side of me began to emerge. I felt my mother, my hero, betrayed me, my father was indifferent to my fate and I was all alone to right my situation as a future woman on this earth. I fought every restriction, every imposition at home and at school and I began to rebel using my older sister as a beacon: she was a cool intellectual and I determined that I would also live the life of women with brains. I assigned to my body the troubles of women. To live without the body, controlling the body, demeaning the body were the early ways I had learned would free your spirit and now I used that strategy to defy my fate as a woman. Hurt and disappointed, I left the church that required of women and of poor people to tolerate their circumstances and to dream of compensation in the world beyond. Well, that wasn't for me. For awhile I imitated my sister: a philosopher and a poet, she was safely agnostic and spiteful of the conventional life of a woman. Like her, I read voraciously in my pursuit of enlightenment. I didn't pick up on revolution because I was born in Argentina and the times had a lesson or two to teach me about revolution. They never involved or improved the situation of women. I knew at an early age that their enslavement benefitted men. I became aware of the dangers of marriage and decided that I was going to live outside the law in that respect, but being unable to dispense with the sensual body I had inherited I was to make sure that I met only men who were my equals and who would defend, indeed admire my love for freedom and justice. During the second World War I was an adolescent in the Lyceum. We identified with the Allies and denounced fascism. My first taste of political involvement and my first acquaintance with anti-semitism took place at this time. Shortly after, in our own country, the terrible experience of dictatorship and terrorism with the coming of Peron into power raised further my awareness. I saw the gradual destruction of democratic rule and although Peron did awaken and support the working class, he did it in a climate of amorality and revenge, of fraudulence and intimidation. For the first time censorship prevented us from knowing what was going on and fear permeated the minds of people everywhere. Control by intimidation was followed by imprisonment of political prisoners, incarceration of those who defied the regime and dismissal of professors at universities that did not go along with "the government." My first public acts of defiance against Peron were in demonstrations where the police charged against us with their horses. I knew then that brutality and violence would eliminate the "weak," women. At those times, friends of mine went to prison, the first students who I knew were tortured. This period was grim, and although I was very scared, I helped in the underground. That was where women were found. The few who defied the regime worked in obscurity; the young men were in the front lines. I saw the corruption that the state of siege caused in people, the way in which they began to lie and to deny reality to stay safe. I realized then that censorship and intimidation and coercion caused a derangement in human functioning, a state of pathological adaptation in most people. The fear of speaking critically against the government gave way to fraudulent speech, an "as if" manner of thinking recognizable in the "sufferers" of that condition. Little did I know then that I would recognize it later in my life in the way psychiatrists spoke to defend the psychiatric diagnosing of women's condition.

Dictatorship and the discovery that the military in Argentina was going to rule one way or another, the awareness that the population would not support those of us who took risks and would not defend democracy made me leave the country as soon as I finished medical school. My future husband and I got scholarships in Paris and I got a contract in the USA to undergo training as a psychiatrist at the famous Menninger Clinic.

After a year in Paris, life in Topeka, Kansas, was hell. The culture shock was exquisitely painful. The flatness and blandness of landscape and people alike, the indifference of–what it seemed to this foreigner–the attitude of its people, crushed my view of the US as the country for women. I had been an admirer of the US, its films and dynamism if not its foreign policy. I thought that Katharine Hepburn and Bette Davis were representatives of American women and their freedom, but when we got to Topeka we thought we were in a prison state: the women seemed deeply unhappy but sported false smiles in faces surrounded by puffed up hair and bodies restrained by garters and corsets. Men wore crew cuts, all of them. The shock of the cultural differences which wouldn't have been so noticeable in a big city like New York, of the striking differences in the views of time, personal relations, work ethic, numbed me and together with the new language, transformed me into a person who seemed to me retarded. To make it worse, my first clinical supervisor was puritanical and sexist and he was a crude introduction to the attitude of white, educated men of the midwest towards professional women. There were only two of us in a group of 36 residents and the two women were foreign. Where were the American women physicians? I soon learned that only one or two got into medical schools and that they had such a hard time that not all of them graduated. At first, the complications of having to learn so many new things made it difficult to discover the cultural shibboleths. What was it: their sexism, racism or my ignorance, my ethnocentrism? I remember, for instance, my disbelief when my supervisor presented me with a grid which looked remarkably close to a cell with bars which he called a "schedule," and announced that I had to fill it up with my activities every hour of the day. If that was a problem for anyone who is not obsessive, it is torture for an Argentinean, raised to accommodate hundreds of unpredictable happenings every day, accustomed to live in the moment and make the best possible use of the opportunities that present themselves in the spontaneous flow of the day. No, these folks in Kansas truly believed that it is you who designs the universe and nothing happens that is not on your schedule. But not everything was wrong in Topeka: the monotony of life resembled that of a monastery but because of it there was plenty of opportunity for learning and reflection and intimate relationships flourished. After a year of having more competent teachers, beginning to understand my psychotic patients and becoming excited with psychoanalysis, I began to sift slowly the cultural weight of my experience in that universe, as a woman and as a Latina. I had noticed how unusual they found it that I had my own opinions, that I wasn't intimidated by men (my five brothers had made that possible). When I looked around me the panorama of women was dismal: there were few women in the work force except as teachers, secretaries and nurses. The tendency to be self-effacing and meek made most women invisible. The few professional women were rendered silent and ineffective. Yet I found in the few of them the mentors that I needed in Topeka: Lois Murphy, an unusually accomplished analyst in research was the only American. A Polish analyst, Micha Fabian, helped me with my first ventures in treating schizophrenic patients. It was Lois Murphy who encouraged me to write and publish my first article ("The Feminine Role: A Case Report" on the loss of IQ points in a gifted little girl when she became a "feminine" adolescent) and it was she who gave me *The Feminine Mystique* to review for the Menninger Bulletin. Friedan gave me the awareness of a native born of the restrictions that I saw in women and their connections with the femininity myths of the culture; she helped me sift my perceptions and strengthen my confidence that I was detecting a myriad of difficulties that women "suffered" that were deeply connected with the environmental forces that I had crudely observed.

I was interested in adolescents at that time and I noticed the restrictions imposed on the women patients' sexual lives. Although in all other respects the clinic had the authority to respectfully prescribe almost anything that it saw fit the patients' needs, they would not prescribe contraceptives and they could not see the double standards that they held. It began to be noticeable that my success with patients, particularly with adolescent girls who were rebellious and defiant of authority, wasn't simply because I liked them. It was obvious that I understood better their needs and their flight from the dismal world of "womanhood" that they were offered. Another sign of the prejudice held about women at the time was the inability to conceive that a woman may want to do work other than rear children. Work was seldom discussed with a woman patient, particularly when many of them did not consider it an option. I was interested in fostering in my patients the examination of their gifts and their desires for work and education which had been seriously restricted even if they belonged to the upper classes. I saw their "pathology" as related to the constraints imposed upon them. My elders had an explanation for my kind of woman: the "masculine protest." Those of us who were inclined to see meaning in serious work were thought to be dissatisfied with our true "feminine" nature and wanted to be men. Rationalizations this simplistic explained with circular logic any deviation from the norm. Although in truth many of them did not believe the penis envy hypothesis, they all found it comforting; seldom did I see anyone examining the possibility that there were gains for men in protecting the status quo, that it was immensely convenient to be thought of as superior and enviable. The blindness and impermeability of men was so intense that I began to think there was an unconscious reason for the necessity to want to see women as deprived and lacking. Later on, my friend Harriet Lerner was to write an enlightening article on the envy of men and their devaluation of women. Armed with de Beauvoir's *The Second Sex*, Phyllis Chesler's *Women and Madness* and Karen Horney's *Feminine Psychology*, I began to notice and record their reactions towards me. Men were noticeably uncomfortable if I became angry or even passionately involved in a discussion. There was what amounted to dread of the anger of women and women reflected this fear: their attitude of meekness and the fear of their own anger cut across all classes. I didn't know it at the time but I had started to explore what would become a major search in my working life. I was very alone. When I started psychoanalytic training in Topeka, which at the time was the aspiration of every psychiatrist in the country, I was the only woman in my class, a situation that I had gotten used to expect. I had bright teachers but they all had such compliance towards the old theories and such idolatrous sentiments towards Freud that only very exceptional ones were willing to hear. I realized then that this was too massive a structure to dismantle by myself. I began to move towards different experiences and an extraordinary opportunity presented itself.

Until the time of the civil rights riots, Topeka had been segregated in such a perfect way that no one ever saw it. African Americans and Mexican Americans, poor and disenfranchised, lived on the other side of town. I was to have an extraordinary experience with them, which led me to integrate many of my experiences of oppression and injustice and that determined the future of my research interests. There were funds to help and encourage developments in segregated populations in coordination with funding from private sources in similar proportions. The Menninger Clinic decided to help integrate health care efforts in segregated neighborhoods and establish links with the Clinic as well as other health care givers. Three of us in the staff of the Clinic volunteered to establish the first links with the African American community. A social worker, a minister trained psychologically, and I were sent from the Department of Preventive Psychiatry. We met at first with a group of community folks to help us see what was needed and wanted. In the middle of the heated discussion I felt an extraordinary sense of being at home, half relieved, half excited. Everyone was talking animatedly at once while they appeared not to be listening to one another. My colleagues were frustrated trying to follow the different trends of the conversation. But I was at ease: everyone was listening in several frequencies at once, not missing a beat. When they finally had consensus it seemed to have come arbitrarily but it had been processed all the way through. I knew it because in Buenos Aires people also interacted at a high level of participation simultaneously but they also could hear what different people were telling each other. It wasn't so much a question of impoliteness; the "group speech" was faster and more efficient and had the advantage of permitting the immediate expression of excitement and enthusiasm. African Americans, I was sure, would be considered less civilized because they didn't speak like whites, because they wouldn't wait their turn. But for an impatient person like me, that speech was music to my ears and I had no trouble following it. I realized how the density and slowness of Kansas speech had deadened me and distracted me from listening.

That was a profound period of growth for all of us. At first the neighborhood used me as a physician. Often in the process of discussing their physical symptoms, in those kinds of intimate and unusual conversations to which physicians had entry, my patients told me what was bothering them, why they didn't consult white physicians and didn't use hospitals or other facilities. Gradually, I earned their confidence and we were involved in liaison with other physicians, community organization and training of indigenous health care workers. Neighborhood community houses were created and I started my first groups of mothers and of adolescent girls. These groups had very practical agendas (contraceptive methods, the perils of hysterectomies, how to prevent pregnancy in daughters or how conception occurred and the differences between girls and boys in sexual response). The girls and women in our groups had important insights and strong opinions and I realized that they seemed more assertive and more able to express anger than their white counterparts. They were excited, I was excited: we were breaking barriers, talking about forbidden subjects, exploring the ways in which poverty and segregation produced alienation and mental illness. I couldn't believe it when after organizing them to request improvements from the local government or to find jobs or when we went about breaking the segregated lines (my first public mission with the girls was to desegregate the Pizza Hut) there was definite improvement in their emotional and psychological states. There seemed to be less despondency, less marital disharmony, less disorganized behavior when unemployment and its sequelae got corrected and when hope, self-determination and control entered their lives. Although I never believed the theory of the time that poor/uneducated people were less able to profit from psychotherapy, I was astounded that we could work in any place (sometimes my client and I had to use the bathroom as a meeting place because it was the only available room) and in the midst of interruptions. I found my patients able to use insight and information fast and to put them into action without delay as well as finish their contacts without lingering when the matter that brought them to consult me was resolved. Problems they presented were serious and always involved an awareness of the social realm. These experiences marked me and helped me see the concrete ways in which poverty, racism and sexism enter the psyches of our patients producing "mental illness" which when diagnosed in isolation from the social conditions in which they lived, prevented the right kind of understanding and action and led to the making of fraudulent diagnosis.

I was to take this "home." I began to incorporate a view of my patients in the social system. This was particularly pertinent to women. I began to see that misdiagnosis, labeling and theorizing about women's condition did not take into account their complex social disadvantage. Unlike blacks or latinos the women in the middle class appeared to enjoy the advantages reserved to whites but when compared with men the inequalities and psychological restrictions and mind confinements made them "deficient," "ill."

When the women's movement began its emergence I was still in Kansas. I remember the excitement of the first consciousness-raising groups we formed. From the very beginning, the support of women directed me into social action, something which the civil rights revolution had given me the skills and experience for. I felt that my energies would be best used in transforming the view of women in my profession and that I could start in our own backyard.

As a student of group process and as a group therapist I noticed with surprise how much faster the leaderless groups were moving than our therapist-led groups and I was intending to learn what were the reasons. These were the first experiences that led to my 15-year research in groups and gender and women's groups that I was to conduct at Michigan State University.

The women's groups gave a voice to this "silent majority" and gave women the chance to seek affirmation from others of their reality and perspective. Once again the role that anger played in their liberation astounded me. These were women who had not dared to complain and who now, supported by others, were raising their voices in protest. I was to spend a lot of my professional life studying the ways in which the expression of anger was at the very core of the prohibitions that our culture enforces in its construction of femininity. What began as the study of a cultural prohibition became a source of understanding of the "pathology" of the most prevalent women's disorders: depression, sexual dysfunction, eating disorders.

To convince others that prohibitions of anger played an important role in the subordination of women and in many of the so-called "psychiatric illnesses" was another matter. I still remember my first paper in a National psychiatric conference on the subject: *Women and Anger: Conflicts with Aggression in Contemporary Women.* The women flocked to my support. They came in large numbers to the podium and also sent letters. The men were indignant, furious, dismissive. This dramatic difference convinced me that I was on the right track, that the silence protecting the awareness of the prohibition about speaking about anger having been lifted, produced the expected massive retaliation by those who supported the status quo and the domination of women.

In 1971, I felt that I no longer could stay in psychoanalytic training. The awareness that in practice, psychoanalysis was committed to the exploitation of women by ignoring the role of social injunctions brought me face to face with the awareness that I had been fighting a useless battle: there were too many important interests at stake and my teachers were men and in their great majority totally hostile to the idea that women needed to free themselves from bias and prejudice. My teachers paid lip service to psychoanalytic understanding about the unconscious need of people to maintain supremacy and control through prejudice and domination, and how this was relevant to the situation of women. Like my leaving the Catholic church at 16, this break also liberated me. Yet, I believed that psychoanalytic theory in its radical aspects had been extraordinarily useful in my clinical work and in the liberation of women and I felt that I would continue to use it. Major transformations had to be made, however, in those aspects of theory and technique that were incongruent with my new knowledge of women and I thought that it would be exciting for me to attempt it.

I began my academic career at Michigan State University, desirous of a place where I could do research and not be hindered by the old theories and idolatries of the psychoanalytic camp. I entered the Department of Psychiatry of a new, exciting medical school. The move to the midwest, to an environment that supported my ideas and respected my training, where colleagues were eager to innovate, having been hampered like me by people too attached to what they knew even if it was no longer valid, proved a godsend. I had a hand at organizing and creating many "first things": the first women medical students groups; my participation in the first admissions committee that would make sure that women and minorities were powerfully represented, recruited and supported; my chairing the first Affirmative Action Committee in the medical school, making sure that we recruited women and minorities for faculty; the first conferences where I could invite my feminist colleagues to teach what we knew about women to students and faculty.

My activity acquired frantic proportions: I was the only woman in the tenure track for awhile and I felt responsible for supporting students and residents, for seeking faculty members who were women, for learning the ropes of how certain things were done. I thrived and learned a lot, I became an advocate of women in my department, my medical school but also the University at large. There were few but exciting feminist sisters around with whom we exchanged information and headed multiple ventures. My friendships with people like Barrie Thorne in Sociology, Marilyn Frye in Philosophy, Michele Fluck in Biology expanded my knowledge, stretched my awareness and led me to other wonderful women and other networks across the country. The women in the social and behavioral sciences taught me, among other things, how to understand social roles and socialization and I began to use and test this understanding in my research and clinical work. My lesbian friends and students further opened my awareness of our "compulsory heterosexuality" and together with them we began a series of small groups of straight and lesbian feminists to learn more intimately what prejudices and fears separated us at times from one another. These gatherings became large, customary "First Fridays" in our little town. My feminist colleagues in Psychiatry like Jean Baker Miller and her close associates at The Stone Center helped me reflect on the devaluation of feminine qualities and helped me reconsider my own defensive suspiciousness of anything "feminine." I ventured with them into all sorts of involvements, public, social, spiritual.

I had the opportunity to train psychiatric residents, and the first ventures in teaching them my perspective on women and gender were difficult because the men had a great resistance to see themselves as oppressors and the women were often scared of offending their male colleagues. I did begin to make an impact and my classes began to be more and more popular. I instituted feminist mores: to make the classroom and the seminar a place of intimacy where hierarchical barriers were erased, to permit all points of view, to rule mostly by consensus and to pay as much attention to the personal and the political. I directed the group training program in the Department and trained residents to do groups incorporating my awareness of gender differences and the way to promote a treatment of women that empowered them by lifting the prohibitions stemming from their social environment. The goal was to use the therapist in the beginning of the group to resolve struggles that the women had with their authority and in expressing their own anger, but phasing out the therapist gradually by training the women in leadership skills and group dynamics. With women psychologists we instituted the creation of groups for "pre-orgasmic women" so successfully started by L. Barbach in California, and we trained women residents and graduate students to co-lead them. We discussed and read about rape and wife battering in rooms hushed by the awareness of the grief in women's lives but enlivened by a new energy and solidarity. Male students and residents were introduced to feminist notions of power and were invited to join the amazing transformation that was taking place.

These were periods of intense work and multiple roles: every week there was a new and exciting development, from the simplest (to have hospitals allow women to wear long skirts on the wards) to the risky (to bring to the first year medical students' classroom new birthing methods practiced by accomplished midwives that were revolutionary because they emphasized the primacy and activity of the woman and the supportive role of the doctor), to the procedural (to alter the ways women were seen and their accomplishments assessed in their seeking of tenure in promotions and tenure committees), to warrior-like protests when inequalities arose or when physicians missed obvious opportunities to correct their prejudicial beliefs.

My courses on the "Psychotherapy of Women," which I taught at my University and in national conferences for psychiatrists, became very successful. Graduate students from other departments began to join our own residents in large numbers. I thought it was most important to teach obstetricians, so crucial if we wanted to provide adequate medical care to women, so I created the OB/GYN consultation-liaison service which I directed for 10 years and which was a crucible and a stirring experience. The resistance to learn about women from a woman and a feminist to boot, was extraordinary, the fear, ferocious. But the time came when in showing a videotape of a patient that I had interviewed, several of these hard core machistas had tears in their eyes. I took up their most bedeviling cases, interviewed the patients on videotape and showed them how I talked to them and what the women said to me. Witnessing our intimate conversations, the physicians could "see" how their patients' "problems" were in large measure connected with the multiple unhappinesses, violence and injustice women found in their environment.

In other areas of our University our presence as feminists began to make a difference: the Women's Advisory Committee to the Provost was composed of all women but of a minority of feminists when I was appointed to it. In two years we had the most radical group assembled the Provost had ever imagined! We were responsible for the first coherent and organized Affirmative Action Plan that passed the university's various approving committees and much of it was adopted finally as the MSU IDEA, a complex series of policies, structural changes and rewards for the enhancement and permanent protection of minorities and women's rights. Those were heady times! We knew what to do, how to fight and succeed and how to contact each other and those outside the University for support, information and consultation.

Simultaneously, my activity in national organizations and my presentations to national conferences were at a peak. I began to teach an annual course at the American Psychiatric Association Annual Meetings with a faculty of brilliant feminists. The success of the courses and the workshops that we presented began to demonstrate that new knowledge in our discipline had profound implications and was not political rhetoric. A coalition of the few feminists to be found in Psychiatry was momentous. It occurred around the boycott of states that had not passed the ERA and led to a powerful boycott of the APA's meeting in New Orleans and the creation of the first women psychiatrists organization, the Association for Women Psychiatrists. We began to be more active in the APA as a result of these political gatherings and several of us decided to congregate in the Committee on Women of the APA hoping to transform the massive unawareness of the APA organization and to protect women's interests by bringing our knowledge and experience to the center of the debate. I worked there with remarkable colleagues: Nanette Gartrell, Jean Hamilton, Judith Herman, Silvia Olarte, among others. During my tenure as a Chairperson of the committee, the famous struggle against the APA's attempt to place several new diagnoses for women in the infamous DSM-III-R, the manual of psychiatric diagnosis, took place. The exhausting and illuminating experience of fighting the psychiatric establishment head on and learning what was truly going on in the sanctum of diagnosis was both exhilarating and extremely depressing. I was very naive to think that psychiatrists of such experience and renown would see the light after we confronted them with their obvious ignorance and prejudice. How they hated us, how horrified they were that we were joining women psychologists to present our data to the press and to criticize them. We won that battle. The diagnoses were not accepted in the "book" although some of them awaited further research findings. But I could never again work with them or present anything at the APA. The place had become for me the symbol of oppression and mendacity.

My battles in the Department of Psychiatry began with a new chairman who maintained that I wasn't a "mainstream psychiatrist" because I did not treat depressed women with drugs and because I was against involuntary hospitalization. I had to defend my position through a grievance which I won, realizing how glad I was that I had tenure. My position in protecting patients who had been victims of therapists' abuse had cost me already a series of disputes with a few faculty members who fought hard to not have a systematic way to find the perpetrators in our midst.

These battles demonstrated to me the violence hidden under the professional demeanor of these men, the virulence in their hatred of women when the men were in danger of being uncovered as sexist. Those were the bitter discoveries I was to make. Since many important changes had come about in the medical school and in the University as a whole, I felt I was ready for a break. I was tired of living

in an environment composed mostly of men with views so divergent
to mine and although I had many supporters and a huge contingent of
students on my side, I knew that the time had come for a venture
where I could build something with people who shared my views.
Two factors facilitated this choice: an extraordinary experience with
women in the Bunting Institute at Radcliffe during my sabbatical
year, my closer association with The Stone Center and my participation the same year in a Mothers' Group in Cambridge where I met
Carol Gilligan. Those experiences convinced me that the environment of Departments of Psychiatry with their arcane views and biological reductionism were toxic to me. I flourished in the contact
with women who created a climate of openness and care. On my
return to Michigan I joined my psychologist colleagues in a new and
unusual educational venture: the creation of a first feminist psychoanalytic institute with a structure and a curriculum that included the
contributions of feminists and their critiques of Freud and other
theorists. A contingent of feminists participated in this conception
which was to allow women to join in large numbers.

To detail in which profound way feminism and the women in it
transformed me and enlightened me would take a book. I was
almost the person I wanted, not the saint but the "woman in my
rightful place" who changed my mother's life. I felt a part of a
larger community committed to liberation and caring concern, my
daily life was meaningful, expanded, my mind open to change. But
if my professional life and what I could do for and with women
changed me so, my personal life was enriched and transformed by
feminism as well. I grew up a child during the Vietnam war and I
put considerable energy and intuition in the making of a new kind
of man, more tender, more available, comfortable with women,
joyful and responsive to those less privileged than himself. I feel
amazed that my husband and I succeeded in such inhospitable times
to rear a child who is now a man I admire and who transformed me
in turn. Feminist principles were also involved in my choosing the
single life as my preferred and most authentic way of living after 22
years of marriage.

To my astonishment, I am not afraid of old age and it is to my
sisters that I owe this continuous rebirthing, this ending of exile.

Women's Psychology, Goddess Archetypes, and Patriarchy:
A Jungian Analyst, Feminist Activist, Visionary Feminist Foremother

Jean Shinoda Bolen
JoAnn Clausson

Jean Shinoda Bolen, MD, is Psychiatrist, Jungian analyst, Clinical Professor of Psychiatry, University of California Medical Center San Francisco, author, activist, and lecturer. She is the author of *The Tao of Psychology, Goddesses in Everywoman, Gods in Everyman, Ring of Power* and *Crossing to Avalon*. She is a Fellow of the American Psychiatric Association and the American Academy of Psychoanalysis and a Diplomate of the American Board of Psychiatry and Neurology. She has chaired the Council of National Affairs of the American Psychiatric Association, is a past member of the Board of the American Orthopsychiatric Association and the Ms. Foundation for Women, and a current board member of the International Transpersonal Association. She is a leader in feminist thinking, in the psychology of women, gender studies and women's spirituality, and an advocate and an activist for women, women's issues, and ethics in psychiatry.

JoAnn Clausson is a graduate student in Clinical Psychology at the University of Vermont. Her research interests include hypnosis, gender differences in depression and the effects of alternative family constellations on children's adjustment. She is presently working on her dissertation on factors affecting hypnotic susceptibility. Her clinical interests span a broad range which includes community mental health, family therapy and the treatment of adult survivors of child sexual abuse.

Correspondence may be addressed to Jean Shinoda Bolen, MD, 2021 Webster Street, San Francisco, CA 94115.

[Haworth co-indexing entry note]: "Women's Psychology, Goddess Archetypes, and Patriarchy: A Jungian Analyst, Feminist Activist, Visionary Feminist Foremother." Bolen, Jean Shinoda and JoAnn Clausson. Co-published simultaneously in *Women & Therapy* (The Haworth Press, Inc.) Vol. 17, No. 1/2, 1995, pp. 71-85; and: *Feminist Foremothers in Women's Studies, Psychology, and Mental Health* (ed: Phyllis Chesler, Esther D. Rothblum, and Ellen Cole) The Haworth Press, Inc., 1995, pp. 71-85; and: *Feminist Foremothers in Women's Studies, Psychology, and Mental Health* (ed: Phyllis Chesler, Esther D. Rothblum, and Ellen Cole) Harrington Park Press, an imprint of The Haworth Press, Inc., 1995, pp. 71-85. Single or multiple copies of this article are available from The Haworth Document Delivery Service [1-800-342-9678, 9:00 a.m. - 5:00 p.m. (EST)].

71

The influence of the women's movement on my life and the development of my thinking about women's psychology have gone hand in hand. When I was on the threshold of my professional life, the United States was on the threshold of the women's movement. I was a resident in psychiatry at the University of California Medical Center in San Francisco from 1963 to 1966. The same year that I entered my residency, two seminal ("ovuminal") publications came into the world, and the response to them began the women's movement. The first was the report from John F. Kennedy's Presidential Commission on the Status of Women; it described the inequities in women's pay for doing the same work that men did, and the barriers to entry and advancement that existed for women. The unfairness and discrimination struck a chord of outrage, and brought into consciousness that the work world was unfair to women. The second impetus was Betty Friedan's book *The Feminine Mystique*; this book articulated the unhappiness of women who had followed culture and Freud's assumptions and were not only unfulfilled but blamed themselves for their unhappiness. Cultural stereotypes and the limitations that resulted for women came into awareness. Consciousness was being raised, groups of women were meeting to tell each other the truth of their lives, and in the decade that followed, psychiatry would be affected.

A MATTER OF TIMING

Meanwhile, I was a resident in a program that was psychoanalytically oriented where women were in a distinct minority, and males in authority considered themselves authorities on women's psychology and were as yet unaware of the relevance of the women's movement on their area of expertise. I was increasingly in cognitive dissonance with the contrast between what I was reading in women's literature and the Freudian dogma I was being taught that said all women suffered from penis envy and were inherently inferior, castrated humans, with a lesser superego, and if we protested, it was evidence of having a masculinity complex. I was inwardly questioning what I was being taught but at that point (and under the circumstances) had not yet found a voice. For instance, I did not challenge the male clinician who said that a statement by a woman patient equating "being a woman with being a nigger" was "a loose association," rather than a perceptive comment.

Times changed due to the women's movement, even in clinical academia, thanks to the activism of the women's movement combined with the articulation of women's situation in some powerful anthologies and other publications which came out toward the end of the sixties and the beginning of the seventies. As a result, male experts on women within psychiatry were becoming increasingly uncomfortable continuing as experts and were becoming shy (unused to being challenged, uncomfortable with women's anger and power, they were "gun-shy" at the thought of confrontation).

In the years immediately after graduating from residency, I was part of the beginning women's movement within psychiatry in that I, along with other women colleagues, formed the Committee on Women of the Northern California Psychiatric Society. It had some of the impact for me of a consciousness-raising group experience. It was the first time that I had been with other women who were like me in being women and psychiatrists. We had come together with attitudes and prejudices towards our own group; each of us had thoughts of being exceptions to a negative image of unfeminine women doctors that we had gotten in our mostly-male training. It was wonderful to look around and see mirrored back, active, bright, attractive, and distinct individuals and to be part of such a group of women.

I had become a clinical instructor immediately upon graduating as a resident. I believe that this would have happened without the women's movement. However, I know that I would not have been invited to teach the sections of women's psychology that I was asked to teach if it were not for the women's movement which made the men who asked me to teach personally uncomfortable presenting themselves as experts on women. The opportunity to teach was an invitation and challenge to bring my personal experience as a woman together with women's movement literature and psychological theories. The "personal is political" perspective of the women's movement is a radicalizing notion–and an empowering one; it would give me the grounding to draw on my own experience and perceptions.

The second unorthodoxy after feminism (mainstream psychiatry was a combination of Freud and psychotropic drugs) was my interest in Jungian psychology. There are hardly any psychiatric training programs where a resident encounters Jungian analysts at all; at the time, the residency I was in may have been the only one. Among the clinical faculty who supervised us, there were a handful of Jungian analysts, and as fate or synchronicity would arrange it, among my supervisors, I would be assigned Jungian analysts and later would actively seek more. The one Jungian course that was offered was a lunchtime elective. Compared to Freud's theories on women, Jung's were "kinder" in degree; they were subtly rather than blatantly sexist. They assumed that both men and women have a contra-sexual element in themselves (animus in women, anima in men). Jung considered all women as primarily receptive and relationship-oriented, and by defining the animus as a less conscious part of a woman, she then is inherently less able to think well or be spiritually developed since these are animus rather than ego qualities. Interested as I was and am in dreams, creativity, and spirituality, I gravitated toward Jung, and sought more training by entering the training program of the San Francisco C. G. Jung Institute. This would be another perspective through which I would see the psychology of women, and it would be another psychology to see through the lens of feminism.

BINOCULAR PSYCHOLOGICAL VISION

I attribute the way of seeing that I quite naturally do as growing out of having had to straddle worlds all my life. Like the physics of binocular vision in which each eye sees the world from a different angle, presenting two images to the brain which then superimposes the two images into one image that now has depth, I have always seen the world psychologically from different angles, which initially had to do with being ethnically Japanese–a sansei or third-generation Japanese in America–in a Caucasian world where I was usually accepted and yet aware of being different; moving from elementary school to elementary school during World War II made me necessarily sensitive. When I entered medicine, I was a woman in a male profession. Because of my ethnicity, then because of my gender, and once in psychiatry because I became a Jungian analyst,

I experience the various worlds I am in, from at least two different perspectives. Wherever I am and whatever I am observing I can see from the majority or mainstream position, but because I am also an outsider or have another way of looking at things, I, in effect, superimpose another perspective upon the situation. I never can unconsciously merge with a collective, when a part of me is aware of being "a stranger in a strange land." In this way my gender and my ethnicity have contributed to a way of perceiving and thinking which is the basis of all of my contributions to theory. I see things from two perspectives at the same time, which adds depth to what I perceive.

BECOMING A FEMINIST ACTIVIST
IN THE AMERICAN PSYCHIATRIC ASSOCIATION

As I mulled over what my particular contributions have been that put me into the group of feminist foremothers, I realized that my activism as a feminist within organized psychiatry needs to be included, is significant, and significantly contributed to perceptions that shaped my thoughts.

Participation at the national level in the American Psychiatric Association was part of my continuing education in the psychology of discrimination; of racism, sexism, homophobia; of negative stereotyping and disempowerment. Within the council and committee structure, in the informal alliances and friendships, my awareness grew. That I was there at all, I attribute to the activism of Black psychiatrists and to the women's movement. The Black Caucus fostered an awareness of the need for affirmative action on the American Psychiatric Association, an organization whose leadership and membership, like all medical specialty organizations, were primarily white men. At the national level, many APA leaders were liberal, and at the top, many were old enough to be influenced by the women's movement through their daughters. As a result of activism on the part of others, I was invited to become a member of the Council on National Affairs in 1975, which was a major appointment to a policy making and policy influencing body of the APA. As a woman and an Asian, I was a "two-fer," or a double minority, and I considered that I was there to give these two "constituencies" a voice as well as to add color and gender. I subsequently proposed the formation of the Task Force of Asian-American Psychiatrists which became the Committee of Asian-American Psychiatrists, now a formal part of the APA. I became part of a growing, creative, political network of women in psychiatry who were making an impact at the national level, on policies, appointments, and presentations at the annual meetings. Meanwhile, a backlash within the membership was forming, with the American Psychiatric Association's support for the Equal Rights Amendment the issue. A referendum was passed in opposition to support for the ERA, just months before the 1981 annual meeting in San Francisco.

At the time, the APA was 89% male and two-thirds of our patients were female. Inequality, discrimination, and stereotyping affect self-esteem and limit opportunities for women; that psychiatrists who treat women did not support the ERA was appalling. I knew that if there were to be a protest against this in San Francisco, it would be up to me to organize it. There wasn't anyone else here in a position who could. I knew that silence is consent, and that all it would take for this particular evil to triumph would be for women to do nothing, and knew that this particular woman, me, had to become an activist, a protestor, and an organizer.

I organized PFERA–Psychiatrists for the Equal Rights Amendment. I invited Gloria Steinem to come and address members of the American Psychiatric Association at an event we would sponsor, and I pulled out all of the journalistic, public relations and political savvy that I had acquired, most prior to becoming a psychiatrist, and drew on talented people and contacts I had in San Francisco. The protest, which included an informational picket line, a publication, ERA-YES buttons, the support of those men at the top with feminist-daughters and younger psychiatrists with feminist-wives, and the involvement on the scene of the network of women psychiatrists that had been growing over the years, was a major success.

As a result of these endeavors, the Board of Trustees voted to pull the next annual meeting out of New Orleans (a non-ERA ratified state), contribute twenty-five thousand dollars to political efforts to ratify the Equal Rights Amendment, and voice support for the ERA as a mental health issue. A bare six weeks later, the board responded to the angry backlash from anti-ERA members, reversed their position, and decided the organization would hold its next convention in New Orleans after all. That made me an activist for another year, this time leading a boycott of the New Orleans meeting, with leadership shared by Alexandra Symonds, MD, in New York and Jean Baker Miller, MD, in Boston.

The net effect was wonderful in what it did to raise consciousness within psychiatry. A boycott meant that every member of the APA had to make a personal, political, and ethical decision whether or not to go to this particular annual meeting. That women patients could know if their psychiatrists went to this boycotted meeting became a possibility when Gloria Steinem announced that she would make the names of the psychiatrists who went to this meeting known through *Ms Magazine*. Now the relationship of sexism, the Equal Rights Amendment and women's mental health that had been raised at the national level, was brought to almost every department of psychiatry and every district branch of the APA, as well as to other psychiatric societies and organizations. Women psychiatrists all over the country found themselves in the position I was in as the annual meeting was coming to San Francisco: it would be up to them to raise these issues, and they did.

There were direct and indirect consequences. The boycott had an effect which was felt, yet we remained within the APA and had opened new dialogue, many more individual women became involved at all levels of psychiatry, and a permanent new organization was formed that grew directly out of Psychiatrists for ERA. Under the leadership of Alexandra Symonds, who had been the Co-chair, the Association for Women in Psychiatry was formed. Two years later, the American Psychiatric Association elected its first woman president. Through organizing Psychiatrists for the ERA, I met Gloria Steinem, which led to me becoming a member of the board of the Ms. Foundation for Women.

Becoming an activist had the effect of taking an advanced, experiential course in feminism (and patriarchy), which was further enhanced by sitting on a board with women, some of whom had founded *Ms. Magazine*, and others who had major roles putting feminism in practice, perceiving and meeting needs. As Gloria Steinem says, "Before the women's movement, there were no words for wife-battering, date-rape, sexual harassment—(and many other enumerated issues, that I can't recall)—it was just called life."

ARCHETYPAL PSYCHOLOGY AND FEMINISM:
NEW THEORY IN GODDESSES IN EVERYWOMAN

I was in Washington, D.C., for the meeting of the Board of Trustees of the American Psychiatric Association in June 1981, at which support for the Equal Rights Amendment was rescinded, when my literary agent called with the news that I had a contract to write *Goddesses in Everywoman: A New Psychology of Women*. As a result of these events, I made a commitment to write a book and lead a boycott on the same day. It was a symbolic coincidence, a synchronicity, that underlined the link between my feminist activism and psychological perspectives on women.

I had previously authored *The Tao of Psychology: Synchronicity and the Self* (1979). *Goddesses in Everywoman* was published in 1984, followed by *Gods in Everyman* (1989), *Ring of Power* (1992), and *Crossing to Avalon* (1994). They are all still in print and are all at heart deeply feminist because every book emphasizes the need to trust inner knowledge, to seek meaning, and speaks for the necessity for each person to be her or his own authority. I see this interior stance as a spiritual and psychological position that is in opposition to obedience to exterior, hierarchal authority which is the basis of patriarchy. The right to define ourselves becomes a political issue, when men in power and patriarchy claim to have this right.

Goddesses in Everywoman: A New Psychology of Women described the archetypal patterns in women's psyches, based upon the Greek goddesses, each of whom has particular qualities, strengths, susceptibilities for psychopathology, and possibilities for growth. It is a psychology that explains the complexity within individual women, as several archetypes may be active in the same woman and they may be in conflict with each other; and it also accounts for the diversity among women. Normality encompasses a wide range and depth in this theoretical model. Beginning with Freud and Jung, theories on the psychology of women present us with one model of all women, with deviation from the one model equated with pathology. In my own experience of women, as friends and patients, and my own sense of myself, the one model psychologies fit some but not all women.

In *Goddesses in Everywoman*, I introduced the idea of a psychological perspective that developed out of having "binocular vision": as a feminist and a Jungian analyst, I was aware of two powerful forces–archetypes and stereotypes–that shape the individual woman, whether or not she is conscious of them. Archetypes are sources of being and behaving; they can be compelling, unconscious, and predetermining; they are sources of meaning when they are fulfilled and can be sources of symptoms and distress under other circumstances. Some archetypal patterns fit family and cultural expectations and are welcomed, and given opportunity to be developed and lived out fully. Other archetypal patterns are rejected by family and culture, leading to a lowered self-esteem and difficulties. When archetypes are not allowed expression and denigrated, the women in whom these archetypes are active come into conflict with others and within themselves. In *The Feminine Mystique*, Friedan described the emptiness of women's lives as "the problem with no name"; which I attributed to the lack of depth and authenticity that follows when women try to be what others expect of them and these roles are not rooted in their archetypes.

In *Goddesses in Everywoman,* I described seven archetypal patterns that I put into three categories: The Vulnerable Goddess Archetypes (Hera, Demeter, Persephone) need others to be fulfilled and are vulnerable to symptoms and dysfunctional relationships, just as these goddesses were in their mythology. The Virgin Goddess Archetypes (Artemis, Athena, Hestia) are the "one-unto-herself" aspects of women that enable women to set their own goals, think strategically, enjoy solitude; they do not depend upon others to be fulfilled; as goddesses they were not victimized in their mythology and as archetypal patterns have more to do with character patterns than symptoms. The Alchemical Goddess Archetype (Aphrodite) has to do with transformation, creativity, and sexuality; as an archetype, there are aspects of vulnerability and of autonomy.

Each of these categories has a characteristic energy: diffuse, focused, or alchemical, and expression of each category (or each goddess archetype) has been either supported, repressed, or punished depending on the values of that particular time. As archetypes are as inherent as talent, intelligence, or instinct, women with certain archetypes thrive or not, in some historical times more than others. For example, in the 1950s when early marriage and many children were the ideal, the pendulum swung toward the Vulnerable

Goddess Archetypes. Times changed by 1970s, women entered careers, zero population growth was an ideal, and the Virgin Goddess Archetypes were expressed and supported.

Just as the goddesses of Greek mythology existed in an Olympian patriarchy with Zeus as chief god, which is reflected in their mythology, so are expressions of these archetypes in contemporary women shaped and limited by the patriarchy.

When I wrote *Gods in Everyman,* I said that instead of two separate books, I should have written one larger volume called *Gods and Goddesses in Everyperson.* While women usually have a preponderance of goddess archetypes, both male and female archetypes exist in each of us, and most women will find that at least one of the male archetypes is active in them, the awareness of which completes the picture. For example, in the writing, lecturing and traveling that I enjoy doing, I am very much aware that the archetype in me that is being expressed through these activities is a male archetype, Hermes the Messenger God, the communicator archetype for whom words are important, who in his most profound aspect was called the guide of souls.

In an effort to bring forth the detrimental effects of patriarchy on men, I further described and developed my understanding of patriarchy, of male archetypes that shape men and in turn are rewarded or not. In *Gods in Everyman,* the contribution of archetype to sacred experience was further delineated. In the two books, a complete system of understanding the psychology of personality based upon archetypes and culture, applicable to both women and men, was completed. I brought together insights from Jungian psychology, feminism, and clinical practice in two books written for the general public, rather than for a professional audience. I am more interested in helping people grow, to look inward and trust their own intuitive wisdom, to seek depth and meaning and thus have the possibility of leading a personal meaningful life, than in laying claim to territory by writing in journals. What I have to contribute would also lose its essence, which is much more of the soul than of the mind, if it had to be written in conformity to the requirements of professional journals.

In the realm of Jungian theory on the psychology of women and men, I have put forth a coherent and complete descriptive system based upon archetypes as personified by the Greek goddesses and gods. While it grows out of Jung's major contribution on the arche-types of the collective unconscious, I am maintaining that his anima/animus theory does not apply to everyone, while a theory based on the range of archetypal patterns which also takes culture into consid-eration, does. I also described in *Goddesses in Everywoman* how Jung's theory on anima/animus, where each gender has a less con-scious contra-sexual component, and a dominant and more conscious (and stereotypical) male or female orientation, is inconsistent with his theory on psychological types which has no gender basis or bias. In his psychological type theory, a woman can be a thinking type, which means that thinking would be her primary conscious function; while his anima/animus theory attributes a woman's thinking to her animus, which by definition is less conscious than the thinking func-tion in men. A woman with a well-developed Athena archetype can think well. She takes after the goddess Athena who was the best strategist, the clearest thinker of all the Olympians, who did not lose her head while others were caught up in the emotions of love or war. She uses her fine mind to accomplish what she focuses upon; a less conscious male part of her does not do her thinking for her.

In *Goddesses in Everywoman,* I also took issue with feminists, who maintain that traditional roles are imposed upon women by patriarchy. While patriarchy certainly does this, by not taking arche-types into account, feminism fails to understand that the roles of wife and mother are inherently meaningful to women in whom these archetypes live regardless of the culture. This can perhaps be understood when fulfillment of these particular archetypes goes against traditional (patriarchal) values, because of sexual orienta-tion, or because a woman is a single, unmarried mother. The arche-type of Hera the wife is fulfilled in a committed, monogamous relationship, whether it is with another woman or with a husband; marriage for her is a source of wholeness and a sacred commitment, and when betrayed exposes her to being overwhelmed by jealousy and rage. The archetype of Demeter the mother is expressed by having a child, not a spouse. In a patriarchal, fundamentalist cul-ture, traditional roles for women are defined by their being in subor-dinate relationship to men; they fulfill the needs of men by these roles. When a woman lives these roles out of her archetypal depth, however, they have a deeply personal meaning, regardless of the circumstances.

DYSFUNCTIONAL FAMILY PSYCHOLOGY
AND FEMINIST THEORY–RING OF POWER

Feminist psychology as I see it is as much about the effects of patriarchy upon women as it is a psychology of women. The necessity from the beginning of the women's movement was to become aware of how we were being defined by others (men and patriarchy) as well as to define ourselves and our own experience. To make conscious choices, we need to become conscious of what affects us from within and without; to do this we need words, concepts, and images that fit our experiences and reality. In 1992, I wrote *Ring of Power: The Abandoned Child, The Authoritarian Father*, and *The Disempowered Feminine*, which furthered the work I had brought forth in *Goddesses in Everywoman* and *Gods in Everyman*. Once again I wrote about archetypes and their interaction with patriarchy, this time focusing on the dysfunctional family, and how power is the ruling principle in patriarchy and how it is expressed in families, institutions and society, and has major detrimental effects on individuals. I defined a dysfunctional relationship as any relationship in which it is not safe for us to express how we feel and what we perceive. In such relationships, co-dependency to authority happens as a matter of structure and power.

Ring of Power was inspired by Richard Wagner's *The Ring of the Nibelung*, a compelling four-opera cycle comprised of *The Rhinegold, The Valkyrie, Siegfried*, and *The Twilight of the Gods*. In the *Ring Cycle*, I saw the archetypes I described in my previous books, now with names from Germanic and Norse mythology, enacted as opera and covering three generations. I now added concepts and words from the recovery movement and Alice Miller's *Prisoners of Childhood: The Drama of the Gifted Child* to the psychology of archetypes and patriarchy. Anyone and everyone who is required to be an extension of a parent's ambitions or needs, which was amply and horribly demonstrated in the *Ring Cycle*, instead of being loved for herself and seen as having her own purpose, destiny, talents and yearnings, is, in my definition, an abandoned child. As seen in real life as well as in the *Ring*, the authoritarian father in families and in society leads to a disempowered feminine and tragedy for all concerned.

It is the archetypal figure of a father's daughter who suffers and transforms herself and the story in the *Ring Cycle*. It is a role I see individual women taking, and in as much as I empower women and men to become conscious of what they know and feel, and then in their moments of truth, act upon what they know is true for them, I bring an element of activism to the psychology I write about. Feminist psychology is a psychology that leads to making changes; it is an activist psychology.

THE SPIRITUAL DIMENSION OF FEMINISM: CROSSING TO AVALON

In *Crossing to Avalon: A Woman's Midlife Pilgrimage* (1994) I described a pilgrimage I took to sacred sites in Europe, and the reflections upon my own experience that this journey evoked. In the midst of a midlife transition, I had received an unexpected invitation to go on this journey which began with a private audience with the Dalai Lama. In my mind were *The Grail Legend* and *The Mists of Avalon*, a novel that had made me think of the grail from a goddess perspective.

I wrote that any woman, no matter how privileged, is oppressed in a culture where there is no Goddess. To change patriarchy, theology must be changed. For patriarchy is based on a male sky god theology and hierarchy, which gives men (because they are created in the image of divinity, which is male) dominion over women, children, animals, over everything including the planet. Women's psychology, self-acceptance, self-esteem, and self-determination have been shaped by theology.

For 25,000 to 5,000 years before patriarchy, divinity was in the image of woman. The goddess as Great Mother was the creator. There is a realm of embodied spirituality which women know that is not acknowledged by patriarchal theology; there are sacred experiences to do with pregnancy, delivery, nursing an infant at the breast, making love, touching, healing, and comforting, in which we experience the Goddess, or are ourselves in that moment an embodiment of the Goddess. The Goddess comes through women and Nature, through personal experience. For me to tell what I know and perceive, required me to write a very personal and spiritual book.

I think that women's spirituality is the last and most significant wave of the women's movement. If theology changes and divinity is experienced as both male and female, God and Goddess, spirit and soul, eternal and in matter, then psychology and culture will change. Bringing about a shift in the theological perspective will have an enormously positive effect on the psychology of women. At this time, the Goddess is emerging through us, in dreams, visions, intuitions, and sacred experiences as an aspect of divinity; there is a re-membered quality to these experiences, as if from a repressed, dis-membered and excised past.

Crossing to Avalon is an extension of feminist principles that emphasizes the personal and experiential. The experience of God/ Goddess/divinity is very personal; a numinous, synchronistic, meaningful, or sacred moment is a subjective event. Most patriarchal religions, in contrast, are based upon authority and obedience. The Word is emphasized, as are obedience and belief. A divinely inspired book or text or revelation is given to a patriarch, a hierarchal organization forms, and followers must believe in the words and experience of the authority; in most religions, submitting to divine authority vested in men is required.

I think that anyone who insists that: "the final authority of what is meaningful, sacred, or matters to me, is me," is an empowered feminist. Every one of my books beginning with *The Tao of Psychology: Synchronicity and the Self,* is empowering in providing the means through which a reader has an Aha! reaction; when this happens, my words have articulated what the reader knows is true but did not have the concept, perspective, or words for. In doing so, consciousness is raised, which is another priority and characteristic of feminism. To have the right to be fully and particularly who we are is a feminist goal that might be called "the right to individuate." This is an underlying assumption in my writing.

I think women have found that getting a share of patriarchal power has its satisfactions, but it is not fulfilling in itself. It is better than being oppressed, it is better than being paid less, and it's better than a lot of things, but the result is not a meaningful life. Meaning has to do with finding a way to express our active archetypes and integrate our experiences of the sacred into life; this in turn depends a great deal on our freedom to be who we are, voice what we know, and act from our convictions. For this we need to free ourselves from our particular Ring cycles, which *Ring of Power* addresses. In the process of personal transformation, I believe that we also contribute to transforming the patriarchy.

PERSONAL TRANSFORMATION
AND THE TRANSFORMATION OF PATRIARCHY

In both *Ring of Power* and *Crossing to Avalon,* I suggest that we change more than ourselves when we become conscious and make changes, or bring what we know into consciousness; we contribute to changing the world. Our actions and growth in awareness contribute to a morphic field through morphic resonance, which in turn makes similar changes or growth easier for others. This is theory proposed by Rupert Sheldrake, a theoretical biologist. His theory provides the mechanism through which C. G. Jung's archetypes of the collective unconscious can evolve. It is this possibility or actuality that makes me feel that we are engaged in creating a post-patriarchal world each time we speak the truth of our feelings and perceptions, transform dysfunctional relationships into egalitarian ones, or bring what we have experienced of the Goddess into consciousness.

Notes of a Feminist Therapy "Foredaughter"

Laura S. Brown

When I first received the letter that invited me to participate in this special volume, I had an immediate response of "who me?" This is not because I do not think that my work has an important impact on the field of feminist therapy; that would be a level of false modesty impossible to sustain (plus, my friends would laugh at me!). But a "foremother"? Me? I have never thought of myself as a feminist foremother. Rather, I have seen myself as a well-loved and cared-for older daughter of many other feminist therapy foremothers (Brown, 1994b) whose role as a prominent theoretician and "eldest sister" of feminist therapy has owed much to that older generation of women who have mentored me and made the way

Laura S. Brown, PhD, practices feminist clinical and forensic psychology in Seattle, WA, where she has lived since 1976. She holds a Diplomate in Clinical Psychology, is a Fellow of APA and APS, and is Clinical Professor of Psychology at the University of Washington. Active in both feminist and mainstream psychology, she has written and taught extensively on issues of feminist therapy theory, ethics, assessment, and practice, and on psychotherapy with lesbians. She has co-edited three books on feminist therapy, and recently completed her first authored book, titled *Subversive Dialogues: Theory in Feminist Therapy* (Basic Books, 1994).

Correspondence may be addressed to Laura S. Brown, 4527 First Avenue NE, Seattle, WA 98105-4801.

[Haworth co-indexing entry note]: "Notes of a Feminist Therapy 'Foredaughter.' " Brown, Laura S. Co-published simultaneously in *Women & Therapy* (The Haworth Press, Inc.) Vol. 17, No. 1/2, 1995, pp. 87-95; and: *Feminist Foremothers in Women's Studies, Psychology, and Mental Health* (ed: Phyllis Chesler, Esther D. Rothblum, and Ellen Cole) The Haworth Press, Inc., 1995, pp. 87-95; and: *Feminist Foremothers in Women's Studies, Psychology, and Mental Health* (ed: Phyllis Chesler, Esther D. Rothblum, and Ellen Cole) Harrington Park Press, an imprint of The Haworth Press, Inc., 1995, pp. 87-95. Single or multiple copies of this article are available from The Haworth Document Delivery Service [1-800-342-9678, 9:00 a.m. - 5:00 p.m. (EST)].

open for me to do my work. It has been a shock to my system in the last few years to encounter feminist graduate students coming up to me at conventions with the same appreciation for my work that I could once be found directing towards Hannah Lerman or Nancy Felipe Russo or Adrienne Smith or Lenore Walker or Barbara Wallston or a score of other incredible thinkers and doers in the fields of feminist psychology and feminist therapy. From these more recent encounters with students and younger colleagues, I begin to get the notion that whether I accept it or not, I have become an authority figure to someone.

But when I approach the question posed by the editors about how I came to make my contributions to feminist therapy theory, it is that older daughter position that emerges continuously as the one defining my experience of that process. I was born in 1952; most of the women who are now my professional peers and were once (and to some degree still) my personal mentors in the field of feminist therapy are at least ten years older. Largely because of some quirks of fate (I got into kindergarten a year earlier than my late December birthday should have allowed; I skipped my senior years of high school and college; I pushed myself through my doctoral program very fast) combined with my tendency to think out loud and in print with more chutzpa than most people, I have appeared to be a peer of sorts to the women who I think of as my feminist and feminist therapy foremothers. I have also benefitted from the privileges of race, class, and culture; as an upper-middle class white Jewish woman who comes from a family in which women's intellect and education were specifically valued and encouraged (and whose maternal grandmother was a strong feminist before she had words to name it), I came to the field of feminist therapy with a sense of intellectual entitlement and a heritage of intellectual analysis and concern with ethical and theoretical matters that have made it easier for me to showcase my ideas. We live in a society that privileges those who, like myself, are quick of tongue, "articulate," and who live in the world of words; that privilege is another facet of the political and social milieu that grew me.

The circumstances that led me to make my contributions to feminist therapy thus have their roots in the ways in which social context has given meaning and value to my individual talents, skills, and propensities. But none of this would have ever expressed itself without the supportive presence of several organizations and the feminist women (and a few men) who made those organizations my professional and political home. In my first year of graduate school, I became involved with the Association for Women in Psychology, a national feminist organization. Because it was feminist, it was profoundly non-hierarchical, and graduate students like me had the opportunity for close and peer-like contact with what I called "the grown-ups": feminist psychologists with PhDs who were out working in the field and generating new knowledge. I also had the chance to be taken seriously immediately as a feminist thinker and feminist therapist, and to take on responsibilities for organizational management.

Going to the AWP annual conventions in those early years of the 1970s was like attending a large and continuous consciousness-raising group, in which feminist analysis of psychology and psychotherapy went hand-in-hand with presentations on exciting new feminist topics. This atmosphere would continue in AWP suites at the annual APA conventions; I and other poor students would rent sleeping-bag space on the floor for a few dollars a night, then bask in the presence of the luminaries of feminist psychology holding their discussions in front of our eyes, and including us in. I first met Hannah Lerman in an AWP suite in 1974 as she passionately debated some long-forgotten man about why sexual abuse of clients had to be specifically declared unethical in the APA code. I first met Adrienne Smith at the initial AWP conference in Ft. Wayne, Indiana when she emerged as the first openly lesbian psychologist I had ever known. Neither these, nor any of the other feminist psychologists that I met in this context ever treated me as other than a peer, never offered me anything but utter encouragement to develop and present my ideas. Feminist egalitarian principles were truly the hallmark of AWP and the women I met there.

The Feminist Therapy Institute emerged from AWP when Adrienne (who died of cancer in 1992) began to agitate for the creation of a meeting for the more advanced and experienced clinicians, and I was somehow included in the list of women who were invited to attend a meeting that was organized by Lenore Walker in Vail, Colorado in May of 1982. The Vail Advanced Feminist Therapy

Institute (AFTI) has become a hallmark in the heritage of feminist therapy. For four heady days, a group of sixty women sat in a windowless room and talked about feminist therapy practice at a level of sophistication, politically and psychologically, that I had found almost nowhere else in aggregate. I wrote my very first feminist therapy ethics paper for that meeting, and in that setting first began to think of myself as someone for whom the development of theory in feminist therapy was an interest.

The other context that allowed me to make the contributions that I have made was the practice I was doing. In 1979, I became, as far as I know, the first *openly* lesbian licensed psychologist in Seattle (there were other lesbian psychologists who preceded me, but none who were out to their colleagues or consumers). This circumstance provided me opportunities to work with a range of clients and to become involved with a lesbian community in ways that immediately began to highlight some of the ethical and professional challenges for persons like myself, lesbians who lived and worked in the same community as many of our clients and whose social networks and extra-therapeutic social roles also overlapped. I also began to practice in the context of a scandal in our community that involved the disintegration of a therapy cult created by one of the first openly lesbian therapists in town, a woman who had become sexual with one client, gone into business with others, and in general attempted to control women's lives.

These factors awakened an interest in therapy ethics as they applied to feminist and lesbian therapists. Since the moment I had read *Women and Madness* (Chesler, 1972), I had been actively working on the problem of sexual abuse in psychotherapy, but had seen it as a problem of men oppressing women. The lesbian communities that made up my life and my practice "catchment area," as it were, gave me an entirely new view of this issue.

The themes that emerge from those formative experiences define what I consider to be my two meaningful contributions to the field of feminist therapy. The first major area of impact (the editors told me not to be modest, so here goes) of my work has been in the development of feminist therapy ethics, and the creation of complex and sophisticated conceptual models for understanding the ethical dilemmas arising for feminist therapists, especially the many of us who practice in small communities; the social and psychological small towns of lesbian communities, communities of color, of faith, of shared politics. I wanted to understand the ethics of how we "set the fee as a feminist" (Luepnitz, 1988), so I wrote about business issues; money, barter, sliding scales, accessible office spaces, class differences between therapist and client. Because I felt dissatisfied with the answers that standard ethical codes provided to feminist therapists who were faced with questions such as how to share the only lesbian/gay synagogue or only feminist women's gym or only women-of-color support group with their clients, I began to write articles and book chapters about my ideas about how to attempt solutions to these quandaries.

I also took on, head-first, the problem of sexual abuse of women clients by their women therapists. Spurred by what had happened in Seattle, and by the cases of prominent feminist therapy teachers from Colorado and Minnesota who had brought entire training programs crashing down in ruins because of sexual relationships with clients, I began to try to understand and work to prevent this painful problem. As with other forms of woman-to-woman abuse, my exposure of this was not always greeted with joy, and was also difficult to fit into the then more simple models held by feminists for explaining sexual exploitation. Some of my most valuable contributions have been on this topic, and in the work that has emerged from my attempts to grapple with and understand the explosive combination of the intensity of therapy, the imbalance of power therein, and the close social proximity created by overlapping roles in small communities.

My development of the concept of a continuum of boundary violations (Brown, 1988, 1990) and the paradigm of all therapists as being at risk to move along that continuum helped move feminist thinking on ethics and boundaries into a less dichotomous, more inclusive model that aided all of us in understanding how we could be at risk, and what we could do to prevent risk to clients, communities and ourselves. More recently, and flowing from that work, I have argued for a more conceptual and less concrete framework for understanding violations of boundaries (Brown, 1994a) that specifically empowers feminist therapists as ethical decision-makers and active participants in the development of feminist therapy ethics in their own work.

Finally in the area of ethics, and closest to my heart, has been the work I have done to develop a paradigm of anti-racism as an ethical action and imperative for feminist therapists (Brown, 1991, 1993). My introduction to anti-racism and other forms of anti-domination work, which occurred as the Feminist Therapy Institute struggled with this dynamic in the late 1980s, made me see that in the crucible of fighting racism in ourselves, our theories, and our practice, the politics of the matter were also calls to ethical action. Following Val Kanuha's call (1990) for feminist therapists to examine our racism as a matter of ethics, I have worked to show how core feminist ethical principles of respect, mutuality, and egalitarianism could not exist absent a commitment by the therapist to anti-racist and other anti-dominant strategies. I think that my work on this topic has helped to expand what feminist therapists mean by ethics.

The second area of my major contributions has been in the creation of feminist therapy theory. Along with other women in FTI, the development of a theory for feminist therapy has become a passion for me. Hannah Lerman (1986) was the first feminist therapist that I know of to set forth what have become consensus criteria for theory in feminist therapy, and I have had the good fortune to be included in her thinking process and have my own nourished by hers. Just before starting this piece, I finished the final copyediting work on a complete book of feminist therapy theory, one that I hope will be a major contribution to our dialogues and debates in the field, and which expands on a great deal of other work that I had done previously (Brown, 1994b).

But before writing this book, I have been an active (sometimes too-loud) voice in the endless discussions between and among feminist therapists and feminist critics of therapy about what is it that makes feminist therapy truly feminist (Brown, 1992). I think that I have made some valuable contributions with my analysis of the ways in which feminist therapy is an act of social transformation, distinguishing therapy, or any sort of practice for that matter, done with feminist analysis and contextualization from "women therapists working with women" which is neither a necessary nor sufficient set of descriptors for feminist therapy. I have helped the field to have a definition, and clarity of boundaries.

How has this changed my life, the editors asked? Well, it's hard to imagine my life at all without this work! But specifically, the first and most important thing that has resulted from my participation in the creation and development of feminist therapy theory and ethics is that I had to learn to use and love computers. Hannah Lerman and Lynne Bravo Rosewater were the first people I ever knew to own personal computers; I can recall sitting at the 1982 AFTI in awe of this fact. Then I got one in 1984, and discovered how indispensable a tool this was for a writer; and then I fell in love with anything with microchips. My entire relationship to the burgeoning world of cyberspace would never have happened had I not wanted to find an easier way to write all the articles and book chapters that my fertile little brain was giving birth to in the fecund milieu of the feminist therapy world.

And I became a writer because I was a feminist therapist with a computer and something on my mind. My CV is very telling; there are something like six articles before 1984; then it gets to be more like six or eight or ten every year. Becoming a writer, discovering my voice on the keyboard, and the enormous exhilaration that attends on seeing my own words in print–being invited into the vast conversation on paper that is the creation of theory and ethics in feminist therapy–and then first editing and then finally writing a book; all of these have completely changed my image of myself and my visions for my future. I had never thought of myself as a writer; now I spend almost every weekend, for at least part of one day, sitting with the computer in my lap, tapping away, happily oblivious to everyone but the dog who takes up residence on my foot (and my partner who is sitting at her own computer, as well). The more I write, the more opportunities I am given to write, and the more chances I have to play with and expand the ideas of my previous work.

But how do I put into words the experience of knowing how in my own way I am part of feminist revolution? How to talk about the energy that I feel when I see the impact of one of these ideas on a client, student, colleague; the effect on me when a straight white male colleague comes up to me after a talk and tells me that he is going to have to rethink his entire intro psychology class because what I said turned the lightbulb on? How do I tell you the ways in which this has changed my life? It's difficult, almost impossible, because this *is* my life; I stumble, become tongue-tied at moments like this, think "changed from what?" I cannot imagine that I would have been able to survive in psychology had I not found feminism and feminist colleagues there from my very first month of graduate school; I cannot envision working, thinking, writing as other than a feminist. Once having read *Women and Madness* in the year before graduate school, I did not feel myself to have a choice to be other than a feminist therapist if I truly wished to do good. My doing of my work, the writing and teaching, the therapy and forensic practice, has given me the chance to meet and know amazing human beings who I might have never otherwise encountered; that certainly has changed my life. My work in feminist therapy has been the door that opens other doors; but who would I have been had I never opened that first door in 1972 when I read *Women and Madness* and was permanently transformed? I do not know.

I can only say honestly that by being a writer, teacher, scholar of feminist therapy, my life has been profoundly enriched. I have had chances to meet and confront my own internalized domination (Pheterson, 1986) and oppressiveness; I might have come later to this, or avoided it, were not my pride so great and my self-righteousness so powerful that I could not stand in a role of teacher and not face the challenge to do this work against racism and domination. I have had the privilege to see the plethora of ways in which a feminist analysis can extend to the practice of psychology, be it supervision, forensic work, community psychology, teaching or consultation. And I have been gifted with the friendship of remarkable people who I know I might have never met otherwise: my feminist foremothers, my peers and colleagues, and the students, clients, and trainees that I have worked with along the way, many of whom came to me because I had done some of the work that constitutes my contributions.

Feminist ideas and analysis came to my life at a crucial developmental stage, just as I was entering young adulthood and beginning my professional education. Nothing of who I am professionally, and little of who I am now personally, would exist without that. Perhaps the best answer is to say that feminist theory, and the work of feminist therapy, has allowed me to live my life. It has given me a raison d'être that has sustained me in the face of knowledge of the horrors of oppression, as well as at times of personal pain and difficulty. Feminist therapy has joined at the root with my Jewish heritage so that, an hour at a time, a life at a time, I can participate in the revolutionary activity of "Tikkun olam," healing the world through the transformative work of feminism that takes shape for me in the practice of feminist therapy.

REFERENCES

Brown, L.S. (1988). Beyond thou shalt not: Thinking about ethics in the lesbian therapy community. *Women & Therapy, 8,* 13-26.

Brown, L.S. (1990). Confronting ethically problematic behaviors in feminist therapy colleagues. In H. Lerman & N. Porter (Eds.) *Feminist ethics in psychotherapy* (pp. 147-160). New York: Springer Publishing.

Brown, L.S. (1991). Anti-racism as an ethical imperative: An example from feminist therapy. *Ethics and Behavior, 1,* 113-127.

Brown, L.S. (1992). While waiting for the revolution: The case for a lesbian feminist psychotherapy. *Feminism and Psychology, 2,* 239-253.

Brown, L.S. (1993). Anti-domination training as a central component of diversity in clinical psychology education. *The Clinical Psychologist, 44,* 83-87.

Brown, L.S. (1994a). Boundaries in feminist therapy: A conceptual formulation. *Women & Therapy, 15,* 29-38.

Brown, L.S. (1994b). *Subversive dialogues: Theory in feminist therapy.* New York: Basic Books.

Chesler, P. (1972). *Women and madness.* Garden City NY: Doubleday.

Kanuha, V. (1990). The need for an integrated analysis of oppression in feminist therapy ethics. In H. Lerman & N. Porter (Eds.) *Feminist ethics in psychotherapy* (pp. 24-36). New York: Springer Publishing.

Lerman, H. (1986). *A mote in Freud's eye: From psychoanalysis to the psychology of women.* New York: Springer Publishing.

Luepnitz, D.A. (1988). *The family interpreted.* New York: Basic Books.

Pheterson, G. (1986). Alliances between women: Confronting internalized oppression and internalized domination. *Signs: Journal of Women in Culture and Society, 12,* 146-160.

Spiritual Dandelions

Zsuzsanna Emese Budapest
Kathryn T. Downey

Z Budapest believes that women must become more like dandelions. The noble dandelions travel on the wind, catch and multiply

Zsuzsanna (Z) Budapest is the first genetic witch to join feminism and witchcraft that sparked the worldwide Women's Spirituality Movement, otherwise known as the Goddess Movement. As High Priestess, she led the first feminist coven, the Susan B. Anthony Coven Number One, which became a role model for many feminist covens in the USA and abroad. Z's first book, published in the early seventies, *The Feminist Book of Lights and Shadows* received wide readership and was re-released by Wingbow Press, Berkeley, into a larger volume called *The Holy Book of Women's Mysteries.* Her other books are *The Grandmother of Time* and *Grandmother Moon* by Harper & Row, San Francisco, which is about lunar holydays and festivals from around the world. Z's latest books, published by Harper/Collins, San Francisco, are *The Goddess in the Office* and, published Valentine's Day, 1995, *Goddess in the Bedroom.* Other firsts include the first Goddess TV show "13th Heaven," created by and starring Z, and the First International Goddess Festival, organized by Z and the Women's Spirituality Forum, held in 1994 at the May full moon. Z lives and works in the San Francisco Bay Area, and travels throughout the world teaching workshops for women.

Kathryn T. Downey is a graduate student at the University of Vermont pursuing a doctorate in Social Psychology. She is currently finishing a meta-analysis on obesity and its effects on self-esteem. Kathy's research and teaching interests include the psychology of women, social cognition and statistics.

Correspondence may be addressed to Zsuzsanna Budapest at Women's Spirituality Forum, P.O. Box 11363, Oakland, CA 94611.

[Haworth co-indexing entry note]: "Spiritual Dandelions." Budapest, Zsuzsanna Emese, and Kathryn T. Downey. Co-published simultaneously in *Women & Therapy* (The Haworth Press, Inc.) Vol. 17, No. 1/2, 1995, pp. 97-102; and: *Feminist Foremothers in Women's Studies, Psychology, and Mental Health* (ed: Phyllis Chesler, Esther D. Rothblum, and Ellen Cole) The Haworth Press, Inc., 1995, pp. 97-102; and: *Feminist Foremothers in Women's Studies, Psychology, and Mental Health* (ed: Phyllis Chesler, Esther D. Rothblum, and Ellen Cole) Harrington Park Press, an imprint of The Haworth Press, Inc., 1995 pp. 97-102. Single or multiple copies of this article are available from The Haworth Document Delivery Service [1-800-342-9678, 9:00 a.m. - 5:00 p.m. (EST)].

© 1995 by The Haworth Press, Inc. All rights reserved.

in small places, take strongholds, and grow from small clusters to oceans of yellow blooms. Every little piece of a dandelion can actually make a complete, new plant. Dandelions are beautiful, healthy to eat and full of life's green energy. They are indestructible. But they are hated, for they are not valued by those who erroneously believe dandelions interfere with the "natural course" of the lawns of the universe.

I first became aware of Z Budapest's work while browsing through an occult section at a small bookstore. (Yes, even as little as five years ago, her books were placed in the "occult" section instead of the psychology section.) At that time in my life, I was searching for nontraditional, woman-centered books on spirituality. I was not fulfilled with traditional religions that focused on men, hierarchies, and punishment. I purchased *Grandmother of Time* and devoured it from cover to cover.

After reading *Grandmother of Time*, I became alive with the knowledge of rituals that made me feel special, connected and powerful. I replaced old views of spirituality with eclectic beliefs in reincarnation and animism. Z helped me to discover ways that I could bond with other women through special ceremonies and rituals. It also made me feel that being female was beautiful and should be celebrated every day. Women do have a special niche in the universe. Z made me realize this.

But I did not know how her strong woman-centered spirituality would affect me until I shared my beliefs with others. I chose to "come out" in a class on Death and Dying. The professor asked all of the students to discuss their views on religion and the afterlife. I enthusiastically told my peers of my recent awakening and of the wonderful books that they should read. I shared with my class the visions I was having at the time, that I did not subscribe to a certain religion and that I practiced spiritual rituals. After they picked their jaws off the floor, they reciprocated the sharing by being amazed at my lack of morals, my naiveté, and my weirdness. By telling me my worldview was incorrect, they felt they were trying to save me. They felt they were helping me; instead, they alienated me. This only made me more curious about non-mainstream spiritual beliefs. Like a dandelion, being crushed underfoot made me generate into a stronger, more complete flower.

During a conversation with Z, she told me of her influences, her journey to America and to feminism, and her contributions to women's spirituality. Z also described her process towards becoming a more complete person by branching into different environments and growing strongholds.

Z has always rooted herself in her spirituality and her connections with other women. However, the crises that she has encountered made her question her assumptions and made her stronger and more complete, like a dandelion. She has always looked to women for inspiration. Z was raised by three very strong women: her grandmother, mother, and her still-living Aunt Titi, the elder sister of her mother. These women are the cornerstone of Z's spiritual knowledge, for in her family, the women have been spiritually strong for generations. For example, Z's grandmother was a suffragist. Masika Szilagyi, Z's mother, was an artist and a famous sculptor in Hungary. Masika was born a psychic and was spiritually adopted by the witch who saved her life. She also learned about witchcraft from the women in the Hungarian countryside. Z grew up in a temple-like house full of goddess statues, goddess stories and mythology: the Queen of Swords and Hearts and the Triple Goddess who are the Fates. Z did not inherit her mother's mediumistic abilities, but she does see spirits on rare occasions. On even rarer occasions, she sees ghosts of family members who have passed over.

Growing up in communist Hungary, Z was surrounded by women who took equality seriously. However, in reality the women did not have the same social or economic powers as men. Sexism was unnamed and very much alive. In addition, the brighter women in general were still very male-identified, but Z's mother took inspiration from Goddesses. Outside her home, there was oppression, while in her home her family created a spiritual oasis.

Z became a political refugee from Hungary at the age of 16. With most of her family staying in Hungary, she escaped after the Hungarian revolution and came to America. Z believes that this bloody civil war and following migration made her adaptable to life's future changes. Like a dandelion, Z traveled on the wind and took a new stronghold.

After coming to America, she read much Jung and found the

White Goddess by Robert Graves. At this time there were few books on European paganism. There were many books on folklore, but little on spiritual ceremonies, especially for women. Z organized the women around her who, together with Z, created their own rituals. This became the basis of *The Holy Book of Women's Mysteries*. Learning mythology through her family, self-education and instinctual improvisation, she managed to reclaim a female culture as a path to empower women.

When Z first started writing, the word "Goddess" was scandalous and powerful. At that time, women could not relate to Goddesses and men found them threatening. "Goddess" is much more than the female equivalent of "God." "Goddess" is indicative of female-based spirituality that does not rely on hierarchies. This type of spirituality is very accepting and nurturing. It is a liberating, not a constrictive word. Using the term "Goddess" validates women's power in the universe. With more women using the term "Goddess," women's spirituality has become a grassroots practice today.

Z felt a need to create an environment where Goddesses are discussed and prayed to and where her family witchcraft is directed and applied to all Goddesses around the world. Only feminist psychologist and activist Phyllis Chesler talked openly about Goddesses in *Women and Madness*. Z read Chesler's work not only through a psychological perspective, but also with a spiritual perspective. To Z, Chesler explained the psychological need for female divinity. After reading *Women and Madness*, Z met Chesler and they became lifelong friends.

When Z felt the crush of oppression she turned to the women around her as she had done when she was a child. Her inner world was filled with strong women while the outside world was a harsh environment. Working at the Women's Center in Los Angeles in the early seventies, she experienced two years of intense growing and awakening. She also became a lesbian. She was part of a tight-knit group of people, whom she saw as the sisters she never had. They together organized political events, went to marches and published a newsletter called "Sister."

Z was drawn to feminism in two ways: by moving away from negative heterosexism and hierarchies and by reaching toward a positive, woman-loving environment. When she did find feminism, she felt it was like a homecoming. Her spirituality and her worldview finally merged. She felt fulfilled in ways that she did not know before. She found her mission.

However, there is still no general support from the political side of feminism for the spiritual side of feminism, such as Z's work. There is still a schism between the "political" feminists and the "emotional/spiritual" feminists. Z believes the root of oppression is a spiritual poisoning, and until political feminists respect spirituality as the spiritualists respect politics, women will not be whole.

For Z, the spirit is an important focus. Maintaining spiritual health is integral to mental health. Feminism has been slow to accept spirituality because of male identification and the deep wounds suffered from patriarchal religions. However, women are the main supporters of all denominations of religion/spirituality. According to Z, women "hold up all of the sky." People cannot take spirituality away from women in exchange for politics alone. Women will always find the spirit in which to believe. Spirituality is inherently important to women and it is suicidal not to include it in political work.

Unfortunately, integrating feminism and spirituality is a difficult task. This debate has been raging since the suffragist movement in the last century. Elizabeth Cady Stanton took on the Bible to show how women's inferiority is created by men, not by God. Z would like to see a blending of the political and the spiritual in the feminist movement. Z thinks blessings or rituals could be done at political meetings, which would give women a focus, a blend of intellectual, emotional, and spiritual power. Being spiritual includes verbal hygiene. For example, using "Oh Goddess!" instead of "Oh God!" for "God." In addition, people should use female positive language.

Z's contribution to us is the introduction and revival of Women's Mysteries in the US. This includes the practice of female-centered/ Goddess improvisational spirituality. She teaches her American students how to pray to their own bodies, their ancestors, and the global Goddess, and how to get in touch with their own divinity. She brings a wealth of lore into knowledge about the Goddess, such as Diana, the Goddess of the Forest and the Moon. Z has inspired thousands of women to open their minds to different types of spirituality, especially rituals that are created out of love for women.

Z's political spirituality is her life. This is her gift to the feminist movement. In return, Z's life has changed due to feminism. Feminism awakened a connection with other women that Z needed. Z has multiplied her strengths through her spiritual daughters who carry on her teachings.

Z always wanted to be the great Hungarian novelist, writing strong female characters. Instead she has written seven non-fiction books on female-centered rituals. Currently, she wants to write short stories and essays, but her heart is in the theater. She wants to write screenplays with spiritual themes, where women are the heroes.

REFERENCES

Chesler, Phyllis (1972). *Women and Madness.* Garden City, NY: Doubleday.
Graves, Robert (1972). *White Goddess: A Historical Grammar of Poetic Myth.* New York: Octagon Books.

The Fitting Room

Sandra Butler

In 1950, when I was twelve years old, I was 5'5" tall, exactly the average height for a girl. By my thirteenth birthday, I had grown to a height of six feet. Now I was an average size girl in a six-foot-tall body, a body that it would take me 25 years to grow into. Without feminism, maybe I never would have.

At thirteen, I was convinced that I had a rare disease, convinced that I would continue to grow and grow, convinced that I was doomed to be different, an outsider, marked by my body. I developed a complicated series of strategies. I stood very straight and tall to contradict my awkwardness about my out-of-control body. My real experience was to be private, unshared. Instead, to compensate, I made myself small in my personality, my hungers and my behavior. I tried to be inconspicuous, unnoticed and unmarked for the derision that I was sure would be the result of being so big. I spent most of my time alone reading, mostly about outsiders and outcasts, those who were, in some way, marked by their bodies as different.

Sandra Butler is the author of *Conspiracy of Silence: The Trauma of Incest* and co-author of *Cancer in Two Voices* which won the Lambda Literary Award for Non-Fiction in 1991. In addition to her work in the fields of child sexual assault and the politics of women's health, she is co-founder of the Institute for Feminist Training.

Correspondence may be addressed to Sandra Butler, 6114 LaSalle Avenue #299, Oakland, CA 94611.

[Haworth co-indexing entry note]: "The Fitting Room." Butler, Sandra. Co-published simultaneously in *Women & Therapy* (The Haworth Press, Inc.) Vol. 17, No. 1/2, 1995, pp. 103-112; and: *Feminist Foremothers in Women's Studies, Psychology, and Mental Health* (ed: Phyllis Chesler, Esther D. Rothblum, and Ellen Cole) The Haworth Press, Inc., 1995, pp. 103-112; and: *Feminist Foremothers in Women's Studies, Psychology, and Mental Health* (ed: Phyllis Chesler, Esther D. Rothblum, and Ellen Cole) Harrington Park Press, an imprint of The Haworth Press, Inc., 1995, pp. 103-112. Single or multiple copies of this article are available from The Haworth Document Delivery Service [1-800-342-9678, 9:00 a.m. - 5:00 p.m. (EST)].

In 1955, during my first and last semester of University, this strategy and my love for jazz led me straight to the Negro students and townies, men and women who shared my love for and knowledge of jazz. By that first Thanksgiving, I was dismissed for "consorting with undesirable elements." I had, without ever intending it, in my longing to fit in and to be known, again stepped outside the borders of white, middle-class female life of the mid-1950s.

The only imaginable alternative way to enter a successful adulthood, now that I had failed at the University, was on the arm of a successful man. In months, I had found that arm. Within three years, when I was only twenty-one, I had a fourteen-room house, two daughters, a gardener, carpool responsibilities and carefully clipped recipes that I used to entertain my husband's business clients. I was inside, at last, but inside an enormous golden cage, which quickly slammed shut behind me, dwarfing me, compelling me to remain small and hidden within it.

In fewer than five years, the constraints of being muted, except for acquiescent murmurs and smiles, had become unbearable. I was beginning to strain at the confining borders of small and appropriate behavior. Not far from our home were several embassies of newly-emerging African nations. In front of each was a grinning ceramic Sambo standing in solitary isolation on a manicured emerald lawn with outstretched arms that held either a lantern or a house number. These symbols of colonialism and racism became as unbearable as my own neatly manicured life. I began a mission of liberation—theirs and mine.

I would cross the border and steal a Sambo late at night, returning to hide it in our cellar, a stop on my own private underground railway. After each theft, I wrote a letter to the local newspaper explaining my outrage over this racist symbol. None were ever printed. Aside from the frustrated anger of my kind husband, bewildered by my flailing discontent, there was not a ripple of response to my increasing protests. I left my marriage, everyone said, without a good reason. Except that I had rattled the cage so much that it slowly began to come apart.

I moved to an apartment in New York City with my two small daughters and went to work as the "girl" in a one-girl dental office. It was 1963, and the civil rights movement was gathering momentum in the south. In New York City, its local expression was the sharply polarized busing struggle for integrated schools. That and the early organizing against the war in Vietnam shaped my political vision. I became involved locally in dismantling the racial divisions in my daughters' classrooms and in the city-wide organizing efforts to mobilize the resistance against the growing war in Vietnam. I engaged both in the microcosm of personal unfairness and the macrocosm of structural injustice. I spent the rest of the 1960s doing what my grandmother called "sticking up for everybody," without ever noticing that my own life and my own experiences as a woman were not in my politics. I had not yet begun to "stick up for myself," still afraid I would stick out. I knew that there was a "woman question" and believed that it would and should be addressed, but only after the more urgent needs of revolutionary activity had been completed.

During these important years, I was learning to organize, to speak up at meetings and to disagree with other organizers. I was drawing attention to myself, but slowly it became purposeful. I was beginning to grow into my size. When early feminist activism began to take shape in 1969, I immediately recognized that its shape was mine, that it would be a center from which I could continue to live my politics. Fully. On a large scale.

My earliest feminist activist work was with rape crisis. It was as the Director of the Sexual Trauma Center in San Francisco that I began to hear disclosures of incestuous assault from one woman after another. Women who had been brought by police to the hospital emergency room after having been raped. Women who were ashamed to be in this brightly lit examining room after the dim cars, apartments and parks where they had been raped and often battered. Eyes lowered, they faced me. I, armed only with police reports and good intentions, listened carefully to their halting voices, as they vacantly and politely answered my well-rehearsed crisis counseling questions. All too often, somewhere in the telling, their voices would change and their bodies shift in the uncomfortable orange plastic chair. In a flood, they would tell me of an earlier abuse, only first remembered in that moment. Undigested and as shocking to them as it was to me. "Please, Daddy. Don't make me. I don't want to. Don't. Please." Imploring, terrified, their words would rise to a crescendo of urgency, then fall again, into the muted, well-modulated tones of women in shock.

The first time I faced a middle-aged woman who had, before my eyes, become an eight-year-old girl pleading for mercy from an unnamed grown-up, I thought I had witnessed a unique moment. Soon there were others. African-American housewives. Young Indian children. Asian adolescents. Disabled women. Sex workers. Married and divorced women. I was witnessing something for which I had no name, no words of comfort and no training.

I tried to understand, as I thought I was supposed to do, by looking up "incest" in the card catalogs (there were no computer searches in 1977) and beginning to read. I found monographs written by male psychiatrists carefully explaining that incest happened in one in a million families. It was a consequence, they opined, of immigrants transplanting village cultural norms to America as a way of comfortably assimilating. It was caused, they went on, by mothers abandoning daughters and colluding with fathers. It was done, they concluded, to girls seductive and eager for sexual contact with their fathers. I read everything and knew, that as a feminist and as a woman, I would have to look elsewhere for my answers.

I received a small grant from an activist church, and began to travel and interview child protection agency administrators, researchers and educators. Seated behind their highly polished desks, they would smilingly murmur, "Not here. Perhaps on the other side of town where 'they' live, you will find a higher rate of abuse." In each city, each other side of each town, there were different races, ethnicities and classes of "theys," but it was always the "theys" who were the ones who committed and experienced incest. Not the "us" whom the smug child protection agencies assumed they served.

I realize now that if I had understood that I was doing research to write a book, one that would change my life and create, along with other writings, a movement, I probably would have been frozen in intellectual self-doubt, would have felt overwhelmed by the size of such an undertaking and would have encouraged other women, women more suited, I would have said, to take on this work. But I didn't stop to think about what I was doing. Something very wrong and shockingly common was occurring in the lives of girls and women, and I set out to see what it was. In so doing, I received the rest of my education.

Thousands of miles later, frustrated and angry, I remembered the early experience of my first consciousness-raising group. Eight women sat in a circle and talked about the nature of our daily lives. After the "telling" came the analysis and then the theory. Not before. I had forgotten the earliest lesson of feminism. It was then that I returned home, stopped searching libraries and interviewing "experts" and instead listened to ordinary women in ordinary lives. Lives where sexual abuse was itself a frequent and painfully ordinary occurrence. I began, woman by woman, to create small moments over a cup of tea or in a pause on a park bench where they could tell me about their childhood abuse. I was clearer now about where the information was stored, how to unearth it and just who the real experts were. The words of those women led to the publication of *Conspiracy of Silence: The Trauma of Incest* published in 1978, the year I became forty. I expected the book would be well received by movement women and anticipated perhaps 1000 copies would be sold. Perhaps I would have some small notoriety.

Several pivotal events shaped that fortieth year. My youngest daughter graduated from high school and left to find her way in the world. I moved out of San Francisco, out of an apartment that had been my home for many years to a one-bedroom cottage in a distant suburb, where I got another in a long series of jobs in dental offices, jobs that had supported me during those years alone with my daughters. But this job was one where I could ride my bike to and from work. I began to run each morning. I read the Stanford catalogue for classes I might audit. I checked out the Jewish Community Center for interesting lectures. I was starting over. I knew that. I just didn't know yet the shape "over" would take.

My birthday party was a gala event that celebrated both me and the publication of the book. My apartment was filled with friends, family, colleagues, extravagant food, exuberant music, and in the center, there I was in a blue velvet dress. I couldn't take my eyes off the book that was propped up next to the large cake that was placed in the center of the table. I was so proud of what I had accomplished in just five years.

In five years, I had returned to college and completed both my bachelors and masters degrees. They were years in which my world opened, my long-buried hungers surfaced, and time flew. I worked and studied, read endlessly and wrote with both determination and the beginnings of skill. Friends would marvel at what they called my "discipline"–to be able to work a 40-hour week, then write papers, analyze eight or ten books a week, attend seminars, care for my children (then in their teens) and maintain some semblance of a household. But it never felt like discipline to me. It was the hungers surfacing, the hungers I had kept banked all my life. They fueled me, gave me energy, sleep and nourishment. I never felt either disciplined or driven, but just, finally, in my own life. At my own desk. In my own thoughts. My own passions. Moving towards my own size.

Several months after *Conspiracy of Silence's* publication, I was asked to be the keynote speaker at a conference. Me? A keynote speaker? That was something "real" experts did. Famous people. Important thinkers and activists. These women who didn't seem to understand that I was none of those things wanted to know my availability, my fee, the topic I would most like to address. After sleepless nights and waves of insecurity, I wrote back accepting their invitation. Having no one to ask such things, I made up a fee.

I spent the next months returning from the dental office each evening to painstakingly work on my first public talk. I had entitled it *The Politics of Outrage.* I had no idea it would change the trajectory of my life. Three months later, I got on a plane to Harrisburg, PA, and settled back to review my carefully typed speech. It had begun. This was my introduction to a world of women eager for expertise and information, validation of their frontline work and a radical and feminist view of our shared task. I was both terrified and eager to oblige.

I entered a small, cohesive and exhilarating world of radical feminists who had dedicated their political lives to ending violence against women. In those early years, we who were providing counseling and advocacy to victimized women understood the need to expand the psychological body of knowledge already developed by feminist psychologists in a way that would be respectful of the political and personal nature of the experience of sexual assault. We needed to establish medical and legal protocols, train workers, create research, funding, resources and programs for women.

Nothing that sexually victimized women needed existed, so we had to create it. And we did. It was that uncomplicated and that passionate. From the first whispered stories of abuse, feminists coalesced and created a movement. Those were generative years for those of us who were organizing rape crisis centers, battered women's shelters or incest survivors' groups. Ending violence against women was then a political, not a psychological, movement. There was so much to do and we were so determined to do it all. "Children tell the truth," we insisted. "Women are the experts on their own experience," we declared. We were optimistic, enthusiastic and certain we would prevail. In the respectful company of other women, I grew in my capacity to think rigorously, feel deeply and communicate both.

During the decade from 1978-1988, I stayed outside the professional world of psychotherapy, proudly identifying myself as an outside agitator. I began to trust that I, too, could create political theory, psychological analysis and healing practice with other women. I was still tentative, still apologetic with more formally trained feminist theorists and psychologists, but with each year I grew more confident. I reminded audiences of women that had grown to proportions that astonished me that none of us could do social change work and be socially acceptable in the same lifetime, that they were mutually antithetical activities, and should be; that, to the degree that we still had longings to be acceptable, we would be less effective in ending violence against women or in changing the nature and practice of gender. I was speaking the very words I needed to hear. My voice, my effectiveness and my passion were expanding, deepening and broadening. I was trying to ask the biggest questions, to hold the largest vision. I wrote articles, consulted with programs run by women with university training, coaxed feminists back to the outrage, to the biggest, the most expansive, bravest and strongest in themselves. And as I led them, I followed.

"We live in a world that mass produces victimized women and children," I said in my speeches, workshops, trainings, retreats and meetings. As feminists, in a racist, sexist, homophobic, classist world, what do we mean by healing? What would be described as wellness? What is a healthy woman? Who decides? Why are women all over the world unsafe in their bodies from birth to death? Is this about women or about men? Who is responsible? How can we make fundamental, social, political and psychological change skillfully, collaboratively and passionately? I was growing. Growing to meet myself.

In 1985, I spoke at a national conference in Canada where over one thousand feminists had gathered. I was to open and to close the gathering. I began my keynote speech by suggesting that moving in our therapeutic and political language from victim to survivor was a step in the right direction from our early beginnings, but not nearly far enough. Sexual abuse could not become an identity. It was an experience, a political and psychological experience. "We are more than our pain," I called out to them. Our healing strategies have to incorporate that knowledge. For the first time, I never once looked at my notes. I knew what I needed to say and let the words take shape.

At the conclusion of the conference, I was asked to offer my thoughts about where we go from here, as a movement, as a discipline and as individual women. But, as I had observed the three-day gathering, I saw women who felt unheard, unseen, disregarded and invisible. Women of color. Lesbians. Disabled women. Old women. Women who had spent much of their lives in prison. There were too many women, too few amplified voices, too much expertise. Without anxiety, preparation or even thought, I invited women to line up behind the microphones that were scattered throughout the large ballroom. I asked each woman to remember the name of someone whose life was changed because of how she lived her life and expressed her political and psychological vision. It was a way, I suggested, to honor themselves, their choices and their skill. As I encouraged them to acknowledge their pride and sense of accomplishment, I did the same and together we filled that room to become even more brazen, impolite and determined female selves.

By the end of the 1980s, there was not only the need to remember the successes, there was also the avalanche of failures. By then, we had all lost so many women and children: women for whom the pain of their life experience was intolerable; children lost in the maze of services designed to help, but that all too often, entrap and further wound; adolescents who had run from abusive homes and were locked in worlds of flesh, drugs and loneliness; women and children who might have been us. Their measure of pain is ours.

There were few public or private avenues created for discussion about the experience of such exhausting "atrocity work." Places where each of us could describe the accumulation of years spent listening to abused women. Knowing they needed to assure us that their bruises were an exception to an otherwise uneventful marriage. Knowing they needed to believe that in order to return. Knowing that they needed to return because they had no place to go. Knowing they had no place to go because they had dropped out of school or lost a job or had too many children or just one child who was ill or any of the thousands of reasons women tell themselves stories in order to endure the lives that entrap them. Sitting with a woman whose father had convinced her that his sexual assault was her idea or her fault or her desire. How she deserved it or enjoyed it. How he was teaching her how to be a good wife when she grew up.

The repetitive experience of grief that was the result of feeling, of seeing and of knowing that women and children are lost to male violence over and over left me shrinking again, trapped and feeling impotent. I needed to find a way to fully experience the grief that was an authentic reflection of my political and psychological choices and not be immobilized by it. I needed to find some way to incorporate it into my work and into my life as a radical feminist woman. I had to create a way to turn my grief into activism, my despair into action in the world, to build a bridge from personal loss back to political passion; a bridge to a fuller and deeper level of activism, a fuller and deeper level of passion and a fuller and deeper level of outrage. A bridge strong enough to keep me steady on it. I needed to expand to embrace this, too. The sense of outrage and grief, success and failure that informs my feminism is the core from which I live. Finally I needed to grow even larger to take it all in.

My feminism is a practice, not an ideology. It is no longer about success and failure, but instead is a way of life that is demanding, scrupulous and unsentimental. Feminism requires me to engage with every moment and every interaction, understanding that not only is feminism a practice, it is a discipline, a way of living with the consequences of consciousness in every moment. It is a holy dailiness. As a secular Jew, this consciousness is my relationship to the sacred. I have come to understand that each moment shimmers with the possibility of tikkun olam, which is to live in the knowledge that each moment contains within it the possibility of mending, repairing and transforming the world.

"Weak Ego Boundaries":
One Developing Feminist's Story

Paula J. Caplan

Why this title? Because it refers to a key event in my development as a feminist and psychologist, and because it raises a theme
that I keep running into as feminist psychology develops and deep-
ens. It comes from my first year of graduate school, from an experience which, when it happened to me, I thought had only ever
happened to me, regarded as my fault, and could subject to no
feminist analysis until years later. I tell this story not just because it
happened to me but because I know that such appalling things still
happen to women, and at my age (48) I don't feel inclined to guard
the dirty little secrets of the men who mistreated me. Obviously, I
hope that hearing about my experience will reduce the isolation and
self-blame of those who have had similar ones.

When I graduated from Radcliffe/Harvard in 1969 and started the
doctoral program in clinical psychology at Duke, I had been deeply

Paula Joan Caplan, PhD, is clinical and research psychologist, teacher, writer,
and speaker. She has taught both psychology and women's studies and has been
Full Professor of Applied Psychology at the Ontario Institute for Studies in
Education and a Visiting Scholar at Brown University's Pembroke Center for
Research and Teaching on Women. Her children are Jeremy Benjamin Caplan, a
Brown graduate in Physics, and Emily Julia Caplan, a Brown student.

Correspondence may be addressed to Paula J. Caplan, 77 St. Clair E., Toronto,
Ontario, Canada M4T 1M5.

[Haworth co-indexing entry note]: "'Weak Ego Boundaries': One Developing Feminist's Story."
Caplan, Paula J. Co-published simultaneously in *Women & Therapy* (The Haworth Press, Inc.) Vol. 17,
No. 1/2, 1995, pp. 113-123; and: *Feminist Foremothers in Women's Studies, Psychology, and Mental
Health* (ed: Phyllis Chesler, Esther D. Rothblum, and Ellen Cole) The Haworth Press, Inc., 1995, pp.
113-123; and: *Feminist Foremothers in Women's Studies, Psychology, and Mental Health* (ed: Phyllis
Chesler, Esther D. Rothblum, and Ellen Cole) Harrington Park Press, an imprint of The Haworth Press,
Inc., 1995 pp. 113-123. Single or multiple copies of this article are available from The Haworth
Document Delivery Service [1-800-342-9678, 9:00 a.m. - 5:00 p.m. (EST)].

113

affected by the police bust of my undergraduate classmates' occupation of Harvard's University Hall the previous spring. I had opposed the Vietnam War before that, but the bust had jolted me into awareness of such issues as wealthy property owners' treatment of their tenants and the need for an Afro-American Studies program. My awareness of and interest in feminism, however, were still to come. Even so, during that first year of graduate school, I arranged to do an independent study about sex-differences research (remember that in 1969-70, that was considered unusual). In a course about theories of psychotherapy that year, when the time came to choose a term paper topic, I decided that I would take the bits and pieces that Freud and the other "great men" of psychotherapy had written about women, stick them together, and see what that could help us understand about women. I don't recall feeling angry that so little had been said about women except to pathologize us, but I do remember feeling a bit wistful, longing for someone to write about our lives. I had no idea that anyone else felt that way and certainly no clue that feminist critiques of personality theory and therapy were about to surge forth on a massive scale. Recently, I reread my paper, and it is very mild, but when the professor, Marty Lakin, returned it to me, he had scrawled on the front, "How many times in this century is Freud to be attacked for his views on women?" Several pages into the paper, you can still see his pen's indentation from what was apparently the intensity of feeling with which he wrote that comment.

Lakin's response astonished me, but I had no time to try to understand it, because I was kicked out of the clinical program that April. I could stay in the Psychology *department* and take courses in theory and research but couldn't go near the clinical program and work with people, they said. The reason they gave was that I had weak ego boundaries. The first time I ever recounted that publicly was in the Popular Feminism Lecture series at the Ontario Institute for Studies in Education in 1986, and when I did, the audience of women laughed. I then said that in 1970 I would not have dreamed I would ever tell that story and hear my listeners laugh, because in 1970 I was devastated. Having been what a Harvard psychologist had described as a Kellogg's Cornflakes, All-American-type girl in high school and much of college, and having profound respect for teachers, I assumed that my Duke instructors must be right and decided I had better strengthen those ego boundaries. First, though, I had to find out what in the world "weak ego boundaries" meant. I went to see most of the eleven clinical psychology faculty, all of whom were white men, and nine said they didn't know me very well and had relied on the judgment of my two primary instructors. So, I went to see them. One of them, John Coie, was my advisor. I was terrified but walked into his office, slammed his door, and said, "Didn't I come to you back in November and say I was getting funny feelings about how the faculty felt about me? And you said to me, 'That's just first-year, graduate student paranoia.' Well, what the hell happened between then and now?" He replied that my weak ego boundaries had led them to kick me out. When I asked what that meant, he said, "We have the sense that if a depressed patient came to see you, you would probably say, 'Oh, you poor dear' and leave it at that." I asked why on earth they would assume that, when in the interviewing course, he and the co-instructor Phil Costanzo had told me my interviews were good. "Oh," he replied, "that was because we knew you were not able to take criticism." Then I said, "Wait a minute. Do you remember after my interviews, when you said they were good, and I thanked you but said I'd like suggestions about how to improve next time, and you said, 'We don't have any suggestions; you were really good." He replied, "You see, we sensed even then that you were not able to take criticism."

I raced back to my apartment and phoned Bruce Baker, the only clinical psychologist with whom I had studied at Harvard, and said, "Bruce, you gotta tell me straight. Did you find you had to be careful about criticizing me?" He said, "No, it's quite the opposite." I had great respect for Bruce's judgment and began to wonder whether maybe, just maybe, the problem was not in me.

Still believing that I needed to work on myself, I went to see Marty Lakin, because he taught the Group Process course. I told him that I needed his permission to take that course the upcoming year. He asked why I wanted to take it, and I said that I had heard that one learned there to see oneself as others see one. I pointed out that my view of myself seemed to differ considerably from that of the faculty, and so I felt it was important for me to try to understand how I came across to others. He responded that he couldn't let me take the course. "Why not?" I asked. "Because you would destroy the group," he said. Quite a shocking thing for a Kellogg's Corn-flakes type to hear. I went to the Veteran's Administration Hospital across the way to ask Arnold Krugman, a psychologist with an appointment in the Duke department, if I could study with one of the hospital therapists. To my amazement, Krugman–with whom I had had no previous contact–said, "I know what you've called me. I know that you've called me a fascist pig." At that time, I had never called anyone a fascist pig. To call this series of events Kaf-kaesque would not be inappropriate, I think.

Working with Marcel Kinsbourne in the Duke Hospital Learning Clinic, I learned a great deal and managed to finish my Master's thesis, and then I actually got my Ph.D. from Duke through working with the social psychologists. My degrees were in Psychology, mind you, not Clinical Psychology, but I had had a great deal of clinical experience through my work with Marcel. After doing a one-year internship through the delightfully more sane University of North Carolina at Chapel Hill, I was set to qualify for my official psychologist's registration after some supervised work in Toronto later on. But it took some years of reading DeBeauvoir and Friedan and Phyllis Chesler's *Women and Madness* and after receiving the wonderful support of Toronto feminists like Kathryn Morgan and Jeri Wine, not to mention my parents, Tac and Jerry Caplan, before I finally made some sense of my expulsion from the Duke program. I came to understand that Coie's remark about my allegedly weak ego boundaries reflected the all-male faculty's discomfort with a woman who was expressive rather than detached and formal, as they thought therapists should be. It further reflected, I believe, the traditional tendency of men to feel that expression of feelings is immature and inappropriate in a wide variety of contexts. Thanks to thinkers like Rachel Josefowitz Siegel, Janet Surrey, Jean Baker Miller, Judith Jordan, Alexandra Kaplan, Irene Stiver, and Carol Gilligan, hordes of us have now learned that what others call women's "dependency," "neediness," and "overemotionality"–and "weak ego boundaries"–are often instead our capacities for interde-pendence, connection, relationships, and a life rich with emotions. Understood in this way, I believe that what the Duke clinical psychology faculty called my "weak ego boundaries" were the interest in and relishing of human connections that led to much of my feminist work.

Reading Friedan's *The Feminine Mystique*, I was deeply moved by the awful tragedy of the isolation of the unhappy housewives, each of whom thought she was the only crazily "selfish" stay-at-home Mom who didn't find fulfillment in furniture polish and novel ideas for hors d'oeuvres. The theme of breaking down isolation and finding commonalities among people who believe they are different and who feel powerless, with the aim of empowering them to make political and social change, is dear to my heart. A second theme that I have found deeply absorbing, as well as useful in figuring things out, has been that of myths and Catch-22s. Usually, when I find myself perplexed by an issue, it is because myths are clouding my view. Then, conversely, naming and exploring the nature of those myths leads to clearer vision and often to empowerment: If you can see what is happening, it is easier to change it for the better.

For many years, every time a relationship I was in was ending, I wrote something. For instance, when my first, brief marriage ended, it was my Master's thesis, and when my second marriage ended, I wrote *Between Women: Lowering the Barriers* (1980). As I write this article, it occurs to me that, in part, my writing at those times has been a way to deal with the loneliness, loss, and increased isolation by imagining connecting with people who might later read what I wrote.

Between Women came to be because I had audited University of Toronto philosopher Ronnie deSousa's course on "Philosophy and Psychoanalysis," and in rereading Freud was struck both by the fact that Freud dignified mother-daughter relationships by at least trying to understand them and by how far afield he went in making that attempt. "His writing about women just doesn't ring true, somehow," I remember saying. As a feminist, I was particularly interested in identifying socially caused barriers between women, so that we could overcome them and work together more easily and effectively. After jotting down some ideas on the subject, I spoke to my mother on the phone and asked her if my ideas seemed idiosyncratic. She said they did not. I told her I was thinking of writing a paper about them, and she replied, "Good. But that doesn't sound like a paper. It sounds like a book." My heart pounded with fear, but what she said felt right. So I wrote it, and it was essentially about my view that most problems between mothers and daughters, or between any two women, are either created or exacerbated by one or more of the myths that our sexist culture purveys about females. *Don't Blame Mother: Mending the Mother-Daughter Relationship* (1989) was an expansion of some themes from that book.

My interest in *The Myth of Women's Masochism* (1985, 1987, 1994) grew partly from my disgust with the psychoanalytic notion that women suffer *because* they enjoy it–and that if they don't admit that they enjoy it, that only means that their masochism is unconscious. It also grew from feeling fed up with people telling me and other women I cared about that whatever problems we had–with relationships, health, or work–must be because we were "our own worst enemies" and "needed" to suffer and to fail. I considered that theory both to be untrue and to be what feminist psychologist Nikki Gerrard (1987) calls a "terminal" idea. Terminal ideas are those that halt progress, that show no way forward from where one is. If we are in a terrible job or an abusive relationship, and a friend or therapist "teaches" us that our unconscious need for misery is what created that situation, we learn to be helpless, for why should we consider leaving the job or relationship, when our unconscious masochism would indubitably propel us toward yet another job or relationship in which we would be badly treated? In the 1994 edition of that book, I proposed in a preface some guidelines for identifying emotional/psychological abuse, an area that has been explored very little, partly because women are so afraid that they are only feeling emotionally abused because they are overly sensitive and too immersed in the victim's role. I believe that the vast majority of women have been psychologically abused, if only by the deceptively innocuous-sounding "sex-role stereotypes," and that we have been trained to ignore both the abuse and the soul-killing effects it can have on us.

My friend Kathryn Morgan, the brilliant feminist philosopher, recommended me to the Status of Women Committee of the Council of Ontario Universities, when the Committee was looking for someone to write a "survival guide for women in academia." That became *Lifting a Ton of Feathers: A Woman's Guide to Surviving in the Academic World* (1993), and as I began to work on it, I began to see it, too, as an attempt to bring women together, to focus on some commonalities–in this case, the set of myths, Catch-22s, and unwritten rules in academia that lead us unjustifiably to blame ourselves when we don't succeed or even when we don't feel welcome on campus.

The next book on which I worked–and co-authored with my son, Jeremy–developed from a seed that had been planted in 1979. Kathryn Morgan and philosopher Ronnie deSousa had conceived of a core course in Women's Studies for the University of Toronto, to be called "Scientific Perspectives on Sex and Gender." Ronnie was heading the Women's Studies program and asked me to coordinate the course and give the one-third of the lectures that were to be about psychology, the other two-thirds being about biology and anthropology. I said I would do that if the course could be aimed at making the students informed consumers of claims they might hear about research on sex and gender. From the beginning, the other teachers and I emphasized critical thinking, showing students how to use common sense, logic, and some knowledge of the histories and methodologies from the different disciplines to critique research. Through my own experience and those of other women, I had learned that most people teaching psychology of women and psychology of sex differences courses had had little or no training in those areas. Most of us felt it was all we could do to pull together a mass of material and convey it to the students. Most of us were already overworked and had little time to do much critical thinking ourselves about the studies, never mind teaching the students to do so. For years, I had wanted to write a book that would present a lot of sex-and-gender research from various critical thinking perspectives. The summer that Jeremy was 16, I had decided that that was the summer I had to finish the book. Realizing that I could not possibly do it alone, I asked myself who could write clearly, think logically and carefully, grasp the material, and understand what I was aiming for. Jeremy came immediately to mind, but he turned out to be even easier and more fascinating and thought-provoking to work with than I had hoped, and we wrote *Thinking Critically About Research on Sex and Gender* (1994). My daughter, Emily, did the line editing for the book, so it was a family affair.

In and through these and other pieces of writing and my teaching on campuses and to community groups, as well as through various kinds of clinical and court-related work and political and social action, I began to notice a recurring theme over the years. Again, it turned out to involve isolation and powerlessness. The theme was that, in more than 25 years of participating in a wide variety of systems and institutions, sometimes as a so-called authority or expert, sometimes as a consumer, and sometimes as both, I had observed that the experts in all these areas use many of the same techniques to make consumers feel stupid and powerless. This is not news to us children of the '60s, but what worried me was the way we could see so clearly when these techniques were being used against other people, but when they were used against us, we often couldn't see. And then, we would blame ourselves, wondering, "Why is my mother's doctor treating her so badly? Have I been too aggressive with him? Have I not been assertive enough? Have I been too ill-informed to know what questions to ask him? Or have I been so well-informed that he thinks I am trying to tell him how to do his work?" It occurred to me that making a simple list of (what turned out to be 20 of) the most commonly used techniques, naming them succinctly and giving examples of each could make these techniques more accessible to our consciousness. That is what I did in *You're Smarter Than They Make You Feel: How the Experts Intimidate Us and What We Can Do About It* (1994). My goal was for readers, after inspecting the list and reading some examples and then feeling stupid or powerless in relation to a doctor or therapist or lawyer or plumber or government agency official, would *not* blame themselves but instead would check the list and realize, "Oh, that person is using technique number 14 on me." At the very least, I hoped that that would prevent people from indulging in unwarranted and ineffective self-blame, and at most, I hoped it would lead some of them to organize for social and political change.

As I write this paper, I have just finished *They Say You're Crazy: How the World's Most Powerful Psychiatrists Decide Who's Normal* (1995). It is an exposé of the way the American Psychiatric Association's handbook, the *Diagnostic and Statistical Manual of Mental Disorders,* which has been called the mental health Bible, is purported to be based on solid science but is actually the product of scandalously unscientific and political, including sexist, decision-making processes. In this case, too, my wish is to empower consumers and potential consumers of mental health services with the knowledge that "normality" and "mental disorder" are constructs that are laden with value judgments and political content, so that if anyone decides they are abnormal, they will be in a position to question the how and the why of that decision. These issues are especially important to women because of the systematic tendency for the producers of the handbook to pathologize women far more than men.

I want also to mention an early piece of research that I did. As an undergraduate, I had taken a course with Erik Erikson and thought him quite wonderful in many ways. But sometime later, after Emily was born and Jeremy was starting nursery school, something Erikson had said came back to my mind. He had said that his research had shown that girls build enclosures and boys build towers, that this was evidence that the shape of our genitalia affects the way we perceive and organize space, and that a woman cannot have a sense of her identity until she knows who will fill her inner space. Goodness, I thought, if that is true, it is very important, and someone must have tried to replicate it. For the first time, I read the original article in which Erikson reported the tower-enclosure research. For his class, we had only been assigned the book in which he referred to his "discovery." In the original article, I found that children of both sexes had built far more enclosures than towers, that hardly anyone of either sex had built a tower, but that of those few who had built towers, slightly more had been built by boys. I tightened up his methodology, redid the research with my son's nursery school class (Jeremy was the only child who refused to participate), failed to find what Erikson had claimed (wrongly) to have found, and wrote a paper about it (1979). That experience was important to me because, although I hated criticizing Erikson, I learned that, if one reads research carefully, one often finds that what are taken to be truths often have no basis in fact, especially if the truths are asserted by famous, respected people. That, plus the encouragement and training in critical thinking that I received from my uncle, Bill Karchmer; my parents, Tac and Jerry Caplan; and my teachers, Jack Bush (Greenwood High School, math), Donald Stanton (Greenwood, speech and debate), and Bruce Baker (Harvard, psychology), have led to my relishing of the process of thinking questioningly about what I am told.

The editors of this volume asked me to describe how my life has changed because of this work. One profoundly important change has been that work in feminist psychology has been deeply absorbing both intellectually and emotionally. It is a joy to do work with which I feel connected on a daily basis and which is intended to bring about social and political change. And as more new work about women appears, it becomes increasingly necessary for me to keep abreast of what is happening in a delightfully huge range of fields. This helps me feel alive and fresh. Very much related to those feelings is the joy of getting to meet and work with so many interesting women–and to some extent, increasingly–some men who care about the kinds of issues that matter to me. But another consequence is that, at parties, I am often having perfectly lovely conversations with men, but as soon as they learn that I am a feminist and/or a psychologist, they need to go freshen their drinks and never return. Just being a psychologist–even though I almost never do therapy–seems to endanger me in relationships with men, and I have heard similar tales from other women therapists. The typical scenario is that the woman psychologist is voicing a legitimate concern or grievance to the man, and he narrows his eyes suspiciously and says, "Don't you psychologize me! Stop analyzing me!" These are what Nikki Gerrard (1987) would, I suspect, call terminal orders.

In closing, I want to thank Phyllis Chesler, Ellen Cole, and Esther Rothblum for honoring and surprising me by considering me a feminist foremother.

REFERENCES

Caplan, Paula J. (1995). *They Say You're Crazy: How the World's Most Powerful Psychiatrists Decide Who's Normal.* Reading, MA: Addison-Wesley.

Caplan, Paula J. (1994). *You're Smarter Than They Make You Feel: How the Experts Intimidate Us and What We Can Do About It.* New York: The Free Press.

Caplan, Paula J. (1993). *Lifting a Ton of Feathers: A Woman's Guide to Surviving in the Academic World.* Toronto: University of Toronto Press.

Caplan, Paula J. (1989). *Don't Blame Mother: Mending the Mother-Daughter Relationship.* New York: Harper and Row.

Caplan, Paula J. (1985). *The Myth of Women's Masochism.* New York: Dutton.
—Paperback edition with additional chapter about the American Psychiatric Association's pathologizing of women: New York: Signet, 1987.
—New edition with new preface: Toronto: University of Toronto Press, 1994.

Caplan, Paula J. (1981). *Between Women: Lowering the Barriers.* Toronto: Personal Library. Published earlier as *Barriers Between Women.* Jamaica, NY: SP Medical and Scientific Publications.

Caplan, Paula J. (1979). Erikson's concept of inner space: A data-based re-evaluation. *American Journal of Orthopsychiatry, 49,* 100-108.

Caplan, Paula J., & Caplan, Jeremy B. (1994). *Thinking Critically About Research on Sex and Gender.* New York: HarperCollins.

Gerrard, Nikki. (1987). Guilt is a terminal word: A critical analysis of guilt in relation to women with a focus on mothers and daughters. Unpublished paper, Ontario Institute for Studies in Education. (Available from author at: 1904 Pembina Ave., Saskatoon, Saskatchewan, Canada S7K 1C3).

Judy Chicago,
Feminist Artist and Educator

Judy Chicago
Laura Meyer

Judy Chicago is an artist, writer, and educator who played a leading role in the feminist art movement of the 1970s. She received an MFA in sculpture from the University of California, Los Angeles, in 1964. In 1970, she established the nation's first feminist art education program, focusing on non-traditional art media and subject matter as a means of empowering women. Her monumental collaborative installation, *The Dinner Party,* is arguably the most famous and most controversial artwork to come out of the early feminist movement. Ms. Chicago is the author of *Through the Flower: My Struggle as a Woman Artist, The Dinner Party: A Symbol of Our Heritage, Embroidering Our Heritage: The Dinner Party Needlework,* and *The Birth Project.* Her most recent artwork is the *Holocaust Project.* Ms. Chicago is married to photographer Donald Woodman and lives in Albuquerque, NM.

Laura Meyer is a doctoral student in Art History at the University of California, Los Angeles. Having experienced the early years of the Women's Movement from a "child's-eye-view," she is currently studying feminist art in the context of social change in the U.S. in the 1970s. Her MA thesis, "The 'Essential' Judy Chicago: Central Core Imagery vs. the Language of Fetishism in *Womanhouse* and *The Dinner Party*" (U.C. Riverside, 1994), analyzes Chicago's early work in the light of current feminist debates over so-called "essentialist" and "deconstructive" strategies for representing female identity. Ms. Meyer lives in Los Angeles with her husband and daughter.

Correspondence may be addressed to Judy Chicago, Through the Flower, P.O. Box 5280, Santa Fe, NM 87502-5280.

[Haworth co-indexing entry note]: "Judy Chicago, Feminist Artist and Educator." Chicago, Judy, and Laura Meyer. Co-published simultaneously in *Women & Therapy* (The Haworth Press, Inc.) Vol. 17, No. 1/2, 1995, pp. 125-140; and: *Feminist Foremothers in Women's Studies, Psychology, and Mental Health* (ed: Phyllis Chesler, Esther D. Rothblum, and Ellen Cole) The Haworth Press, Inc., 1995, pp. 125-140; and: *Feminist Foremothers in Women's Studies, Psychology, and Mental Health* (ed: Phyllis Chesler, Esther D. Rothblum, and Ellen Cole) Harrington Park Press, an imprint of The Haworth Press, Inc., pp. 125-140. Single or multiple copies of this article are available from The Haworth Document Delivery Service [1-800-342-9678, 9:00 a.m. - 5:00 p.m. (EST)].

Judy Chicago played a pioneering role in the feminist art movement of the 1970s, working to empower women in all walks of life by giving women increased "control over . . . the recording of history, the disseminating of information, [and] the transmitting of new values" through the creation, viewing, and discussion of art (Chicago, 1975, p. 173). In 1970, she founded the nation's first feminist art education program, a unique combination of feminist consciousness-raising and radical artistic experimentation that laid important groundwork for feminist artworld activism in the coming decade. During the early 1970s, she played an instrumental role in the development of Womanspace gallery, a Los Angeles cooperative dedicated to the exhibition and critique of women's artwork in a female-controlled environment, and helped establish the Los Angeles Woman's Building, which for nearly twenty years served as an important arts center and political base for women in Los Angeles and nationwide. During the latter half of the decade, Chicago led a team of some four hundred women and men in the creation of her most famous artwork, *The Dinner Party,* a monumental paean to women in history executed through the labor-intensive, traditionally "feminine" crafts of embroidery and china-painting. The opening of *The Dinner Party* at the San Francisco Museum of Modern Art in 1979 drew record-breaking crowds of mostly female viewers, and generated intense controversy among critics and art historians. Since that time, Chicago has continued to make artwork addressing highly charged personal and political issues, including childbirth, the social construction of male power, and the Holocaust.

Judy Chicago was born Judy Cohen in 1939, in the city (Chicago) she later adopted as her namesake. She credits her politically left-wing parents—her father was a labor union organizer—with providing her with an "early knowledge about oppression" (Chicago, 1994). While her father's political activism was grounded in a materialist ideology, however, Chicago's artworld activism has stressed the primacy of myth in shaping human society. She states that

A species makes myths that correspond to its needs and allow it to act on the needs that are momentarily paramount. I believe that myth, at its base, has to be challenged before economics or sociology or philosophy will change . . . I believe in the power of art to change consciousness. (Chicago cited in Lippard, 1980, p. 115, 125)

Chicago's awareness of the profound sexism inherent in modern art institutions, including art schools, art museums, and even art "styles," developed gradually during her years as a student and young artist in Los Angeles in the 1950s and 1960s. When Chicago began art school at the University of California, Los Angeles (UCLA) in 1958, the artistic "style" that predominated in the United States was Minimalism, an abstract form of painting and sculpture that stressed simple geometric shapes, monumental scale, and the precise, "high-tech" handling of industrial materials like metal and Fiberglas. Modern art, as defined by leading critic Clement Greenberg and others, was supposed to "confine itself to what is given in visual experience and make no reference to any other orders of experience" (Greenberg, 1965, p. 74). Thus, art was defined ideally as a completely neutral visual phenomenon, devoid of narrative content and social significance. The unstated subtext of Greenberg's definition, however, was that art should concern itself with the mastery of technical procedures and abstract thinking, both skills that were typically associated with male prowess in the 1950s, and should exclude the personal, emotional side of life that was then considered the exclusive domain of women. As Chicago has pointed out, since most women in the 1950s did not grow up taking "shop" classes and working with tools like their male peers, when confronted with a typical introductory sculpture assignment to make something out of a couple of two by fours, they "would probably get the message that sculpture was just not for them" (Chicago, 1975, p. 87).

Although she recalls that at UCLA in the 1950s, "the respected members of the studio [art] faculty were all male . . . [and] most of the serious students were men," the fiercely ambitious Chicago nevertheless determined that "art has no gender," and sought success by imitating her male peers (Chicago, 1975, p. 27-28). Abandoning her early interest in biomorphic, body-oriented painting, Chicago switched to sculpture and learned to manipulate heavy equipment and industrial materials like the other "serious" (men) students. Eager to fit in with the distinctly macho art crowd in Los

Angeles (the prominent artists represented by Ferus gallery referred to themselves only half-facetiously as "The Studs"), she adopted an exaggerated masculine costume and demeanor, and took to smoking cigars and attending motorcycle races. Recalling her college years in her autobiography, Chicago expresses special regret for having bypassed the opportunity to work with the two women art instructors at UCLA, and for even having "joined in [with the men] . . . putting other women down, calling them 'chicks' and 'cunts' " (p. 27-28). The path to success seemed to require being " 'different' from other women," and Chicago recalls having felt "a warm glow of pride in my 'specialness' and . . . the status that I had as the result of being the only woman [the men] took seriously" (p. 27-28).

Yet even as her professional life flourished after she graduated with her B.A. and M.A. from UCLA in 1964, Chicago felt increasingly alienated from her work. By 1966, she had had a solo exhibit at the Rolf Nelson gallery in Los Angeles, and one of her sculptures was included in the "Primary Structures" exhibit at the Jewish Museum in New York. She exhibited a series of twenty-foot-high Fiberglas "Ten Part Cylinders" in the "Sculpture of the Sixties" show at the Los Angeles County Art Museum and the Philadelphia Art Museum in 1967, and in 1969, the Pasadena Museum (now the Norton Simon) held a one-person exhibit of her large and small-scale Minimalist sculpture. Despite her professional success, however, she faced continual sexual harassment from art dealers, supply salesmen, and even artist friends who apparently felt threatened by her "unfeminine" ambition. Even worse, in order to maintain her professional standing, she found it necessary to "neutralize" the content of her work, suppressing any symbolic references to her sexual identity and her personal experiences as a woman. "I began to realize," she wrote, "that my real sexual identity had been denied by my culture, and this somehow represented the entire sense of denial I had been experiencing as a woman artist. I felt that if I could symbolize my true sexual nature, I could open up the issue of the nature of my identity as a woman through that symbolic statement" (p. 50).

In 1970, Chicago decided to "sneak" some of her developing feminist concerns into her abstract artwork, and showed a series of small acrylic "Domes," ring-shaped "Pasadena Lifesavers," and photographs of billowing pyrotechnic "Atmospheres," all of which she associated with female anatomy and the sensation of orgasm, in an exhibit curated by Dextra Frankel at California State University, Fullerton. To highlight the feminist meaning of the exhibit, she posted an official announcement that she was changing her name from Gerowitz, her first husband's surname, to Chicago: "*Judy Gerowitz* hereby divests herself of all names imposed on her through male social dominance and freely chooses her own name *Judy Chicago*." Yet when critics continued to interpret her new work in the same formalist terms they had applied to her earlier Minimalist abstractions, Chicago decided that stronger action was necessary: "[t]he full impact of my alienation struck me. I had tried to challenge society's conception of what it is to be a woman. At the same time, I had, in trying to make myself into an artist who was taken seriously in a male-dominated art community, submerged the very aspects of myself that could make my work intelligible . . . I realized that if the art community as it existed could not provide me with what I needed in order to realize myself, then I would have to commit myself to developing an alternative, and that the meaning of the women's movement was that there was, probably for the first time in history, a chance to do just that" (p. 65-66).

The developing women's movement strengthened Chicago's determination to define her identity and her artwork on her own terms. As she has described her reaction to the early feminist literature she discovered around 1970,

> When I read it, I couldn't believe it. Here were women saying the things I had been feeling, saying them out loud . . . I identified with all the material in those early tracts as I had never identified with anything in my whole life . . . realizing that at last there was an alternative to the isolation, the silence, the repressed anger, the rejection, the depreciation, and the denial I had been facing. If these women could say how they felt, so could I. (p. 59-60)

In the fall of 1970, Chicago left Los Angeles to found a new educational program for women artists at California State University in Fresno, at a distance from the constricting standards of the mainstream Los Angeles art establishment. Chicago's goal for the Fresno Feminist Art Program was to challenge every type of cultural limitation placed on women artists–from society's low expectations for female achievement, to traditional definitions of the appropriate subject matter for art. Believing that creative, successful women must move beyond the limits of what she then referred to as "female role," she pushed her students to develop what were traditionally considered "masculine" skills. The Fresno class's first assignment, for example, was to locate and rebuild an off-campus studio space, a task that involved learning to negotiate business transactions and developing advanced construction skills. At the same time, however, Chicago encouraged her students to draw on their most personal experiences as women for the content of their artwork, thereby challenging the Modernist rule that art should be abstract, free from narrative content, and made on a grand scale from industrial materials associated with masculine technical prowess.

During the early months of the program, Chicago and the Fresno students engaged in extensive feminist consciousness-raising activities. According to participant Faith Wilding, who has since written extensively about her experiences in the Feminist Art Program, consciousness-raising focused on "what we would today call socially constructed female experience," allowing the students to locate their personal histories within a larger social and political context:

> As each woman spoke it became apparent that what had seemed to be purely "personal" experiences were actually shared by all the other women: we were discovering a common oppression based on our gender, which was defining our roles and identities as women. In subsequent group discussions, we analyzed the social and political mechanisms of this oppression, thus placing our personal histories into a larger cultural perspective. This was a direct application of *the* slogan of 1970s feminism: The personal is political. (Wilding, 1994, p. 34)

Topics addressed in consciousness-raising sessions included "work, money, ambition, sexuality, parents, power, clothing, body image, [and] violence" (p. 34). Several students revealed histories of serious abuse. Chicago was often surprised and frightened by the emotions unleashed in consciousness-raising, not knowing how to respond to a process that seemed to develop its own momentum once she had set it in motion. For the most part, she encouraged the women to channel their feelings into their artwork. In this way, consciousness-raising became a method for determining artistic subject matter, which the students were then free to carry out in a variety of unconventional media, including fabric, glitter, plastic flowers, and other household "crafts" materials, as well as performance, drawing, painting, and sculpture.

Among the most important topics addressed by Chicago and her students in the Fresno Feminist Art Program, both in their artwork and in consciousness-raising sessions, was the theme of female sexuality. One crucial reason for the importance of sexual imagery in the early feminist art movement was that images of women's bodies had historically been used in art (and in advertising, film, etc.) as a sort of "blank canvas" onto which male fantasy, desire, and even ownership could be projected. Chicago and her students wanted to symbolically reclaim the female body as a vehicle for *female* power and expression, conveying women's own thoughts and feelings as experienced in their bodies. As Patricia B. Richgels stated in a 1992 issue of *Women & Therapy*, "The control of female sexuality is the cornerstone of other forms of social oppression of women. Questions of sexual desire and pleasure are also intrinsically questions of power and oppression. Creating our erotic heritage is fundamental to women's liberation" (p. 134).

The Fresno students' forceful sexually-themed artwork attested to startling depths of anger and desire. In one performance addressing sexual exploitation and violence, for example, a performer dressed as a man led a young woman to a milking machine and forced her to "milk" blood out of her breast until she had filled a pitcher. Then, against a backdrop of slides showing meat and mutilated cattle, and the sounds of a tape-recording describing the proceedings at a slaughterhouse, the "man" poured the blood/milk that the woman had "given" over the woman's body (Chicago, 1975, p. 89-90). The local slaughterhouse provided materials for a more dreamlike, open-ended artwork by student Faith Wilding, as well.

Wilding created a tableau featuring an effigy of her own body heaped with cow intestines, lying on a red velvet dais, and surrounded by bloody sanitary napkins. The installation literally placed the female body on a pedestal, but simultaneously linked the monthly reproductive cycle to images of death and decay, highlighting the sense of shame and fear that women had been taught to feel about their normal bodily functions.

The students also produced exuberant images expressing pleasure and pride in their sexual identity. Reclaiming as a symbol of pride the dreaded word "cunt" that Chicago herself had previously used to demean women, Chicago and her students now asserted that "cunt is beautiful," in much the same spirit that the Civil Rights Movement proclaimed that "Black is beautiful." Inspired by a cut paper "cunt alphabet" Chicago was working on in the program studio, the Fresno women, as Wilding remembers, "vied with each other to come up with images of female sexual organs by making paintings, drawings, and constructions of bleeding slits, holes, gashes, boxes, caves, or exquisite vulval jewel pillows" (Wilding, 1994, p. 34). Students Cay Lang, Vanalyn Green, Dori Atlantis, and Susan Boud spontaneously elected themselves the Feminist Art Program cheerleaders, donning pink and red satin costumes that spelled out the word C-U-N-T, and leading ribald, witty public cheers to women. According to Wilding, "making 'cunt' art was exciting, subversive, and fun, because 'cunt' signified to us an awakened consciousness about our bodies and our sexual selves"(p. 34).

Another important cornerstone of Chicago's Feminist Art Program was the ideal of collaboration among women. Believing that they could best empower themselves by avoiding dependence on men, Chicago encouraged her students to develop connections with women, both past and present. Students read and discussed feminist literature and did research on women artists whose work had been ignored by mainstream art history, seeking to learn from the insights of others as well as to develop a sense of pride in their female heritage. Reaching out to the community beyond Fresno, they published a special issue of *Everywoman* magazine documenting their activities, and held a number of well-attended open houses at the end of the year including displays of student artwork, student performances, slide shows of women's artwork, and public discussion groups. One frequent visitor to the program, artist Miriam Schapiro, was so excited by Chicago's ideas that she invited Chicago to join her at the prestigious California Institute of the Arts outside Los Angeles, where the two would co-direct an expanded Feminist Art Program with state-of-the-art facilities.

When Chicago and the Fresno students joined Schapiro at Cal Arts in the fall of 1971, however, the promised facilities had not yet been completed. Meeting adversity with aplomb, the group convened in the apartments of students and staff to brainstorm ideas for a major collective project that could be completed off-campus. Perhaps inspired by their temporary institutional homelessness, they decided to make a home, women's traditional "place," both the site and the subject of their first project. The result was *Womanhouse,* an abandoned Hollywood mansion that the artists transformed into what the *Womanhouse* catalog describes as a "repository of the daydreams women have as they wash, bake, cook, sew, and iron their lives away" (p. 3).

Making use of traditional homemaking crafts like sewing and crochet, as well as sculpture, painting, costume and performance, the young creators of *Womanhouse* confronted the domestic role historically reserved for women in modern American society with a complex mixture of longing, nostalgia, horror, and rage. The "Dining Room," for instance, a collaborative project carried out by five students along with Miriam Schapiro, commemorated women's traditional nurturing activities with a richly colored feast of papier-mâché foods, laid out before a sumptuous mural of fruits and flowers. Vicki Hodgetts and Robin Weltsch, on the other hand, evoked the sinister aspect of selfless service in their pink-painted "Nurturant Kitchen," where the ceiling and walls dripped with rows of fried eggs that gradually transformed into drooping severed breasts. Upstairs, in a 19th-century style boudoir inspired by Colette's novel, *Cheri,* students Karen Le Coq and Nancy Youdelman took turns acting the part of an aging courtesan, ceaselessly applying, removing, and reapplying heavy makeup in a desperate attempt to disguise the signs of age. The most confrontational installation in the house, Chicago's "Menstruation Bathroom," featured a white, antiseptic bathroom filled with douches, deodorants and other manufactured products designed to hide the "shameful" signs of menstruation, which nevertheless escaped in the form of blood-stained sanitary napkins spilling over the sides of the bathroom wastebasket like an angry red scream. Chicago's "Menstruation Bathroom," like Le Coq and Youdelman's performance, highlighted the damage inflicted on women through society's impossible standards of feminine beauty and "purity," and insisted that women's bodies and emotions be confronted in their totality.

By transforming the private domestic space of a home into art-work, *Womanhouse* challenged the institutional barriers separating the elite, quasi-sacred realm of art from the rest of society, and insisted that art is never "neutral" and cannot be separated from the rest of life. Addressing formerly taboo or supposedly "trivial" topics, *Womanhouse* accorded new importance to the daily rituals of shared domesticity, making ordinary people's lives every bit as compelling as the lives of popes and politicians. While honoring traditional women's emotional and material contributions to human culture, it simultaneously protested the historical confinement of women's creative energy to a narrow domestic sphere of expression.

Womanhouse made a tremendous impact on the feminist art community, especially on the west coast. With her talent for public relations, Chicago had scheduled the installation's opening in February 1972 to coincide with the West Coast Conference of Women Artists, hosted by West-East Bag (WEB), a national artists' network organized by Chicago and others. Films documenting the installation were broadcast on public television and distributed through the feminist film community, while a photo-essay in *Time* magazine brought images of *Womanhouse* to millions of general readers (Littman, 1972; Demetrakas, 1972; *Time*, 1972). As the earliest large-scale example of what came to be referred to as "female imagery" in the 1970s, *Womanhouse* served as a model for much of the feminist artwork and performance that developed over the course of the decade.

Chicago's teaching experiments in the feminist art programs at Fresno and Cal Arts also had a profound effect on her own artwork. Having met with enthusiasm for her ideas in an educational setting, she began to work more assertively to integrate the themes of women's experience, women's sexuality, and women's visual traditions into her own brand of abstraction. Fascinated by the women's "hobbyist" china-painting tradition, Chicago determined to do something "different," with the medium, using it as a vehicle to convey women's historical oppression, as well as their creativity and drive. While she admired the beauty and precision of a well-painted china plate, she also saw such domestic crafts as a historical means of containing and trivializing women's creativity:

> I remember one particularly poignant experience of visiting a china-painter's house and seeing, as Virginia Woolf once said, that the very bricks were permeated with her creative energy. All the chairs had needlepoint cushions; all the beds were covered with quilts; all the pillowcases were hand-embroidered; all the walls were covered with oil paintings; all the plates were painted with flowers; and the garden was planted with the kinds of flowers that were painted on the plates. This woman had done all that work, trying as best she could to fit her creative drive–which could probably have expanded into mural-size paintings or monumental sculptures–into the confined space of her house, which could hardly have held another piece of work.
>
> The china-painting world, and the household objects the women painted, seemed to be a perfect metaphor for women's domesticated and trivialized circumstances. (Chicago, 1979, p. 11)

Chicago's experiments with china-painting ultimately led to the conception of her most famous, most monumental artwork, *The Dinner Party*. At first she planned to make a series of abstract "portraits" of creative women on porcelain plates to be hung on the wall–an early working title for the project was "Twenty-five Women Who Were Eaten Alive." Ultimately, however, she settled on a more complex and more explicit format, a huge (48' × 48' × 48'), open, triangular table laid with thirty-nine place settings honoring thirty-nine women who had made important contributions to western civilization and the well-being of women. *The Dinner Party* was conceived as a symbolic alternative to standard history books and art, illuminating the accomplishments of important women who previously had been "written right out of history"

(Chicago cited in Demetrakas, 1980). As Chicago's ambitions for *The Dinner Party* expanded beyond the power of one artist to execute, she solicited the help of many collaborators, some of whom were paid a small salary, but many of whom volunteered their labor over a period of up to five years. Before it was completed, some four hundred women and men from all walks of life had contributed their time and expertise to the creation of *The Dinner Party*. Chicago, however, retained artistic control over the project (Chicago, 1979; Lippard, 1980; Wachtel, 1981).

The Dinner Party's thirty-nine handmade porcelain plates, representing "dinner guests" ranging chronologically from prehistoric goddesses to Roman philosopher Hypatia, 17th-century astronomer Caroline Herschel, and modern painter Georgia O'Keeffe, were painted and sculpted into various abstractions of the female sexual organs. The female sexual organs were in this way shown to be beautiful and well-made, and female sexuality, or "femaleness," was represented as a source of creativity and accomplishment. Chicago also associated the plates' motif with flowers and butterflies–both symbols of growth and transformation–and as the guests progressed in chronological order around the table the imagery rose in increasingly three-dimensional forms like butterflies breaking free from the surface of the plates.

Each place setting was laid with a painstakingly hand-embroidered runner, executed in the needlework style of the honored guest's historical period, and referring to important events in her life or society. Symbolizing Chicago's idea that success can be achieved only within a supportive context, the porcelain floor beneath the table was painted with 999 names of other women who had contributed to the fields of endeavor represented by the women at the table. Additional historical information, as well as documentation of *The Dinner Party* workers and the history of the project, was provided in museum brochures, documentary panels, and a *Dinner Party* book.

The Dinner Party opened at the San Francisco Museum of Modern Art in March, 1979, to record-breaking crowds of mostly women viewers. The exhibit represented a major event in American society, documented in the national media through television coverage and stories in popular magazines like *Life* and *Mademoiselle,* as well as numerous underground feminist publications. As one viewer recently described the impact the piece had on her in 1979, "What *The Dinner Party* did was so new it was beyond shocking. It put us on entirely different ground. I had always just assumed that society worked as much for my benefit as for the benefit of men. Now I realized that things were profoundly different for women. *The Dinner Party* said, "We are here and we must be reckoned with" (Marges, 1994). At a subsequent exhibit of *The Dinner Party* in Brooklyn in 1981, journalist Eleanor Wachtel interviewed a gray-haired woman she noticed weeping on the steps, who explained that she was crying "because women have been eliminated from history . . . because it's so exciting to see them here . . . but it's painful too . . . this was done with such loving care, by women working together in a woman's way" (Wachtel, 1981, p. 38).

As much as *The Dinner Party* was loved by general viewers, however, it was reviled by leading conservative art critics, both male and female, who denounced the project as a "crass . . . vulgar . . . libel on the female imagination," and "the ultimate in 70s kitsch" (Kramer, 1980; Muchnic, 1979). Art Museums in Seattle and Rochester, New York abruptly canceled their plans to exhibit the work; it continued to tour North America and Europe throughout the 1980s, however, largely due to the efforts of grassroots women's groups that managed to raise the funds to bring the enormous installation to alternative exhibition sites in their cities. Even as late as 1990, when Chicago attempted to donate *The Dinner Party* to the University of the District of Columbia in Washington, D.C., conservative members of Congress objected to the donation on the grounds that *The Dinner Party* was "clearly pornographic," "weird, sexual art," and introduced a bill to cut the university's federal funding if it should accept the gift (Rep. Dana Rohrabacher and Rep. Stan Parris cited in Lippard, 1991, p. 43). The bill was eventually defeated, but the negative publicity surrounding the Congressional hearings forced Chicago to withdraw her offer, and today *The Dinner Party* remains without a permanent home.

The controversy surrounding *The Dinner Party* raises provocative questions about the nature of art and its importance in society. Who does art serve? Who decides what is "good" art? How do ostensibly disinterested judgments about artistic "quality" work to regulate the expression of different points of views and different values in society? As Chicago sees it, a monumental, feminist work of art like *The Dinner Party* is perceived as a threat to conservative values because "art is a symbol system that gets passed into the future" (Chicago, 1994).

Ironically, *The Dinner Party* has also become a focus of controversy among feminist artists and writers in recent years. In the 1980s, as a second generation of feminists attempted to integrate feminist values into a broader cultural base, early feminist art was frequently criticized for "ghettoizing" or "essentializing" women; by focusing attention on women's bodies and on domestic themes, feminist art of the 1970s was seen as reinforcing stereotypes about women as sex objects and selfless nurturers. More recently, however, feminists and art historians looking back over the past twenty-five years of feminist activity have begun to reassert the importance of early feminist efforts to redefine female identity on women's own terms. Early feminist artworks like *The Dinner Party,* regardless of inevitable flaws and shortcomings, strengthened women's sense of freedom and self-determination, and laid important groundwork for subsequent feminist activism. Such artworks also asserted the importance of intimacy and nurturing in the lives of both women and men. An exhibit of *The Dinner Party* at UCLA's Hammer Gallery, scheduled to open in April, 1996, will reexamine the significance of Chicago's work in the history of the feminist art movement from the 1970s to the present.

Since completing *The Dinner Party,* Chicago has continued to address issues of sexual identity, power, and dominance in her artwork. *The Birth Project,* consisting of about 150 woven and embroidered images of the rarely pictured subject of childbirth, was created between 1980 and 1985 by several dozen needleworkers who interpreted and implemented Chicago's designs. In contrast to *The Dinner Party,* which was completed in a large communal studio in Santa Monica, CA, *The Birth Project* was pieced together by women working in their own homes. Chicago made a point of soliciting the participation of women from diverse socioeconomic and ethnic backgrounds for the project, perhaps in response to some viewers' objections that *The Dinner Party* project had been inaccessible to poor, working women, and gave short shrift in its imagery to women of color.

Chicago's 1986 *Powerplay*, her first non-collaborative project in many years, took the social construction of male power as its subject. According to Chicago, this series of paintings explored "the faces men present to the world to cover up the sadness they are not allowed to show . . . I wanted to show [men] as *human*, but acting in ways that are intolerable . . . Women focus too much on themselves as victims and not on men as perpetrators. We as women can look out on the world and we have a gift to give . . . Sometimes men don't see themselves too realistically" (Chicago cited in Carroll, 1991, p. 17; Chicago, 1994).

Her most recent artwork, the *Holocaust Project*, grew out of research that she and her husband, photographer Donald Woodman, undertook in the late 1980s to learn more about their Jewish heritage and the Holocaust. After traveling to concentration camps, massacre sites, and memorials, studying photographic archives and drawings created by camp inmates, and viewing numerous films and documentary exhibits, Chicago worked with Woodman and a team of needleworkers to create an educational exhibit on the Holocaust combining photography, painting, and needlework. Holocaust educator Isaiah Kuperstein has described the project as a valuable extension of previously available information, that "recompose[s] the standard litany on the Holocaust story . . . showing women's experiences on these very same issues. Thus women assume an egalitarian position of equal weight in Holocaust history" (Kuperstein cited in Carroll, 17, 19). The *Holocaust Project* opened at the Spertus Museum in Chicago in October, 1993, and will travel to museums around the United States through 1997.

In a recent interview, Chicago expressed the hope that her life and artwork might function as "a testament to [the importance of] believing in yourself and finding the courage to risk being who you are," asserting that "one person *can* make a difference" (Chicago, 1994). For the future, she stresses the importance of inclusivity, and according all people an equal voice through the making, viewing, and discussion of art, in defining human experience.

REFERENCES

Carroll, Alberta (1991). "Judy Chicago and her Art," *Minneapolis Women's Press,* May 22-June 4, 1991.

Chicago, Judy (1975). *Through the Flower: My Struggle as a Woman Artist.* Garden City, New York: Doubleday.

Chicago, Judy (1979). *The Dinner Party: A Symbol of Our Heritage.* Garden City, New York: 1979.

Chicago, Judy (1994). Interview with Laura Meyer.

Chicago, Judy and Miriam Schapiro (1972). *Womanhouse* catalog.

Demetrakas, Johanna (1972). *Womanhouse* (film).

Demetrakas, Johanna (1980). *Right Out of History* (film).

Greenberg, Clement (1965). "Modernist Painting," *The New Art: A Critical Anthology,* ed. Gregory Battcock (1966). New York: E.P. Dutton.

Kramer, Hilton (1980). "Art: Judy Chicago's 'Dinner Party' Comes to Brooklyn Museum," *The New York Times,* October 17, 1980, Section C, p. 1, 18.

Lippard, Lucy (1980). "Judy Chicago's 'Dinner Party' " *Art in America* 68, n. 4.

Lippard, Lucy (1991). "How Washington Lost 'The Dinner Party,' " *Art in America,* December 1991.

Littman, Lynne (1972). *Womanhouse Is not a Home* (film).

Marges, Dawn (1994). Interview with Laura Meyer.

Muchnic, Suzanne (1979). "An Intellectual Famine at Judy Chicago's Feast," *Los Angeles Times,* April 15, 1979, Book Review.

Richgels, Patricia B. (1992). "Hypoactive Sexual Desire in Heterosexual Women: A Feminist Analysis," *Women & Therapy* 12, n.1/2.

Time (March 20, 1972). "Art: Bad Dreamhouse," p. 77.

Wachtel, Eleanor (1981). "This Is Judy Chicago," *Homemakers,* November, 1981.

Wilding, Faith (1994). "The Feminist Art Programs at Fresno and CalArts, 1970-75," *The Power of Feminist Art,* ed. Norma Broude and Mary Garrard (1994). New York: Harry Abrams.

Becoming a Feminist Foremother

Nancy J. Chodorow

It is a little over twenty-five years, about a generation, since I first became involved with feminism. My women's group, organized by the first women's group in the Boston area, started meeting in December, 1968. So it should not be surprising that I have gone from being a daughter, or feminist daughter, to a mother, or feminist foremother. Yet one's professional and political daughter identity (one's personal daughter identity as well) does not easily disappear, as my own writings attest (Chodorow, 1978; Chodorow & Contratto, 1982). I had turned to the study of early women psychoanalysts, after all, partly as a search for my own psychoanalytic foremothers (Chodorow, 1986, 1989 and 1991). I fully expected that my contribution to a volume on feminist foremothers would again place me as a daughter. I would write, perhaps, on Melanie Klein or Karen

Nancy J. Chodorow, PhD, is Professor of Sociology at the University of California, Berkeley, a faculty member of the San Francisco Psychoanalytic Institute, and a psychoanalyst in private practice. She is the author of *The Reproduction of Mothering* (Berkeley and Los Angeles: University of California Press, 1978), *Feminism and Psychoanalytic Theory* (New Haven: Yale University Press and Cambridge, UK: Polity Press, 1979) and *Femininities, Masculinities, Sexualities: Freud and Beyond* (Lexington: University Press of Kentucky, and London, UK: Free Association Books, 1994). She is working on a book currently titled *The Power of Feelings: Personal Meaning and the Psychoanalytic Encounter.*
Correspondence may be addressed to Nancy J. Chodorow, PhD, 5305 College Avenue, Oakland, CA 94618.

[Haworth co-indexing entry note]: "Becoming a Feminist Foremother." Chodorow, Nancy J. Co-published simultaneously in *Women & Therapy* (The Haworth Press, Inc.) Vol. 17, No. 1/2, 1995, pp. 141-153; and: *Feminist Foremothers in Women's Studies, Psychology, and Mental Health* (ed: Phyllis Chesler, Esther D. Rothblum, and Ellen Cole) The Haworth Press, Inc., 1995, pp. 141-153; and: *Feminist Foremothers in Women's Studies, Psychology, and Mental Health* (ed: Phyllis Chesler, Esther D. Rothblum, and Ellen Cole) Harrington Park Press, an imprint of The Haworth Press, Inc., 1995, pp. 141-153. Single or multiple copies of this article are available from The Haworth Document Delivery Service [1-800-342-9678, 9:00 a.m. - 5:00 p.m. (EST)].

141

Horney, or on one of the other early women psychoanalysts who wrote about and treated women. Or I would write about these remarkable women as a collectivity of active women professionals who challenged women's traditional roles. But I am glad to place myself in the feminist maternal lineage, myself looking back to those I consider my own feminist foremothers, yet also standing as a foremother to those of succeeding generations.

Both personal and cultural circumstances, I believe, led me to feminism, and in particular to psychoanalytic feminism and feminist psychoanalysis. I would say that I was in the right place at the right time: I was in graduate school, in the New Left, in my midtwenties, without family or career commitments. Feminism found me, as much as the reverse. But I know from my own research and reading on successful women that women often attribute their accomplishments to luck and circumstance; it saves them from admitting ambition, aggression, self-assertion and skill. I was also driven by inner passions, some of which I can articulate, but some of which, I believe, were at the time and probably remain unconscious. I resonated, certainly, to the feminist critique of personal life and the objectification of women. The empirical truth of feminist observations of inequality was indisputable. Male dominance (in personal relationships, in the polity, and in the economy) and women's economic and psychological dependence on men seemed ubiquitous.

But I would have to admit, with hindsight, that politics do not move me from within. For many of my generation, political activity arose out of a centering and motivating passion for fairness and justice. As I later realized, many of my generation loved to participate in political groups, in political organizing, in demonstrations. These were activities I joined and ethically believed in, but my participation did not arise out of a political passion, and I did not particularly enjoy political activism. What was key for me in early feminism was a movement and analysis that required a psychology, an analysis and transformation of inner life. It was a movement whose politics spoke directly to felt tensions and internal conflicts, in the claim that the personal was political and in political practices that included consciousness raising as well as more traditional political activities in the public sphere.

My own academic background supported such a movement and analysis. I had been guided toward psychological anthropology by discovering, early in college, Erik Erikson's *Childhood and Society* (1950), Oscar Lewis's *Children of Sanchez* (1963), and Ruth Benedict's *Patterns of Culture* (1934), all books that focus on how the individual creates a self, psyche, and life in particular cultural and social conditions, and how these conditions shape, constrain, and limit psychological experience. These interests in the exact place where the individual meets culture and society, this extensive attention to psychological experience, met an almost intuitive and at the time unarticulated fascination on my part, a fascination that is still with me. Feminist theory and practice—enacted in intensely personal women's groups, focused on the complicated felt dynamics of being a woman, of relations among women, of relations between women and men—called upon these early interests and, in a sense, relegitimated them: I had, influenced by both intellectual fashion and political challenge, moved away in my work from psychological concerns.

What about my own contributions to feminism? Again, I begin with the circumstances that led to my specific involvements with feminist psychology. During this early period of feminism, I was in graduate school in sociology at Brandeis University. For a variety of reasons (see Thorne, forthcoming), Brandeis fostered critical thinking of all sorts and in particular feminism and many feminists. In a seminar on family dynamics, we found many readings on father-son, father-daughter, and mother-son relationships, but we were frustrated by our inability to find theories about or studies of mothers and daughters. In response, several of us formed "the Mother-Daughter Group." This group, a few graduate students in sociology enlarged to include some friends and students in other fields, took as its task the analysis of mother-daughter relationships. Everyone in the group was a daughter, a few were also mothers, and there were some (prized) mother-daughter pairs. Mothers and sisters of group members joined meetings when they were visiting; pre-teen and early teenage daughters were invited to meetings at their own houses.

The Mother-Daughter Group intuitively focused on emotionally-charged issues, and we created a method of discussion and analysis that combined consciousness-raising, psychodynamic understanding, and phenomenological bracketing. We discussed shame, guilt, anger, varieties of family alliances and constellations, siblings, our fantasies and wishes about maternal presence or absence during illness or when facing abortions, family menstrual traditions, and family secrets. During a particularly explosive meeting, many ex-teenagers in their twenties and thirties found themselves unable to empathize with a group member worried about her own teenage daughter's weight gain. We also individually drew from the group in our work: films were made, short stories written, training as a therapist undertaken. My own writing on mothers and daughters, and especially my understanding of psychological separation and connection in the mother-daughter relationship and in female identity and selfhood, began in that group. This understanding was confirmed as I began to read the psychoanalytic literature on women.

Although my involvements with and contributions to feminism have, of course, developed and changed, they were set in this environment of collective, self-reflective analysis, reading, and concern with issues that are personally meaningful. I describe the Mother-Daughter Group, then, not only because its substantive topic helped to generate some of my founding feminist theorizing. I focus on it also because I believe it is easier and more customary in describing one's development to focus (as I do above) either on personal individuality (whether psychodynamic, familial, or intellectual) or on larger political and cultural conditions. In my case, and I suspect in the case of many feminists of my generation, face-to-face supportive interpersonal networks of friends, colleagues, and "sisters" have been equally important (prefaces and acknowledgements are good everyday places to find this level of fostering feminist process).

Another potential contribution of this kind of collectivity, central for all of us who teach, is in teaching. As we were building our teaching repertoires, several of my cohort at Brandeis for years shared syllabi, course notes, and entire sets of course lectures with one another. Barrie Thorne and I still ritually exchange syllabi at the beginning of each semester. For years, we two ex-anthropologists thought of this exchange as our private kula ring, patterned after

Malinowski's classic analysis of how men's exchange networks in the Trobriand Islands create Trobriand society (Malinowski, 1922). However, inspired by Annette Weiner's feminist reanalysis of Trobriand society (1976), we now consider it a banana-leaf skirt exchange.

I began publishing comparisons of male and female psychology, as these related to gender inequality, in 1972 (in Chodorow, 1989). In "Being and Doing: A Cross-Cultural Examination of the Socialization of Males and Females," an article that drew on my undergraduate training as a psychological anthropologist and my beginning reading as a psychoanalytic sociologist, I set myself a double task. I wanted at the same time to challenge claims for the biological basis of gender personality and role differences (the language of roles is not one I would use today) and to understand the nearly universal secondary status, power, and devaluation of women. I developed the idea that femininity was more easily attained, and attained through a more continuous process, than masculinity. The more difficult task for female development was coming to terms with cultural devaluation. Masculinity was achieved through "doing" rather than "being," performance rather than identity. Masculinity also–and here it tied closely to the devaluation and secondary status of women–responded to a dread of women and active rejection of the feminine. As has been characteristic of my work since, I drew from a variety of sources: anthropological studies, psychoanalytic articles, psychological research, theory of various sorts. It was in making connections among these sources and moving beyond them that my contribution lay.

Some of these ideas were continued in "Family Structure and Feminine Personality" (1974, in Chodorow, 1989), the article that laid out briefly some of the core insights that would later form *The Reproduction of Mothering* (1978). Again I set a pattern characteristic of my later work, in which I wish both to retain and to challenge a psychoanalytic perspective. Theoretically, "Family Structure and Feminine Personality" argues for a psychoanalytic understanding of gender; at the same time, it introduces a non-traditional approach to this understanding, drawing upon psychoanalytic object-relations theory and challenging both the substance of Freud's account and his drive-based approach to gender. Substantively, I claim for feminist theory that we need to notice that women mother, and that there are consequences to this fact (Dinnerstein, 1976, also elaborates this fact for a feminist psychology and social critique). I give an account of female (and male) development in terms of the changing intra-psychic (preoedipal and oedipal) relationship to the mother, and I introduce into feminist discourse the claim that feminine personali-ty, or the female self, is defined or founded on relation and connec-tion (1989, pp. 45, 57), or what I later call a "self-in-relationship" (1978, pp. 169, 200, 209).

Throughout the 70s and early 80s, I continued to generate a psychoanalytic feminism that revised psychoanalytic understand-ings of gender. I argued against traditional drive and anatomic ap-proaches to gender psychology and for a revaluing of feminine psychology and a problematizing of masculinity. I also continued to explore the nature and psychological consequences of women's mothering, in what I have sometimes called a "matricentric" psychology (1989, 14). I remained steadfast, in the face of much feminist unease with both psychology in general and psychoanaly-sis in particular, that psychoanalysis had much to offer feminism (1987, in Chodorow, 1989).

The Reproduction of Mothering was key here. In that book, I develop in detail an account of the preoedipal, oedipal and adoles-cent creation of a female self intrapsychically connected to mother and also involved in a complex and shifting bisexual oedipal triangle, and of a male self that in its intrapsychic development comes to be increasingly preoccupied with differentiation, rejection of dependence, and separateness. I argue, implicitly against psycho-analytic ego psychology and popular psychologies, that separate-ness and individuation can be a defense rather than an achievement. I also investigate the relations between masculinity and male domi-nance and describe how prevalent tensions in male-female relation-ships, what I call "heterosexual knots," can be understood in terms of the psychologies of gender I have described.

Although many readers have not thought so, I think it can be claimed that this book is careful in its generalizations. I state force-fully and unequivocally that women mother, or that, universally, men do not do primary child care. As with all universal claims, there are probably exceptions here, but the claim for cross-cultural, cross-historical and cross-racial-ethnic near universality of women's mothering is probably not to be challenged. I am also specific when I refer to what I (and many contemporaneous writers) call the "Western middle-class"–when my generalizations are not meant to be universal claims. I am also careful to note in an "Afterword" that the outcomes I describe are not universal but prevalent–that there are numbers of reasons why individuals may themselves for social or psychological reasons create a different psychology than the one I describe. This specificity, I believe–my distinguishing between a psychoanalytic method that investigates the relations between inner and outer worlds and the contents of particular self-constructions or unconscious fantasies–is why it is possible to "apply" my understandings and approach to a variety of different cultural and social groups, so that the contemporary feminist interest in differences among women specifies, but does not vitiate, my argument. (I address questions of generalization and differences among women in Chodorow, 1989, "Introduction," and Chodorow, 1994 and 1995).

I note another particular contribution from this period. Susan Contratto's and my article, "The Fantasy of the Perfect Mother" (Chodorow & Contratto, 1982; in Chodorow, 1989) has been important on many fronts. We cautioned feminists to be careful about their idealization and blame of their own mothers and mothers in general, noting the difficulties even thoughtful, articulate feminist writers had in sustaining an even-handed attitude toward maternal subjectivity and mothers. The cautions we described can also be applied to culture in general and to psychological practitioners, and indeed Contratto has been active in arguing within psychology and in the therapeutic community for better understanding of mothers (see, e.g., Contratto, 1984, 1985, and 1992; and Buttenheim & Contratto, 1994).

"The Fantasy of the Perfect Mother" also specified what had been implicit in all my psychoanalytic feminist writing. A psychoanalytic account, focusing on unconscious psychodynamic processes and outcomes, is not in itself enough, nor are unconscious psychological outcomes a justification for behavior. Psychoanalysis and all dynamic psychologies assume that change is possible and desirable, and makes individuals agents (albeit unconscious agents) of their own psychology. By differentiating unconscious from conscious, and primary process from secondary process, psychoanalysis shows how intention and motivation work, and how these can be altered. If feminism requires change, and if we believe that some of that change is psychological and emotional, then feminism requires a psychodynamic psychology.

These early writings had and continue to have a wide impact across many academic disciplines and for feminist therapy and psychology. *The Reproduction of Mothering* won an award from the American Sociological Association, has been translated into seven languages, and was the subject of symposia at professional meetings in a number of different disciplines. Both that book and *Feminism and Psychoanalytic Theory* led to interviews and focused articles on my theories here and abroad. They provided guidance and interpretive guidelines for psychotherapists treating women, who needed new ways of understanding what their patients or clients were telling them. They enabled those committed to psychoanalysis to conceive a different but still psychoanalytic way of understanding and treating patients. They provided self-recognition for many readers, who could see themselves in the intense mother-daughter relationships and tangled heterosexual knots I describe. My writings on the mother as subject and my co-authored essay with Contratto articulated what many women who were mothers, and many therapists who read the therapeutic maternal-blame literature, felt.

For theorists and writers, these writings provided both a model and tool kit. As a model, they said that women (indeed young women–I was in my late 20s and early 30s when my writings through *The Reproduction of Mothering* were published) could forcefully take on theoretical giants and unquestioned dogma and could think logically and analytically about ideas and theories that had been largely the province of men. As a model, they provided an alternate theory. As a tool kit, they provided underpinnings for studies in feminist epistemology, literary criticism, literary biography, folklore, politics, theology, ethnography and philosophy. I have always been particularly grateful for attention and interest beyond the academy, especially because my writing is so clearly academic. Although my ideas have been drawn upon extensively by numbers of popular psychological writers–to the extent that they have almost passed into common parlance, sometimes beyond the point where specific attribution is given—I am myself not at ease (or would not be if I tried) writing for a more general audience in more popular forms.

Both my life and my feminism have changed, as a result of my own intellectual, personal, and interpersonal involvements and development, and, I am sure, as a result of the changing times. I have said that my early passions and fascinations were with the psyche, that I believed fully from my earliest feminist involvements in the importance of individual consciousness. Such beliefs were consonant with early second-wave feminist practice and theory. Beginning in the mid-1980s, I undertook psychoanalytic training, and I now practice as a therapist and analyst as well as continuing my work as an academic. Further to address psychological conflict and ill-ease, beyond the understandings I had already gained in my work for *The Reproduction of Mothering* and *Feminism and Psychoanalytic Theory,* required that I know the psyche firsthand. Not illegitimately, moreover, it seemed necessary myself to have clinical experience if I wished to have a real impact on those who treat women and men concerning gender and sexuality, as well as concerning the other aspects of emotional and fantasy life which construct a self and interact with or generate this gender and sexuality. I was not mistaken and not unrewarded: I find my clinical work to be, minute by minute, among the most meaningful work I do.

I do not know if I can say that this change is a result of my involvement with feminism. I can certainly say it is a result of my commitment to the view that personal psychology is central to a desirable life and well-being. This well-being includes a life that can (to the maximal extent possible) sit comfortably in the probably inevitable internal demands, tensions and contradictions (certainly the demands, tensions and contradictions found in our problematically gendered and sexed world) of forging gendered subjectivity, meaningful relations, and embodied and sexual selfhood. I do not privilege personal psychology over economic, social or political conditions or treatment, and I do not at all mean to minimize poverty, discrimination, or being battered in this country and the almost unspeakable treatment we read, hear about and see of women (and men and children) in the many war zones of our world. It just happens to be the arena in which I think I can make a sustained contribution to change. It is my own personal solution to the praxis question since, as I note earlier, I am not by nature a political activist.

Currently, then, my feminism is expressed in three areas. In my teaching, I teach feminist theory, feminist methods, psychoanalytic feminism, and gender to both graduates and undergraduates. I want my students to understand especially the complexity and multiple constructions of each woman's life, and the methodological care we must bring to capturing and respecting this as we study women. In my clinical work, I find the particularity of each person's gender, sexuality, and selfhood and help to change individual lives.

My writing (Chodorow, 1994 and 1995) now reflects and expands upon the knowledge I have gained on the one hand in the classroom and the academy and on the other in the clinical consulting room and psychoanalytic world. Responding to the challenges of a multicultural classroom and multi-racial-ethnic feminism, I pay more explicit attention to diversity and variability among women. Drawing from my clinical work, though also addressing the claims of postmodern feminism, I have begun to question the generalizations about gender and sexuality that psychological theorists, researchers, and popular writers, both feminist and otherwise, still make.

As I read these largely monocultural literatures, it seems to me that there is still an attempt to find gender differences, and to focus on what characterizes women versus men, to claim (as I have also done) that "women are," or "men are." Such generalizations, as guidelines to treatment or understanding, can be useful, but I don't think that these literatures in recent years have been responsive enough to the racial-ethnic and international feminist critique of universalizing difference and to attempts to see the more contextual, constructed, contingent multiplicity of individual, cultural, and racial-ethnic genders and sexualities. The non-psychological feminist literature, as well as clinical experience, teach that gender and sexuality are personally expressed and constructed, drawing on pieces of the cultural or social setting, aspects of cultural meaning, and the power relations that underpin and create gender and sexuality. Gender and sexuality are inflected individually with unconscious fantasy and individual emotional tonality and in culturally and familially specific ways. For practitioners, it is also clear that gender cannot be separated from other aspects of selfhood, identity, and psyche (on this, see Harris, 1991, and Dimen, 1991). One strategy in this context is to simplify and abstract out commonality; another is to make respect for complexity and individuality a theoretical, empirical and clinical goal. At this point in time, it might be useful for feminist psychologists and therapists to pay more attention to how individuality develops and is expressed and less attention to assertions about gender difference.

My contribution, then, comes partly from my feminist (multi) location. I am still very much centered in academic feminism, which itself takes its lead currently from poststructuralist trends in the humanities, from epistemology and philosophy, and from theorizing by U.S. women of color and international feminists. My impression is that these trends do not find their way into a very different feminist world, that of feminist therapy and psychology, where I also find myself. In turn, these academic feminist worlds, unfortunately, do not seem much aware of what feminist psychologists are doing, perhaps because psychology is seen as too empiricist, too atheoretical, or too much locked into a kind of theorizing about difference that has been eschewed. I have been forced to consider these two different locations and to situate myself within both.

Finally, I also see myself very much in the psychoanalytic world. I try to bring insights about gender inequality and the pathologies of normal gender and sexuality to this world–to rethink psychoanalytic theory–and to bring, as I have done for the past twenty years or more, psychoanalytic perspectives to the worlds of academic feminism and feminist psychology and therapy. My recent writing (1994, whose title, *Femininities, Masculinities, Sexualities,* explicitly pluralizes) crosses with this psychoanalytic world, as I respond to two feminist criticisms of psychoanalysis. The first criticism (which academic feminism might also make of feminist psychology) concerns the psychoanalytic and psychological tendency to overgeneralize or universalize claims about gender. The second criticism (one that feminist psychology shares with academic feminism) is that psychoanalysis normalizes a problematic gender and sexuality, and especially, that it has traditionally treated as unproblematic and normative male-dominant heterosexuality, while at the same time making problematic and abnormal other sexualities.

Different feminisms locate themselves differently. As is clear, I still locate myself and see my contribution in dialogue with what many would consider quite traditional discourses and institutions. I believe that psychoanalysis, read not as Freud gave it to us but as revised by both psychoanalytic and feminist theorists, remains the most powerful account we have of the psyche, including the gendered, embodied, and sexual psyche. Psychoanalytically-informed treatment has the potential to promote self-understanding, psychological change and emotional well-being, which by definition includes aspects of self and psyche intertwined with gender and sexuality. So, I have felt it important to stay not only in the psychoanalytic feminist dialogue, but also in the feminist dialogue with psychoanalysis as a theory and practice. And I believe in these dialogues I have had some impact.

REFERENCES

Benedict, Ruth. *Patterns of Culture*. Boston, Houghton Mifflin, 1934.

Buttenheim, Margaret and Susan Contratto. "Family Secrets and Twisted Relationships: Distortions in the Mother/Daughter Relationship Arising from Father/Daughter Incest." Unpublished paper presented to The Michigan Society for Psychoanalytic Psychology, 1994.

Chodorow, Nancy J. "Being and Doing: A Cross-Cultural Examination of the Socialization of Males and Females." 1972, in *Feminism and Psychoanalytic Theory*.

Chodorow, Nancy J. "Family Structure and Feminine Personality." 1974, in *Feminism and Psychoanalytic Theory*.

Chodorow, Nancy J. *The Reproduction of Mothering: Psychoanalysis and the Sociology of Gender*. Berkeley and Los Angeles, California, 1978.

Chodorow, Nancy J. "Varieties of Leadership Among Early Women Psychoanalysts." In Leah Dickstein and Carol Nadelson, eds., *Women Physicians in Leadership Roles*. Washington, D.C., American Psychiatric Press, 1986.

Chodorow, Nancy J. "Feminism, Femininity and Freud." 1987, in *Feminism and Psychoanalytic Theory*.

Chodorow, Nancy J. *Feminism and Psychoanalytic Theory*. New Haven, Yale, and Cambridge; UK, Polity, 1989.

Chodorow, Nancy J. "Seventies Questions for Thirties Women: Gender and Generation in a Study of Early Women Psychoanalysts," 1989. In *Feminism and Psychoanalytic Theory*, 1989.

Chodorow, Nancy J. "Where Have All the Eminent Women Psychoanalysts Gone? Like the Bubbles in Champagne, They Rose to the Top and Disappeared." In Judith R. Blau and Norman Goodman, eds., *Social Roles and Social Institutions: Essays in Honor of Rose Laub Coser.* Boulder, Westview Press, 1991.

Chodorow, Nancy J. *Femininities, Masculinities, Sexualities: Freud and Beyond.* Lexington, University Press of Kentucky, and London, UK, Free Association Books, 1994.

Chodorow, Nancy J. "Gender as a Personal and Cultural Construction." *Signs* 20, 1995, in press.

Chodorow, Nancy J. and Susan Contratto. "The Fantasy of the Perfect Mother." 1982, in *Feminism and Psychoanalytic Theory.*

Contratto, Susan. "Mother: Social Sculptor and Trustee of the Faith." In Miriam Lewin, ed., *In the Shadow of the Past: Psychology Portrays the Sexes.* New York, Columbia University Press, 1984.

Chodorow, Nancy J. "Psychology Views Mothers and Mothering, 1897-1980." In Victoria Petraka and Louise Tilly, eds., *Feminist Revisions: What Has Been and Might Be.* Ann Arbor, University of Michigan Press, 1985.

Chodorow, Nancy J. "The Illusive Father-Everywhere/Nowhere: A Reply to the Notion of the Uninvolved Mother in Father-Daughter Incest." Unpublished paper presented to the Meetings of the American Psychological Association, 1992.

Dinnerstein, Dorothy. *The Mermaid and the Minotaur.* New York, Harper and Row, 1976.

Erikson, Erik. *Childhood and Society.* New York, Norton, 1950.

Lewis, Oscar. *Children of Sanchez.* New York, Vintage, 1963.

Malinowski, Bronislaw. *Argonauts of the Western Pacific.* New York, Dutton, 1922.

Thorne, Barrie. "Brandeis as a Generative Institution: Critical Perspectives, Marginality and Feminism." *Theory and Society.* Special issue: *Gender, Agency, and the Development of Feminist Sociology.* Forthcoming, 1996.

Weiner, Annette. *Women of Value, Men of Renown.* Austin, University of Texas Press, 1976.

Pauline Rose Clance:
The Professor from Appalachia

Pauline Rose Clance
Amy J. Ojerholm

When asked what circumstances led her to contribute to feminism and women's mental health, Pauline Rose Clance went directly back to her childhood in the Appalachian hills of Virginia. She was born in 1938 and raised in a tiny coal-mining town where money and educational opportunities were limited and women almost took domestic violence for granted. This was not the case in her own family, however, where her parents were seen as caretakers

Pauline Rose Clance, PhD, is Professor of Psychology at Georgia State University, Atlanta, GA. She is Associate Director of the Psychotherapy and Behavior Therapy Clinic. Her research and writing have focused on the development of human potential and actualization, women and barriers to success, body image issues, and the psychotherapy process. She is author of *The Impostor Phenomenon: Overcoming the Fear That Haunts Your Success*. She has been in practice for 25 years, working with individuals, groups, and intimate systems. She also supervises students and consults with other therapists, employing the methods of both existential and Gestalt psychotherapy.

Amy J. Ojerholm is a graduate student in her second year of the Clinical Psychology Program at the University of Vermont. Her research and clinical interests include lesbian mental health, fat oppression and body-size acceptance.

Correspondence may be addressed to Pauline Rose Clance, PhD, Department of Psychology, Georgia State University, University Plaza, Atlanta, GA 30303.

[Haworth co-indexing entry note]: "Pauline Rose Clance: The Professor from Appalachia." Clance, Pauline Rose, and Amy J. Ojerholm. Co-published simultaneously in *Women & Therapy* (The Haworth Press, Inc.) Vol. 17, No. 1/2, 1995, pp. 155-162; and: *Feminist Foremothers in Women's Studies, Psychology, and Mental Health* (ed: Phyllis Chesler, Esther D. Rothblum, and Ellen Cole) The Haworth Press, Inc., 1995, pp. 155-162: and: *Feminist Foremothers in Women's Studies, Psychology, and Mental Health* (ed: Phyllis Chesler, Esther D. Rothblum, and Ellen Cole) Harrington Park Press, an imprint of The Haworth Press, Inc., 1995, pp. 155-162. Single or multiple copies of this article are available from The Haworth Document Delivery Service [1-800-342-9678, 9:00 a.m. - 5:00 p.m. (EST)].

of the community and who served as important role models for
Pauline. Her mother acted as a midwife and healer when people in
the community couldn't afford the doctor or couldn't wait for him
to arrive, and her father often made sure that if the doctor did make
it in time, he was paid for his services. Pauline was the youngest of
six children, and she recalls that as well as caring for her and her
siblings, her mother also took in boarders, raised vegetables and
milked the cows. Despite her mother's strength and power, her
father was the one who received the largest proportion of respect
from most other people, and this disparity was one of Pauline's first
experiences with sexism.

Pauline's development as an activist began early in her life. She
recounts a story of how she learned the importance of fairness and
equality for people in general:

> My brother had gone into the service and was going to be
> shipped overseas, so my mother and father took a bus to Ala-
> bama to see him before he left. My mother told me about being
> in the bus station where there was a Black woman waiting to
> get on the bus to go see her son. She had been waiting for three
> days to board the bus, but had been repeatedly put to the back
> of the line because the buses were very crowded due to the war.
> My mother talked about the fact that this woman's son was
> going away just like everyone else's and that she thought it was
> wrong that she was getting bumped. My mother put the woman
> in front of her, despite the fact that my father told her not to get
> involved. I know it had an impact on her because she talked
> about it when she came back. My mother didn't ever talk spe-
> cifically about women's rights, but she tried to look out for
> people when for whatever reason things weren't going very
> fairly for them—I think what I did was just take it and apply it to
> women.

During her high school and college years, Pauline experienced
encouragement and success as she became involved first with public speaking around political issues for the Democratic party and
later as a speaker about civil rights issues. She was unaware of any
limitations imposed upon her because of her gender and took full
advantage of many opportunities to participate in political debates

and to work for civil rights. Her first major career goal was to become a lawyer. When the Brown decision to integrate schools was passed down during her second or third year of high school, she was shocked and puzzled by the amount of hate she observed, even among members of her church who had taught her as a child to love everyone. As a result of trying to understand the origin of such hatred and anger, Pauline shifted her focus to psychology during her college years. During college, she also wrote articles for the student newspaper, was involved in dialogues about civil rights issues, and participated in the ecumenical movement of trying to bring together members of different religious groups.

Amidst her involvement in the politics of civil rights, Pauline read Simone de Beauvoir's classic work, *The Second Sex,* only a few years after its publication in the early fifties. She experienced a "critical kind of awareness and awakening that had a significant impact on my life" and for the first time took a hard look at the struggle of women, which had not yet developed into an active movement on college campuses. Interestingly, her "awakening" occurred only a short time before her first experience with blatant sexism. This experience occurred when she was applying to graduate school in psychology.

> I was told by one graduate school, directly, which is fascinating, "We'll only look at your application if you're twice as good as any male candidate. Women drop out." Other women were told, "If you aren't married and you want to enter graduate school, we don't want you because you will get married and drop out," or, "If you are married, we don't want you because you'll have children and drop out." You couldn't say you were a lesbian because psychologists still thought that lesbians were ill, so essentially there was no way out. That really hit me hard because of how I had been treated by my professors in college. Because they encouraged me to go on and believed I could succeed without any trouble, I was unprepared for the overt discrimination that I faced.

Pauline's experience with graduate school interviews was only the beginning of the discrimination she was to face throughout her graduate career. The students in the counseling centers were unwilling to obtain therapy from women therapists, thinking men were better. There was little mentorship available to women students apart from peer support, which the women students did provide for each other. The psychoanalytic tradition was THE tradition, and any woman who argued against the existence of "penis envy" was told that since she raised the issue, she was an example of it.

Although she was experiencing the effects of sexism in her own life more noticeably than ever before, Pauline continued to put a large proportion of her efforts into civil rights activism.

> I think that somehow there was more permission to do that for other oppressed people than for ourselves, and I think there's still some of that, frankly. One of the things that I see happening here in Atlanta is that a huge amount of the work done with AIDS is being led by lesbian doctors. I think until just the last year or two, we've not had near the mobilization for women and breast cancer, for example, which has been a deadly epidemic for a long time. The AIDS fight and the breast cancer fight are both critical. I'm not quite sure how that consciousness for others becomes more important than consciousness for women. I don't think it should be either/or, because my civil rights work has been integral and very important, but it is fascinating how there was more permission to work for others—it was almost like relationships with others could be attended to more than oneself.

In focusing a great deal of her energy on civil rights, Pauline began to see that such efforts could produce change. During graduate school, she participated in boycotts and sit-ins that were successful in integrating restaurants and movie theaters, and she saw things changing all over the South as well. It was exciting and encouraging to see that things could change, and she was motivated and optimistic that similar changes could occur in the condition of women.

Pauline earned her PhD from the University of Kentucky in 1969. Women's issues weren't yet accepted by APA for convention programs, so some of the most fascinating exchanges of ideas took place in the hospitality suites where women got together and discussed issues like women's personality development, women in therapy, discrimination and oppression, marriage and children, and sexual preference. It seemed as if women's issues had finally begun to enter onto the scene.

She worked at a Veteran's Administration hospital following graduation while the Vietnam War was going on. Her patients were all men, and she worked to develop programs that met their needs. Meanwhile, she was very active in the anti-war movement and was also beginning to talk about women's issues at a Unitarian church in Ohio, running seminars and leading discussions.

Discouraged by the treatment of Vietnam veterans, Pauline left the V.A. and accepted a position at Oberlin College in Ohio. Oberlin was the first coed college in the country and she imagined it would be a great haven for women.

> Well, it wasn't. It wasn't at all. There were very few women faculty, and they didn't have much power, and the ones that were there were often employed as instructors or assistants, instead of in tenure track positions. Even though the student enrollment was 50/50, all the people in power were still men, and it was shocking, similar to the shock when I went to graduate school–I still had not quite gotten it.

It was at that point that she started getting very actively involved in women's issues at the college. The president created a committee on the status of women, and she served on the committee with women faculty, students, and town residents. The committee eventually had a big impact, but in order to do so had a lot of strategy meetings where they learned how to work in the system.

> A contribution I feel I have made for women in psychology is really emphasizing the political, and working with women students and faculty to get political in APA and within existing academic systems. Regarding politics–I don't think we can wash our hands and say we don't want to be political. We have to learn how to do politics and do them well. I think I have been instrumental in teaching women how to do that, once I learned how to do it at Oberlin.

Pauline became aware of the impostor phenomenon while she was at Oberlin. She and Dr. Suzanne Imes co-developed and described the phenomenon in 1978. Pauline had had similar experiences herself, especially in graduate school, but thought it was because of her educational and socioeconomic background. They found that other women at Oberlin who had outstanding grades, SAT scores, and recommendations were experiencing the same thing. That made them think, "Whoa, what is happening here?" They realized then that it was not just a personal phenomenon. Although the client population at the counseling center was 60% women and 40% men, the women were talking about their imposter feelings much more, leading Pauline and Suzanne to describe it as a phenomenon primarily affecting women. Later, after researching the topic, they found that men experienced it as well.

> We're still struggling with this issue, because all along it's been very important for us not to have this be another "defect" in women or a pathologizing of women, that's why we called it a phenomenon rather than a disorder. Our guess is that when men experienced similar feelings, they were given a lot of encouragement to go ahead in spite of their fears, whereas when women had these fears, the fears were supported by the societal view of them. It seemed to women that it was reality instead of just a way of interpreting experience.

Pauline observed that discrimination and other social forces impacting women made the imposter phenomenon more powerful. Some women were coming in and saying, "They asked me to do an honors thesis, but I'm not going to, because if I do they're going to find out all I don't know." She began to investigate and found a very significant difference between the number of men and women doing honors at Oberlin, even though when the women entered, their records were stronger. She believed that there was also probably some discrimination in that women weren't being asked to do honors theses as often. One way she could directly address the problem was by helping the women who were being asked to recognize and transcend their imposter feelings. "We started doing workshops for women, and the very next year after that we had a big increase in the number of women doing honors work. It was very rewarding."

Pauline's most significant contributions have been made at several levels. Therapeutically, she has attempted to apply new understanding about women to the therapy process; professionally, she has emphasized the development of feminist therapy by challenging traditional policies and presenting new work in professional organizations; academically, she has devoted a lot of energy to getting good female students admitted, providing mentorship to these students and working with them to legitimize the study of women's issues.

We focused on feminist scholarship, held the personal as political, and emphasized the sacredness of the everyday. Judith Jordan says empathy occurs in the particulars, and for me, a lot of what I have done is just that basic and ongoing support of women–in terms of feminist scholarship and empowerment, in terms of raising issues in supervision, raising gender and feminist issues in faculty meetings and in hiring policies, trying to get women to be full professors, and then by continuing to work for racial and gay and lesbian equality. I think that if I took a broader view, my work has been in trying to undo–one step at a time–the effects of oppression. Feminism and anti-oppression are so closely related that, in a way, all my work has involved fighting against oppression and has been very much dedicated specifically towards trying to undo the oppression of women. Regarding your question as to how my life has changed as a result of my work in women's issues, I don't really know how to answer it, because since about 1970, it would be difficult to separate the two–that the personal is political and the political is personal. Feminism is an integral part of my life, a part of my self-definition, a part of my way of being. Anti-oppression and working in all the big and little ways is a lot of what I'm about. I think there is something about the importance of the everyday–you do occasionally do big things, but it's that day-to-day, hour-to-hour, week-to-week, moment-to-moment, person-to-person awareness and support and change that is so critical.

BRIEF PROFESSIONAL SKETCH

Editorial Board, 1992-1993, *Women & Therapy.*
Elected as Publication Board Member, Division 29, American Psychological Association, 1988-present.
Editorial Board Member, *Psychotherapy: Theory, Research, and Practice,* 1984-present.
Editorial Board Member, *Journal of Couples Therapy,* 1990-present.

SELECTED BIBLIOGRAPHY

Budd, B., Clance, P.R., & Simerly, D.E. (1985). Spatial configurations: Erikson Re-examined. *Sex Roles, 12*, 571-577.

Clance, P.R. (in press). Commentary, in E. Tick, & J. Flosdorf (Eds.), *My Father was Shiva*. Norwood, NJ: Ablex Publishing Corporation.

Clance, P.R., & Imes, S.A. (1978). The impostor phenomenon in high achieving women: Dynamics and therapeutic intervention. *Psychotherapy: Theory, Research, and Practice, 15*, 241-247.

Clance, P.R., & O'Toole, M.A. (1987). The impostor phenomenon: An internal barrier to empowerment and achievement. *Women & Therapy, 6*(3), 51-64.

Holmes, S.W., Kertay, L., Adamson, L.B., Holland, C.L., & Clance, P.R. (1993). Measuring the imposter phenomenon: A comparison of Clance's IP Scale and Harvey's I-P Scale. *Journal of Personality Assessment, 60*(1), 48-59.

Langford, J., & Clance, P.R. (1993). The impostor phenomenon: Recent research findings regarding dynamics, personality and family patterns and their implications for treatment. *Psychotherapy, 30*(3), 495-501.

Matthews, A., & Clance, P.R. (1985). Treatment of the impostor phenomenon in psychotherapy clients. *Psychotherapy in Private Practice, 3*(1), 71-81.

Rachelson, J., & Clance, P.R. (1980). Attitudes of psychotherapists toward the 1970 APA standards for psychotherapy training. *Journal of Professional Psychology, 18*, 261-267.

Feminist and Activist

Florence L. Denmark

MY FEMINIST BEGINNINGS

Although I didn't know it at the time, circumstances which led toward my interest in and subsequent contribution to feminism and feminist mental health began early in my childhood. My family placed a high emphasis on female achievement. Along with my older sister I was motivated to achieve by my mother who encouraged my educational and professional development. My father, who was an attorney, also exerted an influence and was extremely pleased when we achieved. I followed my father's example by being a voracious reader and excelling in mathematics and enjoying history, but I must admit that it was my mother's prompting and support which spurred me on to my accomplishments. Perhaps that

Florence L. Denmark received her PhD in Social Psychology from the University of Pennsylvania. She had been the Thomas Hunter Professor of Psychology at Hunter College of the City University of New York, and at present is the Robert Scott Pace Distinguished Professor of Psychology at Pace University, where she is Chair of the Department of Psychology. A past president of the American Psychological Association and the International Council of Psychologists, she has edited and authored numerous books and articles on the psychology of women and has been the recipient of many professional awards and honors.

Correspondence may be addressed to Florence L. Denmark, PhD, Department Chair, Psychology Department, One Pace Plaza, New York, NY 10038.

[Haworth co-indexing entry note]: "Feminist and Activist." Denmark, Florence L. Co-published simultaneously in Women & Therapy (The Haworth Press, Inc.) Vol. 17, No. 1/2, 1995, pp. 163-169; and: Feminist Foremothers in Women's Studies, Psychology, and Mental Health (ed: Phyllis Chesler, Esther D. Rothblum, and Ellen Cole) The Haworth Press, Inc., 1995, pp. 163-169: and; Feminist Foremothers in Women's Studies, Psychology, and Mental Health (ed: Phyllis Chesler, Esther D. Rothblum, and Ellen Cole) Harrington Park Press, an imprint of The Haworth Press, Inc., 1995, pp. 163-169. Single or multiple copies of this article are available from The Haworth Document Delivery Service [1-800-342-9678, 9:00 a.m. - 5:00 p.m. (EST)].

is because she had abandoned her own career as a concert pianist in order to raise my sister and me. This may have resulted in a frustration of her own ambitions and consequent desire to have her children succeed.

I was an "A" student throughout my entire years in elementary and high school, and graduated from high school as class valedictorian. Immediately following high school graduation, I enrolled at the University of Pennsylvania where I pursued a double honors major in both history and psychology. As an undergraduate in psychology, my research honors thesis was on leadership, comparing female and male leaders. At that time, when gender stereotypes were prevalent in psychology as elsewhere, my results were surprising. Thus, contrary to expectations, women leaders were found to be less authoritarian than male leaders, and women followers were less likely to conform than were male followers to their leaders' positions. The results of this study served as an impetus for my future investigations on leadership. My history honors thesis was about Amelia Bloomer who felt women should not be constricted by long skirts and "invented" bloomers. This also foreshadowed my interest in women and women leaders. These latter topics continue to be of personal interest to me in my research pursuits.

After college I went to graduate school to obtain a doctorate and develop a professional career. This was during a time–the 1950s– when most women were not pursuing postgraduate education. This pattern changed years later when many of my former female college classmates became "reentry" women–either in returning to school or to the workforce. I have to admit, however, that I was influenced in my choice of graduate schools in a more "traditional" sense. My decision to attend Duke University (my first choice among graduate schools to which I was accepted and offered a fellowship) was reversed, and I opted instead to remain at the University of Pennsylvania where my then fiance was a dental student. Happily, I was awarded a teaching and research assistantship at the University of Pennsylvania.

As a graduate student in psychology I found that there were few female mentors and role models. Hardly any women were on the faculty, and the only tenured woman was a long-term *assistant* professor close to retirement. Many barriers to women in psychology existed at this time. Relatively few women were in graduate psychology programs, and women were clearly steered away from specific areas such as industrial psychology. I failed to advance from graduate assistant to assistant instructor despite three years' experience, while many male graduate students were upgraded after only one year. I did eventually manage to obtain my promotion after confronting the department chair and assuring him of my competence, "despite being a woman."

Following completion of my graduate training in 1958, I did not immediately seek full-time employment since I was pregnant and later involved with raising three children. I worked part-time from 1958 to 1964, teaching psychology courses as an adjunct instructor and working in the Testing and Counseling Center at Queens College of the City University of New York (CUNY). In addition I was conducting research and publishing. Although I spent more hours at Queens College than did full-time faculty, full-time employment by mothers during this time period was not considered appropriate–in fact, even working part-time was looked at askance.

In 1964 I sought full-time academic employment at Hunter College (CUNY). A male faculty interviewer inquired as to whether I was married and what my husband's occupation was. Not realizing at the time the reason for his inquiry, I replied that my husband was a dentist, thinking that this would demonstrate my stability and little likelihood of relocation. While I was offered a faculty position, I later learned that the information that I had a husband with a profession was used to place me at the lowest rank for someone with a doctorate, i.e., instructor, with the lowest salary available. Knowing what I know now, I should have said that my husband was a bedridden invalid! A male colleague, hired at the same time as myself, had a wife who was a biology professor–he was never asked about his wife's occupation and given the rank of assistant professor.

Ironically, my first marriage deteriorated as my husband was unable to appreciate my career advancement. I met my present husband, publisher Robert Wesner, who signed my first book, *Woman: Dependent or Independent Variable?* which I co-edited with Rhoda Unger (1975). Bob continues to be encouraging and supportive of my goals and professional aspirations.

Long before the women's movement began, I had research interests in reentry women college students in addition to women as leaders. The women's movement served to foster my motivation to pursue investigations pertaining to women and their/our particular situations as well as to promote equality for women.

Teaching also contributed to my involvement with feminism. As I gained recognition through publishing and giving presentations on women's issues, I became known as a pioneer in the psychology of women. I was a foremother of the Association of Women in Psychology. My involvement has, I believe, helped to establish and shape this subdiscipline. I taught the first graduate course ever given in the psychology of women at the City University of New York Graduate Center. This was a feminist course with a strong feminist mental health component. I find teaching students, particularly those who will go on to do research and/or teach in this field, to be especially rewarding personally and professionally. It is equally satisfying to instruct those students who will later become clinicians and employ feminist therapy and strive to empower women.

After twenty-five years at CUNY, I was offered the position of Robert Scott Pace Distinguished Professor and Chair of the Department of Psychology at Pace University. In addition to my administrative responsibilities at Pace, I work directly with students as instructor and mentor. I especially enjoy working with my female graduate students whom I encourage to reach their highest career aspirations. I am also currently co-teaching a graduate course on multicultural and gender issues in professional psychology. Our students are given every opportunity to enrich themselves culturally, and last year I was influential in enabling one of my graduate assistants to fulfill her externship requirements on the Northern Cheyenne Indian Reservation in Montana.

MY FEMINIST CONTRIBUTIONS

Much of my research and much of my time have been devoted to breaking down the barriers to women's achievement, and I have dedicated myself to writing about and making presentations encouraging women to realize the full potential of their abilities. My work has been printed in numerous publications, including the *Psychology of Women Quarterly, Sex Roles*, and the *American Psychologist*, to name a few. Some of my scholarly contributions include my American Psychological Association (APA) presidential address, *Psyche: From rocking the cradle to rocking the boat* (1980), *Guidelines for avoiding sexism in psychological research* (1988), and *Engendering psychology* (1994). I co-edited (with Michele Paludi) the first handbook on the psychology of women, entitled *Psychology of women: A handbook of issues and theories* (1993).

I've been honored by the American Psychological Association (APA), and the New York State Psychological Association (NYSPA). Among the many APA awards which I've received are the 1985 Distinguished Leader for Women in Psychology Award granted by the Committee on Women in Psychology, the 1987 Distinguished Contributions to Education and Training in Psychology Award, the 1992 Distinguished Contribution to Psychology in the Public Interest Award, and the 1992 Centennial Award for Sustained Contribution to the Public Interest Directorate. In 1980 I received an Outstanding Women in Science Award from the Association for Women in Science, and in 1987 a Distinguished Career Award from the Association for Women in Psychology (AWP). In 1992 I was given the APA's Carolyn Wood Sherif Award for mentoring and scholarship. I have also been honored by my inclusion in the O'Connell and Russo text, *Models of achievement: Reflections of eminent women in psychology* (1988). The awards which I am most proud to have received are those which have recognized my efforts to promote the advancement of women and all underrepresented groups in psychology, as well as activities designed to include the new scholarship on women and cultural diversity in the education and training of psychologists.

ACHIEVEMENT AND LIFE CHANGES

I believe it is important for those of us women who have contributed and succeeded to serve as role models for students and fledgling psychologists. We need to encourage students to aspire, even in areas which may at first be new and challenging. I like to believe that students can look at me and say, "Here's a woman who has taken risks, has reached her professional goals, and has been successful. She is a woman we can emulate."

As women I believe we can be more nurturing than our male counterparts in encouraging students to reach their educational, professional and career goals. I've always been a goal setter and feel I can support others in similar efforts. I was influenced by women psychologists. Mary E. Reuder gave me my first postdoctoral position at Queens College. Virginia Staudt Sexton exposed me to psychological organizations and encouraged my involvement in them. As a result, I've learned to become politically active and have held the presidencies of the American Psychological Association, Division 35 of the APA (the Division of the Psychology of Women), Eastern Psychological Association (EPA), the New York State Psychological Association, and Psi Chi.

I believe my own advancement was a natural evolution. I have always been an activist and will continue to be one. I believe in being active in any endeavor I undertake–academically and professionally.

I believe in empowering other women. This is a way I can contribute having already "made it." This is important to me. Appreciation from my students and colleagues is perhaps my single greatest reward. In the words of one of my graduate students, Karen Nielson, (personal communication, September 14, 1994), "Florence has been a personal source of inspiration for me in her untiring commitment and dedication to the discipline of psychology and to her students. Her broad mindedness has enabled me to expand myself personally and professionally, and I am grateful to her and to her supportive friendship in many ways." It is my lasting hope that I can continue to inspire others (students, women, and minorities) by advisement, instruction, and example to reach their highest potential. I am supportive of the creation of new areas of study within psychology as well as in assisting students and colleagues to achieve their own personal visions within the discipline. I hope my students and younger colleagues will in turn reach out to help other women.

REFERENCES

Denmark, F. L. (1980). Psyche: From rocking the cradle to rocking the boat. *American Psychologist, 35*, 1057-1065.

Denmark, F. L. (1994). Engendering psychology. *American Psychologist, 49*, 329-334.

Denmark, F. L., & Paludi, M. (Eds.). (1993). *Psychology of women: A handbook of issues and theories*. Westport, CT: Greenwood Press.

Denmark, F. L., Russo, N. F., Frieze, L. H., & Sechzer, J. A. (1988). Guidelines for avoiding sexism in psychological research. *American Psychologist, 43*, 582-585.

Denmark, F. L., & Unger, R. (Eds.). (1975). *Woman: Dependent or independent variable?* New York: Psychological Dimensions.

O'Connell, A. N., & Russo, N. F. (1988). *Models of achievement: Reflections of eminent women in psychology* (Vol. 2). Hillsdale, NJ: Lawrence Erlbaum Associates.

Fighting Sexual Abuse

Andrea Dworkin
Teri Brooks

Teri Brooks: How would you describe your connection to feminism?

Andrea Dworkin: I am a writer with a political commitment to writing and to activism. I believe in direct confrontation with male power through demonstrations, civil disobedience, leafletting, and all kinds of dialogue, including argument and conflict. I also believe in direct action through changing the legal system so that women are primary subjects, not victims, in the legal system.

I have published, I think, ten books—it might be eleven. The reason that it's iffy is that I published a couple of books of poetry before I was in any way a feminist writer. It always seems to me that feminism came into my life very late. I had always been very active politically. I was committed to opposing the Vietnam War very

---

Andrea Dworkin is a radical feminist activist and the author of ten books, including *Intercourse, Pornography: Men Possessing Women, Letters From a War Zone*, and the novels *Mercy* and *Ice and Fire*.

Teri Brooks is a feminist graduate student in the Clinical Psychology program at the University of Vermont. Her interests in women, diversity and sexuality have led her to become involved in several feminist projects including participation in a lesbian research group, collaboration on a book chapter on coming out that will appear in *Dyke Life*, and co-authoring a review of the book *Rape: The Misunderstood Crime*. Clinical and research interests center around developing and implementing prevention programs targeted to adolescents, particularly with regard to sexuality issues.

[Haworth co-indexing entry note]: "Fighting Sexual Abuse." Dworkin, Andrea and Teri Brooks. Co-published simultaneously in *Women & Therapy* (The Haworth Press, Inc.) Vol. 17, No. 1/2, 1995, pp. 171-185; and: *Feminist Foremothers in Women's Studies, Psychology, and Mental Health* (ed: Phyllis Chesler, Esther D. Rothblum, and Ellen Cole) The Haworth Press, Inc., 1995, pp. 171-185; and: *Feminist Foremothers in Women's Studies, Psychology, and Mental Health* (ed: Phyllis Chesler, Esther D. Rothblum, and Ellen Cole) Harrington Park Press, an imprint of The Haworth Press, Inc., 1995, pp. 171-185. Single or multiple copies of this article are available from The Haworth Document Delivery Service [1-800-342-9678, 9:00 a.m. - 5:00 p.m. (EST)].

early on; and committed to racial equality and justice when we still had *de jure* segregation in the South. Feminism came to me in the early 1970s but I was not in this country so I was not part of the early women's movement here, which is probably different from the experience of most of the women that you are talking to.

Teri Brooks: Which country were you in?

Andrea Dworkin: I was in Holland at the time.

Teri Brooks: And is that where you first became involved in feminism?

Andrea Dworkin: Yes. I had left the United States in 1968, I think, disgusted with the Vietnam War. This was the second time for me. I first left in 1965, for the same reason, really, except that the first time I had participated in an anti-war demonstration and been jailed in New York City's notorious prison, the Women's House of Detention. While I was there, just for a few days, I was hurt very badly by two doctors, a physically brutal internal examination, the first such examination I ever had. I was very traumatized when I came out of jail but protested what had been done to me in the prison. There was no women's movement then, in the sense that no one dealt with sexual abuse or the women in that prison and why they were there. I left the country after several months of trying to do something about how women were treated in that prison.

I returned to the United States sometime in 1966 and left again sometime in 1968. In Holland, I married a politically active and radical man, and he began to batter me. It was through the help of feminists, individual feminists, that I eventually escaped and began to change my consciousness and to develop a political commitment to women. Before that time I didn't see the issue of women as a political issue. In other words, I could see Vietnam politically. I could understand racism in the United States politically. I could even be outraged and act politically on behalf of women in the Women's House of Detention. But I didn't see women as a political class of people, or as a group of people who had important experiences in common that were, in fact, political oppression by any standard: things that happened to us because we were born women. And so I really came into contact with feminism through being a woman in trouble, not through being any politically inspired savant.

Teri Brooks: Right–through actually experiencing the oppression.

Andrea Dworkin: Yes. I mean, I think that most feminists do, but that may have been lost in these last twenty years because we've developed a kind of professional political elite. In the early days, from what I know, I think there was a sense of outrage over injustices that one experienced as a woman as well as a sense of excitement, discovery, and solidarity. I think we may have lost the sense of a women's movement that includes all kinds of women in it because they've experienced discrimination or violence or what it means to be put down because you're a woman. That basic reality of what the women's movement is–what it has to be–has perhaps been lost and so now we have women who think feminism is a lifestyle or who are basically antifeminist–they think women have nothing in common, they believe that violence against women is not politically significant or, for instance, that date rape isn't really rape. They don't believe women's testimony; they don't care about women; and the media identifies them as feminists.

Teri Brooks: Really? I hadn't had the same impression. How do you get that sense?

Andrea Dworkin: Two obvious examples are Camille Paglia and Katie Roiphe. They don't believe that women are oppressed and at the same time they claim to stand for feminism. Paglia does warmed-over Aristotle–and he wasn't a feminist the first time around. She says men make culture, women make babies. This is a very old worldview, and feminism rose up in opposition to it. Roiphe says that women claim they have been raped by dates when, in fact, they have just had what she calls "bad sex." Maybe she means unpleasant sex. But she claims that feminists are basically lying. Certainly this is a version of "Women lie when they say they have been raped." A political word, *feminist,* replaces the old biological word, *women.* But the meaning is that women lie about rape, especially women with feminist ideas.

In the early stages of the women's movement, great numbers of women finally began to understand deep and basic truths about their own lives. I was one of those women. One of the horrible aspects of being battered as a woman is that when you try to escape, people will refuse to help you. They justify this refusal to help by saying that you wanted to be hit or hurt or that you provoked it or that you deserved it. That's when you are *running away*; they have the audacity to tell you it's your fault. I knew that really was not true; but it was only with the help of a couple of women who said they were feminists that I was able to undertake the extremely dangerous process of escaping for good. I mean, we know now, as we didn't back then, that a battered woman is more likely to be killed by the batterer when she does escape. With two decades now of experience in helping women get out, we know that. What distinguished the feminists from everyone else I asked for help–all politically very advanced and lovely people–was that they did not consider me the agent of violence; they considered the perpetrator the agent of violence. It is a remarkable thing to realize that most people still do blame the woman who is being hurt for the violence. Feminists don't. These feminists brought me into contact with a whole bunch of feminist ideas and books that I had missed by leaving the United States–especially Kate Millett's *Sexual Politics*, Shulamith Firestone's *The Dialectic of Sex*, and *Sisterhood Is Powerful* edited by Robin Morgan. Those books were extremely important to me, because I really fought with them. I was a committed sixties sexual liberationist and I had a deeply leftwing point of view about what politics was and what oppression was–so those books really changed the way I thought about women, and eventually the way I conceptualized politics altogether.

Teri Brooks: You've talked about how you developed a woman-identified sense of awareness and an interest in the women's movement, but what activities exactly did you become involved in and how did you become an activist?

Andrea Dworkin: The first thing that happened to me was that in the process of escaping–literally while hiding–I started writing my first feminist book, *Woman Hating*. I made a list of phenomena that I thought had had an impact on me and on what I had internalized about being a woman, on the constituent parts of being a woman. I made that list in a dark, dirty, dank basement in Amsterdam; and it became the table of contents of *Woman Hating*, which was published in 1974 but which I had started writing, as I said, literally in the process of escape, in 1971. I had a draft of it, a partial draft, before I finally escaped from Amsterdam to come back to the United States, which I did in November 1972. At that time I became involved in trying to find a publisher for it and trying to finish it. I also began to take myself seriously as a writer: to learn how to discipline myself to write, how to rewrite–in other words, writing as a form of communication rather than merely self-expression. I also began to change the focus of my political activities from Vietnam, which I was still organizing against, to feminism. When I came back to the United States in November 1972, I wasn't part of anybody's idea of the women's movement. I was a totally destitute woman who had been battered, who was often in a state of terror, still hiding. I went to lots and lots of demonstrations. One of the first I remember was for the Three Marias of Portugal. They had written a feminist book and had been arrested for it. We did a lot of organizing here in New York to try to dramatize the fact that they had been arrested for breaking the silence around women's lives. I was in some of the earliest lesbian demonstrations. I spoke at lesbian pride rallies. I just did as much activism as I possibly could while at the same time trying to write and having many different jobs.

Teri Brooks: Did you have any particular focus or priorities in your activism or your talks or in your writing that was guiding you?

Andrea Dworkin: I think I was being guided by a different set of priorities than most of the women in the women's movement and that over time those different priorities ripened and became a new kind of influence in the women's movement. I saw violence against women as political–and if that sounds familiar, that's the good news, that now it sounds familiar. In the early 1970s, people were having theoretical arguments about which was more important: economic oppression or sexual oppression or social oppression. There were all kinds of theoretical, ideological divisions inside the women's movement and from my point of view the arguments were very abstract. I didn't have time or patience for abstract arguments. I still don't.

When I was living in Amsterdam and being helped by these women who called themselves feminists, which was my first contact with committed feminists, I became very aware that I had experiences that they didn't have, that were different, partly be-

cause of the poverty in my life. When I came back to the United
States, the women's movement appeared to be pretty solidly middle
class. And my experience was more than just economic poverty,
because I had spent several years on the streets doing prostitution. I
had been homeless. I didn't understand the ramifications of all this
but I did understand that I saw things differently about what being a
woman was and what the focus of oppression was than the middle-
class women I was reading and meeting and demonstrating with. At
the time, of course, I was still very much learning from other
women. This isn't an either/or proposition. I think it was true of
everyone I met during those years that the conversations we all had
were very excited conversations and there was a quality of discovery in them that was wonderful. I was twenty-six when I escaped
my marriage finally (twenty-five when I got out of the marital
home) and I had lived a radical, committed political life since I was
a child, and no ideas about feminism had ever been part of my life.
Women's writing was really suppressed, and the women's movement was uncovering and bringing out all kinds of work and writings by women. Some of the writings were from the nineteenth
century, and none of us had ever seen them, even if our field was
American history, because it was never taught–the history of
women wasn't taught. Stuff by women really didn't exist in the
society at large so that even if you were a voracious reader you still
didn't read novels by women that had any kind of stature or standing, and if you were interested in philosophy or history you never
encountered work by women. Everything was new.

But I think I had a different point of view than anything I encountered. I believed that I had a contribution to make and I didn't know
if it would matter very much. I didn't have any idea of the consequences. But I knew something was missing in the women's movement and I knew that I had at least some kind of clue as to what it
was. It had generally to do with the ways in which women are
marginalized who are poor and it had to do with the fact that
violence against women was political and systematic–that one
could not talk about the equality or inequality of women without
taking into account that women were being hurt because we were
women. To me that had a political meaning and I think it is fair to

say that at the time it did not have a political meaning for most feminists.

Teri Brooks: As you were saying that, I was thinking that it's remarkable to me how you were able to take your experience and to view it through a political lens and to share that with the rest of the women's movement and really make such an impact. It seems that is a very valuable part of what you have been able to do for the women's movement.

Andrea Dworkin: Thank you. I hope so. I feel also that a kind of political methodology evolved from the focus on marginalized women and violence against women, which is very much in harmony with most women's ideas of feminism but probably not with the practices of many women. I myself am very suspicious of any kind of feminism that is abstract and merely based on ideas. I think that feminism must be about women's real lives, including, of course, the lives of middle-class, white women. If one looks at violence against women, at battery, incest, rape, everything except for prostitution, the devastation is across class and across race. There are more modes of denial, or lying, available to middle-class, white women. In my political practice, I try to be extremely concrete in how I understand problems. I put a very high value on women's testimony, on what women say has happened to us. I don't believe that experts have a right to talk us out of our own experience. I also put a very high priority on concrete organizing rather than endless ideological arguments, which I think are fairly worthless.

Teri Brooks: Could you talk about some of the concrete things that you have done or the priorities that you are setting now, the activities that you do?

Andrea Dworkin: In terms of concrete activities: pornography is a major political target because it is a concrete phenomenon, which is to say that there are magazines and videotapes there. If you and I are deciding we want to do something–for instance, we want to do something against rape–it is hard for us to find a target that is concrete. That's not true when we talk about pornography, which promotes rape and other sexual abuse. I think of pornography as the

DNA of male supremacy. It is the geography of male supremacy and as such it is a map of rape, of battery, of incest, of prostitution, of the ways in which women are sexually exploited and dominated. It is also concrete in the way that it is produced and marketed and distributed; and it is concrete in its impact on women's lives. It is a concrete target because it is a profit-making business. One fights an industry, not abstract ideas about women. One fights the embodiment of woman hating in women's bodies that are sold by pimps for money. One can, in a way that is very clear, delineate what sexual exploitation is and one can target the exploiters. This is a very useful way of trying to communicate what it means for women to be second class. For instance, I would point to all of the demonstrations against the film *Snuff,* a 1976 film that had major distribution all across the country in first-run cinemas. It was shown in a major motion picture theater in New York City, not in some sleazy porn joint. It was supposed to be the evisceration of a woman's body–the man climaxes on her uterus as it is pulled out of her body. While it turned out that the film was a hoax, we found out during that time that there were snuff films, that they were being made, that women were being killed, and that the films were being sold in the United States. So we organized against *Snuff,* picketed every day and leafletted every day, tried to stop people from going into the theater.

Another form of concrete activism to which I am committed is Take Back the Night marches. The first one in the U.S. was in San Francisco in 1978. There were thousands of women at that march. I spoke there. It was also our first conference on pornography. The thousands of women who demonstrated in the Take Back the Night March closed down the whole pornography district in San Francisco for one night. That is another concrete way of protesting and it shows you what you can do if you organize. Take Back the Night marches, I am happy to say, are still going on all over the country. I think that they have been effective in helping women to speak out about the violence that is kept hidden in this society–and they have helped bring rape out into the public domain, not from the point of view of the rapist, as so much media do, but from the point of view of the victim.

It is important that women organize around what they know. College-age women, for instance, are more likely to have been direct victims of incestuous rape or date rape than to have experienced battery in marriage. Although it seems that boys are beating up on girls in romantic relationships with more frequency now, mostly battery is not an experience of college-age women; but date rape is. So the exposure of date rape becomes a priority at colleges.

In the kind of politics that I'm involved with, there is a great deal of emphasis on exposing the perpetrator, on holding the perpetrator responsible for what he has done. Out of this kind of activism comes a strong, grassroots movement, very deep and very wide. It is virtually never reported as such in the media and when it is mentioned it is because it is being reacted against. I will tell you what I mean by that. College students organize against sexual abuse all across the country. Every year they have a meeting, a national conference, for those who are working against sexual abuse. I have never seen national news coverage of this annual conference or this organizing. I have never seen a news magazine cover about it. Instead, Katie Roiphe writes a book that says date rape doesn't exist. She is angry because Take Back the Night marches happen every year, all over the country; she identifies them as rites-of-passage for college-age youth and denounces them; she denounces students organizing against sexual abuse on campuses and the measures that have been taken to educate students and faculty on the subject. She is treated as if she is news. She isn't news. What she is reacting against is the news. The media tend to define reality for so many people and, at the same time, there is a separate reality that has to do with what people experience and know to be true–for instance, date rape; because even all of the antifeminism of the media has not begun to have an impact on stopping grassroots feminist organizing against violence. No matter how much is erased and no matter how much opposition is spotlighted, the organizing continues–and I think that's terrific. That's what I'm part of. I'm part of that grassroots movement that exists in the U.S. and in Canada and, really, in most of the world. To me, that's where the future of the women's movement is. It is not in whatever media manifestations a small, elite group of us (and that probably at this point includes me) is able to do. Those appearances are insignificant up against the grassroots organizing that is ongoing.

Teri Brooks: You talked about how initially you became part of the women's movement and that your focus really was violence against women, which had come out of your experience, and you've also talked about pornography. How did your focus change or did it just sort of evolve and how did that process happen?

Andrea Dworkin: First, let me be clear that if it had not been for the experiences of other women and my knowing about those experiences through many conversations, it is very unlikely that I would ever have written about, for instance, my own personal experience, or thought that what had happened to me was important. I think that that is true of most women. I think that it's remarkable how we continue to blame ourselves for the bad things that are done to us, and about the only way around that, or through it, is political organizing that actually brings you knowledge of other women's lives. Then you find out that you're not the only one that happened to. I didn't initially write about anything that had happened to me in a direct, personal way. But I had a focus because of it. I had an understanding that it went somewhere in the picture, the political picture; and my experience sort of drove my perceptions and my choices about what to do.

Now, pornography became important partly because I'm very interested in how culture affirms violence against women and suggests that violence against women is a good thing, not a bad thing, and how the institutions of this society are complicit in protecting rapists and batterers and men who use prostitutes. I come from a generation that had a lot of experience with pornography so that, in contrast to what people are saying, or in contrast to a lot of criticism that is published, women of my age are anything but Victorian women. We are probably the first generation of women who sexually did whatever we wanted. We came into sexual adulthood exactly at the moment that birth control became available. Abortion was illegal but at some point it became legal. So we didn't have a lot of the hindrances that our mothers had had or women older had had. I was able to see, although I didn't necessarily trust my own perceptions, the use of pornography in acts of violence against women, in abuse, in controlling women and dominating women, in getting women to do things in the counter-culture that women didn't want to do. *Woman Hating* is constructed, in a sense, on that generational experience: first we have sex roles in fairy tales, in the world of children; in pornography we have sex roles in the world of adults, in the explicit sexual behavior of adults. What you find is that the woman is still annihilated for any independence or self-determination or any real repudiation of male control of her life. Because I wrote about pornography, women started to talk with me about pornography. They started to tell me about all kinds of ways in which it had been used against them, especially in kinds of sexual assault, including stranger rapes, but especially rapes that took place inside the home. I found myself with a body of information about sexual abuse and the relationship of sexual abuse to the male use of pornography that I didn't know what to do with, because nobody took pornography seriously and it wasn't seen as being in any way related to the status of women, or even related to sexual violence against women. It was simply seen as a kind of speech that was maybe illegal and maybe not, but that had some radical, liberating dimension to it. I began to understand pornography in a different way and try to honor both my own experiences with it and the vast amount of information I was getting from other women by trying to pursue the actual impact of pornography on women's lives.

I found that if you challenged pornography, talked about it as an important form of male dominance, people started fighting with you. Male supremacy could remain staggeringly indifferent to political attack but, strangely enough, when you began to be activist about pornography, men and the institutions that they run became very angry and tried to stop you.

That indicated to me that, yeah, male supremacy is a brick wall, a big brick wall, but it had this one soft spot, because if you tried to put your fist through the wall at that exact point called pornography, someone would start fighting back. That meant that someone on the other side of the wall, the boy side, felt threatened. It also meant that the wall was soft there, right there. It meant that there was a point of vulnerability. It became clear that in forcing men to defend their use of pornography–what they thought about women, how they saw women, how they saw their entitlement to women–they couldn't keep all that stuff hidden, secret, known only to them: the world of pornography, a world that women didn't see but in which women were used; a world made by men for men using women so that women did what men wanted women to do and women were what men wanted women to be. Attacking pornography also meant that there was a way of bringing all of the sexual abuse that pornography itself countenances and affirms out into the public. Attacking pornography was a politically viable way of doing that. So that's sort of the beginning of it, the combination of women's real experiences with a beginning understanding of the role that pornography was actually playing in maintaining male supremacy–reproducing male supremacy, continuing to create it.

Teri Brooks: We have covered a lot of your contributions to feminism, but if you were to add anything that we haven't talked about, what would you add?

Andrea Dworkin: Well, I think that I've created a body of literature that is probably my real contribution. Even though my books don't sell very well and I have a very hard time surviving as a writer, they appear to have had an enormous impact way beyond any numbers that they sell. I've been able to keep pushing on that dynamic of male domination over women, especially in the sexual arena, with sexual domination at the center of the ways in which women are kept down. So I think that the body of literature that I've created is very important; and I think that now my work is just beginning to be understood because people are now comprehending that violence against women is systemic. People are always prepared to be outraged by individual acts of violence, but I'm talking about the schematic reality of violence against women. So I think that body of literature is very important.

I also think that through my work a whole new group of women consider themselves to be part of the women's movement. They're the women who have been in prostitution, in pornography; they're the women that middle-class women, frankly, did not want to go near, did not want anything to do with. I think that's important.

Finally, I believe that the civil rights ordinance that Catharine A. MacKinnon and I drafted for the city of Minneapolis in 1983, which recognized pornography as a violation of women's civil rights, is very important. That act of legislation is now being taught in law schools all over the country and has been introduced into the legislatures of several foreign democracies–for instance, in Sweden, a very rich country, as well as in the Philippines, a very poor country. I think that the anti-pornography civil rights legislation will eventually be passed and used and accepted in the United States and that when that happens, the status of women inside the legal system is going to change. The legislation is an important contribution because it redefines pornography in a way that has to do with human rights abuses, not as a speech or censorship issue, a formulation that always left women invisible as human beings while being exploited in front of everyone's eyes. The legislation enables women who have been hurt by pornography to sue the pornographers and hold them responsible for the harm that they do; defines that harm essentially as inequality, the creation of civil inequality. It's a whole new way of looking at how you get social equality for women and it is a commitment to being concrete about which institutions compromise civil equality for women. So I think the legislation is very important.

Teri Brooks: You had talked a lot about your activist endeavors, speaking in talks and marching in marches and really voicing your ideas at these collective activities of the women's movement. Yet you didn't mention organizing or direct action as one of your major contributions.

Andrea Dworkin: Well, because for a long time it has been the case that many of the things I attend or contribute to have been organized by other people. The organizing is theirs. They are doing the real work. I did a lot of organizing when I was younger against the Vietnam War. Organizers are always the invisible people who have put together the opportunity for the rest of us to come out and try to do something. So, if we were talking about Vietnam, I would say that one of the things I did was to organize lots of political demonstrations, a conference, and so on; but my activism in the women's movement has much more been being able to mobilize and motivate crowds of people once they've already been organized to be in a certain place at a certain time for a certain purpose. I think that it is really important, at least politically in one's own understanding of how a movement works, to give enormous credit to the people who do the actual organizing. I haven't done organizing as such in a very long time.

Teri Brooks: Let's talk about how your work has changed your life. You've talked a lot about things that you've done and it seems that they're integrally bound with your life, but if you were to be able to sort of tease apart how your life has actually changed, how would you describe that?

Andrea Dworkin: Feminism was an enormous change for me. I mean, it was a total transformation of my life, certainly the politics and certainly the activities. I've learned an enormous amount from other women that has also helped me to change my life and to understand those changes. The initial impact of feminism on my life, of course, was that I both escaped from the marriage I was in and at the same time began to question my economic reliance on men. I also made the determination, a vow, almost like taking an oath, that I didn't want to be involved in prostitution any more, and that's in the literal and metaphoric sense.

Feminism is also responsible for making me take myself seriously as a writer and for helping me to understand that a lot of the impediments to taking oneself seriously had to do with sexism, had to do with trivialization of one's heart and one's mind by a culture that hates women. Therefore, for me the discipline of being a writer is very connected to feminism: to the recognition, for instance, that women are afraid to be alone and how important being alone is to being a writer able to write. Writing requires a good deal of solitude and strong nerves, especially to be able to sustain a book, which takes a long time to do.

All of those changes were a big part of my early years as a feminist. They were personally transforming years.

My whole way of life has changed. I have become a writer. That is how I spend most of my time: doing writing projects that in some way or another advance the cause of women. I also do a lot of lecturing. The whole economic base of my life is different than it was even though I have enormous trouble publishing, and I still have enormous economic difficulties. The fact of the matter is that I live my life as a writer and a lecturer. My books are published in languages all over the world, which is something that would have been beyond my imagination twenty years ago. Probably for me the most astonishing thing is that I can go to any city or town in the country and there will be women in that city or town who basically are my family, who care about my safety, who are completely committed to stopping men from hurting women. That's an enormous difference.

And I think that not just the substance of my thinking has evolved in a way that is complex and important over these years, but my ability to think has evolved because of the other changes in my life, because of taking myself seriously, because of feeling that I have a vocation, a calling.

One of the things that I both learned from feminism and brought to feminism is this idea that the one thing any woman can do, no matter who she is, no matter what her resources are, is to learn from her own experience about how the world around her works. I have done that, and I have pushed myself to do that very hard and very far. I think that is very important.

Bridging Feminism and Multiculturalism

Jessica F. Morris
Oliva M. Espín

Oliva M. Espín, PhD, was born in Cuba, received a BA at the University of Costa Rica, and a PhD at the University of Florida, Gainesville. She is a Full Professor in the Department of Women's Studies at San Diego State University, and part-time core faculty at the California Professional School of Psychology in San Diego. She has also taught at the graduate level at McGill University, Boston University, and Tufts University. Her teaching focuses on multicultural issues in the psychology of women. In 1979, she started a masters level counseling women specialization at Boston University in collaboration with other colleagues. Her therapy practice has been primarily with women from different cultural backgrounds and lesbians, who have also been the focus of her writings. She received a fellowship from the National Institutes of Mental Health from 1981-1983, while she was a visiting Fellow at Harvard University. Among other awards, she has received a Distinguished Contribution Award from the American Psychological Association (APA) in 1991. She was also cited by the APA's Division of Psychology of Women as one of the 100 women who have made significant contributions to psychology in the last 100 years.

Jessica F. Morris is a PhD candidate in Clinical Psychology at the University of Vermont and a graduate of Vassar College. Her research, writing, and clinical work concentrate on the psychology of women, and are particularly focused on lesbians. Other areas of interest include multicultural feminism, female cocaine abusers, and women in the Antarctic. Her dissertation project is titled *Lesbian Mental Health and the Coming Out Process*. Most recently, she has worked as a Research Fellow, Graduate Teaching Fellow, and Therapist.

Correspondence may be addressed to Oliva M. Espín, Department of Women's Studies, San Diego State University, San Diego, CA 92182.

[Haworth co-indexing entry note]: "Bridging Feminism and Multiculturalism." Morris, Jessica F., and Oliva M. Espín. Co-published simultaneously in *Women & Therapy* (The Haworth Press, Inc.) Vol. 17, No. 1/2, 1995, pp. 187-193; and: *Feminist Foremothers in Women's Studies, Psychology, and Mental Health* (ed: Phyllis Chesler, Esther D. Rothblum, and Ellen Cole) The Haworth Press, Inc., 1995, pp. 187-193; and: *Feminist Foremothers in Women's Studies, Psychology, and Mental Health* (ed: Phyllis Chesler, Esther D. Rothblum, and Ellen Cole) Harrington Park Press, an imprint of The Haworth Press, Inc., 1995, pp. 187-193. Single or multiple copies of this article are available from The Haworth Document Delivery Service [1-800-342-9678, 9:00 a.m. - 5:00 p.m. (EST)].

Speaking with Oliva about her life and accomplishments, I was struck, quite strongly, by the memory of a favorite poem. Oliva, too, is familiar with this poem. Since Oliva is a published poet herself, in Spanish, her native language, I thought it appropriate to include an excerpt from the poem we had discussed. The Bridge Poem, *by Donna Kate Rushin (1981), is the basis for the title of* This Bridge Called My Back: Writings by Radical Women of Color, *an early and influential book in the areas of feminism and multiculturalism.*

This bridge I must be
Is the bridge to my own power
I must translate
My own fears
Mediate
My own weaknesses

I must be the bridge to nowhere
But my true self
And then
I will be useful

Oliva Espín has often been in the position of bridging two worlds. Who she is, is inextricably intertwined with the experience of "uprootedness." She has lived in many countries and has carried with her a sense that she does not fully belong in any of them. The irony is that most of the time she is not even aware of this feeling and, in fact, lives a reasonably happy life. For Oliva, this is what it means to be an immigrant, that you never fully belong and you are not fully aware that you do not. This is how she describes her feelings of uprootedness.

It was only upon leaving Cuba that Oliva realized how much growing up in a dangerous situation had affected her life. She had learned to live immersed in a situation of constant danger without being consciously aware of that fact. This struck her quite suddenly while watching a movie soon after leaving Cuba for a short while in 1958. Overcome by this realization, she was aware that it was actually possible to enjoy the movie without the fear that a bomb might explode. Although Oliva, herself, had never been injured by a bomb, or arrested, she had witnessed this happen to others, including friends. It was this incident in a theater in Madrid, Spain, which brought to her awareness that she had learned to always be alert without even knowing that she had learned it.

In 1984, Oliva returned to the country of her birth for the first time after an absence of 23 years. At that time, she had lived half her life in Cuba and half away from her country. This journey was an emotional pilgrimage. She became aware of the fact that she had been going through a grieving process all those years. A great need had driven her to return to Cuba and when she arrived she was filled with the sense that everything was "as it always was and as it was always supposed to be," a deep sense of belonging in a place that is, at present, inaccessible to her. Curiously, before her journey, she had felt as if her memories "had no geography," but during this visit she had a profound experience about the reality of physical space where she grew up and its continued existence beyond her memory.

In addition to her experiences as a refugee woman, and the prevailing sense of "uprootedness" that she carried with her, Oliva also was always a feminist and interested in politics. She was convinced of the idea of feminism before she had a label for it, even though she was not living in the United States in the sixties and was not part of the "women's movement." At that time, she was in Latin America working with women through a Catholic organization. This organization, run by the women members, aimed at conveying to all women the sense that a college education was important to obtain and encouraged them to develop to their full potential. She had been part of this group in Cuba and then worked directing these groups in Panama and in Costa Rica. When she came to the United States after her divorce and a period of time in Europe, she went to graduate school at the University of Florida.

Going to graduate school to study Counseling Psychology, Oliva was able, in her first year, to take Psychology of Women as an elective. This was an important experience, especially because it put theory to what she had been doing for the last 10 or more years. The class allowed her to put together what, in her gut, she knew was true about the lives of women in all cultures. In her doctoral program, she specialized in counseling women. Because of a series of fortuitous circumstances, she taught a class on counseling women while still in graduate school. This, too, was an important learning experience, particularly because of all the material she read in preparing the course. Although in her department there were only male professors, one sponsored her to teach the class.

At the time she did not realize how unusual such a class was but also how unusual it was to have institutional support for such an endeavor. Oliva's dissertation was also focused on the experiences of women. The study compared college educated Latin American women with women from the United States, with a specific eye toward critical incidents in which they felt they had been treated differently because they were women.

During this time, in the mid-seventies, the women's movement still showed little awareness of cultural differences. There was not much of an understanding within feminism that women from ethnic minority groups had much to offer to feminist theory and practice. At the same time, many women of color were thinking that feminism was about getting jobs for white women, and since many Latina and African American women were already working outside the home, they felt that they did not need feminism. There was not much of an understanding, among white feminists, of cultural difference. Nor did women of color sense that feminism had anything to offer them. Oliva had a sense that there was a need to bridge both communities (white feminists and women of color communities) and worked in her practice and research to facilitate that goal. As *The Bridge Poem* indicates, it was through being this bridge that Oliva felt a sense of purpose professionally and contributed to both psychology and feminism.

The major contributions that Oliva has made in feminism and psychology are in the area of multicultural issues. Strongly influenced by her own background, she has continually sought to bring feminism to multicultural studies, and issues of culture into psychology and women's studies. For example, at Boston University, in 1976, she developed one of the first courses in the nation on cross-cultural counseling and psychotherapy. At that time, such a course was considered unnecessary. The prevailing sentiment was that all human beings are the same, no matter what culture they come from and so there was no need to pay attention to cultural factors in the training of psychologists. She taught the class with a feminist perspective, which then, as now, is rare.

During the same time period, also at Boston University, she

participated in federally-funded programs to train ethnic minority students, at the masters and doctoral levels, in psychology and in a program that provided job counseling and basic math skills to women in five ethnic neighborhoods in Boston. In collaboration with other colleagues, she created a masters level counseling program for the training of counselors and therapists of women at Boston University. She served as the program's codirector for seven years. Multicultural issues were considered very important in the program. This program served as a model for many others and received a number of awards during the 10 years it lasted. In addition, in 1977, in Boston, she and other women in Womanspace, a feminist collective, put together a conference for therapists about cultural issues in feminist psychology. At the time this was quite unprecedented. But for Oliva it made sense. She was already used to bridging cultural issues with feminist psychology.

In 1991, Oliva received a Distinguished Contribution Award from the American Psychological Association, a significant and important honor. The citation for this award articulately enumerates Oliva's accomplishments:

> With zeal for scholarship and service, Oliva Espín has made outstanding efforts to assure that our field takes into account all the factors that constitute a true psychology of humankind. She has worked forcefully to advance cross-cultural communication, gender issues, human sexuality, international awareness, and cultural factors as critical elements in the knowledge base of psychology. Her contributions have been especially valuable to understanding and providing psychological services for Latina women, immigrants, and lesbians. An exemplary scholar, teacher, speaker, writer, mentor, and therapist, she has made a precious difference in individual lives and in the teaching and practice of psychology.

Nevertheless, there is not one specific event that is Oliva's major contribution to feminism or feminist mental health. Rather it is a combination of small events, such as constantly bringing up the issues of feminism and multiculturalism at department meetings, professional conferences, and women's gatherings. By bringing up these issues continually, she was challenging the status quo. The path Oliva has traveled is not considered the standard one, rather it is one she has invented for herself.

When working in the development of new areas of knowledge, such as feminist multicultural studies, the ideas are not as well developed as those in very well established fields. Further, the prevailing theories may not be as sophisticated. Consequently, there were no outlets for publication of feminist multiculturalism throughout much of the time that Oliva has worked on these issues. Nevertheless, Oliva persisted in making these ideas central in her career in the academy. For example, from 1981 to 1983, she was a National Institute of Mental Health Fellow at Harvard University doing research on the psychological development and life histories of Latina women healers in urban centers in the United States.

Throughout her career, Oliva had a private psychotherapy practice. Her clients have been Latina, African American, and Asian women, some of whom are also lesbians. A lot of what she knows she feels she has learned from the experience of working with women in therapy. Oliva has been able to share in the process of their lives and in their development. This therapy practice has informed what she teaches her students as well as all other aspects of her work. In addition, her personal experience has also had a significant impact. As an immigrant Latina, she was able to make a unique contribution to the study of the psychology of Latina women in the United States.

The experience of being the only one to bring up multicultural issues continued as Oliva became involved with lesbian psychology. Her often cited chapter in the Boston Lesbian Psychologies Collective's book *Lesbian Psychologies* about the identity development of Latina lesbians was one of the few chapters in this book that discusses ethnic minority women. She is presently doing research on lesbian and heterosexual women immigrants from all over the world in several cities in the United States.

Oliva does not know where she would be without feminism. She thinks she probably would have felt unable to be a psychologist. This is because the world of psychology was ignoring fundamental experiences of women from all cultures and backgrounds. Feminism has been very important as a way of understanding the world of her clients and of understanding her own life. It is within feminism that she has been able to have a language to bridge multiculturalism, psychology, and feminism, itself. Perhaps it is the feeling of uprootedness which she carries with her that allows her to be such a bridge.

SELECTED BIBLIOGRAPHY

Cole, E., Espín, O.M., & Rothblum, E.D. (Eds.). (1992). *Refugee women: Shattered societies, shattered lives.* New York: Harrington Park Press.

Espín, O.M. (1984). Cultural and historical influences on sexuality in Hispanic/ Latin women. In S. Vance (Ed.), *Pleasure and danger: Exploring female sexuality* (pp. 149-164). London: Routledge and Kegan Paul, (2nd Edition: London: Pandora, 1994).

Espín, O.M. (1987). Issues of identity in the psychology of Latina lesbians. In Boston Lesbian Psychologies Collective (Ed.), *Lesbian psychologies: Explorations and challenges* (pp. 35-55). Urbana: University of Illinois Press.

Espín, O.M. (1987). Psychological impact of migration on Latinas: Implications for psychotherapeutic practice. *Psychology of Women Quarterly, 11* (4), 489-503.

Espín, O.M. (1988). Spiritual power and the mundane world: Hispanic women female healers in urban U.S. communities. *Women Studies Quarterly, 16* (3-4), 33-47.

Espín, O.M. (1990). Roots uprooted: Autobiographical reflections on the psychological experience of migration. In F. Alegria & J. Rufinelli (Eds.), *Paradise lost or gained: The literature of Hispanic exile* (pp. 151-163). Houston, Texas: Arte Público Press.

Espín, O.M. (1992). Women's diversity: Ethnicity, race, and class in theories of feminist psychology. In L.S. Brown & M. Ballou (Eds.), *Personality and psychopathology: Feminist reappraisals* (pp. 88-107). New York: Guilford Press.

Espín, O.M. (1993). Giving voice to silence: The psychologist as witness. *American Psychologist, 48,* 408-414.

Espín, O.M. (1994, August). *Crossing borders and boundaries: The life narratives of immigrant lesbians.* Presented at the 102nd Annual Convention of the American Psychological Association, Los Angeles, California.

Espín, O.M. (1994). Feminist approaches [to therapy with women of color]. In L. Comas-Diaz & B. Greene (Eds.), *Women of color: Integrating ethnic and gender identities in psychotherapy* (pp. 265-286). New York: Guilford Press.

Espín, O.M. (1994). *Latina healers: Power, culture, and tradition in urban centers in the United States.* Encino, California: Floricanto Press.

Espín, O.M. (1994). Traumatic historical events and adolescent psychosocial development. In C. Franz & A.J. Stewart (Eds.), *Women creating lives: Identities, resilience, and resistance* (pp. 187-198). Boulder, Colorado: Westview Press.

"Fag Hags," Firemen
and Feminist Theory:
Girl Talk on Amtrak

Judi Addelston
Michelle Fine

We wrote this piece together–sometimes in person, sometimes apart. Trying to create a cross-generational language of feminism, psychology and activism, across our passions and our worries. Our narrative is filled with questions of feminism, asked at the borders of Self-Other, intellect-passions, 20-something-40-something, activism-the academy. This is an essay constructed on the hyphens.

Michelle Fine is Professor of Psychology at the City University of New York, Graduate Center, and the Senior Consultant at the Philadelphia Schools Collaborative. Her recent publications include *Chartering Urban School Reform: Reflections on Public High Schools in the Midst of Change* (1994), *Beyond Silenced Voices: Class, Race and Gender in American Schools* (1992), *Disruptive Voices: The Transgressive Possibilities of Feminist Research* (1992), and *Framing Dropouts: Notes on the Politics of an Urban High School* (1991).

Judi Addelston spent her formative feminist years at Brooklyn College facilitating The Women's Action Movement, a feminist student organization. Currently a doctoral candidate at The City University of New York Graduate School, she is working on her dissertation about men's gender identity.

Correspondence may be addressed to both authors at The City University of New York Graduate School, Box 325, 33 West 42nd Street, New York, NY 10036.

[Haworth co-indexing entry note]: "'Fag Hags', Firemen and Feminist Theory: Girl Talk on Amtrak." Addelston, Judi, and Michelle Fine. Co-published simultaneously in *Women & Therapy* (The Haworth Press, Inc.) Vol. 17, No. 1/2, 1995, pp. 195-203; and: *Feminist Foremothers in Women's Studies, Psychology, and Mental Health* (ed: Phyllis Chesler, Esther D. Rothblum, and Ellen Cole) The Haworth Press, Inc., 1995, pp. 195-203; and: *Feminist Foremothers in Women's Studies, Psychology, and Mental Health* (ed: Phyllis Chesler, Esther D. Rothblum, and Ellen Cole) Harrington Park Press, an imprint of The Haworth Press, Inc., 1995, pp. 195-203. Single or multiple copies of this article are available from The Haworth Document Delivery Service [1-800-342-9678, 9:00 a.m. - 5:00 p.m. (EST)].

195

We conducted the first interview on the Amtrak Metroliner to Philadelphia where we are on our way to run a focus group on masculinity. This is not unusual for Michelle, all meetings are usually conducted at a brisk pace, often in innovative locations, with the next person waiting to see her at the door. Between meetings, introductions are made all around, in a style Michelle has that puts people at ease and creates a community of folks dedicated to activism and each other. A generation apart, we weave our versions of feminism into the fabric of our professional and personal lives. Michelle teaches not only traditional and transgressive psychology, but daily life lessons braiding the personal, intellectual, and political throughout.

We settle into our seats and I ask how she feels about being solicited as a feminist foremother–"It's embarrassing!" She delights in a feminism that speaks through generations of lots of women. She feels indebted to women who have come before her, and obligated to the next generation of now teenage feminists (Fine & Macpherson, 1994).

I revel in her concern, being one of the "next generations" that she worries about; I ask who *her* feminist foremothers and mentors were. "We have to unpack the notion of mentor. Really I had no exposure to *strong* women. I had to re-imagine, re-invent the older women in my life *as if* they were strong. I'm always struck by the question of mentor. It assumes a kind of behavioristic model who supported me in my outrage. I think few of us had real mentors. My feminism came more likely from witnessing unhappy women than from mentoring by 'successful' women" (Fine, 1992, pp. i, xi).

Witnessing, naming and telling are very important to Michelle. She received her BA in 1975 and her PhD in 1980. "I was a student in the first women's studies course. When I was in college my eyes opened. I was called a fag hag–but didn't know it was a compliment. I was thrilled at the social margins of outrage and desire, I got to see how women and gay men invented *the power of naming* as we recast social injustices that my mother and grandmother simply called 'life'."

Michelle wrote in the preface of *Disruptive Voices*: "Rebecca, my grandmother, bore eighteen children in Poland. The last of them was my mother. Rebecca was a woman who smiled often, loved much, expected (and got) little, and would, I can only imagine, be shocked to hear that marital rape, sexual harassment, or safe abortions have been legally encoded (and eroded) during the past twenty years. In the next generation my mother, Rose, was born, when Rebecca had reached fifty-two (or fifty-six, depending on which relative you chose to believe). She lived under the rule of her oldest brother, who fiercely controlled family resources, movements, and family talk. In her early twenties, my mother married my father, Jack, a onetime Lower East Side horse and buggy junk salesman. I remember as a child watching my mother cry at the kitchen table. Second-wave feminist outrage was undoubtedly well nourished. So many of us witnessed, from under or beyond the kitchen table, the swelling of maternal depression across the 1940s and 1950s.

"Most profoundly, I remember the ways in which my mother harbored secrets from her friends, kin, and maybe herself, as if her not telling would somehow render her experiences untrue. Her secrets could not have differed much from what most women struggled with during the 1950s–their marriages, loneliness and isolation, finances, children, disappointments, worries about health, and probably even their passions. But my mother told me her secrets. Then I carried her silences. And, since adolescence, I have voiced our outrage. As a child, I must have vowed I would tell and invite other women to tell" (Fine, 1992, pp. i, xi).

GENERATIONS, LEGACIES AND FOOTPRINTS IN THE SAND

Teaching at the University of Pennsylvania, in the "Ed School" for 12 years, watching too many friends denied tenure, it took Michelle a long time to decide to come back to psychology. "As a person who doesn't aspire toward marriage, I thought that feminism and psychology had gotten married, and feminism took his name." But she is now glad to be back within social psychology, having created a "safe space" with colleagues and students at CUNY. Social research has regained its heart in our work. "Take for instance the upcoming 1994 APA meetings. Los Angeles promises to be one of those amazing moments. At the APA conference, 8 to

10 students working on questions of social justice are presenting work on politics, bodies, gender, race/ethnicity, class relations, sexuality.

"They are a wonderful set of students, each struggling to make peace amidst personal passions and intellectual intrigue within the very narrow sardine cans that social psychologists have allowed them to play in. At CUNY, and beyond–at Penn, Harvard and the New School–these students have spun a diaspora of smarts, critique and comfort. When they fall back, they catch each other. They've practiced their papers too many times, analyzing brilliantly the nuances of social psychology as it saturates bodies, social consciousness, relationships and social movements.

"This next generation of social psychologists carry proudly the legacies of feminism, civil rights and gay/lesbian activism, voicing elegantly their chi squares, ANOVA's and inter-rater reliability. I kvell [Yiddish: swell with pride]. They are bi-lingual, in politics and scholarship, and code switch as needed. They know so much from being in so many closets, and are now in the position to proudly analyze the keepers of the closets, the delicacies of the hangers, and the campy fun of hiding, flaunting, coping and coming out–through gender, race, ethnicity and sexuality. Instead of creating 'zippered identities', in which a repressed professional is socialized separately from her vibrant lived critique, they make their passions smart. In L.A.–they'll knock their socks off."

I ask what legacy she wants to give to her students. "Intellectuals have an obligation to name and participate in the transformation of inequities. At CUNY, we've created a community of smart, active inquirers, committed to social change. For me, that is the only interesting reason to 'do' social science. My nightmare is working with students who study, but feel no pain; the ones who can sleep well at night. My legacy? I guess I want students to *feel* dis-comfort every time they attend fancy conferences to speak on questions of injustice–and maybe not sleep so well."

INTERRUPTIONS

"As a girl child, I was always told I was too loud, spoke too much, or interrupted too often. This will sound familiar to feminists." At our departmental colloquia, Michelle is famous for asking the questions many of us are thinking but do not have the guts to speak. When I ask what she sees as her main contributions to psychology, she almost reads my mind: "That I am willing to go to the edge in scholarship and begin to say what other people seem to be scared of. Piercing the unspoken political and intellectual text; prying open treacherous territory. While my mother and grandmother choked on 'personal' or 'family' secrets–I divulge, study, write a book about it. Today, or maybe always, it seems desperately important for feminist researchers to see ourselves centrally as activists–to press, provoke and unbalance social inequities that choreograph relations of gender, race, class, disability, and sexuality.

"Over the past five years, my most engaging work has been done with and on social movements. With students, I've worked with the ACLU gathering up evidence for why Shannon Faulkner, a young woman from South Carolina, is entitled to attend The Citadel, an all-male public college. We run focus groups with African American men to understand spirituality and community and interview white working-class firemen, trying to understand how they construct Self so markedly in opposition to white women and people of color. We have hoagies and sodas with white upper-class men who constitute the corporate elite of America, to excavate the forms of masculinity available to and sculpted by the upper class. We've met with activist nuns to figure out a Latina homeless empowerment project, and observed the trials of elite gang rapists and high school principals accused of racist comments and behaviors. Making visible the institutional policies and practices which enable the reproduction of social hierarchies, we force an 'upwards' accountability for social institutions (Fine, Genovese, Ingersoll & Roberts, 1994; Fine, Weis & Addelston [forthcoming]; Fine, Pastor & MacCormick; Fine, Weis & Wong [forthcoming]). Most importantly, we braid theory, research and political practice in ways that are irrefutably rigorous and compelling. We exploit psychology as a tool to reframe the atrocities of social injustice as a site for social analysis" (Fine, 1988; Fine & Addelston, in press; Fine & Asch, 1988; Fine, Guinier, Balin, Bartow & Sachtel, 1993).

COURT-ING THE MARGINS

Asked what her favorite/most critical works are, Michelle says that the best part of her job is teaching, learning with students and friends, and doing expert testimony in court. "It is the opportunity to put scholarship to political use. I can lend the language of social science to legal struggles for justice." Her testimony is usually about her research on gender, race, and education. Her most recent testimony was in *Shannon Faulkner and the United States of America v. James Jones et al. for The Citadel*, the military college of South Carolina, where she testified as to the benefits of admitting women into a prestigious all-male college.

"We all flew in for Shannon, women and men academics who didn't know each other or her. Not because we were great supporters of the military or because we were staunch gender equality advocates. But because a young woman took the message of second-wave feminism seriously. Shannon said, 'I was a young girl who did it all right, and I thought I should go to the best college in South Carolina I could find. It's a public school–are they telling me there is no constitution?' We owed it to her to deliver the institution and the State.

"At one point, when The Citadel boys were being particularly severe to Shannon, sitting in a circle with steel blue eyes and ironic buttons that read, 'Save the Males', I turned to [feminist educator] Pat Campbell and said, 'At some point, we have to get her out of here.' Pat said, 'This is like people who pull other people out of rivers and save them from drowning. We are hers for life.' And so we are.

"It is that thread among us, those delighted that feminism has arrived in the academy and those traumatized that academic feminism has been so coopted. Those who cherish the opportunity to embroider intellectual passions with politics, and those who insist that the two shall remain separated by a canyon of objectivity. That is the community of feminist scholars, cross races and ethnicities, sexualities and politics, who have created a powerful chorus among ourselves–a delicious di-census–with the women of the past, and the young women and men of the future. We are the feminist fore- and after-mothers, watching the rich mutations of politics work their way through the intellectual work of the academy and always back on the streets."

GROUNDING IN GIRL GROUPS

We chat about that chorus. "Since 1971, when I was in the college, I have always been in a women's group. I, like other adult/ aging women, need to be around young women, the next generation, to help me think through the legacy of feminist and anti-racist work that was so vibrant during the 1960s and 1970s, so quiet during the 80s and 90s. Young women ground my mind, and my heart. They are the ones who make me see how desperately they refuse to be victims; how much they appreciate what 'we' did for 'them' since gender inequities have *apparently* been cleared up. They are the ones who look at 'our' lives and 'our' troubles–and wonder if it was worth it. Girls' groups keep my intellect alive and my juices flowing. *They* need a history and *we* need to hear where they have taken feminism. It is not that they reject, but they do not parrot our words. We forgot that what was exhilarating in the 1970s was *inventing* the names, the frames and the atrocities. Their *inheritance*, of those names and frames, forced them into a stance of victimization, and they're saying 'no.'"

"I worry, though, about the gutsy feminists of the next generation, like Shannon and others. They carry such a deep sense of entitlement (to what boys have), but an unsophisticated sense of the dangers they are about to wander into. Is it possible to carry both a sense of entitlement and a reasonable dose of fear? When [graduate student] Jennifer Pastor found that young adolescents of color who are most astute about racism also voice the most *depressed* aspirations for themselves, we realized that we had to rethink how to teach social critique, and inspire a sense of entitlement and help to create a vision of collective possibility. Our work is cut out for us."

THE PERSONAL IS POLITICAL AND INTELLECTUAL

How do ideas emerge for intellectual work? Some sneak in from home. "With David Surrey, I am raising our 7-year-old white son,

Sam, and helping to raise a 17-year-old African American teen, Demetrius. Wrestling with male culture–in all its racial tints–I feel the yawning space between feminist and civil rights analysis and the 'praxis' of parenting. With Sam, we're trying to figure out how he can participate in, consume, and resist the world of white boyhood, a culture of hierarchy, and put downs (it is not unusual for him to ask what he should say when an older boy calls him a girl!)."

On the way back, as we enter Newark train station, Michelle continues–"I watch Sam delight in play–with all the smiling entitlement of a sweet little white boy who expects the world to adore him, and I watch, even here at the train station, police and commuters eye Demetrius, watching for trouble, and he expecting a confrontation. I grab his arm and all relax. We beat back, for a moment, gendered racism. This becomes a place which now fuels my work with Judi, Michael Reichart, and others, trying to imagine how to pry open institutional constructions of, and confrontations with, gender and race."

CONCLUSION

"As for myself as a feminist foremother, it's both too grand and too individualistic. We are a generation of women who witnessed too much pain to believe and persist in the footprints of our mothers. We knew we were entitled to whatever the boys got–so we, too, got tenure, started smoking, developed heart attacks, acquired sexual harassment complaints, earned accusations of elitism, lost our connections to activism at the same time as we stayed passionately connected to social change. Surviving in *their* world while creating *our* own, feminist academics added new depth to the notion of life at the hyphen. We can be nasty to each other, more than we should, but we will watch each other's backs, because we know no one else will. As I look back, I have few complaints. Struggling at these hyphens with a bunch of noisy, rowdy women and men, is perfect work for me!"

REFERENCES

Fine, M. (1988). Sexuality, schooling, and adolescent females: The missing discourse of desire. *Harvard Educational Review, 58,* 29-53.

Fine, M. (1992). *Disruptive voices: The transgressive possibilities of feminist research.* Ann Arbor: University of Michigan Press.

Fine, M., & Addelston, J. (in press). The discursive limits of "sameness" and "difference." In S. Wilkinson (Ed.) *Contemporary feminist social psychology.* London: Sage Publications.

Fine, M., & Asch, A. (1988). *Women with disabilities: Essays in psychology, culture and politics.* Philadelphia: Temple University Press.

Fine, M., Genovese, T., Ingersoll, S., Macpherson, P., & Roberts, R. (1994). White li(v)es: Looking for a discourse of male accountability. In M. Lykes, A. Banuazizi, & R. Roberts (Eds.). *Unmasking social inequities: Victims and resistance.* Philadelphia: Temple University Press.

Fine, M., & Guinier, L. with Balin, J., Bartow, A., & Sachtel, D. (1993). Becoming gentlemen: The education of women at the University of Pennsylvania. *University of Pennsylvania Law Review, 141,* 1001-1082.

Fine, M., & Macpherson, P. (1994). Over dinner: Feminism and adolescent female bodies. In H.L. Radke, & H.J. Stam (Eds.). *Power/gender: Social relations in theory and practice.* London: Sage Publications.

Fine, M., Weis, L., & Addelston, J. (forthcoming). (In)secure times: Constructing white hetero-masculinity in the 1980s and 1990s.

Lesbian Feminist
Fights Organized Psychiatry

Nanette K. Gartrell

My journey to lesbian-feminist activism began when I was an undergraduate at Stanford during the Vietnam war. That was the era of "free love" (translation: women weren't cool if they said "no" to men who came on to them), and great political sacrifice (translation: women were expected to help the antiwar effort by servicing male activists. As a lesbian I had little to offer). Mine was the typical dual-track education of the late sixties: one in humanities and sciences, the other in heterosexism. Not that I had a keen understanding of what this last term meant at the time. But in an environment of daily sexual harassment, a lesbian learned quickly.

During the first few weeks of college, I found that it was dangerous for women to ride their bikes alone at night on campus, or even

Nanette K. Gartrell, MD, is Associate Clinical Professor of Psychiatry at the University of California, San Francisco, where she teaches ethics and feminist psychotherapy theory. She is a lesbian feminist psychiatrist, teacher, researcher and organizer. She has been documenting sexual abuse by physicians since 1982 and conducting a national longitudinal lesbian family study since 1986. She has a private psychotherapy practice in San Francisco.

Dr. Gartrell would like to thank Mary Eichbauer, Susan Kennedy and Joan Lester for their assistance in the preparation of this article.

Correspondence may be addressed to Dr. Gartrell at 3570 Clay Street, San Francisco, CA 94118.

[Haworth co-indexing entry note]: "Lesbian Feminist Fights Organized Psychiatry." Gartrell, Nanette K. Co-published simultaneously in *Women & Therapy* (The Haworth Press, Inc.) Vol. 17, No. 1/2, 1995, pp. 205-212; and: *Feminist Foremothers in Women's Studies, Psychology, and Mental Health* (ed: Phyllis Chesler, Esther D. Rothblum, and Ellen Cole) The Haworth Press, Inc., 1995, pp. 205-212; and: *Feminist Foremothers in Women's Studies, Psychology, and Mental Health* (ed: Phyllis Chesler, Esther D. Rothblum, and Ellen Cole) Harrington Park Press, an imprint of The Haworth Press, Inc., 1995, pp. 205-212. Single or multiple copies of this article are available from The Haworth Document Delivery Service [1-800-342-9678, 9:00 a.m. - 5:00 p.m. (EST)].

to visit the library stacks without a friend in tow. I enrolled in a Karate class and got in the habit of looking over my shoulder, but these strategies were useless when it came to more institutionalized forms of oppression. When I sought counseling at the student health center, for reasons unrelated to my lesbianism, I was told I needed long-term psychotherapy because I was unwilling to explore my resistance to heterosexuality. Paid university staff–so-called "counselors"–routinely preyed on freshwomen in the "encounter groups" we were encouraged to attend. I found myself living in a constant state of hypervigilence. At some point, my wariness shifted to anger, which led me to action.

I wrote a series of term papers advocating increased social tolerance of lesbianism. In reviewing the psychiatric literature, I found that unbiased, nonhomophobic studies on lesbians were nonexistent; instead, the literature was replete with case histories "demonstrating" lesbian psychopathology. Having already experienced the lesbianism-as-illness model of psychotherapy, I knew how dangerous it could be. I decided that it was time to generate data rigorous enough to challenge the homophobic status quo. In 1971, during my senior year, I launched my first study.

I surveyed members of the American Psychiatric Association (APA) and found that most considered lesbianism a normal variation of sexual expression (Gartrell, Brodie, & Kraemer, 1974). I then proceeded to lobby my senior research advisor, who was the APA's Program Committee chair and later became its President, to include nonbiased presentations on homosexuality at APA annual meetings. These early speakouts helped pave the way for the removal of homosexuality from the *Diagnostic and Statistical Manual of Mental Disorders (DSM)* in 1973.

Shortly after I began my first study, a report that gay men had lower testosterone levels than heterosexual men hit the press (Kolodny et al., 1971). It was accompanied by considerable speculation that homosexuality was biologically determined. My advisor and I quickly assembled a group of gay male Stanford volunteers. Using the same research design and analysis as the widely-publicized report, we found that gay men had significantly *higher* testosterone levels than their heterosexual counterparts (Brodie, Gartrell, Rhue, & Doering, 1974). As a medical student at the National Institutes of

Health in 1975, I conducted the same study on lesbians: all subjects had normal testosterone levels (Gartrell, Chase, & Loriaux, 1977). Neither of these studies received much media attention, undoubtedly because they were inconsistent with the pathological view of homosexuality. However, they helped dispel the homophobic notion that homosexuality could be "cured" by an alteration in testosterone levels.

I did my psychiatric residency at Harvard from 1976-1979. In 1978, I accepted an honorary fellowship to serve on an APA task force, hoping I would be able to steer organizational policy away from the heterosexism which had permeated my educational experiences. The task force had been constituted to develop a curriculum on the psychology of women for psychiatric residency programs. When we submitted our detailed 200+ page proposal two years later, APA officials were incensed over a single sentence written by me: "Homosexuality is a normal variation in sexual expression."

The magnitude of the backlash surprised me. Never mind that homosexuality had been eliminated from the *DSM* six years previously, or that, by then, the APA had an official policy of nondiscrimination against lesbians and gays. Prominent female psychiatrists pressured me to delete the sentence, warning that my professional career could be ruined if I did not comply. Meanwhile, several male psychiatrists rewrote my sections and submitted their versions for publication under my name. I was also subjected to a long-term smear campaign. (Among the rumors launched to discredit me, my favorite was that I had been asked to leave the Boston Psychoanalytic Institute because I was so emotionally disturbed. This slander was particularly remarkable as I had never even considered applying! Moreover, no analytic institute in the U.S. had yet admitted an out lesbian.)

Despite these tactics, I refused to capitulate. I resigned from the task force, withdrew my contributions to the curriculum, and removed my name from authorship. Many of my colleagues followed suit. Sadly for women psychiatrists who eagerly awaited our assistance in revamping patriarchal training, the curriculum was never published. I became completely disillusioned about the possibility of making any changes within organized psychiatry without major resistance.

In spite of protests by many APA officials who disliked my sexual orientation and politics, I became chair of the APA's National Women's Committee in 1982. Our mandate was to advocate women's mental health issues within the U.S. Phyllis Chesler had called our attention to psychiatric sexual abuse in *Women and Madness* (1972), yet no efforts had been made within the psychiatric community to deal with offenders. I knew that the APA would never sponsor educational programs on psychiatric abuse unless its prevalence had been documented. As chair of the Women's Committee, I called for an APA-sponsored investigation into the problem. No surprises this time: I encountered massive resistance everywhere I turned. I was told repeatedly that documenting psychiatric sexual abuse could destroy the credibility of the psychiatric profession! I responded that abusive psychiatrists were responsible for the damage, not those of us who were attempting to stop the exploitation.

When it became clear that the APA intended to stall my investigation indefinitely, I conducted a series of studies independently. Six percent of psychiatrists surveyed in 1985 acknowledged sexual involvement with one or more patients; 65% of respondents had treated patients who had been abused by mental health professionals (suggesting that the 6% self-reported prevalence was a conservative estimate); and the patients involved were devastated by the abuse (Gartrell, Herman, Olarte, Feldstein, & Localio, 1986; Herman, Gartrell, Olarte, Feldstein, & Localio, 1987; Gartrell, Herman, Olarte, Feldstein, & Localio, 1987; Gartrell, Herman, Olarte, Feldstein, Localio, 1988; Gartrell, Herman, Olarte, Localio, & Feldstein, 1988). In 1990, I surveyed internists, obstetricians, gynecologists, surgeons, and family practitioners. Sexual abuse by these physicians turned out to be as prevalent and harmful as abuse by mental health professionals (Gartrell, Milliken, Goodson, Thiemann, & Lo, 1992).

Data from these studies were used to develop criminal statutes prohibiting sexual abuse by health professionals, to support malpractice claims by victims, to educate consumers about nonabusive medical care, and to develop preventative educational programs in medical and mental health training. In addition, despite considerable opposition, the AMA and the APA have amended their ethics codes to specify that sexual contact with current or former patients is unacceptable. Progress is still fitful, however. In 1988, the APA supported the defense of Dr. Jason Richter, a Colorado psychiatrist who acknowledged sexually abusing his patient, Melissa Roberts-Henry (*PBS Frontline*, 1991). Defense tactics condoned by the APA included hiring detectives to tail Roberts-Henry (further victimizing her), as well as assassinating the character of the woman psychiatrist who subsequently treated Roberts-Henry. This tactic was so successful that this psychiatrist was forced to close her practice, change her name, and leave the state. In 1989, I publicly resigned from the APA in protest of its participation in Richter's defense. I could no longer work in an organization that refused to be accountable for the damage done to countless female patients by male psychiatrists.

As I later found out, one of those patients was my own mother. In 1992, she told me that she had been sexually abused by the psychiatrist she had seen when I was a child. This was the psychiatrist who had hospitalized her for depression when I was 11 years old, and had insisted on seeing her five or more times per week for 15 years at $35 per hour (an unmanageable hardship for a family of five living on my father's blue collar $8000 annual salary). This psychiatrist also held and fondled my hand as he led me around his new office complex when I first met him at 16. He employed my mother as a bookkeeper while treating her, sexually abused her while treating her, urged her to kill my father while sexually abusing her, then raped her when she attempted to terminate with him. This psychiatrist is a former President of the World Association of Social Psychiatry. He has prevailed in every claim filed against him by other abused patients.

Words cannot communicate the rage I have felt since having my worst suspicions about my mother's psychiatrist confirmed. All my efforts on behalf of other victims cannot possibly erase the devastating impact on my own family. I can no longer speak or write about psychiatric sexual abuse without reexperiencing my own pain.

I have encountered power-abusing health professionals at every turn: from my mother's psychiatrist, to the counselors at Stanford, to my Harvard residency training director (who was apprehended on multiple counts of sexual harassment), to my outpatient supervisor (who sexually abused clients while directing Harvard's student mental health services). What upsets me more than anything is that my experiences are not unique. Even though my work has forced the medical community to acknowledge the prevalence and severity of physician exploitation, and has alerted consumers internationally to this heretofore unanticipated "risk" of healthcare, I still receive anonymous communications from victims of psychiatric abuse who are too frightened to identify themselves. These heartbreaking documents have even included photographs of children conceived as a result of the abuse. Nevertheless, I remain optimistic that exploitation by health providers will eventually be curtailed as women gain greater power to set and enforce standards of professional conduct.

I spent 11 years on the Harvard Medical School (HMS) faculty before returning to my native California in 1988. This transcontinental move was accompanied by several major life decisions concerning my work. I decided to limit my medical school affiliation to clinical status, which means that I can now teach, write, and speak about whatever topics I choose without risking University censure. I fund all my own projects because my work has always been too radical for traditional funding agencies. As it turns out, I can earn more money through my private practice than I would receive from alternative sources, and in less time than it takes to prepare grant applications. Finally, I take on projects only if they are both meaningful and fun. One of my most enjoyable fundraising projects has been a comedy tennis tournament featuring lesbian mixed doubles (butch-femme) for Lyon-Martin Women's Health Services, one of the few clinics in the U.S. specializing in healthcare for lesbian and bisexual women.

Over the years, I have devoted considerable effort to organizing lesbian physicians. My activities have ranged from establishing newsletters, to holding potlucks, to setting up support groups, to organizing for demonstrations. As the first out lesbian professor at HMS, I networked among local lesbian physicians, encouraging them to come out and speak out. Eventually, I expanded my efforts nationally, urging lesbian physicians to make themselves more visible. I presented the keynote speech at the first national lesbian physicians' conference, organized the second national conference, and provided ongoing support. It has become the largest annual gathering of women physicians in the U.S. My mission has always been to increase the visibility and power of lesbian physicians so that lesbian patients can receive nonhomophobic, quality health-care.

In 1986, I began a national, longitudinal lesbian family study with friend and colleague Jean Hamilton. This project will carry us into the next century as we follow 85 children conceived by donor insemination into adulthood. It is the only study of its kind, and it promises to deliver meaningful, exciting, and useful data concerning child development and family evolution. It will also serve as an important guide to healthcare professionals, public policy analysts, and legal experts in deliberations concerning child custody, adoption, definitions of parenthood, and nontraditional families.

In looking back over my life, I find that lesbian feminism has focused me, anger has fueled me, and friends, colleagues and lovers have sustained me. I am tempted to name all the women who have supported me in the work I have done, but the list would probably occupy as many pages as the preceding text. Due to space limitations, I will restrict myself to a few. Thank you, Dee Mosbacher (my partner of 20 years), Joan E. Biren, Marny Hall, Judy Herman, Karen Johnson, JoAnn Loulan, Silvia Olarte, Minnie Bruce Pratt, and Jasna Stefanovic for holding my hand, suggesting new strategies, and gently, lovingly, sending me back to the front.

REFERENCES

Brodie, H.K.H., Gartrell, N., Rhue, T., & Doering, C. (1974). Plasma testosterone levels in heterosexual and homosexual men. *American Journal of Psychiatry*, 131(1), 82-83.

Chesler, P. (1972). *Women and Madness*. New York: Avon Books.

Gartrell, N., Brodie, H.K.H., & Kraemer, H. (1974). Psychiatrists' attitudes toward female homosexuality. *Journal of Nervous Mental Disease*, 159(2), 141-144.

Gartrell, N., Chase, T., & Loriaux, L. (1977). Plasma testosterone levels in heterosexual and homosexual women. *American Journal of Psychiatry*, 134(10), 1117-1119.

Gartrell, N., Herman, J., Olarte, S., Feldstein, M., & Localio, R. (1986). Psychiatrist-patient sexual contact: results of a national survey. i. prevalence. *American Journal of Psychiatry*, 143(9), 1126-1131.

Gartrell, N., Herman, J., Olarte, S., Feldstein, M., & Localio R. (1987). Reporting practices of psychiatrists who knew of sexual misconduct by colleagues. *American Journal of Orthopsychiatry*, 57(2), 287-295.

Gartrell, N., Herman, J., Olarte, S., Feldstein, M., & Localio R. (1988). Management and rehabilitation of sexually exploitive therapists. *Hospital and Community Psychiatry*, 39(10), 1070-1074.

Gartrell, N., Herman, J., Olarte, S., Localio, R., & Feldstein, M. (1988). Sexual contact between psychiatric residents and educators: results of a national survey. *American Journal of Psychiatry*, 145(6), 690-694.

Gartrell, N., Milliken, N., Goodson, W.H., Thiemann, S., & Lo, B. (1992). Physician patient sexual contact: prevalence and problems. *Western Journal of Medicine*, 157(2), 139-143.

Herman, J., Gartrell, N., Olarte, S., Feldstein, M., & Localio, R. (1987). Psychiatrist patient sexual contact: results of a national survey. ii. attitudes. *American Journal of Psychiatry*, 144(2), 164-169.

Kolodny, R.C., Masters, W.H., Hendryx, J. et al. (1971). Plasma testosterone and semen analysis in male homosexuals. *New England Journal of Medicine*, 285, 1170-1174.

PBS Frontline, "My Doctor, My Lover." First aired: November, 1991.

A New Voice for Psychology

Carol Gilligan
Lori Farnsworth

I am listening to Carol Gilligan's voice. Not surprisingly, I hear an extraordinarily compelling voice. What she might describe in another as embodied-resonant. Such an open and direct voice is unexpectedly refreshing when compared to the dominant voice of the field in which disconnection between thoughts and feelings, though changing, is still the norm. What I hear most prominently is a gifted writer with the ear of a musician–tuned to the nuances and

Carol Gilligan, PhD, is a writer and a psychologist, the author of *In a Different Voice: Psychological Theory and Women's Development*, and "Joining the Resistance: Psychology, Politics, Girls and Women." A founding member of the Harvard Project on Women's Psychology and Girls' Development, she has edited and coauthored numerous books with other project members, including *Meeting at the Crossroads*, with Lyn Mikel Brown; *Women, Girls and Psychotherapy: Reframing Resistance*, with Annie Rogers and Deborah Tolman; and the forthcoming, *Holding Difference, Sustaining Hope: Women and Girls, Race and Relationship*, with Jill McLean Taylor and Amy Sullivan. A Professor at Harvard in the Human Development and Psychology Program, Graduate School of Education, she was a visiting Professor at the University of Cambridge from 1992 to 1994.

Lori Farnsworth is currently a PhD candidate in the Clinical Psychology program at the University of Vermont. She received her master's degree in Counseling from Harvard University Graduate School of Education in 1992.

Correspondence may be addressed to Carol Gilligan, 503 Larsen Hall, Harvard University, Cambridge, MA 02138.

[Haworth co-indexing entry note]: "A New Voice for Psychology." Gilligan, Carol, and Lori Farnsworth. Co-published simultaneously in *Women & Therapy* (The Haworth Press, Inc.) Vol. 17, No. 1/2, 1995, pp. 213-228; and: *Feminist Foremothers in Women's Studies, Psychology, and Mental Health* (ed: Phyllis Chesler, Esther D. Rothblum, and Ellen Cole) The Haworth Press, Inc., 1995, pp. 213-228; and: *Feminist Foremothers in Women's Studies, Psychology, and Mental Health* (ed: Phyllis Chesler, Esther D. Rothblum, and Ellen Cole) Harrington Park Press, an imprint of The Haworth Press, Inc., 1995, pp. 213-228. Single or multiple copies of this article are available from The Haworth Document Delivery Service [1-800-342-9678, 9:00 a.m. - 5:00 p.m. (EST)].

texture of language—its rhythm, tone and color. Carol begins by describing herself as "first, deeply a writer."

I also hear in her voice a social activist; aware of the power of voice to transmit, politicize and to construct a culture. Carol has worked for social justice and awareness for the last 30 years on issues ranging from feminism and registering African-American voters, to working on nuclear disarmament.

It is also the voice of a woman embedded in relationships. A daughter and mother raised "as a Jewish child during the holocaust," now a mother of three, taught to "always stand up for what you believe in." And an academic who realized early in her career the power of collaboration, especially with students, such that in psychology, as in political resistance, "you don't work alone and you form a group."

Ultimately, I hear in the voice of this ground-breaking developmental psychologist and feminist scholar a woman deeply connected to honoring and integrating all of these ways of being in the world. A profound sense of curiosity about human nature as it is expressed through the voice and, in turn, through relationship, permeates our discussion.

It is, of course, Carol Gilligan who has so eloquently invited countless other women to do the same; that is, to struggle to stay in genuine connection with themselves, and with others, by speaking from a place of courage and authenticity. As feminists, she has encouraged us to hear the absence of women's and girls' voices in this culture. And challenged us to begin to wonder with her about how the inclusion of these voices might bring a "different voice" not only to psychology, but to society as a whole.

We are speaking together in her office at Harvard in early August. It's one of those oppressive days that sends Bostonians down to the Cape, or out to the Berkshires in droves, but Carol, wearing black, with her long, thick hair down around her shoulders, seems unaffected by the heat. She is animated as she describes the weekend retreat from which she has just returned, part of a project she co-developed. These ongoing, experiential workshops bring girls from the community, including "at risk" girls, together with women to learn from one another about sustaining and strengthening connection (or reconnecting) to their own voices in a culture that more often supports what Carol has called "a kind of dissociation" from voice. She has only recently returned to this Cambridge from Cambridge, England where she has been a visiting professor for the past two years.

As a former student of Carol's I am excited to be back at Harvard to speak to her about how she came to make her contributions to the fields of psychology and to feminism. For Carol, the "truth" about what led her to "notice, hear and then write about" what she saw and heard in this culture lies "somewhere in the convergence of my life, the historical moment, and where I happened to be at that particular time." Since she was a child, Carol has been passionately involved with music and language. As an undergraduate at Swarthmore, she studied literature; then she pursued clinical psychology in graduate school.

From the beginning, the voice in the field of psychology, and the way of talking about human lives was problematic for me. It seemed to me very flat. The kind of descriptions you pick up in case presentations, like "mother was . . . " or "father is. . . ." No person can be described adequately in that way. At that time, I had a sense of a disparity in the way I thought about human experience. My own experience, other people's, and the ways I knew in great novels and poetry and theater were so different from what I was coming across in clinical psychology. I wrote my thesis about that disparity. It was called, "Responses to Temptation: An Analysis of Motives."

I got my PhD from Harvard, and I was supposed to finish my clinical internships, and I just thought . . . I can't do this. I can't go on talking *about* people in this way. Then I left the field. I became more involved in the arts and was a member of a modern dance company. I was also active in the civil rights movement. And I was the mother of a small child. We had moved to Case Western where my husband was in medical school, and I found myself in a kind of international women's community, living in student housing where we all kept each other company while we cared for our children.

In 1965-66 Carol returned to psychology as a junior faculty member at the University of Chicago . . .

At that time, grades were going to be used for deciding who would go to Vietnam and who would be exempt from the draft. A group of us, almost all very junior faculty, refused to turn in our grades if they were going to be used as a basis for deciding who would live and who would die. I remember one faculty meeting that was an incredible lesson to me. Of the whole faculty, it was mainly those of us who were the lowest of the low who spoke out. I sat there thinking, all of these people with tenure have nothing to lose. We had everything to lose.

When she returned to the East Coast, Carol went back to Harvard and taught with Erik Erikson, in his course on the Human Life Cycle, and then in Lawrence Kohlberg's class on Moral and Political Choice.

Here I was, teaching with Erikson and Kohlberg, and still hearing the voice of the field as hypothetical in some sense, different from the ways in which people actually experienced their lives. Or at least that is how I thought about it at the time: as a difference between the hypothetical and the real. With a group of graduate students, I set out to do a small piece of research on the ways people actually experienced a sense of self, and how people responded to real situations of moral conflict and choice, where they had to live with the consequences of their choices. I was teaching the theories of Erikson and Kohlberg and also listening to the ways in which people actually spoke of themselves and their lives, their experiences of conflict, crisis, distress.

My background in literature and music led me to listen for voice and also for language or key. I also was affected by the historical moment: the political was so present in the early '70s, and questions about morality and values. And then I was teaching with the people who had created the theories, so I could see the relationship between the life and the work. These theories were human constructions; they didn't seem so awesome to me. I saw how Erik's work on identity came right out of his life. He was a man who had not known who his father was; he had named himself. And moral dilemmas ran all through Kohlberg's life, beginning in his childhood. So I saw the connection with both of these men, between their experiences and their theories. Psychological theories were not carved in stone, or written on tablets that came down from the heavens.

So then, in essence, I began to connect my life and my work, and this connection turned out to be very radical in all kinds of ways.

Because it revealed the absence of women's voices and women's experiences, and also a problem in the conceptual framework: a disconnection from women and a misrepresentation of relationship. I started by doing what I thought of as basically a clinical study: talking with people who were in the midst of crisis and who were facing an actual turning point in their lives. I had begun a study of Harvard students and was planning to follow them to the point where as college seniors they would face the Vietnam draft. But then Nixon ended the draft. I enlarged my sample to include women and interviewed these students more generally about their sense of self, their experience of moral conflict, and how they were thinking as college seniors about the perennial questions of how to live and what to do in life. I was interested in how a sense of self came into play in the making of life choices, and also their moral and political concerns (because these were students who had elected to take a course on moral and political choice) affected the choices which they were making in their lives. I began to follow the relationship between the questions, "What am I going to do next year?" and "What do I want to do next year?" and "What should I do next year?" to see how a sense of self was interwoven with desire and a sense of moral purpose or agency or responsibility.

Then the Supreme Court legalized abortion. I thought, aha, here's another place where people have to make a difficult choice with real consequences in a finite period of time, and they come to a public place. With Mary Belenky, I tied in with a variety of pregnancy counselling services and abortion clinics and we interviewed women of different social classes, different cultures, different races, religions and ages.

At the time, I had noticed that many women had dropped Kohl-berg's course on moral and political choice. Something like 15 of the 25 women who initially signed up for that course dropped it even though it had taken a lot of work to get into the class. And of the 50 or so men, only 5 dropped. There was this huge gender difference in students' responses to the class. I remember women who stayed in the class asking burning questions about what Kohl-berg's theory had to say about the starvation in Bangladesh and what to do, knowing that people were starving. And there was no good answer, based on the theory. I remember thinking, that's a really good question, but then I would realize the framework within which I was teaching and I would have to say, well, that's a really great question–but that's not what we are talking about here. In fact, I felt constantly that I had to put my experience to one side and remember how does Erikson talk about motherhood, or how do Object Relations Theorists talk about mother-child relationships. The women students had to do what I had done in teaching, which is to put aside their own experience and learn Kohlberg's way of talking about moral development, or they were going to do what many of them did, which was to leave the class. With a graduate student, I contacted these women who had left the class and interviewed them; we wanted to know how they thought about morality and what experiences they construed as moral conflicts and choices and whether their approach was at odds with what was taught in the class.

I was sitting at my kitchen table one day, reading through the interviews with women from the pregnancy/abortion decision study, and finally it crystallized: this thing that had been bothering me in one way or another for a long time but which I had not initially named as having anything to do with feminism or with women. My friend Dora Ullian came over and I said, "You know Dora, women are defining the whole problem differently, their sense of themselves is different, and that's what's wrong." It was the missing piece. What was going on here? I remember she said, "Why don't you write about that?"

I sat down and wrote out the counterpoint I was hearing between the women's voices and the voice of psychological theory. I wrote, "The arc of developmental theory leads from infantile dependence to adult autonomy, tracing a path characterized by an increasing differentiation of self from relationships with others and a progressive freeing of thought from contextual constraints." But the men who framed these theories of development–Freud and Erikson, Piaget and Kohlberg–all had a similar problem: the problem of women, whose sexuality seemed more diffuse, whose sense of self was more tenaciously embedded in relationships with others, whose thinking was insistently contextual and whose moral judgments were more influenced by emotions. They solved the problem by saying that women were deficient in their development. So I asked, if women's voices are different from the voice of psychological theory, is the problem in the women or in the theory?

And basically the answer was both. There was a problem in theory and also a problem in women's development. The key that unlocked this for me was being there at a historical moment when the framework shifted slightly; the Supreme Court, in legalizing abortion, gave women the deciding voice in a decision that affected their own lives and the lives of other people, that involved ultimate questions of life and death. Legally, if not psychologically, women suddenly found they could speak and also have an effect. The psychology of that moment was fascinating because of the shifting relationship between inner and outer worlds. To begin to hear women speaking in different terms about the sense of self and the experience of moral conflict and choice clarified a problem that was embedded in psychological theory and also in the legal and political system. A set of assumptions that were belied by women's experiences.

All of the preparation from my own life, from the historical time, from the women's movement and the fact that I was interviewing women and was at that time a mother of three young children, made the issues very real to me. I think that it was a moment where I faced a choice: either I was going to listen to the women, including listening to myself and my responses to the women, or I was going to listen to the theories. I mean, I went with the women.

It was the first time that I wrote something just for myself. It was the winter of 1975; I sat down and wrote, "In a Different Voice: Women's Conceptions of Self and of Morality," and I remember writing in a kind of rush–just sitting down with the feeling of seeing something and wanting to write it down. I wrote this 50-page paper, and then put it aside. The following year, when I went back to Harvard to teach, I showed it to some students as part of an ongoing conversation we were having about psychology and about women, and one of the students who was on the board of the Harvard Educational Review asked it he could take it to them.

They came back and said, this is wonderful but we really don't know what it is. Is this psychology? They rejected it but said that I could revise and resubmit it. The second time, they said, well, we'll accept it, but we want you to rewrite it in short, declarative sentences. And I said no, that I couldn't do that; that you couldn't write Faulkner's novels in Hemingway's prose. The voice of the piece was complex, was contrapuntal, and the sentence structure was elaborate because my point was not a simple or straightforward point, but had to do with different voices and different ways of seeing and speaking. So at every step it was a struggle.

I ask Carol how this early work was received by Kohlberg, Erikson and others.

Basically, it didn't occur to me to discuss this with Erikson or with Kohlberg. I wasn't working with Erikson at the time, and I wasn't really working with Kohlberg, although he was a colleague. I was working with a very active group of graduate students who had similar questions. Initially, Kohlberg was very dismissive of my research with women and basically ridiculed my abortion decision study, getting his class to vote that abortion was not a moral problem and telling my research seminar that I had confused gossip with research. At the same time, he was also very collegial and personally friendly, so it was a complicated double message. I remember having a sense of political theater, that I could get my class to vote that abortion was a moral problem and by that time, I knew that the research which Kohlberg was defending had included no women.

I had a sense of how to hear the kinds of things he was saying about my work and not to take it in. I had been involved in enough political struggles and because of the way I grew up and my experience, I heard these kinds of comments as political statements. There are a lot of reasons, you could say, why I was someone who would go against the grain. I knew that it was important to maintain a sense of my own integrity and not just to listen to somebody else saying you can't do this. You know, when we didn't turn in our grades at the University of Chicago, the world didn't come to an end. Having always had one foot in the arts and one foot in academia, and having a life outside the university, I was just enough on the edge that I was in a good position to take a risk. And I had economic backup from my husband and my parents, so I could afford to lose my job.

I did find Erikson's and Kohlberg's work interesting and important, but I knew that they had an investment in a way of looking at the world that was not mine. As long as they could incorporate my work into their theories or regard it, as Larry used to say, as a kind of interesting cross-cultural research–a study of this other culture, called women–then everything was fine. But when listening to women implied changing their theories, then there was a problem. So I began to write about the fact that Freud and others were saying that they had a psychology of love and a theory of sexuality and they didn't know about women. What did this say about their psychology of love or theory of sexuality? And what is it like for women living in a world where this kind of thing can be said and not heard as a problem?

It's just astonishing now to realize how many psychological studies that included no women or girls were funded and passed peer and editorial review and were published, even co-authored by women and men. After *In a Different Voice* was published and I went around giving talks, I heard a kind of testimony from psychologists who said that initially they had included girls or women in their studies of motivation or creativity or development or whatever, but that they could not make any kind of theoretical sense out of the data they had collected. So, they simply did not report the data and forgot to mention this in their publications. There was a massive cultural blindness; neither men nor women were seeing the omission of women as a significant omission in psychological research or hearing women's silences in psychoanalysis or therapy. But there also was a major theoretical challenge: how to make sense of women's psychology, and how to interpret evidence of difference. I argued for a different voice, a new psychology, new research methods, changes in clinical practice; I saw an opening within the field and also in the larger society, in the political system and the culture as a whole. Others saw the omission of women and the silences as a little problem and said in effect, "now we are including women, we have made some small adjustments in our theories and everything is just fine. It turned out not to be a problem after all."

I ask Carol, what do you consider your contributions to the field?

First of all, a different voice. Secondly, an analysis of women's psychological development. And then, a theory of development and a method of research. *In a Different Voice* revealed that psychology had a voice and that the voice was out of relationship. The key was separation, and bringing in women's voices changed the voice or the key. Now everyone speaks about relationships. If the representation of human experience is dissonant with the experience of being in relationship, then the people who live in relationship are going to experience a kind of dissociation. Many women became selfless or voiceless. When women brought their voices into relationship and felt that this was psychologically or morally necessary in order to be responsive in relationship, they often felt or were told that they were selfish or bad or hurtful or crazy women.

The first part of my work was to expose this structure and analyze its psychological dynamics. So instead of dismissing women as enmeshed in relationships or not having a sense of self or not knowing what love or morality is, I showed how listening to women's voices led to a different understanding of self, relationship, morality and love–based on an understanding of responsive relationship rather than on the achievement of separation. It is sort of extraordinary that the implicit voice in most psychological theories (clinical and developmental) up to that point, was a male voice, in a male body, and that the patriarchal nature of society and culture was taken for granted or represented as natural. And therefore, at this particular moment in time, and in this particular culture, women's voices will bring into psychology certain realities of relationship that otherwise remain unspoken and unseen. For this reason, listening to women changes the voice of psychology–the way of speaking about the human world.

As *In a Different Voice* was being published, I found that I was really tired of an argument about difference that seemed to me to be going nowhere. I also felt that I couldn't be heard. The question about difference that people were obsessed with was, "Is it nature or is it nurture? Is it biology or socialization?" It was a question of who or what to blame. To me, given the particular society we live in and given that the psyche is in some relationship with the body and the culture, I thought that it would be extraordinary if there were no psychological differences between women and men in the present social, cultural and historical context. And if differences in the body, in the embodiment of sexuality, in relationships, in society and culture have no psychological ramifications, then the psyche is, in some sense, encapsulated or sealed off from experience. But it felt impossible to be heard and it would keep coming back to, "Are you saying that it's biology? Is this essentialism?" So I wanted to get out of this argument.

I had a question from *In a Different Voice* which had to do with women's development. The girls in that book did not seem to be on a continuum developmentally with the women. Sharry Langdale who was working with me at the time kept talking about this, and I thought that she was absolutely right. Then the 1980 *Handbook of Adolescent Psychology* came out saying that adolescent girls "had not been much studied," and I decided to do what I thought of as a straightforward piece of developmental research. I would study women's psychological development not by comparing women with men but by connecting women with girls. I would go backward through developmental time into girls' adolescence and girls' childhood.

So, the second contribution has to do with what we learned from working with girls in a variety of settings over a period of years. It was amazing and we were unprepared for the strengths that we heard in listening to girls. A child's knowing is like a naturalist's; built upon specificity and detail. And girls know the human world in this way; they describe the complexity of relationships, the range of emotions, including both positive and negative feelings without feeling that they have to choose either/or. I realized that the psychology of women had been oddly disconnected from girls and that this mirrored the dissociation that many women carry from their own earlier experience. Not to make this dissociation challenges the psychological structures that maintain and are maintained by a patriarchal social order.

I got very excited because I felt that we were coming to understand the dynamics of something that had been observed clinically by psychologists for over a hundred years and that also was registered in epidemiological data. Girls showed greater psychological strength and resilience than boys throughout childhood but then something happened at adolescence. Freud described it as a "fresh wave of repression"; more recently it has been called a loss of resilience or self-esteem. What our research uncovered was a crisis of relationship; girls had to move out of relationship or out of connection as part of their initiation into womanhood. And girls were resisting losing relationship; they were struggling to keep their voices in relationship.

I felt that I was seeing into the joining of psychology and culture; that I was witnessing how a patriarchal social structure or culture takes hold psychologically, or is taken in psychologically so that it structures psychology and becomes replicated over time. It was really exciting to me to see girls' resistance and girls' courage. Girls are not just socialized passively into womanhood. They are not simply victims of genetic or social engineering, but people with voices and desires for relationship. And they fight for their voices and their desires, however effectively or at whatever cost. We saw some very valiant and also creative strategies. The psychological struggle for psychological health became a political struggle to change relationships in ways that seemed psychologically beneficial to both women and men, because it represented a move away from various forms of disconnection and dissociation.

I am indebted to the students with whom I worked so closely throughout this time. Working in collaboration became essential when the evidence of our research went against what we thought we knew and led into places of real discovery. Because at these moments, we had to work against the forces of our own dissociation and self-deception. The students also were crucial in helping me to make explicit a way of working which I implicitly followed, involving listening for voice, following shifts in voice, picking up changes in rhythm or key, paying attention to the unspoken, and so forth. Some of this came from my work in clinical psychology, but I also was drawing on what I knew as a writer and a musician. It is a way of listening to the human world that is so close to me that I didn't see it as a method but just how I worked. Voicing an interview text like a piece of choral music, picking out four or five lines and following their interweaving. The voice-centered method we developed is a way of capturing the layering or polyphony of psychological processes, and it also offers a way of maintaining difference and representing the relationships which are at the center of psychological inquiry. Rather than blinding ourselves to these relationships and their effects or voicing over people's voices and blurring cultural differences. The method offers a way of holding difference and maintaining relationship. And I see this as essential in psychological work, necessary for a good psychology or a psychology that is good science.

The theory of development takes evidence of asymmetry with respect to time of heightened psychological risk as a basis for conceptualizing psychological development within a cultural framework. For a long time, psychologists have known that boys are more at risk than girls in childhood, and girls are suddenly at risk psychologically in adolescence. The evidence we gathered from listening to girls elucidated a crisis of relationship, which then corresponded with long-standing observations about young boys. I saw early childhood for boys and adolescence for girls as analogous in that these were times of relational crisis and potential dissociation. To put it another way, these were times of initiation–psychological initiation into a patriarchal order of relationships, as defined by the conventions of masculinity and femininity which directly affect the sense of self or self-worth. The pressures to solve this relational crisis by some form of dissociation, some compromise between voice and relationships, were great, but there was also evidence of resistance and courage on the part of both young boys and adolescent girls. The developmental difference meant that girls' resistance was more grounded in experience, more robust, and more articulate. The heightened psychological risk could be seen as a direct function of the dissociation, which weakens psychological resilience and undermines the ability to act. So it contributes to a sense of helplessness and powerlessness in the face of distress.

To undo dissociation, you have to move associatively. You can't do it logically. Being in the presence of girls, hearing girls' voices, picking up the kinesthetic cues from the way girls move in their bodies begins to undo women's dissociation and brings forgotten memories and desires and hopes up for women again. Working with girls and staying with one another in the process, we found ourselves entering what my colleague from the theater, Normi Noel, calls "the undiscovered country," or what feels like a lost time.

I ask Carol where she hopes to go now with her work and how her work has changed her life.

I'd like to go into a deeper understanding of the psychological and cultural processes involved in dissociation–not knowing or feeling what in another sense one feels and knows. And I am interested in the power of voice and the rhythms of psychological change. Where my own work is going–I am writing and that is always a process of discovery. I am intrigued by the potential for psychological and social change that lies in the asymmetries between women's and men's development. I am fascinated by the phenomenon of resistance, by the truth that lies in resistance, and also by the many meanings of resistance–immunological, psychological, political. I'm not sure where I will go next.

I hope that the findings of the Harvard Project research can provide a new grounding for efforts at preventing psychological suffering. Our findings explain feelings of loss and psychological disconnections that have been taken as necessary or even seen as desirable, but which are very costly psychologically and also to society. And our research indicates how these problems could be prevented.

My life has been profoundly changed by the work that I and other women have done. I can understand my own struggles to speak and be heard; I can hear my voice as different now without feeling discouraged from speaking. And I can make sense of a problem that was affecting me and many other people; a problem that seemed at once pervasive and elusive. The work with girls led to times of such pure joy, and brought back all kinds of memories. Through that work, I came to a very different understanding of my own life and the lives of other women. I also have come to a deeper understanding of men's struggles in this culture–what Freud called men's discomfort with the culture they have created. I found myself picking up such strong resonances in novels and poems and plays, and it led me to wonder how I could have missed these before. So I also ended up with a much sharper awareness of the power of psychological processes such as dissociation, and the brilliant but costly moves that people make psychologically to preserve what feels most essential.

I have come to see psychology as a very powerful science, capable of revealing the structure of the human world. It offers a talking cure, and women are in a very powerful position. But it is also easy to cover the psychological world; to not know, in part by not feeling. I think that voice is a powerful channel connecting inner and outer worlds. The work on voice is just a beginning; it leads to a very radical psychology, in the sense of getting to the heart of things. I am writing a book, which I sometimes call "Recovering Psyche" and sometimes I call it "The Birth of Pleasure," depending on whether I want to emphasize the cyclical process of uncovering psychological truths and then covering them over again, or whether I want to point toward the potential for a new story, one that is about pleasure rather than about tragedy. As long as there has been civilization or patriarchy, there has been resistance to the disconnections and dissociations that are built into that structure. And women's voices are particularly revealing, as many writers know. So what would it mean to join the resistance and fight for voice and relationship? It seems to me it would be a move toward psychological and societal health.

Before all of this, I was raising three children, teaching part time, taking dance classes, playing some music, working for nuclear disarmament. It never occurred to me that my life would go in the way that it has. And when I wrote *In a Different Voice,* breaking what had been a long silence, I wanted to take my book and plant it in my garden. I had a large organic garden at that time, and it seemed like a good place for my voice. I did not think that the book would bear fruit in the world. I actually did not think it would be heard or understood. So that was a big surprise to me; the extent to which what I said resonated with other people and the generosity of their responses. The attacks I expected, and the misunderstanding. That was why I wanted to bury the book, because I cared about what I said and it rang true for me.

Now I like it that I did what I wanted to do, in the sense of writing what I wanted to write, and I ended up with tenure at Harvard, because I think it holds this possibility for other women: that you don't necessarily have to give up what you want or work in some way that you don't believe in or that doesn't ring true. To know the psychological world, to expose that world is very radical because it exposes people's vulnerability–their relationships, their feelings, their hopes and fears. I hope that what I have done will encourage others to go further, to work in collaboration with others, to use a voice-centered method, to be courageous and take the kind of risks that are part of any creative work. Because you don't know.

It's satisfying also to see the people I've worked with over the years writing their own books now and doing original and creative work. I like to think that at our best, we maintained individual voices within a group, like a chorus. And now when I hear these voices developing further, it gives me great pleasure, and also frees me to move in new directions in my own work. I remember at one of the AWP meetings where there were several presentations by members of the Harvard Project, and the voices were all different but the project had a distinctive voice. You could tell it when you entered the room. I felt that we were bringing a new voice into psychology. And this was very hopeful to me. What is most moving to me always in my own work is when somebody says, I read your book and I can hear myself where I didn't before: it changed the way I listen to myself and other people.

SELECTED BIBLIOGRAPHY

Carol Gilligan. *In a Different Voice: Psychological Theory and Women's Development.* Cambridge, MA: Harvard University Press, 1982 (with new preface, 1993).

Carol Gilligan. "Joining the Resistance: Psychology, Politics, Girls and Women." *Michigan Quarterly Review,* 29,(4), 501-536.

Carol Gilligan. "Teaching Shakespeare's Sister: Notes from the Underground of Female Adolescence," in Carol Gilligan, Nona Lyons, and Trudy Hanmer, eds., *Making Connections.* Cambridge, MA: Harvard University Press, 1990.

Carol Gilligan. "Women's Psychological Development: Implications for Psychotherapy." in Carol Gilligan, Annie Rogers, and Deborah Tolman, *Women, Girls and Psychotherapy: Reframing Resistance.* NY: The Haworth Press, Inc., 1991.

Carol Gilligan. "Remembering Iphigenia: Voice, Resonance, and the Talking Cure," in Edward Shapiro, ed., *The Inner World in the Outer World,* forthcoming.

Work of the Harvard Project:

Carol Gilligan, Janie Ward, and Jill McLean Taylor, eds. *Mapping the Moral Domain.* Cambridge, MA: Harvard University Press, 1988.

Carol Gilligan, Nona Lyons, and Trudy Hanmer, eds. *Making Connections.* Cambridge, MA: Harvard University Press, 1990.

Carol Gilligan, Annie Rogers, and Deborah Tolman, eds., *Women, Girls, and Psychotherapy: Reframing Resistance.* NY: The Haworth Press, Inc., 1991.

Lyn Mikel Brown and Carol Gilligan. *Meeting at the Crossroads: Women's Psychology and Girls' Development.* New York: Ballantine Books, 1992.

Jill McLean Taylor, Carol Gilligan, and Amy Sullivan. *Holding Difference, Sustaining Hope: Woman and Girls, Race and Relationship.* Cambridge, MA: Harvard University Press, forthcoming.

On Being a Feminist
and a Psychotherapist

Miriam Greenspan

1969. BECOMING A FEMINIST: FINDING MYSELF

I was a feminist before I was a psychotherapist. In retrospect, this was a determining factor in the subsequent development of my work. My life can be divided into BF (Before Feminist Movement) and AF (After Feminist Movement) consciousness. This momentous personal and historical shift in consciousness came in the year 1969. I had just left Columbia University with a Master's degree in English and Comparative Literature, a doctoral drop-out. Though I could not exactly explain why (because in BF time there were no

Miriam Greenspan, MEd, MHC, is a psychotherapist in private practice in the Boston area, a consultant and internationally known lecturer and workshop leader, and a writer. A leading voice in the field of feminist therapy and women's psychology for the past twenty years, her book, *A New Approach to Women and Therapy* (McGraw-Hill, 1983, Tab Books/McGraw-Hill, 2nd Ed., 1993) has been described as a "landmark" work in the field. Her writing has appeared in *Ms. Magazine, Socialist Review, Women & Therapy,* and other journals. She is currently counselor for the Episcopal Divinity School in Cambridge, MA, and working on a second book, *Healing Through the Dark Emotions: The Alchemy of Grief, Fear, Anger and Despair.*

Correspondence may be addressed to Miriam Greenspan at 27 Moraine Street, Jamaica Plain, MA 02130.

[Haworth co-indexing entry note]: "On Being a Feminist and a Psychotherapist." Greenspan, Miriam. Co-published simultaneously in *Women & Therapy* (The Haworth Press, Inc.) Vol. 17, No. 1/2, 1995, pp. 229-241; and: *Feminist Foremothers in Women's Studies, Psychology, and Mental Health* (ed: Phyllis Chesler, Esther D. Rothblum, and Ellen Cole) The Haworth Press, Inc., 1995, pp. 229-241; and: *Feminist Foremothers in Women's Studies, Psychology, and Mental Health* (ed: Phyllis Chesler, Esther D. Rothblum, and Ellen Cole) Harrington Park Press, an imprint of The Haworth Press, Inc., 1995 pp. 229-241. Single or multiple copies of this article are available from The Haworth Document Delivery Service [1-800-342-9678, 9:00 a.m. - 5:00 p.m. (EST)].

229

words for what in AF time would be named as the emotional abuse women suffer in patriarchal institutions), I felt I had to leave the university. I had been drawn to the study of literature because it offered some clues to the mysteries of human suffering, but as a grad student of literary criticism I felt my soul shriveling. Despite academic honors and financial rewards, I thought of myself as a fraud and a failure who didn't have the right stuff to hack it in academia.

At this juncture, a trusted woman friend called to invite me to join a group. "It's a group of women talking about their lives, like in group therapy, but it's *not* therapy. It's not like anything you've heard of before. It's called consciousness-raising."

The spontaneous combustion of the women's movement, passing along woman to woman, propelled me to check out this c-r group for myself. What I experienced changed my life irrevocably. Here was a group of women who talked with unrefined honesty about their lives, looking for areas of commonality in their stories. They broke ranks with the self-policing, self-silencing and self-subordination that defined the way women were supposed to act. They talked with integrity—as though their lives were meaningful in a way that had bearing on the state of the world and vice versa. They talked as though their stories mattered not only as individual narrative but as collective social history.

I remember Laurie, a professional photographer, speaking about her work. "I'm paid to be a photographer, yet I can barely call myself one. My boyfriend takes a couple of photos and—bam—he announces he's a photographer!"

Zap! It was the first jolt of consciousness-raising, a harbinger of all the zaps to come. I had a sudden realization of all the ways in which I didn't take my work or mind seriously, instinctively comparing myself to and falling short of a standard which, for the first time, I recognized as a distinctly *masculine* standard, and which seemed always just out of my reach. I realized why my choice to leave Columbia felt like a failure and saw the seed of strength in trying, despite the external pressures to do otherwise, to find my own way and honor my own voice. Later on, looking for the seed of strength in what conventional psychology labelled deficit or pathology became one of the cornerstones of my approach to women in therapy.

The juxtaposition of conventional psychology and feminism in my life in this era was itself a consciousness-raising experience. I embarked on my first trial as a patient of individual psychotherapy at around the same time that I joined my first Boston c-r group. In the women's group, we told our stories, listened respectfully, and honored these stories as a source of knowing. The healing of this kind of speaking and listening was immediate and powerful. It stood in sharp contrast to my frustrating plight as a patient of therapy, where I felt that my story could not stand on its own merit but was forever being interpreted, pathologized, reduced and demeaned by the professional who sat across from me—whom I eyed with a combination of deferential rescue fantasy and strong resistance. (The difference between the BF *psychological* meaning of the term resistance and the AF *political* meaning of the same word is a telling one.) For a long time, I resisted my therapist, our therapy sessions degenerating into political debates about the value of radical feminism: was it legitimate or was it simply my "defense" against the curative knowledge that only he could bring me? When I trusted myself enough to realize that I was paying this man each week when he should be paying me for a crash course in radical feminism, I dumped him. The most empowering thing I did in this therapy was to leave it. Since then I have taken some nachas (the Yiddish word for delight and pride in others' accomplishments) from the fact that dozens of women have written me that they were similarly empowered to leave an incompetent, maddeningly distant, sexist or abusive therapist after reading *A New Approach to Women and Therapy.*

I credit the movement with curing my depression, anxiety, and career panic. I remember thinking that the feminist movement saved my life. For me, this was more than a movement for social justice. Emotionally and spiritually, it was a foundational source of personal healing. In finding feminism, I found myself and my work. From this experience I knew that powerful and enduring personal transformations were possible through means other than psychotherapy. All of this profoundly affected the ways in which I would later come to think about female psychology and to practice therapy. It made me permanently skeptical about narrow and rigid definitions of professional propriety and about dogmatic theories of psychology. And it made me a die-hard feminist.

In short, my active participation in the early days of feminism as a social movement rather than an academic theory has been the ground of being from which my work as a psychotherapist has grown and for the particular vision I tried to articulate in *A New Approach to Women and Therapy.*

1972. BECOMING A PSYCHOLOGY TRAINEE: THE COLLISION OF RADICAL FEMINISM AND PROFESSIONALISM

By 1972, I had found my vocation. The vision I had of myself as a therapist was as a catalyst for change–someone who could help women use the pain of their lives to bring about personal and social transformation. The year I started my psych internship program was also, happily, the year *Women and Madness* hit the stands. Reading it was like a shot of fresh energy mainlined to the heart, soul and brain. Though it was a scholarly piece of work which incorporated research and had a thousand footnotes, it read like the book of an angry, impassioned woman who wasn't disguising her voice for the sake of demure professional etiquette. It integrated the scholarly and the activist, the scientific and the spiritual, speaking in the authentic voice of the prophetess.

This essay seems a good opportunity to publically thank Phyllis Chesler for her groundbreaking work. As far as I'm concerned, Phyllis is the mother of all feminist foremothers in the field of psychology. *Women and Madness* was the first and remains one of the best and most consciousness-raising works of feminist scholarship, feminist social analysis, and feminist vision that we have.

With *Women and Madness* in the air, the woman's movement in full swing, the discovery of my newfound calling in life, with a great and naive passion and the energy of a Totally Committed Feminist, I became a student of counseling and started out as a psych intern at a large Boston hospital.

This part of my life reads like Feminist Wild Woman meets the Psychology Establishment and has a Rude Awakening. While being trained to diagnose a "borderline personality"–and to ignore or deny that most of these women were abused and angry–I was also participating in feminist and socialist-feminist women's conferences where I had an intellectually challenging, emotionally profound and fun-filled experience of bare-breasted women changing the world. While being taught how to do an intake interview in which I pigeonholed a person's emotional, social and spiritual suffering into pseudo-medical categories, I was also being followed by FBI agents after staging a sit-in and takeover of a Harvard building with a group of women who in this fashion created one of the first Women's Centers in the country, peering into my cervix with the early health feminists, living in an urban commune, and making what we liked to call the "cultural revolution."

That which was most enlivening and healing in my life was grist for the "shrink" mill and irksome to my psych supervisors. All of it was reduced to a psychological "issue," amusing at best and troublesome at worst. My problem, I was told, was that I was "ambivalent about my professional role." Indeed–but whether you saw this as a deficit or an asset really depended on your point of view. The problem was I asked troubling philosophical and political questions about the received wisdom of psychological theory. This kind of questioning, I was told in no uncertain terms, was behavior unbecoming to a *professional*. It was not *appropriate*. The words *professional* and *appropriate* have remained, to this day, suspect words in my eyes, words that hold a silent tyranny and that we should examine and question very closely.

My trials and tribulations as a feminist trainee with AF consciousness in a BF internship program became part one of my book. Here is where I got to immortalize stories of being told by my supervisors that professionals (if they are female) must wear brassieres, that the etiology of homosexuality had to do with too powerful mothers, that excessive anger in a woman is a sign of a character disorder, that an inordinate preoccupation with spiritual matters is a symptom of schizophrenia, that too much empathy is a serious lapse in professionalism, that too much compassion is an impediment to one's expertise as a psychotherapist.

Having learned in training how *not* to practice therapy, I was determined to create another way that would be in keeping with what I knew about women and healing from the women's movement.

1974. GRASSROOTS FEMINIST THERAPY

When I started my therapy practice, therapists who openly called themselves feminists were a small group and we communicated with each other–studying and working together, holding conferences, and questioning everything. What was most precious to me in these years in the mid-1970s was the sense of belonging to an ongoing cultural questioning and critique of received wisdom, the emotional/intellectual buzz of collective feminist enterprise, the creation of new words and new ways. And the empowerment that came from being enlivened by the words, feelings and thoughts of other women. This was grassroots feminist therapy at its best.

But I don't want to whitewash these good old days. If sisterhood was powerful, sisterhood was also painful. I remember with sadness the doctrinaire disputes between cultural feminists and socialist-feminists, between lesbians and straight women. I remember the anti-semitism of some of my sisters. I remember being publicly trashed and witch-hunted by the tyranny of political correctness which was an endemic part of all the progressive social movements of the era.

Nevertheless, the best and most important contributions of the grassroots feminist therapy movement deserve to be credited here. To me, these are: the unabashed and outright rejection of Freudianism and of the medical model as a basis for understanding and treating women; trusting ourselves to be the experts in our own lives; developing theory from the ground of our own experience; understanding empowerment as a *social* and not simply individual psychological process; the openness to different voices, different modes of working, trying things out in a "beginners' mind" sort of way; the rejection of professionalism as defined by the medical model and the psychiatric establishment; the efforts to work collectively rather than hierarchically, developing models of work and study, theory and practice in which degrees and credentialization were less important than learning from one another and treating each other with equality and respect, regardless of our rung in the professional hierarchy.

In many ways, these contributions seem as important today as they were 20 years ago. The original foundations of feminist therapy could still serve as a guidepost by which to evaluate our work.

1983. A NEW APPROACH TO WOMEN AND THERAPY

I wrote *A New Approach to Women and Therapy* because I wanted to consolidate the best of grassroots feminist therapy in the form of a book that women could use as both providers and consumers of therapy. I wrote it because I had faith that what I had learned from the vantage point of a feminist activist about healing and change could be applied to how we think about and treat women in therapy. I wanted to take up where Phyllis Chesler left off. If the abuse of women was built into the practice of psychiatry and psychology, how could therapy be liberating rather than oppressive, healing rather than harmful? I passionately believed then–and still do–that the entire enterprise of psychiatry and its way of going about viewing and treating people was bound to result in psychological casualties–male as well as female. I wanted to address and expose the terrible tyranny of the medical model of psychotherapy, which in a positivist, materialist, and scientistic culture, is taken to be the sole model of truth. I wanted to expose, in a way that was readily accessible not only to educated professionals but to consumers of therapy, the biases of the traditional model of therapy practice (intrapsychic bias, the medical model bias and the bias of white male expertise). I wanted to speak in my own voice and offer a model of psychology and therapy practice that was rooted in the ground of feminist consciousness. I wanted to openly credit c-r, rather than academic theory, as my epistemological base. And finally, because I knew firsthand the power of women's authentic narratives to transform self and world, I wanted the book to be told largely through women's stories.

I was not setting out to write a scholarly, heavily-researched book. My audience, as I imagined it in the course of writing, was largely an audience of women consumers of psychotherapy many of whom had been, were still, or would be casualties of the traditional system. My intention was to write an accessible book that would be a source of encouragement to women by presenting clearly what was wrong with the traditional system, and by mapping out and minutely illustrating an alternative model of care which grew out of a feminist vision of the possibilities of psychotherapy. When I started to write *A New Approach* and when it was published in 1983, I knew of no other book that attempted to do this.

I wanted to validate a way of working in which the female strengths that were devalued in patriarchy–the skills of nurturance, empathy, intuition, relationality, the ability to recognize another's emotion and to support its expression–were recognized as the cornerstones of therapeutic work. I wanted to validate women who were trying to do therapy in a feminist way and struggling with the internalized voice of patriarchy in their heads. I wanted to redress the imbalance of male-defined systems of thought and treatment by putting out a model of care that was clearly woman-identified and woman-oriented. And my most modest goal was to incite women to rebellion, free-thinking and outright feminist revolution.

In my vision, the foundational myth of the practice of psychotherapy was not an image of Man as Scientist but of Woman as Midwife. Psychotherapy could be seen as an extension of the tradition of wisewomen called witches who preceded the male white-coated Doctor as community healers and physicians–the tradition which had been persecuted, destroyed and co-opted by a coalition of State, Church and the rising male-dominated medical profession between the 13th and 19th centuries.

In contrast to the scientific myth of "objectivity" I wrote about a distinctly pro-woman model of therapy, one that was up front about its feminist values and ethics. For me, these values can be summarized as follows: (1) that therapy, at the very least, should do no harm. Therefore, it must be based on a non-patriarchal model of work which takes into account the power dynamic of the psychotherapy situation; (2) that therapy, if it is to be non-abusive, needs to be based on an ethic of *mutuality* rather than hierarchy, *connection* rather than (male-style) distance, *compassion* rather than separation; (3) that therapy should empower rather than pathologize; (4) that therapy should embody the values which we want to see reflected in the rest of society, e.g., not rampant male-style individualism but collective mutual responsibility for one another.

The empowerment model of therapy I described and illustrated was based on: (1) re-thinking diagnosis and moving from a medicalized view of women's intrapsychic "disorders" divorced from social context to a social view of the roots of women's emotional pain in women's social condition; (2) looking for the seeds of strength in what traditionally gets labelled "pathology"; (3) working with victim psychology, male-identification and women's anger in a compassionate woman-identified framework; (4) redefining the individualistic ideal of mental health and moving to a more holistic definition which included the struggle for social and spiritual wholeness; (5) having a balanced view of both how women are socially victimized by patriarchy and how women have resisted and brought great emotional, mental, and spiritual resources to bear on our social predicament.

The feminist psychology of women presented in *A New Approach to Women and Therapy* took shape just prior to and roughly in the same period as the developmental theories of women's psychology emerging from the Stone Center at Wellesley College. The model of therapy I wrote about, with its emphasis on an empowering and real, mutually enlivening relationship was similar to the model Jean Baker Miller elaborated with her colleagues at the Stone Center. Certainly grassroots feminist therapists everywhere were deeply influenced by Jean's gem of a book, *Toward a New Psychology of Women*. Jean's presence in my life was a strong and vital source of inspiration. As she did with so many other women, Jean mentored me when I was a member of the Brookline Women's Counseling Group, reading my manuscript in its earliest form and offering much needed assistance and encouragement.

After book publication, I took my work on the road, presenting countless workshops, papers and panel discussions throughout the U.S. and abroad. Of all the things that the book has brought to me, the most important has been the sense of an ongoing conversation with women around the world. I have met many wonderful, daring, creative, gifted and inspiring healers. I have seen how feminism has changed the face of psychology and I have been privileged to be part of this change.

1983-PRESENT. BEYOND A NEW APPROACH
TO WOMEN AND THERAPY

The birth of *A New Approach to Women and Therapy* coincided with the birth and death of my first child. Aaron taught me about the limits of any particular view of reality, including my own. Through Aaron, I had come to a bodily-grounded realization of the sacred gifts that can come even from the most painful, sundering experience. Though my awareness of the injustice of women's suffering in patriarchy stayed constant, I came to a different understanding of the spiritual dimensions of suffering. I came to think of therapy in more overtly spiritual as well as political terms.

I began to work with much more traumatized women with a greater sense of ease and safety in the work. I ran groups which I called "Healing Through the Dark Emotions" groups. These were designed to be shared initiations for women who were willing to journey together into their most "negative" emotions—sorrow, fear, anger and despair—to find the authentic sources of knowledge, power and energy that emerge when these emotions are allowed to take their course. Through my own experience, I had come to see the alchemy of painful emotions into healing energies and I wanted to help create a milieu in which this became possible for women in a group setting. For the past few years, I have been working on a book called *Healing Through the Dark Emotions: the Alchemy of Grief, Fear, Anger and Despair* in which I present a holistic theory of emotional transformation embedded once again in women's narratives.

In general, it has been my pleasure in recent years to focus my work on the integration of the political and the spiritual in psychotherapy. I have also been working with other therapists who are interested in broadening the parameters of psychotherapy to include the self-earth connection. The connections between feminism, ecology and psychology are a growing concern for those of us who are aware of the fact that the ecocidal threat to our planet is, as Joanna Macy says, "the pivotal psychological reality of our time."

1994. FEMINIST THERAPY: WHERE ARE WE?

Writing this nostalgic review of how feminism has influenced my life and work, I find myself wanting to end with some musings about the fate of feminist therapy in the 1990s. In a quick, bird's eye view of feminist therapy history, it can be seen that the 1970s was the decade of grassroots feminist therapy as a part of the overall social movement for women's liberation. And the 1980s can be seen as the decade that academic feminism entered the mainstream. A decade after the social movement came the academic discourse. The latter gained some respectability for ideas that originated in the movement, many of which were discredited at the time.

Looking at feminist psychology and feminist therapy as a field of inquiry and practice, I fear that we are in some danger of forgetting our (grass)roots in the feminist movement. For one thing, while there are numerous pockets of cultural resistance and rebellion, there is no social movement per se to speak of. Everything has become de-centered and de-constructed. Feminist therapy seems to coexist quite happily in the capitalist marketplace of therapeutic commodities. Feminist therapists can be purchased along with all the other brands of therapists in the ever-expanding multi-million dollar new age/recovery/therapy/healing industry. So it's easy to lose our sense of where we come from, or that we ever had a vision of changing the world.

For another thing, feminist professionals have been blessed with some (meager) modicum of acceptability in the mainstream. There are tremendous gains in this hard won respectability. But there are also hidden perils. One is the tendency to develop historical myopia. The fact is that without the social movement of women 20 years ago, none of this would have been possible. This was, to begin with, a radical movement for social change. If we forget this, I believe we stand to lose a great deal not only in terms of our continued struggle for social power, freedom and equality, but in terms of our practice as helping professionals.

It seems to me that this potential loss is most evident where feminist therapists have adopted a code of professionalism that looks much like the dominant ethic of psychiatric psychotherapy that the grassroots feminists rejected so heartily 20 years ago. The

current controversy around professional "boundaries" in psychotherapy highlights this issue.

This is not the place to go into the complexities of what we mean
by professional "boundaries." But it might be the place to ask some
questions: In response to the pervasive problem of therapist sexual
abuse of patients, have we adopted a knee-jerk embrace of standard
professional ethics which stress "boundaries," separation, and distance at the expense of the core feminist values of empathy and
connection? In the context of a profession that–in an effort to stave
off therapist abuse–is drawing stricter and more rigid guidelines
about professional "distance," have we become so fearful of being
seen as unprofessional that, ironically, we are willing to adopt an
innately abusive ethic of power–one that stresses a rigid, unyielding
inequity of power in its dogmatic faith in so-called "boundaries?"
In my view, the re-infusion of the male medical model with the
blood of feminist support with the misguided idea of safeguarding
against patient abuse is one of the things we most urgently need to
address as a community.

It was a sobering moment for me when I realized that I felt more
endangered in my practice of feminist therapy in the past 5 years
than I have felt in all the time since 1974. At no other time have I
worried as much that many of the things I most prize about my
work–my ability to connect with clients, my use of the art of self-
disclosure, my gifts in breaking down the wall of separation between Patient and Expert, could be so misconstrued as "unprofessional" and therefore ipso facto abusive. At no other time have I
feared as much that other feminists might be the first to condemn
any therapeutic work that involves physical touch–work which I
feel is vital to trauma survivors who want to experience the difference between abusive touch and respectful, nurturing connection.
At no time in the past 20 years have I felt more tempted to silence
myself, to hide what I do and to go underground. This tells me a
great deal about the current climate of fear which exists in the
profession.

It seems to me that now, more than ever, the core values for
feminist therapy that I wrote about–the values of connection, intuition, empathy and compassion–are suspect as "unprofessional." I
am by no means suggesting that we don't need professional stan-

dards. But if what we are looking for is an ethic that will curb power abuses in therapy, then what we need is to stand by our power analysis of psychotherapy. What we need are stricter feminist ethics, not stricter "boundaries" in therapy. If what we mean by "boundaries" is an unshakable respect for the client, then I'm all for it. But often it comes to mean a fear-driven, pseudo-objective distancing that I believe is stultifying to creative work in therapy and damaging to clients, particularly to trauma survivors. It saddens me to feel that the best and most important contributions of grassroots feminist therapy are now so suspect in the field, even to many feminist therapists themselves.

Twenty years of being a feminist and a therapist has reinforced my faith in feminism as a visionary capacity to see through patriarchy to what we have been and what we can be as women. Now more than ever, I believe that the future of healing ourselves as women and of bringing healing to the earth itself, lies in expanding–not constricting–our models of work. Expanding the boundaries of our hearts so that we become more, not less, connected to those who entrust themselves to us. Expanding the boundaries of our understanding so that we can see the connections between self, society, earth and cosmos in our work. All the juice of the early feminist therapy movement–its creativity, its boldness, its willingness to speak up and speak out–is needed today as much as it was all those years ago.

Judy Herman:
Cleaning House

Judith L. Herman
Amy J. Ojerholm

Amy Ojerholm: What were the influences that led you to contribute to feminism and women's mental health?

Judith Herman: It's often hard for me to figure it out because it seems as though everything is relevant. There were influences that were important in getting me involved in movements for social change more generally, and my involvement in the women's movement grew naturally out of that. I grew up in Manhattan, NY. My parents were academics and intellectuals who were children of Jewish immigrants from central Europe, and I was raised in a tradition that emphasized intellectual contributions and the need for social

---

Judith L. Herman, MD, is Associate Professor of Psychiatry at Harvard University in Cambridge, MA. She is also the Training Director of the Victims of Violence program in the Department of Psychiatry at Cambridge Hospital. She is the author of *Father Daughter Incest* and *Trauma and Recovery.* She has written numerous articles and lectures widely about sexual and domestic violence.

Amy J. Ojerholm is a graduate student in her second year of the Clinical Psychology Program at the University of Vermont. Her research and clinical interests include lesbian mental health, fat oppression and body-size acceptance.

Correspondence may be addressed to Judith L. Herman, 1675 Massachusetts Avenue, Cambridge, MA 02138.

[Haworth co-indexing entry note]: "Judy Herman: Cleaning House." Herman, Judith L., and Amy J. Ojerholm. Co-published simultaneously in *Women & Therapy* (The Haworth Press, Inc.) Vol. 17, No. 1/2, 1995, pp. 243-250; and: *Feminist Foremothers in Women's Studies, Psychology, and Mental Health* (ed: Phyllis Chesler, Esther D. Rothblum, and Ellen Cole) The Haworth Press, Inc., 1995, pp. 243-250; and: *Feminist Foremothers in Women's Studies, Psychology, and Mental Health* (ed; Phyllis Chesler, Esther D. Rothblum, and Ellen Cole) Harrington Park Press, an imprint of The Haworth Press, Inc., 1995, pp. 243-250. Single or multiple copies of this article are available from The Haworth Document Delivery Service [1-800-342-9678, 9:00 a.m. - 5:00 p.m. (EST)].

reform. My family and religious community had the perspective of a minority that had been persecuted, and took a wary, critical stance toward the society that we were in. Those were very formative influences when I was growing up. When I was a young teenager in the fifties, my parents were investigated by Senator McCarthy because my mother had been a communist. The daily dinner table conversation included discussion of who had been summoned and who had testified, and we got a very close look at whether people stood by their principles or not, and how people rationalized their cowardice. I was also exposed to the kind of accommodation that people made with injustice and with political movements that looked for scapegoats. I remember a lot of the fear at that time. People feared going to jail, losing their jobs, having their passports taken away, because it was apparent that fascism could happen anywhere–there was no illusion that it couldn't happen here. You had to fight it, you had to critique it, you had to be aware of it, and you also had to be ready to flee, if necessary. There was a funny mixture of assimilation and critical distance, along with a very strong kind of emphasis on the life of the mind, on trying to appeal to people's better nature, because that was about all you had to counter not only brute force, but people's tendency to bully.

My mother was educated at Barnard, then went into psychology to pursue academic research and teaching. When she was blacklisted and couldn't get an academic job, she took her little bit of inheritance from her father and got analytic training, and became a practitioner, really as second choice. It was unusual at that time to have that model of a mother who worked and was a professional and was as serious about her life and her politics and her choices as my father was. When I came of age and got involved first in the civil rights movement and then the anti-war movement, it wasn't a break in any way from the tradition in which I'd been raised. I was also raised with the expectation that I would become a professional–that expectation was very strong in my family. Fortunately I had the temperament or the ability to fulfill those expectations. High expectations can be a burden, but being a parent now and seeing how people raise their kids and what kids struggle with, I'd rather see them struggle with high expectations than low expectations, or none.

I was also lucky to come along at a time when there was a movement to get involved with–first in civil rights and then the anti-war movement, and there was a natural evolution from that to the women's movement. After a certain amount of time had been spent fighting for some kind of vision of greater equality or greater justice, the women in the movement woke up and noticed that the way we were being treated by our "brothers" didn't make us feel very good. The light went on–and getting involved with the women's movement just made sense. It was as though everything people believed in on a larger scale suddenly connected with everything personal–the smallest details of personal experience–and once you had that insight, it was overwhelming and an enormous amount of energy was released. It was so freeing to see suddenly that it wasn't an abstract principle–it was about your daily existence, and every relationship that you had was touched and affected by it. It felt overpowering to realize that we were immersed in the deep structures of those kinds of power relationships, but it also meant that any place one started was fine.

How I came to contribute to the psychology of women was really a function of the time in my life when I was making a career decision. I chose to go to medical school and then to go into psychiatry, and I was also in a consciousness-raising group. My feminist awakening occurred just at a time when I was finishing my medical training and my internship, and beginning my psychiatry residency. Everything fit in a certain way–psychology seemed to be absolutely relevant to discussions of the relations of the sexes, how people were socialized, how people came to internalize what were essentially social and political constructs about superiority and inferiority, and how relationships should be conducted. My consciousness-raising group was organized by a feminist umbrella organization called Bread and Roses, which organized a conference in the fall of 1970 for people who had already been in consciousness-raising groups and wanted to organize around specific topics or issues. I joined a group of women who were in training in various mental health professions. Our group became the Women's Mental Health Collective.

The Mental Health Collective originally had very grandiose ambitions in terms of really re-thinking the psychology of women from scratch and changing the practice of psychiatry and psycho-therapy—we had such a sense of energy and possibility. I might have been the first vocal feminist at my particular workplace, but once one person spoke up, people made their sympathies known, and as I said, with the way I'd been raised, being in a minority, a critical role was nothing new. Many other women who came to the women's movement had a bigger distance to travel in terms of being prac-ticed at taking a critical stance or speaking out, whereas the tradi-tion in which I'd been raised tended to glorify and admire that.

Amy Ojerholm: How did you get involved in your work with trau-ma?

Judith Herman: It seemed to flow naturally from my residency. My first year I had two women patients who were incest survivors who came into the hospital after serious suicide attempts and were very depressed. One was a woman in her 40s, the mother of 5 kids, whose husband was very abusive. It seemed to me that she over-dosed because it was the only way she could escape the battering. There were no services for battered women at that time, and the hospital really served as a refuge for her. Her therapy consisted of helping her understand that she didn't have to tolerate the abuse and that she could actually get a divorce. It turned out that the incest played an important role in keeping her trapped in the marriage, because her husband knew her secret and she felt blackmailed by that. She believed that she was a "fallen woman" and he'd been decent enough to marry her, so she had to put up with whatever was being dished out to her.

   The other patient was somebody who was classically "border-line"—she self-mutilated, overdosed, got herself involved in all kinds of abusive situations, was emotionally volatile, very self-de-structive, and had very stormy, off-again, on-again relationships. Her incest history was documented because she had been in foster care, but it wasn't made the centerpiece of her treatment. I had a male supervisor who encouraged me to explore the incest with her, not in a feminist way in terms of examining the dynamics of male dominance, but in a relational way in terms of what it had done to this person's sense of self, sense of trust, and the price that she felt she had to pay to be in any kind of a relationship. Both of those were successful therapies, and I saw how taking on the incest as a central issue really made a huge difference in their recoveries.

When my training was complete and our group became the Mental Health Collective, we decided that we didn't want to just go ahead and get jobs in the system or start private practice, and instead wanted to work in an alternative women's setting and create a different type of women's mental health care. We went to work at a free storefront clinic, the Somerville Women's Health Project, and began our practice there. The medical clinic only survived until 1976, but the Mental Health Collective has survived up to the present. It was in that context of being in an alternative institution that took women seriously that we saw more and more of the same kind of stories that I had seen with my first patients in my residency–incest case after incest case. I was doing peer supervision with Lisa Hirschman, who was then a graduate student in psychology, and we were both seeing so many incest cases that we asked each other, "What is this? Is there something wrong with us? Why are we getting all these incest cases? Or is this an epidemic? If it is an epidemic, why isn't somebody writing about it or saying something about it?" After a certain amount of sitting around and waiting for someone to say something, we decided that *we* should say something. We collected twenty cases between us, and wrote our first paper in 1976. We knew at this point that we were onto something, because we started getting letters from around the country from people who had read the manuscript. The letters said "I've never told anyone and I thought I was the only one"–classic lines of people who need a movement and don't know it. As soon as they knew it they had that same moment of insight and connection that we had experienced in consciousness-raising. It was now being transmitted through the writing, and that's when I realized that this was what we had to do.

Amy Ojerholm: Can you summarize what your main contributions were to the field of feminist mental health?

Judith Herman: I've contributed towards raising awareness in the women's movement and more generally about sexual and domestic violence as central and paradigmatic issues for women's liberation. Specifically, I've been able to make a contribution along the intersection of the dynamics of power and oppression and the dynamics of human relationships or psychology–in other words, the whole issue of sexual and domestic violence, which I see as basic methods by which men as a group keep women as a group subordinated.

Another area that I've contributed to has been in the arena of psychological development–in the formation of the self in relation to others. I've been able to use my education and training to articulate insights that many people have had about the way that this particular abuse of power affects women's lives, and that led to the writing of *Father Daughter Incest,* which crystallized and articulated the importance of understanding incest as a way of shaping women's psychology.

My path went in two directions from there. One was coming back to the area of personality disorders–some of the most prejudicial concepts in psychology had come to roost in that area. It was the most value-laden, the most subject to social prejudice, and I felt it imperative to rethink some of those concepts. We reframed borderline personality disorder as a post-traumatic condition and got rid of self-defeating personality disorder and masochistic personality disorder as constructs. This work was a way of rooting out one of the last bastions of intransigent sexism in psychological theory. In practice, it was everywhere. The other thing that I took on during the 80s with Nanette Gartrell and Sylvia Olarte was the issue of incestuous behavior within the profession, that is, the sexual exploitation of patients. All three of us were members of the Committee on Women of the American Psychiatric Association. We tried to point out that the dynamics that led some fathers to feel entitled to have sex with their daughters were exactly the same dynamics that led a certain minority–probably about the same percentage–of psychiatrists or other mental health professionals to feel entitled to have sex with their patients. The rationalization and the excuses were exactly the same, the blaming of the victim was exactly the same, and the cover-up within the profession was exactly the same as what we'd find in an incestuous family, so it was very easy to make that analogy. We had a lot of fun doing our national survey of sexual involvement with patients, and watching the reactions. We proposed this to the American Psychiatric Association, and watched them waffle and duck and hide. Each time we tapped into some area that had been taboo and hidden, there was an outpouring of response from people who had been ashamed and had kept these things secret. In all fairness, there were many people within the establishment who were willing to be swayed if you made your case persuasively, if you concentrated on presenting hard data and an analysis of the evidence. It was an uncomfortable, embarrassing and difficult issue to talk about, but the only thing worse was not to talk about it.

In terms of summarizing my contributions, the first major one was *Father Daughter Incest*. During the 80s, my main work was on personality disorders and the house cleaning within psychiatry in terms of the diagnostic concepts and in terms of the most egregious practices. In the meantime, I had found two new collaborators–Mary Harvey, who started the victims of violence program with me, and Bessel van der Kolk, with whom I worked on the borderline study. He brought the perspective of somebody who'd worked with combat vets and saw psychological trauma from that perspective, and he helped me expand my ideas. I saw that trauma was trauma whether you were talking about men or women. It was those two collaborations that led to *Trauma and Recovery*, which was a synthesis of psychological trauma from a broader perspective. Mary and I had built a program, and we were doing what I had originally hoped the Mental Health Collective would do, which was to create a setting that was not just a refuge for women to come and practice differently or get a different type of therapy, but was also located in a teaching hospital–a city hospital that was committed to taking care of poor people. We were able to have students and be part of an intellectual community where we not only made innovations in our practice, but could turn them into model programs that could be tested, written up and disseminated. We could also train the next generation of practitioners. Having students cuts down on the bullshit considerably, because whatever you offer them, they test out, and if it doesn't work, you hear about it.

Amy Ojerholm: How did your life change as a result of your contributions?

Judith Herman: For the better, mostly. It has been wonderful to have the sense of community with people all over the country and all over the world, and the chance to connect with so many people who care about the same things that I care about in a passionate way. It's been enormously rewarding and enriching in that sense, and I have felt able to integrate my professional life with working for social change. That is an enormous privilege, and has given me enormous satisfaction, which I haven't even had to pay a large personal price for. I've had more professional recognition than I'd ever dreamed of. My only regret is that I wish we were much further along in what we had to offer. It's hard to turn around to people who are suffering and injured and say to them, "What you need isn't out there, you have to go organize it," and to deflect their anger. The women's movement seems to be at a point now where people take certain amounts of progress for granted, and they want to know why what they need isn't out there. Sometimes I get grumpy about it and think, "You should have seen what it was like 20 years ago," but that's on bad days.

Revolutionizing the Psyche of Patriarchy

Shere Hite
Melissa J. Perry

THE BASIC IDEAS

Sometimes I read something, and I think, I have made a contribution to history! I can hardly believe it myself, this is so exciting. It is hard to realize. Wow! No matter what happens to me, I feel fulfilled to have interacted with thousands–no, millions–of people around the world, and made a difference. This is a great pleasure to know. The Hite Reports are published in over thirty countries, though banned in most of the Arab world, only published for the first time in South Africa in 1994, and even today, restricted in India, among other places, by postal censorship.

I hope that my current theories in *The Hite Report on the Family:*

Shere Hite has an MA in history and conducted work for her PhD at Columbia University. She is the award-winning author-researcher of numerous best selling books including *The Hite Report on Female Sexuality* (1976), *The Hite Report on Men and Male Sexuality* (1981), *Women and Love: A Cultural Revolution in Progress–The Hite Report* (1987). Her most recent book is *The Hite Report on the Family: Growing Up Under Patriarchy* (Grove-Atlantic Books, 1995).

Melissa J. Perry, PhD, is Research Assistant Professor in Psychology at the University of Vermont and a previous contributor to *Women & Therapy*.

Correspondence may be addressed to Shere Hite at Grove-Atlantic Books, 841 Broadway, New York, NY 10003.

[Haworth co-indexing entry note]: "Revolutionizing the Psyche of Patriarchy." Hite, Shere, and Melissa J. Perry. Co-published simultaneously in *Women & Therapy* (The Haworth Press, Inc.) Vol. 17, No. 1/2, 1995, pp. 251-263; and: *Feminist Foremothers in Women's Studies, Psychology, and Mental Health* (ed: Phyllis Chesler, Esther D. Rothblum, and Ellen Cole) The Haworth Press, Inc., 1995, pp. 251-263; and: *Feminist Foremothers in Women's Studies, Psychology, and Mental Health* (ed: Phyllis Chesler, Esther D. Rothblum, and Ellen Cole) Harrington Park Press, an imprint of The Haworth Press, Inc., 1995, pp. 251-263. Single or multiple copies of this article are available from The Haworth Document Delivery Service [1-800-342-9678, 9:00 a.m. - 5:00 p.m. (EST)].

251

Growing Up Under Patriarchy will help revolutionize psychology, the way my first book, *The Hite Report on Female Sexuality,* helped revolutionize the understanding of female sexuality. In 1976, the Masters and Johnson theory that if a woman did not have an orgasm during "penetration" (i.e., coitus), that she was "frigid" or had a "sexual dysfunction," was believed by nearly everyone. Only Anne Koedt and Albert Ellis questioned this,[1] but with no body of evidence.

I began, in 1971, using my own scarce money (mostly borrowed from friends), to do a five-year research project investigating female sexuality. At the time I was on leave from graduate school (the Department of History at Columbia University) and an active member of the New York chapter of the National Organization for Women, Image of Women in Media committee. There was very little discussion of sexuality in 1970-71 in the women's movement; we, like other women, were shy and did not like disclosing our personal means for orgasm, the stimulation we needed, nor if we masturbated or had orgasms during sex with our partners. I thought one way to overcome the lack of dialogue on this subject was to write an anonymous questionnaire and distribute it. I used essay questions, since I believed that using the much simpler multiple choice items would mean I was imposing my own categories of answers on others. Further, I felt that as women we had never had a chance to speak for ourselves on the topics of orgasm, sexuality and "the politics of the bedroom," and thus essay questions would give a chance for women to write in their own words, in their own way.

This research, which took over four years and in which over 3,000 women of all ages and walks of life, from all over the United States, participated, legitimated most women's need for clitoral stimulation in order to have orgasm. These and other findings encouraged me to speak out for women's right to orgasm, as well as the right not to have sex, or to have sex with another woman, or to un-define sex. I explained that "sex" as we know it is a reproductive activity, one which is socially constructed, narrowed, to fit a certain philosophy, not a biological given.

It had been said that a woman was "not normal" if she did not orgasm from intercourse. Kinsey, Masters and Johnson, the society at large–all said or implied that a "normal woman" should orgasm "with no hands" from simple coitus, in the same way men did.

Never mind that most also noted that it was "more difficult" for women to orgasm "that way" than men. I concluded, that it was not women who had a problem having orgasm, but society which had a problem in not accepting the ways in which women do have orgasm. Why should "sex" be defined as "foreplay," leading automatically to "intercourse"; with the grand finale being the male orgasm? This is simply a reproductive definition of "sex"; which should be un-defined. Of course, this was extremely controversial to say in 1976! (And part of it still is today, i.e., that sexuality should be undefined, not always including coitus, etc.)

One of the innovations in my research was distributing questionnaires in such a manner that I could be sure to protect the complete anonymity of those participating. In most research, people are asked questions over the telephone or in face-to-face interviews, and the interviewer knows the name, address, and telephone number of the respondents. By using a written questionnaire, distributing it through clubs and organizations, churches and colleges, then asking people not to sign their essay answers (to over one hundred questions) but only to inform me as to their age, occupation, religion (if any), income and so on, people knew they could feel free to write anything they wanted; they need not hide anything.

In my works, I also provided statistics on many new topics that were not considered "research areas" before–starting with "How does orgasm feel?" and "How do you masturbate?" going on to such subjects as "Who broke up first?" "When were you the loneliest?" and, "What does love feel like? Is love passion or caring? Which is more important?" . . . and hundreds more, which can be found in the appendices to my books.

The final innovation of my research methodology was to not only present my own analysis of the findings, but to allow those participating to debate topics within the books in which I present my findings. By presenting the actual voices (written statements) of those participating–and 90% of the books are composed of these testimonies–we gain first, the richness of people's own voices, and secondly, readers can judge for themselves which points of view they prefer. Readers need not agree with my conclusions or point of view, but may prefer to take a point of view of one of the participants. Only after presenting all the points of view received in answer to my questions do I proceed to draw what I believe are the appropriate conclusions. This, as I am aware, is never or almost never done, especially in research with large samples, such as mine.

Sometimes in psychological papers something like this is done. However, typically, these studies use small numbers, often a handful of graduate students, for analysis. (Freud, in fact, generalized about women from a sample of three upper-class Viennese women.) However, I feel that small samples are inappropriate for psychological studies, since to generalize from limited samples means that one believes that "human nature" or behavior is universal, not culturally bound or socially constructed. I try, by having an extremely large and diverse sample, to include a broad range of voices and points of view, and thereby underline the cultural nature of much of thinking and feeling.

On the other hand, by publishing for a large audience (because I wanted as many people as possible to be involved in the debate of re-thinking our way of life), sometimes I note with pain that I am not cited in academic papers (by people who should know better), although my ideas are clearly in evidence. I was once told by a female graduate student that she wanted to cite me, but couldn't, because in order to get her doctoral thesis accepted, she could not cite anyone as "controversial" and "popular" as me.

THE RESEARCH: TRYING TO DISSECT THE IDEOLOGY AND CREATE A NEW UNDERSTANDING

Here is a brief synopsis of every Hite Report, with its year of publication. (Concise excerpts of the first three Hite Reports can be found in *Women as Revolutionary Agents of Change.*) Of course there are many more ideas and research findings in these works than can be summarized here.

(1976) The Hite Report on Female Sexuality

"Sex" is cultural. We have a reproductive definition of sex, designed by patriarchy. It is not "naturally ordained"; otherwise, why the warnings and rules against everything else, such as cunni-

Some excerpts from:

The Hite Reports:

Charting an Ideological Revolution in Progress[1]

Naomi Weisstein, University of Buffalo

Published internationally with widespread influence, these books comprise complex and fascinating portraits of a crucial fifteen-year period in American culture–a period in which society came into an extraordinary confrontation with the traditional ideas of home and family.

This confrontation is examined in the Hite Reports by looking at what really is there–i.e., documentation consisting of the responses of thousands of people to anonymous, open-ended questionnaires–rather than at what reigning theory tells us should be there, and by a debate carried on sometimes among the participants, sometimes between Hite and the participants, a debate based on a coherent theoretical perspective. Perhaps we will look back and say that what is documented here is ideological revolution of the end of the twentieth century.

. . . Hite's theoretical framework for understanding what is happening today in personal relationships and in the culture is neither Freudian or Marxist, but builds on feminist analyses of patriarchy. . . Hite, like many feminists, believes that the society we have, with so much emphasis on aggression and competition, is not necessary–we simply don't have to live this way–and what is needed to change it is a complete understanding and revision of the ideological system at hand. It is to this that her books are dedicated.

1. From Hite, S. (1987). *Women and Love: A Cultural Revolution in Progress–The Hite Report*. New York: Knopf.

lingus, lesbianism and homosexuality? Why did the classical
Greeks have to pass a law saying that men had to have coitus with
their wives at least three times a month?

Most women, two-thirds, can orgasm easily during some form of
clitoral or exterior stimulation, but not from coitus alone; over 90%
of women can masturbate easily to orgasm; only 2% use penetration
during self-stimulation. It is not women who have the problem with
"sex," but the society that has the problem with the way it is
defining sex, and with women's bodies. Women having sex with
other women generally have a higher rate of orgasm.

If women don't generally have orgasm simply from coitus, this is
not a terrible mistake of nature, but shows that the definition of sex
is too rigid and should be made more individual and varied. Various
forms of sexuality and touching should always be possible (this
sounds innocuous now but it certainly wasn't when I first said it!).
Sex should be redefined and undefined to include many more types
of touching than we have today, with various levels of intensity and
intimacy, affection should be possible without "going all the way,"
and eroticism and sensuality are valid experiences in themselves.

Why is Michel Foucault being given credit for saying that the
definition of "sex" is cultural and not biological? Kate Millett,
Andrea Dworkin, I, and others were published before and during
the same year (even in France) that Foucault was.

(1981) The Hite Report on Men and Male Sexuality

Seven thousand men of all ages debate who they are, sexually
and emotionally. Male sexuality is not only a "drive for penetra-
tion-reproduction," but also a longing to be entered: to take and be
taken.

My findings on male psychosexual identity showed that most
men don't marry the women they most passionately love. Not only
that, but also they are proud of this, and often feel they "made the
right decision." (The questions this leaves unanswered are brought
up again and answered in The Hite Report on the Family.)

The paperback edition of this book in the U.S. (Ballantine, 1982)
also contains some very important drawings of clitoral anatomy, by
Suzanne Gage, which I asked her to do specifically for this book
and which we presented together at an annual meeting of the Soci-

ety for the Scientific Study of Sex in the 1980s, in California. (These drawings are also reproduced in *Women as Revolutionary Agents of Change*.)

I had never found an adequate drawing of the clitoris and interior sexual structure to use in the Hite Report on Female Sexuality. After hearing about Suzanne through the women's movement, I asked her to make one. She investigated the topic thoroughly and produced her own elegant drawings, full of new information.

(1987) *Women and Love: A Cultural Revolution in Progress–The Hite Report*

I am particularly proud of *Women and Love: A Cultural Revolution in Progress*. The most complex of my works and least understood (at least to date), I feel it took the cultural perception of who women are ("women's psychology") in romantic relationships, and dragged it to another level. The study asked, "Is love real, or just a way women are manipulated?" My interpretation of the debate between women, presented in the book, shows that what women are doing in love is frequently heroic; rather than "clinging" or "masochistic," as women's actions are so often portrayed.

This work should make it possible for women to examine the emotions of love more profoundly, as well as take pride in emotions rather than blaming themselves for problematic situations, and to cease feeling guilty if they want to leave a love relationship. It examined some differences between heterosexual and lesbian relationships, and also clarified the terms of what I call the unstated "emotional contract."

I became interested in the topic of love as an ideology after hearing Ti-Grace Atkinson say that love was the ideology used to control women. Still, "falling in love" did seem to happen–even to Ti-Grace! So my research asked women whether they thought love was important, and if so, which kinds? Passion or caring?

This book was violently trashed by parts of the media–so violently that Kate Millett, Gloria Steinem, Barbara Seaman, Phyllis Chesler and Karla Jay, among others, signed a statement in my defense and held a press conference. Why? Because the book, for the first time since the Crimes against Women tribunal in the Hague in the 1970s, opened the doors of the bedroom and private life, and let women state the emotional battering and crimes against them which men had done in the name of love. Just ten years before this, in the 1970s, the world had been surprised by the extent of the newly presented statistics on physical battering in marriages; with *Women and Love*, many women testified to widespread emotional battering—yet this was called "male-bashing" by portions of the U.S. press.

In fact, the book did many things: it applied everyday human rights standards to private relationships, it spoke of an outdated "emotional contract," it let women debate in its pages the meaning of love—whether passionate love or more low-key, stable, caring concern makes for a better love relationship—and whether "love," that category by which women were defined for so many centuries, would still be as important to women as it had been. Thus, the subtitle: "A Cultural Revolution in Progress." Many women, the book said, were beginning to take their friendships with other women just as seriously as their relationships with men. The ideology of "love," with women as the caretakers, the love-givers, was being questioned. *Women and Love* contains lengthy and important sections on friendship between women, as well as lesbian relationships—as does the original 1976 *Hite Report on Female Sexuality*.

In this sense of redefining themselves, I concluded that women were changing from being what Simone de Beauvoir called "the Other" to what I called "the Seer"—those who can see the society for what it is more clearly, most clearly, for being and having been on "the outside," looking in and observing. Suddenly the larger picture seen by the "outsider" is more valid and helpful than the narrow perspective of someone who can only see inside the system.

(1993) Women as Revolutionary Agents of Change: The Hite Reports and Beyond

This is a book of essays from *The Hite Reports*, with appendices of speeches I have given at academic conferences, plus speeches or papers presented by others about my work.

(1994) The Divine Comedy of Ariadne and Jupiter

This is a fictional political satire, in which the main character, my dog, has the ability to take me away to heaven where I get advice on

Some excerpts from:

Women and Love: Towards a New Feminist Methodology[1]

Nancy Tuana, University of Texas

In her first study, *The Hite Report on Female Sexuality,* Shere Hite was an important founder of a methodology now central to the feminist tradition–listening to women's own voices. She was one of the first researchers to develop a model and theory of female sexuality arising out of women's OWN experiences, rather than attempting to force a preconceived model upon our experiences. This methodology of listening to women's voices is the foundation of Carol Giligan's later study of women's moral reasoning in her *In a Different Voice,* and of women's self-image, in *The Woman in the Body.*

Just as Hite discovered through her first report that the then accepted models of sexuality were lacking, so other theorists, employing the same methodology, have now discovered that our philosophical and psychological accounts of reason and morality have been distorted by the omission of women's perspective. Hite's third study, *Women and Love: A Cultural Revolution in Progress,* demonstrates that our models of intimacy must be reexamined–and begins to identify the socio-political structures that ground and reinforce unidentified patterns, a context we must be aware of in order to hear and understand women's voices, as well as to discover ways to transform these patterns. Hite's works are an invaluable resource to scholars.

1. From Hite, S. (1987). *Women and Love: A Cultural Revolution in Progress–The Hite Report.* New York: Knopf.

Excerpts from prefacing statements on:
Women as Revolutionary Agents of Change[1]
Dale Spender

Shere Hite has made history. She has helped to shape the beliefs and behaviors of western society. At a time when women were asking—*who are we, and what do we want?*—Shere Hite started out by trying to find some of the answers, and she did this by getting women to speak for themselves. In the early 70s she listened to the questions and the responses of women, to the spoken and the unspoken, to the individual and the community meanings. And she carefully, conscientiously, and creatively put all the pieces together, and returned to women their collective voices in *The Hite Report on Female Sexuality* in 1976. If ever there was an example of the interactive process, Shere Hite and her research on women's physical and emotional relations would have to be it.

But her contribution did not stop with the documentation of women's attitudes and actions: Shere Hite understood that women's expressions about their physical and emotional reality raised a range of crucial issues about men, male values, and manhood. And in 1981, *The Hite Report on Male Sexuality* was published—and gave substance to the suspicion that sex, sexuality, and society, meant very different things (and often incompatible things) to women and men.

"A Cultural Revolution in Progress" was the apt subtitle of *Women and Love*, the third Hite Report, published in 1987. It was because she had been taking soundings of women's experience for more than fifteen years that Shere Hite was able to show in this remarkable and reverberating study, not just what women were thinking, but how women's thinking was changing. There *has been a revolution*, it is one which continues and one in which Shere Hite has played a crucial part. Throughout this period of rapid change, Shere Hite has both monitored and molded women's ideas and aspirations; in her three significant volumes, she has not only identified the issues, and chronicled the critical changes, she has constructed a framework for their interpretation.

1. From Hite, S. (1993). *Women as Revolutionary Agents of Change: The Hite Reports and Beyond*. London: Bloomsbury.

the possibility of social change on earth–and speculate (with Cleopatra's help) on where we are headed.

(1994) The Hite Report on the Family: Growing Up Under Patriarchy

The Hite Report on the Family finds a completely different landscape of childhood than mapped out by Freud, saying that "puberty" doesn't exist for girls in the sense that it does for boys–reproductive puberty, yes, but not a puberty of sexual-awakening. This was total surmise on Freud's part; this is not at all what my research over almost twenty years has shown. Puberty is not "puberty"; the psychology of the culture *uses* puberty with its changes in body and social (reproductive) status to teach its desired roles and power behaviors. Girls have no puberty, according to my research. That is, girls have a reproductive puberty (they develop the ability to reproduce, including breasts and menstruation), but they have no sexual puberty, since girls can have orgasm long before the ability to reproduce (puberty), and long after menopause (all of life). Girls have no "sexual awakening" because they are always sexual. In fact, many girls' alienation from other women starts here, when girls cannot see or discuss their sexual anatomy with their mothers or other girls at school.

With regard to boys, Oedipus should be allowed to continue loving his mother, according to my research, because the forcing of him to bond with boys against girls (and his mother) tears him apart psychologically, and forms a dangerous tendency toward male-pack-bonding (or male-pack-fear) which carries over into adult life, and keeps men bonding like herds against women who try to enter–either a business with them, or their hearts and bodies. The social practice of forcing dissociation from the mother, and in fact mother-hate (woman-hating, as Dworkin has labelled it) should be done away with.

Another finding of *The Hite Report on the Family* is that children at "puberty" feel no stronger sexual attraction for an opposite-sex parent than for a same-sex parent. This is documented in particular with relation to girls and their mothers.

Finally, in *The Hite Report on the Family,* I pointed out that having a hierarchical biological family (reproductive-unit, actually

Some excerpts from:

Who's Afraid of Shere Hite?

Jennifer Gonnerman, *Ms.*, September/October, 1994

When Shere Hite revealed that women had better and more frequent orgasms on their own than with a partner, a chorus of angry critics tried to silence her. Now, 18 years later, it seems that backlash may have temporarily succeeded—at least in the United States.

Several years ago, Button bought the U.S. rights to *The Hite Report on the Family: Growing Up Under Patriarchy* from Bloomsbury, Hite's British publisher. Late last year, Dutton sent out news of the book's upcoming release, but it abruptly canceled the book several months later for "editorial reasons." Dutton and Bloomsbury refuse to give details.

Letters to the Editor, *Ms.*, September/October 1994

The Hite Report on the Family: Growing Up Under Patriarchy—the latest book by groundbreaking researcher Shere Hite—could be a major contribution to the U.S.'s ongoing debate over high divorce rates and "family values." Unfortunately, you cannot get a copy of this book in the U.S., although it has already been published to favorable reviews in Australia, Canada, Great Britain and the Netherlands. The fact that this work, by an author that has sold millions of books over the last two decades, is being withheld by the U.S. publisher suggests that the backlash against feminism is far from over.

Phyllis Chesler, Naomi Weisstein, Jessie Lernisch, Barbara Seaman, Barbara Ehrenreich, Kate Millett, Ruby Rohrlich, Andrea Dworkin, Gloria Steinem, Susan Faludi, Stephen J. Gould the mother and father are not biologically related, of course) with the father as the head, trains the children psychologically to keep on repeating the cycle of putting men on top in society and family, no matter what. The authority of the biological parents, without the children having any options for leaving and living in a group home or going to other relatives, ingrains in them, and all of us, a tendency to not ever question authority or power, but rather always to feel that we should "make our peace with the powers that be," understand "you can't fight city hall," and so on. Yet we expect these same children-citizens to think independently and indeed to question those in power at every election. Thus the traditional authoritarian, or hierarchical, family system is not good for, or compatible with, democracy. We are creating "human nature" in the family as we have structured it; if we change and diversify—democratize—the family, we will change human nature.

NOTE

1. Rhonda Gottlieb, "The Political Economy of Sexuality" in *Review of Radical Political Economics* 16(1): 143-65.

WORKS BY SHERE HITE

The Hite Report on Female Sexuality. Macmillian, 1976.
The Hite Report on Men and Male Sexuality. Knopf, 1981, Ballantine, 1982.
Women and Love: A Cultural Revolution in Progress–The Hite Report. Knopf, 1987.
Women as Revolutionary Agents of Change: The Hite Reports and Beyond. Bloomsbury, 1993, University of Wisconsin Press, 1994.
The Divine Comedy of Ariadne and Jupiter: The Spectacular Adventures of Ariadne and Her Dog Jupiter in Heaven and Earth. Ullstein, 1993, Peter Owen, Ltd., 1994.
The Hite Report on the Family: Growing Up Under Patriarchy. Bloomsbury, 1994, Grove-Atlantic Books, 1995.

Feminism:
Crying for Our Souls

bell hooks

Contemporary feminist movement moreso than any other liberation movement in the United States radicalized the notion of mental
health. Among black women Sister Toni Cade Bambara was one of
the first to tell the world at a time when black liberation and women's
liberation were hot, that revolution begins with the self. In the self,
the individual is the basic revolutionary unit. She must be purged of
poison and lies that assault the ego and threaten the heart. That
hazards the next larger unit–the family or cell. That puts the entire
movement at peril. Feminist understanding that women would need
to heal from the psychological wounds inflicted by sexism and sexist
oppression created a cultural revolution. It does not matter that the
energy for self-help and self-recovery generated by feminist movement was appropriated in the most offensive ways by a whole genre
of self-help books by women for women that devalue us and pretend

bell hooks is the author of numerous books, including *Ain't I a Woman: Black
Women and Feminism* (1981), *Black Looks: Race and Representation* (1992),
Breaking Bread: Insurgent Black Intellectual (1991), *Feminist Theory From Mar-
gin to Center* (1984), *Sisters of the Yam: Black Women and Self-Recovery* (1993),
Talking Back: Thinking Feminism, Thinking Black (1989), and *Yearning: Race,
Gender and Cultural Politics* (1990), all by South End Press.
Correspondence may be addressed to bell hooks at 291 W. 12th Street, Apt. 4,
New York, NY 10014.

[Haworth co-indexing entry note]: "Feminism: Crying for Our Souls." hooks, bell. Co-published
simultaneously in *Women & Therapy* (The Haworth Press, Inc.) Vol. 17, No. 1/2, 1995, pp. 265-271;
and: *Feminist Foremothers in Women's Studies, Psychology, and Mental Health* (ed: Phyllis Chesler,
Esther D. Rothblum, and Ellen Cole) The Haworth Press, Inc., 1995, pp. 265-271; and: *Feminist
Foremothers in Women's Studies, Psychology, and Mental Health* (ed: Phyllis Chesler, Esther D. Rothblum, and Ellen Cole) Harrington Park Press, an imprint of The Haworth Press, Inc., 1995, pp. 265-271.
Single or multiple copies of this article are available from The Haworth Document Delivery Service
[1-800-342-9678, 9:00 a.m. - 5:00 p.m. (EST)].

we will be satisfied by just getting healthy so we can serve the patriarchy better. What these books did for me (everybody read them) was show me that if feminist movement really wanted to have an impact on the masses of women and men in this society we would have to take the issue of mental health seriously and create therapeutic strategies for change that would merge feminist political thought with movements for self-recovery. This led me to write *Sisters of the Yam: Black Women and Self-Recovery.*

It had become more than evident that individual black females suffering psychologically were not prepared to go out and lead the feminist revolution. Even before we could begin to talk about revolution we had to share with women the power and pleasure of studying and learning feminist thought. We had to educate for critical consciousness in ways that would enable women and men to see that patriarchy promotes pathological behavior in both genders and that our wounded psyches had to be attended to not as a secondary aspect of revolutionary struggle but as a central starting point. Those of us engaged in feminist therapy as practitioners and/or clients know that when women are in pain it is not difficult to convince us to seek healing. The difficulty comes when the pain–the disease–has been thoroughly diagnosed and the individual resolutely refuses to engage the practice of healing, that is to say, to take concrete steps in their daily life to be well. There is no doubt in my mind that feminist movement has successfully brought home to every American female some understanding of sexism, of sexist exploitation, and oppression. I make a distinction between sexism that is about the basic notion that males and females differ and must be treated differently (for example: that men should open doors for women, etc.) and sexist exploitation and oppression which presume that gender differences justify coercive male domination of women by men, using any means necessary whether it be economic subordination–paying us less–denying us access to jobs or via sanctioned regimes of male violence (i.e., domestic violence, rape, sexual harassment, etc.). Unfortunately, many women and men feel that they can live quite happily with gender discrimination.

Working with women, especially black women, I have found that many of us are willing to acknowledge the evils of sexism, the way it wounds and hurts everyone, but are reluctant to make that conversion to feminist thinking that would require substantive changes in habits of being. This is the dilemma of feminist movement in the United States right now. More women and men than ever before are concerned about sexism, yet most of us remain unwilling to link that concern with a concrete political practice that would change ourselves, our families and communities, and this society.

While therapy has become a widely accepted way to confront problems and seek healing, feminist therapy has not become an accepted norm. Indeed, the false assumption that any professional woman who has made it in a man's world must be feminist, so popular in the public imagination right now, means that many women seek help without even considering the gender politics of their therapist. For example: A few years ago one of my sisters, married, not working, began to experience extreme agoraphobia as well as unhappiness in her marriage. Against the will of both her husband and parents she sought therapeutic help. Initially, she saw women practitioners. All the strategies for change they offered her were based on the assumption that she was the problem and that by simply conforming more to the status quo and changing her behavior she could resolve her dilemmas. It was only when, quite by accident, she went to see a progressive black male therapist that she was able to confront the link between sexism and the difficulties she was facing at home. With the help of this caring therapist she was able to resist domination in the domestic household in useful ways, to finish college, and overcome her fear of open spaces. Yet when he suggested to her that she might one day need to leave this relationship to continue growing towards self-actualization, she stopped seeing him. In time, most of the problems in this marriage worsened and she began to lose touch with the awakening feminist consciousness that was providing her with a way to understand the power dynamics in their domestic household. Observing her experience, I begin to see the enormous difficulty women face trying to transform their sexism within the context of the patriarchal family. Even if they succeed as an individual it only makes them desperately unhappy since it puts them at odds with everything that is familiar to them.

Future feminist movement has to evolve in ways that allow us to create constructive strategies for feminist change which concretely intervene on the circumstances in individual lives. Too many women feel that they cannot simply give up everything familiar and lead the "feminist" lifestyle. One of those undermining aspects of contemporary feminism has been the shift away from political action to lifestyles. Certainly feminist therapy should be a place where individuals, female and male, can discover what is needed to transform their lives.

So many individuals used feminist movement as a catalyst to change their lifestyle (and in some cases that did mean moving away from sexist men) without remaining committed to a political struggle to end sexism. Liberal individualism seemed to preclude a sense of accountability to a world beyond the privatized self. Instead of feeling that it was important to stay engaged in a larger feminist movement, many feminist women simply used appropriated opportunities created by feminist interventions. This seemed to me directly related to issues of mental health, particularly self-esteem and the capacity to be fully self-actualized. It occurred to me that feminist therapy might have an enormous role to play in providing women and men with ongoing strategies for coping with conversion to feminist politics. Those of us committed to feminist therapy know that when we begin to live our lives against the grain of the culture, we can begin to feel isolated, alone in struggle. At times that isolation can lead to depression or even the feeling of being crazy.

I saw this with my sister. On the one hand she was willing to engage in feminist thinking. She raised her consciousness but then felt she was left empty-handed without concrete strategies for coping, for sharing her newfound awareness and habits of being in a domestic household where neither her husband nor her children wanted to welcome them. There is a particular psychic pain women feel when they begin to learn feminist thinking but are unable to translate what they are learning to "real" life.

Seeing again and again these gaps in feminist theory pushed me to consider writing more about mental health. While feminist thinking has benefitted in some ways from academicization, the push to create feminist theory that will be legitimized within patriarchal institutions really took the focus away from building mass-based feminist movement, from the need to invent strategies for change that would address everyone.

Masses of women and men will never convert to feminist thinking unless they can see ways that the practice of feminism positively transforms lives. Those of us who long ago converted to feminist thinking know that initially it may not feel as though it is making life better. For a time this process of change and transition may lead to extreme feelings of alienation and unresolved woundedness. During this period of transition from allegiance to sexism and the patriarchal, individuals often need support and guidance. It concerned me that so many feminists were smug and content about the way feminism had positively changed their lives and to some extent felt themselves to be a better class of people than the unenlightened. To these folks, feminist resources (and that includes feminist strategies for improving mental health) were to be hoarded and not shared. I did not want to become a self-indulgent feminist, pleased about all the wonderful changes feminist thinking and practice had brought into my life and not caring that so many black women and men were still not taking the struggle to end sexism seriously.

Writing a self-help book was one of the ways I hoped to bridge this gap–to share. By writing *Sisters of the Yam: Black Women and Self-Recovery,* I was able to share the positive power of feminist thinking and practice–of feminist politics. Through my testimony and that of other women I could talk about the ways it improves the quality of our lives. Having written six other books that were aimed at academic audiences as well as the feminist reading public, I was challenged by the desire to write a book that would really seek to reach black women in all walks of life. Although I wanted to keep the language simple and clear, I wanted the ideas to be complex, to challenge in a caring way, to make the readers stretch their minds.

In my life, from the time I was seventeen until the present day, I have always used therapy as a way to assist me in my struggle to be self-actualized. Over the years, I found that self-help was often more therapeutic for me than the time I spent in offices with therapists. Often the books focused more on concrete change rather than simply learning new and different ways to describe or understand dilemmas intellectually. As an avid reader of self-help books and working in the academy, I was often stunned by the extent to which my peers and colleagues held such literature in contempt, seeing it as really useless. I remember when I first began to say to colleagues

that I really–really–wanted to write a self-help book, I was subjected to laughter and ridicule. I persevered because I knew from
my experience that choosing to work on self-actualization either in
the therapist/client setting or with self-help books could be a space
of healing. *Sisters of the Yam: Black Women and Self-Recovery* and
other self-help books are not a substitute for seeing a therapist.
When they are used in a constructive way, they empower women
and men so that they have the capacity to know whether or not their
mental health needs could best be met in a therapeutic setting.

Progressive self-help books that centralize the issues and concerns of people of color are especially useful in breaking down the
barriers many of us feel in relation to caring for mental health. I
discussed *Sisters of the Yam* at the Studio Museum of Harlem.
During the dialogue individual black women in the audience gave
personal testimony about the way in which this book had helped
them in times of dire psychological crisis. One woman courageous-
ly confessed that she had been so deeply troubled that she tried to
share her sense of anguish with friends and family who primarily
encouraged her to seek healing through prayer, through giving her
troubles over to a Higher Power. No one wanted to hear her say that
this was not working for her. When she broached the subject of the
therapy she received no support. Someone she knew shared their
copy of *Sisters of the Yam*. It validated her experiences, affirmed her
need to receive care, and gave her a sense of where to start. When I
hear testimony like hers, usually in letters, I feel so blessed because
it affirms to me that we can as feminist thinkers share the resources
that empower us to be healthy–to be well in our souls.

The dialogue this book opens up between me and women of all
races (but especially black women) breaks through any isolation I
might feel and restores my sense of community and possibility. It
gives me hope for the future. The past twenty years of my conscious
commitment to feminist thinking and practice have shown me that
so many women and men feel so wounded about the issue of gender. When feminist thinking, via critical interventions into mental
health care, addresses that pain the possibility for transforming this
society so that sexism and sexist exploitation and oppression are
eradicated is strengthened.

Many black males have written to me expressing that they found comfort and solace in reading *Sisters of the Yam* and they want to know why there are not more books of this nature written for black males. I encourage them to be the writers of such books because they have already shown both interest in and commitment to self-recovery. So many of the relatively few self-help books that address black men and women are not written from a progressive perspective on gender. Usually, they advocate systems of benevolent patriarchy, encourage black folks to assume traditional sexist roles with a spirit of respect and kindness. Yet when relationships between black males and females (whether parents, siblings, lovers, or spouses) are already troubled by issues of gender domination and struggle for power, they cannot be healed by the reinforcement of patriarchal thinking.

Today many more black females and males are thinking seriously about sexism, about ending abuse in domestic households, about adult domination and violence towards children. My work has helped to educate for critical consciousness. It continues to grow and change as I evolve spiritually–emotionally. Oftentimes I express this conviction that mental health must be one of the new fronts of our revolutionary struggle. We must acknowledge that all systems of domination–racism, class elitism, sexism, imperialism–wound the spirit. Damaged spirits rarely choose liberation. When I first heard the Brazilian educator Paulo Freire declare "we cannot enter the struggle as objects in order later to become subjects," I realized that to be subjects we must pay attention to self-actualization. We must be able to use our imaginations to create self against the borders of the imposter identity forced onto us by those who would keep us in a state of subjugation and dehumanization. Any liberation struggle to end domination is fundamentally about a revolution in mental health. Feminist thinkers remain a vanguard among those visionary souls who not only recognize this truth but offer it as necessary bread that we may break and carry together. This vision of sweet communion calls us to rejoice that we are making a world where all can be well with our souls. In the southern black church of my upbringing we would sing the lyrics: "Is it well with your soul? Are you free–free and made whole?" As we care for the soul, we create the cultural context for transformation of self and society.

Progress Notes

Ellyn Kaschak

I was the kind of child who was always in trouble. I was said to be "out of control" by the adults who were designated by society to control me. I talked too much and laughed too much at school and saw too much everywhere I went, especially for a girl. Paradoxically, this was called "not paying attention" and I was always in trouble for not paying attention. Although I had many friends and many adventures, I was considered a socialization failure. Measured against the standard of consciousness-lowering that society and most adults call socialization, I was one.

I was a child who found friends not only in the streets and the schools of a long-gone Brooklyn of the 1940s and 1950s, but in the libraries and corner candy stores that offered up all imaginable forms of fiction and fantasy from Russian drama to comic books. I owe whatever I have become as an adult woman as much to books

Ellyn Kaschak, PhD, is Professor of Psychology at San Jose State University, Fellow of Divisions 35, 12 and 45 of the APA and winner of the Distinguished Publication Award of the Association for Women in Psychology for *Engendered Lives: A New Psychology of Women's Experience*. She has been the Chair of The Feminist Therapy Institute and the Committee on Women in Psychology of the American Psychological Association and is a co-founder of the Institute for Feminist Training.

Correspondence may be addressed to Ellyn Kaschak at the Psychology Department, San Jose State University, San Jose, CA 95192.

[Haworth co-indexing entry note]: "Progress Notes." Kaschak, Ellyn. Co-published simultaneously in *Women & Therapy* (The Haworth Press, Inc.) Vol. 17, No. 1/2, 1995, pp. 273-282; and: *Feminist Foremothers in Women's Studies, Psychology, and Mental Health* (ed: Phyllis Chesler, Esther D. Rothblum, and Ellen Cole) The Haworth Press, Inc., 1995, pp. 273-282; and: *Feminist Foremothers in Women's Studies, Psychology, and Mental Health* (ed: Phyllis Chesler, Esther D. Rothblum, and Ellen Cole) Harrington Park Press, an imprint of The Haworth Press, Inc., 1995, pp. 273-282. Single or multiple copies of this article are available from The Haworth Document Delivery Service [1-800-342-9678, 9:00 a.m. - 5:00 p.m. (EST)].

273

as to my friends and comrades, as much to the childhood hours spent with Little Lulu, that intrepid adventurer and storyteller who would not take "no" for an answer, would not respect that the clubhouse was for boys only, as to the most complex epistemological analysis. As much to Dr. Doolittle as to Dr. Freud, to *The Secret Garden* as to Dostoevsky. To the reading that I was repeatedly admonished would "ruin" my eyes. True enough, my eyes were ruined. I was early on, a socialization failure with ruined eyes that saw too much of what I was not supposed to see. I was destined to become a feminist.

In *Engendered Lives,* I wrote of the importance of being aware, as a clinical psychologist, that each woman's story is uniquely her own and, as a feminist, that no woman's story is just her own. So is my own both unique and inseparable from the many feminist women of my generation. Mine is the story of being, at the same time, academic and activist, clinician and researcher, writer and speaker, mainstream psychologist and contrarian. It transcends the dichotomies and disciplines that men have devised to create borders in their lives. Women's lives have never fit neatly into men's categories and so is mine not a neat story either, but one of a woman, a feminist, a psychologist. It is not just about having a full feminist psychotherapy practice, but also about the fullness and dailiness of the practice of feminism. And for me it has been a daily practice, a way of living and understanding each moment, each woman as fully as possible. A way of paying attention to what I was never supposed to notice.

As difficult as it is to sum up a life in just a few pages, I can at least make a beginning, for now we have some of the words we need. I began as a feminist before we had words. Words like sexual abuse or molestation or battering. Before we had shelters or our own conferences or our own therapy. We were the first to speak them, to name our own experience and then to insist upon it. The world changed every time we spoke those words aloud.

How could it have been possible that we could not speak of and did not know our own experience? Hadn't we been paying attention? Those of us who were students or professionals looked to our fields, our disciplines for the answers to these questions. We not only did not find the answers in psychology or literature, sociology or biology, but we did not even find women's questions. Instead we found the ways that men understood women to be. We found penis envy; we found mothers who caused schizophrenia, autism, homosexuality and generally bad attitudes in the rest of the family members. We found analyses of women's desire to be raped and the seductiveness of little girls, which caused their fathers to molest them. We found violence against women in the very systems that were supposed to treat them.

And we all too often found expressions of anger and ridicule when we tried to bring these issues to the attention of our professors, male colleagues or administrators. For example, in the graduate program in which I was enrolled, the women students wrote a petition requesting a seminar on the psychology of women. This was a graduate program that emphasized individual initiative, creativity and innovation and was designed so that each student could develop her or his own program of study. The class was to be self-directed as a study group and would cost them nothing–financially, that is. In 1970, there was no one qualified to teach a course on the psychology of half the world.

What did these faculty members do with this petition from their female students? They corrected the grammar and spelling and returned it to us. We were stunned, as we had innocently expected a positive and enthusiastic response. Yet they had understood more of what we were asking for than we had. We were their students and they had taught us an important lesson, a life altering lesson at that, for we had begun to understand what lay ahead of us and how this struggle was going to disrupt any sense of trust or order that had gone before. We would change a lot more than the grammar before we were done.

The second wave of feminism found me in Ohio and washed me up in the San Francisco of 1971. Revolution was in the air, on the streets and in the homes, in the bookstores and the cafes. It was also in the psychotherapy offices, and the critique, the possibility of remaking psychotherapy, caught my imagination just as it caught the imagination of many other women of my generation. I was in San Francisco as an intern at the Palo Alto Veterans Administration hospital, there to learn the application of the various systems of treatment that I had been studying. And there it was. Everything that was wrong with the institution. The institution of psychotherapy. The institution of the hospital, the clinic, the medicalization of human suffering. The personalization of the political. Some of us would dedicate our lives to reconnecting it to the political. Healing the real wounds. Patching up broken hearts.

Women and Madness was the first and best statement of the problem. It ignited a generation of feminist psychological thought. I became interested in psychotherapy in a completely new way. Before it had always seemed too small, too personal, too practical. It demanded much more patience than I could summon up. The politics of it, the theory, the epistemology is what captured my mind long before the work captured my heart. My interest was not in practicing the masculinist psychotherapies that they were teaching us in the hospital, but in questioning every detail, in dismantling and reinventing psychology and with it psychotherapy.

In 1972, after several long and intense meetings with a group of feminists, psychologists and social workers by training, several of us decided to form The Women's Counseling Service of San Francisco. Our discomfort, alienation and fragmentation finally had a name. So did the solution. We would develop and offer feminist therapy. We would dismantle the master's house and, while we were at it, his hospital and clinic, his well-appointed office where he practiced so privately. We would reinvent psychology and psychotherapy. A grand enough scheme. Yet we knew we were right and we knew we were not alone anymore.

So we did what was done in 1972. We printed up some notices and called a meeting. We rented a room at the local Unitarian Church and put up the notices on bulletin boards and telephone poles all over the city. On 24th Street where all day every day there was a line of people waiting for Bud's ice cream, on Sanchez and on Castro. Wherever there were women. What Is Feminist Therapy? Come find out. We prepared to speak to the 10 or 20 women that we expected. We decided to charge $2 apiece–enough to pay for the rental of the room and a pot of coffee for us to share.

7:30 P.M. A Tuesday night in August, 1972. At seven, we opened the door to some 200 women, eager–no, thrilled to be there. To witness the invention of a feminist therapy. The Women's Liberation Movement reinvents psychotherapy, it might have read, had we known, had there been a road map telling us where we were going. Yet we all did know it–in our bones and in our hearts. There was no map yet and we didn't need one. We knew where we were and where we were going. No map could have led us there. Only we could lead each other.

And so we did. The Women's Counseling Service. A few other groups, one in San Francisco, others in Boston and New York. It was the next thing to do. We used the money to buy an answering machine, one of the first–a big cumbersome wooden box with a reel-to-reel tape inside it that failed almost as often as it succeeded to record the calls that began to come in on a daily basis.

And that's how it began. Psychology intern by day, subversive by night. Isn't that the way of women? Women's ways of knowing.

The next year, in 1973, I taught the first formal class in feminist therapy at the University of California, Berkeley. Not the Psychology Department proper, for we were not proper, but the Extension Program tacked on for the stragglers, the academically marginal. We were, of course, in the margins, the subversion even in Berkeley.

There was enough to read, enough to say about feminist therapy in 1973 to fill ten weeks. Yet once the students began to speak, it became clear that ten weeks were just a beginning. Those students had their hearts in it, for they had had their hearts, but not their spirit, broken by psychotherapy. They wanted to tell of the horrors they had experienced in the name of psychological intervention. The consignment to a locked ward for disagreeing with a husband, who had only to find a doctor to agree with him and to sign the commitment papers. The shock therapy for having sought an abortion. The drugs to kill the memory of a husband's infidelity or to pave the way for its continuation. We could barely believe ourselves. No one else had.

In 1974, my dissertation completed, I received my Ph.D. Time to look for a "real" job, the academic job that I had prepared for all these years. A year when there were almost no jobs, when Ph.D.'s drove taxis, as they used to say then. Yet a position appeared at San Jose State University as if someone had written it just for me. Half time teaching Marriage and Family Therapy and the other half in activist-oriented Community Psychology. Community in San Jose in 1974 meant Chicana(o)/Latino(a), and as the result of my years in Costa Rica, my fluency in Spanish served me well.

Having satisfied themselves as to my academic credentials, the San Jose faculty arranged for me to be interviewed by members of the community with whom I would be working. Could I work with them, among them? This time my irreverence and political analysis served me. They were as suspicious of academia as I was. We spoke a common language, the language of outsiders. We tried to decode their language. "What are they up to?" "What is their real agenda?" We worked hard to decode each other's also. The questions from the margins. "What is really going on here?" It is never what it seems. Never "Is there danger?" but "Where is the danger to us hidden and how can we subvert it?" Those of us assigned to the subversion come by our questions honestly. We are natural subversives.

Yet the dangers for them and for me were very different. After the interview, after expressing their opinions, the community members all returned to their communities. This community of white male academic psychologists would become mine, but I would never be theirs.

The judgment of the community members differed from that of my colleagues, who would repeatedly question my collegiality over the years to come. This would be used in countless university departments across the country as a justification to deny tenure and promotion to women. It would become the focus of grievance procedures. "She's just not one of the boys." Of course, it would not be said straight out like that, but in code. It was my problem from the beginning. There were two ways to play it and I refused them both. I was not one of the boys or one of the girls. I was still a socialization failure.

Yet I did play in my own way. I published and I taught and I spoke, but it was all about feminist critique or feminist theory or feminist therapy. In 1976, my first publication on feminist therapy in a mainstream journal was published: *Sociotherapy: An ecological model for psychotherapy with women.* Many more articles, chapters and conference presentations were to follow. I would serve on local and national committees and eventually on international ones. I would serve as Chair of the APA Committee on Women in

Psychology and as national Chair of the Feminist Therapy Institute. I became one of a new and instantly anomalous breed, a radical feminist in a mainstream academic institution.

In the twenty years that I have now been at San Jose State University, I have been a professor, chaired a graduate program in Marriage and Family Therapy, directed a university family counseling clinic and trained a generation or two of therapists. During many of those years, I did not discuss feminism with my students. This is one of the odd strategies of a radical feminist psychologist in a mainstream institution–particularly during the decade of the 1980s. In fact, when *Engendered Lives* was published in 1992, many of the therapists I had trained commented, "I had no idea that we were learning feminist therapy. I thought it was just good therapy." Exactly.

My professional and personal lives have, for more than twenty-five years, spanned two continents and two San Joses, the other the capital of Costa Rica, where I have also taught, written, conducted feminist research and trained family therapists in feminist approaches. In the 1960s, when I first visited Costa Rica, I knew neither the culture nor the language. I was repeatedly admonished, as a woman, never to leave the house unless in the company of a male or I would be both ridiculed and endangered. Any male would do and, for the occasion and despite my many protests, I was provided with a 16-year-old boy to escort me. Over the years, I have made many more trips to this country and have both viewed and been involved in the advent of feminism and the development of a culturally-based feminist psychology. As I became fluent in the language and at home in the culture, I became involved in conducting cross-cultural research and clinical training. With Costa Rican colleagues, I developed the Spanish language Latin American Sex Role Inventory. By 1987, a colleague and I were able to introduce the first postgraduate course in feminist family therapy and in 1989, I was invited to deliver a public address on feminist psychology and epistemology sponsored by the University of Costa Rica to the–by now–significant feminist community. In 1993, I participated in an international feminist conference which included a march and demonstration supporting the rights of women in Costa Rica and globally. We marched from the university to the center of San Jose, thousands of women unescorted by even one male, although there were some in the local crowds that cheered us on. I marched, accompanied by both North American and Costa Rican female comrades, in that very city in which I could not walk down the street in earlier years without the protection and legitimization of a male.

I have also spoken and conducted training in feminist psychology in Europe, South America, Mexico, Canada and Asia and found eager and enthusiastic students and colleagues in all these places. I was never alone. My collegiality was never among the important questions, never questioned at all. I know because I was paying attention.

In all my travels and cross-cultural studies, I have been interested in the ordinary and the quotidian, in the lives of women, in the embeddedness of gender in every moment in every culture. My work, if it is anything, is a psychology of the ordinary. The question of *Engendered Lives* is not "What happens when things go wrong?"–but "What happens when things go right?" Our psychology begins with our own questions. In the right to ask the questions and to have one's questions matter lies the first moment of real power. Our theories and our practice depend entirely upon who asks the questions, for our questions come from ourselves and lead right back there. Our lives are determined first by epistemology and only after that by the answers, the political and psychological justifications for the laws, the wars and the acts that control our societies and individuals. My work and our work has been to Take Back The Questions.

As a feminist psychologist and psychotherapist, I have traveled on many roads without a map and been a guide on other people's journeys. As a visitor from another psyche, from inner space, I have been able to use the dual perspective of insider and outsider, mainstream professor and contrarian. I have been fortunate enough to be part of a generation of feminists, so that my adventures have not been lonely, but filled with the richness of ideas, of passion, of students and clients, of colleagues and comrades. We practice a psychology that is not the same as we found it.

And yet . . . On an ordinary day in San Jose, California, one of my most promising students comes to class very agitated. She speaks faster and faster about finally understanding what it means for her to be Asian and to be a woman. She interrupts when anyone else talks. She has to speak, has to be heard. She cannot stop herself. She doesn't try to and neither do I. Not fully realizing the literalness of it, I let her go. And she does go. Frightened, her family places her in captivity. The institution that we should have dismantled is still in place. Her problem is judged to be a medical one and they medicate her. The smallest solution of all. In the name of help, she should be sedated. Somehow make her as sedate as she used to be.

Later that week, from the pay telephone on the locked ward, she calls me to say, in a voice so rapid that it pulls her thoughts along behind it, "You know what happened. I read your book and something clicked inside me. And as soon as it clicked, it snapped. Now I need your help so that everything I understand won't drive me crazy."

I've seen it too many times by now, a woman trying to run faster than the speed of sorrow. We have the words to speak to each other now, but often what we have to say with those words is still unbearable. We are paying careful attention, but what we see not only ruins our eyes, it can break our hearts.

Yes, we have the words to speak to each other now. Yet completing a draft of this paper, I absentmindedly access the spelling check program on my computer and it stops immediately at the word "foremother"—and changes it to "forefather." There is no such word as "foremother." Again, there is no word for us and again we will prove them wrong, for here we are, still inventing the words to speak of ourselves and to ourselves.

SELECTED BIBLIOGRAPHY
OF MOST RELEVANT PUBLICATIONS

Kaschak, E. *Engendered Lives: A New Psychology of Women's Experience,* Basic Books, 1992.

Kaschak, E. How to fail as a family therapist: A feminist analysis. *Feminist Ethics in Psychotherapy,* Springer, 1990.

Kaschak, E. The reciprocal relationship between limits and boundaries: toward a complex psychology of women. *Women & Therapy,* Winter 1989.

Kaschak, E., & Sharratt, S. Gender roles in Costa Rica: the effect of the presence of males or females. *Interamerican Journal of Psychology,* 22:1 and 2, 1988, 67-74.

Kaschak, E. Integrating information about the Psychology of Women into the curriculum. The case for clinical psychology. In Denmark, F. L. (Ed.), *Social/ Ecological Psychology and the Psychology of Women*. North-Holland, 1985, 379-386.

Kaschak, E., & Sharratt, S. El sexo en Latinoamerica, *Revista Nacional de la Nacion*, August 1985.

Kaschak, E., & Sharratt, S. A Latin American Sex Role Inventory. *Cross-Cultural Psychology Bulletin,* February 1985.

Kaschak. E. Psychotherapy and women. In Kimball, G. (Ed.), *From The Right Hemisphere*. Scarecrow Press, 1982.

Kaschak, E. Feminist therapy: The first decade. In Cox, S. (Ed.), *Female Psychology, The Emerging Self.* New York: St. Martins Press, 1981.

Kaschak, E. Another look at sex bias in students' evaluations of professors: Do winners get the recognition that they have been given? *Psychology of Women Quarterly,* Summer, 1981.

Kaschak, E., & Sharratt, S. Sex roles and androgyny in Latin America: A psychological perspective. *Reportorio Americano,* Spring, 1979.

Kaschak, E. Role playing "reality": A technique for training family therapists. *Marriage and Family Counselor's Quarterly,* Spring, 1978, 2:3.

Kaschak, E. Therapists and their clients: Clients and their therapists: Two views of the process and outcome of psychotherapy. *Professional Psychology,* Spring, 1978.

Kaschak, E. Sex bias in students' evaluations of professors' teaching methods. *Psychology of Women Quarterly,* 1978, 3:3, 135-143.

Kaschak, E. Sexist ratings. *Human Behavior,* November 1976, 50-51.

Kaschak, E. Sociotherapy: An ecological model for psychotherapy with women. *Psychotherapy: Theory, Research and Practice,* Spring, 1976, 61-63.

Logan, D. D., & Kaschak, E. Sex roles and mental health. *Psychology of Women Quarterly,* Spring, 1980.

Working with Feminist Foremothers
to Advance Women's Issues

Gwendolyn P. Keita
Adele Jones

Gwendolyn Puryear Keita, PhD, is Director of the Women's Programs Office and Associate Executive Director of the Public Interest Directorate of the American Psychological Association. As Director of the Women's Programs Office, she encourages the generation, dissemination and application of psychological knowledge on issues of importance to women, promotes the equitable and just treatment of women through the science and practice of psychology, and monitors and develops strategies to assure representation of women within APA and the profession. Dr. Keita also coordinates the activities of the Committee on Women in Psychology. Dr. Keita has written extensively and given numerous presentations on issues ranging from women and depression, violence against women, women's health, mental health issues affecting women and ethnic minorities, and occupational stress and workplace wellness. Dr. Keita has testified before government officials and Congress on issues of women and depression, women's health, violence against women and occupational stress. She has convened two national conferences of occupational stress and workplace wellness and the first major conference addressing psychosocial and behavioral factors in women's health. Prior to joining the staff of APA, Dr. Keita was Assistant Director of the Howard University Counseling Service in Washington, DC. She holds a PhD in Personality and Social Psychology from Howard University and has completed coursework for a postdoctoral degree in Clinical Psychology at George Washington University, Washington, DC.

Adele Jones, an Asian-American feminist, is currently a graduate student in Clinical Psychology at the University of Vermont. She hopes to practice feminist therapy with the broad spectrum of women's issues.

Correspondence may be addressed to Gwendolyn P. Keita, American Psychological Association, Women's Programs Office, 750 First Street NE, Washington, DC 20002-4242.

[Haworth co-indexing entry note]: "Working with Feminist Foremothers to Advance Women's Issues." Keita, Gwendolyn P., and Adele Jones. Co-published simultaneously in *Women & Therapy* (The Haworth Press, Inc.) Vol. 17, No. 3/4, 1995, pp. 283-290; and: *Feminist Foremothers in Women's Studies, Psychology, and Mental Health* (ed: Phyllis Chesler, Esther D. Rothblum, and Ellen Cole) The Haworth Press, Inc., 1995, pp. 283-290; and: *Feminist Foremothers in Women's Studies, Psychology, and Mental Health* (ed: Phyllis Chesler, Esther D. Rothblum, and Ellen Cole) Harrington Park Press, an imprint of The Haworth Press, Inc., 1995, pp. 283-290. Single or multiple copies of this article are available from The Haworth Document Delivery Service [1-800-342-9678, 9:00 a.m. - 5:00 p.m. (EST)].

Gwendolyn Puryear Keita, the current Director of the Women's Programs Office and Associate Executive Director of the Public Interest Directorate at the American Psychological Association, was born July 28, 1948. Her early years were spent between South Carolina and New York, growing up in an all-female household which included her mother, aunt, grandmother, and cousin. With both mother and aunt divorced, and grandmother widowed, Gwen grew up believing that women can do anything they want to do, and that they have to be able to take care of themselves. She also grew up with a high regard for education. "Many of the feminist issues, of independence and equality, are old hat for me. I grew up living them. There was always the feeling that everybody should be treated equally and that women could do most anything. This wasn't about being feminist, but about being Black and poor. My family had to work to make ends meet and we all learned everything we could to save money."

In 1966 Gwen enrolled at Bennett College, obtaining a degree in psychology in 1970. Her graduate work was done at Howard University where she earned a doctoral degree in personality/social psychology in 1978. Additionally she completed training at the Washington School of Psychiatry in group processes and psychotherapy, and coursework for a postdoctoral degree in clinical psychology at George Washington University. Before coming to the APA, Gwen spent 13 years at the Counseling Service at Howard University where she was the Assistant Director for Research and Institutional Testing. Additionally she was one of the original members of the first Task Force on Black Women in Psychology. This was later to become the section on Psychology of Black Women, Division 35, and Gwen was later to become President.

My major function at the APA, and primary contribution to feminism, has been as one of organizer and facilitator–pulling together, and working with, groups of women on major projects of importance to women psychologists and women consumers of psychological services. The topics I have covered include violence against women, women and depression, psychosocial and behavioral factors in women's health, and the effects of work stress and the work family interface on women's physical and mental health. Although my particular focus has been on African-American women, I have always been concerned about African-American women and men, and about the status of all women.

In an office where I am responsible for all issues dealing with women I obviously cannot focus only on those pertinent to African-American women. However, it remains a large part of what I do within many of the topic areas in which I work. For example, on a recent violence against women project, I was a key contributor on describing violence against ethnic minority women.

I originally entered the field of psychology because I fell in love with social psychology and felt that I could have an impact on society through social research. I was attracted to action research as a forum where one thought of ways to change attitudes and behaviors and then put the ways to work. I grew up nurtured by my community in South Carolina, and there learned a clear lesson that you have to give something back. This developed, for me, into a commitment to giving back, and a concern about moving African-American people forward.

While in graduate school I worked with Dr. Martha Mednick, who was my advisor and mentor, and got involved in the whole area of achievement motivation and feminist thought and scholarship. Dr. Mednick had a lot to do with some of my early thinking on those issues. Later, at the University Counseling Service, I was influenced by Dr. Carolyn Payton and became very interested in the whole issue of mental health. I became intrigued by what was known and not known about treating African-Americans.

I felt then, and still do feel, that psychology is important as a field to help African-American people. This is especially so because mental health issues such as low self-esteem play an important role in keeping African-Americans back. However, many minorities weren't taking advantage of mental health services for a number of reasons, including stigmatization and past negative experiences of their own or acquaintances. Moreover, many therapists, black and white, held biases against treating black clients or were inadequately trained to address their needs.

At Howard University we were doing so much good work with African-American clients while so many others were saying that this group would not come in for therapy. As psychologists, we needed to look at the context in which services were provided, and we needed to make African-American clinicians interested in doing research so that we could better understand the issues involved as well as effective treatments. For example, we found that group psychotherapy was a very effective treatment modality for African-American women and men.

I also did some of the early work on the connection between achievement and relationships in the lives of African-American women. For instance, for African-American women, fear of success was not as important an issue as it was for white women. African-American women saw work as an integral part of their role, moreover, many wanted less work responsibilities. They were very concerned about their relationship to African-American men and the effect of the recent stereotypes of black women as castrators of black men. Many psychologists didn't understand the importance to African-American women of these negative messages nor the impact these messages were having on the black family.

One of my main contributions to feminist health while at APA was my work with the Women and Depression Task Force, and the ensuing published report, *Women and Depression: Risk Factors and Treatment Issues*. The work accomplished by this task force did a great deal to help de-stigmatize psychotherapy and depression. The book (of which I am a co-editor), a mini-convention during the APA annual convention, the public lectures, and participation by members of the task force on television talk shows and radio programs all helped to get the word out to women that they were not alone, and that treatment did work. A major contribution of the Women and Depression Task Force Report was that it showed the connection between violence against women and depression. Although the task force was not the first to find it, that connection was very much ahead of its time, and changed a lot of people's thinking about the impact of violence in women's lives.

I also organized and was a member of the Male Violence Against Women Task Force; its report was published in July 1994. Based on that work, major testimony on the Violence Against Women Act was provided to members of Congress and to a number of individuals in states where legislation was pending. The major purpose of this report was to educate policy makers, psychologists, and other professionals about the prevalence of violence against women and its impact on mental and physical health. For example, the report highlights the fact that a number of women in mental institutions have been victims of child abuse, either physical or sexual, and many also are victims of domestic violence. Sexual harassment was also included as part of the focus of this task force since it is a part of the continuum of violence against women.

Aside from organizing women to work on issues of importance, another role I fulfill is as a resource to APA members and consumers. Often the Women's Programs Office does not do the original work but finds information and disseminates it to the public. I offer information directly to callers, can refer them to the experts in the different areas, and can bring together people who can provide testimony to Congress, federal agencies, and others who develop policy.

While for the most part it is psychologists and consumers who call, an important part of being a resource is also responding to the media. Many people will call to find out what psychologists are saying about current issues, and the Women's Programs Office makes sure that the feminist perspective is communicated. For instance, for many reasons, including the O.J. Simpson case, there is currently an emphasis on domestic violence. The Male Violence Against Women Task Force Report and task force members have readily-available information. Likewise, when Anita Hill's case contributed toward having sexual harassment in the news, one of the key witnesses on the scientific research about sexual harassment was a task force member. We didn't make the news, but we have the information to ensure that the psychological perspective is heard and that a feminist view is provided.

Not only is the Women's Programs Office asked to respond to current national issues, but it can have an influence on what is actually considered newsworthy. For instance, I believe that the Women and Depression Task Force Report had a major impact on the media attention given to depression and the positive slant toward treatment. The open discussion of the issues went a long way toward de-stigmatizing depression.

In addition to responding to the media, the Women's Programs Office also offers the psychological perspective in legal and public policy arenas. For example, while sexual harassment and violence against women in general are important on many levels, the Women's

Programs Office helps focus attention on how these issues are viewed from a psychological perspective. For instance, I organized psychologists to work with lawyers on a major brief in the last Supreme Court case of sexual harassment, Harris vs. Forklift, and much of what was said in that decision came directly from the APA brief, including the difference between how women and men view harassing situations. We have used psychological research to put things in context in ways that have made a difference for women.

Another area in which I have continued to work is with the Committee on Women in Psychology (CWP) and its focus on making sure that women are fully represented in the publication process to ensure that feminist thought and research are integrated into the publications. CWP has worked to increase the number of women reviewers and editors of journals and to increase attention to sexist language and its impact on women (a section on non-sexist language is in the APA Publications Manual). Prior to my coming to APA, some of these things were being addressed by CWP, but this is an issue of continuously raising awareness. For instance, we just looked at the fact that six new journal editors have been selected and none of them are women. Again, it is important to raise awareness that women are not represented, to try to identify the issues that continue to keep women from being fully represented as editors of journals, and to make sure that people know why it's important that there be representation. Many women say "I don't want to be a journal editor," but it is an important issue because for women in academia, number and placement of publications contribute a large part to promotion and tenure decisions. Having feminist women in publishing really does help give recognition to feminist issues. There was a time when women who published research on women's issues were told that their research was less scholarly and therefore their publications in these areas were devalued. Women still call and say this is happening and ask what they can do. Recognition of women is important. When an approach that devalues women's work is raised during tenure decisions, that is discrimination and we let people know that it is and provide information to combat this practice.

I find the APA, for the most part, committed to women and minorities. There is a recognition that diversity is important if we are to have a psychology and psychological training that are representative of all people. Without information on women and minorities in our books and training programs, psychologists would not be fully trained. As with any discipline, people really need to be pushed and monitored or they can easily revert to past bad habits. Many people say that psychology continues to be a sexist and racist field. In comparison to other fields, I think we do relatively well but we cannot rest because I think there has been some backsliding. The minute we think we are doing well and can rest is the minute we start sliding back down this slippery slope to disadvantage.

We currently have more women in the pipeline of psychology. Approximately 60% of people completing PhD programs are women and there are growing numbers of women APA members. However, I definitely don't think we have arrived. There are still too few women at the top, heading departments and agencies, editing journals, and determining policy.

More women need to be involved in leadership activities. We need to train and mentor younger women in leadership, as well as improve our own skills. As we begin to represent increased percentages of the field, we are going to need to work to make sure that the status of women and the status of the field continue to be high. Racism and sexism are very much alive and they are powerful influences, both subtle as well as direct.

Women have not consistently been in positions of power. However, there are a growing number of women who are interested in leadership so we are going to have increasing numbers of women in these positions.

Overall I enjoy my current position very much and I enjoy the opportunities I have had to be a mentor to a number of young people and to have an impact on people's lives. Basically I can't think of anything I'd rather be doing at this time in my life.

SELECTED BIBLIOGRAPHY

Puryear, G.R., & Mednick, M.T. (1974). Militancy, fear of success and affective attachment. *Journal of Consulting and Clinical Psychology, 42*, 263-266.
Mednick, M.T., & Puryear, G.R. (1975). Motivational and personality factors related to career goals of Black college women. *Journal of Social and Behavioral Sciences, 21*, 1-30.

Mednick, M.T., & Puryear, G.R. (1976). Race and fear of success in college women: 1968 and 1971. *Journal of Consulting and Clinical Psychology, 44*, 787-789.

Puryear, G.R. (1980). The Black American women: Liberated or oppressed? In B. Lindsey (Ed.), *Comparative perspectives on Third World women: Social, educational and economic patterns.* New York: Praeger.

Keita, G.P., VandenBos, G.R., Jones, J.M., & Granick, L.W. (1989). Forward. In C.I. Hall, B.J. Evans, & S. Selice (Eds.), *Black females in the United States: A bibliography from 1967 to 1987* (pp. vii-xi). Washington, D.C.: American Psychological Association.

Keita, G.P., & Muldrow, T. (1990). Carolyn Robertson Payton. In A.N. O'Connell & N.F. Russo (Eds.), *Women in psychology: A bio-bibliographic sourcebook.* New York: Greenwood.

Keita, G.P., & Jones, J.M. (1990). Reducing adverse reaction to stress in the workplace: Psychology's expanding role. *American Psychologist, 45*, 1137-1141.

McGrath, E., Keita, G.P., Strickland, B.R., & Russo, N.F. (1991). *Women and depression: Risk factors and treatment issues (Final report of the American Psychological Association's National Task Force on Women and Depression).* Washington, D.C.: American Psychological Association.

Keita, G.P., & Sauter, S.L. (1992). *Work and well-being: An agenda for the 1990's.* Washington, D.C.: American Psychological Association.

Goodman, L.A., Koss, M.P., Fitzgerald, L.F., Russo, N.F., & Keita, G.P. (1993). Male violence against women: Current research and future directions. *American Psychologist, 48*, 1054-1087.

Goodman, L.A., Koss, M.P., Fitzgerald, L.F., Russo, N.F., Keita, G.P., & Browne, A. (1994). *No safe haven: Male violence against women at home, at work and in the community.* Washington, D.C.: American Psychological Association.

Keita, G.P., & Hurrell, J. (1994). *Job stress in a changing workforce: Investigating gender, diversity and family.* Washington, D.C.: American Psychological Association.

Enlightened, Empowered
and Enjoying It!

Jane Knowles

I was born just after eight in the morning on the 30th of October 1949. The birth was traumatic, my mother being in an iron lung suffering from polio. My mother's illness was not the only trauma in the family. My brother of two years seniority had recently been diagnosed as having cerebral palsy as a reaction to a vaccination. A healthy young toddler, the brother I would never know had been cruelly transformed into a child who could not walk or talk, and needed help to eat or sit, the brother I was to know for nine years until his death.

My father, too, was far from healthy, being back from a Japanese prisoner of war camp only four years earlier. Our doctor of the time commented that my father seemed to be an unlucky man, an under-

Jane Knowles, MBBS, MRC Psych, is Consultant Psychotherapist and Medical Director to a National Health Service Trust in Berkshire, United Kingdom and an Associate of the Group Analytic Practice in London. She is a member of the Council of the Institute of Group Analysis and Treasurer to the Society for Psychotherapy Research (SPR) U.K. Dr. Knowles lectures and acts as a senior tutor to psychotherapy courses in Oxford and London. She is married with two adult sons, studying for a History of Art University Certificate, and interested in travel, tapestry and growing herbs.

Correspondence may be addressed to Jane Knowles at 7 Albert Road, Caversham, Berkshire RG4 7AN, United Kingdom.

[Haworth co-indexing entry note]: "Enlightened, Empowered and Enjoying It!" Knowles, Jane. Co-published simultaneously in *Women & Therapy* (The Haworth Press, Inc.) Vol. 17, No. 3/4, 1995, pp. 291-299; and: *Feminist Foremothers in Women's Studies, Psychology, and Mental Health* (ed: Phyllis Chesler, Esther D. Rothblum, and Ellen Cole) The Haworth Press, Inc., 1995, pp. 291-299; and: *Feminist Foremothers in Women's Studies, Psychology, and Mental Health* (ed: Phyllis Chesler, Esther D. Rothblum, and Ellen Cole) Harrington Park Press, an imprint of The Haworth Press, Inc., 1995, pp. 291-299. Single or multiple copies of this article are available from The Haworth Document Delivery Service [1-800-342-9678, 9:00 a.m. - 5:00 p.m. (EST)].

statement if ever there was one. In those days nobody knew about post traumatic stress disorder but that did not stop him experiencing the symptoms.

In retrospect I can see that many would consider this an inauspicious start to life and yet, perhaps strangely, I find myself feeling grateful. It allows me a resonance with the human condition which I have never found frightening, and now, thanks to years of training analysis both individually and in groups, I can feel to be creative and caring rather than painful. I suspect that all "natural" therapists come out of similarly pressurized molds, a career which fate chooses for you, a pathway which represents survival of the soul.

My early life is a mystery to me except for family mythology and dimly whispered memories. I was a quiet and undemanding child, who observed the world but at a distance. I can feel this reservation in me even today when most of my friends would think of me as wholeheartedly extrovert. That infant time has left me aware of the "aloneness" of life, an existential fact I knew too early for comfort. But, nonetheless it is part of what allows me to operate alone, to go out on philosophical limbs where wiser people fear to go and to stand against others when I believe them to be wrong. Alongside those brave moments I have also come to recognize a deep need for female closeness which has been magically met in its adult form by friendships with women that span generations, continents and cultures.

I was offered a model of adults who coped with whatever life threw at them by my parents. Although sometimes exasperated by the inappropriateness of their strength, I love and respect them for it, too. The more I trust in the power of psychotherapy to heal, the more I see its limitations, the more I realize we have to come to terms with who we are and not yearn for whom we might have wished to be. Accepting that for yourself means also accepting it for parents, children and friends. Acceptance need not mean collusion. I think that forgiveness grows when we cease to feel manipulated to collude on the one hand and yet accepting of each other's personal limitations on the other.

I am not sure when I first realized I was clever. I do remember feeling that it was a problem for a teenage girl to demonstrate any brains, however. Perhaps it was my sensitivity to this that ensured that I always went to girls' schools, ten in all as my father travelled in the British Army and I followed on. I rejected the idea of girls' boarding schools although it might have made education more easy. They concentrated on cookery and deportment and I knew, as young as eleven, that these were not things I wanted to learn. An inspirational headmistress once told me that men should be seen as hobbies and not full-time occupations. For a girl growing up surrounded by women who considered marriage and motherhood their full-time work this was little short of revolution. Being a female child in the Army was an uneasy experience. The war had not long been won and soldiers were still seen as divinely important. Returning from Malta in 1960, the men on one troop ship and the women and children on another, it was the one carrying me and my mother that got detoured out into mid-Atlantic to rescue a boy with appendicitis from a weather ship in a force nine gale: the men in the other ship were seen as too valuable to put at risk! This sort of experience left a deep well of anger at injustice in me. I am still fuelled by this at times, making me crash into "battle" against injustice when giving up or staying quiet would be the easier answer to hurdles and threats.

In the mid-60s I read Betty Friedan's book *The Feminine Mystique* and knew that across the Atlantic were women who were thinking as I was beginning to think. That knowledge was crucially sustaining throughout the long years of higher education. I entered the oldest medical school in the world in the Autumn of 1969. Barts has trained doctors since the twelfth century, on the same site in the City of London, next door to St Paul's Cathedral. I was in awe of all that had gone before me of which 99% was male. This made it hard to find a feminine identity within medicine, a task which took me almost twenty years before I felt completely comfortable.

Misogyny was in the very air we breathed. Only recently has it felt safe to talk over with women friends who were sister students just how hard those days were. On top of the normal harshness of long days, much study and no money, were the inevitable and endless jibes of sexism, the attacks verbal and physical and the sense of having to be something or someone else in order to "get through." I think the first real achievement of my adult life was to survive this, to have fun sometimes, and to emerge, not brainwashed, but strengthened. Helen Reddy's song "I am Woman" was, for me, an anthem, throughout the mid-70s to my survival and that of the women who shared the ordeal and are truly sisters.

During these years of my life I also began the struggle to make sense of my feminism on the one hand and my heterosexuality on the other. It was hard to find arenas in which to talk feminism when not only the men but also most of the women I knew wanted nothing to do with it. Books became an intellectual lifeline as I submerged into heterosexual relationships and at 22, marriage. As students in the same year, an early and in retrospect superficial equality was possible within the marriage but all that changed in the tidal wave of life events which surrounded my 25th birthday. We had our first child, a son, just eight weeks before we were both due to sit medical finals. We celebrated our qualification, the baby, Ben's, christening in St Paul's and my 25th birthday just a few weeks later. "A productive year" my parents wrote in their habitually understated fashion in their card to me.

To become either a mother or a doctor are major upheavals in both the inner and outer world. To do both at the same moment felt like a "make or break" situation. Given my background how could I do less than "make"? And so I went to work, with a nanny and Ben often accompanying me into the operating room or the ward, at all times of the day and night. Because it was so unusual I met delight, support, and encouragement from most of my colleagues, but hostility, even hate, from most of the women I socialized with. To be in a situation where I felt so different from other women was terribly painful. I still grieve when I hear the work vs. home arguments. Although Freud got many things wrong, I think he was right to say that mental health depended on adults knowing the glories of both love and work. To base many years of adulthood on only one side of that balance is, I think, to miss the point. What I learnt from these years was the skill of prioritizing, although for many years that skill only extended to a capacity to prioritize the needs of others. In recent years I have extended that skill to include my own needs, too.

I also learnt that it was possible to improve the environment in which women could make decisions about their careers and families, simply by being a model of the fact that my choice worked at least as well as anyone else's. Of course I labored under maternal guilt: would my children suffer from maternal deprivation in my absence? Now, with sons who are young men, who seem at least as stable as anyone else's, and who like and respect women as much as men, it is good to be able to be sure about the wisdom of my early choices. By the time my younger son, Sam, started school many of the women around me worked, too. Instead of feeling attacked for my choice I found myself consulted on how to manage the impossible balancing act. A change had happened in the mid-late 70s in British attitudes, it was a new beginning for any mother who wanted choice and I had the wonderful knowledge that I had been one of those on the first peak of that wave. It had been frightening and lonely at times but it had also been a liberation, a shaking off of what society had instructed me to think and do, an establishing of myself, my right to mother in a way that suited my children and myself. The greatest casualty was the marriage. In retrospect I cannot regret either going into it or coming out of it. And so, aged 29, I had an emerging career as a psychiatrist, two small sons and a large financial debt! In fact, although I did not realize this at the time, I had everything I needed to enable me to make the internal decision to succeed, to get to the top and change things from a position of power.

Within three years of starting my psychiatric and psychotherapeutic training, I was becoming known as a feminist. I tried hard to neither hide nor flaunt it but rather to weave it throughout my work. A male colleague once referred to me as the acceptable face of feminism and I have never been sure whether or not that is a compliment. I have always felt sensitive to a syndrome in which the men you work with pay lip service to feminism and women-at-work success stories but then go home and take out their backlash on the wife and daughters. The real problem with any form of backlash is that it hits out and hurts those still too weak to protect themselves from its fury. In promoting the rights of women I would hate to be the indirect cause of greater pain to any woman and yet I fear that it is impossible to progress without making some waves, taking some risks, including stirring up the opposition.

After a visit to the London Womens' Therapy Centre in 1981, I returned to Nottingham to start a Womens' Therapy Centre there. A small group of women gathered to work together, to develop skills and theory together, and to support each other at work and play. This group was one of three or four such groups in the Midlands and north of England which have since dispersed like fertile feminist therapy seeds across the country.

Having completed an individual therapy training I returned to the south of England, a consultant job in Berkshire and a second marriage. The fact that I was marrying a man eighteen years older, an African and a Muslim, made many of my feminist friends weep! None the less they came and danced at the wedding, as we have danced so many happy times since. One of the true advances of feminism since my mother's younger life has been a reestablishing of the right of women to have fun together without their menfolk. How good it always feels to be together. How much laughter and love women can generate. How lucky to be a part of this generation and enjoy it.

There had been no provision of psychotherapy within the National Health Service in Berkshire previously. A population of a million people only had access to private therapy and hundreds of patients, mostly women, had their distress diagnosed and treated with little regard for their real complaints, dilemmas and conflicts within the limitations of a much-stressed psychiatric service. My task was to establish and then run a high standard service, a service which could use feminist principles as its bedrock for women and men, on the sort of shoestring budget for which the NHS is famous.

Now, nine years later, I can look with pride on a service, still beleaguered by more demand than resource, but renowned for quality and caring. The service has treated more than 4,000 clients of whom 75% are women. These women come from all social groups, have widely various experiences of education, relationships, love or abuse. Some come in crisis, others from long-term needs and neglect. We try hard to meet each and every one on the same basis of personal respect, and egalitarianism between therapist and client. The supervision and training needs of the staff are a high priority, too. The need for social change as well as individual change is enshrined in our philosophy.

And, for me, a metamorphosis took place, initially stimulated by the need to write about my experience of motherhood and then sustained by friendship with Esther Rothblum in the USA and Glenys Parry in Britain. Their determination to write and to publish has been inspiring. I thought back to the central role that books had played in supporting me in younger times and knew that I wanted to add to that growing mountain of written work. Now, three books (*Motherhood: What It Does to Your Mind, Know Your Own Mind,* and *Love: a User's Guide*) and many papers that seek to insert feminist thoughts into mainstream journals later, I have a very real sense of achievement.

Motherhood: What It Does to Your Mind was an attempt to look at the early days of mothering psychoanalytically from the woman's point of view. As most analytical literature only views this phase of development from the infant's position with mother relegated to some object who should meet all needs and will, of course, be bound for failure and blame, I wanted to shift the balance and make mothers' needs an open topic. Basically my hypothesis is that happy fulfilled women make good mothers. If we really want to improve the quality of mothering we should put all our energies into making women happier rather than criticizing them for doing their best in difficult circumstances.

Much of the pleasure has been in the feedback from all corners of the world. One talk-in radio program to Melbourne, Australia, satellited from a studio in London will stay with me until I die. Woman after woman from the other side of the world talked of reading *Motherhood* and feeling supported and understood. I left the building in tears of joy and relief to be so close to women geographically so far away.

Know Your Own Mind was a real labor of love. A reference book of all you need to know about mental health, mental illness and the varieties of theories about and cures for it, I wanted to empower those who suffer from mental health problems with a wide range of knowledge. So often they feel powerless and without options. I hope this book can be their friend and mentor and offer new options back to health.

My first meeting with Esther Rothblum came on a sunny morning in 1986 at Gatwick Airport, with me holding up a card with her name. Although I had never met her, having read some of her work I had taken the liberty of inviting her and Laura Solomon to visit

England on a month's teaching tour. My faith was richly rewarded as I travelled with them and watched them, time and time again, produce the "goods" for audiences of women from Southampton, to London, to Manchester. Friendship flowered and before long we were planning the Motherhood conference in Vermont which finally happened in September 1988. What a wonderful experience those three days were as we enjoyed the hospitality and planning of Ellen Cole at Goddard College and shared the experiences that formed the basis of *Motherhood: A Feminist Perspective* that Ellen and I co-edited. A love affair which I started with the USA when I first read Betty Friedan came to fruition for me as I talked with the women gathered there and felt embedded and sustained by them.

In the late 80s I qualified as a Group Analyst and was soon invited to join the prestigious Group Analytic Practice in London as their first overt feminist. I felt honored and recognized, not just for myself but also for all of those who have labored to produce feminist ethics in analysis. My work in the NHS has also been supported and I have recently become a medical director to a wide range of services, a new challenge for my mid-40s.

Love: A User's Guide is about intimacy from birth to death. It explores the various forms love can take and all those emotions that exist alongside of it. Love is so much a central theme in life and yet most of us find that it is in our loving relationships that we have much stress and disappointment, too. I hope this book will provide a basis for discussion of this paradox.

Now for the future: I think that feminism still has miles to go. Life, though changed, is still ripe for more change. It is my experience that it is harder to make feminist changes in personal arenas than it is out in the big wide world. Much needs to be done before women will be equal inside of their homes and this is a difficult area to infiltrate and change on anyone else's behalf. I would like to work towards a world where women can feel safe at home, not over-burdened by domestic responsibilities and not at risk of violence. How we achieve this is difficult to see. There has to be a combination of empowering women socioeconomically and of making sure that boys and girls grow up with super-egos that demand equality.

I would like to see more monuments to women of the past. We owe them most of the freedoms we enjoy and I want to see that honored. Perhaps if we each chose one woman deserving of recognition and worked towards a suitable public statement, be it a monument, a garden or a scholarship for her, then we could catch up on our neglect of this duty to our foremothers as quickly as possible.

Finally I want to see more links of working together and friendship across cultures. American and British feminism have always seemed to me to be different movements, sometimes going in different directions and with different aims. I have no problem with that as long as we can share the total richness rather than end up at odds with each other. Friendship is fertile soil for a growing understanding of and tolerance to what I hope to see as a blossoming and much larger feminist movement by the time I die.

Feminist Reflections
from the Wheat Fields

Harriet Lerner
Dana Osowiecki

I recently had the opportunity to speak with Harriet Lerner from her home in Kansas. She has worked to reach out to women through her writings on issues ranging from scholarly revisions of psychoanalytic theory to popular works aimed at understanding the experience of women in relationship. She has developed her own unique, powerful voice of necessity, responding to an initial lack of acknowledgment from her immediate intellectual community. She uses that voice to speak clearly and simply to her audience, in a language that is accessible, and informative for women of all walks of life. The experience of not being heard is unfortunately all too common for women and ironically the experience of not being heard can lead to a kind of deafness as well. As Harriet related "I

Harriet Lerner, PhD, a staff Psychologist at the Menninger Clinic, is the author of *Women in Therapy,* and the trilogy, *The Dance of Anger, The Dance of Intimacy,* and the *Dance of Deception.* She writes a monthly advice column for *New Woman* magazine and lectures widely on the psychology of women.

Dana Osowiecki is a graduate student in Clinical Psychology at the University of Vermont. Her current research focus is on health psychology, with a special interest in women's issues.

Correspondence may be addressed to Harriet Lerner at Menninger Clinic, Box 829, Topeka, KS 66601-0829.

[Haworth co-indexing entry note]: "Feminist Reflections from the Wheat Fields." Lerner, Harriet and Dana Osowiecki. Co-published simultaneously in *Women & Therapy* (The Haworth Press, Inc.) Vol. 17, No. 3/4, 1995, pp. 301-308; and: *Feminist Foremothers in Women's Studies, Psychology, and Mental Health* (ed: Phyllis Chesler, Esther D. Rothblum, and Ellen Cole) The Haworth Press, Inc., 1995, pp. 301-308; and: *Feminist Foremothers in Women's Studies, Psychology, and Mental Health* (ed: Phyllis Chesler, Esther D. Rothblum, and Ellen Cole) Harrington Park Press, an imprint of The Haworth Press, Inc., 1995, pp. 301-308. Single or multiple copies of this article are available from The Haworth Document Delivery Service [1-800-342-9678, 9:00 a.m. - 5:00 p.m. (EST)].

301

credit feminism with allowing me to pay attention to many voices that I had not paid attention to, my own included." The desire to speak and be heard reminded me of a favorite Marge Piercy poem "Unlearning To Not Speak": [excerpt] . . . Phrases of men who lectured her / Drift and rustle in piles: / Why don't you speak up? / Why are you shouting? / You have the wrong answer, / the wrong line, wrong face. / They tell her she is womb-man, / baby machine, mirror image, toy / earthmother and penis poor, / . . . She grunts to a halt. / She must learn again to speak / starting with I / starting with We . . .

In this interview I had the opportunity to explore how this feminist foremother found her own true voice and what her message has been. The following are excerpts from that interview.

Dana Osowiecki: What were the circumstances that led up to your contribution in the area of feminist mental health, what made you become interested in this area?

Harriet Lerner: Moving from Berkeley to Topeka radicalized me. When I lived in California–and before that in New York–I was slow to "get" feminism. But when I started post-doctoral training at the Menninger clinic in 1972, necessity became the mother of comprehension. At that time women had hardly begun to tell the truth about female experience, not even to themselves, and those women who departed from narrow conventional norms were diagnosed as envying or imitating men. The theoretical formulation that I was learning had fit little with the experience of real women and when women differed from the theories it was the women, not the theories, that were brought into question. I began to write out of personal necessity because when I would speak out I wasn't heard.

Dana Osowiecki: Writing it down was a validation?

Harriet Lerner: Yes. And it moved me out of a position of isolation and non-productive anger. Publishing also allowed me to network with other feminists around the country. Feminist psychiatrist Teresa Bernardez "discovered" the first paper I published and invited me to present with her at a professional meeting. In addition to her friendship, she generously introduced me to her feminist friends and colleagues. My feminist connections were my lifeline.

Dana Osowiecki: What was the response when you started publishing your work?

Harriet Lerner: Well, from whom? Some colleagues diagnosed me with penis envy and saw me as "one of those angry women." Or they viewed my feminist perspective as a narrow, biased, subjective, particularized perspective. To some extent this was true, since we all see reality through a filter that excludes more than it includes. But for me feminism was an enlarging perspective.

In my own institution, I was the only identified feminist back then, and I took it upon myself to address every injustice. I soon lost my effectiveness and became encapsulated in a role that made it impossible for me to be heard. So writing allowed me to be heard, to make a difference, to find an intellectual community among women who supported me. Writing also helped me to clarify and deepen my own thinking.

Eventually, I stopped dissipating my energy trying to convert my colleagues or turn them into feminists. In time other women spoke up, and more effectively than I had. My friend and colleague Marianne Ault-Riché was very courageous and made a big difference at Menninger. As did others, over time.

Dana Osowiecki: What do you think that your major contributions have been?

Harriet Lerner: My first contributions were feminist revisions of psychoanalytic theories of women. When I later became interested in family systems theory, I tried to integrate feminist, systemic, and psychoanalytic thinking. These publications appeared in professional journals and subsequently in my book, *Women in Therapy.* There is a false dichotomy between "individual theory" and "family theory" in our field. The more I have learned about multigenerational family theory, the better able I am to help individuals.

Jean Baker Miller was the person who most inspired me to write accessibly in plain English. It's a risky business because one's colleagues, including feminist ones, are likely to write you off. But at this point my greatest passion is to make theory accessible and useful to "just plain folks." I'm best known through my "Dance" trilogy, *The Dance of Anger, The Dance of Intimacy* and *The Dance of Deception. The Dance of Anger* was a five-year project accompanied by much personal anguish. The shift from professional to popular writing was more difficult than I ever could have imagined. First, I had to unlearn everything I had learned as an academic writer. Second, I was forced to face all my unclarity. If I wrote, "The child became the carrier of mother's unconscious projections," my editor would say, "What is this? What exactly is happening between this mother and child and describe it in plain English!" When I would try to describe the family emotional process in plain English, I faced what I did not know, what had been obscured by abstractions and jargon.

People who think that it's simpler to write simply have never done it, or have never done it well. I learned a huge amount writing my first book, *The Dance of Anger.* It took me five years of endless revisions and much anguish in the face of repeated discouragement. I could wallpaper the largest room in my house with rejection slips from that book. When it finally saw the light of day in 1985 I thought no one would read it besides my mother and my seven best friends. But over time I learned the meaning of that maxim, "Success is the best revenge." The book has become an international bestseller and is still flying off the shelves. The process around my first book was so painful, that I swore I'd never do it again, like a woman in labor. But the extraordinary response from readers amazed and inspired me, so I kept writing.

I also have a monthly advice column in *New Woman* magazine, and I have a strong feminist voice in this publication. At first I felt uneasy about this work because women have always had more than enough experts telling them what to do. But I've managed to avoid recipes for success, quick-fix solutions and blueprints for relational bliss.

Dana Osowiecki: So, what do you view as your current contributions?

Harriet Lerner: I'd say the clarity of my voice and my ability to translate complex theory into useful and accessible prose, that can be read at multiple levels. My "Dance" books are used in professional training programs and then these same professionals give the books to clients with little formal education.

Dana Osowiecki: Are you also writing journal articles at this time?

Harriet Lerner: No. Although I'm working on a book. Journal writing is very important, and I value what I've done in this arena. But at this point in my life, I want to write in my own voice about what matters to me. I don't want to conform to journal style. I also enjoy writing short pieces, like one I recently published called "Hating Fred." It's about the Rev. Fred Felps, a minister and disbarred attorney who has made it his full-time job to eradicate homosexuality from the planet, and has begun his work in my home town of Topeka, Kansas. The article is about the community response to Fred, and how much easier it is for folks to point the finger at Fred's outrageous form of homophobia, than to look inside themselves. I'm writing about whatever is important to me these days.

And who knows. I may begin to miss academic writing some day and do it again. But I'm definitely allergic to jargon. It's disheartening to me when I read scholarly feminist papers and I can't understand what I'm reading. I can only conclude one of two things. Either I'm stupid or the authors are not writing clearly. Of course, I prefer the latter interpretation. I still teach nationally and present workshops and lectures to professionals, but I avoid technical language because it obscures from us what is no longer clear in our thinking, or never was.

Dana Osowiecki: What part of your success is most enjoyable?

Harriet Lerner: It's a privilege to get paid for what I love to do and to have a voice in my field that matters. I'm in a position to empower other women and that's a wonderful feeling. I have some clout to speak to issues of who is included and who is not and in what relative numbers. One way that I personally meet this challenge is to be a pest. I push myself to ask difficult questions. I say, for example, "Look, women are 53% of the population, why is there such a token representation of women on this workshop staff, on this board, on this administrative council." Or I say "You've put together this reading list, or panel, or curriculum and there is no gay or lesbian perspective, or there is no Latino or African-American scholarship or faculty included." So I try to use my status and privilege to move us toward a more fair world, not only because this is the democratic and polite thing to do, but also because I agree with Robin Morgan who says that "pc" stands for "plain courtesy." And issues of inclusion have profound implications for the construction and deconstruction of knowledge in our field.

Dana Osowiecki: And what kind of response do you receive when you put yourself out on a limb and point out to people that they aren't being inclusive?

Harriet Lerner: I usually get a positive response, in part because I'm the "invited expert." People don't listen as well to feminists in their own institution. Sometimes I'll make a point, say at a psychiatric hospital, that women have been saying over and over in that same institution and they haven't been heard. It takes an "outside" person with some clout to exceed the threshold of deafness of those in charge. It's how it is, it isn't a matter of bad intentions.

Dana Osowiecki: So, it seems to you that people exclude groups more on the basis of misunderstanding rather than deliberately not attending to a group or an issue?

Harriet Lerner: When it comes to issues of exclusion, most people I meet don't have bad intentions. If they're hiring staff, planning a workshop, or putting together a reading list, they do not have the intention to exclude. They're not sitting around in smoky rooms with maps and pins, plotting to keep out gays and lesbians, or African Americans or any other group. It's just that the dominant group takes itself to be "it."

Dana Osowiecki: Do you think that it never occurs or do you think that there is also an element of discomfort that makes people stay away from certain groups or issues?

Harriet Lerner: Of course people are anxious about differences. Dealing with differences is the greatest of all human challenges and many people are more comfortable huddled together with people just like them. It's also a fact that no dominant group has ever relinquished power independently. Change happens only when members of subordinate groups join together as a powerful social and political force to be reckoned with.

But it's also the case that being dominant in any way just puts one to sleep. For example, when I became a serious feminist, I always noticed when women were not included in significant numbers. I couldn't not notice this. But during this same time period I would, say, co-direct a women's conference entitled "Mothers and Daughters." It didn't even occur to me that the conference was really about white, middle-class, heterosexual mothers and daughters. I had no intention to exclude anyone. I was asleep. Luckily people came and hit me over the head.

Dana Osowiecki: It must be a good feeling to be able to speak out and feel that your voice is being heard, especially since you had the experience earlier in your career when you were speaking out and feeling that you weren't heard.

Harriet Lerner: Right, it is a great feeling.

Dana Osowiecki: I know there are times I've spoken up with no power or privilege and not been sure if I've been heard or not.

Harriet Lerner: Well, sometimes you think you're not heard but there is some other person sitting there and what you're saying makes a huge difference to them, although you may never know it. Or five people speak out and aren't heard. But the sixth person is heard because of the previous five. Everyone's voice makes a difference. And sometimes we speak even if we are discounted because it is important to speak.

Dana Osowiecki: How do you feel that your life has changed as a result of your feminism?

Harriet Lerner: Feminism has allowed me to see past a "reality" that I had once taken as a given. It has transformed how I experience myself and the world. It's allowed me to pay attention to countless voices, my own included, that I had been taught "don't count." Feminism allows me to maintain hope. My debt to the feminist movement is simply incalculable.

Dana Osowiecki: When were you exposed to the feminist movement?

Harriet Lerner: In Berkeley, in 1970 and before that in New York. But my reaction was, "What does this have to do with me, I'm getting my Ph.D, I've never been discriminated against as a woman?" I was sleepwalking, or in a coma. Still today, I keep "getting it" at deeper levels. You think you understand something like "The personal is political," but you could take several lifetimes to achieve deeper levels of understanding of this seemingly simple phrase.

Dana Osowiecki: And you feel like you are better able to help people get feminism through your popular writing now as opposed to your scholarly works?

Harriet Lerner: Popular writing is where my heart is these days. It's what I love to do. But I'm actively involved with clinical work and with professional colleagues.

Dana Osowiecki: Thinking back to when you first felt that you "got" feminism, has your conception of what feminism means changed?

Harriet Lerner: Of course. Early on I had an "equal rights" approach. Later, feminism put everything up for examination.

REFERENCES

Lerner, H. (1985). *The dance of anger: A woman's guide to changing the patterns of intimate relationships.* New York: Harper and Row.

Lerner, H. (1988). *Women and therapy.* Northvale, New Jersey: J. Aronson.

Lerner, H. (1989). *The dance of intimacy: A woman's guide to courageous acts of change in key relationships.* New York: Harper and Row.

Lerner, H. (1993). *The dance of deception: Pretending and truth telling in women's lives.* New York: Harper Collins Publishers.

Piercy, M. (1982). *Circles on the water: Selected poems of Marge Piercy.* New York: Knopf.

Who Ever Thought I'd Grow Up to Be a Feminist Foremother?

Bernice Lott

The invitation to contribute to this volume on women who have played some part in influencing the development of feminist psychology, and to be part of the group of distinguished sisters whose essays appear here, makes me feel older than is comfortable

Bernice Lott earned her PhD in Social Psychology from UCLA and taught at the University of Colorado and Kentucky State College. At the University of Rhode Island she served as Dean of University College and currently is Professor of Psychology and Women's Studies. She was a visiting scholar at Brown University's Center for Research and Teaching on Women, Stanford University's Institute for Research on Women and Gender, the Department of Psychology of Waikato University, New Zealand and, most recently, visiting professor at the University of Hawaii at Manoa. She received the University of Rhode Island's Excellence Award for scholarly achievement in 1988 and was elected President of the American Psychological Association's Division 35 (The Psychology of Women) in 1991. She is the author of numerous theoretical and empirical articles, chapters and books on issues relevant to women. Her book, *Women's Lives: Themes and Variations in Gender Learning*, is now in its second edition (Brooks/ Cole, 1994), and her latest books are *The Social Psychology of Interpersonal Discrimination* (co-edited with her former student, Diane Maluso) and *Combatting Sexual Harassment* (co-edited with Mary Ellen Reilly).

Correspondence may be addressed to Bernice Lott at the Department of Psychology, University of Rhode Island, Kingston, RI 02881.

[Haworth co-indexing entry note]: "Who Ever Thought I'd Grow Up to Be a Feminist Foremother?" Lott, Bernice. Co-published simultaneously in *Women & Therapy* (The Haworth Press, Inc.) Vol. 17, No. 3/4, 1995, pp. 309-323; and: *Feminist Foremothers in Women's Studies, Psychology, and Mental Health* (ed: Phyllis Chesler, Esther D. Rothblum, and Ellen Cole) The Haworth Press, Inc., 1995, pp. 309-323; and: *Feminist Foremothers in Women's Studies, Psychology, and Mental Health* (ed: Phyllis Chesler, Esther D. Rothblum, and Ellen Cole) Harrington Park Press, an imprint of The Haworth Press, Inc., 1995, pp. 309-323. Single or multiple copies of this article are available from The Haworth Document Delivery Service [1-800-342-9678, 9:00 a.m. - 5:00 p.m. (EST)].

but has also given me the delicious opportunity to do reflective autobiography while tracing the path that propelled me into self-recognition as a feminist social psychologist. Despite the self-focus in this essay, it is important to state clearly at the very beginning that I have never been alone in my work or thinking and to acknowledge the empirical and theoretical work by feminist scholars who continue to enrich our understanding of the multiple meanings and personal/political consequences of "being a woman."

The word feminist was rarely used when I was in high school or college; those of us who qualified for such an identification thought of ourselves as radicals, while some school officials and teachers preferred the term troublemaker. The first time I got into serious difficulty for acting in accord with my values was in junior high school when my homeroom teacher observed one morning that my attention was on a book instead of on her recitation of a New Testament prayer. Her report of my "bad character" led to a semester's delay in my election to *Arista*, an honor society for which my good grades had made me eligible. Later on, at Brooklyn College, I was censured by the Dean for having helped organize a march around campus to protest the administration's cancellation of a scheduled talk by Howard Fast, who had been branded by pre-McCarthyite committees as a "Red."

In the late 40s and throughout the 50s, when radicals spoke about issues relevant to women's lives, as we sometimes did, we were likely to say that we were discussing "The Woman Question." But although my consciousness about gender issues may have been higher than that of many of my peers, it was, of course, influenced by the times and by my own particular life circumstances. I remember boasting, for example, as a very young married graduate student in the early 50s that I would be happy to stay at home with small children and make my political contribution as a PTA mother and community activist. I still remember those words with shock and marvel at the strength of the social forces that led me to believe them.

As it turned out, my personal and professional path was very different from what those words would lead one to expect. To start from the beginning, I was born in 1930, the third living child, and the third daughter of immigrant parents living among other working class families in Brooklyn. My mother had come to this country at 14, alone, from a shtetl in Eastern Europe, just like the one in *Fiddler on the Roof*, and she remained a boarder in her aunt's house on the East Side of Manhattan until she married my father at the age of twenty. Among her friends in the garment industry sweatshops she was known as Red Annie because of her support for the union and her high spirits on the picket line when they were out on strike. She never learned to read and write, except for her signature, but somehow devised ways to get off at the correct subway stops in order to shepherd her children to doctors, clinics, and shops. My mother's greatest satisfactions came from the appearance and accomplishments of her children who were always well fed and well dressed, at what I now understand to have been at great sacrifice. When I was very young, she sang Yiddish folk songs to me, told me stories about the old country, and let me play with her treasured shawls.

My father had been to gymnasium (high school) in a fairly large Polish city that was then part of the Austro-Hungarian empire. He was the son of well-to-do restaurant owners who tearfully let him go off with a stranger on a journey to the United States. My father proudly spoke and read many languages, had served in the U.S. army during World War I, was a strong patriot, and a lover of song and dance. He was also a hard worker. In the midst of the depression, he landed a civil service job which he kept until he retired, supplementing a meager (but steady) salary with second jobs that included making umbrellas, waiting on tables, and selling knishes from a pushcart.

During the nineteen years I lived at home with my family we moved from one rundown neighborhood to another, always looking for something better or cheaper or newly painted. This meant frequent changes of school for me until high school. During most of my teen years, including three years as a commuter college student, we lived across the street from shops and open stalls selling everything from live chickens, to fruits and vegetables, to pickles in brine-filled wooden barrels.

My parents fought with each other loudly and abusively and my two older sisters, who were in the process of gaining their independence and becoming educated, were more actively involved in the outside world than in the family. When I was eight, and my mother thirty-eight, she gave birth to a fourth child, my brother. This immediately changed my family status from that of baby sister to big sister so that I have essentially been both the youngest and the oldest in my family. In addition to taking on responsibilities for care of my brother, I also took on the role of parental go-between and peacemaker.

I had my share of children's city street fun but I became an insatiable reader, ranging from Nancy Drew mysteries and gothic romances to the complete works of Charles Dickens, collected by my mother from stamps offered by the life insurance salesman for premiums paid on time. My greatest joys were going to libraries and museums, taking the subway to Manhattan, going to the movies, eating Chinese food, taking long walks, and going to the Yiddish theater with my parents on those rare occasions when they tolerated each other's company.

I first discovered that I was relatively poor in the last junior high school I attended after one of the girls, who wore plaid woolen skirts and cashmere sweaters and who came to school on a school bus, invited me to her house once, but never asked me back. But school was fun and easy; I skipped second and eighth grades, and graduated from high school at sixteen. During my school years, three negative episodes stand out sharply for me. Once, the school nurse found nits (or lice eggs) in my hair, the treatment for which was kerosene shampoos and fine-tooth combing! For years afterward I dreaded lining up for the annual examination of our hair with a gingerly-held pencil by a grim-faced teacher or nurse. Another experience that disturbed me for a long time was being beaten up after school by a boy I liked, a fellow fifth-grader with whom I had had some words during a class trip to the aquarium. He waited for me after school and pummeled me, hard. Then, at the age of thirteen, I was found to have scoliosis, a curvature of the spine, for which a year in a cast was first proposed. A fortunate encounter led my mother to a more enlightened medical facility where an experimental program of exercise was prescribed. As a result I had to travel into Manhattan every Saturday for the next three years for exercise, x-rays, examinations, and adventurous excursions. I made up a boyfriend, complete with photograph, to explain my weekly absence from the neighborhood and knowledge of the world outside of Brooklyn.

My decision to attend a girls' high school that specialized in commercial education and art, because that was where my non-middle-class friends were going, turned out to be a significant choice. I elected an academic curriculum, took three years of science and math, got heavily involved in dramatics and politics, and was one of a few non-Black student members of the Frederick Douglas Club. How I would have fared in a larger school competing with boys and worrying about clothes, hair, and dates I do not know but I suspect that the outcome for me would have been different.

But, although I won honors and medals at graduation, and had an almost straight-A record, I was never counselled to apply for a scholarship at a private college nor was I encouraged to pursue a particular curriculum. The assumption was that anyone in my situation interested in college had only one option—a free education at one of the City colleges. I was strongly tempted to forego college for the life of a secretary or bookkeeper, but I did take the entrance examination for Brooklyn College, passed it, and decided to give it a try. The year was 1946; veterans were returning from World War II and the City Colleges were using a higher entrance exam score for women than for men, not just a higher score for non-veterans! I suppose this was my first clear introduction to overt sexist discrimination.

Brooklyn College was challenging and exciting. I quickly found sociology, my initial choice of a major, to be jargon-filled and fuzzy, but my very first course in psychology showed me where I belonged. What a joy to discover that there were methods by which I could test the answers to questions about human social behavior. And so, a social psychologist was born!

I left Brooklyn College at the end of my junior year to marry a war veteran six years older than I was, who had been accepted for graduate work in psychology at UCLA. After finishing my bachelor's degree at UCLA I was admitted to the graduate program. The GI Bill paid my husband's tuition, provided him with a stipend, and made us eligible for low-cost veteran student housing. This enabled me to cover the cost of my education through scholarships and part-time jobs which ranged from working for an accounting firm in Beverly Hills that handled the finances of Hollywood stars (making it possible, ever since, for me to do my own tax returns!) to a research assistantship with my major professor.

When I entered the graduate program in UCLA in January of 1951, I was not yet 21 years old. During my first day in the department, the chair, Roy Dorcas, shook my hand and said something like the following:

> While I am pleased to meet you, I'm sorry to see you in this program. Your credentials are excellent, but getting a PhD will be a waste of everyone's time and energy since you will undoubtedly have children in a few years and never work as a professional psychologist.

A few years ago I read a statement by Sandra Scarr (1987) in *Psychology Today* in which she related an almost identical incident with Gordon Allport who had interviewed her in 1960 for admission to Harvard.

I don't know how much the words I heard from Roy Dorcas served as a challenge. I certainly never forgot them. Once past this warm welcome, however, my experiences as a graduate student were positive and exhilarating. I rediscovered the joy of mathematics in my statistics classes, adopted cultural anthropology as my minor subject (it holding the key to an appreciation of human plasticity and variability), and I became thoroughly hooked on behaviorism and learning theory, an addiction which is still with me. My major professor, Franklin Fearing, a Lewinian field theorist, let me go my own wayward way and agreed to a dissertation on the formation and generalization of attitudes, operationalized as color preferences, in a sample of kindergarten children. This study is now treated as something of a "classic."

Graduate school for me was an intellectual adventure in an almost totally male environment. My friends were other students, most of whom were men. The lives of their wives revolved around supporting their husbands financially and emotionally and/or taking care of a home and toddlers while my life was more like their husbands', focused on books, classes, research, part-time work, and exams. Only one member of the Psychology faculty was a woman.

I remember Sarah Fisher as a superb teacher of history and systems, but she was a reserved and private person who did not befriend the women students who might have benefitted from her interest and counsel. A woman who did serve as a model for me was a non-tenured adjunct professor, Evelyn Hooker, who never attained full faculty status at UCLA despite her reputation as an excellent teacher and scholar and her pioneering, non-heterosexist work on homosexuality.

It was at APA conventions that I made further discoveries about the role of women in my chosen field. We women graduate students were courted, ogled in elevators, invited to the bar and to parties, and pursued by the most eminent of men within our discipline. I met all the big names whose work I'd been reading in my classes, simply because I was young, female, and showed how flattered I was by their attention. These contacts were sexist and shallow, but I only partially understood that then.

After defending my dissertation in the summer of 1953, I followed my husband, who had earned his Ph.D. a semester earlier, to his first job at the newly opened Riverside campus of the University of California. Anti-nepotism sentiments were strong so I began teaching through the Extension Division—anything offered to me. Eager for full-time work, I turned to the public school system. Just at that time, California was launching a new program for so-called "educable mentally retarded" children and so I talked my way into a job at the Riverside Junior High School. Despite my Ph.D., I had to take some essential courses in education (like audio-visual methods) to earn a secondary school credential, and for two years I worked as a teacher of 12 mentally retarded adolescents in a classroom that had been converted from a storage room in the basement and that could be entered only from a special door at the rear of the school. At the end of each year my special class prepared and gave a creditable assembly program, just as all other homeroom classes did. Some of my so-called retarded kids were simply hard of hearing, others spoke better Spanish than English, and still others were just "bad" or unmanageable. So I ended up learning indelible lessons about the nature of intelligence and its testing, about creativity, human potential, social myths, and the politics of public education. My principal permitted me to carry out a research project on the job, the results of which I subsequently published in a well-received paper.

In the summer of 1956 I ended my difficult and painful marriage. A legal quirk permitted the marriage to be dissolved by annulment instead of divorce so things moved quickly, and my husband and I divided our meager assets equitably. It is likely that my life would have taken a very different turn at that point, if I had had children. I had gotten pregnant a year after marriage but had been dissuaded from bearing the child by my husband. One of my sisters supplied the name of a legitimate physician willing to make some money on the side by doing illegal abortions on a table in the back room of his office during early morning hours before his "real patients" arrived.

I went to the APA convention that August of 1956 to find a job. B. F. Skinner offered me an assistantship in his lab at Harvard, but I decided instead to accept a temporary one-year assistant professorship at the University of Colorado. They needed to replace their group dynamics expert and, although I really knew next to nothing about group processes, this seemed a good way to learn and to enter the world of academia. So I went back to Riverside, filled my little blue Plymouth with clothes, books and notes and drove off to Boulder, the first time in my life that I had ever driven such a distance all by myself. I was launched on a grand adventure as a gay divorcee and about to do something else I'd never done before—live alone!

On my first day on the job, I met Al Lott who I married two years later. Had I not been hired, he would have gotten the job that I took. Al was four years older than me, but Army service during World War II had delayed his education, while also making it possible, so he was just finishing his dissertation. Another GI Bill success story! My one temporary year in Boulder was followed by another, until the department found the male "star" it had been searching for, launching me on still another phase of my life.

I married and moved to Lexington, Kentucky, where Al, the year before, had joined the University of Kentucky faculty. Almost immediately, I found a job at Kentucky State College in Frankfort, the college for Black students. This was 1958 and Kentucky was tightly segregated in all public facilities and resources. I was hired by the college President, an old-fashioned autocrat who ruled benignly but ruled nonetheless. I stayed at Kentucky State for 11 years; during this time I was the only White person on campus except for occasional visitors.

The years in Kentucky were ones of great personal and professional enrichment. Beginning in 1960, I gave birth to three children within a five-year period. For several years, Kentucky State adjusted my teaching schedule so that I could teach two courses each semester, seminar style, one in the afternoon and the other in the evening of the same day. Looking back on this now, I am awed by the flexibility I was permitted. Many of my husband's colleagues, on the other hand, were aghast by an arrangement that required Al to stay at home one afternoon each week. We had few options in the early 1960s that would permit both of us to work full-time and to raise a family. We convinced ourselves then that the best overall plan was for Al to continue up the traditional tenure-track ladder in academia while I did the heavy-duty childcare, taught part-time, and we both worked together on research grants and projects.

During those years we tried various child-care arrangements enabling me to work and to carry out an investigation of Black and White high school youth. We also succeeded in obtaining federal grants to support our research on group cohesiveness and interpersonal attraction, and in publishing our findings. At the same time we were both actively involved in the Civil Rights movement. After all, this was the sixties and we were living in a segregated southern world. We had meetings, we planned, we marched, we sang, we sat in, sometimes we were threatened and grew frightened, and some of us got arrested, but our small group of Black and White activists, members of CORE, succeeded in turning Lexington around and in integrating those lunch counters, restaurants, movies, and other public places. Of course, federal laws helped us eventually, but we had started the job and had done it well! This hands-on experience in social change has unquestionably influenced my work as a social psychologist and a feminist.

For many years I functioned professionally outside of the establishment and the academic mainstream. I did not move into a full-time tenure-track position in a department of psychology until 25 years past the earning of my doctorate! I do not recommend my career path to anyone, and I am not extolling the advantages of professional hustling, which is what I used to call what I did. But there were gains as well as losses. As an outsider I was able to pursue my interests and retain my theoretical perspective without thinking about potential threats to my career; perhaps I would have done the same as an insider, but I cannot be sure.

Al Lott and I just celebrated our 37th anniversary in June 1995. Our eldest daughter Sara, a writer who has worked in publishing, is currently working on a graduate degree in Denver in international communication. Our second daughter Judith, mother of six-year-old Samone, is an attorney specializing in family law in California's bay area. Our son Joshua, an urban and regional planner for the Department of Commerce, lives in the DC area with his wife, a speech pathologist. I take great pride in my children's values and in the work that they have chosen to do. Like other mothers, I have experienced the pains of watching my children get hurt and make choices that had negative consequences, but I have also seen them grow in competence, confidence, and concern for others, and been heartened by the way they are living their adult lives.

But I was never a traditional mother and homemaker. By the end of 1970, when a new phase of my life and career began in Rhode Island, and my children ranged in age from 10 to 5, I had published 22 good papers and chapters, some jointly with Al, and co-authored a book. We moved to Rhode Island when Al was offered a professorship at URI, although I had just accepted a full-time position in a small college in Lexington. But the move would bring us back to the east coast where we had family, back to ocean and beaches, and it was good for Al. I was confident that I would find something worthwhile since my "hustling" had always paid off in the past. Unfortunately, the southern New England psychological community took little notice of my arrival. As a result, my confidence was jolted but my feminism was strengthened. I made the uneasy discovery that having settled into being second author on our joint publications because Al's name began with A and mine with B was cute but not very smart.

During the two lean years that followed, I was an underpaid, underappreciated sabbatical replacement in the psychology department at URI where I taught the introductory course to 500 students, developed the university's first women's studies course, and continued to do research and to write. By the time I was asked to be the

Dean of a new college for entering students in May of 1972, a
position I then held for six years, I had smartened up and proceeded
to "make a deal." I insisted that I also be given a tenure-track
appointment in the Psychology Department. Later, when I thought
my time for promotion to Full Professor had arrived and asked for
the support of my department, it was not forthcoming. I was told by
my Chair that two of the department's men were going up for
promotion and I was asked to please wait until they had made it. My
reaction included an angry letter to my colleagues detailing my
record which compared more than favorably with any of theirs.
Enough of my colleagues changed their minds and supported me,
and I had no trouble gaining administration approval. Another lesson in sexism, and in what women must do in response to it.

Just as the time and place was right in Kentucky for civil rights
activism, the time and place was right in Rhode Island for a feminist
movement. I became part of a core of women faculty who developed a women's studies major, successfully sued the state and the
university administration for discrimination, were instrumental in
developing affirmative action and sexual harassment policies and
procedures, and who have supported each other through tenure and
promotion, strengthened each other as teachers and scholars, and
seen one another grow personally and professionally. The consciousness raising group I became a part of in 1969 is still functioning.

With regard to the direction and nature of my empirical and
theoretical work, I have been interested from the beginning in social
problems and their expression in interpersonal behavior. I started
off with an interest in attitudes, then saw the relevance of this
concept for understanding group cohesiveness (the mutual liking of
members for one another), and then began to focus specifically on
interpersonal attraction. What followed was a decade or more of
empirical and theoretical work on the antecedents and consequences of liking and disliking, much of it done jointly with Al
Lott.

In the late 70s, and continuing until the present, I began to move
the earlier work in a new direction and to focus on attitudes toward
women. I was particularly interested, however, in how men behaved
in the presence of women rather than in what they said they felt or
in what they believed. I proposed a social psychological model of

interpersonal sexism in which prejudice, stereotypes, and discrimination are conceptually and operationally distinguished, and my empirical work has focused on interpersonal sexist discrimination, defined as avoidance or distancing behavior.

There have been two other major threads in my work during the past 25 years. One focus has been theoretical and integrative, and has included critiques of androgyny, explication of the relationship between the feminist perspective and social psychology, critical analyses of "essentialist" and trait-bound theories of gender, and development of a social-learning, constructionist model. The other is work on sexual harassment, done jointly with my colleague Mary Ellen Reilly from sociology and women's studies.

I have been the fortunate and proud major professor of some two dozen exciting graduate students who have pursued feminist questions empirically and will continue to raise their radical provocative voices in professional journals, in academe, and in areas devoted to practice and application. I have been an APA Fellow since 1971, elected first by Divisions 8 and 9, and later by 35. I have been a member of the Association for Women in Psychology from close to the very beginning of its existence in 1969 and my work has twice won an AWP Distinguished Publication Award. In 1981 the Association for Professional and Academic Women at my university named me Woman of the Year, and in 1991, APA's Committee on Women honored me with its leadership award.

When I was elected to the presidency of Division 35 for the 1990-91 term, I felt that my cup was full. I set as my major goal the encouragement of ethnic diversity in our leadership and as a primary focus of our research and activities. A second objective was to encourage our open and proud identification as feminist scholars and practitioners with important contributions to make to the continued vitality and development of psychology. A related goal was to help bring forward into prominence in APA some of the many deserving women who are worthy of honors, responsibilities, and awards. I took on the special task of reminding our organization's leaders that women expect and deserve a new century in psychology's history that is both non-sexist *and* affirmative in its recognition of women's contributions and interests. Still another of my objectives as Division 35 President was to encourage trust and respect among our members and leaders so that feminist work could be done in feminist ways, cooperatively and creatively, with conflicts aired openly and resolved reasonably. I think I made some progress in achieving each of these goals, and I ended my presidency with great satisfaction.

In thinking of how to bring this essay to a close and remembering Esther Rothblum's words to contributors to this volume, that "this is no time to be modest!," I have decided to share with you the citation given to me by my university as part of the award for scholarly excellence that I received in 1988. I do so to emphasize that recognition can come to those of us who have proudly and uncompromisingly continued to do feminist psychology in our teaching, scholarship, and community action. Our perspective is enriching, empowering, and challenging, and there are many out there paying attention to what we have to say. Here are some of the words in the citation of which I am very proud:

> Bernice Lott. Your pioneering work in the areas of social psychology and women's studies has been instrumental in promoting a positive change in attitudes, moving people away from masculine and feminine stereotypes toward an appreciation of human nature. Entering a field initially greeted with skepticism by traditional psychologists, you have proven . . . to be an inspiring influence on the lives of others and one of the most highly regarded psychologists in this country . . . The high standards you uphold and the expectations you have for your students have created a generation of productive scholars and teachers . . . Through your significant contributions, you have moved many to question and examine their attitudes on equality, sexual harassment and minority issues, and thus to break down barriers of ignorance and build bridges of understanding and enlightenment.

AUTHOR NOTE

An earlier version of this paper was presented on August 1, 1991 in San Francisco at the annual conference of the American Psychological Association as part of an invited symposium "Eminent Women in Psychology–Historical and Personal Perspectives," chaired by Agnes N. O'Connell.

REFERENCE

Scarr, Sandra (1987, May). In Twenty years of growing up. *Psychology Today*, p. 26.

SELECTED BIBLIOGRAPHY

Attitude formation: The development of a color preference response through mediated generalization. *Journal of Abnormal and Social Psychology*, 1955, *50*, 321-325.

The formation of positive attitudes toward group members. *Journal of Abnormal and Social Psychology*, 1960, *61*, 297-300 (with A. J. Lott).

Negro and white youth. 1963, New York: Holt, Rinehart & Winston (with A. J. Lott).

Group cohesiveness as interpersonal attraction: A review of relationships with antecedent and consequent variables. *Psychological Bulletin*, 1965, *64*, 259-309 (with A. J. Lott).

A learning theory approach to interpersonal attitudes. In A. G. Greenwald, T. C. Brock, & T. M. Ostrom (Eds.) *Psychological foundations of attitudes*. 1968, New York: Academic Press, pp. 67-88 (with A. J. Lott).

The power of liking: Consequences of interpersonal attitudes derived from a liberalized view of secondary reinforcement. In L. Berkowitz (Ed.) *Advances in experimental social psychology*. 1972, New York: Academic Press, pp. 109-148 (with A. J. Lott).

Who wants the children? Some relationships among attitudes toward children, parents, and the liberation of women. *American Psychologist*, 1973, *28*, 573-582.

The role of reward in the formation of positive interpersonal attitudes. In T. L. Huston (Ed.) *Foundations of interpersonal attraction*. 1974, New York: Academic Press, pp. 171-192 (with A. J. Lott).

A feminist critique of androgyny: Toward the elimination of gender attributions for learned behavior. In C. Mayo & N. Henley (Eds.) *Gender and nonverbal behavior*. 1981, New York: Springer, pp. 171-180.

Becoming a woman: The socialization of gender. 1981, Springfield, IL: Charles Thomas.

Sexual assault and harassment: A campus community case study. *Signs*, 1982, *8*, 296-319 (with M. E. Reilly & D. Howard).

Learning theory in contemporary social psychology. In E. Aronson & G. Lindzey (Eds.) *Handbook of social psychology, Vol. III*. 1985, Reading, MA: Addison-Wesley, pp. 109-135 (with A. J. Lott).

The potential enrichment of social/personality psychology through feminist research and vice versa. *American Psychologist*, 1985, *40*, 155-164.

Women's lives: Themes and variations in gender learning. 1987, revised ed. 1994, Pacific Grove, CA: Brooks/Cole.

Sexist discrimination as distancing behavior: I. A laboratory demonstration. *Psychology of Women Quarterly*, 1987, *11*, 476-58.

Sexist discrimination as distancing behavior: II. Prime time television. *Psychology of Women Quarterly*, 1989, *13*, 341-355.

Dual natures or learned behavior: The challenge to feminist psychology. In R. T. Hare-Mustin & J. Marecek (Eds.) *Making a difference: Psychology and the construction of gender.* 1990, New Haven, CT: Yale University Press, pp. 65-101.

The perils and promise of studying sexist discrimination in face-to-face situations. In M. Paludi (Ed.) *Ivory Power.* 1990, Albany, NY: SUNY Press, pp. 53-66.

Social psychology: Humanist roots and feminist future. *Psychology of Woman Quarterly*, 1991, *15*, 505-519.

Sexual harassment: Consequences and remedies. *Thought & Action*, 1993, *8*(2), 89-103.

The social learning of gender. In A. E. Beall & R. J. Sternberg (Eds.) *The psychology of gender.* 1993, New York: Guilford, pp. 99-123 (with D. Maluso).

Combatting sexual harassment in higher education. In press, Washington, DC: National Education Association (with M. E. Reilly).

The social psychology of interpersonal discrimination. In press, New York: Guilford (with D. Maluso).

Distancing from women: Interpersonal sexist discrimination. In B. Lott & D. Maluso (Eds.) *The social psychology of interpersonal discrimination.* In press, New York: Guilford.

Global connections: The significance of women's poverty. In J. C. Chrisler & P. Rozee (Eds.) *Lectures on the psychology of women.* In press, New York: McGraw Hill.

When Aphrodite Called I Listened

JoAnn Loulan
Jeanine C. Cogan

During graduate studies in clinical psychology, I chose human sexuality as a minor field, taking courses in the Human Sexuality Department of the University of California San Francisco Medical School. I was surrounded by aficionados and connoisseurs of sex who experimented with and celebrated sexuality in many forms. I came out in this environment where people were so open and adventurous about sex that my being lesbian was seen as just another option.

JoAnn Loulan, MA, is a mother, lesbian, feminist, psychotherapist, author, and lecturer. She is in private practice in Portola Valley, CA. Her books include *Lesbian Sex; Lesbian Passion: Loving Ourselves and Each Other; The Lesbian Erotic Dance: Butch, Femme, Androgyny and Other Rhythms,* all published by Spinsters Books. She is one of the co-authors of *Period,* published by Volcano Press. Ms. Loulan lectures and presents workshops on various topics concerning sex, self-esteem, and power in all parts of the United States and Canada.

Jeanine C. Cogan, PhD, is a social psychologist currently conducting research on the mental health consequences of antigay hate crimes at the University of California at Davis. She has conducted research, published, and presented on the sociopolitical consequences of body hatred which is an umbrella term she uses for things such as body dissatisfaction, the negative impact of the beauty myth, traditionally labeled "eating disorders," and fat oppression. Her primary message is that body hatred is a social construction that serves to isolate and divide women.

Correspondence may be addressed to JoAnn Loulan at 4370 Alpine Road, #106, Portola Valley, CA 94025.

[Haworth co-indexing entry note]: "When Aphrodite Called I Listened." Loulan, JoAnn, and Jeanine C. Cogan. Co-published simultaneously in *Women & Therapy* (The Haworth Press, Inc.) Vol. 17, No. 3/4, 1995, pp. 325-333; and: *Feminist Foremothers in Women's Studies, Psychology, and Mental Health* (ed: Phyllis Chesler, Esther D. Rothblum, and Ellen Cole) The Haworth Press, Inc., 1995, pp. 325-333; and: *Feminist Foremothers in Women's Studies, Psychology, and Mental Health* (ed: Phyllis Chesler, Esther D. Rothblum, and Ellen Cole) Harrington Park Press, an imprint of The Haworth Press, Inc., 1995, pp. 325-333. Single or multiple copies of this article are available from The Haworth Document Delivery Service [1-800-342-9678, 9:00 a.m. - 5:00 p.m. (EST)].

325

When I entered graduate school in 1975, *Gray's Anatomy* (the medical bible of human anatomy) did not have "clitoris" in it. There were few places to get accurate information. What little had been written on women's sexuality was geared toward heterosexual women. The few references there were to lesbians categorized us as sick, wrong, bad, or displaying immature sexuality. At the same time, I was beginning to teach through the Human Sexuality Department and, after giving an hour's lecture on lesbian sexuality, it was not uncommon that I heard comments like "Oh, you're so cute. You could get a man."

After many such reactions I decided it was time to concentrate my focus, and I shifted all my attention and energy to the lesbian community. I wanted to teach lesbians what I was learning. I gave public lectures with Tee Corrine, who writes lesbian erotica. Her *Cunt Coloring Book* (1975), with its black and white drawings of real women's genitals (including labia and vagina), had just been published and was helping women learn about their bodies. I collaborated with Dotty Calabrese in creating a workshop about lesbians and sex. Six times a year we rented a house on the beach and, with about twenty lesbians, conducted weekend workshops on lesbians and sex.

The women who attended the workshops continually suggested I put the information in a book. I wrote down everything I had learned about lesbians and sex in what became *Lesbian Sex* (1984). My goal was to provide accurate and much needed information. I also felt compelled to counteract the negative messages about lesbians while naming the destructive mythology that inhibited the full range of lesbian expression. I felt passionately about knowledge and understood that women had very little of it when it came to our sexuality and our bodies.

The only information available at this time was in three books, *Loving Women* (1976), *Women Loving* (1975), and *Sapphistry* (1980). There were no video tapes and very little lesbian erotica. The only hope for conversation about lesbian sex could be found in bits of poetry. Given this dearth of information, *Lesbian Sex* (1984) sold well and was brought alive during my speaking engagements.

Irony played a major role in my becoming a lesbian sex educator. Though defined by who we have sex with and often labeled as oversexed nymphomaniacs, in reality I began to discover in my work that we were not having much sex! I knew we deserved to have the pleasure and joys of this form of expression. I also thought we merely needed accurate information and permission.

My most significant proclamation about lesbian sex is that, contrary to popular spoken opinion among many lesbians, sex *is* important! Women in general are taught that sex is not vital. For lesbians the negative messages about sex become a double indemnity. Heterosexual women are introduced to the male point of view about sexuality and the permission men receive about sex in this culture. In lesbian relationships, neither woman has been given permission to be sexual much less to explore and celebrate her sexuality.

The consequence of this construction is reflected in a statistic from *Lesbian Passion* (1987), for which I surveyed 1500 lesbians. Among those surveyed, the average length of time in a relationship was three years. Sex dropped off an average of 50 percent by the end of the first year and an average of 75 percent by the end of the third year. Obviously, the women in this group were leaving their relationships when sex wasn't happening.

We have perfected companionship; how to live together; how to create a household. What we are not so good at, however, is continuing to have sex, keeping sex interesting, and considering sex a priority. A common scenario is that once we stop having sex in the relationship, someone else comes along who looks exciting and we move out of the existing relationship into a new one in which the pattern will most likely repeat itself. This can change if we are willing to work on our sex issues with each other.

Another irony which has been a motivating factor in my work is that when I came out as a lesbian in the 70s, though I had been encouraged by my experience in graduate school to be open about sexuality, I entered a community where there was an unspoken taboo around talking about sex, even with one's partner.

Even in 1984, the year I published *Lesbian Sex,* simply speaking about sex, much less introducing the notion that sex among lesbians is important, was controversial. My style of presentation was also controversial–and still is. I am opinionated and challenging. Currently I am being criticized by some lesbians who work in the AIDS field for being an alarmist because I give a lot of practical information to lesbians about safer sex. A fatal disease is, after all, a fatal disease. Let's not have any lesbian die because she didn't have the knowledge necessary to save herself.

My major contribution to the community is that I talk out loud about sex. Through lecturing around the country, I have helped create a dialogue about lesbian sex that wasn't there before. A typical scenario–I am talking about sex in a room filled with 500 lesbians. They buy my book. They want to talk with me in more detail. The momentum builds and soon they are talking with each other. They want to learn about sex; they want to talk about it; they want to do it!

My approach is practical in the hope of providing useful information; i.e., where you put your fingers, how you might use those fingers, vaginal juices, orgasm, etc. I like to offer many concepts because it makes people think. My delivery is funny, so people will be laughing and all of a sudden, I will deliberately say something deep. I always push the envelope, led by my love of women.

Because I lecture to large groups of lesbians and make the tale funny I have been labeled the Dr. Ruth of Dykedom and a stand-up psychotherapist. I write and talk about everything related to consensual, adult, lesbian sex. I convey the critical theme that lesbian sex is good. I have reached more lesbians about our sexuality than anyone before me because I have used major media to relay my message. In addition to writing books (*Lesbian Sex, Lesbian Passion,* and *The Lesbian Erotic Dance*) I have appeared on many talk shows, recorded audio and video tapes, and lectured to more than 75,000 lesbians giving information about sex in a down-to-earth manner. My message is not esoteric; it is simple meat and potatoes. "Okay, this is what you do if you want to have anal sex. Use lots of lubrication and don't put anything in the anus and then into the vagina."

I offer a practicality about sex and the realities of our sexual lives. Sex is not the totality of our orientation. It is only a part of it. Sex is not love. Love does not automatically mean great sex. Sex can be merely fun and intimate. Sexual orientation is a complex construct that includes sex, emotion, how our world is oriented, and many other factors.

I write and lecture about everything I can think of that pertains to lesbian sexuality: the healing of sex for survivors of incest and sexual assault, sex and lesbians with disabilities, lesbian mothers and sex, sex and menopause, the sociological and psychological issues that impact lesbian sex, specific exercises for lesbians having problems with sex. More recently, I have incorporated the role breast cancer plays in lesbians' lives. My thoughts and theories continue to evolve. Most importantly, I am committed to communicating that nothing should serve as a permanent obstacle to fun and fulfilling lesbian sex.

Times have changed in the lesbian community in 25 years. Playing and experimenting with sex is more a part of lesbian culture today. Dildos and vibrators were never discussed except possibly behind closed doors with a lover you knew would never tell anyone. Today we have stores, such as "Good Vibrations" in San Francisco that has a whole wall of dildos! They come in millions of colors, shapes and sizes. Only you decide whether or not to participate.

When I first talked about dildos I was practically booed off the stage. Women were noticeably holding their breath, shocked and even fearful of what they might hear. I used to take dildos and vibrators on stage, showing the audience how to use them. Women flipped out! Today when I do an on-stage demonstration, such as how to use a dental dam over a lover's genitals, women are standing on their seats screaming and yelling. They love it.

We are celebrating our sexuality much more than we used to. It's more of a play time incorporated into our political struggle. I think sexuality *is* political. I feel there is a whole part of our community that has lightened up. There is a noticeably different attitude about how we approach sex: more conversation about it along with an openness to the full range of lesbian sexuality.

This acceptance of diversity of expression is apparent in other aspects of lesbian life as well. There are simply more choices in expressing ourselves today. Look at our dress. When I came out, "good" lesbians didn't wear dresses, make-up, leather, etc. There was a dress code and if you broke it, you were ostracized. Now I see lesbians of all age groups wearing a wide range of clothes styles.

The way we view money and power has changed as well. Today we believe we can make an economic difference in the world and that we have. We believe we can create social service programs that are lesbian-oriented and funded.

As a lesbian feminist for over two decades, I have experienced many notable changes. The biggest change has to do with visibility. When I came out in 1975, I was just behind the wave of women who had come out during very dangerous times. I was the lucky little sister of those who had been on the front lines.

Recently I have had several lesbians in their twenties enter therapy. They are not struggling with coming out to their parents, their advisors, or to their roommates in college. They are not in that struggle. Instead, they take their partners home for the holidays. In contrast, my generation has spent so much time deciding who to come out to and when. Many women of my generation have been rejected and ostracized by their families, lost their children in custody battles, been fired from jobs, discharged from the military, etc. This is not to say that younger women have an easy time being out or that they don't experience real prejudice or discrimination as well. However, these women have a dramatically different world from those of us who still spend enormous time and energy on the issue of being out.

All the legislation and social struggle for lesbian and gay civil rights has resulted in positive change as well. Even the recent minor military policy adjustment of "don't ask, don't tell" would never have been introduced, let alone become part of the national discourse, just three years ago. During this time, Barry Goldwater, one of the conservative arch-enemies of college students in the sixties, said in public that queers should be able to be open in the military. He has an out gay grandson, and like many people of his generation and experience, has been educated. While the current policy is not the positive and empowering legislation we need, the environment is such that we are able to openly fight for our rights.

Popular culture has now incorporated the concept of homophobia. It's in our language, conversations, and on all the talk shows. Even if much of the discussion in the mass media is inaccurate or far from perfect, I believe all publicity is good publicity. At least everyone is being exposed to something that is part of the human condition.

Lesbians are more visible today. I love the Lesbian Avengers' slogan "10 percent is not enough. Recruit, recruit, recruit." I was in New York for the twenty-fifth Stonewall anniversary celebration in June 1994 and attended the Dyke March. It was wonderful marching down Fifth Avenue and encountering straight women on the sidewalk all dressed up and at the end of their shopping day. I went up to them and said, "You know, we recruit." They just stood there dumbfounded, holding their Saks Fifth Avenue bags. The purpose of the Dyke March was to be visible and celebrate our lesbian selves. I always want to give women the opportunity to join us. I am a lesbian cheerleader.

When I reflect on the lesbian community over the years, I always like to ask these questions: "What have we brought to feminism and the culture as a whole?" and "Where do we need to focus our women-loving energies today?"

Lesbians were the first to provide child care at public events. Women's music was and is a movement by, for, and about lesbian feminists. The musical styles, lyrics, and cultural events that have evolved from the movement are lesbian creations. Lesbian events were the first to be made accessible to disabled women as well. Our concerts and rallies were the first to provide on-stage interpreters for those who have a hearing impairment.

We have always been the "wives" of progressive movements. We have labored in the closet on boards and staffs of organizations committed to civil rights, organized labor and the women's liberation movement. For three decades lesbians have provided a wide range of social services for women, largely through volunteer efforts. We brought skills, leadership and boundless energy to the feminist abortion fight, rape crisis hot lines, and women's centers. Interestingly enough, now that some of these agencies and concerns have gone "mainstream," they are run by male-dominated boards and owned by male-dominated corporations. Lesbians are being kicked out of the upper tiers of these institutions even though we created the concept and fueled reality with our efforts.

Much of the sweat and energy that lesbians offer feminism continues to go unrecognized. This is certainly true of our contribution in the fight for safe, legal abortions. We are not identified within the struggle as a constituency of supporters as are labor, people of color, etc. We are acknowledged as feminists but not as lesbians. I would like to have a button that says "Another lesbian marching for straight women's rights." Let's face it, how many lesbians need abortions? I would guess that one in three pro-choice marchers is lesbian.

Lesbian influence and presence in feminist culture and politics is awesome. Yet we continue to be invisible to many people. Becoming visible in this context must be part of our work in the 90s.

I am currently working on a book which explores my theory that the standard female gender stereotype is limited by the dichotomous heterosexual construct. Articulating the complexity of lesbian sexuality renders that limited paradigm obsolete. Lesbians have always challenged gender norms and traditional views of women. Lesbians have pushed against gender boundaries and limits and have never accepted all the rules for women proscribed by the patriarchal culture. Many of us have dressed differently than we were told, have had jobs that were not traditional, fought for our rights against all odds, and expressed our sexual energy differently than we were "taught." We were more able to do these things than heterosexual women because we don't have the same restrictions, conflict of interest and anxieties that these outlaw attitudes create for heterosexual feminists.

Lesbian contributions to feminism are about our lives and our community. They are about living with friends in a culture that is women-loving. It is women giving energy and time to other women. It is such a different way of living. This women-loving culture and lifestyle gives us a unique view of feminism.

Our feminist agenda in the 90s needs to be achievement of equality on all levels–gender, race, class, sexual orientation, etc. To achieve this end, we need to focus on what our children are being taught. I attend children's and young adolescents' movies with my 12-year-old son. I am struck with the overt sexist and heterosexist messages. When we went to see "Little Rascals" I sat next to an eight-year-old girl. I longed to say, "I'm sorry, we struggled for 25 years to eradicate this crap and you are still getting this awful message that boys are better than girls."

It sometimes seems we have gained little ground in the ways boys and girls are portrayed in the media. The anti-gay messages are even more virulent and violent. "Ace Ventura Pet Detective" was one of the most popular films in 1994, yet a woman was shown being stripped and savagely beaten in front of a group of men because "she" was a man. Clearly, all forms of the media need transformation.

We can focus on the media messages children receive through textbooks and reading materials in schools. Teachers are underpaid, overworked, and stressed. It would be unfair to ask them to create an entirely new curriculum. They don't have the time. Instead we need feminist committees in every school district to look at every piece of material children receive. There are plenty of books and materials available today that are non-sexist, non-racist, and non-homophobic. There is no excuse for the sexist, racist, and homo-phobic literature that our children are reading.

My words of wisdom to the budding feminist are simple: one woman can make an impact. I did not think this when I started; I merely followed my passion and my heart. Each of us can have a dramatic impact on our lesbian communities. We need leaders: women with novel, controversial, excellent, loving ideas. An inter-esting paradox that persists in feminist communities is the impulse to be strong and out there juxtaposed with the fear of taking the lead. We believe no one woman should have more power than another. I believe we need to be out there; women need to step out front, be the lightning rods; take the heat. The result is tremendous dialogue and information sharing that benefits everyone. Our com-munity needs that.

Most important, I would say to this young feminist: follow your passion. Follow your heart which will allow you to profoundly touch other lives as well as offer a richness to our lesbian feminist movement. Always remember to open your heart to yourself. You deserve joy.

REFERENCES

Califia, Pat (1980). *Sapphistry: The book of lesbian sexuality*. Tallahassee, FL: Naiad Press.

Corrine, Tee (1975). *The cunt coloring book*. San Francisco, CA: Pearlchild Productions.

Falk, Ruth (1975). *Women loving: A journey toward becoming an independent woman*. New York: Random House.

Loulan, JoAnn (1990). *The lesbian erotic dance: Butch, femme, androgyny, and other rhythms*. San Francisco, CA: Spinsters Book Co.

Loulan, JoAnn (1987). *Lesbian passion: Loving ourselves and each other*. San Francisco, CA: Spinsters/Aunt Lute.

Loulan, JoAnn (1984). *Lesbian sex*. San Francisco, CA: Spinsters Ink.

Nomadic Sisters (1976). *Loving Women*. Senora, CA: Nomadic Sisters.

Learning from Women

Jean Baker Miller
Amy S. Welch

In 1976, Jean Baker Miller, MD, pioneered a new way of thinking about human development, by calling attention to women's formative experiences. Through its exploration of women's lives as they are lived, *Toward a New Psychology of Women* moved beyond traditional psychoanalytic formulations, and offered groundbreaking insights into women's psychological experiences, opening up an avenue for greater understanding of human development generally.

Jean Baker Miller, MD, is Clinical Professor of Psychiatry at Boston University School of Medicine, and Director of Education at the Stone Center, Wellesley College. She has written *Toward a New Psychology of Women,* co-authored *Women's Growth in Connection* and edited *Psychoanalysis and Women,* as well as numerous articles on depression, dreams, and the psychology of women. She is a Fellow of the American Psychiatric Association, the American College of Psychiatrists, American Orthopsychiatric Association, American Academy of Psychoanalysis, and has been a member, consultant to, and teacher of several women's groups.

Amy S. Welch is a clinical research Fellow and doctoral candidate in Clinical Psychology at the University of Vermont, and a member of the Vermont Psychological Association's Committee on Women and Minorities. She is coauthor, with B. E. Compas, J. Connor, and D. Osowiecki, of the chapter "Effortful and Involuntary Responses to Stress" in the forthcoming B. Gottlieb (Ed.) *Coping with Chronic Stress.*

Correspondence may be addressed to Jean Baker Miller at 105 Salisbury Road, Brookline, MA 02146.

[Haworth co-indexing entry note]: "Learning from Women." Miller, Jean Baker, and Amy S. Welch. Co-published simultaneously in *Women & Therapy* (The Haworth Press, Inc.) Vol. 17, No. 3/4, 1995, pp. 335-346; and: *Feminist Foremothers in Women's Studies, Psychology, and Mental Health* (ed: Phyllis Chesler, Esther D. Rothblum, and Ellen Cole) The Haworth Press, Inc., 1995, pp. 335-346; and: *Feminist Foremothers in Women's Studies, Psychology, and Mental Health* (ed: Phyllis Chesler, Esther D. Rothblum, and Ellen Cole) Harrington Park Press, an imprint of The Haworth Press, Inc., 1995, pp. 335-346. Single or multiple copies of this article are available from The Haworth Document Delivery Service [1-800-342-9678, 9:00 a.m. - 5:00 p.m. (EST)].

In this foundational work, Dr. Miller first presented her ideas on relational contexts and modes of being, emphasizing the importance of relationships for both women's and men's emotional growth and development. She also identified and affirmed women's psychological strengths, many of which had been seen as nonsignificant, or even as deficiencies, rather than as qualities essential for maintaining emotional health and well-being.

Since the publication of *Toward a New Psychology of Women*, Dr. Miller has continued to have a substantial impact upon the field of human development. In 1981, she was chosen to become the first director of the newly established Stone Center for Developmental Services and Studies at Wellesley College. The mission of the Center, the prevention of emotional problems, was shaped under Dr. Miller's guidance, and formulated on the basis of her work on relational contexts in women's and men's development. It emphasizes the importance of human connection and of relational modalities, both on a theoretical level, and as a working model for action and research programs. Dr. Miller and her colleagues have worked together to expand their understanding of the relational approach in many areas of human development, publishing numerous papers, some of which were brought together in 1991 with the publication of *Women's Growth in Connection*, of which Dr. Miller is a co-author, along with Judith Jordan, Alexandra Kaplan, Irene Stiver, and Janet Surrey. Presently, she is working with Irene Stiver on a forthcoming book, tentatively entitled *Connections: From Self to Community in Life and in Therapy*.

Jean Baker Miller, MD, is currently Clinical Professor of Psychiatry at Boston University School of Medicine, Director of Education at the Stone Center, Wellesley College, Lecturer in Psychiatry at Harvard Medical School, and Associate Psychiatrist at Beth Israel Hospital. The following is excerpted from a conversation with Dr. Miller:

Amy Welch: So perhaps you could begin by talking about what it was that led up to your work in the area of feminist mental health.

Jean Baker Miller: Well, for years I was practicing psychotherapy, and also teaching psychiatry, and it seemed to me that something was fundamentally wrong with the formulations about women, which were based upon traditional psychoanalytic theories. I thought that they were wrong, but I didn't have a framework for an alternate way of thinking. Also, in addition to thinking that these formulations were wrong, I always felt that the women whom I was seeing in my practice had a lot of strengths. These capabilities, such as making relationships and knowing how to do that, or helping the whole family survive and flourish a little, were extraordinarily valuable. However, in our culture, the women themselves could never really perceive them as being strengths, and so these strengths did not help them anywhere near as much as they should.

Maybe I'll give you an example, which is in the book *Toward a New Psychology of Women*. I worked with a woman whose lawyer husband became more and more seriously addicted and was falling apart. She had been his secretary, and was actually keeping his practice going, by doing the legal work. At the same time, she was also raising three children, trying to cope with all the problems his poor decisions were creating, and attempting to keep up a front, in terms of their social life, so that no one would know about his addiction. So she's doing this overwhelming job and, yet, this woman would tell me that she "couldn't *do* anything." Women did, and to some extent still do, think, "I don't know anything. I don't do anything worthwhile. *I'm* not worthwhile." So that was the kind of thing that I was seeing over and over again, and it was very hard to help women in an atmosphere where none of these experiences were really seen or described or valued.

Then came the Women's Movement and I started to read "the books" by the early writers, like Gloria Steinem, Phyllis Chesler, and Naomi Weisstein. And the other big thing, at that time . . . the early seventies . . . were consciousness-raising groups. They certainly were making a big difference. I lived in New York City, and some of my patients joined these consciousness-raising groups. I remember thinking, "Oh my god, these groups are doing more than I am!" These women were in their twenties, and I was then in my forties. So I was feeling too old. But one of the residents I supervised found a group for me. I remember that there was one woman older than me who was a nurse, and also a teacher, a secretary, and a woman who was working in public relations. The group was really varied, in terms of age, economics, and interests. And it was a force, along with the writings, which led to great personal change. *Ms.* magazine, when it first began, used the word "click," in the sense that something "clicks" and the whole world looks different. Well, that's what happened to me. And so I began to be able to see things, such as the larger framework of what the culture does to women. And then I began to see a path which leads from the culture to what we call "psychopathology."

As I thought more and more about what was happening, though, I felt that there was one tendency in the women's movement that could not be right. That is, it seemed to me that there was the theme of trying to get what men had, and, therefore, trying to be like men, accepting things as they are, just wanting women to get more of it . . . a bigger piece of the pie. I felt that if we really meant what we said about patriarchy being oppressive, then the model which it holds out for men's development can't be the right one. If it isn't right for men, then women should not be trying to emulate it. Instead, I thought we should start from women's experience, which I believed held the seeds of a more enlightened way of life, although never, of course, could women *really* live it, existing under oppressive conditions. But it had the seeds of what we've now come, in our work at the Stone Center, to call "growth-fostering relationships" or "mutual growth-fostering relationships." I was at great pains about how to say that, as women, we shouldn't emulate men, but should look to women's experience–what women actually *do*–and realize that a lot of so-called "deficiencies" can be reframed as the seeds of strength. So that was the main theme of my book *Toward a New Psychology of Women.*

Amy Welch: So, it sounds like your own movement towards feminism and feminist mental health, and the writing of Toward a New Psychology of Women, *was largely based upon both your own personal experience, as well as your work with clients?*

Jean Baker Miller: Yes, definitely. Very much so.

Amy Welch: Prior to that time, had your practice consisted primarily of female clients?

Jean Baker Miller: No. In fact, to show you how bad I was . . . I wasn't totally bad, but I was bad! I had a mix of men and women at that time, and I remember thinking to myself, "I want to keep it about half-and-half because otherwise I won't be a *real* psychiatrist. If I'm just seeing women, it's just women talking, not real psychiatry." That's how much I had internalized the ideas that were around. I never *said* that out loud, but I know that it was in my head.

Amy Welch: Yes. Well, I can certainly understand your thinking that, given the realities of what it must have been like trying to become established in a predominantly male environment at that time. I'm sure that the messages about how one should go about it were pretty clear, if unspoken.

Jean Baker Miller: Yes, that's right. I would never think that way today. And women don't think that way now. Women used to want to go to male therapists. They thought they must be better. But now, women want to go to women. It's certainly a big change.

Amy Welch: Yes . . . definitely a positive one. So, I guess we should move on to the next question, as I'm sure that we will need quite a bit of time for this one! Could you describe what you think have been your major contributions to the field?

Jean Baker Miller: Well, let's see. I think, first, we'll start with writing, perhaps with *Toward a New Psychology of Women*, which I think, again, made two major points. First, it tried to bring to the fore women's strengths, as opposed to looking at women from a "deficiency" model. Second, it sought to offer the beginnings of a relational point of view. This relational framework is, I think, a fundamental shift in how we look at human development, as well as society as a whole, since our society is largely based upon an individualistic and ultimately "power-over" kind of model. So, through this book, and then later on in the writings that I've done with my colleagues at the Stone Center, I've tried to offer a new vision. Having a vision is important because we can get so stuck in the whole culture that surrounds us that it's hard to see that there can *be* any other way. And yet, I think there can be.

I wanted to be able to continue that kind of work, asking questions like, "How does it all look different if we start from women?" Of course, no one ever becomes totally free of the assumptions and the ways of thinking which predominate in our culture. Still, you can try; but it's hard to try if you don't have supporting environments that are really interested in helping you do that. At the Stone Center, we've been able to create an atmosphere that encourages looking at things in a new way. The Center's mission is the prevention of psychological problems. Our programs cover a broad range, from work with school children, to preventing depression in young mothers, to many other areas. It's wonderful to work at an institution that focuses on prevention. And now we're trying to make diversity the core of all of our thinking and our work. Any place that is part of an established institution doesn't have total freedom; yet, we can try to create a context for innovative work. We have tried to do that, and it's wonderful to work in a place where part of your mission is to create new formulations, right or wrong, and to make a central commitment to diversity. There's such pleasure in that.

Amy Welch: Yes. I think that one of the most valuable things about the Stone Center, and the working papers which are produced, is that it creates a forum to present new ideas, which may or may not be "finished products," per se, but which invite comment and collaboration from those outside of, as well as inside, the immediate Stone Center community.

Jean Baker Miller: Yes. You don't have to have a finished product, but you can share something you think is worthwhile while it's developing. That is another aspect of the Center that I feel really good about. So many people have gotten involved, like those whom you would see on a list of authors of Stone Center working papers, and many others. Many people are doing and teaching this work, people who read the papers and attend conferences, and tell us about what they're doing. It's wonderful being able to bring together whole gatherings of people.

Amy Welch: Well, it certainly creates a more relational context . . . a forum for dialogue, rather than isolated scholarship.

Jean Baker Miller: Yes. Well, I don't think I've been optimally good at it, but I have tried to make this a relational kind of work. So when I talk about my contributions, it's not just me; it's a lot of people. And I don't think that's being altruistic. I just think it's so wonderful when you can feel part of a group effort, which is not to say that we don't have problems! It is true that we live in a world that makes it hard to do collaborative work, and many of our institutions make it hard . . . including academia, where there's a great deal of forced competition, as you know. So it's not easy to move towards working in more relational or collaborative ways. If you can do it, though, I find that it really is fulfilling. It's so much better and more fun.

Amy Welch: Well, that collaborative mode of scholarship certainly comes across in all of the writings from the Stone Center.

Jean Baker Miller: I'm glad. Well, I guess another thing that I'd like to mention is a program at the Charles River Hospital, which is a small, teaching hospital that was connected with Boston University Medical School. We set up a program, using a relational model, for women inpatients that really worked. Prior to that time, it felt like the work of the Women's Movement had not really reached those women who were most distressed, those who are in psychiatric hospitals. There is one wonderful place, the Elizabeth Stone House, which provides an alternative to hospitalization, but even they can't take women who are suicidal, or who are severely psychotic. So I was very excited to see people come together and really work to help women who had not been reached by the Women's Movement or outpatient services. And we succeeded, I think, because the women really did do much, much better. This model, at least parts of it, have now been used by other places . . . like the Women's Treatment Network of McLean Hospital, or Synthesis, the inpatient unit for substance abusing women at Metro West Hospital in Framingham, MA. We're now trying to adapt this model for women prisoners in a project with the Massachusetts Committee on Criminal Justice.

Amy Welch: I read your working paper on the program. It sounded as though the project received a lot of support from within the hospital. I was wondering if you encountered any opposition,

*questions as to why women needed something "in addition" to what
the men were receiving?*

Jean Baker Welch: Oh, yes. Very much! At the beginning, there
was a lot of questioning. The hospital administration had several
meetings about whether they should go ahead with it, and I think it
was a close decision. For several years, there were people around, at
every level, who questioned it, from administrators to nurses to
mental health counselors, both male and female. There would be
snide remarks, jokes, and so on. So it was a long process. But we
did go ahead, and as the program proceeded, the questioning
stopped. So there was certainly opposition. Yet, in the overall, it
seems hopeful that the hospital and its leadership were even willing
to try it when no one else had. I feel that it really made a difference
to so many women. And it provided a model to work with in other
settings.

*Amy Welch: I realize that it's a big topic, but I was wondering if
you would say a bit more about the relational approach with regard
to the practice of psychotherapy?*

Jean Baker Miller: It certainly is a big topic! It's a whole different
therapy, right? The essence of it, I would say, is to build mutually
empowering relationships in therapy. The therapist's focus isn't on
interpretations, as such, but on finding ways that she can come
together with clients to build a better connection, helping them to
bring more and more of themselves and their experiences into that
connection, particularly those parts that they have felt that they had
to keep out. And, then, it is creating a framework to understand the
movement in therapy. The therapy is a process, moving from establishing connection, to repeatedly and inevitably moving out of connection, to finding new connection. And the relational approach
provides a kind of framework, a whole way of looking at therapy
that is different. I guess the biggest difference is that the therapist
really has to be there herself, participating in each particular relationship. Which is certainly not to suggest that the therapist's role is
to talk about her own troubles or anything like that!

*Amy Welch: Yes! I think that people have certainly misconstrued
the relational approach in that manner, as it challenges the model*

that is presented in most clinical training programs, which emphasizes professional distance. I certainly think that this is a substantial contribution, because it seems that it is time to talk about how we might do therapy a bit differently . . . in a manner that doesn't involve being in a very distanced, "power-over" kind of a position as a therapist, but which is still attentive to appropriate boundaries and professional integrity.

Jean Baker Miller: Exactly. And I think that we're still trying to find the right ways to say it, ways that don't lead people to think that you just sort of "hang out" together and tell each other your troubles. The relational approach gets distorted so easily. We have to keep finding ways to say it better, I think. But it is definitely clear to us that this approach is more helpful. It made a huge difference for people in the hospital who were in severe distress. In fact, that's another thing I'd like to mention. At the time, it was not widely known or recognized that the overwhelming majority of women coming into psychiatric hospitals had been traumatized. I certainly wasn't the first to see that, but, at Charles River, we published what was, as far as I know, one of the first studies showing that a large percentage of women inpatients had been victims of sexual or physical abuse.[1] So, what I was starting to say is that for women who have been traumatized, it's even more important not to be in this power-over, controlling, distant mode. It's the worst thing for them.

Amy Welch: Yes, I would certainly agree with that. Well, we have one more question to discuss: "How did your life change as a result of your work?"

Jean Baker Miller: I can think of two things right off. First, to continue on with that thought about relational contexts, today I'm working in a much more collaborative way, which really is quite different than what I had been doing before. Years ago, I used to have my own practice and work in a medical school, and there was nothing much collaborative there. I did do some research projects with other people, usually men, because there weren't even that many women around back then, and also some projects and papers with some residents. But it wasn't at all like working with groups of women who are really very consciously trying to change how we think about things and how we go about doing things. That's made a huge, huge difference in my life; it has been so much more fulfilling and satisfying for me. So, for me, personally, to be working in that context, as well as to be helping other working groups get going, at the Stone Center and at Charles River and at lots of other places, all of that makes for a whole different life than what I would have had before.

Amy Welch: Which would probably have meant working primarily in an individualistically-oriented context?

Jean Baker Miller: Oh yes, very much. And also not feeling involved in a kind of joint mission or something that mattered to all of us; I didn't have that at all before. Then, I guess the other thing, which goes hand-in-hand with this new way of working, is my becoming immersed in trying to work out a new theoretical framework, which I find very stimulating. It's just so enjoyable to try to stretch your own thinking and understanding, and to do that together with other people. It's really the interchange with others that makes it possible. You might go home and think of something on your own, too, but it's really come out of feeling that . . .

Amy Welch: Yes, that stimulation of a day-to-day environment that is supportive of talking about new ideas and ways of doing things.

Jean Baker Miller: Right. I think that I'm very fortunate to have it. Otherwise, as women, we're always in a kind of foreign culture, like in graduate school, or, in my case, medical school. It really is, I think, a foreign culture, where you do your best to translate what you're trying to say, and often people still don't get it. And you're not getting that kind of support; you may be getting almost the reverse of the kind of stimulation I was just talking about. You experience sort of an oppression, depending, of course, upon the institution, since some are worse than others. You get demoralized, thinking, "Oh I can't be right. They're all saying this, so I must be wrong." I mean I think that that kind of thinking still goes on; it still goes on for me and I've been at this a long time now. We are affected by what surrounds us. So to have a supportive base for thinking new thoughts is very, very exciting!

NOTE

1. Bryer, J.B., Nelson, B.A., Miller, J.B., Krol, P.A. (1987). Childhood Sexual and Physical Abuse as Factors in Adult Psychiatric Illness. *American Journal of Psychiatry, 144:(11)*, 1426-1430.

SELECTED BIBLIOGRAPHY

Books

Connections: From Self to Community in Life and in Therapy (Tentative title). New York: Basic Books, forthcoming, co-author.
Women's Growth in Connection. New York: Guilford Press, 1991, co-author.
Het Zelf-in-Relatie. Eindhoven (Netherlands): Els Uitgeverig, 1988, co-author.
Toward a New Psychology of Women. Boston: Beacon Press, 1976, and London: Allen Lane and Penguin Books, 1977. Also published in Germany, Spain, The Netherlands, Sweden, Denmark, Greece, Norway, Israel, Japan, Brazil. Second Edition, Boston: Beacon Press and London: Penguin, 1987.
Psychoanalysis and Women: Contributions to New Theory and Therapy (Editor). New York: Brunner/Mazel, 1973. New York: Penguin Books, 1973. London: Penguin Books, 1974.

Papers

Movement in Therapy: Honoring the "Strategies of Disconnection," *Work in Progress, No. 65*. Wellesley, MA: Stone Center Working Paper Series, 1994.
A Relational Approach to Understanding Women's Lives and Problems. *Psychiatric Annals 123*,1-8, 1993, co-author.
The Impact on Families of Changing Roles and Relationships, in A. Tasman & S.M. Goldfinger (Eds.), Annual Review of Psychiatry, Vol. 10. Washington, DC: American Psychiatric Press, 1991, co-author.
A Relational Reframing of Psychotherapy, *Work in Progress, No. 52*. Wellesley, MA: Stone Center Working Paper Series, 1991, co-author.
Psychoanalysis and the Psychology of Women, in M. Meisels and E. Shapiro (Eds.), *Traditions and Innovations in Psychoanalytic Education*. Hillsdale, NJ: Lawrence Erlbaum Associates, 1990.
Revisioning Women's Anger: The Personal and the Global, *Work in Progress, No. 43*. Wellesley, MA: Stone Center Working Paper Series, 1990, co-author.
From Depression to Sadness in Women's Psychotherapy, *Work in Progress, No. 36*. Wellesley, MA: Stone Center Working Paper Series, 1989, co-author.

Connections, Disconnections and Violations, *Work in Press, No. 33.* Wellesley, MA: Stone Center Working Paper Series, 1988. Reprinted in M.M. Burger, (Ed.), *Women Beyond Freud: New Comments on Feminism.* NY: Brunner/Mazel, 1994.

Childhood Sexual and Physical Abuse as Factors in Adult Psychiatric Illness. *American Journal of Psychiatry, 144(11)* 1426-1430, 1987, co-author.

Women and Power. *Women & Therapy, 6,* 1-10, 1987.

Themes in Psychoanalytic Understanding of Women: Some Reconsiderations of Autonomy and Affiliation. *Journal of the American Academy of Psychoanalysis, 14,* 241-253, 1986, co-author.

What Do We Mean by Relationships? *Work in Progress, No. 22.* Wellesley, MA: Stone Center Working Paper Series, 1986.

Women and Mental Health. *Journal of American Medical Women's Association, 39,* 97-100, 1984.

Women's Mental Health: Moving Forward with Awareness and Program Alternatives. *Women & Therapy, 3:*29-37, 1984. Reprinted in *Women and Mental Health: New Directions for Change,* C. Mowbray et al. (Eds.), New York: The Haworth Press, Inc., 1984.

The Effects of Inequality on Psychology, in E. Carmen & P. Rieker (Eds.), *Gender and Psychotherapy,* New York: Plenum Press, 1984.

The Development of Women's Sense of Self, *Work in Progress, No. 12,* Wellesley, MA: Stone Center Working Paper Series, 1984. Reprinted in C. Zanardi (Ed.), *Essential Papers on Female Psychology,* New York: New York University Press, 1990.

The Construction of Anger in Women and Men, *Work in Progress, No. 4,* Wellesley, MA: Stone Center Working Paper Series, 1983.

The Necessity of Conflict. *Women & Therapy, 3,* 3-9, 1983. Reprinted in *Women Changing Therapy.* J.H. Robbins & R.J. Seigel (Eds.), New York: The Haworth Press, Inc., 1983.

Psychological Recovery in Low-Income Parents. *Journal of the American Orthopsychiatric Association, 138,* 1319-1330, 1982. Reprinted in R.H. Moos (Ed.), *Coping with Life Crises: New Perspectives,* New York: Plenum Press, 1986.

Conflict and Psychological Development, in M. Notman & C. Nadelson (Eds.), *The Woman Patient, Volume III,* New York: Plenum Press, 1982.

Aggression: Conceptual Issues and Clinical Implications, in M. Notman & C. Nadelson (Eds.), *The Woman Patient, Volume III,* New York: Plenum Press, 1982, co-author.

Women and Power, *Work in Progress, No. 1,* Wellesley, MA: Stone Center Working Paper Series, 1982. Reprinted in T. Wartenberg (Ed.), *Rethinking Power.* New York: State University of New York Press, 1992, and in T.J. Goodrich (Ed.), *Women and Power.* New York: W.W. Norton & Co., 1991.

Adventures of a Feminist

Kate Millett
Betsy Hinden

The way I "got into mental health" was by getting busted, by psychiatric assault, by being deprived of all my rights and having my life set in ruins about me by a series of stupid, split-second judgements made by a number of people who didn't know what they were doing. You might call it a family disagreement into which state psychiatry intervened–creating havoc. I was involved in a political cause of which my relatives disapproved. They were able to have me imprisoned through a few phone calls and a "visit" to a psychiatrist. The psychiatrist was not, as I had imagined, located in a comfortable, private office, but in a locked facility. I was betrayed

Kate Millett, PhD, is a graduate of the University of Minnesota, Oxford University, and Columbia University. A sculptor, essayist, autobiographer, and teacher of literature and philosophy, she lives in New York City and Poughkeepsie, New York, where she has founded an art colony for women. She is the author of *Sexual Politics* (1970), *The Prostitution Papers* (1971), *Flying* (1974), *Sita* (1976), *The Basement* (1979), *Going to Iran* (1981), *The Looney Bin Trip* (1990), and *The Politics of Cruelty* (1994).

Betsy Hinden is a graduate student in Clinical Psychology at The University of Vermont. She is currently doing research on age and gender differences in depression among children and adolescents. She is grateful to have gone to college after *Sexual Politics* was written and included in university curricula.

Correspondence may be addressed to Kate Millett at 295 Bowery, New York, NY 10003.

[Haworth co-indexing entry note]: "Adventures of a Feminist." Millett, Kate, and Betsy Hinden. Co-published simultaneously in *Women & Therapy* (The Haworth Press, Inc.) Vol. 17, No. 3/4, 1995, pp. 347-360; and: *Feminist Foremothers in Women's Studies, Psychology, and Mental Health* (ed: Phyllis Chesler, Esther D. Rothblum, and Ellen Cole) The Haworth Press, Inc., 1995, pp. 347-360; and: *Feminist Foremothers in Women's Studies, Psychology, and Mental Health* (ed: Phyllis Chesler, Esther D. Rothblum, and Ellen Cole) Harrington Park Press, an imprint of The Haworth Press, Inc., 1995, pp. 347-360. Single or multiple copies of this article are available from The Haworth Document Delivery Service [1-800-342-9678, 9:00 a.m. - 5:00 p.m. (EST)].

into this situation and it changed my life, destroyed for me many years, but it also made me an activist for patients' rights and against psychiatric abuse.

My first experience went back way before that. I worked in a looney bin when I was a college student. I took abnormal psyche with three of my college friends. We had high hopes of getting summer jobs as psychiatric aides because we knew the requirements were minimal; even minimum intelligence wasn't a necessity. We were young enthusiasts, most hopeful of making a difference. We imagined if we were kind instead of brutal, sensitive instead of insensitive, gentle and concerned and so on, the supposed mad would flock to us in droves and we would affect miraculous cures from this strange state, this alienated condition as we saw it.

It was a fascinating and wonderful summer. Of course we didn't convert people en masse to sanity. We learned an awful lot, and read hard. We got divided up: I guess the administration spotted a bad little package coming. One friend worked at what would now probably be called a Developmental Disability Center for young people. I was so appalled on a tour of the place that I could not consider working there, though she bravely did, and stuck it out the whole summer. There were little children in the most vile forms of restraint, creatures who had really become monstrosities–sad and very blank, filthy and shouted at a lot. They ate dreadful food and smelled dreadful and stared out the window all day. It was cruel beyond all imagination.

Instead, I went to St. Peter's, the worst state hospital in Minnesota, reading Don Quixote on the bus, to find my own windmill, I suppose. I was also appalled on seeing this place. It was like the opening of the *Divine Comedy* where Dante gets lost in the wood. The place was truly terrifying. The mad were so vividly mad, and of course they were angry and frustrated. They had some drugs then, but they had not really perfected their chemical straightjacket yet, so they had plenty of real straightjackets, and patients were beaten. The noise was deafening. The patients were patients, inmates, victims, prisoners. They were frustrated in every conceivable way. They couldn't even smoke cigarettes and they could have nothing of their own. They had nothing to do all day long and they had been there 20 years. St. Peter's was a snake pit and I worked on the back wards. The women patients there were simply people who had been dumped there by their relatives many years before and never collected again. Of course they naturally withdrew, as anyone would, trying to find some solace at least in the mind. Finding none, they represented a kind of a continuous state of frustration, chagrin or despair.

Their lives were terribly sad. They were women who hadn't "put out" or wouldn't wash the dishes or owned property which someone else wanted. There were all possible stories, but they were all stories of abandonment. Of course there weren't many people incarcerated then. By now psychiatry has reached many millions more and put them in looney bins, even though they don't stay very long. Afterwards they are paroled to take all those weird drugs which tranquilize and silence them, kill the spirit, and certainly poison the body. While at St. Peter's, I decided that I would die rather than see my mother in such a place. I made such a vow because the place was no more than a dog kennel. Many years later I did rescue my mother from an old age home where they were intending to use an electronic bracelet on her, then restraint and probably drugs. She wasn't "adjusting." She didn't want to be there and had been lied to as was customary in these places: "Just a little while and you'll be home," "when your hip mends" or "as soon as you've recovered from the surgery."

When I was at St. Peter's I yearned to publish something in the local paper. I was convinced that if the City Council or state legislature could simply parade through St. Peter's asylum, they would vote it plenty of money or free everyone. I spent a large part of my salary on tobacco and a tiny rolling machine, because very few things are as deplorable as total destitution. Most of the "responsible parties" who dropped people off there, never to return, didn't give them money either. So patients were unable even to buy a candy bar. Imagine being locked up your whole life and unable to buy a candy bar or a toothbrush or a cigarette or have a cold drink because you lacked a nickel?

At St. Peter's they also did a lot of electroshock and insulin shock. I was ordered to assist at electroshock. After the first convulsions, I looked up at the nurse and said, "I'm awfully sorry but I can't do this. I can't participate in this." Its nearness to torture was so obvious. It seemed a nasty, obscene thing to be doing whether they thought it was a medical procedure or not. They used the shock box an awful lot down there and they had done a good many lobotomies. Lobotomies are dressed up in a new terminology now, as psychosurgery. Very few people realize this is going on. Nor is the public aware of the resurgence of electroshock, used principally upon women and the elderly. We are conditioned to believe in the "helping profession" and by now we have built a gigantic bureaucracy about "mental health." In my village there are probably 20 or 40 listings for such agencies, private and public.

As to my "contribution" to mental health, it came first, largely in the form of skepticism, acquired while working as an aide and wearing the keys, being one of the boors who keeps these poor unfortunates in confinement. I used to wonder, "why am I keeping them in confinement? I have no grudge against them." How enormously powerful is society if one or two individuals merely pronounce you crazy or strange, and you lose your freedom. The state has empowered psychiatry to deprive one of personal freedom, the freedom to come and go. Liberty of person–the most basic liberty of all.

The whole term "mental health" seems a little silly. Presumably, it's intended to parallel "mental illness." Actually, it has replaced the state of grace. As a method of social control, the Therapeutic State is far more effective than religion ever was and has a much closer rein. There are thought crimes and sins of intention and so forth. The invasion of the psyche is pretty entire. As to the term "feminist mental health," it makes no sense to me at all. I suppose you could say there might be such a thing as feminist therapy, that a therapist might be a feminist and be well read in the psychology of oppressions and civil rights history. Yet it is my impression that many in the field do not actually read. One of the unfortunate things about feminist therapy is that often its greatest achievement is the sliding scale. "Feminist Therapy" boosts the private practice of the practitioner, exploiting feminism as a commodity. One has the impression that there's a certain amount of self-serving in all of this. Therapy is a marginal career and difficult to advertise. So, if there's a target group . . .

One of the central problems with psychiatry is that there is no standard of care. If you have a faulty appendicitis operation you can sue the doctor since physical medicine does have a standard of care, whereas psychiatrists are protected as if they are members of some secret clergy–immune. As to therapy, the therapist is always more or less playing god, and the "patient" is playing penitent or inadequate person. So as Jeffery Mason pointed out, there's an inherent inegalitarian balance, which is at odds with a feminist way of doing things. Perhaps peer counseling works better for us. I must say that for all my skepticism, I have certainly gotten plenty of good, useful help from therapists. They can move me along with my life, save me a little time in understanding how and why I act.

On the negative side, however, there is a mountain of evidence against psychiatry, especially as it has affected women. Elaine Showater makes a good case as to how psychiatry has targeted women, particularly institutional psychiatry, and victimized us as a class. It is one of the chief ways in which a female is punished in patriarchy for all the crimes of speaking up or having thoughts or disagreeing about something. She risks diagnosis. There is a veneer surface of respectability, the reception room and the pleasant office; and then you pass into the locked institution and back wards, and the place is a zoo and it stinks. It's a tremendous shame humans are confined this way. The popular superstition is so powerful that people actually go to these places for help, imagining they might get some. But instead one is fed a lot of drugs which are harmful to the body. As to the mind, we are destroyed by the judgement that there is something wrong with our minds. We lose confidence and have an even harder time, captive to a theory with no physiological evidence.

The summer after I worked at St. Peter's I spent very differently, running around in Glacier Park with a cowboy and having a whale of a time. I was finished with saving the world. Yet it's very strange that this experience of the Asylum happened to me when I was a kid, because it's almost as if this were to become my cause, long before feminism did. Many years of feminism elapsed before we started rapping out our little theories about female oppression and psychiatry. The Minnesota mental health central office located in Hastings, Minnesota changed my life utterly, and at a very early age, dedicated me to trying to change a system although I wasn't yet its victim. I carried keys, I was an employee. I could do anything I wanted: exploit, torment, abuse–things like that were done all the time. I was constantly afraid that this brutality would just get into my system. The male attendants were so vicious it was hard to believe their stories: one wanted not to. They talked about their charges as if they were some kind of animals, and were utterly addicted to the use of force upon their helpless victims. There was sexual abuse, drug abuse, rape, beatings, the whole spectrum of prison life, and none of these people had committed a crime. So, when you think of it from a legal point of view, it really is astonishing that the ACLU won't do anything genuine to ensure patients' rights or prevent commitment. So, many years later, when I was busted, I was forced to make a contribution here. Circumstances did this for me. I had to read a great deal more, I had to concentrate and remember what it was like for those 10 days. So often they're just a blur of drugs. So, I suppose working at St. Peter's asylum was the circumstance that led up to my "contribution" to mental health, for although it didn't come back into my life for a long time, I felt a kind of moral responsibility to the people who were there. It was my first cause as a young person.

I suspect my main contribution is to provide an essential skepticism which I feel we have discarded. I wish to expose the fraud of psychiatry. Its inhumanity–asylums are really so dreary, you can't imagine it. St. Peter's was really hell, the cruelest and most stupid way to treat a couple of boxcars of people. Their despair, their sense of betrayal. It isn't expected that they'll live that long. To do this to people and to pretend then that you're helping them or taking care of them, tying them into a straitjacket where they could have a heart attack . . . consider the idea. Consider the sadism.

In addition to this skepticism, *The Loony Bin Trip* is my other main contribution to mental health. I spent 5 years writing it and another 5 trying to find a publisher for it since it is heresy to criticize psychiatry in America. And this book says far more than I can say to you here. Surely the picture of psychiatric fraud and abuse, the narrative, even the humor says it best. Writing it also mitigated what I had suffered and spoke for others who had suffered as well.

In joining the anti-psychiatric movement one is necessarily on the side of imagination and poetry and against irrational thinking and popular superstition. Psychiatry has made the mind questionable, suspect. It narrows the permissible and discourages imaginative experience. I am also struck by how irrational psychiatry is, how incapable of medical logic, physiological cause and effect, scientific evidence such as physical medicine demands. They are a force for social control, but as doctors or men of science–laughable. Many trust therapists much more, assuring themselves, "I can tell her anything and rely on her discretion," but therapists are affiliated with psychiatry. They can lift the phone and get you drugs or get you incarcerated. Getting busted was the greatest catastrophe of my life, yet it did let me see what life was like in the pit, and those are pretty useful things to have an acquaintance with if one is a humanist.

My first memory of being a feminist is probably at age five when I asked my mother why the president, pope and so forth were all men. She said, "It's a man's world" and I said, "I don't find that fair," and she said, "Well, it isn't." Being a feminist in those days was always a form of "maladjustment" because one was supposed to adjust to a man's world. If you didn't, then you should perhaps see a therapist. When I was at Oxford, I came across *The Second Sex,* Simone DeBeauvoir's book, and it changed my life. Here, finally, was someone who agreed with me, and in fact, had really thought about it long and hard long before me. The book was a success du scandale at the time. It was a best seller in France but it was argued about endlessly. It arrived in the U.S. a little later, but it was put out in the 50s, long before there was a second wave of feminism. At Oxford I went to Paris a great deal and I would sit in cafes and argue with people about this book which everyone was reading. The curious thing is that the fellows who were socialist would at least in theory agree with me. They would never, of course, alter their behavior at all. On the other hand, women might agree with the book emotionally, but intellectually they would resort to a whole lot of arguments about nature and "you can't change things" and "perhaps you are maladjusted and perhaps you should see a therapist because the world as it's constructed doesn't satisfy you." I went along being dissatisfied with this construction for a few years in Japan and I came home and read Betty Friedan's book, *The Feminine Mystique,* which explained a great deal to me: for example, why I wasn't being able to find a job in New York with my fancy English degree and my low typing speed. So the *Feminine Mystique* explained America and what had happened since the suffragettes. My own mother voted in the first election and when I presented her finally with *Sexual Politics* she said, "Oh I've known about this all along."

I don't know exactly what my contribution to Feminism might be. . . . When I returned from Japan the civil rights movement was taking place and was part of why I came home. I worked for CORE during Mississippi summer and learned a little bit about the politics of civil rights, its actions and activities. Then I began graduate school at Columbia. The summer before I started graduate school, I saw an advertisement in the Village Voice for a series of lectures at The Ethical Culture Institute, by a man named Tobin from City College. The lectures were titled "Is Women's Emancipation Completed?" or something along that line. I thought "gee," but it cost $75.00, which was a great deal of money at the time. I was living with Fumio Yoshimura then, and he said, "Oh go ahead, somehow we'll find the money." And so I went up on the subway. It nearly reminded me of going to gay bars in that there was something surreptitious or vaguely scandalous about going to these lectures because they were feeding into my "misfit" side. I went to the whole series and was brave enough to ask a question or two and was eventually spotted by some women who came up to me at the last lecture and said, "Would you like to join a civil rights organization for women?" and I said "Oh yes, I certainly would, I always wanted there to be such a thing." So I joined NOW and the people who tapped me were some of its early officers, among them my good friend Anselma Del'Olio. So I went to NOW meetings and then it all just began to happen. Suddenly there was Downtown Radical Women and I joined that. I founded Columbia Women's Liberation with some friends up there, Harriet Zelner, Anne Harris and Sydney Abbot. There was Downtown Radical Lesbians and I joined that and I went to Redstockings. I just went to meetings all the time. I was living in a flurry of revolutionary thought and activity. I was also writing my doctoral thesis for Columbia. I'd since been fired from Barnard where I had been a lecturer for $308.00 a month, for 6 years. My political activities, especially on behalf of the students during the student strike of '68, got me fired. My feminism was probably another problem. They were going to have to advance me in rank because I had finally passed all my examinations for the doctorate and was now writing my thesis. They canned me and I wept and cried because I loved this job even though I was so underpaid. I loved teaching and I loved the students and I actually loved that school. So, I drank martinis in the daytime for a little bit and went off the track. They weren't taking me back and I didn't have quite the gumption or feeling of support to make an issue or call on student support for protest. In those days there was no hope of suing anybody about anything. I just took it on the chin and so there was nothing left to do except write that damn thesis. But it was now a different thesis since I imagined I had no academic future. It was all over after 10 years of teaching. Since I was sacked from Columbia, I probably wouldn't get a job anyplace else. So I sat down and wrote the three passages that *Sexual Politics* begins with, which are three descriptions of sexual intercourse, although I think "fucking" is perhaps a more appropriate term where the subtext is all force, brutality and politics. I read these passages to Fumio and a friend, and we drank a lot of martinis and laughed and laughed. I was growing encouraged. I knew a lady at Doubleday who had refused to reprint *Token Learning,* which was a pamphlet I wrote about women's colleges when I was chair of the Education Committee for New York NOW. I put 500 bucks into it. Anselmo Del'Olio had it distributed. We sold them all and put the money back in and printed them again, but Doubleday was still not interested. It's now an extremely rare book. I myself don't have a copy. At any rate, I showed the publisher my three opening selections and she offered to buy the book for $4,000.00. Since I didn't have any money at the time, this struck me as an awful lot. I got $2,000.00 ahead and $2,000.00 when it was finished and worked like a maniac. I had done a good deal of work on the thesis already. For example, I had read all of Lawrence which takes several years, and so I just went ahead and did it.

At around this time, I was invited to make a speech at Cornell where I got paid 75 dollars and wore my very best dress. I called the speech "Sexual Politics" and it became the second chapter, the "Theory of Sexual Politics." On the way home from Cornell I confessed to my comrades that I'd been fired and so there was nothing else to do but keep writing this book. So I got it all written and the rest is sort of history. It hit at the right time and I got on the cover of *Time*, even against my wishes and the express philosophy of the women's movement. *Time* asked me what would be good for the August 26th cover and I said "maybe a whole group of women in a march or something because we don't like leaders and personalities." Despite this, they used an old photograph and got Alice Neil to paint a portrait because I'd refused permission to be photographed for the cover. The cover is the portrait by Alice Neil, which is probably even nicer, but it did cause kind of a lot of ruckus and Sturm und Drang and embarrassment. There was even a faction of the Women's Movement which thought I should publish my book anonymously. I said, "Well, at least the mistakes are my own." But the book really came out of all those meetings and late nights in New Haven with other graduate students while we tried to figure out the origins of patriarchy and all that kind of stuff.

It came very much out of the context of the times. Fiorika up in New Haven was more insightful than I on the origins of patriarchy, suggesting that it might be a population explosion coming out of the discovery of paternity. I'd read all the texts available and the rest of the time we just tried to reason it out. I had to control my rhetoric a bit, because it was going to be submitted as a thesis. The publisher thought so, too. So I was always cooling it down a little and it does read both ironic and arch. It reads like who I was then, about thirty-five and going to a lot of meetings. It's in a Mandarin kind of English. I wanted to make it less turgid and tedious than American scholarship, more genteel and readable like the British. But it is rather fancy and academic, so it was a wonderful thing to break through into my own voice with *Flying*.

Sexual Politics was published in July and was actually on the best seller list, although I know it didn't sell that many copies. It didn't sell as many copies as things that probably should have been on the best seller list. For example, Billy Graham had a book out at the same time which I'm sure sold a great many more copies. Anyway, by November, *Time* magazine was gunning for me, or the media or the establishment or the powers-that-be or the great conspiracy of the right wing or whatever. I was targeted to be first blown up like a balloon and then burst. So *Time* printed that I was a bisexual and that therefore all my scholarship in *Sexual Politics* was suspect, an interesting jump in logic. The sales of the book fell off terribly. Everybody who was going to my classes at Bryn Mawr stopped coming and there was a whole terrible hassle with the family, who were really very brave about it, but for my mother, the idea of everybody sitting in their dentist's office all over the world reading about how little Katie was a bisexual was rather formidable, especially since she had insurance clients and was always a little nervous about my activities in this direction.

So, from being a celebrity, I became an obscure person over-night. It was reassuring to the extent that I had a private life again and so, could be an artist. Much longer in mediaville and I probably would have gone off the tracks and stayed gone. But it also meant I couldn't any longer talk on television or express my opinions in America or have any effect when there was something I wanted to get done, or somebody I wanted to help, or some cause or principle to stand up about. Naturally, in response to *Time*, we had a wonder-ful press conference, the whole women's movement united, not around the attack on me so much as the attack on the whole issue of homosexuality and lesbianism, and the whole business of having called us dykes from the beginning and now having quote, "discov-ered" we were dykes after all. I had been all this time telling the press that I was a member of Radical Lesbians so it wasn't as if they were just discovering it. It was simply that they decided at that point to print it and to use verbiage like "admitted" and "confessed" and all that sort of nonsense. At any rate, we did make a wonderful statement of principle about how the women's movement and the gay movement were involved with the same issues, with attacking the whole sexist setup and stereotype, the same systems of status and masculine and feminine personality traits, and how they were really just cogs in a whole power scheme of sexual politics and so forth. So we had come now to a position of total support for gay liberation. That was a wonderful occasion for the women's move-ment to make an important ideological statement of unity with the gay movement.

So, I suppose that one of the things that I may have contributed was uniting those two movements and being a pivotal person in bridging between the two. I've tried to do that with other issues, for example, the anti-psychiatric movement or the movement against psychiatric abuse and the women's movement. I've also been very often involved with prisoners' rights. My latest book is about the torture of political prisoners. In that book I perhaps went beyond the contribution I was trying to make as an international feminist by looking at world politics, seeing power politics from a feminist perspective and concluding that cruelty was deliberate state policy throughout this century. We have an amount of torture and a routine use of it that is staggering and far surpasses the Middle Ages and the Inquisition. And unless there is some kind of worldwide movement again for the abolition of torture as there was through the enlightenment, it will simply grow and democracy has very slim hopes.

Betsy Hinden: You seem to be attributing your contributions to the times, the historical context. However, there are many people who aren't courageous, even in courageous times. You stand out . . .

Kate Millett: Perhaps there are people like me who don't really mean to get in trouble but do so anyway. Perhaps because they have a certain penchant for telling the truth or they just happen to be at the wrong spot when things blow up. I was in Iran when the Ayatollah took over. I didn't mean to be arrested and held under tommy guns and I was scared out of my mind, but I had been, for years, involved with the Iranian situation due to the torture of political prisoners; and I had been involved with Iranian expatriates and spoken in their behalf to expose the crimes of the Shah. So the Shah goes and we're going to have a wonderful revolution in Iran and return to the democracy and the constitution of 1905 and all the rest, and instead we get the Ayatollah. I had just gone over to celebrate International Women's Day because I was invited. Little did we ever imagine we'd be having these vast marches as the last cry of women's freedom and of democracy itself in Iran. I never mean to get into all the pinches that I do anymore than I thought I'd be locked up just by going to see a psychiatrist in his office, which is how I understood that afternoon. But there we go. I didn't mean to get fired from Columbia. I believed in academic freedom. A lot of it derives from my naivete, probably.

Betsy Hinden: A willingness to speak the truth is truly courageous. Most people don't take risks. I am still wondering why you think you are the type of person who is willing to take risks?

Kate Millett: I was a rebel in school. I come from an Irish revolutionary background, so it isn't hard to keep it up. I'm also non-violent, so I always figure I know where I'm skating because I'm still a pacifist. But that doesn't always keep you out of trouble, does it?

With respect to the last question regarding how my life changed as a result of my involvement in feminism and "mental health," my life was broken in half by mental health, several times, and repairing it wasn't easy. You lose your credibility. I couldn't get gigs for a long time, speeches at universities. My friends all assumed I was crazy because somebody else said I was and nobody checked. Early on, if the incident were mentioned, I would say, "You wouldn't believe what this place was like, calls itself a hospital, it's really a jail . . . " Others would respond with this sort of pained expression and something of a rebuke: "Well, you must have been there for some reason. You must have done something." After awhile you learn to shut up, and when that won't work, you finally write a book. But think of all the lives destroyed by this idiotic system. The fear of being crazy is crazy-making. Once they've planted that seed of self-distrust, it becomes a kind of self-destruct. It has lead to all kinds of suicides and it certainly put me in that frame of mind a few times.

Feminism changed my life utterly, of course. In many, many ways it really made my life. I think it's been an enormous force in my art, in my visual art as well as my writing. It made my life really fun and exciting because the 70s and the 60s were terrific times of not only wanting to change the world but seeing that you could. And, by the way, how remarkably easy it was. So feminism has been kind of a life force for me. It has brought me lifelong friends and a lifelong interest.

Feminism is an endless movie unfolding. It's been going on forever, but certainly heating up since the middle of the 19th century. I feel very close to the early feminists as one of many, many,

many women taking a certain road. Lots of setbacks and so on. Recently, American feminism has dug in, has become very strong in the economy and has had a real influence on business and also on social life, but it also has gotten stalemated by all those years of Republican rule. The real advances, the excitement to me now, is international and I would love to go to Beijing. Since I can't seem to get invited, maybe I'll just break down and get myself a ticket because feminism is one of the greatest moments of change in recorded history, and we've been lucky enough to play a part and see it happen. Even to the privilege of being instigators and effective. That alone makes for a very exciting life, personally and in every aspect–amorous as well as everything else. Certainly it's made for a tremendous energy and force that's gone into my work and into my art.

Betsy Hinden: You mention that feminism has resulted in the development of lifelong friendships. You seem very committed to your friendships, even under very difficult circumstances where others might have written them off . . .

Kate Millett: Well, you only have one family, so you can't really write them off. I've invested an awful lot in all these friends and they're all terribly important to me. I love them sometimes against my will, but, persevering is a way of reeducating, too, and solving it, you know. Also, feminism has given me the women's art colony which is one of the great things in my life. At times, it really is a paradise. We're having a terrific summer this year. Being able to build buildings, being able to build a community, all of that has been exciting: To restore all these acres, to make the trees support the colony, to share the trees, to have that relationship to nature. To be surrounded by this much beauty all the time, and this much fun. This was the life we dreamed of when we were dreaming up feminism. We get to live it at the farm. Then of course we have to go back into reality, so-called . . .

Foremothers/Foresisters

Ginny NiCarthy

"Who me, 'foremother'?" The term at first brought forth images of old, dead or at least venerable, respectable women, roles I'd never thought to apply for–though I'd made it to "old" without effort. But *Women & Therapy* made the allegation, called me a "foremother" of feminist therapy, so I en-

"FOREMOTHERS/SISTERS/ FATHERS/BROTHERS"

For most of her adult life Ginny NiCarthy has been an activist in civil rights, civil liberties and peace movements, as well as in feminist politics. She practiced Feminist Therapy with groups and individuals for nearly twenty years, specializing in problems of abuse and violence against women. She views her community work as part of her profession of Feminist Therapist. In that context she co-founded and directed Rape Relief, founded and directed the Abused Women's Network, co-directed The Women's Institute, edited the *International Network Against Violence Against Women (INAVAW)* and authored books for women suffering violence, especially in relationships with intimate partners. Her most recent publication is *You Don't Have to Take It! A Woman's Guide to Confronting Emotional Abuse at Work.* She currently lives half-time in Mexico, experiments with new forms of writing and tries to fit as much traveling as possible into her life.

Thanks to foresisters Ruth Crow and Naomi Gottlieb, who once again came through with helpful comments on this manuscript.

Correspondence may be addressed to Ginny NiCarthy at 626 1/2 36th Avenue, Seattle, WA 98122.

[Haworth co-indexing entry note]: "Foremothers/Foresisters." NiCarthy, Ginny. Co-published simultaneously in *Women & Therapy* (The Haworth Press, Inc.) Vol. 17, No. 3/4, 1995, pp. 361-372; and: *Feminist Foremothers in Women's Studies, Psychology, and Mental Health* (ed: Phyllis Chesler, Esther D. Rothblum, and Ellen Cole) The Haworth Press, Inc., 1995, pp. 361-372; and: *Feminist Foremothers in Women's Studies, Psychology, and Mental Health* (ed: Phyllis Chesler, Esther D. Rothblum, and Ellen Cole) Harrington Park Press, an imprint of The Haworth Press, Inc., 1995, pp. 361-372. Single or multiple copies of this article are available from The Haworth Document Delivery Service [1-800-342-9678, 9:00 a.m. - 5:00 p.m. (EST)].

tertained second thoughts about it. I *have* been a long-time activist and Feminist Therapist, perhaps I *have* had some impact on the development of feminist therapy, especially with women who've been battered. I did give birth to feminist projects and promulgated ideas that helped shift women from individual to sociopolitical interpretations of their lives. I've also elaborated and adapted others' ideas and put them in writing, which helped give them a lasting life. I became a kind of Feminist-Therapist-on-the-printed-page.

This volume implies that "foremothers" embody the most positive of mothering stereotypes: nurturing, generative, powerful. We cling to the romance of the family, hopefully reinventing its form despite the fact many of our mothers, fathers, brothers and sisters turned our dreams to nightmares. That strikes me as odd. But okay. I'll reluctantly accept that family framework, with the proviso that we institute the concept, "foresisters," a term at least as appropriate as "foremothers," to honor early innovators and those who carried out their radical ideas. Dozens or more feminist "foresisters" influenced, supported, abetted, enabled my work, as I did for them. Some foresisters are listed on the borders of these pages. "Forebrothers" too. Why not? Naming names is important.

During the second wave of feminist ferment, I became part of the movement against violence toward women. The movement was inflamed by, and helped set off, an explosion of new feminist analyses: of culture, gender, relationships and psychotherapy.

"FOREMOTHERS/SISTERS/ FATHERS/BROTHERS"

Simone de Beauvoir

Betty Friedan

Gloria Steinem

Robin Morgan

Kate Millett

Shulamith Firestone

Joleen

Germaine Greer

Theories and strategies multiplied at a stunning rate. It was as if, on a long holiday from conventional ideas, we waved bouquets of feminist sparklers, which in turn kindled even more radical spins on all that we'd been taught.

In conjunction with other feminists I initiated groups, programs and ideas, especially in relation to rape and battering of women. Sometimes it seemed that the vision was mine alone. But who could tell which woman ignited a particular spark first, in what direction it would fly, which fires it would kindle? Embers–feminist, rebellious, social-change embers–had burned in me for years, taking the form of rage, periodically dying down into depression or despair, then flaming into anger again. Yet I woke up in the eighties to find myself receiving an "Innovator Award" from King County Coalition on Domestic Violence and a Governor's award for my first book, *Getting Free.*

I can't remember a time when I didn't resent the unfairness of arbitrary status discrimination, especially related to gender. I think I must have been born a feminist:

1930s: "It's not fair that I have to do the dishes and Paul just has to dump the garbage, just because he's a boy! It's not fair that I have to wear dresses and can't climb fences!"

1943: "Yes, Sister Mary Wilma. I heard you say that boys can't control their sexual urges, so girls have to set limits." (I don't believe it.)

1954: "Okay, I'll marry you, but I won't cook or do housework. I'll earn our living, Bob, if you'll stay home with the baby."

For me the important click! often came when someone else recognized what I'd perceived, validating the thought, explaining a "crazy" feeling, enabling me to feel relatively sane at last. But more than once I lost sight of feminist understandings. In the early 1960s just as the feminist revolution gained a toe-hold, I slid into the role of depressed "housewife" (with a second, controlling, husband) and stay-at-home mother of pre-schoolers. Once more I was out of sync with the times. But I became a civil rights and peace activist in organizations that reinforced the ideas, hunches and attitudes I'd acquired long before. Like many feminists I learned something about organizing and about how to focus rebellion through work in other radical movements.

As I try to trace the development of my role in feminist therapy, I'm overwhelmed by surfacing memories of dozens, maybe hundreds, of individuals and of social, intellectual and political links forging a loosely coupled train of movement events. Their names should be recorded and so I'm making a start here. In 1972 I was one of the people who started Rape Relief and I became its director. But first came a Speak Out On Rape inspired by an article describing a similar event in New York City. In Seattle the crisis line for rape victims could not have begun had it not been for University YWCA co-directors and board members who had the foresight, financial commitment and willingness to let us initiate our program under its umbrella. It wouldn't have existed without the courage and vision of women who broke away from the YMCA

"FOREMOTHERS/SISTERS/ FATHERS/BROTHERS"

Congress of Racial Equality

American Friends Service Committee

New York Speak Out Organizers

New York Magazine

Univ. YWCA Board

*Univ. YWCA co-directors
  Shelly Yapp
  Jan Knutson*

*Anne Hirondelle:
separated Univ.
YWCA from YMCA*

Law Enforcement

*Assistance
Administration*

in 1971. Possibly we couldn't have sustained it without the support of certain established government institutions and one particular police officer.

It became a cornerstone of Feminist Therapy that no one had the right to have sex with *any* woman without her consent—a radical new perception, suddenly obvious to feminists. Sparks of awareness flickered all over the country illuminating ideas remarkably similar, many adapted from non-feminist sources. Although in 1972 I was not a therapist and had just begun studying social work, I had some familiarity with other radical thinkers. I agreed with professionals of various stripes who determined to re-define therapy.

1950: I'm excited by a book on Marxist psychoanalysis critical of Freudian interpretations. My psychiatrist boyfriend won't listen.

1954: I'm proud to work as a psychiatric aide in a hospital that favors "milieu therapy" and disdains meds for mentally ill patients.

1968: Radical alternative workshops at an Orthopsychiatry conference validate my tentative criticisms of traditional therapy.

1972-3: With encouragement from feminist faculty, I arrange a social work internship at the University YWCA and in a feminist program to release women from jail.

Although I had no real theory to back my beliefs it seemed natural and obvious to follow principles of openness about method, to minimize power differentials between therapist and client and to strongly consider the role of status and socialization. Those ideas

"FOREMOTHERS/SISTERS/ FATHERS/BROTHERS"

City of Seattle Office of Law and Justice:
  Donna Schramm
  Phil Sherburn
Mike German,
Seattle Police Dept.

NOW

KNOW, Inc.

Karen Horney

R.D. Lang

Ari Kiev

Thomas Szasz

Frank Riessman

Carl Menninger

Pinel Foundation

Hoagy Wycoff

Claude Steiner

Faculty:
  Naomi Gottlieb
  Cheryl Richey

Sharon Berlin,
internship supervisor

Jennifer James,
jail project

grew out of political convictions and informal testimonies of women who had been violated by traditional psychiatric systems. But they were also part of a revolution taking place within psychology, among Radical Therapists and others seeking to maximize the "power of the people"–of ordinary people. Feminist activists and therapists like myself carried them over to our work with women who had been battered, sexually victimized as children and raped. We began with egalitarian feminist ideals, plus goals of liberation, and then learned from our clients what they wanted.

By 1976, having waited in vain for *someone who knew how* to lead shelter-based groups for women who had been battered, I finally invented the process, and along with Jane Klassen, began them myself. It soon became apparent that many women who didn't reach shelters needed help, too. So I started a community group, and the women in it began to trade childcare, phone support and lots of other mutual aid outside of our meeting times. I realized that additional advocacy and help in forming alliances would multiply the effects of their interconnections as well as those of other women who couldn't get out of the house for a group. Through the Women's Institute I started The Abused Women's Network, a nonshelter service for those women. At first we had no money and no staff, but through the federal programs CETA and WIN we hired advocates who answered a crisis line and put women in touch with each other by phone and in person.

I began to record what I was learning

"FOREMOTHERS/SISTERS/FATHERS/BROTHERS"

Black Panthers

SDS: Students for a Democratic Society

SNCC: Student Nonviolent Coordinating Committee

Diana Russell

Susan Brownmiller

Robin Morgan

Del Martin

Phyllis Chesler

*Center for Women Policy Studies
    Jane Chapman
    Margaret Gates*

*Shirley Kaplan, Dir:
New Beginnings Shelter
for Battered Women*

Seattle Women's Commission

Susan Crane

*Women's Institute:
    Naomi Gottlieb
    Cheryl Richey
    Molly Moss
    Christie Fisher*

*Abused Women's
Network: Karen Kaur*

from the women, and to hand out copies to others in the group each week. They told me what more they needed and I wrote it up. I began to envision a pamphlet or book small enough to tuck into a purse or pocket and wrote what became my first major book, *Getting Free: You Can End Abuse and Take Back Your Life* (subtitled differently at first). One publisher after another insisted, "There isn't enough need for such a book." Then they said, "No woman would walk out of a bookstore with it because she would be too stigmatized." Twenty-four publishers rejected it.

"FOREMOTHERS/SISTERS/ FATHERS/BROTHERS"

Doggedly I kept writing the book, certain it would fill a necessary gap. There was nothing in print that would help women who had been abused. Eventually I turned to Seal Press, a small feminist press right in. my own town that had published poetry, chapbooks and a biography. They "didn't do" self-help books. Nevertheless they took a chance and Barbara Wilson walked me through many re-writings. *Getting Free* was at first distributed mainly through shelters, then gained a broader audience as the movement against battering grew.

Seal Press:
Barbara Wilson
Hylah Jacques
Rachel de Sylva
Faith Conlan

Leading groups ultimately spawned a co-authored book, *Talking It Out: A Guide to Groups for Abused Women,* for shelter workers and professionals. Women didn't need therapy, we authors said, so much as they needed to listen to *each other.* Listening to group members' histories and trading solutions to problems placed their experiences in a political framework. It resembled a specialized *CR* group, but with a leader who played the role of traffic director and

Talking It Out
co-authors:
Karen Miriam and
Sandra Coffman

presented exercises to help women clarify their situations and options.

During the nineteen-seventies and early eighties, like a lot of other feminists, I was fueled by excitement that bordered on obsession. I began my writing career between 1978 and 1982 by turning out a feminist assertion manual for youth workers, a teacher's guide for a book on sex-role socialization and *Getting Free*. I directed the Abused Women's Network, co-directed the Women's Institute, conducted a private therapy practice and led women's groups on power, risk-taking and numerous other topics.

I taught a summer school Women's Studies class on Women and Power and led second stage groups, designed for women who had stayed away from partners for six weeks or more. Those groups provided continuing sustenance and problem-solving assistance as new and difficult situations arose. In the late nineteen-seventies Ruth Crow, one of the few feminists actively concerned about young women, initiated a feminist program for teenaged women. She persuaded me I could write the assertion manual and train youth workers to use it.

During that period I also met with a group of men and women exploring relationships between therapy and politics and conducted workshops for professionals and shelter workers. Many of those activities were concurrent, which scarcely seems credible. But those were heady days—days when everything seemed possible. Like a lot of other people I waited for others to do what seemed necessary—someone who knew how—and when no such person materialized, I did it

"FOREMOTHERS/SISTERS/ FATHERS/BROTHERS"

Feminist Press
Ruth Rosen

Women's Institute:
* Lenora Mundt*
* Naomi Gottlieb*
* Ruth McCormick*
* Cheryl Richey*
* Sharon Berlin*

Ruth Crow, Director:
New Directions
for Young Women

Judge John Conlan

Dan Kelleher
Jane Klassen

Carol Richards
Karil Klingbeil
Vickie Boyd
Ellen Pence
Betsy Warrior
Susan Schecter

myself. All over the country those actions were being replicated.

I was frustrated at researchers' continual focus on the question, "Why do women stay?" Especially since each week I observed women leaving abusive partners and staying away from them. A more pertinent question, I thought, was *how* women stayed away, which sparked interviews that in 1987 became the book, *The Ones Who Got Away: Women Who Left Abusive Partners.* I wanted professionals and the public to focus on surviving more than victimization, a focus still needed in the movement against violence and Feminist Therapy.

I co-authored an easy-to-read version of *Getting Free* and eventually initiated or encouraged others to establish groups for black women and lesbians who were battered. I helped establish ABBL, Advocates for Abused and Battered Lesbians and co-led groups for lesbians who abused their partners. For six years I wrote a newsletter, *International Network Against Violence Against Women (INAVAW)*, initiated at the U.N. women's conference in Nairobi. Beginning with the U.N. women's conference in Mexico City, which I'd also been privileged to attend, it became more and more clear that women all over the world dealt with similar problems and that we could learn from each other. In all of that work, and in later co-authoring *You Don't Have to Take It! A Woman's Guide to Confronting Emotional Abuse at Work* emphasized the role of socialization, especially the conditioning of women and men into rigid sex-roles.

"FOREMOTHERS/SISTERS/ FATHERS/BROTHERS"

Sue Davidson, co-author: You Can Be Free: An Easy-to-Read Handbook for Abused Women

Addei Fuller: leader of groups for black women

ABBL: Christa Irwin Kathleen Mangan Debra Rutt Merrill Cousin

Ann Harvey, co-leader group for abusive lesbians

Seattle Counseling for Sexual Minorities

INAVAW Newsletter: Sharon Adkins Qiyama Rahman B J. Bryson Ann Nicoll

Co-authors: Naomi Gottlieb Sandra Coffman

Carol Tavris Alexandra Kaplan Sandra Bem Jessie Bernard

As a result of a lecture on battering to a group of American Sign Language interpreters I met Marilyn Smith, who wanted to organize services specifically for deaf women. I said, "Do it!" She said, "I don't know enough yet." I didn't know enough about deafness and she didn't know enough about leading groups. I kept urging and she kept hesitating until we came up with a viable plan. I would provide a series of training sessions for Marilyn and several deaf colleagues, who would then become her support group. The groups evolved into AD-WAS, Abused Deaf Women's Advocacy Services, now serving deaf women rape victims and children molested by family members, as well as women abused by partners. Marilyn conducts national trainings on her work.

There were, of course, some idiosyncratic reasons that I became a writer. I grew up in a family that valued the written word and forced a traditional Catholic education on me, so I'd learned how to write a proper sentence and even to diagram it. Only after many years of chaotic personal stumbling and randomly directed rebellion, did the discipline I'd resisted belatedly take hold. I'm a visionary ("crazy," "unrealistic") and willing to take risks ("foolish," "reckless"), traits that have been useful to me. Just as importantly, I'm focused ("obsessive") and persistent ("stubborn"). Feminists and other political colleagues re-defined my previous labels of "mad," "bad" and "crazy" for me, and I found myself transformed into "imaginative," "innovative"–a respected feminist activist.

"FOREMOTHERS/SISTERS/ FATHERS/BROTHERS"

Murray Straus
Richard Gelles

ADWAS:
Marilyn Smith
Kathy Hoog
Karen Bosley

In the course of those events, especially as a writer, I unwittingly laid the groundwork for the label, "foremother." Part visionaries, part recorders, critics and reviewers, writers are sometimes theoreticians, propagandists and problem-solvers. Writers get noticed. If we continue in the movement or our books last, colleagues and followers may name us "foremothers." Meanwhile numerous "foresisters" who haven't recorded their actions or thoughts are lost to history.

In the seventies many of us feminist movement workers felt personally and politically beleaguered, discriminated against and oppressed. We were right about that. It's also true that most of us were able to participate in feminist anti-violence work in large part because of our education and white middle-class status–that is, as members of the majority class, the class of oppressors. In those days I would have said I had no access to power. Yet clearly I knew people who did have that access. They gave me opportunities and encouragement to contribute to the movement, to learn as I went along, and especially to write. To recognize that privilege is not to indict those of us who used it. Nor does it imply that I and the groups I was part of didn't try to expand our membership, our organizing and our services to include women of color and working-class women. We did exactly that, though our efforts were often too little, too late and inept.

As I look back at our history the themes that stand out for me are the forgotten roles of "foresisters": interconnections with and support of other movements; widespread

"FOREMOTHERS/SISTERS/ FATHERS/BROTHERS"

Susan Schecter: recorder of "foresisters' " work in the movement against woman battering

*Sue Davidson
Ruth Crow*

political foment; the unrecognized roles of white and middle-class privilege; the personally miraculous happenstance for me of ideas and actions once labeled "crazy," "bad," "mad" or "whacko," suddenly being re-named "imaginative," "innovative," "useful." It would be going just a tad too far to say my feminist work has become my life, has turned my life upside down, but it's close. It takes lots of women to hold up half the sky. Feminism has enabled me to hold my hand up there with my foresisters. I wouldn't have missed it for the world.

NAOMI GOTTLIEB: IN MEMORIAM

Having retired from her University of Washington position as social work professor, Naomi Gottlieb served in spring 1995 as a Tel Aviv University guest professor and advisor on development of a women's program. While traveling during the spring break she was hit by a tram in Prague and died May 8, 1995. Brief references to Naomi Gottlieb in the above article scarcely begin to do justice to her contributions to feminist social work, feminist social work education and the ripple effect of her influence on students who continue her work as feminist therapists. Her influence and sisterly critiques of my projects and thinking about many topics significantly furthered my work as a feminist therapist and activist. Naomi lives on in the continuing political struggles of those of us privileged to have known her. And she lives on in generations to come, who may not even be aware of their legacy from her–as foremother and foresister.

Testing the Boundaries of Justice

Suzanne Pharr
Diane M. Felicio

I've always had difficulty in thinking of myself as just a member of the women's movement, or just a member of the lesbian and gay movement. I think of myself most often as an anti-racist worker. It feels to me, that racism permeates all that we do and shapes all of our beings, and I live with the most fervent desire to make that different: to be able to work the best I can, to take the privilege of my white skin, which was given to me without my asking, and to spend that privilege in every way I can to make that change come about.

–Suzanne Pharr, July 19, 1994

Suzanne Pharr is a social and economic justice worker from the South. She is a strategist, organizer, and writer who currently spends most of her time focusing on the insurgency of the Right.

Diane Felicio holds a PhD in Social Psychology from the University of Vermont. Her research on the experiences of women in medical school was recently published in *Basic and Applied Social Psychology*. Her works in progress include an article on feminist ethics in higher education and a book chapter on the dynamics of friendship between lesbian and heterosexual women. She is currently a faculty member in Psychology and Feminist Studies at Goddard College, Plainfield, Vermont.

Correspondence may be addressed to Suzanne Pharr at 1423 NE 28th Street, Portland, OR 97232.

[Haworth co-indexing entry note]: "Testing the Boundaries of Justice." Pharr, Suzanne, and Diane M. Felicio. Co-published simultaneously in *Women & Therapy* (The Haworth Press, Inc.) Vol. 17, No. 3/4, 1995, pp. 373-381; and: *Feminist Foremothers in Women's Studies, Psychology, and Mental Health* (ed: Phyllis Chesler, Esther D. Rothblum, and Ellen Cole) The Haworth Press, Inc., 1995, pp. 373-381; and: *Feminist Foremothers in Women's Studies, Psychology, and Mental Health* (ed: Phyllis Chesler, Esther D. Rothblum, and Ellen Cole) Harrington Park Press, an imprint of The Haworth Press, Inc., 1995, pp. 373-381. Single or multiple copies of this article are available from The Haworth Document Delivery Service [1-800-342-9678, 9:00 a.m. - 5:00 p.m. (EST)].

© 1995 by The Haworth Press, Inc. All rights reserved.

BACKGROUND AND INFLUENTIAL MOVEMENTS

For much of her life, Suzanne Pharr has spent her time thinking, writing and organizing about the interconnection of oppressions. Suzanne's work on racism, sexism, homophobia, violence against women, and the religious right has revolved around her belief that if you look closely at any one oppression you will recognize the presence of others. One outcome of this belief has been a commitment to community education on the interrelatedness of oppressive systems. For example, Suzanne's work with the women's anti-violence movement included workshops on homophobia, and her workshops on homophobia included particular attention to the dynamics of racism. According to Suzanne, "If oppressions are related, then the people who experience oppression are connected to one another, and therefore the solutions have to be connected."

Suzanne's interest in dismantling oppression grew from a host of personal and political influences. Having grown up on a small farm in Georgia during the 1940s and 1950s, she was raised with a strong sense of community and a belief that "community is something worth working for and is life-sustaining." This rural, Southern ethic led to Suzanne's lifelong desire to create community. Further, although she ultimately parted from the Church, Suzanne was influenced by the Christian message of forgiveness and redemption. In Suzanne's mind, the existence of forgiveness and redemption opened up many possibilities, including the possibility that life could be shaped and changed.

Interestingly, the appreciation for community that was being fostered during the early years of Suzanne's life stood in direct opposition to the racial tensions that also existed at the time. As a "white Southerner on the periphery of the Civil Rights Movement," Suzanne developed an appreciation for the inherent contradiction between community building and racism. As a result, she began to develop a strong alliance with the "victims of white power." Through this alliance, she witnessed the work of people willing to give their lives to the cause of justice. These Civil Rights pioneers were committed to a better way of life and Suzanne's exposure to these models gave her a real sense of the strength, endurance, patience, and sacrifice needed to create change. The momentum of the Civil Rights Movement "infused" her life.

Suzanne attributes her heightened sense of injustice in part to the fact that as a closeted lesbian she, too, was an "outsider." In her book, *Homophobia: A Weapon of Sexism,* Suzanne explains that until the age of thirty she ". . . had to be constantly vigilant and lie, primarily through omission but sometimes through commission, virtually every minute of every day." Given the intolerance extended to lesbians and gays during the 1950s and 1960s, Suzanne was forced to hide her sexual identity for the sake of keeping her family, friends, and community.

It was not until 1969 and the burgeoning of the women's movement that Suzanne was able to come out publicly, for the first time. Through her membership in a consciousness raising group that she organized in New Orleans, Suzanne was introduced to the idea that the "personal is political." Until then, she had spent most of her time talking about the political, to the exclusion of the personal. She came to realize that having a full life meant addressing the whole person, and that meant coming out as a lesbian. According to Suzanne, the women's movement offered the integration of life that she was searching for, and the members of the women's movement became her "community of justice seeking people."

CONTRIBUTIONS

Suzanne highlighted five contributions that she has made in her attempt to create community and raise awareness about oppression. In all of this work, the ideals espoused by the Civil Rights Movement and the Women's Liberation Movement remain a strong and constant thread.

Women's Anti-Violence Movement. In 1977 Suzanne co-founded a battered women's shelter in Fayetteville, Arkansas and from 1977-1982 she served as a volunteer and Chair of the Board of Directors. It was through this early work that Suzanne began to see the interconnection of the oppressions: "The women's anti-violence movement brings all of the issues [oppressions] together. It lays them out very clearly, if you're looking, because all the issues are connected in battered women or women who are raped. When you walk into a battered women's shelter, you see the results of societal injustice."

As a result of her work in the battered women's movement,

Suzanne was invited to co-chair the Lesbian Task Force of the National Coalition Against Domestic Violence (NCADV). As the co-chair in 1986, she opposed a United States Department of Justice $600,000 grant designed to provide public education and training about domestic violence. Just before the grant was to be awarded the Coalition came under attack by some powerful conservative organizations, including the Heritage Foundation. These organizations accused the NCADV of being "pro-lesbian" and "anti-family." The Department of Justice responded to these attacks by demanding full approval of all programs funded by the grant. Ironically Suzanne was selected as the NCADV's vice chair to oversee the work of the grant and the relationship with the Justice Department. After much struggle, Suzanne and other members of the National Coalition found these demands unacceptable and as a result rejected the grant and terminated their relationship with the Department of Justice.

Homophobia Workshops. Along with negotiating the terms for the domestic violence grant, as Chair of the Lesbian Task Force, Suzanne conducted homophobia workshops for members of local and state domestic violence programs. These workshops were developed in response to lesbian workers who reported discriminatory treatment by agency workers, including directors and others with decision-making power (e.g., The Department of Justice). The goal of the workshops was to draw attention to the direct connections between sexism, racism, homophobia, economic injustice, violence against women and the patriarchal and economic foundation on which all of these oppressions are based. This work helped pioneer an integrated analysis of homophobia, making gay and lesbian oppression commonly understood.

The Women's Project. Suzanne founded the Women's Project in Arkansas in 1981, served as director for the first ten years and is currently a senior staff member. The mission of the Women's Project is to work against racism and sexism through education, analysis, and community organizing throughout Arkansas and nationally. Suzanne was quick to note that the organization's focus on racism and sexism inevitably leads to an analysis of class, age, disability, and homophobia: "The Women's Project has created some enormously effective programs. I think it has kept a radical agenda alive in the state of Arkansas, and it has kept an analysis that connects oppressions and issues nationally . . . People talk now about the necessity to work across race, gender, class, sexual orientation–that has become the common language and understanding of progressive groups in this country. I don't think we single-handedly did that at The Women's Project, but I think we contributed in large part to it."

Another example of the work accomplished by the Women's Project is the Women's Watchcare Network (WWN). The purpose of the WWN is to monitor racist, religious, anti-gay and lesbian, and sexual violence. Suzanne explained that the WWN was one of the first organizations to introduce the idea that women are the targets of biased violence. Until the Network began collecting factual data on the incidence of hate crimes against women, other organizations around the country had focused their watch only on religious, racial, and homophobic hate crimes. Women were not part of the Hate Crimes Statistics Act and therefore the WWN was the only group in the country collecting evidence about the nature of biased violence against women (e.g., the number of women killed by men, the number of women killed by men who were strangers, etc.) and has been collecting this evidence for the last five years. The reaction to this work has been controversial. Suzanne explained, ". . . we jumped right into the middle of the fire. There was a major resistance to the notion that women are the victims of biased violence. There's still an enormous controversy around that. And so we added a great deal to feminist thought around the country on that issue and it was picked up and talked about–what we and other people added to that collective thinking."

Along with the commitment and dedication needed to maintain such an organization, the success of the Women's Project can also be attributed to its internal power structure. According to Suzanne, the Women's Project serves as "an outstanding example of an organization having integrity in practicing what it advocates." The Board and staff are composed primarily of women of color, people make the same amount of money, and everyone has equal access to decision making and opportunity.

Homophobia: A Weapon of Sexism. Published in 1988, *Homophobia: A Weapon of Sexism* is a book about "connecting." The purpose of the book is to show that homophobia, like racism, sexism, etc., does not exist in a vacuum, but rather is a "necessary adjunct to sexism with its roots in sexism and gender control." In the book, Suzanne uses examples from her homophobia workshops and other political work to demonstrate the patriarchal truths inherent in sexist and homophobic attitudes, beliefs, and behaviors. She theorizes about the imbalance of power and control that is maintained by stereotypic sex roles and the implications of this imbalance for our cultural understanding of sexual identity and freedom. In other words, as long as patriarchal standards of masculinity and femininity continue to govern our perception of what it means to be a man or a woman, those individuals who effectively live in opposition to these standards (viz., independent women, lesbians and gay men) will be subjected to increasing harassment and abuse (i.e., homophobia).

Suzanne reviews several strategies for eliminating homophobia, including using the word lesbian proudly and in public venues, participating in lesbian culture, making lesbian culture visible, and participating in actions and discussions that integrate the oppressions and function to eliminate them all. In concluding the chapter on strategies, Suzanne writes, "We must see that to give no voice, to take no action to end them [the oppressions] is to support their existence . . . There is no middle ground. With an oppression such as homophobia where there is so much permission to sustain overt hatred and injustice, one must have the courage to take the risks that may end in loss of privilege. We must keep clearly in mind, however, that privilege earned from oppression is always conditional and is gained at the cost of freedom."

The Religious Right. Part of Suzanne's work with the Women's Watchcare Network was to monitor hate crimes committed by the Ku Klux Klan and other far right organizations. Through this work she developed an interest in actively combatting the advancement of the religious Right. In the Fall, 1991, the Oregon Citizens Alliance, a religious Right organization, put forth an initiative that would have criminalized homosexuality in the state of Oregon. Passage of this initiative would have wiped out all state money being directed toward lesbian and gay issues and would have prohibited any participation by lesbians and gay men in civic life. A similar version of the Oregon initiative was also being promoted in other states (e.g., Colorado). Because of Suzanne's work with the Women's Watchcare Network she recognized the national importance of this initiative and was asked by the Coalition for Human Dignity and the Lesbian Community Project to work in Oregon to help develop strategies that would prevent the bill from being signed into law.

Suzanne's passion for this work came from her understanding that the initiative being forwarded by the Oregon Citizen's Alliance was not an isolated incident. According to Suzanne the Oregon initiative ". . . was happening in the context of an insurgency of the Right and it was actually about an attack on the gains of the Civil Rights Movement and an attack on democracy itself."

Suzanne's work on the initiative lasted for eight months and she has since continued to write about and organize against the Right. Although the Oregon initiative was defeated, it remains a widely debated issue within the state, and initiatives like it have been passed on the ballot in other states. Suzanne's work now focuses on bringing people and organizations together nationally to develop strategies across the many issues of the Right: immigration, welfare, education, taxation, lesbians and gay men, censorship, etc. Once again, her work is on the connections among the oppressions and the connections among the people who feel their impact and desire a better world.

REFLECTIONS AND FUTURE DIRECTIONS

In thinking about the contributions she has made as a lesbian and as a feminist, Suzanne pointed out that she has not acted alone: "There are not very many isolated individual contributions. I think they're in connection to other people. These things are happening simultaneously. It's not that one person does this one thing and it becomes a singular contribution. We are part of a movement in history, shaped by our time." Most notably, Suzanne explained that because of her work she has accumulated extraordinary friends who treat her with "humor and respect." Her ongoing connection with community activists provides the forum she needs to continue the local and national strategizing that is most important to her.

The more Suzanne has engaged in social justice work, the more she has been confronted with a sense of sorrow about the world. As she described, "The more you work, the more you see . . . I feel like I have witnessed all of my life a tide of racism that has been relentless with no ebb of relief. I feel that I have worked for two decades in the battered women's movement and the women's anti-violence movement and have seen a steady increase in attacks against women, everywhere . . . I have watched the Right in its continued organizing throughout my life, and now it is in an insurgency that threatens the very fabric of democracy."

As much as these experiences have added an element of sadness to the work Suzanne has accomplished, the positive outcomes have been immeasurable. Suzanne made particular mention of the cultural shifts that have taken place over the past few decades that have resulted in the creation of an active feminist culture, an active lesbian and gay culture, and a greater appreciation for racial diversity: "I have seen this country change in its demographics so that it has many more people of color, which is so much more wonderful. And despite the backlash that is currently going on, [I have seen] a remarkable awareness on the part of many people about what it means to harness peoples' lives and dreams and the need for people to have their dignity, worth, and liberation."

As for the future, Suzanne observed that there are at least two political movements that will determine the direction of oppressions work. First, she noted that people seem to be moving away from identity and nationalist politics into more coalition and alliance politics. This shift toward a more collaborative decision-making model is consistent with, and will undoubtedly promote, the values that underlie the anti-oppressions movement. However, Suzanne has also witnessed major efforts to polarize and divide people. For example, her work against the religious Right in Oregon demonstrates that certain political groups have a strong investment in maintaining the status quo, and reversing any progress that has been made toward the advancement of civil rights. Yet, Suzanne remains hopeful: "One of the things that makes me hopeful is the level of ability for people to communicate with each other through the proliferation of books. I love how many books are currently published by some great publishers like Kitchen Table Press. They are getting out wonderful, wonderful, wonderful pieces of writing. We have extraordinary opportunities for learning. I think the issue is how to put one's life to the good. How to be on the side of that which is positive, that which is about justice, equality, dignity and worth, and having every human being count."

Finally, Suzanne spoke of the importance of doing political work that is directly connected to peoples' sense of wholeness. She explained that all of her work on the interconnection of oppressions has been about dealing with the whole person, and being more authentic by speaking to peoples' hearts *and* minds. This commitment to authenticity and wholeness has infused all of Suzanne's writing, speaking, and organizing, and she continues to break barriers by making connections:

This is going to take a lot of cultural organizing. A lot of work on things that I wouldn't necessarily call spiritual, but are about spirit. There is going to need to be more music, more poetry, more dance, more painting of murals, more creation of what we want together, and ultimately more and more creation of relationships and of community.

Words of Honor:
Contributions of a Feminist Art Critic

Arlene Raven
Jean Pieniadz

Arlene Raven is an art historian writing criticism for *The Village Voice* and a variety of art magazines and academic journals. She is East Coast Editor of *High Performance Magazine,* and a member of the editorial board of *Genders* magazine. Her selected essays were published in *Crossing Over: Feminism and the Art of Social Concern* (1988). She was Editor and contributor to *Feminist Art Criticism: An Anthology* (1988), for which she won the Susan Koppelman Award. She was the Editor of, and contributor to, *Art in the Public Interest* (1989). *Exposures: Women and their Art* was published in 1989, and *Nancy Grossman* in 1991. A founder of the Women's Caucus for Art, the Los Angeles Women's Building, and *Chrysalis* magazine, Raven has lectured nationally, taught at major art schools and universities, and curated exhibitions for a number of institutions. She studied at Hood College, George Washington University, and Johns Hopkins University, and holds an MFA in Painting, and an MA and PhD in Art History.

Jean Pieniadz is a clinical psychologist in independent practice at Mansfield Psychotherapy Associates in Burlington, Vermont. She is an adjunct faculty member in the psychology department at St. Michael's College, and is a field faculty advisor at Vermont College of Norwich University. She earned her BS in Psychology and Philosophy at Clark University, and her PhD in clinical psychology at the University of Vermont. She is a member of the Executive Board of the Vermont Psychological Association, and a member of the American Psychological Association Council of Representatives. She is also a member of the Feminist Therapy Institute, and the Society for Research in Adolescence.

Correspondence may be addressed to Arlene Raven at 105 Eldridge Street, New York, NY 10002.

[Haworth co-indexing entry note]: "Words of Honor: Contributions of a Feminist Art Critic." Raven, Arlene, and Jean Pieniadz. Co-published simultaneously in *Women & Therapy* (The Haworth Press, Inc.) Vol. 17, No. 3/4, 1995, pp. 383-389; and: *Feminist Foremothers in Women's Studies, Psychology, and Mental Health* (ed: Phyllis Chesler, Esther D. Rothblum, and Ellen Cole) The Haworth Press, Inc., 1995, pp. 383-389; and: *Feminist Foremothers in Women's Studies, Psychology, and Mental Health* (ed: Phyllis Chesler, Esther D. Rothblum, and Ellen Cole) Harrington Park Press, an imprint of The Haworth Press, Inc., 1995, pp. 383-389. Single or multiple copies of this article are available from The Haworth Document Delivery Service [1-800-342-9678, 9:00 a.m. - 5:00 p.m. (EST)].

I'm an art historian. My contribution, if I define it in terms of helping people, and in the area of mental health, would be in education. In 1972, I was finishing my graduate school course work for my PhD, and I attended a conference, which was the first conference on women in the visual arts on the east coast. There I met two artists, Judy Chicago and Miriam Schapiro. I was extremely interested in what they had to say, because I had been teaching at the Maryland Institute College of Art, and I was wanting to teach a course on women and art at that time. They had a whole program of study they offered in California, and I made arrangements to go there and visit them.

Between the time that I made the arrangements, and the time that I went–which was one week–I was raped. This rape had a profound influence on what happened subsequently. I was completely distressed from having been raped, very brutally, and kidnapped by two people. That was a very politicizing experience for me, and it allowed me to see, in a personal way, what role social institutions were going to play in my life. Here I was getting my PhD, and always feeling that education was going to help me to equality, and I realized that as long as I had a pussy between my legs, that was the only requirement to be oppressed. I was just as vulnerable as anybody else, and that fact was shocking to me. I had been working in the civil rights movement, I had been in the SDS and the Labor Committee, and was a feminist, and I was going to consciousness-raising at the time. Still, I completely changed my life, toward increasing my commitment to feminist/political work.

I was married, I was raising a step-daughter and teaching, while also finishing graduate school. I then moved to Los Angeles, and became the art historian for the feminist program at the California Institute of the Arts. Judy Chicago and I taught at Cal Arts for one year, and then we were joined by Sheila de Brettville, who is now the dean of the school of design at Yale. She ran a women's design program at Cal Arts.

Judy, Sheila, and I established an independent school–the Women's Building–and in this school, we taught women. We came together as a community, and we taught women very practical things: finding out what our real experiences were, and making work from those experiences. Many of our students had been incarcerated in mental hospitals. (I made a count one time, and one-third of our forty-five artists had been in mental hospitals! This was amazingly high, especially because these people were not crazy.) We went from consciousness-raising to making real work and being in the real world, instead of in a school setting. While it was a school, it wasn't exclusively that; deliberately, there wasn't that institutional buffer. We taught women how to write their resumés and get jobs and all kinds of things that you never learned in school. And we did that in the community. I think that that was very good, for my mental health, certainly.

I was also developing my scholarly field at that time. There was very little done in the art history of the 20th century, focusing on women artists. It was a completely open field, and one could be very creative. I did research with my students, about the discovery of women's art heritage. To learn about this heritage was also, in the social sense, a very strong, steadying influence, which counteracted the canon that we had learned in other schools. Namely, this canon left women feeling that they didn't make a contribution to art. In the text which is used for all art history students, there is literally not one woman mentioned. When it was pointed out to the author–Jansen is his name and it's called *The History of Art*–he was so arrogant as to say that no woman had done work that was worthy of being in that book–a completely crazy assertion. I believe that realizations such as those, and working to build that history ourselves, do that art work ourselves, and present it in the public sphere made us new people; it made us redefine ourselves completely. In the process, we challenged our prescribed limitations. In addition, I think the teachers were getting as much education as the students. Many of them already had their graduate degrees and were older students. They were community members. So it was a school, but also a community.

I had an opportunity to make a contribution in California because we *created* the Women's Building, whereas I was just teaching a course in an existing institution here. Our group of feminists in the arts also formed Womanspace galleries, the Feminist Studio Workshop, the Center for Feminist Art Historical Studies, the Lesbian Art Project, the Feminist Art Workers, and the Waitresses. We rented a building, and we went in with other women in the building, a bookstore, a press, a feminist cooperative gallery, a commercial gallery, a cafe–we had a lot of different organizations in the build-ing. The Women's Building existed for 18 years, and it saw many other organizations come and go in that time. It no longer exists as it was, however, because while we still have our corporation, we gave up our physical plant. There's an oral history of the Women's Build-ing, which is becoming somebody's dissertation; we'll have ar-chives.

I now primarily work as a columnist for *The Village Voice*, writ-ing art criticism. And for me, that's working in the mainstream. It's funny that *The Village Voice* is considered a left-leaning paper, but for me, it's very different. I was so highly radicalized elsewhere that I find that some of the things that I've been saying for the last 20 years are still very challenging and startling to people in my current workplace. But I still have to keep saying them.

I feel that I have made a number of contributions to the field of art criticism. I was responsible for writing the theory of the Women's Building and our feminist art-making there. Among other things, the theory states that art-making is intended to raise con-sciousness and invite dialogue, and to lead to action. That's a very different idea of what art is, so it has very different requirements. Part of putting the theory into action meant that our teaching pro-cess was unique at the time. We did a great deal of team teaching, and co-teaching with people who came in as students. This gave us a sense of overall equality, while still respecting that there might be some kind of particular information that each person could impart to someone else. That was very important to me.

I taught by example and participation. I was in work groups with people and I participated in their art, as they participated in mine. I shared my writing with everybody else. In other words, I wasn't simply there as a teacher–I was also there as a participant. I co-created works of art, as well as art critiques, with students. I also did take the responsibility for structuring what was going to happen. That's a hard line to walk. I tried to do that because I felt we hadn't had enough of that kind of experience before. The women who started and taught in these feminist workshops were extremely ar-ticulate, very brilliant, and very visible in the field. Thus, it was a relative kind of equality: if you wanted to go where you were equal, you really had to *go* there, and not stand on how you were different from the others. Professional feminists are prone to making distinctions between themselves and other women, as a way of elevating themselves. While I think that's a very natural, class-bound thing to do, it has to be stopped sometimes, deliberately.

My body of writing is a very unique body, which has also been recognized by the art-critical establishment. I was one of two women, and seven people, who were asked to be part of a special series of essays on art in the 1980s (I contributed to the writing in a book called *Crossing Over,* from that series). I felt grateful to have the quality of my work acknowledged, even though it's far off the "beaten path." My art criticism is artful, and I try to use different forms, either plain or poetic, without jargon.

I employ a feminist process in my art criticism. I think of my work as "writing alongside" the art of other people, and I enter into a reciprocal relationship with the artists whose work I attempt to interpret. Part of this process also means that I struggle to gain an understanding of artists' intentions and assess the fulfillment of their intentions within their audience. The context in which artists both create and exhibit/perform their art is also considered in my work. In addition, I "value" every work I choose to write about according to my known and unknown biases and taste. The way in which I preselect themes and subject matters to review, based on my own preferences, may explain why I don't write so-called bad reviews. Unlike Georgia O'Keefe, for whom color was always more definite than words, I honor the words of art criticism themselves as an art form.

I think the fact that I'm a feminist who has just turned 50 is significant: I have been very steady in my commitments to feminism, and I put them out wherever I am, with a conviction that they're right. I know this is one thing that a number of people in my age group who've been in the movement for a long time can provide. Specifically, there's a certain kind of comfort and steadiness that other people, younger people, can acquire from you; they come to know that this is not just a one-year fight or a ten-year fight, or it's not even a lifetime fight. It's going to continue, and it's bigger than anybody's one lifetime. It's got to be passed down, and I feel some responsibility in that regard.

I was the founder, with other people, of two feminist magazines,

Womanspace Journal, and *Chrysalis.* Womanspace was the first West coast women's gallery space, and that was the first project I worked on in California.

I'm also teaching a new series of workshops in Snowmass, Colorado, at the Anderson Ranch Arts Center. There is a residency program where artists can come, like an art colony, both during the year, and in the summertime. I've been teaching there for about six years, and in that time, I developed a workshop called "Writing for Artists," which involves working with artists *about* their work. It involves learning ways to look at your work, and exploring its various meanings.

In the workshops, I start with–and this is my feminist approach to teaching again–what has been a very negative experience for many people in art school, which is a critique of their own work. Usually the teachers, who are probably not even doing any art work of their own, somehow make the students feel that they're nothing. In these workshops, I try to create a community wherein people start to write about their work by talking about it, and having other people write down what they are saying. They don't really have to take it up as writing, until they've really got more than just a blank page.

It's something that people have found to be a profound experience for them, and I am still very moved by what happens there. I try to conduct it in ways that are constructive for me, as well, i.e., in ways that are extensions of my teaching and writing philosophies.

I think that my ideas, overall, are the contributions of a feminist. In a recent interview in *Art Papers,* I took exception to the attitudes of people in the art world. I think the art establishment is unfair to artists, when there's no reason to be. For example, an artist will send slides to a gallery, and the gallery will throw them in the trash–never call the artist, or say, "I got your slides," or anything, because they don't feel they have to. It's the same with writers and editors. I think these are unprofessional practices, as well as inhumane. I'm therefore breaking with my normal art-world reference group, in that I'm trying to look critically at the art community, and to get people to try to act right. I know I'm not the last word on what's right, but I know what's humane and caring, and I know which things promote creativity and don't squash it.

My life has changed a great deal as a result of my contributions to feminist theory, scholarship and practice. Foremost, I'm a happy person! I attribute this to the fact that my work allows me to express myself, and I have taken, I'm glad to say, the paths that have lead me to do the work I want to do. I've made the sacrifices that I've needed to make and I feel very good about that. There's much internal conflict for individuals in the arts: getting a secure job vs. doing the work you really want to do; being a promoter and dealer of work, rather than being a philosopher of work; choosing to deal with new people, marginalized people, people who haven't had a voice yet (this is what I have chosen to do), as opposed to those who are more "bankable" people. It has been important for me to struggle with these conflicts, because I've been able to succeed anyway for some reason, and that sort of proves to me that I've gone the right way. I've always made those hard choices, and the risk-taking that I've made myself do in my life, as a result of wanting to live my feminism, and having a sense of justice, has been to choose the authentic life.

BIBLIOGRAPHY

Crossing Over: Feminism and the Art of Social Concern. Ann Arbor: UMI Research Press, 1988.

Feminist Criticism: An Anthology (editor and contributor). Ann Arbor: UMI Research Press, 1988. Reissued by Harper Collins Publishers, New York, 1992.

Exposures: Women and Their Art. Pasadena, California: NewSage Press, 1989.

Art in the Public Interest (editor and contributor). Ann Arbor: UMI Research Press, 1989.

Nancy Grossman. Brookville, New York: Hillwood Art Museum, 1991.

New Feminist Criticism. NY: Harper Collins, 1993.

Feminist Anthropologist
Anointed Foremother!

Ruby Rohrlich

As a feminist who bloomed late into a feminist anthropologist, I am honored to be dubbed a foremother in the women's movement. A foremother is "a female ancestor" (*Merriam-Webster*) who, while distinguished for her service to womankind, is dead or very old. For their contributions specifically to feminism, *Women &*

Ruby Rohrlich, PhD, is the author of *The Puerto Ricans: Culture Change and Language Deviance* and *Peaceable Primates and Gentle People*; Editor and contributor to *Women Cross-Culturally: Change and Challenge*, and *Women in Search of Utopia: Mavericks and Myth-Makers*. Her articles are published in the anthologies: *Women in Sexist Society; Toward an Anthropology of Women; Politics of Anthropology; Humanness: An Exploration into the Mythologies about Women and Men; Women's Studies: The Social Realities; Becoming Visible: Women in European History*; and in various journals including *The American Anthropologist, Signs, Feminist Studies, Heresies, Critique of Anthropology, l' Homme, Women's Review of Books*. She is presently writing a book entitled *The Levi's of Turin, Italy: From Ashes Into the Light*, dealing with the lives of Primo Levi, survivor and eminent chronicler of Auschwitz, and Dr. Rita Levi-Montalcini, who survived Fascism/Naziism in Italy to win a Nobel Prize in science in 1986 for her discovery of the Nerve Growth Factor. The protagonists, unrelated but very good friends, grew up in the ancient, culturally significant city of Turin, the center of anti-fascism during World War II.

Correspondence may be addressed to Ruby Rohrlich at 3003 Van Ness Street NW, #520-S, Washington, DC 20008.

[Haworth co-indexing entry note]: "Feminist Anthropologist Anointed Foremother!" Rohrlich, Ruby. Co-published simultaneously in *Women & Therapy* (The Haworth Press, Inc.) Vol. 17, No. 3/4, 1995, pp. 391-405; and: *Feminist Foremothers in Women's Studies, Psychology, and Mental Health* (ed: Phyllis Chesler, Esther D. Rothblum, and Ellen Cole) The Haworth Press, Inc., 1995, pp. 391-405; and: *Feminist Foremothers in Women's Studies, Psychology, and Mental Health* (ed: Phyllis Chesler, Esther D. Rothblum, and Ellen Cole) Harrington Park Press, an imprint of The Haworth Press, Inc., 1995, pp. 391-405. Single or multiple copies of this article are available from The Haworth Document Delivery Service [1-800-342-9678, 9:00 a.m. - 5:00 p.m. (EST)].

Therapy is honoring living women, middle-aged, like Phyllis Chesler, and old, like me; it takes time to become a contributing feminist. The patriarchal designation for an old woman is "hag"–defined (Ibid.) as "an ugly, slatternly or evil-looking old woman"–or crone, "a withered old woman." Early in the women's movement I rejected such designations in favor of a feminist *midrash,* asserted by the Irish-American feminist Mary Daly (1978): "The Great Hags of History lived to be Crones, the long-lasting ones, . . . examples of strength, courage and wisdom." So, hag, crone, female ancestor, foremother, I thank Esther Rothblum who, in asking me to describe my major contributions to the field of feminism, underlined her caveat, *this is no time to be modest.* I need that reminder. "Well into the twentieth century, it continued to be impossible for women to admit into their autobiographical narratives the claim of achievement, the admission of ambition, the recognition that accomplishment was neither luck nor the result of the efforts or generosity of others" (Carolyn Heilbrun, 1988). To form a truer composite, though, this record of triumphs must include trials and tribulations.

To account for my late blooming in anthropology requires my return, circuitous though it be, to early family history, specifically to my father's death when I, the youngest of six children, was little more than a year old. My brother Arthur, sixteen years old, was to graduate from high school the following year, an event as important then as college graduation is now. My mother insisted on it. However, somebody had to bring money in, and since the oldest sibling was in the Canadian Army, it had to be my fourteen-year-old sister Molly. Thus, while Arthur graduated from high school and studied to be an accountant, Molly became a sales clerk, then a stenographer, and went to night school until eventually she, too, graduated from high school. Then, about fifteen years later, when *I* needed another year of high school to graduate, these circumstances repeated themselves, but with a different outcome for a different sex. Struck down by the Great Depression, as deadly in its impact on individuals as a death in the family, Arthur, by this time struggling to support a wife and three children, decreed that I not return for the last year of high school, but get a job. Molly had begun nurses' training, her dream for many years; Anne was married and barely managing; Lou and Hy were off somewhere looking for work. I screamed that I *had* to graduate from high school, so I could go on to college, that I would work and pay my own way. But it was a question of supporting my mother, too, whom I loved and who, God knows, had earned it. Besides, said Arthur, who used to call me, lovingly, Ruby Rubina Rebecca Rohrlich, what good is another year of school; you're going to get married and have a husband to support you. "No, I'm not," I stormed. "I'll go to college, and support myself." I did, six years later.

For the next five years I worked as a stenographer, a secretary and office manager–the start of my "female moratorium . . . a condition marked by a profound sense of vocation, with no idea of what that vocation is, and by a strong sense of inadequacy and deprivation" (Heilbrun, 1988, pp. 52-53). My only rudder in this rudderless time was my intention of getting to college somehow, so I took the courses I needed to matriculate at McGill University, at least as valid as high school graduation. During the divorce proceedings, years later, my husband gibed that I had not even completed high school when we married, implying that my doctorate had been acquired through his good graces.

When I was twenty-one, my mother and I left Montreal for New York City, to live with Molly, who had recently finished nurses' training. I planned to work during the day and go to college at night, which I could not then do in Montreal where there were no evening college courses. The year was 1935, the depths of the depression. It took me a month to find a job, with a company manufacturing uniforms, whose owner brushed against my breasts whenever possible. I detested this job to such an extent that I could say the name of the company only with difficulty when I had to answer the phone. Nevertheless, New York was vibrant and hopeful, and I fell in love with it.

At the end of my first year there I married Milton, whom Molly had adopted as a kid brother at summer camp years before. He had recently graduated with an engineering degree from M.I.T., but this was the first time in its history that M.I.T. couldn't automatically place its graduates, and also the time when the acronym WASP came into being, from the employment ads in the *Herald Tribune* and *Times,* which excluded every one but white, Anglo-Saxon Protestants. Why did I marry him? He was witty and made me laugh.

Also, to be truthful, economic conditions were improving for my family in Montreal, and I wanted to divest myself, as a struggling married woman attending college, of the burden of supporting my mother. I quit my hateful job, and began to attend New York University.

But as an undergraduate I usually had three part-time jobs. At one o'clock, when my classes ended, I would run across the campus, eating my sandwich (and incurring a gall bladder infection in the process) to my job, which also began at one o'clock, in the NYU radio department. Here my work included script-writing, which I enjoyed, for 20 hours a week, at 50 cents an hour, paid by the National Youth Administration. In winter, spring and summer recesses I worked for an advertising agency at 60 cents an hour, and turned down the job they offered me when I graduated, of account executive, who mainly had to find synonyms for "glamor" and "casual."

In my junior year I fell madly in love with anthropology, and my teacher, Adamson Hoebel, who became well-known internationally, noticing that I was an extremely interested student who took notes in shorthand, offered me a job taking notes at a seminar integrating anthropology and psychiatry Friday nights at Columbia University. So enthralled was I by the lectures that I would have done the work gratis, but I received $5.00 for transcribing the notes, which took all day Saturday.

NYU gave me scholarships for half my tuition during my last three years. I was elected to Phi Beta Kappa and the English Honor Society, and graduated *cum laude*. Best of all, Hoebel offered to get me a graduate fellowship through the doctorate at Columbia. I was delirious with joy, but Milton was aghast at my delirium: "How can you think of going away to do fieldwork for possibly two years, when we've been married for such a short time?" He had just been tenured in his teaching job at a vocational high school during a period of superlative education in the New York City high schools, staffed by over-qualified teachers unable to find jobs in their own fields. Sorrowfully, bitterly, I turned down this golden opportunity; I had not yet read about Margaret Mead's unstoppable journey through her doctorate and on into Samoa.

Shortly after the U.S. entered World War II, the Office of War

Information hired me as a propaganda analyst, based on my college transcript and my expertise in French; I had grown up bilingual in Montreal, and had taken advanced French courses at N.Y.U. At the O.W.I., I met Ruth Benedict, who was writing pamphlets about the cultures American soldiers were encountering. She became one of *my* foremothers, this beautiful, grave woman, whose biography I would review forty years later. Only during this period did I not regret that I gave up anthropology. I became editor of the propaganda analysis department, and when the Allies invaded North Africa, the O.W.I. set up an Office of Psychological Warfare in Casablanca, which I was asked to direct. I accepted with great pleasure and anticipation, Milton having decided to apply for a commission with the Navy. The thorough physical examination I had to undergo revealed that I was anemic, and I was given vitamins to correct the deficiency. I had been wanting to have a baby, so we had not been using contraception, but I was not conceiving. Those vitamins must have been powerful; I became pregnant. Foiled by my female biology, there went my second golden opportunity!

However, my predilection for falling in love extended to my son, Michael, and to provide him with a sibling, I had Matthew whom I also loved. We moved to the suburbs, and I stayed home with the children for eight years. When Matthew was in the first grade I began to teach in an elementary school in a neighboring suburb, took courses in the evening and summers leading to a M.Sc. in Speech and Hearing Rehabilitation and became a speech pathologist, at first, in the same school, and later, in the Speech Bureau of the New York City school system, where I worked with Puerto Rican children. I was working to earn money that was needed, but as my children moved into adolescence, I was given to bouts of anger, self-hatred and weeping; I couldn't see my way out of the trap I felt I was in. "Marriage is the most persistent of myths imprisoning women" (Heilbrun, 1990, p. 77). I wanted to be an anthropologist.

When Michael was a senior at M.I.T., Matthew was a freshman at Boston University, so we had two tuitions to pay at the same time, but the following year, at my insistence we sold the house in the suburbs, which provided the money for Matthew's remaining three years of college, and moved back to New York. Milton totally opposed this move, but fortunately the house was in my name, too.

I enrolled again at New York University and gained a doctorate in anthropology in 1969, twenty-nine years after I had received my B.A. My moratorium was finally at an end!

My dissertation combined speech pathology and anthropology in a global study of stuttering, centering on a comparison of the speech and socioeconomic history of Puerto Rican children in San Juan, Puerto Rico, and New York City. Michael, who obtained his doctorate in political science the year after I got my degree, helped me with the statistics, the only course in which I had received a C. Titled *The Puerto Ricans: Culture Change and Language Deviance,* the dissertation was accepted for publication by Colin Turnbull, then editor of the Viking Fund Publications in Anthropology, as #51, the first fifty volumes having been written mainly by established scholars. I did the fieldwork and wrote the dissertation between 1966 and 1968, a time when the new Women's Movement was burgeoning, but the feminist literature was still meager and not yet relevant to my work. However, the feminism that had been brewing in me since kindergarten, according to my Montreal friends, emerged when I dealt with the struggles of Puerto Rican girls and women in the two cultures. The book is widely used in Puerto Rican Women's Studies, in Puerto Rican studies, and by those who study stuttering in its cultural context.

I obtained a job in the Anthropology Department of Brooklyn College, City University of New York (CUNY) to replace a teacher who died early in the semester. After receiving satisfactory evaluations from students and peers, I was fired by the chair, Robert Ehrich, an archaeologist, who couldn't rehire me, he said, because at my age (middle fifties) I could never write the publications necessary to obtain tenure. I came close to fainting dead away. I then applied for a job to teach Puerto Rican studies, but was turned down because I wasn't Puerto Rican. But I had also been "adjuncting" at Manhattan Community College, which needed teachers (CUNY had instituted open enrollment), and Manhattan hired me on a tenure track.

Now began an exciting period of my life. I was exchanging papers, sometimes worn and tattered, not only with feminist anthropologists but with feminists in every discipline. I remember feeling simultaneously overwhelmed and intoxicated by Mead's

Sex and Temperament, Chesler's *Women and Madness,* Millett's *Sexual Politics,* Weisstein's *Psychology Constructs the Female.* I integrated such material for students who were active in the civil rights, anti-war and women's movements, and I learned much from these students. I also learned from my younger son, Matthew, how to write lecture notes on a card, in a sort of shorthand, with a red pencil.

A pioneer feminist anthropologist, my favorite course was my Anthropology of Women, reluctantly approved by my department on the second try, which I taught for more than ten years, beginning in 1971. I was an active member of academic and non-academic feminist groups; in fact, the first meeting of NYWAC, the long-lasting New York Women's Anthropology Caucus, was held in my home in 1972, shortly after my husband and I separated. Our paths had diverged, first, when I acquired the doctorate against his bachelor's degree; second, and primarily, when I became an active feminist. Soon accustomed to the novelty of living alone, I became drunk with my freedom, and was all-out productive. Those of us who experienced those first heady feminist discussions, particularly in consciousness-raising, will concur that they were as nectar and ambrosia to our thirsting souls and minds. My friends now were feminists of every political and social hue; we supported one another in sickness and divorce, in getting jobs and tenure, in our relationships with women and with men.

Not trained as a social/physical scientist to write in the confessional mode, now, inspired by Heilbrun's *Writing a Woman's Life,* to which, fortuitously, I was just introduced, I reveal for the first time that since my undergraduate days, I did everything possible to avoid speaking in public, and when I couldn't avoid it, my speech sometimes bordered on stuttering. I recognize that I was afraid of speaking before a mixed audience, afraid of evoking male hostility even before I declared myself a feminist, and I confided in no one my shame at feeling fear. I began to understand why my female students were much more reluctant than the males to speak up. I am still grateful to the feminists who pushed me into doing research which provided some answers to their questions about how, why and when women were subjugated. They came to listen to what I had to say, approved vociferously of what I said, thereby warming the cockles of my heart and loosening the bonds constricting my speech. I understood why I was drawn to do a dissertation exploring stuttering worldwide, and later, delved into sociolinguistics which, however, didn't solve my speech dilemma.

My article "Women in Other Cultures," published in 1971 in Gornick and Moran's *Woman in Sexist Society,* launched my writing/publishing career and that of many others. This classic feminist anthology includes the early work of Jessie Bernard, Phyllis Chesler, Shulamith Firestone, Vivian Gornick, Kate Millett, Linda Nochlin, Cynthia Ozick, Catherine Stimpson, Naomi Weisstein, as well as all manner of writers: playwrights, novelists, poets. No wonder it is still being used in Women's Studies more than two decades later. My own article, about the egalitarian relations between the sexes and the frequent prominence of women in non-western societies—not what we had learned in either undergraduate or graduate anthropology courses—was widely used by anthropologists reconstructing the authentic status of women.

For the IXth International Congress of Anthropological and Ethnological Sciences I edited an anthology *Women Cross-Culturally, Change and Challenge.* This Congress meets every five years in a different country, and the IXth Congress, which met in the U.S.A. in 1973, was the first ever to hold a feminist seminar on women, which I organized during the two years preceding the meeting. This first international volume on women's status and movements contains papers about women as food gatherers, farmers, potters, weavers, traders, chiefs, miners, industrial workers, union organizers, soldiers, servants and professionals. Victims of exploitation and fighters against oppression, they worked in Bangladesh, Nigeria, Brazil, Peru, Chile, Bolivia, Mexico, the Dominican Republic, Puerto Rico, Israel, the Soviet Union, China and the United States. The three-day conferences in Oshkosh, preliminary to the summations in Chicago, welded the authors into a solidary group. We discussed our work with honesty and empathy, and in the process became fast friends.

The first Conference on the Older Woman, which I helped organize, was held in New York City in the summer, 1972. Ti-Grace Atkinson's keynote address, "The Older Woman as Garbage Heap," was enormously evocative. The women who attended, from

Mexico, Canada, and all parts of the United States, were not only diverse racially but ranged in age from 29 to 79, young single mothers finding more in common with older than younger women. My workshop on the nexus between racism and sexism provided an early forum for Hispanic, black and white women to explore similarities and differences in their situations.

1972 was the Year of the Older Woman, when younger women viewed us with respect and compassion for the vicissitudes of our lives, and acknowledged our ground-breaking feminism with gratitude. It was the year when older women were leaving their husbands in droves, and relating sexually to other women, and to men often younger by far. "Time and trouble will tame an advanced young woman, but an advanced old woman is uncontrollable by any earthly force" (Heilbrun, 1990 p. 124).

The summer our conference ended, I took my first trip to the West coast, visiting various feminist organizations, talking on radio and TV about the success of our Conference on the Older Woman, and learning about the accomplishments of West Coast women. Out of this trek came my paper "The Women's Movement is Alive and Well in Berkeley, Boulder and Albuquerque," published in a Queens NOW newsletter in 1972.

The article "Aboriginal Woman: Male and Female Anthropological Perspectives," which I wrote with two graduate anthropology students, Barbara Sykes and Elizabeth Weatherford, was published in 1975 in Rayna Reiter's early anthology *Toward an Anthropology of Women.* This article was, I believe, the first comparison of the radically differing perspectives of male and female anthropologists on women's roles in gathering-hunting bands. It was also published in *Politics of Anthropology,* edited by Gerrit Huizer and Bruce Mannheim, and in Barbara Schaeffer-Hegel's German anthology *Männer Mythos Wissenschaft.*

Ella Lasky's anthology *Humanness: An Exploration into the Mythologies about Women and Men,* published in 1975, contains my articles "The Older Woman: Her Status and Roles," and "Prostitution and the Patriarchy." I presented the first one, in which I contrast the power of older women in gathering-hunting bands with their powerlessness in industrialized societies, at the first conference of *The Feminist and the Scholar* at Columbia University in the early 70s. In "Prostitution and the Patriarchy" I demonstrate that far from being the oldest profession, prostitution was preceded by the professions of priest, merchant, and soldier, and initiated by patriarchal societies.

Peaceable Primates and Gentle People: An Anthropological Approach to Women's Studies is the title of a module I wrote for the series *Harper's Studies in Language and Literature*, published in 1975, and in Barbara Watson's anthology *Women's Studies: The Social Realities* in 1976. Written expressly for community college students, it was also widely used in four-year colleges, until inexplicably it went out of print, a tactic that publishers have used freely with feminist literature. In this module I refute traditional male anthropological views on the evolution and ways of life of non-human and human primates.

For the summer, 1976, I received an National Endowment for the Humanities (NEH) grant to participate in an eight-week seminar at the University of Illinois, Urbana-Champaign. But I broke an ankle on both sides and was hospitalized for five days. When I returned to the dorm I had students fetch books I had listed during the first two weeks, and spent most of the remaining period with my leg in a cast, able to do little except participate in the seminar and write my article on Crete and Sumer. Catholic nuns taking courses at the university were very kind, and I learned a lot about the democracy of convents.

"Women in Transition: Crete and Sumer" was published in 1977 in Bridenthal and Koonz's excellent anthology *Becoming Visible: Women in European History.* I compare Crete and Sumer, roughly contemporaneous, which started as peaceable, egalitarian, agricultural societies. But while Crete retained egalitarian gender relations as it evolved into a peaceable, ranked matriarchy, Sumer became militaristic and class-stratified as it developed into a patriarchy. This article convinced some people that I was a Marxist; others, that I was a matriarchist. What I did was write the facts I found.

Many CUNY teachers who expected to receive tenure in 1976 were summarily fired after the summer recess, just before they returned to their colleges, New York City being on the verge of bankruptcy. One of the few lucky ones, I was tenured and promoted to Associate Professor. I then immediately applied for, and received, an NEH resident fellowship, for the academic year 1977-78, to participate in a seminar on Western Civilization, at the University of California, Santa Cruz. At this spectacularly beautiful university, situated between redwood forests and Monterey Bay, the same type of academic politics–of racism, sexism, and sexual harassment of female students–existed as at the urban colleges in New York City. I was welcomed by the anthropology department, which is probably the only one in the world with a majority of female members, including two black women, and was chaired by May Diaz, the first female provost of one of the Santa Cruz colleges. I was the only feminist participating in the seminar, and I became involved with the active feminist movement at UC Santa Cruz, including an academic consciousness-raising group of six women, who met regularly and became good friends. I also continued my research on Sumer.

Altogether I wrote three articles on Sumer. The second one, "State Formation in Sumer and the Decline in Women's Status," linking women's subjugation to the evolution of the state, was published in *Feminist Studies,* Spring, 1980. The third, "The Patriarchal Puzzle in Mesopotamia and Mesoamerica," written with June Nash, showing the similarities in the development of male supremacy in two societies 4,000 miles and 4,000 years apart, was published in *Heresies,* Vol. 1, #4, Issue 13, 1981.

In 1980 I directed an eight-week NEH summer seminar with Diane Lewis, a black anthropologist, at UC Santa Cruz, on the "Historical Linkages between Gender Roles and Race Relations." The twelve participants were community college teachers, consisting of three African-American women, two white men, and seven white women. We got along well, considering the possible pitfalls on the issues of gender and race in our heterogeneous group.

For the fall semester of 1981, the first half of my sabbatical year, I won a fellowship in the History and Humanities Program for Community College faculty, directed by Professor Herbert Gutman, author of the brilliant and controversial *The Black Family in Slavery and Freedom.* I owe this historian a great debt for introducing me to important aspects of the history of African-Americans and the working class in the United States.

I spent the second part of my sabbatical year in Montreal, my home town. The Parti Quebecois, in power, had declared French to be the official and only language, and I examined the impact of this edict on Francophone and Anglophone feminists who were attempting to eradicate male supremacy in their respective languages. Many of the changes they suggested were adopted by both the Canadian and Quebec governments. A most interesting change had to do with names. The Quebec government decreed that the birth name was the permanent legal name. If this had been the case in the U.S., my publications would have borne the name of one author instead of three different names. I initially used my ex-husband's name, Leavitt, which I changed after the divorce to Rohrlich-Leavitt, marking the transition back to Rohrlich, my final re-adoption. Margaret Mead never changed her name.

The patriarchy's hold over the mass of people in the U.S., through continued patrilineal predominance, remains strong. Hillary Rodham, for example, discovered that "for the use of the name Rodham she had been viewed . . . in Arkansas as alien, and even subversive" (Connie Bruck, 1994). Phillip Carroll, a senior partner at the Rose Law Firm which Hillary had joined, said: "Intelligent people, friends of ours, were just so exercised about her name. They would say, 'It should be Clinton! But she clung to it so tenaciously'." But in the end, she felt forced to yield. "Giving up her name was surely the most costly of the changes that Hillary made" (Bruck, 1994). My sons cling tenaciously to their father's name, and omit their middle name, which is my (patrilineal) name. Very few men use their mothers' birth names, or have added their wives' names, as women frequently add their husbands' names.

At the 1981 American Anthropological Society annual meeting I included some of my Montreal findings in an article "The Politics of Sexist Language in French Canada," which I presented at a panel I organized with John Attinasi, entitled "Linguistically Marginated: The Transformation of Dominated Speech Varieties." In my paper I discussed the sexism in the English language, the validity of Black English, and the need for Hispanic children to learn Spanish as well as English in the schools.

During my final year of teaching, before I was forced to retire at the age of 70, I was a member of a class action suit brought by the female professors against CUNY. A male member of my department was promoted to full professorship ahead of me, a bare two years after he received his doctorate, and with no publications, while I had my doctorate when I began teaching years before, and by this time, had more publications than did Robert Ehrich, who had fired me. We won the suit, and each of us received a cash settlement but, despite the tremendous expense incurred by CUNY, which had prolonged the suit for ten years, the inequities between the male and female faculty remained substantially the same.

My book *Women in Search of Utopia: Mavericks and Myth-Makers* (with Elaine Baruch) was published by Schocken in 1984. The great advantage of being published by Schocken was that their books allegedly never went out of print–until Schocken was purchased by Random House. I was amazed to learn that the book was not only out of print but also out of stock; nor did Random House inform me of this in advance, so that I could order copies. This anthology was, I believe, the first collection of articles by women on utopias organized by women, and in which women predominated. Since then, a number of books on women's utopias have come out.

In 1985 Eleanor Leacock and I spent three months in American Samoa and Western Samoa, following Derek Freeman's attacks, several years after Margaret Mead died, on her early research in Samoa. We met people who still remembered Mead and confirmed her findings, but conditions had changed greatly since her time there sixty years earlier. The socioeconomic, political and gender differences between American Samoa and independent Western Samoa are vast and deserve a full-length book. I miss my friend Happy Leacock, who died on a return trip to Samoa. Her contributions to the literature on race and gender are extremely important.

In March, 1989 *New Directions for Women* published three pages of my twelve-page review essay, "Ruth Benedict, Feminist Anthropologist," of Margaret Caffrey's biography *Ruth Benedict, Stranger in this Land.* This book disclosed the lesbian relationship, revealed earlier in Margaret Mead's papers, between Benedict and Mead, women who contributed uniquely, brilliantly, to anthropology and other disciplines.

In June, 1990, in *Women's Review of Books,* I wrote a review essay, "Prehistoric Puzzles," of *The Language of the Goddess,* by the feminist archaeologist, Marija Gimbutas, in which I criticized her interpretation of Paleolithic art as "the language of the god-dess." Nevertheless, the book is a magnificent collection of the art of our Paleolithic and Neolithic ancestors.

For the past several years I have been writing a book tentatively entitled *The Levi's of Turin, Italy: From Ashes Into the Light,* and have spent much time in Italy. My protagonists are Primo Levi, survivor and chronicler *par excellence* of Auschwitz, and Rita Levi-Montalcini, persecuted under Fascism/Naziism in Italy, and the winner of a Nobel Prize for her discovery of the Nerve Growth Factor. Primo and Rita were friends whose lives were significantly linked growing up in the ancient city of Turin, a center of anti-fascist activity, which figures prominently in the book.

Since her ordeal fifty years ago, Rita has lived in the world of science. In the chapter of my biography of Rita entitled "Rita and Rosalind: Women Scientists in the Male World of Science," I introduce Rosalind Franklin, an English scientist, to provide a more comprehensive, cross-cultural view of the obstacles confronting women scientists during the period 1930s-1950s. This biography is a fitting place to recover Rosalind, who has been brushed aside because of the distortion of her personality and character by James Watson, who filched her crucial contribution to the knowledge of the structure of the DNA molecule, for the "discovery" of which he got a Nobel prize.

I submitted this chapter as a paper in 1992 to the Association for Feminist Anthropology, the unit of the American Anthropological Association which decides on material with feminist content for the annual meetings. The AFA rejected my paper, but I believe it would have been accepted had it dealt with Third World women scientists rather than Jewish women scientists. Although an AAA board member intervened and brought about its acceptance for the 1993 meeting, this is a painful example of anthropology's neglect of Jewish culture, Judaism, anti-semitism.

In 1981 the International Interdisciplinary Congress for Women was organized in Haifa, Israel, and meets every three years in a different country. I attended the third meeting in Dublin, Ireland, in 1987, where I presented my paper on "Law and Disorder: The Impact of the Early Laws on Women in Mesopotamia and Mesoamerica." This paper, dealing with the first codification of laws to validate the military power of despotic rulers, has been referenced in articles by women lawyers, delighted to have information not taught in law schools. I also attended the fifth meeting in 1992 in Costa Rica where I gave my paper on "Rita and Rosalind: Women Scientists in the Male World of Science." The sixth meeting will be held in 1996 in Adelaide, Australia.

At the 1994 AAA meeting I read my paper on the phenomena, mentioned previously, which prevented the writing of my doctorate until midlife, in a panel of older women anthropologists reading papers on this subject. If these personal narratives are published as a book, the problems that women experience in gaining a foothold in academic disciplines will be more convincingly revealed than by statistical surveys.

In "Margaret Mead and the Question of Women's Biography" Heilbrun points out that Catherine Bateson's testifying, in her biography about Margaret Mead, "so believably to the praise and honor . . . she feels for her mother is not only an important tribute, but the herald of an important change in the hearts of women as they look back upon their women predecessors." The publication of this volume, *Feminist Foremothers*, is a model of just such a "change in the hearts of women" which I hope will permeate feminism. Heartfelt thanks, Phyllis, Ellen, Esther!

PUBLICATIONS CITED

Connie Bruck, "Hillary the Pol," *The New Yorker,* May 30, 1994.

Mary Daly, *Gyn/Ecology*. Boston: Beacon Press, 1978.

Carolyn G. Heilbrun, *Writing a Woman's Life*. New York: W.W. Norton & Co., 1988; "Margaret Mead and the Question of Women's Biography," in *Hamlet's Mother and Other Women*. New York: Ballantine Books, 1990.

Reminiscences, Recollections
and Reflections:
The Making of a Feminist Foremother

Lynne Bravo Rosewater

INTRODUCTION

Being asked to contribute to this volume on feminist foremothers is an honor; it's a difficult task to be asked to share your contributions to feminist therapy, because it seems pretentious to list your accomplishments. It's harder I think for women to "brag," to honor ourselves. It seems quite fitting to have this volume created with the express purpose of having "feminist foremothers" discuss our work and our contributions. Feminism, to my mind, is about collab-

Lynne Bravo Rosewater, PhD, is a licensed psychologist in private practice in Cleveland, Ohio. She is a founding mother both of the Center for Prevention of Domestic Violence in Cleveland, Ohio and the national Feminist Therapy Institute. Lynne is the Co-Editor of *Handbook of Feminist Therapy: Women's Issues in Psychotherapy,* and author of *Changing Through Therapy* and *New Roles/New Rules: A Guide for Transforming Relationships Between Women and Men.* She has also written numerous chapters on issues regarding misdiagnosis of battered women, use of the MMPI in courtroom testimony for battered women who kill, counseling battered women and feminist therapy applications.

Correspondence may be addressed to Lynne Bravo Rosewater at 23360 Chagrin Boulevard, Beachwood, OH 44122.

[Haworth co-indexing entry note]: "Reminiscences, Recollections and Reflections: The Making of a Feminist Foremother." Rosewater, Lynne Bravo. Co-published simultaneously in *Women & Therapy* (The Haworth Press, Inc.) Vol. 17, No. 3/4, 1995, pp. 407-417; and: *Feminist Foremothers in Women's Studies, Psychology, and Mental Health* (ed: Phyllis Chesler, Esther D. Rothblum, and Ellen Cole) The Haworth Press, Inc., 1995, pp. 407-417; and: *Feminist Foremothers in Women's Studies, Psychology, and Mental Health* (ed: Phyllis Chesler, Esther D. Rothblum, and Ellen Cole) Harrington Park Press, an imprint of The Haworth Press, Inc., 1995, pp. 407-417. Single or multiple copies of this article are available from The Haworth Document Delivery Service [1-800-342-9678, 9:00 a.m. - 5:00 p.m. (EST)].

orative effort, about helping create new frontiers for women and giving one another support for that process.

I am proud to have twice been a "founding mother," first of Women Together, Incorporated in 1976, the first shelter for battered women and their children in Ohio and the third shelter in the United States, and then of the Advanced Feminist Therapy Institute in 1980. The greatest tribute to my insistence on developing process and procedures is that both of these organizations have grown and flourished without my remaining in a leadership position. It is from my active involvement in both of these organizations that many of my contributions to feminist therapy have sprung.

These contributions include: addressing the issues of misdiagnosis of battered women and the need for feminist test interpretation; opposing misogynistic diagnoses proposed for the revision of the *DSM-III-R* and questioning, with others, whether new or expanded diagnoses weren't needed to describe accurately the dynamics of survivors of interpersonal violence; helping to expand the concepts that delineate what feminist therapy is; articulating the concept of feminist advocacy and helping to develop the strategies used for expert testimony about Battered Women's Syndrome in the courtroom; and writing about the concepts described above both for the academic press and the lay press.

HOW I BECAME A FEMINIST

The birth of my feminism coincided with the birth, twelve months and two weeks apart, of my children. Becoming a mother changed my life totally, while it seemed to change my husband's not at all. I had never before been forced to confront so forcefully the indoctrination I had absorbed. I loved my children desperately, but I felt something was missing and that something was me. Starting that search to find myself was the beginning of a changed consciousness that defined me as a feminist and a feminist therapist.

In many ways I had the making of a feminist since childhood. While I was raised in a traditional home, gender was not a discriminating variable in the treatment of the three children, an oldest son and twin daughters. I was raised with a reverence for justice and a moral outrage at the abuse of power, both, to my mind, very feminist traits. More importantly, I was never given limits about who I was or what I could be. Those restrictions were acquired outside my home in the milieu of a sexist world that gave strong messages about what girls could or couldn't be.

I look back and mourn the girl I was, who so easily gave up her dreams: in high school I was "talked out" of going to law school because I would be "taking the place of a man who would need to provide for his family"; I gave up my desire to teach high school history because I was "too small to control high school students." I suffered monthly cramps that incapacitated me and tolerated the view that it was "all in my head," and even sadder, downgraded my labor pains as "just cramps" rather than acknowledge that monthly my uterus had gone into contractions. As a feminist therapist, I understand the power of indoctrination. I am not mad at the girl who acquiesced, but rather at the culture that saw nothing wrong with the restricting demands that limit who girls can grow to be. And it is this reframing which I think summarizes best my contribution to feminist therapy: the need to see behavior as a normal reaction to an abnormal occurrence, rather than pathologizing the response.

WHAT IS NORMAL?

Traditional psychotherapy has been based on so-called norms which really reflect the standards for white middle-class men. Behavior is viewed as pathological according to the majority view of societal needs. But the question feminist therapists ask is, "*Who* decides what is pathological behavior?" (Rosewater, 1984). This question has been central to several of my contributions to feminist therapy: looking at the misdiagnosis of battered women and other survivors of interpersonal violence; advocating for feminist test-interpretation; and fighting the misogynist proposed diagnoses for the *DSM-III-R*, which included Masochistic Personality Disorder (later changed to Self-Defeating Personality Disorder), Premenstrual Dysphoric Disorder (later changed to Late Luteal Phase Dysphoric Disorder) and Paraphelic Rapism (later changed to Paraphelic Coercive Disorder).

MISDIAGNOSIS

My research with the Minnesota Multiphase Personality Inventory (MMPI) to develop a battered woman's profile (Rosewater, 1985a) showed that battered women presented personality traits that traditionally would be viewed as dysfunctional: significantly elevated scores on the clinical scales that measure anger, confusion and paranoia, as well as significantly low scores on the scales that measure internal strength and belief in one's ability to manage. However, these behaviors are more indicative of a response to trauma than to signs of internal pathology. Labeling these traits as indications of psychosis or of borderline personality disorder when there is a history of physical and/or sexual violence is, I have theorized, misdiagnosing (Rosewater, 1985a). Further, the behavior responses found with battered women can–and should–be viewed as appropriate adaptive responses. This logic explains why Post-Traumatic Stress Disorder is a more appropriate diagnosis for women suffering from Battered Woman's Syndrome (Walker, 1989b). Post-Traumatic Stress Disorder deals with behavioral symptoms as a means to reacting to a recognizable stressor "that would evoke significant symptoms of distress in almost everyone" (APA, 1980, p. 238). The most current definition of Post-Traumatic Stress Disorder (*DSM-IV*) is that an individual has to be exposed to a traumatic event in which both of the following were present: "the person experienced, witnessed, or was confronted with an event or events that involved actual or threatened death or serious injury, or a threat to the physical integrity of self or others; the person's response involved intense fear, helplessness or horror" (APA, 1994, pp. 427-428). This definition is much more descriptive of a victim's response to interpersonal violence, whether that is physically being beaten and/or sexually assaulted or raped.

How symptoms are seen dramatically affects both diagnosis and treatment. Because standardized tests have traditionally been seen as both sexist and racist, many early feminists argued that feminists should not use traditional standardized tests (Brodsky & Hare-Mustin, 1980, Wilkinson, 1980). While the criticisms of standardized tests are certainly valid, I have argued that it is the *interpretation* rather than the test itself which is most problematic (Rosewater,

1985b). The dynamics of a standardized test are like the behavior symptoms presented in therapy: they need to be seen in context of the client's life. Important issues like custody and competency are based on these standardized test results. It is critical that feminists offer alternative interpretations that explain the test results in a manner that does not add to the revictimization of survivors of interpersonal violence and that interprets their test results as depicting a *normal set of reactions* to an *abnormal situation*.

This pathologizing of normal behavior is the root of many of the criticisms I (Rosewater, 1987a) and others (Caplan, 1987; Walker, 1987) had to the proposed diagnosis of Masochistic Personality Disorder (changed to Self-Defeating Personality Disorder). As I stated in a paper given at the American Psychological Association (Rosewater, 1987b), "There is a difference between seeing symptoms as a sign of pathology and acknowledging them as signs of adaptive solutions to societal oppression." One of the original criteria proposed for Masochistic Personality Disorder was "remains in relationships in which others exploit, abuse or take advantage of him or her, despite the situation." This criterion is based on a victim-blaming bias and ignores the fact that battered women are most at risk for serious injury or death when they leave an abusive situation (Browne, 1987, Walker, 1989b). To describe a victim of interpersonal violence as either "masochistic" or "self-defeating" implies that the abuse is the victim's, not the perpetrator's, fault. "It also assumes the therapist can attribute a self-defeating motivation to behaviors which women may adopt simply because they lessen the risk of being harmed" (Rosewater, 1987a, p. 190).

The proposed criteria for Masochistic Personality Disorder and the adapted criteria for Self-Defeating Personality Disorder, while all couched in non-sexist language, described behaviors that reflect the cultural conditioning experienced by females, leading myself (Rosewater, 1987a, 1987b), as well as others (Brown, 1988; Kaplan, 1983; Landrine, 1987) to question whether personality disorders label as pathological what is actually sex-role socialization. Further, personality disorders, as defined by the *DSM-III* (APA, 1980), are used to describe behaviors that are "generally recognizable by adolescence or earlier" and continue throughout most of adult life as "enduring patterns of perceiving, relating to, and think-

ing about the environment and oneself" (p. 305). Yet many of the
behaviors used to describe a personality disorder are traits that are
"reactive responses to victimization and tend to disappear or lower
in frequency when the abuse is eliminated and women feel safe"
(Rosewater, 1987a, p. 193).

This criticism of personality disorders is an especially important
feminist contribution, because personality disorders, as they have
been traditionally defined, posit that the behavioral characteristics
are irreversible; diagnoses like Post-Traumatic Stress Disorder, on
the other hand, define behavior developed in response to trauma as
being recoverable. The movement by feminist therapists such as
myself to broaden the definition of Post-Traumatic Stress Disorder
or to contemplate new diagnostic categories such as Oppression
Artifact Disorders (Brown, 1988) or Disorders of Extreme Stress, Not
Otherwise Specified (DESNOS) (van der Kolk, Davidson & Roth,
1992) is an important shift in the phenomenology of diagnosis.

My involvement with critiquing the proposed diagnosis of Masochistic Personality Disorder led me, along with many other feminist therapists, to question both how diagnoses are created and how
scientific was the process. Two other proposed diagnoses for the
DSM-III-R shared a misogynistic bias: Premenstrual Dysphoric
Disorder, which made PMS a psychiatric disorder (and one only
women could have) and Paraphelic Rapism, which would have
made predisposition to rape a mental illness. Rather than focusing
on the arguments against these diagnoses, I want to focus on the
feminist strategy to fight these diagnoses.

As an expert on domestic violence I know that the importance to
prevention is to hold the perpetrator accountable for his criminal
behavior. The feminist therapy community, spurred by The Committee on Women of both the American Psychological Association
and the American Psychiatric Association, formed a coalition to
fight the proposed new diagnosis. Our original title–which I wish
I'd fought harder to keep–was the Committee Against Ms. Diagnosis. The Committee to revise the *DSM-III-R* disavowed any responsibility for the diagnoses they were creating, but the Committee
Against Misdiagnosis contested that claim. We argued that to create
diagnosis that would be detrimental to women, especially after the
Committee had been specifically warned about the dangers, created

a liability both for the Committee to Revise the *DSM-III-R* and the American Psychiatric Association. It was this argument (along with outcries from across the country, including the Assistant Attorney General) that helped eliminate Paraphelic Rapism (later changed to Paraphelic Coercive Disorder) as a proposed Diagnosis and created the exemption of current victims of physical, sexual or psychological violence from a diagnosis of Self-Defeating Personality Disorder. Our picketing the American Psychiatric Association Meeting in Washington D.C. gave further publicity to the justified concerns about the proposed new diagnoses. The actions of the Committee Against Misdiagnosis also raised the awareness of the professionals and the public that the alleged nosology of the American Psychiatric Association was neither scientific nor value-free.

ARTICULATING WHAT FEMINIST THERAPY IS

I was an active member of the Feminist Therapy Group at the first National Conference on Feminist Practice and Training held in Boston in 1993. We defined feminist therapy as consisting of a viewing lens of feminist principles that must be present for the therapy to be feminist. Techniques may vary, but not the tenets. Our group defined sixteen tenets.

As I've stated earlier in this chapter, I feel a key element of feminist therapy that I have helped articulate is to look at behavior, especially that of victims, as a *normal* response to an *abnormal* occurrence. I have also defined feminist therapy as one that looks for health rather than illness, one that calls for action and change rather than adjustment and continuity (Rosewater, 1984). This concept was defined as Tenet 7: *Feminist therapy's primary focus is on strengths rather than deficits; therefore women's behaviors are seen as understandable efforts to respond adaptively to oppressive occurrences.*

Feminist therapists, I believe, have an obligation to help create change. Agreeing with Brown (1985) that feminist therapists have an obligation to use their power and privilege, I have defined feminist ethics as being proactive rather than reactive (Rosewater, 1990). Traditional ethics prohibit wrongdoing; feminist ethics demand more than merely doing no wrong. They demand the therapist address abuses in the community that add to victimization. One example I gave was, with my client's permission, contacting the chief of police to address the lack of protection given my client by the police. In addition the therapist has an obligation not to misuse her power and privilege in the context of the therapy relationship. This notion is discussed in Tenet 10: *Feminist therapy is based on the constant and explicit monitoring of the power balance between therapist and client and attention to the potential abuse and misuse of power within the therapeutic relationship.*

The issue of power and privilege is also central to my notion of an egalitarian relationship. Like Douglas (1985), I feel that defining the therapist/client relationship as equal denies the reality of the situation in which the client seeks and uses the services of the therapist. I have defined an egalitarian relationship *as equal in respect*, that the expert on the client is always the client herself. This concept is addressed in Tenet 8: *Feminist therapy strives towards an egalitarian and non-authoritarian relationship based on mutual respect.*

Equal respect in the therapy relationship is also dependent upon giving equal weight to the client's input. Such therapy "is not aimed at adjustment as defined by the authorative therapist, but rather at facilitating change. The client, not the therapist, defines change for her" (Rosewater, 1984, p. 271). This concept is addressed in Tenet 9: *The goals, direction and pace of feminist therapy are developed in a collaborative process.*

ADVOCACY

Advocacy–working toward the empowerment of individual clients–is an essential part of the feminist process (Rosewater, 1990). Much of the advocacy work I have done as a feminist therapist revolves around the issues of domestic violence. Helping to fund Women Together (the battered woman's shelter) I participated in two ground-breaking concepts: I helped convince United Way to give money for the running of the shelter and I helped with the passage of a law that increased the marriage license fee and used the proceeds to fund battered women's shelters.

My longest struggle–over a decade–involved getting expert testimony on Battered Woman's Syndrome admitted in Ohio courts. (During this time the decision to allow expert testimony was at the discretion of the individual judge, so that my work was key in the favorable plea bargains offered clients so that a precedent would not be set.) In the course of this battle, I helped develop, along with other groundbreakers in this area like Walker (1989a), the role of the expert, which is twofold: to educate the judge and jury about the dynamics of domestic violence and why the battered woman who killed would have a heightened perception of her imminent danger; and to educate the lawyer about how to present the necessary issues as part of the legal defense. There are two critical issues I believe the expert has to address for the jury: why the battered woman stayed in an abusive relationship and why she believed herself to be in fear of imminent bodily harm at the time she killed. I pioneered the use of the MMPI in the courtroom (and in writing reports for others to use in the courtroom) to substantiate a woman's claims of abuse and her diagnosis of suffering from Battered Woman's Syndrome.

I am currently in the process of developing a pilot Court Watch Program to monitor the Cleveland Municipal Courts to see how appropriately the courts are handling domestic violence cases. It is my hope that this project can be replicated on a national basis.

FEMINIST WRITINGS

I have made two contributions in the field of feminist writing of which I am especially proud. *The Handbook of Feminist Therapy* (Rosewater & Walker, 1985) is a unique volume in that all the women who presented their work at the first Advanced Feminist Therapy Institute (AFTI) were given the opportunity to present their work in writing, whether or not they had good writing skills. This commitment to disseminating ideas and finding others to help the women with their writing is to my mind truly feminist. This book also set the precedence for the work of AFTI to be chronicled in other edited books.

While I have written numerous chapters for academic books, I am most proud to have written two books for lay audiences that present feminist ideas "generically." The first book, *Changing*

Through Therapy (1987c) describes the process of change in therapy. One chapter is devoted to clients' writings about how they experienced this change. The second book, *New Roles, New Rules: A Guide to Transforming Relationships Between Women and Men* (1992) addresses the need to change the sex-role stereotyped rules that underpin heterosexual relationships. In explaining the problems with violent relationships I tried to show that these relationships are problematic precisely because of the sexist rules on which *all* heterosexual relationships are based.

Being a feminist therapist is an ongoing saga. I look forward to the work I have yet to do.

REFERENCES

American Psychiatric Association. (1994). *Diagnostic and statistical manual of mental disorders* (4th ed.) (*DSM-IV*). Washington, DC: Author.

American Psychiatric Association. (1980). *Diagnostic and statistical manual of mental disorders* (3rd ed.) (*DSM-III*). Washington, DC: Author.

Brodsky, A. M., & Hare-Mustin, R. (1980). Psychology and women: Priorities for research. In A. M. Brodsky & R. Hare-Mustin (Eds.), *Woman and psychotherapy*, pp. 385-409. New York: The Guilford Press.

Brown, L. S. (1985). Ethics and business practices in feminist therapy. In L. B. Rosewater & L. E. Walker (Eds.), *Handbook of feminist therapy: Women's issues in psychotherapy*, pp. 297-304. New York: Springer Publishing Co.

Brown, L. S. (December, 1988). *Feminist therapy perspectives on psychodiagnosis: Beyond the DSM and ICD.* Keynote address presented at the International Congress on Mental Health for Women, Amsterdam, the Netherlands.

Browne, A. (1987). *When battered women kill.* New York: The Free Press.

Caplan, P. J. (1987). The psychiatric association's failure to meet its own standards. *Journal of Personality Disorders, 1* (2), 178-182.

Douglas, M. A. (1985). The role of power in feminist therapy. In L. B. Rosewater & L. E. A. Walker (Eds.), *Handbook of feminist therapy: Women's issues in psychotherapy*, pp. 241-249.

Kaplan, M. (1983). A woman's view of DSM-III. *American Psychologist, 38* (7), 786-792.

Landrine, N. (March, 1987). *The politics of personality disorders.* Paper presented at the annual convention of the Association of Women in Psychology, Denver.

Rosewater, L. B. (1984). Feminist therapy: Implications for practitioners. In L. E. Walker (Ed.), *Women and mental health*, pp. 267-279. Beverly Hills: Sage Publications.

Rosewater, L. B. (1985a). Schizophrenic, borderline or battered? In L. B. Rosewater & L. E. A. Walker (eds.), *Handbook of feminist therapy: Women's issues in psychotherapy*, pp. 215-225. New York: Springer.

Rosewater, L. B. (1985b). Feminist interpretation of traditional testing. In L. B. Rosewater & L. E. A. Walker (eds.), *Handbook of feminist therapy: Women's issues in psychotherapy*, pp. 266-273. New York: Springer.

Rosewater, L. B. (1987a). A critical analysis of the proposed self-defeating personality disorder. *Journal of Personality Disorders, 1* (2), 190-195.

Rosewater, L. B. (August, 1987b). *Personality disorders: The dinosaurs of the DSM-III?* A paper presented at the annual meeting of the American Psychological Association, New York, August.

Rosewater, L. B. (1987c). *Changing through therapy.* New York: Dodd, Mead & Co.

Rosewater, L. B. (1990). Public advocacy. In H. Lerman & N. Porter (Eds.), *Feminist ethics in psychotherapy*, pp. 229-238. New York: Springer Publishing Co.

Rosewater, L. B. (1993). *New roles/New rules: A guide to transforming relationships between women and men.* Pasadena: Trilogy Books.

Rosewater, L. B. & Walker, L. E. A. *Handbook of Feminist Therapy: Women's issues in psychotherapy.* New York: Springer Publishing Co.

van der Kolk, B. A., Davidson, J., & Roth, S. (June, 1992). *Defining post traumatic stress for the DSM-IV.* A paper presented at the World Conference of the International Society for Traumatic Stress Studies, Amsterdam, The Netherlands.

Walker, L. E. (1989a). *Terrifying love: Why battered women kill and how society responds.* New York: Harper Perennial.

Walker, L. E. A. (1989b). Psychology and violence against women. *American Psychologist, 44* (4), 695-702.

Walker, L. E. (1987). Inadequacies of the masochistic personality disorder for women. *Journal of Personality Disorders, 1* (2), 183-189.

Wilkenson, D. Y. (1980). Minority women: Social cultural issues. In A. N. Brodsky and R. Hare-Mustin (eds.), *Woman and psychotherapy*, pp. 285-304. New York: The Guilford Press.

From Suburban Housewife
to Radical Feminist

Florence Rush
Nicole Rich

It is with some trepidation that I, as one of the next generation of fledgling feminists, attempt to tell the story of a "feminist foremother." Even with the non-hierarchical beliefs of feminism entrenched in my psyche, I came away in awe of the richness of Florence Rush's life. Whether within the civil rights movement, the anti-war movement or lobbying for progressive legislation, she has a history of both personal and political activism. Over the long span of her existence, Florence was rarely passive in dealing with the events of her life. She was inclined to examine her own behavior, decisions, relationships, and interaction with the world around her. When offended, she confronted; when in doubt, she questioned, and when she sensed or experienced injustice, she challenged.

Florence Rush, MS, CSW, is the author of *The Best Kept Secret: Sexual Abuse of Children* and many articles and lectures related to the status of women and children. She has been a feminist activist since 1970 and recently, due to personal loss, has combined her feminism with AIDS activism.

Nicole Rich is a fourth year clinical graduate student at the University of Vermont. She considers herself a budding feminist and has been active in the areas of the sexual abuse of women as well as reproductive freedom. Her dissertation will examine gender differences in social and physical risk-taking.

Correspondence may be addressed to Florence Rush at 61 Jane Street, New York, NY 10014.

[Haworth co-indexing entry note]: "From Suburban Housewife to Radical Feminist." Rush, Florence, and Nicole Rich. Co-published simultaneously in *Women & Therapy* (The Haworth Press, Inc.) Vol. 17, No. 3/4, 1995, pp. 419-424; and: *Feminist Foremothers in Women's Studies, Psychology, and Mental Health* (ed: Phyllis Chesler, Esther D. Rothblum, and Ellen Cole) The Haworth Press, Inc., 1995, pp. 419-424; and: *Feminist Foremothers in Women's Studies, Psychology, and Mental Health* (ed: Phyllis Chesler, Esther D. Rothblum, and Ellen Cole) Harrington Park Press, an imprint of The Haworth Press, Inc., 1995, pp. 419-424. Single or multiple copies of this article are available from The Haworth Document Delivery Service [1-800-342-9678, 9:00 a.m. - 5:00 p.m. (EST)].

During the 40s, 50s, and 60s, Florence functioned primarily as a social worker, suburban housewife, and mother. Originally she enjoyed these roles which, applauded by family and friends as appropriate occupations for one of her sex, gave her a sense of identity and belonging. However, when her world became saturated with Freudian thinking and other forms of popular psychology, pressure to conform infiltrated her world and impacted her individual psyche, requiring intervention from five days a week on the psychiatrist's couch to regular participation in trendy "touchy-feely" sensitivity programs. She went along with this for awhile but her tendency to confront, question, and challenge eventually led her to conclude that social, cultural, and media manipulation was a greater source of human disorders than an embattled unconscious.

Despite her conclusions, in order to keep up with the demands of her job, Florence studied Freud, Adler, Jung, and other notables in the field of the behavioral sciences. Her supervisors guided her in the techniques of "curing" clients of unresolved emotional conflicts rather than dealing with concrete social impediments. She was uneasy with questionable theories of "penis envy" and "conflicting unconscious impulses." Later, under President Johnson's "war on poverty," Florence accepted a job in a local Neighborhood House. Here she developed programs for pregnant teenagers, teenage mothers, a birth control clinic, a shelter for homeless men, and was able to organize demonstrations for much-needed housing, health services, and the humane treatment of welfare families.

As a mother, Florence learned from Anna Freud, Melanie Klein, Margaret Ribble, Gerald Kaplan, and others that commonplace childhood behavior such as bed-wetting, temper tantrums, or delayed toilet training reflected disturbed mothering. Filled with self-blame, she was driven to a psychiatrist for a 50-minute hour and to group therapy to exorcise the "bad" mother in herself. It finally dawned on Florence that these experts knew nothing about child rearing or mother-child relationships, and that most of them had no children of their own and those who did encountered the same, if not more, problems than herself. After a while she discontinued her own therapeutic entanglements and rescued her children from the egos of incompetent practitioners.

These insights were not popular within her profession or domestic world. In the very early 70s she discovered the Women's Liberation Movement and with it a community to support and validate her values and judgement. Her role as housewife terminated in divorce followed by a move from suburbia to New York City. Her children, now grown, went their own way. Consciousness raising (CR) replaced speculation on the unknown workings of the psyche but no matter how radicalized Florence had become, she found that the past could never entirely be discarded; it flowed into the present just as the personal flowed into the political.

Florence Rush is probably best known for her groundbreaking work *The Best Kept Secret: Sexual Abuse of Children* published in 1980. Well before that time she made up for her "late in life involvement" by participating in many activities concerning the status of women. In 1970, her grown daughter, Eleanor, returned from a woman's conference with glowing descriptions of feminists, their ideals, and stacks of literature. Florence was thus introduced to the Women's Liberation Movement. She immersed herself in the papers and pamphlets produced by The Feminists, New York Radical Feminists and Boston women from Cell 16; she turned to the work of Shulamith Firestone, Kate Millett, Phyllis Chesler, and the mind-boggling contributions of so many brilliant women. Florence attended consciousness-raising groups, women's meetings and conferences and came to the realization that, "I finally found a movement which addressed itself to my life experience, my discontents, and gave me a cause of my own." In Westchester she organized CR groups for "women who were nibbling at the Women's Movement." There they found a community by sharing common experiences in marriage, motherhood, and their sex life. A suburban Women's Movement was born but it was in New York that Florence became firmly grounded in feminism.

In 1971 New York Radical Feminists invited Florence to do a presentation on the sexual exploitation of children at their forthcoming Rape Conference. She refused at first, but when told that a male professor of "human sexuality" had agreed to cover the subject, she quickly changed her mind and accepted. Her presentation was very well received and later expanded into her book. This work still remains the only documentation of the long history and tradition of the sexual use and abuse of children. Florence's pivotal chapter on Freud, published long before Jeffrey Mason's exposé of Freud's renunciation of the problem, has become a model for subsequent studies of Freud's misogyny and his denial of the reality of the sexual violation of children and father-daughter incest.

Florence continued her work on this subject through lectures, interviews, and articles. As most of her interests were usually motivated by the patterns of her life, she became involved in other areas of sexual politics. As an older woman she became one of the founders and organizers of the early Older Women's Liberation Movement (OWL). As a social worker, housewife, mother, and female, Florence felt subordinated by prevailing sexual inequality, discrimination, and sex role stereotyping imposed by the strong socializing arm of the media. To counter the dangerous eroticization of women and children, she joined Women Against Pornography (WAP) and later became the coordinator of the Media Committee within the New York City chapter of the National Organization of Women (NOW). Florence was especially concerned with the images of mothers which reinforced unjust burdens of blame, guilt, and demanding self-sacrifice. Her slide show "From Mother Goddess to Father Knows Best," offered an overview of the relentless depreciation of mothers and motherhood from ancient mythology to present-day advertising, films, and media representations. Her article "Woman in the Middle" illustrated the hardships endured by women caught between the grinding problems of aging parents and grown children. With "Who's Afraid of Margaret Ribble" Florence focused on our culture where all human difficulties are attributed to "bad mothering."

Freeing her from domestic obligations, the Women's Movement had certainly changed the course of her life. But when her son, Matthew, age 36, told Florence in the summer of 1987 that he was infected with AIDS, her feminism was relegated to the back burner. All of her energy centered on her grown child "as though he was five years old." Florence was determined "to make him better" and this responsibility doubled when she became involved with her son's lover, Ron, who was also infected and had been abandoned by his homophobic "Christian" family. She reverted to "putting them first" and assuming responsibility for their well-being. It was as though she had never left being a mother. In spite of all evidence that they suffered from a fatal illness, she became versed in all aspects of the disease in the hope of finding a cure. Realizing that she needed help and support in this monumental task, she attended a Mother's Support Group (mothers of adult children with AIDS) where she found equal compassion, caring, and understanding. From them she obtained the courage and endurance to sustain the pain, suffering, and the inevitable reality. Ron died in June 1990 and Matthew's death followed six weeks later. Towards the end, one mother said to Florence, "No matter what you do it will make no difference. Try to make them and yourself as comfortable as possible." She tried. Later she participated in a mother's bereavement group where, along with these women, she experienced and survived the depths of loss and mourning.

Despite her return to motherhood, the "feminist" in Florence surfaced. After talking and listening, she was struck by the lack of support available to these overburdened, grieving mothers. The stigma of the disease fell on them as well as their sick children; many (not all), whether married, divorced, widowed, or remarried, discovered that some of their husbands or ex-husbands, including biological fathers, gave no or little help financially, emotionally, or as caregivers. Often this lack of support extended to siblings, relatives and friends who resented a mother's redirected concern and energy to her afflicted offspring or who later were critical of what they decided was "unnecessary prolonged mourning." Florence came to understand that a mother's devotion and anguish does not exempt her from the denial of respect and sympathy to so many women. "I came back to feminism through AIDS," she said.

Florence also noted over this span of seven years that the alarming increase in infected heterosexual women is generally the result of their inferior financial and social status. So many women and children, deprived of resources and opportunities and dependent on men for their economic survival, do not have the power to negotiate for "safe sex" or protection against this sexually transmitted disease. Whether in marriage, whether a girlfriend or lover; whether trapped in the lucrative industry of pornography, prostitution or various forms of sexual slavery; whether victims of rape, sexual harassment, child sexual abuse and incest, their existence is determined, in Western as well as other societies, by machoism and male-dominated cultures. Florence insists that "AIDS is a feminist issue."

Florence is now in the process of recording in a forthcoming book what she has been through, what she has learned from other mothers and the terrible toll this epidemic has been on women due to their subordinate status. Yes, AIDS is, indeed, a feminist issue.

Politicizing Sexual Violence:
A Voice in the Wilderness

Diana E. H. Russell

FROM SOUTH AFRICAN REVOLUTIONARY
TO RADICAL FEMINIST

It is hard to imagine less fertile ground for political activism than my family of origin. White, upper-class, and South African, they subscribed whole-heartedly to the patriarchal code that separated Blacks and whites, men and women. Nor was my immediate environment any less hidebound. I attended an elite Anglican boarding school for girls, whose motto was "Manners maketh man." I stumbled into college by accident after dropping out of the cooking and sewing classes recommended by my mother. I was raised to be a useless appendage to some rich white man, and to carry on the exploitive tradition of my family.

The dormant rebel in me made her debut during my college

Diana E. H. Russell, PhD, is Professor Emerita of Sociology at Mills College, Oakland, California. She now works full-time doing research, writing, speaking, consulting, and serving as an expert witness. She is the author, editor, or co-editor of 13 books, and currently is completing her fourteenth entitled *Behind Closed Doors in White South Africa: Incest Survivors Tell Their Stories.*

She would like to thank Marny Hall for her editorial assistance with this article.

[Haworth co-indexing entry note]: "Politicizing Sexual Violence: A Voice in the Wilderness." Russell, Diana E. H. Co-published simultaneously in *Women & Therapy* (The Haworth Press, Inc.) Vol. 17, No. 3/4, 1995, pp. 425-434; and: *Feminist Foremothers in Women's Studies, Psychology, and Mental Health* (ed: Phyllis Chesler, Esther D. Rothblum, and Ellen Cole) The Haworth Press, Inc., 1995, pp. 425-434; and: *Feminist Foremothers in Women's Studies, Psychology, and Mental Health* (ed: Phyllis Chesler, Esther D. Rothblum, and Ellen Cole) Harrington Park Press, an imprint of The Haworth Press, Inc., 1995, pp. 425-434. Single or multiple copies of this article are available from The Haworth Document Delivery Service [1-800-342-9678, 9:00 a.m. - 5:00 p.m. (EST)].

425

years. At the age of 23 I joined an underground revolutionary movement called the African Resistance Movement that sabotaged government property as a form of protest. Ten years was the typical prison sentence at that time for members of such organizations who were apprehended by the police. By the time most members of the ARM had been arrested or escaped in 1964, I was in my second year of graduate school at Harvard University. My dissertation was on revolution, an unlikely topic for a PhD in Social Psychology (a mistaken choice), but accepted nevertheless by that bastion of patriarchy.

Anti-apartheid politics remained my primary political commitment until I moved from Princeton University where I was hired as a Research Associate, to San Francisco to live with my husband. The extreme misogyny at Princeton started me on my feminist path, but it was child's play compared to the crash course in sexism I received when incarcerated in my three-year marriage. Divorce heralded the beginning of my creative life as an active feminist and researcher. When deciding on what research to do, I always tried to choose topics that I believed to be potentially groundbreaking for feminism.

My own experiences of sexual abuse as a child and an adolescent have undoubtedly been vital motivators for my enduring commitment to the study of sexual violence against women. My research and activism exemplify how personal trauma can inform and inspire creative work. I believe these personal experiences have also contributed to my unwavering rejection of all victim-blaming explanations of sexual violence.

REVOLUTIONIZING OUR UNDERSTANDING OF SEXUAL VIOLENCE

Documenting the High Prevalence of Sexual Violence

In 1977 I received funding from the National Institute of Mental Health to study the prevalence of rape and attempted rape. Personal interviews were conducted with a multi-ethnic probability sample of 930 women 18 years and older who resided in San Francisco. In order to be able to compare my findings with those of the official statistics, I applied the legal definition of rape in California in 1978, i.e., penile-vaginal intercourse achieved by force, threat of force, or when the woman/girl was unable to consent because she was totally physically helpless in some way, as well as attempts at these acts.

Following this very conservative definition, 41% of the women in this sample reported being the victims of rape and/or attempted rape at least once in their lives. When wife rape (still legal in California in 1978) was included in the definition, 44% of the sample reported being victimized by rape/attempted rape, and 24% by completed rape.

Using conservative definitions of incestuous and extrafamilial child sexual abuse limited to contact or attempted contact experiences, and further limited for extrafamilial child sexual abuse to rape or attempted rape between the ages of 14 and 17, 38% of this sample of 930 women disclosed at least one experience of child sexual abuse (either extrafamilial or intrafamilial), while 16% disclosed at least one experience of incestuous abuse before the age of 18.

My survey was the first to thoroughly and rigorously document the fact that rape and child sexual abuse have directly affected the lives of so many women in a major U.S. city.

The Scope of My Research

My research has spanned many different forms of misogynist violence against women and girls and illuminated the connections between them. Aside from rape (including wife rape and lover rape), incestuous abuse and extrafamilial child sexual abuse, I have conducted research on woman battering, sexual harassment, sexual torture, femicide (the misogynist killing of females), pornography and its relationship to violence against women, male violence and the threat of nuclear war, and sexual and nonsexual forms of violence against women detained in prison.

Looking back on the work I have done, I have made many contributions of which I feel proud. I have been the first, or among the first, to provide a feminist analysis of several different forms of sexual violence against females. For example:

My book, *The Politics of Rape* (1975), was among the first to provide a feminist analysis of rape. After presenting the poignant stories of over twenty rape survivors, I argued that rape is not a deviant act, but one that is inherently sexist and which conforms to patriarchal notions of masculinity.

The Secret Trauma: Incest in the Lives of Girls and Women (1986) was based on the first study to obtain knowledge about incest from a large-scale probability sample of women. The prevalence rates of incestuous abuse and extrafamilial child sexual abuse that emerged from this study have become the most widely accepted prevalence statistics on child sexual abuse in the United States. *The Secret Trauma* received the 1986 C. Wright Mills Award–the most prestigious award in sociology in the United States–for "exemplifying outstanding social science research on a significant social problem." I'm told that it is still considered to be the definitive work on incest internationally.

Rape in Marriage (1982), based on the same probability sample as my incest research, was the first book ever published on marital rape. For a while it provided the only scientific data available to many of the campaigns organized to criminalize rape in marriage in different states.

Sexual Exploitation: Rape, Child Sexual Abuse, and Workplace Harassment (1984) was the first book to document the widespread prevalence of rape and child sexual abuse, as well as to emphasize the causal connections between these three different forms of sexual violation and sexual harassment.

Against Sadomasochism: A Radical Feminist Analysis (1982), which I co-edited with three other women, was the first feminist book to offer numerous critical perspectives on this phenomenon, particularly as it has manifested in the lesbian community.

My edited anthology, *Exposing Nuclear Phallacies* (1989), was named as an outstanding book on human rights by the Gustavus Myers Center in 1990. It was among the first to analyze the role of patriarchy in the development of a nuclear world, in the proliferation of nuclear weapons, and in the threat of nuclear war.

"Femicide" is a new concept that I first used in *Crimes Against Women* (1976) to distinguish misogynist killing of women from other types of homicide. *Femicide: The Politics of Woman Killing* (1992), a co-edited anthology on femicide in the United States,

Britain, and India, is among the first feminist books on woman-killing to illuminate the misogynist motivation in many murders of women by men–a reality that is obliterated by the gender-neutral term "homicide."

I was also among the first to provide a new feminist analysis of pornography that emphasizes the particularly potent sexism and woman-hatred embedded in this medium (my first essay on pornography was published in 1977). My first book on pornography, *Making Violence Sexy: Feminist Views on Pornography* (1993), was followed by my self-published book entitled *Against Pornography: The Evidence of Harm* (1994). *Against Pornography* is the first book to present a large number of visual examples of pornography (over 100) in a critical and scholarly context. This book also includes a review of the scientific literature on pornography's harmful effects, and a comprehensive explication of my own theory of how pornography causes rape. The pornographic pictures in this book were reprinted without obtaining permission. This placed me at risk of being sued by the pornographers for breach of copyright laws.

My book, *Lives of Courage: Women for a New South Africa* (1989), is among the first feminist books to be published in South Africa. Although the focus of this book is on women's many unsung contributions to the anti-apartheid struggle, many of the 22 women whose personal stories are included also condemned sexism, including male violence. Because the majority of the women in *Lives of Courage* are black, this book served to undermine the prevalent South African myth that only white, middle-class women are concerned about women's oppression, including violence against women.

Despite these accomplishments, the price I have paid for my radical feminism has been high. Most academics in the U.S. who are considered high achievers are rewarded with money, grants, job offers, fellowships, and the like. I have rarely been rewarded in any of these ways. I did not receive a single academic job offer during my 22 years on the faculty at Mills College. I was also shabbily treated by key members of the Mills administration, which contributed to my early retirement in 1991 at the age of 53. Although I have applied for research grants many times, I have received only two substantial grants to date. Once out of graduate school, I have been turned down for every fellowship I ever applied for. In order to do my research and writing, I had to teach half-time and fund my work on my half-time salary. In general, far from earning me money, my research and writing have cost me. I sometimes wonder what I might have accomplished had I received the rewards that a man with my curriculum vitae would have enjoyed.

Despite the many penalties I have undergone for failing to serve the patriarchy, I don't regret my choices most of the time, particularly when I remember that my work has been helpful to many women. I have received many wonderful accolades over the years, the most gratifying of which comes from feminist law professor, Catharine MacKinnon (1993), which I cannot resist citing here.

> Professor Russell is the recognized academic expert on the empirical study of sexual violence against women in the United States, and a leading authority on this subject throughout the world. None of the conceptual, factual, political, or legal advances in understanding, documenting, and opposing violence against women in this country, including my own work, would have been possible without her ground-breaking studies and scholarly publications.

RADICAL FEMINIST ACTIVIST

Although most of my time is spent at my desk, I have also engaged in a variety of feminist actions to combat violence against women. For example:

I was arrested in London in 1974 for protesting the 20-year sentence handed out by a U.S. court to Inez Garcia for killing one of her rapists.

I was one of the founding members in 1976 of Women Against Violence in Pornography and Media (WAVPM)—the first feminist anti-pornography organization in the United States.

I was arrested and jailed in 1990 for tearing up pornography in a porn store in Bellingham, Washington.

In 1993 I started Women United Against Incest—an action group in Cape Town, South Africa—to try to improve the treatment of incest survivors in that country.

In 1974 I conceived the idea of an "International Tribunal on Crimes against Women"–a global speak-out on all forms of oppression and discrimination against females. I became a major organizer of this international women-only conference, which took place in Brussels, Belgium, in 1976. About 2,000 women from all over the world participated in this event, many of them testifying about violence against women. Referring to the International Tribunal as "a great historic event," Simone de Beauvoir concluded her opening statement with an unforgettable tribute: "I salute this Tribunal as being the start of a radical decolonization of women." Of all my activities, I feel the greatest sense of accomplishment for my role in this action, not least because I consider myself a rather inept organizer.

A VOICE IN THE WILDERNESS

I was very surprised to be selected as a foremother of feminist therapy/psychology/mental health because my attempts to communicate about my work to mental health professionals have often been very poorly received. The interest of many of these women appears to be limited to improving their skills as therapists.

I certainly believe in the importance of trying to help incest survivors to heal (I will focus here on this form of sexual violence). I'm a particularly enthusiastic advocate of self-help survivor groups like those developed in Norway that are free, therapist-less, and run according to principles that have been worked out over several years. However, I get extremely disturbed when therapists ignore the political context of incestuous abuse and other problems that they treat.

Mental health professionals must take responsibility for their shameful history of victim-blaming. Despite being privileged to learn about sexual abuse directly from the mouths of victims and survivors, most of them remained trapped in the sexist myopia of their victim-blaming predecessors, of whom Sigmund Freud is the most notorious example. Although many women therapists, particularly feminist therapists, finally learned to see incest victims/survivors in a new way, they learned their new perspective from the feminist movement–not their clients. It took survivors speaking out about their experiences inside and outside the feminist movement to start to revolutionize our understanding of incestuous abuse. Women in the mental health profession must learn from this failure, not repeat it.

As long as therapists confine themselves to treating the relative handful of casualties of the patriarchal system who can afford therapy, they will contribute little or nothing to changing the male-dominated family structure and other social institutions that place so many female children at risk of sexual violence. As long as they work within a narrow psychopathological framework–even though it may be a revised one–they may succeed in enjoying an affluent lifestyle, but they won't succeed in diminishing the prevalence of incestuous abuse.

Individualizing sexual victimization depoliticizes it. It also disempowers survivors by encouraging them to focus on their problems rather than their strengths, and motivating them to seek solutions within themselves. Many therapists of the family dynamics persuasion even insist on "helping" their clients to see the role they played in becoming victims. This is victim-blaming in modern dress.

The widespread overemphasis on the importance of personal healing–the excessive "therapizing" of sexual assault–has also deflected many survivors from being at the forefront of the struggle to change the conditions that caused or contributed to their victimization in the first place.

The psychological health of many women was greatly improved when the feminist theory that accompanied the rise of the second wave of feminism in the United States provided us with an understanding of how sexism had contributed to our personal problems. Many middle-class women walked out of their therapists' offices and into the feminist movement. The often modest achievements of therapy were greatly surpassed for many of these women by the healing that occurred from their involvement in this movement.

Similarly, survivors are likely to benefit greatly from understanding incest as a sociopolitical issue, not merely a problem that existed in their own family and a few other equally unfortunate families. Some may also benefit from understanding that they can empower themselves by taking action to combat incestuous abuse.

Becoming an activist can be therapeutic in a very different way than having individual sessions with a therapist, as well as contributing to the *social* healing of this traumatic experience.

While there are movements against rape and woman battery in the United States, there is no comparable movement against incestuous abuse. I believe the responsibility for this fact falls squarely on the shoulders of the mental health profession—for individualizing, pathologizing and "therapizing" the widespread problem of incestuous abuse. Unless therapists spend time on prevention efforts, they must face the fact that they are financial beneficiaries of incestuous abuse. The more incest there is, the more in demand they will be, and the higher they can set their fees. Effective prevention requires understanding the social and cultural causes and context of incestuous abuse and getting beyond a tunnel-vision preoccupation with how best to treat victims and survivors.

After delivering two speeches to mental health professionals, most of whom were treating adult incest survivors, a therapist and I were asked to answer any questions the audience wished to ask us. The next hour went by without a single question being directed to me. It appeared that my ideas were of no interest to these women compared to the opportunity to get tips from a therapist on how to improve their survivor-treatment skills. When I told them why I deplored their narrow-mindedness and launched into some version of the critique explicated above, the angry organizers reprimanded me for being rude (echoes of "manners maketh man").

I'll end with an offer: I'm willing to accept being labelled a disagreeable, rude foremother, if the indictment of the mental health profession that I have articulated here will help to bring about some of the much-needed changes in this profession.

SELECTED BIBLIOGRAPHY

Radford, J., and Russell, D.E.H. (Eds.). *Femicide: The Politics of Woman Killing.* New York: Twayne Publishers, 1992.

Russell, D.E.H. *Against Pornography: The Evidence of Harm.* Berkeley, California: Russell Publications, 1994.

Russell, D.E.H. (Ed.). *Making Violence Sexy: Feminist Views on Pornography.* New York: Teachers College Press, 1993.

Russell, D.E.H. *Lives of Courage: Women for a New South Africa.* New York: Basic Books, 1989.

Russell, D.E.H. (Ed.). *Exposing Nuclear Phallacies.* New York: Teachers College Press, 1989.

Russell, D.E.H. *The Secret Trauma: Incest in the Lives of Girls and Women.* New York: Basic Books, 1986.

Russell, D.E.H. *Sexual Exploitation: Rape, Child Sexual Abuse, and Workplace Harassment.* Newbury Park, California: Sage Publications, 1984.

Russell, D.E.H. *Rape in Marriage.* Bloomington, Indiana: Indiana University Press, 1990. First edition, 1982.

Russell, D.E.H., with R. Linden, D. Pagano, L. Star (Eds.). *Against Sadomasochism: A Radical Feminist Analysis.* San Francisco, California: Frog in the Well, 1982.

Russell, D.E.H., and N. Van de Ven. *Crimes Against Women: The Proceedings of the International Tribunal.* East Palo Alto, California: Frog in the Well, 1984. First edition, 1976.

Russell, D.E.H. *The Politics of Rape.* Chelsea, Michigan: Scarborough House, 1989. First edition, 1975.

Russell, D.E.H. *The Long Term Effects of Incestuous Abuse: An Exploratory Study.* Pretoria, South Africa: Human Sciences Research Council Publishers, 1995.

A Feminist in the Arab World

Nawal El Saadawi
Mary E. Willmuth

It was my pleasure and privilege as the second author on this paper to interview Dr. El Saadawi. She was extraordinarily articulate and clear while being patient and helpful as I tried to make sure that I was understanding her correctly. I have attempted to report what she said in her own words, with as few changes as possible. I did not think what she said needed explication or interpretation. She speaks for herself here in her own voice, through her own thoughts and feelings, as she always has:

The word feminist is not an Arabic word. In Egypt we talk about the liberation of women and about women who are active and fighting for liberation. We don't use the word feminist as it is used

---

Nawal El Saadawi is an Egyptian physician and novelist who has written over thirty works of fiction and non-fiction about the problems and struggles of women in the Arab world. After rising to the position of Director of Public Health in Egypt she was dismissed from this position and jailed. Fearing for her safety she now lives in North Carolina where she continues undeterred to write and teach as a visiting professor at Duke University.

Mary E. Willmuth, PhD, is a psychologist who works primarily in rehabilitation. She has particular interest in gender issues in health psychology. She is a Clinical Associate Professor in the Departments of Psychiatry and Psychology at the University of Vermont.

[Haworth co-indexing entry note]: "A Feminist in the Arab World." Saadawi, Nawal El, and Mary E. Willmuth. Co-published simultaneously in *Women & Therapy* (The Haworth Press, Inc.) Vol. 17, No. 3/4, 1995, pp. 435-442; and: *Feminist Foremothers in Women's Studies, Psychology, and Mental Health* (ed: Phyllis Chesler, Esther D. Rothblum, and Ellen Cole) The Haworth Press, Inc., 1995, pp. 435-442; and: *Feminist Foremothers in Women's Studies, Psychology, and Mental Health* (ed: Phyllis Chesler, Esther D. Rothblum, and Ellen Cole) Harrington Park Press, an imprint of The Haworth Press, Inc., 1995, pp. 435-442. Single or multiple copies of this article are available from The Haworth Document Delivery Service [1-800-342-9678, 9:00 a.m. - 5:00 p.m. (EST)].

435

by readers and publishers in the West. I think that my being selected as a feminist foremother, however, is more or less realistic because since I was a little girl I was always a feminist in the sense that I felt there was something wrong with the established system. When I was a little girl I was very good in school, more intelligent than my brother who was one year older than me. But, as a male child, both the family of my father and the family of my mother loved and spoiled him. At the end of the year I passed the examinations very well and he failed. He was rewarded for his failure by playing and eating, I was rewarded by working in the kitchen and the house with my mother. I was angry and felt this was unjust. I asked everyone in the two families why this had happened. They told me that was the way God said it should be. I felt that God should either be just or I could not believe in him. To me this is feminism.

My sisters and my friends also had the same feelings but they were so afraid to speak up. We were silenced by our families and inhibited the questions. I started to pray and to fast and to be a very good Muslim and to believe in God. I forgot that period in my history when I was very little and not yet afraid. I think this happens to all girls after a certain age with socialization and training and education. I think all women are born feminists but the fear inhibits these ideas and they inhibit the feminism.

I am writing my autobiography and wondering why this fear did not continue with me. I was very lucky to meet the wrong man. If I had met the right man from the start I could have been married happily with children and maybe have submitted to the moral code. Our separation exposed me to life. I had been protected by my family and my education, but suddenly I was exposed. It reminds me also of my experience when I went to jail. When there is a crisis we really start to see the system and to know that it is wrong. That's the positive aspect of failure.

I married against the will of my family and when I left my husband I had no family behind me. So I started to question everything and to remember my childhood. But this is a process. Every day something happens, some little event that illuminates the injustice of the system. When I walk in the street and some man says an ugly word to me, when male colleagues are promoted though I am more effective it reminds me of the discrimination and the injustice.

But feminism for me is not just the oppression I felt as a woman or as an individual. I was very politically aware that my country was occupied by foreigners. I felt that Egypt was not independent, was a colony, and I felt colonized by men and by the marriage laws. That's why I was politically active when I was a student. I remember in 1951 there was a big demonstration that came out of the medical college and I was almost the only female student. We were shouting about the independence of Egypt: "Independence! Freedom! Freedom!" When we shouted "Freedom!" I was shouting for the country but also wanting to be free myself. So there was a sort of continuity between the fight to free the land, the people, the country and the fight to free myself.

In fact, I do not look to feminism as just something related to religion or sex or gender, I think feminism is related also to class, to colonialism. It is much broader than just the liberation of women or sexual liberation. I didn't need to read books to understand that. It came from practice, from daily life. After I was in medical school I started reading and there was confirmation. But even in high school I used to sit for hours in the library. My father was professor of Arabic so I read a lot of Arabic books about history and Arabic literature. I read about the history of ancient Egypt, our female goddesses and the status of women. I realized that there were goddesses of knowledge, of medicine and of justice who were female. I used to ask myself how it could be that six thousand years ago the head of the courts in Egypt was a woman and now women were prevented from being judges. We also had women doctors in ancient Egypt. I was fascinated and inspired by those women. It gave me a reference. When I tried to say women should be doctors or writers, both men and women in my family would say: "No, women are created to be mothers and wives." They would quote from the Koran and the prophet Mohammed. I could tell them about women and the goddesses in ancient Egypt. It gave me a lot of power to argue with people when they said that women were created just to be wives and servants to men.

I was also lucky to be smart and to have a brother who did not do well in school. My father had six daughters and three sons. It was a big burden and the eldest girl must marry first or the others cannot. He wanted me to marry at ten years old. But my mother was ambitious, a feminist in her own way, and wanted me to compensate for her frustrated ambitions as a girl. She tried to help me and to save me from a very early marriage. My father also believed in me and was disappointed in my brother. He transferred his hopes onto me.

So in a way I was lucky to have an unsuccessful brother. This helped me to survive until I went to medical school. In Egypt the best students, male or female, go to the medical college. This is one of the paradoxes of life in Egypt. There are remnants of the past high status of women. In Egypt we never lose our name in marriage and women can be doctors. Egypt also lost a lot of this heritage with colonialism, the Turks, the British, the Greeks, the Romans. Our female goddesses and much of the matriarchal system were lost to colonialism over the years. But there is still something dormant. We don't lose our names by marriage, the husband has no authority over the money of his wife. I can open a bank account in my name and if I have high grades I can go to the medical college or into engineering. But for many years women were not admitted to Cairo University. So there are many contradictions and paradoxes.

It is through writing that I have been most influential. I began writing very early about what I observed and thought. I write in Arabic. I have been publishing now for almost forty years and my books have been disseminated throughout the Arab countries. There are now almost four generations of women who have read and been influenced by my books, both fiction and non-fiction, and by the articles I have written. My work has been censored in Egypt, particularly under Sadat, which was also when I lost my job and was sent to jail. Nevertheless my books have traveled everywhere in the Arab world. When the censors prevented my books from being published in Egypt I started to publish elsewhere, in Lebanon, in Morocco, in the Sudan, in Algeria. My work was even smuggled into Saudi Arabia, Libya and Iraq. I receive a lot of mail from women and also from men commenting on my books. Some young men have written to me to say that I changed their lives. I have written about men's sexuality, about sadism and about how the patriarchy destroys the character of both men and women. In a way my work has affected thousands of people in the Arab world, and I think that is my major contribution to feminism.

The effect of the books has been considerable. They are bestsellers and have met a great need for such information and knowledge. I was almost the first woman in the Arab world to speak out and link sexual oppression to political and economic oppression. As a doctor I was not afraid to speak about such topics as female circumcision, virginity problems, and abortion and to link them to the economic and political situation in Egypt and to the effects of colonialism. These books were almost the first to link sexuality to politics.

I have been influential in other ways, however. I was not only a writer, I was politically active, too. As a medical doctor I founded and organized the Health Education Association. I edited a magazine called *Health*. The government closed it down because I tried to link health to politics and spoke about women's health and sexuality and the harm done by female circumcision. The Ministry of Health closed the magazine and the association. This happened in the early 70s. It was when I was sent to jail. Sadat came to power and said there was democracy. I believed him and started being openly critical of his policies.

I also tried to organize the Arab Women's Solidarity Association and what we called the International Arab Women's Solidarity Association. We were the first Arab women's association to gain status with the United Nations as a non-governmental association. This happened during the early 80s. It was also closed by the government in 1991 along with our magazine *Noon*.

There have been attempts to silence me concerning everything I have tried to do. I established what we called the Women Writer's Association in 1971. I have tried to organize and establish organizations in different areas of my life, with regard to medicine through health education, in the area of writing by bringing together women writers and in relation to women in general by participation in the Arab women's solidarity movement. In each area the government was after me all the time until I left the country in 1993. This has been a great source of frustration for me, that I was often unable to reach the people I wanted to reach. After the closing of the Arab Women's Solidarity Association, the government put security guards around my house twenty-four hours a day, and a bodyguard to follow me. The guards came to my house during the late 80s after the publication of my novel, *The Fall of Imam*, and then again in

1992 after the assassination of one of the Islamic Fundamentalists. The government said I was threatened by the Islamic Fundamentalists but some people told me I was really in danger from the guards and the government. I was in a very, very awkward situation and my life was in danger. So I left the country and since then have been a visiting professor at Duke University. I feel the danger even in the United States as I think we are governed by an international policy involving a class system. I don't feel safe anywhere at all, but there is immediate danger at home. In my country, in my region, I am a threat to the system and here I feel like a fish out of water.

In some ways I am a person who is never satisfied. I have written more than thirty books, many of them translated into other languages, and yet I always have the feeling that what I am doing is just a drop in the ocean. The system is so well established it takes great efforts to change it. So I work very hard and I write books because I feel that we need to work hard. Also I have a feeling all the time that I have never written the book in my head. There is a part of me that is inhibited, a little fear that I did not overcome. There is a lot of censorship even in the West. I cannot really publish the book I want to. I am limited by the publishing market, especially since I write first in Arabic. For example, my last novel was called *The Innocence of the Devil,* in Arabic. I couldn't publish this book in Egypt and in Lebanon my publisher changed the title. He told me he could not publish a book with a title like that. So I am always in a battle to publish what I want. Even in Lebanon or here I am always fighting with the press. They quote me in the wrong way. Sometimes they take what I say and distort it so I am always angry and dissatisfied. But I also have to say that I feel deep inside me that I did a lot and it gives me pleasure to read reviews of my work, or when I read my mail, when I go back to Egypt, and when I see people around me who love me. So there is a lot of pleasure in my life.

I have a daughter and son. My daughter is a very accomplished and well-known writer. Her name is Mona Helmi and she has published five books in Arabic. She has had some problems because she is my daughter but she proved herself and now she is one of the very few women writers in Egypt. That is a big, big pleasure. I also have a son whose name is Atef Hetata. He is a very accomplished film director and his latest film is called *The Bride of the Nile*. It is a feminist film and it won six international prizes. So this is a great source of pleasure also. Those are my biological son and daughter. I also have thousands of men and women who have done their Masters degrees about my work. They quote my work in the Arab world and it has affected many students. So I have many daughters and sons in a way and this is also a source of pleasure. And there is also my husband. We co-teach together, he is also a visiting professor. He is a novelist and a doctor, too. He spent thirteen years in jail, so he is also a political fighter.

One of my difficulties comes from dealing with feminists from the West. Whenever I meet feminists from America or Europe, at international conferences for example, I have a problem with them. First of all, they do not understand that we live in different countries, that the politics, the culture, the religion are different. So they try to dominate, they try to teach us what to do. They think that the American feminism is the only feminism, that everything American is international and should be the standard of everything. If women here speak about something we should do the same thing. I have a lot of difficulty with that and that is why I usually quarrel with them at conferences. It is another form of oppression and colonialism, the colonialism of Western feminists. We have been so busy fighting at international conferences that this point could not be heard. I hope that the feminists in the West are now changing and beginning to understand that feminism is not exclusively American.

Western feminists also think that feminism is a Western invention, that if I am a feminist it is because I have read Western books. I became a feminist without knowing English. I was inspired by our history. That is why in our Arab Women's Solidarity Association we call ourselves historical socialist feminists. We depend on our history in our analysis of ideas. We are inspired by those great women in our history. We say we are socialist because we are against class oppression and colonialism. We call ourselves feminists because we are against patriarchy and male oppression. So usually we use these three words to describe ourselves. And we believe and say that we have a feminism that is original and not copied from the West. It is important that this be mentioned and understood.

SELECTED BIBLIOGRAPHY

Works Published in English

Fiction:

El Saadawi, N. (1980). *The hidden face of Eve*. London: Zed Books.
El Saadawi, N. (1982). *Woman at point zero*. London: Zed Books.
El Saadawi, N. (1984). *God dies by the Nile*. London: Zed Books.
El Saadawi, N. (1984). *Two women in one*. London: Al Saqui.
El Saadawi, N. (1985). *Death of an ex-minister*. London: Methuen.
El Saadawi, N. (1985). *Memoirs of a woman doctor*. London: Al Saqui.
El Saadawi, N. (1986). *Circling song*. London: Zed Books.
El Saadawi, N. (1987). *The fall of Imam*. London: Methuen.
El Saadawi, N. (1987). *She has no place in paradise*. London: Methuen.
El Saadawi, N. (1988). *Searching*. London: Zed Books.
El Saadawi, N. (1992). *The well of life*. London: Methuen.
El Saadawi, N. (1994). *The innocence of the devil*. London: Methuen, and California University Press.

Non-fiction:

El Saadawi, N. (1985). *My travels around the world*. London: Methuen.
El Saadawi, N. (1985). *Memoirs from a women's prison*. London: Feminist Press. Reprinted 1994 by California University Press.
El Saadawi, N. (in press). *Autobiography*. London: Methuen.

A Late Awakening

Rachel Josefowitz Siegel
Elisabeth Traumann

It feels appropriate that I should be reviewing my work as a feminist therapist during this busy and joyous summer of my seventieth birthday. Aware of the immense and profound changes that I have experienced in my life and in my world, I feel an almost urgent wish to remember and to tell. The wish is tempered by a persistent

---

Rachel Josefowitz Siegel, MSW, is a feminist therapist. She writes and lectures about Jewish women, old women, and the intersection of various biases and prejudices. Until midlife, she was a full-time faculty wife, mother, and community volunteer. She entered graduate school at the age of forty-seven. Born in Germany in 1924, of Lithuanian Jewish parents, Rachel attended schools in Switzerland before emigrating to the United States in 1939. She has been a feminist activist within the Jewish community and a Jewish activist among feminists.

Elisabeth Traumann is a mother, wife, student of social work, mental health worker with the Portuguese Mental Health Team at Cambridge Hospital, writer of stories and poetry. This is her first publication and she's honored to have worked with Rachel. She grew up in a Jewish German town in Southern Brazil, and has been in this country for 14 years.

Elisabeth wants to thank her mother for teaching her to be aware of inequalities. Her mother's decency and outrage inspired Elisabeth's years with the Boston Area Rape Crisis Center, and continue to inform her writing and her work in the mental health field where–not surprisingly–most clients turn out to be women.

Correspondence may be addressed to Rachel J. Siegel at 11 Spruce Lane, Ithaca, NY 14850.

[Haworth co-indexing entry note]: "A Late Awakening." Siegel, Rachel Josefowitz, and Elisabeth Traumann. Co-published simultaneously in *Women & Therapy* (The Haworth Press, Inc.) Vol. 17, No. 3/4, 1995, pp. 443-458; and: *Feminist Foremothers in Women's Studies, Psychology, and Mental Health* (ed: Phyllis Chesler, Esther D. Rothblum, and Ellen Cole) The Haworth Press, Inc., 1995, pp. 443-458; and: *Feminist Foremothers in Women's Studies, Psychology, and Mental Health* (ed: Phyllis Chesler, Esther D. Rothblum, and Ellen Cole) Harrington Park Press, an imprint of The Haworth Press, Inc., 1995, pp. 443-458. Single or multiple copies of this article are available from The Haworth Document Delivery Service [1-800-342-9678, 9:00 a.m. - 5:00 p.m. (EST)].

443

residue of social shyness, self-doubts, and learned inhibitions about boasting and self-exposure. Who am I to be counted among "feminist foremothers?" The invitation to participate in this volume brings on a mixture of humility and pride, fear and pleasure, and gives me permission to reminisce in public.

Elisabeth Traumann: I met Rachel through her article "Turning the things that divide us into things that unite us" (Siegel, 1990d). Rachel's article gave a forum for the disquiet I felt about the privileges of being raised middle-class in Brazil, of being white, straight, able-bodied. I also grew up within the pain of a town made up of German Jewish Holocaust refugees and survivors, disempowered women, and the hard, hard-working poor. Only after reading Rachel's article, did I realize that sympathy needn't be a scarce commodity. So, I wrote a letter to Rachel–and she wrote back! Later, she invited me to co-author this article.

Rachel Josefowitz Siegel: Our first meeting embodied some of the central themes in my professional and personal life. It was the day before my fiftieth Simmons College reunion in Boston. I felt like coming full circle when I talked with Elisabeth, a graduate student at the Simmons School of Social Work, about working together.

We were strangers of different ages, different backgrounds, at different stages of our social work careers. Elisabeth's respectful curiosity about the linkages between my personal and professional life made me feel that she would understand the tensions I have felt between work and family.

This encounter, like so many others, was based on a belief system that guides much of my work, finding its source and strength in a combination of Jewish and feminist values that emphasize community, collaboration, and self-scrutiny. Thus, on that memorable weekend of reunion with former classmates and meeting with Elisabeth, I was following my usual pattern of seeking allies in my work. I was reaching across the span of age and time, and other differences, in order to build bridges, to connect, to integrate, and to find my own sense of self within the context or the absence of my relationships with others.

The connections between my work and my personal growth are

not accidental. The first forty years of my life were spent in creating a family, becoming Americanized, and being a frequently depressed yet energetic and dutiful faculty wife. The next ten years involved a soul-searching and somewhat painful mid-life adjustment, moving through serious para-professional volunteer activities to a masters degree from the Syracuse University School of Social Work. Since then, both in my work and in my own self-awareness, I have moved slowly and sometimes painfully from a focus on the immobilizing effects of various oppressions, to a more joyful appreciation and discovery of the strengths and creativity that are involved in coping with the worst and the best in life.

Elisabeth Traumann: Have you thought about yourself as a leader?

Rachel Josefowitz Siegel: Yes and no. I am trying to absorb the fact that others see me as a "foremother" in my field, while I have been more aware of my good fortune in interacting with the "real foremothers" most of whom are younger than I. Yet I began taking leadership positions as a young homemaker, within some traditional women's organizations, and have continued to do so in my professional work. Early on, as president of my local Hadassah chapter, I taught leadership training courses. During those years of volunteer work, I acquired some of the leadership and organizational skills that still serve me well, especially while organizing professional conferences and workshops.

Elisabeth Traumann: Who were some of the women who influenced you?

Rachel Josefowitz Siegel: I am deeply grateful to the pioneers in feminist thinking, some of whom have become my friends. Among these, I count Paula Caplan, Lenore Walker, Hannah Lerman, Laura Brown, Adrienne Smith, Phyllis Chesler, Jean Baker Miller, and the many friends and colleagues at the Feminist Therapy Institute. I wish I could name them all.

I learned a great deal about my own heterosexual assumptions from Adrienne Rich when she spent some time at Cornell. My interactions with Evelyn Torton Beck, and the members of the National Women's Studies Jewish Caucus have sharpened my thinking and encouraged me to pursue and develop my own interests in the mental health of Jewish women. My five years on the Women's Studies Board at Cornell University exposed me to feminist thought and process in other disciplines.

Paula Caplan has been friend and mentor. Her work on the myth of women's masochism and on mother-blaming is constantly of use to me in understanding and analyzing clinical and policy situations, as well as the situation of women in general.

Elisabeth Traumann: You freely acknowledge that your work has been nourished by the work of others.

Rachel Josefowitz Siegel: Of course. The most ongoing and constructive inspiration and support, since 1980, have come from the members of FTI, the Feminist Therapy Institute, and the editors of *Women & Therapy*, Ellen Cole and Esther Rothblum. Before that, it was the Ortho Women's Institute that gave substance to my earliest experiences in feminist approaches to therapy.

I remember certain moments or events as significantly associated with key concepts. One of these occurred at the Washington, DC Ortho Women's Institute (1979), focusing on Women and Creativity. For the first time, I was among women who acknowledged and explored the fact that speaking our own truth as women, in a world that denies our truth, is difficult and crazy-making. The concept that emerged was that women's creativity can only truly blossom within the supportive environment of like-minded women. The sense of working collaboratively, and in sisterhood, was–and still is–tremendously important to me. It was here that Jean Baker Miller, in her concluding remarks, said: "The only difference between those of us on the speaker's side of the podium, and those of you on the listening side, is that we have presented during the past two days; each of you can also do that." Although I had deeply envied women who could write and speak their truth in public, I had until that moment never dared to think that I could still learn to do so. I was 54 years old.

The following year, in Toronto, I presented my first paper on mid-life (Siegel, 1982b). I also proposed to collect and edit the papers that had been presented at the Ortho Women's Institutes; Joan Hamerman Robbins offered to be my co-editor. Joan and I, both novices in editing, collaboratively produced *Women Changing Therapy: New Assessments, Values and Strategies in Feminist Therapy* (Robbins & Siegel, 1983), which was one of the earliest books in the field.

We agreed on a commitment to feminist process and feminist content. This meant sharing the profits with our authors, letting the authors know what was happening as we went along, and encouraging women who had never written before, so that the book would include timid new writers as well as established authors. We looked for a range of styles and a variety of voices, actively reaching out to include some early writing on lesbian realities and on working with incest survivors.

This was the first of a number of collaborative writing projects each of which has presented me with new challenges and satisfactions. In the beginning, working together gave me courage; now that I live alone, it also cuts through my loneliness.

Elisabeth Traumann: This all occurred pretty early on in your career as a feminist therapist, right?

Rachel Josefowitz Siegel: Yes, I do remember a surge of "post-menopausal zest" during my mid to late fifties. Within the first ten years of professional practice I had also begun my active involvement in national feminist organizations. Together with Alexandra Kaplan, I co-coordinated the 1981 and 1982 Ortho Women's Institutes; I then joined the first Steering Committee of FTI.

Meanwhile, I had been working as a feminist therapist in my own community, at a time when feminist therapy was still considered a radical, questionable, and overly biased model. In 1975 I offered the first workshop on menopause at the Women's Community Building in Ithaca, breaking the silence and taboo surrounding menopause.

Earlier still, I initiated the first women's group in town, at a women's walk-in center. The staff at the Mental Health Clinic, where I worked, was concerned about the effect this would have on my reputation as a new practitioner. Reflecting the general attitude among practitioners at that time, they feared that I would be seen as biased because I was focusing on women (as if existing therapies were unbiased). Within another year, I had full approval from the same colleagues for starting a women's group at the Clinic. It was a period of exciting changes and emerging consciousness of women's needs.

Elisabeth Traumann: How did you become a feminist? Or maybe the question should be, how did you become a feminist therapist?

Rachel Josefowitz Siegel: The two are closely intertwined. I went back to graduate school in 1971, about twenty-five years after getting my undergraduate degree. Despite my volunteer experiences with and for women, I had resisted my daughter Ruth's efforts to expose me to feminist thinking. When Betty Friedan came to speak at Cornell in the early '70s I did not attend the lecture, I did not read her book.

My political views–although I would not have called them that–began to change during my fieldwork in graduate school. My first clients made me aware of how insulated I had been, and how little I knew about the world of women who were not as protected as I was.

Although I had suffered severe migraines and a fair amount of depression during the child-raising years, I had not attributed these symptoms to anything but my own imperfections. I had never been exposed to battering, I had not known of any overt domestic violence. I had felt the subtle ridiculing and powerful silencing of women when men spoke, but had no name for it. I had taken my privileged position for granted and been unaware of the general oppression of women. When I first listened to women who came in with histories of severe beatings, economic powerlessness, and overt emotional abuse, I was deeply shocked.

My exposure to the traumas of other women caused what today might be labeled secondary traumatization. My sense of understanding the world as it is was shaken at the core. It was a painful period of awakening to my own discomfort as well, even within a "good marriage" to a remarkably sensitive man.

The transition from a mainly homemaking self to a professional self required constant, and sometimes minute but significant, adjustments in my personal and married life. It was a time of major life changes and intense personal growth. I decided to go back into therapy, this time with Robert Seidenberg in Syracuse. He had a sophisticated awareness of women's issues and power issues that was very helpful to me, and it was a safe place for me to explore my inner gropings toward a feminist consciousness.

I was gradually realizing that a psychodynamic approach was not sufficient in understanding or helping women, and that gender and power represented significant factors that needed to be included in the therapy.

My first moment of awakening and confirmation actually occurred in an airport bookstore, when I discovered *Psychoanalysis and Women*, edited by Jean Baker Miller (1973). I read it with tremendous interest, finding confirmation for some of the confusion that I had felt in relating psychoanalytic theory to myself and to the women that I had begun to treat as a therapist. When *Toward a New Psychology of Women* (Miller, 1976) came out, I could not put it down. I went on to read Phyllis Chesler's *Women and Madness* (1972), and Gornick and Moran's *Woman in Sexist Society* (1971).

I experienced yet another crucial moment at the San Francisco Ortho Women's Institute in 1978, organized and led by Jean Baker Miller. It was my first encounter with a substantial group of well-established and experienced professional women who did not question the validity of approaching our work from a woman-centered perspective.

Elisabeth Traumann: It suddenly occurs to me as I hear you speak, one can't overestimate the importance of these conferences: the novelty of women's solidarity, the ferment generated by the interaction of audience and presenters–and the novelty of the information that was being disseminated. I don't suppose there was much written material on women at that time at all.

Rachel Josefowitz Siegel: True! In 1976, when we at the Task Force for Battered Women in Ithaca began our first efforts at informing ourselves about battered women, the only piece of literature that was available to us was an unpublished chapter identifying the cycle of violence, which later appeared in *The Battered Woman* (Lenore Walker, 1979).

Elisabeth Traumann: Was this the beginning of your involvement with the battered women's movement?

Rachel Josefowitz Siegel: Yes, I was on the board of the local Suicide Prevention and Crisis Service at that time when reports came in about a number of calls in which women reported acts of violence. In response to these calls, Nina Miller, as Director of SPCS, initiated the community organizing that led to the formation of the local Task Force for Battered Women. I was one of a small group of therapists among the grass-roots activists, who began to provide services to battered women. We took on the task of informing ourselves and our colleagues about the needs of battered women; we led workshops for professionals, and established the first support groups for battered women. I co-led the first group with a formerly battered woman, and went on to train and supervise or consult with later group leaders. The work of Lenore Walker, and my ongoing involvement with the Task Force have been central in my understanding the impact of male domination on the development of girls and women in our society. I'm firmly convinced that no psychology of women can be correct or complete without integrating the effects of a culture of violence and oppression on the lives of women.

Elisabeth Traumann: You talk about special moments of awareness; were there any others in your evolution?

Rachel Josefowitz Siegel: The First International Interdisciplinary Congress on Women, in Haifa, Israel at the end of December of 1981, had a profound impact on my thinking. Jessie Bernard's keynote address remains clear in my mind. She spoke of the importance of having separatist space for women where we could generate our own truths and strategies in our own world, while also learning to function and to gain power within the male-dominated establishment, being careful not to become co-opted by it. She spoke eloquently of being able to move in and out of both worlds, needing to function within both worlds, and the dangers of doing either one without the other.

My first AWP (Association for Women in Psychology) meeting in Boston, around 1980, was another turning point in my immersion in feminist therapy. I had never before been among so many Lesbians. I was amazed to discover that Lesbians were not only people with problems, but also women with a rich and joyful culture of their own. I have to smile at my own ignorance, when I remember thinking that I was not homophobic. Now I know, that no matter how long I work on it, I will never completely get rid of the heterosexual and homophobic assumptions that surround us all.

Elisabeth Traumann: And, you've worked a great deal with lesbian clients since then, right?

Rachel Josefowitz Siegel: Since then, and before. My presentation at the first Feminist Therapy Institute in 1981 was about my work with lesbian clients. As far as I know, it was the first time that a non-lesbian feminist therapist had ever talked about or written about working with lesbian clients. At that time, there was not a single openly identified gay or lesbian therapist in my community. I had worked hard to inform myself about the sensibilities of lesbian clients, and had become acutely aware of my previously unacknowledged heterosexual privileges. Since I like to do groups, I had facilitated a group of lesbian couples. It probably was of some value to the three couples, who were not completely "out" and had not had opportunities to talk with other lesbian couples. For me, it was humbling in terms of how little I knew and how much I needed to learn. When I think back, I am amazed at my own naiveté. That's what I talked about when I presented the paper at FTI that was later published (Siegel, 1985) in the first FTI publication, the *Handbook of Feminist Psychotherapy*. Though I would write the paper differently today, I take a certain amount of pride in this article, because I stuck my neck out in writing it, and in opening a subject that had not been aired before.

Elisabeth Traumann: I know that you were one of the founders of the Feminist Therapy Institute, but I really know very little about it. Can you talk about your history with FTI?

Rachel Josefowitz Siegel: That, too, is part of the reservoir of special moments in my feminist evolution. At the Boston AWP, I attended a small gathering of women who wanted to talk about feminist therapy at an advanced level. This is when I met Lenore Walker, Adrienne Smith, and the Ruth Siegel who is not my daughter. Later that year, I received an invitation to join fifty feminist therapists who were to meet in Vail, Colorado in March of 1981.

Lenore Walker was the prime organizer of that first gathering, where each of us handed out a written work in progress and spoke about it for 10 minutes. The following year, FTI became an organization.

FTI has been the primary source that replenishes my creative energies. It has been the place where I have been able to present fresh ideas, still in the process of being developed. At FTI, I have found the challenge of brilliant minds and the emotional support of caring feminists. We have repeatedly addressed difficult topics at a very sophisticated level, before they were presented elsewhere. We have come together once a year, intensely seeking the kind of feminist affirmation that many of us cannot find in our own communities. The going has not always been smooth, we have had internal strife and disagreements, but we have also made profound and important personal and professional connections with each other.

Elisabeth Traumann: Why do you think I have not heard as much about FTI as I have about the Stone Center and Carol Gilligan? Is it because the relational model is more "acceptable," somehow?

Rachel Josefowitz Siegel: That is an interesting question. We may not be as well known as a group, because FTI is not connected to an institution, we are a small and loosely formed organization. We have not attempted to develop a unified theory, choosing instead to say that our feminist thinking is in process, encouraging each other to develop a variety of theoretical models. Our Code of Ethics (FTI, 1987) is our only unified statement. The Stone Center relational model is more easily identified, has institutional backing, and may be more acceptable to mainstream thought and psychology, because it can easily be misconstrued as pushing women back into an exclusively relational life.

Elisabeth Traumann: As you know, I very much appreciate your writing. The discourse itself feels like a living example of the personal being political. How do you think about your writing?

Rachel Josefowitz Siegel: Much of my writing has been in response to or grown out of my own life experience, as well as a combination of clinical observations, and other feminist writings. All the factors of my personal life and circumstances are unavoidably as well as deliberately woven into my writing and my theorizing. My Jewishness, my age, my return to graduate school when I was 48 years old, my European childhood, my bridging of several cultures, my immigrant history, even my marital and parenting experience, and now my recent widowhood, have all fueled and been present in my writing. My style has become more and more personal as I have made a conscious decision to act on the feminist principle of "the personal is political" and the "political is personal." I have long ago stopped denying the fact that I use all of who I am when I do therapy. I cannot be a blank mirror to my clients. In the same way, I cannot be an invisible presence in my writing. So, it feels important to share with the reader who I am.

I have also found it difficult to write about the people who come to see me in therapy. While I know that clinical cases have been successfully and respectfully written about, particularly by Laura Brown (1986), I have not been able to make that happen as successfully. Having written only one piece using disguised case material without asking the client (Siegel 1982a), I decided that the use of clinical cases made me ethically uncomfortable.

One of the options then, was to write of who I am as a woman and a therapist and use myself as an example. While my experience may well be valuable in reverberating with the experiences of others, I have been mindful not to assume that I could generalize from it. Such personal writing, modeled by Karen Horney and Sigmund Freud, is well within the tradition of therapy as well as within current feminist theory.

In my research on women in their sixties (Siegel 1993), I used a different model. The women that I interviewed agreed to being taped, and had a choice about being named. I included myself as participant observer, and the interviewees had veto power over what I said about them or how I quoted them.

Elisabeth Traumann: So that, too, is a kind of collaboration. What part of your work do you think has had the greatest impact?

Rachel Josefowitz Siegel: Like most therapists, I have touched many lives. I like to think that my work with individual clients and with women in groups and workshops has made a significant difference in some of their lives.

In my writing and public speaking, I believe that my primary contributions have been in the three areas of women and aging, Jewish women, and the compounding intersection of all oppressive biases such as anti-Semitism, racism, sexism, ageism, and homophobia. My article on dependency (Siegel, 1988) seems to have struck a chord for men as well as women; it does not fit into the above categories. My writing has been controversial, and has elicited mixed responses.

In the area of aging and ageism, Jeanne Adleman, Theo Sonderegger, and I were among the first to introduce these topics at FTI and AWP; Shevy Healy's early work encouraged me to start several groups for women over sixty, including my own support group that is now in its tenth year. While I often get negative reactions from women who get angry when I use the word "old," even in a positive context, other women have been eager to discuss their own aging and to read my articles (Siegel, 1990a, 1990b, 1990c, 1993; Siegel, Choldin & Orost, in press; Siegel & Sonderegger, 1990; Siegel, Sonderegger & Connoley, in press) letting me know how much these mean to them.

In the area of Jewish women, I feel deeply touched and honored by the fact that the Jewish Caucus at AWP has selected me to be the first recipient of their annual award for my "contributions to the field of Jewish women in psychology." This award is a recognition of my integration of Jewish issues into the feminist professional world.

I was one of the founders of the Jewish Caucus in 1989, and have been instrumental in introducing and promoting the presentation of professional papers and workshops on the topic of Jewish women at AWP conferences and at the 1992 First Conference on Judaism, Feminism, and Psychology. These presentations have had a cumulative impact on Jewish and non-Jewish mental health professionals as well as readers and clients of many backgrounds, opening a discourse that had previously been conspicuously absent.

My first published article was *The Jew as a Woman* (Siegel, 1977), and my article on *Antisemitism and Sexism in Stereotypes of Jewish Women* (Siegel, 1986) preceded the more popular recognition of the problem. The publication of *Jewish Women in Therapy,* which I co-edited with Ellen Cole (Siegel & Cole, 1991) coincided with a wave of new and vibrant interest among Jewish women in North America wanting to explore their identities, and wanting to be heard. The book and the readings, workshops and presentations that have grown out of it, have introduced the notion that the Jewishness of Jewish clients and therapists is an important aspect of therapy and has a significant impact on self-esteem. I have found that many of the Jewish issues around gender anti-Semitism were also of concern to Jewish men, and I have begun to explore these areas as well.

Elisabeth Traumann: How has this book been received?

Rachel Josefowitz Siegel: While many Jewish women have been enthusiastic about it, and have found it very meaningful, the book has also received a kind of non-recognition, non-response, from the Jewish establishment, that is in effect a negative response. We made it less appealing to traditional Jewish groups by including articles about Jewish women who do not fit the idealized Jewish woman image, such as Jewish Lesbians, and battered women. The visibility of Jewish Lesbians, in four of the nineteen articles, was perceived as over-visibility by some heterosexual readers who felt confused and excluded, asking me if all Jewish feminists were Lesbian.

My writing on the struggle to overcome various biases has overlapped with my interests in Jewish women and old women (Siegel, 1990d, 1992, 1994; Siegel, Greene & Kaschak, 1995). This work was fueled by the early attention to diversity and anti-racism at FTI and AWP conferences. I am grateful to Anne Ganley, Laura Brown, Beverly Greene, Clare Holzman, Natalie Porter, Jan Faulkner, Kitch Childs, and Jeanne Adleman who kept us alert and sensitive to the racism within ourselves and among each other.

Elisabeth Traumann: How has your feminist thinking affected or interacted with your family life?

Rachel Josefowitz Siegel: It is not possible for me to separate my family self from my professional self, my feminist self from my Jewish self, and I have tried to maximize rather than avoid these interactions. In my writing, I have been careful not to expose my family, even when I write about myself, just as I have avoided exposing my clients. When I have referred to my family, I have tried not to speak for them, but to focus on my experience of them, perhaps risking the appearance of self-centeredness while attempting to protect their privacy.

I believe I have always been woman-centered in many ways, and I see no contradiction in saying that I deeply love the men in my life: my father, brothers, husband, sons, grandsons, and now my great-grandson. There was a period when I tried to explore what choices I might have made had I grown up without the heterosexual impera-tives of my generation. I know now that my lasting marriage was based on genuine heterosexual attraction and on the kind of person I married. He was a man of very high ethical standards, who was able—not immediately, mind you—to go along with my feminism out of his sense of justice, and also out of his love for me. My immersion in women's issues and in feminist thinking has at times aligned me with my daughter, and appeared to distance me from my sons, yet strange as it may seem, it has also led me to understand both sons' and daughter's gender issues in a more sophisticated way.

I have gone through stages in which my priorities moved from family to career and back again; I will probably be struggling with this balancing act until the day I die. As I enter the final years of life, time feels more limited and my energy level is lower than it used to be. Living alone for the first time in my life, I still feel the tension between wanting to make the most of my family and friend-ship relationships, wanting to have more leisure and companion-ship, and wanting to keep doing the work that means so much to me. I am profoundly grateful that I have been able to participate in some small way in the enormous changes that women have initiated in my lifetime.

REFERENCES

Brown, L. S. (1986). Ruth: A case description and From alienation to connection: Feminist therapy with post-traumatic stress disorder. In E. D. Rothblum & E. Cole (Eds.), *Another silenced trauma.* (pp. 7-12, 13-26). New York: Harring-ton Park Press.

Chesler, P. (1972). *Women and madness.* New York: Avon Books.

Feminist Therapy Institute, Inc. (1987). *Feminist Therapy Code of Ethics.* San Francisco: Feminist Therapy Institute.

Gornick, V., & Moran, B. K. (Eds.). (1971). *Woman in sexist society.* New York: Basic Books, Inc.

Miller, J. B. (Ed.). (1973). *Psychoanalysis and women.* New York: Brunner/Mazel, Inc.

Miller, J. B. (1976). *Toward a new psychology of women.* Boston: Beacon Press.

Robbins, J. H., & Siegel, R. J. (Eds.). (1983). *Women changing therapy: New assessments, values and strategies in feminist therapy.* New York: The Haworth Press, Inc.

Siegel, R. J. (1977, Winter). The Jew as a woman. *Jewish Spectator,* pp. 40-42.

Siegel, R. J. (1982a, Spring). The long-term marriage: Implications for therapy. *Women & Therapy, 1*(1).

Siegel, R. J. (1982b, Spring). A midlife journey from housewife to psychotherapist. *Voices: The Art and Science of Psychotherapy, 18*(1).

Siegel, R. J. (1985). Beyond homophobia: Learning to work with lesbian clients. In L. E. Walker & L. B. Rosewater (Eds.), *A handbook of feminist therapy: Psychotherapy issues with women.* New York: Springer Publishing Co.

Siegel, R. J. (1986). Antisemitism and sexism in stereotypes of Jewish women. In D. Howard (Ed.), *Dynamics of feminist therapy* (pp. 249-257). New York: The Haworth Press, Inc.

Siegel, R. J. (1988). Women's "dependency" in a male-centered value system. *Women & Therapy, 7*(1), 113-123.

Siegel, R. J. (1990a). Old women as mother figures: Ageism and mother blaming. In E. Cole & J. Knowles (Eds.), *Woman defined motherhood* (pp. 89-97). New York: The Haworth Press, Inc.

Siegel, R. J. (1990b). Love and work after 60: An integration of personal and professional growth within a long-term marriage. In E. Rosenthal (Ed.), *Women, aging and ageism* (pp. 69-79). New York: The Haworth Press, Inc.

Siegel, R. J. (1990c). We are not your mothers: Report on two groups for women over sixty. In E. Rosenthal (Ed.), *Women, aging and ageism* (pp. 81-89). New York: The Haworth Press, Inc.

Siegel, R.J. (1990d). Turning the things that divide us into strengths that unite us. In L. S. Brown & M. P. P. Root (Eds.), *Diversity and complexity in feminist therapy* (pp. 327-335). New York: The Haworth Press, Inc.

Siegel, R. J., & Cole, E. (Eds.). (1991). *Jewish women in therapy: Seen but not heard.* New York: The Haworth Press, Inc.

Siegel, R. J. (1992). Fifteen years later: Am I still an immigrant? In E. Cole, E. Rothblum, & O. M. Espin (Eds.), *Refugee women and their mental health: Shattered societies, shattered lives.* (pp. 105-111). New York: The Haworth Press, Inc.

Siegel, R. J. (1993). Between midlife and old age: Never too old to learn. In N. D. Davis, E. Cole & E. D. Rothblum (Eds.), *Faces of women and aging.* (pp. 173-181). New York: The Haworth Press, Inc.

Siegel, R. J. (1994, Spring). An immigrant again: This time in a country called widowhood. *Lilith: The independent Jewish women's magazine, 19*(1), 25-27.

Siegel, R. J., Greene, B. A., & Kaschak, E. (1995). Three perspectives on racism and antisemitism in feminist organizations. In J. Adleman & G. Enguidanos (Eds.), *Racism in the lives of women: Testimony, theory and guides to practice.* New York: The Haworth Press, Inc.

Siegel, R. J., Choldin, S., & Orost, J. H. (1995). The impact of three patriarchal religions on women. In J. C. Chrisler & A. H. Hemstreet (Eds.), *Variations on a theme: Diversity and the psychology of women.* (pp. 107-144) Albany, NY: State University of New York Press.

Siegel, R. J., & Sonderegger, T. (1990). Ethical considerations in feminist psychotherapy with women over sixty. In H. Lerman & N. Porter (Eds.), *Feminist ethics in psychotherapy* (pp. 176-183). Springer Publishing Co.

Siegel, R. J., Sonderegger, T., & Connoley, J. (in press). Life span issues: Conflict in care. In C. Larsen & E. Rave (Eds.), *Ethical dilemmas: Feminist therapy approaches.* New York: Guilford Publications.

Walker, L. E. (1979). *The battered woman.* New York: Harper & Row.

Count Me In

Theo B. Sonderegger

"Mother," my law-student daughter's voice murmured over the telephone, "why is your salary so much less than every other professor at your rank in the Psych Department?"

She caught me unawares and all I could do was mumble, "Ummm . . . ahhh. . . . is it? I didn't know that. Who told you?"

I was shocked beyond belief. How could that be? I was a productive researcher, publishing as much as most of my colleagues, getting my share of kudos for presenting papers, serving on committees, working in the community (including serving as President of the Nebraska Psychological Association and on the State Board of Examiners for Psychology) and doing the myriad other things that keep a university professor working 6-7 days a week, 12-14 hours a day. But, that much less salary! Diane's information must be wrong.

Theo B. Sonderegger, PhD, is Professor of Psychology at the University of Nebraska-Lincoln and Professor of Medical Psychology at the University of Nebraska Medical Center in Omaha. She is a feminist therapist licensed to practice in Nebraska and California which she does from time to time. Her research interests are in the fields of aging and in the effects of drugs on development. A widow with three adult, feminist children, she lives in Lincoln with two dogs, a cat, a bird, her 93-year old mother, and her companion of 24 years. For more lurid details, read the Sonderegger inclusion in this volume.

Correspondence may be addressed to Theo B. Sonderegger at 1710 S. 58th Street, Lincoln, NE 68506.

[Haworth co-indexing entry note]: "Count Me In." Sonderegger, Theo B. Co-published simultaneously in *Women & Therapy* (The Haworth Press, Inc.) Vol. 17, No. 3/4, 1995, pp. 459-467; and: *Feminist Foremothers in Women's Studies, Psychology, and Mental Health* (ed: Phyllis Chesler, Esther D. Rothblum, and Ellen Cole) The Haworth Press, Inc., 1995, pp. 459-467; and: *Feminist Foremothers in Women's Studies, Psychology, and Mental Health* (ed: Phyllis Chesler, Esther D. Rothblum, and Ellen Cole) Harrington Park Press, an imprint of The Haworth Press, Inc., 1995, pp. 459-467. Single or multiple copies of this article are available from The Haworth Document Delivery Service [1-800-342-9678, 9:00 a.m. - 5:00 p.m. (EST)].

459

My department wouldn't do that to me. Or would it? What was happening?

Maybe that conversation with my daughter almost twenty years ago wasn't the beginning of my feminism, but from that point onwards I was AWARE of gender inequities. Since then I have tried whenever and wherever possible to change the status quo for women for the better.

Shortly after my awakening, I relished the chance to teach a course in "Psychology of Women." Here I could disseminate and discuss with other women some of my newfound information. By then I realized I was a feminist–*a person who believes in equal valuing and equal opportunities for all people*–and I was forever committed to acting on this belief.

I am honored to be included in this volume. Contemplating the issues which brought me here brings to mind long-past events, some pleasant, some not so great. I've structured my comments around the questions suggested by the editors, but before answering them, have begun with a brief background sketch.

EVENTS THAT LED TO BECOMING A FEMINIST

Thinking back, I realize how fortunate my childhood experiences were in shaping my life. My bookkeeper mother loved math and I grew up with no math anxieties. My father's jobs took him, and us, to many places. I attended 12 different grade and high schools (and had just about memorized the Stanford-Binet since each new school gave me a placement test!). I was assured I could be anything I wanted to be when I grew up, but I knew from the beginning I wanted to be a "scientist."

My early "experiments" involved various colored liquids and dyes in the backyard wash tubs. White sheets and towels, shirts and shorts turned gorgeously multi-hued, to my mother's consternation. Here, too, I learned about cause and effect; actions and reactions, the latter involving peach tree switches deftly applied to posteriors of young scientists.

I learned about gender discrimination as valedictorian of my high school graduating class. A doting father, stung by his son's second place rank, prevailed with the graduation committee to permit his son to lead the march of graduates down the aisle to the auditorium stage, the position normally taken by the class valedictorian, not the salutatorian. On what did he base his argument? That his son was 6 ft. tall and male and would make a better visual impression than the 5'2", 95-lb. "little girl" who had earned the right to lead. My counselor and friend, the math teacher, discovered the travesty before we marched. I remember the smile on her face as I passed her seat first in line with a 6-ft.-tall, handsome boy slouching along behind me and the rest of the graduating class following us down the aisle. Sometimes right *does* prevail, but often not without a female touch.

At Florida State College for Women (since converted to coed and university status), I majored in chemistry and then went on to graduate school at the University of Nebraska in Lincoln (UNL) where I obtained an M.S. in physical chemistry before halting my education to marry a returning World War II veteran. In due time, we had two sons and a daughter, wonderful children all (who turned out to be feminists, surprise, surprise). What did I know about rearing children? What formula does one use for rearing healthy, happy kids?

Under the mistaken impression that books and professors knew all, I resumed my education, this time taking the psychology courses I never had as an undergraduate. I didn't learn much about child rearing in school the next few years, but I was intrigued by the experiments with behavior which were every bit as exciting as those I had conducted in the chemistry laboratory. Encouraged and supported by the sole woman in the department, Dr. Katherine Baker, I obtained a Master's degree in experimental psychology and a Ph.D. in clinical psychology. Five other women also were resuming their education in the department at this time. At our monthly gatherings at Kay Baker's house, I learned the value of a women's support group, networking, and the endorsement of a sympathetic professor.

A growing-up family kept me in the Lincoln area after I received my Ph.D. and clinical license. I practiced one day a week in the Nebraska Psychiatric Institute, taught at Nebraska Wesleyan University and when Kay Baker left UNL in 1968, returned to teach in the UNL Psychology Department where I remain today. At first, like Kay, I was the only female professor in the department, but today we are 7 women in a total faculty of 25.

One by one my children left, returned, and finally left home for good. As my mothering responsibilities lessened, I ventured farther afield. I divided the time of my first sabbatical between Northwestern University and UCLA. In the Medical School at UCLA I met Emery Zimmermann, a physician and neuroendocrinologist with whom I have collaborated ever since on studies of the long-term effects of drugs on development. Both of us firmly believe that information should be exchanged freely between clinicians and researchers and we have chaired several national meetings bringing the two groups together.

Because I was spending so much of my time in California during summers, vacations, and sabbaticals from UNL, I added a California clinical license to my Nebraska certification and did some therapy work from time to time. Part of my responsibilities at UNL included supervision of clinical graduate students.

This, then, is my background. I am an academician, an activist, and a feminist therapist teaching and doing research on drugs and development and on aging. Currently, I am a Professor of Psychology at UNL and a Professor of Medical Psychology in the University of Nebraska Medical Center.

QUESTION 1. HOW DID YOUR LIFE CHANGE AS A RESULT OF BECOMING A FEMINIST?

After I began teaching a course in the Psychology of Women and read more and more of the literature, I became aware of, and was angered by, the treatment accorded women not only in psychology, but throughout all aspects of society. In these early years of the feminist movement, we were all angry. I designed my course to open women's eyes and, apparently, from the student comments I get, it continues to do so.

At this time, too, I joined Committee W (women's issues) of the American Association of University Professors (AAUP) and met on a regular basis with local members of the group. As a result of our joint efforts, we were able to institute on campus a Women's Studies Program of which my course became a part.

My teaching principles are honed and focused by feminism and I hold dear the following assumptions: (a) women need support systems comprised of other women with whom they can share experiences; (b) women students need women role models; (c) clinicians need to recognize that many problems experienced by women are created by society and not by the shortcomings of the women; (d) success in a profession requires active participation in and contribution to the profession, i.e., one has to add to, as well as take from, the pot.

QUESTION 2. WHAT ARE YOUR CONTRIBUTIONS TO FEMINISM?

At UNL. In keeping with the beliefs stated above, I have acted to bring the campus women together to support one another. As a bench-scientist/researcher, I always had tied myself to the laboratory between teaching and committee obligations to spend long hours there collecting data. As I became immersed in feminism, I realized a great many women working alone in laboratories and libraries all over the campus could help one another survive and prosper in the academic world if they would pool their strategies and share their ideas and techniques. Graduate Women in Science was one group that resulted through the joint efforts of several of us. Later, when I became Chair on campus of AAUP Committee A (academic freedom) I worked primarily with women faculty having promotion and tenure problems. Clearly, women need the support and help of other women.

Groups comprised of women faculty and students serve a double purpose: they provide support and opportunities for informal exchange of information among their members. All-women parties or pot-luck suppers at faculty members' houses seem to be especially liked, but a weekly meeting at a public coffee house or other student gathering place serves as well.

When Natalie Porter was a colleague in the UNL Psych Department, we had a successful women's Friday afternoon support group that included primarily Psych grad students although often student and faculty women from other departments attended. One year we wheedled funds so that eleven students, Natalie and I could attend an AWP national meeting in Seattle where we and the students presented a program on "Scaling the Walls of Academe." What an experience, especially being snowbound for 24 hours in the Denver airport while the gifts of frozen salmon melted in the carry-on baggage. Now *that* was female bonding!

As the number of women in our department has increased, I have promoted monthly meetings of the female faculty, not only for networking support, but to provide a forum where new members can learn informally the written (and unwritten) rules and lore of academe.

Students need role models and need to see professionals in action, not only academics, but all sorts of career women. There are few senior women academics on campus—only 37 women in a total of 497 are full professors at UNL—which sends a chilling message, I'm sure, to those women who have chosen an academic career. For years I have sought university and other sources of funds to bring outstanding women professionals of national stature as speakers to campus. I also invite women with various roles and degrees of prominence in the Lincoln community to speak to my Psych of Women class. As Chair of the 1984 Nebraska Symposium on Motivation, I invited women to give all eight of the presentations, women professionals of such stature that no one could argue with their credentials, thus doubling in one year the total number of female presenters. (In the previous 32 years of annual Nebraska Symposia, there had been 184 male and only 8 female participants.)

Honorary degrees are another way to call attention to the achievements of women. Year after year UNL honorees have been men, until some committee on committees made the mistake three years ago of making me Chair of the Honorary Degrees Committee. Yes, indeed, Nebraska women have made commendable contributions. UNL now has recognized two native daughters, Mary Gray, known for her work both as a mathematician and as an attorney who works for human rights, and Bernice Neugarten, famous as a researcher and theoretician in the area of aging.

I have also worked hard to serve as a mentor, when asked, to younger faculty women and as an advisor to students at all levels. I have enjoyed especially working with the older women students returning to school later in life as I once did.

I am deeply gratified that I have received recognition for my work in the form of two awards: the Lincoln YWCA Tribute to

Women Award in 1985 for my contributions in helping the women of the area and in 1994, the first ever Chancellor's Commission for the Status of Women Award for work in improving the status of all women at the University of Nebraska.

At the National Level. One can keep things going in one's backyard for a time, but mingling regularly with others from different sites is good for the soul–and for bringing fresh ideas to the local milieu. A great deal of networking and learning takes place among women serving together on committees. I have enjoyed working on many committees for Division 35 (Psychology of Women) of the American Psychological Association (APA) and have chaired several Task Forces. I particularly appreciated and learned much from serving as the Division 35 Executive Committee Representative to an American Psychological Society Human Capital Initiative Committee designed to identify research priorities in the area of aging.

As a consequence of my drug research-clinical work, I served over eleven years as a member of several grant review boards for the National Institute of Drug Abuse (NIDA), particularly those dealing with AIDS research. When I started, women were rarely proposed as research subjects. This has changed over the years, in part because we board members repeatedly called attention to the need for accurate information about women whose physiologies, morphologies and behavior patterns are NOT the same as men's. This is one area where the generic "people" does not apply. Today, research proposals submitted to NIDA and other agencies must have appropriate gender representation or, if not, reasons acceptable to the review boards for the exclusion of women must be clearly presented.

It was gratifying to work with women in the Society for Neurosciences who recognized early on the need to develop their own group, appropriately called WIN (Women in Neuroscience). It is now a very active group and I'm proud to have served for a time on its Steering Committee.

Feminist Mental Health. In 1981 I had the good fortune to attend a gathering of feminist therapists from several states and Canada at the first meeting of the Advanced Feminist Therapy Institute (AFTI). What a tremendous experience to meet other women therapists with feminist concerns who thought and felt as I did. I left the meeting euphoric. I served later on the Steering Committee and as Editor of the newsletter, the *Feminist Therapy Interchange*. An important activity of the group has been development of the Feminist Therapy Code of Ethics, an extremely valuable document for all psychotherapists.

Research on Aging. During one of the early AFTIs, I met Rachel Josefowitz Siegel. Her practice includes psychotherapy with old women and she and I share many of the same concerns about their plight. Rachel and I believe that "old" is an honorable, not a disrespectful, adjective to use in describing the sixty-plus aged woman. We have collaborated frequently in presentations, articles and book chapters, combining clinical and theoretical views. We hold that old women deserve recognition as wise old crones and that they should be respected as individuals unburdened with ageist stereotypes.

Research on Drugs and Development. Laboratory research has occupied a significant place throughout my career and I believe many of my findings are among the most important contributions I've made for feminism and feminist mental health. I began working on motivation as a graduate student, then moved to the effects of brain stimulation on maternal care using animal models. Later, my interests turned to perinatal drug effects, the area in which I continue to work. The latter research involves treating rat pups during the early postnatal period with drugs such as cocaine, morphine, and alcohol, then using behavioral and neuroendocrine measures to study the effects in the treated animals and sometimes, their offspring. This postnatal treatment time in the rat is a period of rapid brain growth comparable to that of the human infant in the third trimester of pregnancy.

My collaborators and I have found that exposure to drugs early in life can impair some types of learning and can damage neuroendocrine and reproductive system functions. Unfortunately, too, some of the effects are found in untreated second generation offspring. Of particular importance is my and others' finding that paternal as well as maternal drug exposure can affect their offspring adversely.

The implications of these data in our drug-taking culture are serious and disturbing. Putting drug-abusing, pregnant women in jail while ignoring the fathers' drug-taking transgressions is unjust, yet courts are attempting to do so today in litigations involving fetal vs. maternal rights. Treatment, not punishment of the pregnant woman, is the most cost-effective answer to parental drug abuse. I have expressed these views in numerous articles, books, symposia, Congressional briefings, conferences, and meetings over the years. The public needs to understand what drugs, especially recreational drugs, can do not only to parents of both genders, but to their potential offspring as well. For my work in perinatal drug research I was very pleased to receive the 1991 Outstanding Scientist Award from the Nebraska Chapter of Sigma Xi.

QUESTION 3. WHAT IDEAS OR HOPES DO YOU HAVE ABOUT CURRENT NEEDS AND FUTURE DIRECTIONS?

I'm about to retire as a professor and have two unfulfilled academic goals. Foremost of these is to establish an adequately funded, Honorary Chair for a woman scholar on the UNL campus. It will be named the Leta Stetter Hollingsworth Chair in honor of the Nebraska native who is a foremother of the Psychology of Women and who received a degree in English from the University of Nebraska.

Secondly, I'm concerned about the way old women are treated in this country, particularly now that I fit the category. My experiences on local and national committees on aging, as well as with my own mother, show me that new, innovative strategies are needed and that feminist viewpoints are required. We need more data about the capabilities of this age group. We have a way to get the information disseminated. The University of Nebraska Press recently initiated a book series entitled "Agendas for Aging." As Series Editor, I hope to publish manuscripts from many of you, particularly descriptions of how old women learn to assume and use their power. No novels, please.

Reclaiming the Sacred

Starhawk
Jennifer Connor

Growing up in the United States, even those of us not part of any official religion are likely to be raised according to Judeo-Christian principles. From this traditional background, we learn about the proper subordinate role of women and the essential maleness of God. Although much has changed in the past decade, with women

Starhawk is the author of *The Spiral Dance: A Rebirth of The Ancient Religion of The Great Goddess* (Harper & Row, 1979, 1989), *Dreaming The Dark: Magic, Sex, and Politics* (Beacon, 1982), and *Truth or Dare: Encounters with Power, Authority and Mystery* (Harper & Row, 1987). A feminist and peace activist, she is one of the foremost voices of ecofeminism, and travels widely in North America and Europe giving lectures and workshops. She holds an M.A. in Psychology from Antioch West University and since 1983 has been a lecturer at the Institute for Culture and Creation Spirituality at Holy Names College in Oakland. She consulted on the films *Goddess Remembered* and *The Burning Times*, directed by Donna Read and produced by the National Film Board of Canada, and co-wrote the commentary for *Full Circle*, a third film in the same Women's Spirituality series. Her first novel, *The Fifth Sacred Thing*, was published by Bantam Books in 1993. She lives in San Francisco, where she works with the Reclaiming collective which offers classes, workshops and public rituals in earth-based spirituality.

Jennifer Connor is a second year graduate student in the Clinical Psychology program at the University of Vermont. Her interests include feminist therapy, ecofeminism, and the prevention of aggression and depression in children and adolescents through community intervention programs. In her spare time she works for Amnesty International.

[Haworth co-indexing entry note]: "Reclaiming the Sacred." Starhawk and Jennifer Connor. Co-published simultaneously in *Women & Therapy* (The Haworth Press, Inc.) Vol. 17, No. 3/4, 1995, pp. 469-476; and: *Feminist Foremothers in Women's Studies, Psychology, and Mental Health* (ed: Phyllis Chesler, Esther D. Rothblum, and Ellen Cole) The Haworth Press, Inc., 1995, pp. 469-476; and: *Feminist Foremothers in Women's Studies, Psychology, and Mental Health* (ed: Phyllis Chesler, Esther D. Rothblum, and Ellen Cole) Harrington Park Press, an imprint of The Haworth Press, Inc., 1995, pp. 469-476. Single or multiple copies of this article are available from The Haworth Document Delivery Service [1-800-342-9678, 9:00 a.m. - 5:00 p.m. (EST)].

assuming positions of power in many established religions, and many religions becoming more inclusive of women, it is still true that everywhere we turn, we still see signs indicating that spirituality is a man's domain.

Since the seventies, Starhawk has been challenging accepted beliefs about religion and spirituality. Known primarily for her work in reclaiming ancient Goddess traditions, her work goes far beyond merely reconsidering the gender of the supreme being. Through her work she radically questions not only what and how we worship, but our very understanding of spirituality and the sacred. Traditional Western religious thought accepts as axiomatic a dualistic universe, with soul and spirit superior to body and nature. Such thinking leads both to a model of domination, man over woman, human over nature, and to an unnatural fragmentation of our being into body and mind. In her work, Starhawk calls for an integration of the different facets of our lives, demonstrating that spirituality is not and should not be separate from our bodies, politics, feminism, or psychology. The different facets of our lives are joined by a web of interconnections; when we sever these connections, we are not whole.

The following pages are excerpts from a telephone conversation with Starhawk. Although topics ranged widely, covering areas including political action, writing, and communal living, I have focused on Starhawk's elaboration of the relationships between politics and spirituality and definitions of the sacred and our daily lives. We began the interview by talking about the circumstances which first led her to identify herself as a feminist.

I got involved, not so much in feminist spirituality, but in Wicca, before I knew anything about feminism. Back in the late sixties, I was a freshman at UCLA and I was doing an anthropology project on Witchcraft. I met some real Witches who began to talk to me about the Goddess tradition. It was an amazing revelation to me to think about having female images of God, or of the sacred. I was raised Jewish, and female imagery was something very foreign. I had never encountered it before, and found it amazingly liberating.

It wasn't until a couple of years later that I encountered feminism. I was travelling with my boyfriend in Europe, and I was sick with the flu and I spent a day in bed in a youth hostel in Frankfurt reading Kate Millett's book, *Sexual Politics*. The book was a revelation. Suddenly all these lights went on. For example, I was an art student, and at that time the art department at UCLA was about seventy percent women undergraduates, about seventy percent men as graduate students, and about ninety-nine percent men in terms of teachers and professors. There were all of these things that you just weren't supposed to notice, or to think about how they affected you and how seriously you could take your own work. So I came home and joined a consciousness-raising group, got very involved with a women's center, and started to think of myself as a feminist.

At that point it occurred to me that having a religion with a Goddess in it had something to do with feminism and something to say to women who were feminist. But there was very little support for that idea. The only woman who was talking about it was Z Budapest. But as the seventies wore on, the feminist movement began to look at spirituality and religion, both to critique patriarchal religion and also to explore other possibilities.

I would say my major contribution has been articulating questions of the sacred from a feminist perspective, and maintaining that the issues and the questions that feminism deals with are questions of the sacred and questions of the spirit, as well as strictly political questions. In other words, I try to link the spiritual and the political in both directions. One of the great gifts is a spiritual connection, because without it, it's very hard to stay in political action for ten years, twenty years, thirty years, a lifetime. Political action tends to not be very rewarding in the sense that it's rare that you do something and immediately see a result that you want. You don't go blockade somewhere and then have Reagan turn around the next day and say, "Oh, I was wrong about those nukes, here's all these dedicated people, willing to go to jail to express their opinions." It doesn't happen like that, it's a long, long process. And oftentimes you can only see the results many many years after it's over, so you have to do something to sustain yourself. And for me that comes out of the spiritual connection.

I think many people felt such a sense of enormous urgency around all the political issues that it was very easy to say, "Oh, let's put aside our personal lives, let's put aside our own health, our own needs and just do this, or we'll be dead. The world will end, something horrible will happen." And that kind of energy can sustain you for awhile, but again, if you're thinking about political action as something you're going to be engaged in for a lifetime, you can't just suspend your life for a lifetime.

One example of a political ritual is the one I organized with Elias Farajaje-Jones at the Holocaust Museum, the same weekend as the big lesbian, bisexual, gay freedom march in Washington. The ritual focused on the lesbian and gay victims of the Holocaust. What happened to the homosexual community in the Holocaust was an enormous tragedy. The survivors faced prejudice when they were liberated from the camps, and many were thrown back in jail by the U.S. forces, who maintained that they were not political prisoners, but criminals jailed for activities that were criminal in the U.S. Many of the victims were so ashamed and so ostracized by being branded as homosexuals that they were never able to talk about their experiences or be reconciled with their families.

For the ritual there were several thousand people in the park. We began with speeches and some education by the people who had done research about the issue for the museum. All the participants had candles and we held them to the four directions, and then we had a litany read by four different voices that described some of the experiences that people had in the camps. It ended with the voice of a man having a vision as he's being beaten to death in the camps that someday the pink triangle that was a badge of shame will become something that people wear with pride, and imagining thousands and thousands of people in the streets. We ended the ritual with each person taking a pink flower and making a huge pink triangle at the steps of the museum.

Reclaiming, the group I work with in San Francisco, always does several big rituals for Halloween, including a traditional Spiral Dance that may involve over a thousand people. For the last couple of years we've also done a women's ritual at this season. In 1992, we decided to focus on choice as the issue. And so we did a ritual with a guided trance meditation where women were walked through their lives as if their lives were an orchard and they were picking the fruits of their choices from the trees, placing them in a basket, and then taking them to the Goddess as the old crone in the center of the circle and giving them to her, giving to her cauldron, giving her the fruits of their painful choices and the fruits of their joyful choices and the fruits of our confusion, the choices where we're never sure if they were the right one or the wrong one, and the fruits of our rage. Then we transformed that rage into power with our voices, raising power for women's right to choose, to make choices about our bodies. And that was a very powerful ritual.

For about five years I've been working with a multicultural ritual group that looks at issues around racism, and all the different isms in the context of creating ritual together. We also do a ritual during the Halloween season to celebrate the ancestors of many cultures. We create altars to represent all our different cultures with art work and candles and food and offerings and cloth and weaving. You get a sense of the real richness of the different cultures as you go around and look at all the altars. During part of the ritual people tell their personal stories, sometimes in poetry, sometimes in music, sometimes very simply, sometimes in very polished forms. We do a guided meditation where we go back and face some of the not-so-nice parts of our ancestors, and clean up the mess they've left us, acknowledging that every culture has ancestors that were oppressors. But every culture also has people we can be proud of, people who struggled against the injustices of their time in whatever way they could. It's important to do both, to know what history gets in the way between us and other people, and also to claim our own pride in our heritage. We give people strips of cloth, which they take from the different altars that represent different ancestries, and we tie them together and make a long, long strip of cloth. And out of that we weave a giant basket, and then dance a spiral.

The multicultural group has been really exciting for me in the last few years. We've learned so much about each other. One of the most important things we've learned is that a ritual has to come out of a living community. We can't meet once a year to make a ritual, we have to meet throughout the year to do ritual together. And so we've begun to feel more like family and community than just a bunch of stray people getting together around this particular thing. I've learned a lot more about dealing with racism and unlearning it from creating ritual with that group than I ever have from any political analysis of the subject.

In my third book, *Truth or Dare: Encounters with Power, Authority, and Mystery,* I look at questions of psychology most closely and extensively. My thesis in that book is that we live in a society that's based on the principle of domination and power over, and that we all in different ways internalize that principle. We internalize it as images, as energy patterns, as ways of thinking and ways that we respond to the world, to ourselves and to each other. And that principle is what makes us sick, what keeps us in distress.

Psychology has focused so much on the individual family level. That's important, but in some ways that focus creates the illusion that there exists this wonderful world of health and normality and your dysfunctional family somehow doesn't fit that. When the reality, I think, is that the whole society is toxic and your family might express that in more or less harmful ways, or even compensate for it. This focus just on childhood and just on families, tends to distract us from looking at the larger issue of our society, and saying, "Is this working? Do our institutions work for us? Is this a system in which people can grow up and be fulfilled and be at peace with themselves?"

One of the analogies I used is that of trying to heal people who live at Love Canal who are ill, by looking at the nutrition that they got as infants. We would probably find that people who were well-fed as infants had more resistance to toxicity, and people who were malnourished might be more susceptible to damage, but the point is that people would still be living in a toxic environment and that's the immediate overwhelming problem. So my focus on healing has moved from looking at our historical pain more into looking at the way we are internalizing structures around us, and discovering what kinds of counter structures we can create that won't be toxic, but will encourage us to respond and to grow in different ways. As human beings, we are collective and communal creatures. We can't heal in isolation, we need a sense of community and connection. That's why in the women's spirituality movement, women's circles, or covens are so important, because they create islands of possibility.

Today we're at a cultural crisis point centered around the question of what is sacred—in the sense of what is most important to us, what defines our values. We've had hundreds of years of patriarchal religions telling us that the sacred is outside the world. Now we have all these different groups rising up and saying, "No, wait a minute, the sacred is in the world." That's a very radical concept, because if you start saying the sacred is in the world, that our bodies are sacred, that the earth is sacred, then you can no longer exploit the earth. Our authority to make choices about our own bodies becomes a sacred authority. The real question around abortion is about who has the authority to make life and death choices about your own body. Is it an external God, or is it inherent in your own living being? And of course if you say it's inherent in your own living being, then there goes the whole hierarchial chain of command.

If the sacred is embodied in the earth, it means that we don't have the right to exploit nature in the ways that we are accustomed to doing. An old growth forest has a kind of value that can't be computed on scales of dollars and cents and profit and loss. Nature has a value that goes beyond the usefulness we find in it. Indigenous people have been telling us this, it is a concept they haven't ever lost in their cultures, but I think the problem is not limited to industrialized society. It just reaches its most extreme form here. The Puritan agrarian society, for example, was in some ways just as disconnected from a sense of a sacred nature. But I do think that people having to live close to nature, having to contend with it, probably had more of an intuitive sense than many of us have today.

If you think about it, even on the purely practical level of food, up until the last couple hundred years most of the time people ate food that they had some kind of relationship with. You walked outside of your house, you saw what was ripe in the fields and what wasn't. Everything you ate literally came from the land, was an expression of your relationship with that land. And now, we're entirely disconnected from the food that we eat. We don't know where it comes from, what it's been through, what's been done to it, who grew it, what conditions it was grown under, what happened to the soil that grew it. And that's just one of the ways in which we've become alienated from some of the very basic processes of life.

Last year a woman in New York was interviewing me and she didn't quite seem to understand why we would go to the risk and trouble of getting arrested for blockading to protect the old growth forest at Clayoquot Sound, where my husband and three of my step-daughters and I got arrested in the summer of 1993. Finally she said, "Well, you know, the thing is, the environment is sort of unreal to most New Yorkers." I laughed, but I think it's very true. And it's exactly why we're in the mess we're in. Not just to New Yorkers, but to people who make the decisions about what happens to the earth, the earth is a kind of an abstraction. It's not something they really have a close personal relationship with.

I think one of the most important, most political and spiritual things we can do is to develop a personal connection with the earth. Whether that's growing a garden or whether that's just getting out of Manhattan, or whether it's learning about things like the falcons that live on the skyscrapers and the pigeons that they eat. Without that, politics is very disconnected from reality, from what actually supports us. And with that understanding I think we also have a connection we need to sustain us in doing political work and working for change.

REFERENCES

Millett, Kate. (1970). *Sexual Politics* (1st ed.). Garden City, NY: Doubleday.
Starhawk. (1987). *Truth or dare: Encounters with power, authority, and mystery* (1st ed.). San Francisco, CA: Harper & Row.

Steps Toward Transformation:
A Conversation with Gloria Steinem

Gloria Steinem
Anna Myers-Parrelli

*When I was offered the opportunity to write with Gloria Stei-
nem about her contributions to feminism, I jumped at the
chance. Actually, the question struck me in the same way as if*

Gloria Steinem is one of the country's most widely-read and critically-ac-
claimed writers and editors. She travels as a lecturer and feminist organizer, and
appears frequently on television and radio as an interviewer and spokeswoman on
issues of equality. She is especially interested in the shared origins and parallels of
caste systems based on sex and race; in non-violent conflict resolution; and in
organizing across national boundaries for social justice and peace. From 1979 to
1985, Steinem was voted the leading social activist by the World Almanac. In the
fall of 1993, she was inducted into the National Women's Hall of Fame in Seneca
Falls, New York. Gloria Steinem is currently an editorial consultant and writer for
Ms. Magazine. Her most recent book, *Moving Beyond Words*, was published by
Simon & Schuster in the spring of 1994.

Anna Myers-Parrelli is a writer and a student in the Clinical Psychology PhD
program at the University of Vermont. She writes short fiction and poetry, and her
professional research has focused on the psychology of women and issues in
community mental health. Anna Myers-Parrelli lives in Burlington, Vermont,
with her partner, Jo Myers-Parrelli.

Correspondence may be addressed to Gloria Steinem at *Ms.* Magazine, 230
Park Avenue, New York, NY 10169.

[Haworth co-indexing entry note]: "Steps Toward Transformation: A Conversation with Gloria
Steinem." Steinem, Gloria, and Anna Myers-Parrelli. Co-published simultaneously in *Women & Thera-
py* (The Haworth Press, Inc.) Vol. 17, No. 3/4, 1995, pp. 477-488; and: *Feminist Foremothers in
Women's Studies, Psychology, and Mental Health* (ed: Phyllis Chesler, Esther D. Rothblum, and Ellen
Cole) The Haworth Press, Inc., 1995, pp. 477-488; and: *Feminist Foremothers in Women's Studies,
Psychology, and Mental Health* (ed: Phyllis Chesler, Esther D. Rothblum, and Ellen Cole) Harrington
Park Press, an imprint of The Haworth Press, Inc., 1995, pp. 477-488. Single or multiple copies of this
article are available from The Haworth Document Delivery Service [1-800-342-9678, 9:00 a.m. - 5:00
p.m. (EST)].

477

*the University of Vermont had asked, "Would you care for
some grant money?" It was an offer I could not refuse.*

*In another way, though, writing about Gloria Steinem's
contributions to feminism seemed a strange exercise. To me, a
twenty-six year old woman, the name Gloria Steinem is a
household word, and the definition of the word is: "feminism."
Trying to tease out Steinem's "contributions to the feminist
movement" and the ways in which "feminism changed her
life," I thought, would be like trying to eat just the chocolate
out of a pint of chocolate ice cream.*

*Gloria would not let herself be put on a pedestal, though. To
the suggestion that she is a "feminist foremother," she quickly
replied, "We're all founding mothers. It's an endless chain–not
any kind of hierarchy. We each communicate feminism to the
others around us."*

*Thus, with both of our places on this chain established,
Gloria and I settled into a comfortable dialogue–about Steinem's entry into feminism, her various contributions, and
where she sees feminism taking us–and us taking feminism–in
the future. Grab some ice cream and dig in.*

–Anna Myers-Parrelli

During the late 1960s, "when the national light bulb of feminism
was beginning to come on," Gloria Steinem was already an adult
woman with a career as a journalist. In 1969, she reported on a
speak-out for women who had obtained illegal abortions. The article she wrote in response for *New York* magazine, entitled "After
Black Power, Women's Liberation," signaled her entry into the
feminist fray.

What was it about this meeting that so changed the course of
Steinem's life? "Hearing women stand up and tell the truth in
public," she says. "I went there as a reporter, and I was blown away
as a woman. It made sense of my life for the first time. While I was
growing up, and as an adult, I constantly identified with the 'wrong'
groups. I was a white person. I had become middle-class. But I kept
emotionally identifying with all the less powerful groups. No one
had ever told me that women were a less powerful group. Until that
hearing, I didn't understand my own feelings of humiliation, or

helplessness, or 'outsiderness'. I had an abortion and never told anyone. So had all these women. Why couldn't we speak about it? It was just the beginning of my realizing that we were not crazy; it was the system that was crazy–which is both the foundation of revolution and mental health."

After the *New York* article was published, Steinem's commitment to the feminist movement solidified. "The response from my male colleagues [to the article] was instructive," she recalls. "Nice men, they would still draw me off into a corner and say, 'You've worked so hard to be taken seriously. Don't get involved with these crazy women.' It made me realize that they didn't know who I was. They couldn't know, really, because I hadn't been speaking my own experience.

"I began to read everything I could lay my hands on, and to go and avidly listen to other feminists speak. It was contagiously, immensely illuminating and exciting. And that has never stopped. There are realizations every week and month that are of the same intensity."

While one could argue that Steinem has made her greatest contributions to feminist theory through her writing and the print media, in the 1970s it was difficult for her to get those ideas published. Publications which had accepted her work before would not publish feminist articles. She recalls, "It forced me–the caring on my part–forced me to communicate in other ways. I had never spoken in public in my life. I was so desperate, that even though I was in the Olympics of fear of public speaking, I decided I had to." Steinem asked a friend, an African American woman named Dorothy Pitman Hughes, to speak with her. Together, the pair drew larger audiences than either could have alone, and reached a more inclusive group of women.

After her entry into the movement, did Steinem ever look back? "*No.* In a word. If feminism hadn't been in the culture, I suppose I would have remained privately rebelling and hoping no one would notice. I would have continued to write darting, tentative rebellions in articles. But–how has feminism changed my life? It's given me life. And saved my life. It's as if I had been looking at the world with one eye closed, and then opened the other eye. Seeing the world *as if women mattered* changes everything."

Reflecting about her contributions to the feminist movement, Steinem remarks that she is not sure what her major contributions are. "We have to take such care with what we do every day–try to make our actions a reflection of our values. Because we really don't know what is going to be influential. Sometimes what seems to be the most trivial is what has the greatest impact."

I press her. Surely there must be certain contributions that stand out? What is she proud of? First, there are the organizations. There is the National Women's Political Caucus, a group formed in 1971 to assist feminists in gaining elected and appointed political office. There is Voters for Choice, a non-partisan political action committee supporting pro-choice candidates, both women and men. There is the Ms. Foundation for Women, started by *Ms.* magazine but as a completely separate entity, which has a number of emphases. Among these are the Economic Empowerment Movement, a group of cooperatively owned businesses among formerly low-income women; the National Girls Initiative, which gave birth to, among other things, Take Our Daughters to Work Day; and a national women's fund offering "seed grants" to a wide variety of cutting-edge grassroots projects. Finally, there is *Ms.* magazine itself, which Steinem helped create in 1971, and of which she is still Consulting Editor.

Steinem hoped that *Ms.* would be "a sort of portable friend that women could find on their neighborhood newsstands." Like so many women, though, *Ms.* suffered from a lack of financial resources and support. "We were always running on two pennies," Steinem recalls. Too many advertisers shunned the feminist magazine, and *Ms.* was eventually sold to two feminists from an Australian publisher, and then finally went bankrupt and was taken over in 1989 by Lang Communications. The present-day *Ms.* contains no advertising, "and it is doing wonderfully!" Gloria celebrates. "That's what is so gratifying–after all these years of the media saying, 'Women don't want a feminist magazine; that's why you're always in financial trouble,' we can finally demonstrate that women do want it. They want it so much that they will pay more for it."

With four organizations under her belt, Steinem says, "I think I have one organization left in me. I would love to contribute to a school for feminist organizers. Being an organizer is like being an entrepreneur of social change. The few who exist now rarely get paid, but they could. We should have a couple hundred traveling organizers salaried by the movement, as they did during the suffragist wave. Their training could be like a course in which people go from one project to the next. . . . Another idea I'm working on with a woman from California–a gifted teacher named Andrea Johnston, who also pioneered action against sexual harassment in schools–is weekend consciousness-raising meetings for girls from 10 to 15. We talk about times when society was pre-patriarchal, pre-monotheistic–when there were ceremonies celebrating menstruation. They come for a day or two and have a way of keeping in touch afterwards. Girls really blossom with this kind of support for their dignity and their imaginations."

Steinem's consistent community organizing and leadership is thus another of her major contributions to feminism. She states, "I love being an organizer. For 25 years, I've spent half my life going out on the road in the same way that Susan B. Anthony and the Grimke sisters and Sojourner Truth and everybody else did. Outside organizers are actually an excuse for everybody to get together and discover they don't really need one anyway.

"I also enjoy working in the electoral system. Social change doesn't start in the electoral system by any means; it starts at the bottom. But it can be stopped at the top, if we don't make sure there are good people there." True to her word, Steinem spent the weeks during which this article was being written out on the road, "stumping" for various feminist candidates, mostly women but also some men.

To many women, though, Gloria Steinem's name stands out not as a community activist or as a founder of organizations, but as a writer and contributor of ideas to the ever-expanding realm of feminist thought and action. She has gifted us with *Outrageous Acts and Everyday Rebellions, Marilyn: Norma Jeane, Revolution from Within,* and most recently, *Moving Beyond Words,* in addition to countless other articles filled with nuggets of feminist wisdom and humor.

For Steinem, writing is a celebration of the truth of women's lives. "In general, to trust our own experience over [the myth about what women's lives are supposed to be like], to speak our experi-

ence as honestly as we can, instead of believing the myth, is the
most important thing any of us can do. Getting people to believe a
myth and mistrust themselves is the basis of everything from gender
roles to totalitarianism: the theft of the self. But once you start to
trust actual experiences instead of comparing yourself to an impossible myth–that is liberation."

Steinem's writing attempts to build bridges of empathy among
women in order to create a non-oppressive future. "I enjoy trying to
find language and to put phrases together in a way that is different
enough to allow women to come together and to spark a new vision," she says. "For example, I'm not sure if I was the first to use
the term 'reproductive freedom', but I did my best to popularize it.
The term allowed us to join together. Women of color experiencing
forced sterilization were included, along with women trying to have
babies and women seeking abortion. It put the power in the individual–not the system, as the term 'population control' had done. I
want to make language that allows us to come together across
boundaries, without losing our individuality or the nurturing parts
of our cultures.

"I suppose I have an underlying motive in writing, which is to
write in a way that would have been helpful to me when I was 16 or
17 and sitting in Toledo. The main problem with the media today is
that it is negative. It presents problems without solutions, and that
makes people crazy. What we can do as writers is to present problems with some choices of solutions. Of course, we each need to
make those solutions our own, but at least [good writing] takes the
concrete block off your brain. You can begin to see the possibility
of change. You can make a place in the imagination for a different
future. The first step toward transformation is to imagine it."

Writing can also be healing, Steinem points out, if we use writing
to speak the truth about our lives. "The last step of healing is to use
your experience to help others," she says. "I wrote a piece about
my mother after she died. At the time I wrote it, I thought it was an
extremely self-indulgent thing to do, because everyone wants to
write about their mothers. I thought, 'Who else would be interested
or derive any comfort from me writing about my mother?'

"Actually, that essay got as much or more response than the
others. It turned out that a lot of us had crazy mothers, because our

mothers were driven crazy. The response was healing and instructive, and brought a sense of closure. I hope my experience helped to make others feel less alone. I also realized that our lives don't need to be that way. Women don't need to be broken-spirited so that their daughters are deprived of strong mothers. To that extent, women have been motherless, and the women's movement has been a way for us to become each others' mothers."

Whenever Steinem writes, she is sure to make her writing accessible to and inclusive of as many women as possible. "My one remaining bias is against academic language," she complains. "It makes me crazy. Academia seems to be a place where your value is measured in inverse proportion to your understandability. What's the point? If people don't have information, they can't act on it. Even Freud realized this. [His theories] were an unmitigated disaster, but he did understand that people should be able to read what he wrote. His case histories were little novels!

"I think the division between intellect and emotions, between the academic and experiential, is really a division built on the masculine/feminine one that we want to get rid of."

Gloria Steinem's writing brings us the world as seen through her own eyes, once she began to take off the patriarchal lens. I wonder how she sees the world today in comparison to 1970. What does she think of the assertion that we are now beyond feminism, in the post-feminist era?

" 'Post-Feminism' is a word that was invented by the *New York Times* editorial page," she retorts. "It's like saying 'post-democracy'. I mean, what does that mean? The first way of dealing with social change is to say that people aren't interested. Then, after it turns out that people *are* interested, the next phase of resistance is to say that it used to be necessary, but not anymore. We once published in *Ms.* this compilation of headlines saying that feminism is over. The first one was published in 1969!

" 'Post-feminism' is just wishful thinking. The suffragist movement lasted almost 150 years. Even if [today's movement] is shortened by mass communication, I'd say we have about 70 years to go."

Does Steinem see women organizing today in the same way they did in the 1970s? "You find feminist consciousness-raising groups

today," she asserts, "but they are called book clubs now. Or networking groups. There are no longer just twelve crazy women in
every town who are feminists and are all in one group. Now they are
gathered together by their profession or neighborhood. There aren't
enough of these small groups, which we need in addition to big
organizations, but they do exist. They are the stuff of revolution,
because they support personal transformation *and* collective action."

If we need to get more women involved, what can we do to
encourage young women to become feminists? "I think life does it.
You can't do it artificially. In general, men are more radical in youth
and get more conservative as they age. Women tend to be more
conservative in youth and get more rebellious as they age. But the
other important thing to remember is that there are actually more
young feminists now than there ever were. There will be even more
feminists when today's young women are in their forties. We did
have twelve years of Reagan and Bush making feminism a dirty
word. Now we have Rush Limbaugh talking about 'feminazis'. But
a 1986 Gallup poll showed that about 60% of all women identify
themselves as feminists and one this year was over 70% when the
dictionary definition of feminism was added. Even the lowest poll
I've seen–remember, it depends upon how and in what context you
ask the question–was about a third of all women. That's about the
same amount that identify themselves as Republicans, but critics
just never compare it to that. Also, from the first poll to the 1995
one, women of color have been more likely to consider themselves
feminists–and to support issues of female equality–than white
women. This makes sense, since they're not only more likely to be
in the paid labor force, but more likely to know discrimination
when they see it. Yet the critics seem to think that only white,
middle-class women *can* be feminists."

If women get more rebellious as they age, I wonder, how has
Steinem become more radical? She comments, "[In the past] I
wanted to fight the system, so I did. But that wasn't the limit of
what I wanted to do as an individual. I tried to make a world in
which women could create and write, but I wasn't saving time to
create and write myself–to take personal risks. I used to have a big

sign on my wall that said, 'Express–Don't Persuade'. Well, now I express more and persuade less.

"I think that when you are on this long plateau of life that is the feminine role, say from 13 to 50, even if you are fighting against [the role], you are still enmeshed with it. After 50, it ends. There is no map. Then you get to figure out who you are and what you actually want to do. . . . Now there's a revolutionary thought!"

I comment that one could look at Steinem's writing and say it is less radical. For example, she moved from talking about "outrageous acts" to women and self-esteem. "I think self-esteem is *more* radical, actually," she responds. *Revolution from Within* "was just a normal progression of emphasis. Every social justice movement has everything to do with self-esteem, because injustice takes away our self-authority in order to get us to obey external authority. No oppressive system can work unless it has been internalized by the oppressed to some degree.

"In the beginnings of feminism, we analyzed the politics of our daily lives. All of this was part of the personal is political. But as the movement widened and deepened, we began to look not only at the politics of our current lives, but at the politics of our childhoods, and of textbooks, and of therapists. But since internal concerns are seen as 'feminine', they aren't taken as seriously. Even in our style of revolution, we're supposed to imitate the male style of what's 'radical'. In fact, self authority is at the root of rebellion. That idea wasn't new, it just broadened and deepened from the idea that the personal is political."

If self-esteem is at the root of rebellion, it seems to me that what Steinem is saying has implications for feminist therapists. I ask what she thinks of therapy, and of women in therapy, in particular. Says Steinem, "When I was in my twenties and thirties, therapy was so Freudianized that it never occurred to me that it would be helpful. Sending a woman to a Freudian seemed like sending a Jew to an anti-Semite. Now it's very different. I am so grateful to the women who have fought this battle inside very difficult, biased, professionally rarified organizations. Of course, feminist therapists have also suffered denigration from some political feminists, who say, 'Forget about internal life. We have to worry about the tangible.' What I think is that this division, the inner/outer, intellectual/

emotional, personal/political division, is a remnant of the masculine/feminine division. There's really not a division at all, but a circle. The inner reality is not more important than the outside, but it is not less important either. Each either strengthens the other in a spiral of progress, or weakens the other in a regression spiral. We can try to separate the internal from the external, but it just doesn't work. That way lies burnout or just plain bad tactics.

"What would be wonderful is if the enormous expertise of feminist therapists could be made more public, so that it is brought to bear on public problems as well. For instance, Reagan, the child of an alcoholic father, was the King of Denial–and he took the country into a disastrous denial of its problems. Or look at the Clintons. If Hillary were in the Senate on her own, she would be getting much less hatred and criticism. What that tells us is that the Clintons both are being penalized for presenting a more equal partnership between a man and a woman. That equality is threatening. So let's name it. Let's talk about that. We need to go public with wisdom garnered in the therapeutic setting–carry it into the public sphere.

"I do wish we had, and I believe we could have, a network of free, populist, neighborhood self-help groups–even bigger than the twelve-step network–that was a feminist network. We need groups that encourage an activism that's fueled by honest, internal work–and vice versa."

I reflect upon Steinem's earlier statement, that "the first step toward transformation is to imagine it." What else, I wonder out loud, does Gloria imagine for us? How else does she see the world changing in the next seventy years of this "revolution?" She replies:

"I think in a psychic sense, we now have half the insight. We believe, and so we have convinced most of the country, that women can do what men can do. But we don't yet believe, and therefore we haven't convinced the country, that men can do what women do. There are an awful lot of women out there still assuming they have to be more responsible for the kids *and* work outside the home. And so instead of getting angry and energized by this injustice, they accept it and get depressed if they can't 'do it all'–which is impossible. Women won't be able to be equal *outside* the home until men are raising children, and cooking, and housekeeping as much as women are *inside* the home. And that has barely begun.

"We have to redefine marriage. It's already changing. For instance, it used to be impossible to make an equal marriage. You lost your name, your credit rating, your legal residence, almost all your civil rights. That's not true anymore. Now the inequality comes when you have children. Men don't take care of children as much as women do—which may be the understatement of all time—and we're also the only country in the world without some national system of childcare.

"We've had the courage to raise our daughters more like our sons, which is good. There are more women now who are more whole people. But fewer of us have had the courage to raise our sons like our daughters. We need to raise sons to raise children—to develop the so-called 'feminine' qualities of empathy, flexibility, compassion, patience, and so on.

"We also need to reflect changed values in our economic structure. We need to attribute value to childbearing, childrearing, home maintenance, and all other kinds of work now considered valueless because it is done by women. All productive work has to have value. We need to attribute value to the environment. Otherwise, all economic incentive is toward destroying the environment. When you cut down trees, it should be recorded as asset depletion. Now it's just seen as profit. Our economic mega-system is just a system of values, and we need to change those values.

"I also think we need to question nationalism as a crazy way of organizing the world. No pollution of the air or water—nothing is stopped by an artificial boundary. Global environmental concerns, or global economic concerns, or refugee concerns—they give a lie to national boundaries. We are trapped in our minds by thinking nationalism is the only form of human organization.

"So I would say: thinking beyond gender, thinking beyond nationalism, thinking beyond the current economic structures . . . Those are all enormous challenges. In a more intimate sense, so is eroticizing equality. The reason feminists are being perceived wrongly as being anti-sex is because sex is now perceived as male-dominated or active/passive—even in some same-sex pairs. If you are against male-dominance, they think you are against sex. That's not true. We need to think about eroticizing equality. I'm telling you, cooperation beats submission every time!"

This last image strikes me as particularly amusing. I try to imagine myself in Steinem's vision. I tell her, "You seem confident that all this–that feminism is going to continue."

"Oh, yes," she replies. "Of course, we need to get out there and do it. Every time we fail to say what we're thinking, or swallow our anger, or go along with the system, we've weakened ourselves, missed an opportunity, and failed each other. We've been moving the barriers and clearing more territory, which is a great victory, but the barriers are still there. We just have to keep pushing them back until finally, they're off the map."

Gloria Steinem invites us–she has always invited us–to share her vision of the future. She welcomes us to share in creating the solutions she proposes. She also inspires us to create visions and solutions of our own, as we each bring our unique talents to the challenges that women face. Finally, like a good feminist foremother, Steinem cautions us to attend to ourselves and to our own needs, even as we address the needs of others and our society. She advises us to see that the "Golden Rule" women need is usually: "Treat yourself as well as you treat others." As we end our conversation, she adds: "Feminism is not only equality between sexes and races, but a balance between internal and external, uniqueness and community. Everything is a balance between two opposites that are not really opposite, but just opposite points on a circle. . . ."

REFERENCES

Steinem, Gloria. (1983). *Outrageous Acts and Everyday Rebellions*. New York: Holt, Rinehart, and Winston.

Steinem, Gloria. (1992). *Revolution from Within*. New York: Little, Brown & Co.

Steinem, Gloria. (1994). *Moving Beyond Words*. New York: Simon and Schuster.

Catharine R. Stimpson:
Charting the Course of Women's Studies
Since Its Inception

M. Kay Jankowski

As an extremely gifted thinker and writer, Catharine R. Stimpson has been a leader at the forefront of the feminist movement for over 25 years. As the current Director of the Fellows Division of the MacArthur Foundation in Chicago, she is on leave from her position as University Professor at Rutgers, the State University of New Jersey/New Brunswick. From Summer 1986, to Summer 1992, she served as Dean of the Graduate School and Vice Provost for Graduate Education at Rutgers. Stimpson is editor of a book series about women in culture and society for the University of Chicago Press and served as the founding editor of *Signs: Journal of Women in Culture and Society* from 1974-1980. She was the founding director of the Women's Center of Barnard College and of the Institute for Research on Women at Rutgers. Her professional interests are in culture, literature, women's studies, and education. The editor of

M. Kay Jankowski is a graduate student in the Doctoral Training Program in Clinical Psychology at the University of Vermont. Her research interests include interpersonal violence and women's mental health.

Correspondence may be addressed to M. Kay Jankowski at the Department of Psychology, John Dewey Hall, Burlington, VT 05405.

[Haworth co-indexing entry note]: "Catharine R. Stimpson: Charting the Course of Women's Studies Since Its Inception." Jankowski, M. Kay. Co-published simultaneously in *Women & Therapy* (The Haworth Press, Inc.) Vol. 17, No. 3/4, 1995, pp. 489-493; and: *Feminist Foremothers in Women's Studies, Psychology, and Mental Health* (ed: Phyllis Chesler, Esther D. Rothblum, and Ellen Cole) The Haworth Press, Inc., 1995, pp. 489-493; and: *Feminist Foremothers in Women's Studies, Psychology, and Mental Health* (ed: Phyllis Chesler, Esther D. Rothblum, and Ellen Cole) Harrington Park Press, an imprint of The Haworth Press, Inc., 1995, pp. 489-493. Single or multiple copies of this article are available from The Haworth Document Delivery Service [1-800-342-9678, 9:00 a.m. - 5:00 p.m. (EST)].

seven books, author of a novel and over 150 monographs, essays, stories, and reviews, she has also lectured at approximately 300 institutions and events in the United States and abroad.

Various circumstances have influenced and led up to Stimpson's contributions to feminism. First, her family environment while growing up was one in which women and their accomplishments were valued. Women in her family including two aunts and her mother worked outside the home. One aunt was a chemist, the other worked for the Red Cross, and her mother ran a small insurance company until Catharine was born. Although traditional in some ways, her family situation was one in which "feminist ideas would not be alien." Stimpson's feminist thinking and desire to pursue a nontraditional role for women were further advanced by reading books about women of accomplishment including Susan B. Anthony. Stimpson also credits her years as an undergraduate at a women's college for shaping her interest and lifelong commitment to feminism and women's studies. She believes women's colleges provide a supportive environment that is conducive to producing leaders.

Stimpson was working in New York during the rebirth of feminism as a member of the faculty in the English Department at Barnard College in the late 1960s and 1970s. She described the time and place as "a wonderfully exciting urban environment when feminist ideals were breaking open." Being in such a stimulating setting was another contributing factor to her own scholarship in feminist studies and her founding of institutions for the advancement and dissemination of feminist ideas.

Stimpson has made a multitude of contributions to the feminist movement. "I think my contribution has probably been as an interpreter of the field of women's studies and as an editor." This seems an understatement given the power that her words carry. Her wit, wisdom, and eloquence are striking. For the past 20 years Stimpson has offered general overviews of women's studies that capture the general evolution of the field as well as the evolution of feminist studies. Her approach to feminist psychology is no different. Her overviews have demonstrated the importance and relevance of a multidisciplinary approach to the study of women. In addition, they have provided an analysis of the progression of the feminist movement in general and in more specific areas such as feminist theory and women and education. Stimpson writes and speaks to audiences about where the movement has come from, giving it an historical context, and where she would like it to be headed in the future. One is struck with the breadth of the knowledge base from which she draws support for her arguments in her overviews. She has given numerous lectures and consistently published these overviews for both academic and nonacademic audiences. In terms of her work addressed to nonacademic audiences, she has been a contributor to *Ms.* Magazine, and chaired the first Board of Scholars for the magazine from 1981-1992. The purpose of the Board was to bring academic Women's Studies to nonacademic audiences.

As one of the founding leaders of the field, Stimpson writes that she loves and celebrates women's studies. "I hope always that the truth and achievements and promise of women's studies will be reflected in all institutions having to do with our social and intellectual lives." She first began teaching courses on women in culture and literature in the very early 1970s, as a young, not-yet tenured professor. It was a time when the field of women's studies was just beginning, long before it was accorded any respect by more traditional academic disciplines. Stimpson believes women's studies is a field where diversity has been respected and explored, setting it apart from nearly all other fields. It offers society "a moral vision of a just and equitable educational community. The moral vision of community pictures access to learning for rich and middling and poor alike, mutual respect among all learners, and policies that serve all learners."

It is not surprising to Stimpson that the field has met with plenty of opposition. Women's studies has had its problems. Often it has been "reductive and prone to labeling." Women's studies has "indulged in vulgar games of identity politics," an oversimplification assuming that there is no difference between people's racial, ethnic or sexual identity and their views, ". . . a grievous flaw of identity politics is its quickness to insist that each of us belongs to one group; that our identity (our sense of self and self-in-the-world) flows solely from membership in this group; that we must remain with the group—come thick or thin, hell or high water; and that we must look at everything through a lens this group has ground."

However, Stimpson states that the mistakes women's studies has made cannot account for the extent of the opposition. Two reasons she mentions for the resistance to the field are: one, the widespread belief "that women of all races, like minorities of both genders, are irrational, castrators of reason, by nature nonacademic"; and two, the reality that as thinking about women changes, so will come change in their social and subject positions, which will result in disturbances of the status quo.

One task for women's studies, Stimpson writes, is to continue dialogue between the various groups that make up the field, and for each group to "enter into thoughtful coalitions with others." In this way, the field must "struggle against the bad differences and celebrate the good."

Writing more generally about women and higher education, she believes that the situation for women is mixed. Women have made great strides, but still have a long way to go. "Women are at once inside and outside of the precincts of higher education; comfortable and bruised, confident and anxious, cheerful and angry, on edge." Writing about the effects of the backlash against women and its effects on higher education, she states "assassins of the dreams of education for us all oil and cock their weapons. Of course, the assassins would have nothing to do if the dreams were not moving closer to reality." She gives a wonderful historical perspective on the struggles of women to be educated and to become "knowing women." That is, "women who know, women of active and assertive consciousness, women who are a lively part of the give-and-take of information."

Another major contribution Stimpson has made to feminism is through her work as editor of *Signs: Journal of Women in Culture and Society* from 1974-1980. She and her colleagues founded *Signs* with the express purpose of representing new scholarship on women and bringing together work from disciplines and fields as varied as the social sciences, humanities, natural sciences, law, health, and education. This interdisciplinary approach allows for important connections to be made between work on women that is being done in independent disciplines. *Signs* has always stood as one of the most prestigious journals in women's studies.

Stimpson highlights three crucial articles for psychology published while she was editor. Gertrude Lenzer's, "On masochism: A contribution to the history of a phantasy and its theory" (Vol. 1, #2) is a study of the concept of masochism and was "an attempt in a very sophisticated way to show the importance of Freud." In this way, it differed from many other feminist critiques of Freud. Another important essay for psychology that she and her colleagues published was Mary Parlee's major review essay on women and psychology (Vol. 1, #1). The third article published by Stimpson and crucial to psychology is Judith Herman and Lisa Hirschman's groundbreaking work on father-daughter incest (Vol. 2, #4).

Stimpson is currently the editor of a book series on women in culture and society published by University of Chicago Press. Although the books have not represented psychology, she states that some of the work in the social sciences published in the series "has great resonance for psychology." One in particular is Marjorie Devault's sociological study of food preparation and women's role as food providers.

When asked how her work and accomplishments have changed her life, Stimpson replied that doing feminist work has been her profession. She has made it the organizing principle of her working life, providing her with happiness and surprise.

I believe Stimpson's work has much to offer the field of psychology. Her overviews and the series that she edits offer a much needed broader context in which to understand women's lives. It is crucial that we as psychologists take an interdisciplinary approach to our work and not rely exclusively on knowledge within the confines of the field of psychology.

Quotations have been taken from an interview with Professor Stimpson and from the following articles:

" 'Wild Boars and Such Things': Pains, Gains, and the Education of Women," *Furman Studies,* 36 (June 1994), 1-36.
"Dirty Minds, Dirty Bodies, Clean Speech," Annual Senate Academic Freedom Lecture, University of Michigan, 1993. Published in *Michigan Quarterly Review,* 23, 3 (Summer 1993), 317-337.
"How Did Feminist Theory Get That Way," in *Politics, Theory, and Contemporary Culture,* M. Poster, (Ed.) New York: Columbia University Press, pp. 13-44.

A Woman Undaunted:
Bonnie R. Strickland

Kathleen M. Shanahan

Kathleen M. Shanahan is a doctoral candidate in Clinical Psychology at the University of Massachusetts at Amherst. In addition to teaching Psychology of Women at the University of Massachusetts, she has focused her clinical work on the impact of violence on women's mental health. Her research interests have been inspired by the ways in which individuals establish, negotiate, violate, and repair the boundary between self and other. Within this framework, she has considered individuals' self-conceptions and moral reasoning, sexual violations within the therapeutic relationship, and the transgenerational transmission of trauma.

Bonnie R. Strickland received her PhD in Clinical Psychology from Ohio State University in 1962. She has been on the faculties of Emory University and the University of Massachusetts at Amherst as teacher, researcher, administrator, clinician, and consultant. A Diplomate in Clinical Psychology, she has also been in clinical practice for over 30 years. Dr. Strickland has served as President of the American Psychological Association, the Division of Clinical Psychology and the American Association for Applied and Preventive Psychology. She was a Founder and on the first Board of Directors of the American Psychological Society. Dr. Strickland has been a long-time public advocate for women and minorities, testifying before the US Congress and serving on numerous national Boards and Committees. She has over a hundred scholarly publications, including two Citation Classics.

Correspondence may be addressed to Kathleen M. Shanahan at Department of Psychology, Tobin Hall, Box 37710, University of Massachusetts at Amherst, Amherst, MA 01003.

[Haworth co-indexing entry note]: "A Woman Undaunted: Bonnie R. Strickland." Shanahan, Kathleen M. Co-published simultaneously in Women & Therapy (The Haworth Press, Inc.) Vol. 17, No. 3/4, 1995, pp. 495-505; and: Feminist Foremothers in Women's Studies, Psychology, and Mental Health (ed: Phyllis Chesler, Esther D. Rothblum, and Ellen Cole) The Haworth Press, Inc., 1995, pp. 495-505; and: Feminist Foremothers in Women's Studies, Psychology, and Mental Health (ed: Phyllis Chesler, Esther D. Rothblum, and Ellen Cole) Harrington Park Press, an imprint of The Haworth Press, Inc., 1995, pp. 495-505. Single or multiple copies of this article are available from The Haworth Document Delivery Service [1-800-342-9678, 9:00 a.m. - 5:00 p.m. (EST)].

495

My father and mother both
used to warn me
that "a whistling woman and a crowing
hen would surely come to
no good end." And perhaps I should
have listened to them.
But even at the time I knew
that though my end probably might
not
be good
I must whistle
like a woman undaunted
until I reached it.

–Alice Walker, *Horses make a landscape more beautiful*, 1984

Relaxing on the deck of her lakeside home in the quiet woods of the Pioneer Valley, Bonnie Ruth Strickland exudes an energy and ingenuousness that belie her status as a feminist "foremother." Although it is twilight, and the hour well-suited to reverie, her recollections are punctuated with new interests and a vision of work yet to be done. There is an edge of excitement in her voice as she contemplates the synergism of strong women working together. "Women are writing a different history about being in relationships," she exclaims, her soft, Southern drawl filling the quiet evening. "There's a spark. You just make yourself available and things happen!"

Bonnie should know. At a time when feminist theorists are drawing attention to connection as a vital force in women's experience, Bonnie's life and work stand as a testament to the effectiveness of collegiality. For over thirty years, as an educator, clinician, researcher, and administrator, she has been making herself available–to students, clients, colleagues, and society at large–asking what she calls "big questions," listening to people who haven't been listened to, and challenging the deficiency model which traditionally has characterized much of the research on marginalized populations, particularly women. Her life's story, like the stories of the women whose lives she has touched, nurtured, illuminated, and shared, speaks to the coming generation of women in psychology, those whose challenge it remains to "whistle like a woman undaunted," as they in turn continue the work so skillfully and so passionately begun.

Bonnie Ruth Strickland comes from a long line of strong, independent, often struggling, always fascinating women. She proudly recounts that through her paternal grandmother she is a descendent of the Lees of Virginia, though she's quick to add in a conspiratorial whisper that all Southerners are. Her maternal forebears include a great-grandmother who ran off with her sister's husband, and a grandmother who eloped with a local ne'er do well and lived to bear and raise thirteen children through two additional marriages. Bonnie's own parents, Roy Elkins Strickland and Willie Whitfield, were married after a whirlwind courtship, and struggled to raise their two children in the waning years of the Great Depression. When her parents' marriage ended in divorce, seven-year-old Bonnie and her three-year-old brother, Roy, remained with their mother in Birmingham, Alabama, though summers were spent with the extended Whitfield family in the Appalachicola River swamps of Northwest Florida.

Growing up in a single parent household, Bonnie learned at an early age the necessity of collaboration. She assumed responsibility not only for assisting with household chores, but also for supplementing the family income with a part-time job at the local library. Her spare time was devoted to playing sports of all kinds, and she excelled in tennis, earning an Alabama State Girls' title and national ranking at the age of sixteen. Upon the recommendation of Louise Pope, the first of many mentors, Bonnie chose to attend Alabama College for Women, where her athletic prowess earned her a physical education scholarship. While there, a game of tennis with one of the college's two psychology professors led Bonnie to reconsider her choice of career, and under the guidance of Herbert Eber and Katherine Vickery, Bonnie was offered and accepted a research assistantship with Julian Rotter in the clinical psychology program at the Ohio State University. Some twenty-five years later, she would be named Alumna of the Year by her Alma Mater, an honor she would accept with special pride.

Ohio State, with its strong program in personality theory and diverse student body, proved a stimulating environment for Bonnie.

Indeed, her life-long commitment to the scientist-practitioner model of clinical psychology can be traced to the extensive training in research and clinical practice she received during her years there. Her early research on need for approval (Crowne & Strickland, 1961; Strickland & Crowne, 1962, 1963) and internal-external locus of control (Strickland, 1970) became the cornerstone and catalyst for a program of research concerning the role of internal versus external locus of control beliefs in shaping and modifying behavior (see Strickland, 1989). Her clinical and internship training was equally significant, exposing her to a variety of patients, training facilities, supervisors, and treatment modalities, including fixed role therapy with George Kelly, social learning theory with Albert Bandura, group work with Ruth Cohn, and family therapy with Gregory Bateson and Virginia Satir. She recalls with amusement one young aide with whom she worked with chronic schizophrenic patients at the Palo Alto VA; the aide, Ken Kesey, who could often be seen taking notes there, would eventually make the ward famous in *One Flew Over the Cuckoo's Nest.*

Bonnie's return to the South as a member of the psychology faculty at Emory University in 1962 coincided with the rise of the Civil Rights Movement. Her position there placed her at the center of a Zeitgeist of social activism, and among her acquaintances were leaders of the movement, including Catholic activists, Quaker pacifists, and Martin Luther King, Jr. Her research, usually in collaboration with colleagues and students, reflected her personal commitment to social justice. During this period, for example, Bonnie did extensive research on racism, prejudice, resilience, and social activism (Proenza & Strickland, 1965; Sank & Strickland, 1973; Strickland, 1965, 1971; Strickland & Weddell, 1972). Of particular note was her study of Southern Student Non-Violent Coordinating Committee activists (Strickland, 1965). She found that African American males involved in dramatic civil rights activities were significantly more likely than a matched group to hold internal locus of control beliefs. This study, the first to use a personality dimension to predict social activism, was eventually named a Citation Classic. A forerunner in the gay and lesbian civil rights movement as well, Bonnie also was involved in one of the first studies to challenge the then prevailing view of homosexuality as an illness, demonstrating that there was no significant difference between the mental health status of a non-clinical sample of gay men and lesbian women and a heterosexual control group (Thompson, McCandless, & Strickland, 1971). The first to include a large sample of lesbian women, this study established a more inclusive standard for research within the gay and lesbian population. A third focal point in Bonnie's research at Emory was the development with Steven Nowicki of a reliable and valid scale with which to measure internal versus external beliefs in children. With the resulting Nowicki-Strickland Children's Locus of Control Scale (Nowicki & Strickland, 1973), Bonnie was able to demonstrate that internal locus of control is an adaptive mediating variable for children's behavior (Strickland, 1972, 1973; Zytkoskee, Strickland, & Watson, 1971). In addition to earning her a second Citation Classic, the Nowicki-Strickland Locus of Control Scales across age groups continue to be widely used, and are among the most frequently cited references in the *Journal of Consulting and Clinical Psychology.* Equally at home in classroom and laboratory, Bonnie was chosen to receive Emory's Outstanding Faculty Award in 1969.

In the midst of this extremely productive period of research, Bonnie served for three years as Dean of Women. As Dean, she was responsible for all non-academic activities of the women students, including residence life. She remembers one conservative first-year student in particular, who, faced with the 11:00 p.m. curfew required of women, quietly submitted, convinced that "We can't change the rules." "Four years later," Bonnie recalls, her iconoclastic streak adding a note of pride to her voice, "she went on to graduate school at Ohio State and shut the University down!" Under Bonnie's guidance, many of the women whom she came to know at Emory chose to pursue graduate studies in psychology and related disciplines, and have since made significant contributions of their own to the field of feminist studies. These former students and colleagues (including that first-year student, now the Executive Director of a major academic/professional association) remain an integral part of the ever-widening circle of women and men whom Bonnie proudly counts among her friends. Still, there have been losses as well, and in a story one might wish were apocryphal, Bonnie recalls two former students who touched her life one week in Spring a few years back. One was being interviewed for the position of Chancellor of the University of Massachusetts at Amherst; the other was murdered–by the father of her baby.

Although her years at Emory were satisfying and fruitful, decisions regarding her promotion and tenure were delayed, a situation not uncommon among women working in predominantly male institutions at that time. Not one to submit to inequity, Bonnie informally began a job search, and was pleased to accept a position as full professor in the Department of Psychology at the University of Massachusetts at Amherst in 1973. Her move meant more than a change in climate; she went from being one of "less than a handful" of women faculty members at Emory University to being one of fifteen women faculty members in the UMass Psychology Department alone. Her research, too, focused more directly on women's issues, particularly women's health. During this time, for example, her investigation of the relation of locus of control beliefs to health (Strickland, 1977a, 1977b, 1978, 1979, 1984, 1989; Strickland & Janoff-Bulman, 1980) led her to examine gender differences in locus of control orientation (Strickland & Haley, 1980) and in depression (Strickland, 1983, 1992). Intrigued by her findings there, she began to explore affective/cognitive interactions in depression (Hale & Strickland, 1976; Haley & Strickland, 1986; Strickland, Hale, & Anderson, 1975), with special attention focused on the impact of food and chemical sensitivities on mood (Strickland, 1981, 1982). Ultimately, this body of research, along with her own bout with illness, led Bonnie to recognize the essential interdependence of physical and emotional health, and resulted in a series of articles addressing mind-body interactions (Strickland, 1984, 1988a, 1988b; Strickland & Kendall, 1983).

Dedicated to sharing her expertise on women's health issues with the public at large, Bonnie has added a demanding lecture schedule to her activities, presenting at nearly 200 conferences and colloquia in the past ten years alone. Invested, too, in the dissemination of research, she has served for several years on the editorial boards of a number of psychology journals, and is presently a member of the editorial board of *Women & Therapy*. At the same time, Bonnie has retained her popularity among students, and her courses on the

Psychology of Women and Lesbian Studies are typically over-en-rolled.

Bonnie's move to UMass also meant a growing recognition by her colleagues of her administrative skills; while on the faculty at UMass she served the University community as Chair of the Faculty Senate Committee on the Status of Women, Director of Graduate Studies in Psychology, Chair of the Psychology Department, and Associate to the Chancellor of the University. In recognition of her numerous contributions to the University, Bonnie was awarded the Chancellor's Medal for Distinguished Service in 1984.

Extensive administrative experience, along with a reputation for scholarship and a commitment to feminist values, soon led to a succession of leadership positions on the national level. In 1975, she was selected to chair the first Equal Opportunity and Affirmative Action Committee of the Division of Clinical Psychology. Five years later she helped to establish the Section on Clinical Psychology of Women within Division 12, and in 1986, the Section on Ethnic Minority Clinical Psychology. During this time, she also chaired the Board of Professional Affairs of the American Psychological Association (APA), and in 1983 was elected president of the Division of Clinical Psychology, the fourth woman in forty years to serve in that capacity. In addition, she served on numerous national committees, including the Advisory Council of the National Institute of Mental Health, the Executive Committee of the National Coalition for Women's Mental Health, and the Science Advisory Board of the Depression, Awareness, Recognition, and Treatment (DART) Program sponsored by NIMH, a position she continues to hold today. In 1985, Bonnie was chair of the Policy and Planning Board of APA, and in 1985 was elected president of the American Psychological Association, one of only seven women in the more than 100-year history of APA to have held that office.

As president of APA, Bonnie's influence was felt far beyond the confines of the association. She continued to be an advocate for the disenfranchised, testifying before Congress regarding the need for increased funding for social and behavioral science research and mental health training, the AIDS Federal Policy Act, and women's health research priorities. Motivated by her personal commitment to women's health issues, Bonnie appointed and served on an APA

Task Force on Women and Depression. The report generated by the Task Force (McGrath, Keita, Strickland, & Russo, 1990) underscored the role of social and environmental risk factors such as poverty and violence in the etiology of depression, and did much to increase public awareness of depression and the potential for treatment. Since her tenure as president, Bonnie has served on the Board of the American Psychological Foundation and is currently co-chair of the half-million dollar Wayne Placek Trust Fund established to support "research to alleviate the stress gay men and lesbians experience in this and in future civilizations."

Deeply committed to education and training, and to the scientist-practitioner model of clinical psychology (Strickland, 1985, 1987a, 1987b, 1991), Bonnie was a key planner and participant in three national conferences on graduate education in psychology. Moved by a growing concern that APA was neglecting the discipline of psychology and the scientific foundation upon which application and practice depend, Bonnie attempted to reorganize APA to streamline the governance and to reflect the interdependence of science and practice. When her efforts failed to bring about the changes she envisioned, she and a small group of others determined to create a new organization, the American Psychological Society, designed to nourish the discipline of psychology and its research base. As she recalls those early, heady days of its founding, her voice is filled with wonder. "We wrote the bylaws here," she asserts, her eyes scanning the lakeshore by which she now sits. "APS started here on the deck in Belchertown, Massachusetts!" She has reason to feel pride in her efforts; from that early steering committee meeting in Belchertown, APS attracted over 7,000 members in its first year, and now has over 15,000 members. This same commitment to the scientist-practitioner model also motivated Bonnie to be one of three founders of the American Association for Applied and Preventive Psychology, and in 1992 she served as president of AAAPP.

In recognition of a lifetime of service, Bonnie was honored with the 1992 Leadership Citation for distinguished leaders for women in psychology from the American Psychological Association's Committee on Women and Psychology. The committee cited her development of "a successful model of power based on the value of

people, on connection and on inclusion, which has greatly benefitted all women. Her vision, courage and direction have promoted
and forwarded the cause of women in psychology."

Women's stories, writes Bettina Aptheker, in *Tapestries of Life*
(1989), "reveal that women have not been exclusively or primarily
victims, crushed by circumstances, but survivors and creators, their
artifacts of beauty arising as it were from nothing" (p. 45). Bonnie
Ruth Strickland has not only survived, but has thrived, dedicating
her life's work to celebrating the creativity and resilience of the
disenfranchised. Throughout her career she has been in the vanguard of a campaign to correct psychology's misrepresentation of
African Americans, gays, lesbians, and women of various ethnicities and orientations. Still, the work is far from over, and she remains deeply invested in the task. "It is very liberating, very exciting," she says, with her characteristic enthusiasm, "still to be
involved in the human rights movement and reconnecting with a lot
of interesting people." Ultimately, there is good reason to expect
that with the passing of time, Bonnie still will be in the vanguard,
working hard to shake things up. "To will implies delay," she's
fond of saying, invoking Alexander Pope. "Therefore now do."

REFERENCES

Aptheker, B. (1989). *Tapestries of life: Women's work, women's consciousness,
and the meaning of daily experience.* Amherst: University of Massachusetts.

Crowne, D. P., & Strickland, B. R. (1961). The conditioning of verbal behavior as
a function of the need for social approval. *Journal of Abnormal and Social
Psychology, 63*, 395-401.

Hale, W. D., & Strickland, B. R. (1976). Induction of mood states and their effect
on cognitive and social behaviors. *Journal of Consulting and Clinical Psychology, 44*, 155.

Haley, W., & Strickland, B. R. (1986). Interpersonal betrayal and cooperation:
Effects on self-evaluation in depression. *Journal of Personality and Social
Psychology, 50*(2), 386-391.

Kesey, K. (1962). *One flew over the cuckoo's nest.* NY: Viking.

McGrath, E., Keita, G. P., Strickland, B. R., & Russo, N. F. (Eds.). (1990). *Women
and depression: Risk factors and treatment issues.* Final report of the APA
National Task Force on Women and Depression. Washington, D.C.: APA.

Nowicki, S., & Strickland, B. R. (1973). A locus of control scale for children.
Journal of Consulting and Clinical Psychology, 40, 148-154.

Proenza, L., & Strickland, B. R. (1965). A study of prejudice in Negro and White college students. *Journal of Social Psychology, 67*, 273-281.

Sank, Z. B., & Strickland, B. R. (1973). Some attitudinal and behavioral correlates of a belief in militant or moderate social action. *Journal of Social Psychology, 90*, 337-338.

Strickland, B. R. (1965). The prediction of social action from a dimension of internal-external control. *Journal of Social Psychology, 66*, 353-358.

Strickland, B. R. (1970). Individual differences in verbal conditioning, extinction, and awareness. *Journal of Personality, 38*, 364-378.

Strickland, B. R. (1971). Aspiration responses among Negro and White adolescents. *Journal of Personality and Social Psychology, 19*, 315-320.

Strickland, B. R. (1972). Delay of gratification as a function of race of the experimenter. *Journal of Personality and Social Psychology, 22*, 108-112.

Strickland, B. R. (1973). Delay of gratification and internal locus of control in children. *Journal of Consulting and Clinical Psychology, 40*, 338.

Strickland, B. R. (1977a). Approval motivation. In T. Blass (Ed.), *Personality variables and social behavior* (pp. 315-355). Hillsdale, NJ: Erlbaum.

Strickland, B. R. (1977b). Internal versus external control of reinforcement. In T. Blass (Ed.), *Personality variables and social behavior* (pp. 219-280). Hillsdale, NJ: Erlbaum.

Strickland, B. R. (1978). Internal-external expectancies and health-related behaviors. *Journal of Consulting and Clinical Psychology, 46*, 1192-1211.

Strickland, B. R. (1979). Internal-external expectancies and cardiovascular functioning. In L. C. Perlmuter & R. A. Monty (Eds.), *Choice and perceived control* (pp. 221-231). Hillsdale, NJ: Erlbaum.

Strickland, B. R. (1981). Psychological effects of food and chemical susceptibilities. *Voices: The Art and Science of Psychotherapy, 17*, 68-72.

Strickland, B. R. (1982). Implications of food and chemical susceptibilities for clinical psychology. *International Journal of Biosocial Research, 3*, 39-43.

Strickland, B. R. (1983). Depression as a concomitant of physical disorders: Difficulties of differentiation. *International Journal of Biosocial Research, 4*, 43-50.

Strickland, B. R. (1984). Levels of health enhancement: Individual attributes. In J. D. Matarazzo, N. E. Miller, S. M. Weiss, J. A. Herd, & S. M. Weiss (Eds.), *Behavioral health: A handbook of health enhancement and disease prevention* (pp. 101-113). NY: John Wiley & Sons.

Strickland, B. R. (1985). Over the Boulder(s) and through the Vail. *Clinical Psychologist, 38*, 52-56.

Strickland, B. R. (1987a). On the threshold of the second century of psychology. *American Psychologist, 42*, 1055-1056.

Strickland, B. R. (1987b). Perspectives on clinical, counseling, and social psychology. *Journal of Social and Clinical Psychology, 5*, 150-159.

Strickland, B. R. (1988a). Sex-related differences in health and illness. *Psychology of Women Quarterly, 12*, 381-399.

Strickland, B. R. (1988b). Forward. In E. A. Blechman & K. D. Brownell (Eds.) *Handbook of behavioral medicine for women* (pp. xiii). NY: Pergamon Press.

Strickland, B. R. (1989). Internal-External control expectancies: From contingency to creativity. *American Psychologist, 44*, 1-12.

Strickland, B. R. (1991). Commentary: The viability of the discipline of psychology: A plea for integrating science and practice. In C. R. Snyder & D. R. Forsyth (Eds.), *Handbook of social and clinical psychology: The health perspective* (p. 82) NY: Pergamon Press.

Strickland, B. R. (1992). Women and depression. *Current Directions in Psychological Science, 1*(4), 132-135.

Strickland, B. R., & Crowne, D. P. (1962). Conformity under conditions of simulated group pressure as a function of need for approval. *Journal of Social Psychology, 58*, 171-181.

Strickland, B. R., & Crowne, D. P. (1963). Need for approval and the premature termination of psychotherapy. *Journal of Consulting Psychology, 27*, 95-101.

Strickland, B. R., Hale, W. D., & Anderson, L. K. (1975). Effect of induced mood states on activity and self-reported affect. *Journal of Consulting and Clinical Psychology, 43*, 587.

Strickland, B. R., & Haley, W. E. (1980). Sex differences on the Rotter I-E Scale. *Journal of Personality and Social Psychology, 39*, 930-939.

Strickland, B. R., & Janoff-Bulman, R. (1980). Expectancies and attributions: Applications for community mental health. In M. S. Gibbs, J. R. Lachenmeyer, & J. Sigal (Eds.), *Community psychology: Theoretical and empirical approaches* (pp. 97-119). NY: Gardner.

Strickland, B. R., & Kendall, K. E. (1983). Psychological symptoms: The importance of assessing health status. *Clinical Psychology Review, 3*, 179-199.

Strickland, B. R., & Weddell, S. C. (1972). Religious orientation, racial prejudice and dogmatism. *Journal of Scientific Study of Religion, 11*, 395-399.

Thompson, N. L., McCandless, B. R., & Strickland, B. R. (1971). Personal adjustment of male and female homosexuals and heterosexuals. *Journal of Abnormal Psychology, 78*, 237-240.

Walker, A. (1984). *Horses make a landscape more beautiful.* NY: Harcourt Brace Jovanovich.

Zytkoskee, A., Strickland, B. R., & Watson, J. (1971). Delay of gratification and internal versus external control among adolescents of low socioeconomic status. *Developmental Psychology, 4*, 93-98.

Some Contributions to Feminist Research in Psychology

Sandra Schwartz Tangri

It is extremely flattering and an honor to be asked to contribute to this volume on feminist psychology's foremothers. Sometimes I think I was just in the right place at the right time although I like to think that some of the work I've done has been useful.

I became a psychologist, a feminist, and a mother at exactly the same time, and this coincided with the new wave of feminism. I was in graduate school, not having time to read the newspaper, when my then-husband read about this new organization that he thought we should join: The National Organization for Women. I had already picked my dissertation topic which focussed on women (see following), but immersion in the new feminist literature fired up a strength of commitment and a theoretical perspective that would not otherwise have been there. These were aided and abetted by the dislocat-

Sandra Schwartz Tangri received her PhD in 1967 from The University of Michigan's interdisciplinary Social Psychology Program. She has taught at Douglass College (Rutgers University), Richmond College (City University of New York), and Howard University (Washington, DC). Between academic jobs, she was Director of the Office of Research for the U.S. Commission on Civil Rights for four years and Senior Research Associate at the Urban Institute for three years.

Correspondence may be addressed to Sandra Schwartz Tangri at the Department of Psychology, Howard University, 525 Bryant Street NW, Washington, DC 20059.

[Haworth co-indexing entry note]: "Some Contributions to Feminist Research in Psychology." Tangri, Sandra Schwartz. Co-published simultaneously in *Women & Therapy* (The Haworth Press, Inc.) Vol. 17, No. 3/4, 1995, pp. 507-515; and: *Feminist Foremothers in Women's Studies, Psychology, and Mental Health* (ed: Phyllis Chesler, Esther D. Rothblum, and Ellen Cole) The Haworth Press, Inc., 1995, pp. 507-515; and: *Feminist Foremothers in Women's Studies, Psychology, and Mental Health* (ed: Phyllis Chesler, Esther D. Rothblum, and Ellen Cole) Harrington Park Press, an imprint of The Haworth Press, Inc., 1995, pp. 507-515. Single or multiple copies of this article are available from The Haworth Document Delivery Service [1-800-342-9678, 9:00 a.m. - 5:00 p.m. (EST)].

ing experience of being on the job market while visibly pregnant. I have been able to work nearly exclusively on topics related to women since then, and have experienced both advantages and disadvantages because of that. This is because I did not stay in academia the entire time. It is thanks to my line of research that I landed the most prestigious job that I've had: Director of Research for the U.S. Commission on Civil Rights. It is also thanks in part to my line of research that I lost the job at The Urban Institute that I would have liked to keep, because the Reagan years dried up funding for what I was doing.

Along those lines I think three of my research efforts have made some difference to the field of feminist psychology. As a social psychologist, I cannot say whether these have been specifically useful to therapists or clients, although each certainly has implications for women's well-being.

LONGITUDINAL RESEARCH ON WOMEN'S CAREER DEVELOPMENT

My first line of research began with my dissertation, using mostly data from the Michigan Student Study (Gurin, 1971). My interest was in women's occupational goals, and specifically in understanding what kinds of women were willing to articulate aspirations that were uncommon for college women at that time (these women received their BAs in 1967, and I refer to them as Role-Innovators).

The main value of the findings was that they countered some of the stereotypes of the "career woman" that were (and to some extent still are) prevalent. For instance, the Role-Innovators were not "wallflowers"; they hadn't identified with the "wrong" parent (i.e., their fathers instead of their mothers); they did not score on the masculine end of the bipolar "masculinity-femininity" scale (this was before Bem's critique of such scales).

Chipping away at stereotypes is always useful. But I think another reason this research has been cited so often is that it set a tone for investigating women's choices and women's lives that was frankly friendly to change, and therefore invited more research that would validate and legitimize a broader range of lifestyles for women. The dissertation was completed in 1969 and partly published in 1972

(Tangri, 1972), as the second wave feminist movement challenged existing sex-role prescriptions, and soaked up information that supported arguments for social change. So the impact it had is also related to the historical times in which it was done. The Special Issue *New Perspectives on Women* (Mednick & Tangri, 1972) of the *Journal of Social Issues* that Martha Mednick and I edited, helped greatly to disseminate my and others' work (including Matina Horner's work on Fear of Success, Broverman et al.'s work on clinicians' gender biases, etc.), and was the first "special issue on women" put out by any of the professional journals in the social sciences. I think that was a watershed in the Psychology of Women field, and for some time it was the best-selling issue of that Journal.

A third reason for its impact is that my dissertation was fairly broad. Although the research question was tightly focussed, the variety of predictor variables was large. Therefore, much subsequent work on women's occupational choices and career development could refer back to something in this study as a reference or corroborative evidence–especially since the major findings held up very well through subsequent studies.

Finally, the study took on a life of its own as I and other researchers continued to follow these women at irregular intervals after they left college (as funding and circumstances permitted). Because the first (1967) and second (1970) waves of data were archived at the Henry A. Murray Center at Radcliffe College, they drew the interest of then-graduate students Sharon Rae Jenkins at Boston University and Jan Hitchcock at Harvard University, who used them for dissertations, and Josephine Ruggiero in the Department of Sociology at the University of Rhode Island. The four of us collaborated on launching the third wave of data which was collected in 1981 and is now also archived at the Murray Center. It was Jan Hitchcock who suggested calling the project the Women's Life Paths Study. Sharon Rae Jenkins supervised the coding and data entry (Hitchcock, 1984; Jenkins, 1982; 1987; 1989; in press a; in press b; Ruggiero & Weston, 1988).

The longitudinal data supported our contention that women's occupational aspirations should be taken seriously and were worthy of social investments. This was at a time when it was still common for universities and employers to consider white, middle-class women marginal to the labor force and only working for "extras"(Tangri & Jenkins, 1986; 1993).

Still another wave of data has just been collected (1992-93) in collaboration with Abigail Stewart at the University of Michigan and her graduate students, Elizabeth Vanderwater, Liz Cole, Joan Ostrove, Jill Allen, Alyssa Zucker, Myra Crittle, and Allison Climo. It, too, will eventually be archived at the Murray Center, making it accessible to other investigators.

There are so few studies that have done this kind of longitudinal follow-up with college-educated women that Kathleen Hulbert and Diane Schuster were able to gather them all into a single book: *Women's Lives Through Time* (1993). Their opening and closing chapters for that book make clear the unique contributions that such longitudinal studies can make to understanding educated women's lives.

The limitations of class and race that these studies share is significant, however, and must be addressed. Toward that end, Martha Mednick, Veronica Thomas and I have launched a new longitudinal study at Howard University, with the assistance of Debbie Wade, Hester Hicks, Askhari Hodari, Deborah Mangold, Judith Lee, and Stephanie Hayes. This is a study of African American women who graduated with Bachelor's degrees between 1958 and 1968. It is hoped that the Howard University Women's Life Paths Study will begin to fill some of the enormous gaps in knowledge that exist regarding the lives of educated African American women. Other studies are clearly needed to fill other gaps.

SEXUAL HARASSMENT

The second area of my work that I believe has had a significant impact is the study of sexual harassment in the federal workforce that I did with Martha R. Burt and Leanor B. Johnson. It was, I have to say, a tremendous opportunity. The U.S. Merit Systems Protection Board (USMSPB)—watchdog of the civil service—was charged by Congress to find out whether sexual harassment was a problem in the federal workforce, for whom, to what extent, in what manner, and with what consequences. At the time, it was the first comprehensive study of sexual harassment in a national representative sample of any size, and it presented many conceptual and methodological challenges (Tangri, Burt, & Johnson, 1985).

We were able to establish for the first time a reasonable estimate of the incidence and prevalence of sexual harassment in a large, complex workforce across the country. A subsequent study of the same workforce done a few years later found (unfortunately) nearly identical incidence rates, i.e., 42% of the women (and 15% of the men) reported experiencing sexual harassment at their government jobs during the preceding 24 months (USMSPB, 1981). The list of behaviors that we asked respondents to identify as unacceptable and as harassment has been used by many researchers since, as is the important distinction between co-worker and supervisor as the source of harassment. These and other aspects of that survey influenced much subsequent research, but the finding that probably most influenced organizations to take sexual harassment as a serious personnel problem was the estimate of the cost to the employer (the U.S. Government): $189 million in just a two-year period. That cost, plus the favorable turn in court decisions, were strong motivators for organizational change.

The theoretical article that we published in *The Journal of Social Issues*, edited by Marilyn Brewer and Richard Berk, developed a threefold classification of theories that has also been used by subsequent researchers: We organized the available literature on the causes of sexual harassment into three models: Natural/Biological Models, Organizational Models, and Socio-Cultural Models. We also used the USMSPB data to test, insofar as possible, predictions derived from each of the three models (Tangri, Burt, & Johnson, 1982). The theoretical framework is currently being updated (Tangri & Hayes, in press).

A FEMINIST ANALYSIS OF POPULATION PROGRAMS AND NEW REPRODUCTIVE TECHNOLOGIES

The third piece of work that has had some impact is the theoretical work using feminist principles to raise and evaluate ethical issues in population programs, and in new reproductive technologies. The former (Tangri, 1974) was given a Distinguished Publication Award by the Association for Women in Psychology, and the latter was an invited address to that Association in 1987, co-authored by Janet Kahn and later published (Tangri & Kahn, 1993). It is harder to evaluate this contribution because it was, and remains, more controversial even within feminist circles than any other work I've done.

An interesting sidelight to the first article is that it began as an invited commentary on a paper given in 1973 by Robert P. Lapham at a national conference on the Ethics of Intervention. Lapham's paper did a very good job presenting the "standard" ethical concerns raised by population programs, and I did not feel that there was much to critique. So I used my time to present another, feminist, set of concerns about population programs. The major points I made had to do with the importance of women's participating in the process of designing and implementing programs directed at women, of giving priority to women's ability to control what happens to their own bodies, and the centrality of childbearing to women's status in many developing nations (the site of most such programs). I also argued that such programs should reduce barriers to other avenues (e.g., education, employment) for women to attain the social standing that would be lost by reduced childbearing.

One of the criticisms directed at the article was that it presumed to impose Western feminist perspectives on women in other parts of the world (Germain, 1977; Tangri, 1977). When the edited proceedings of that conference were finally published in book form (long after *Signs* had published the original), the editors' commentary used my paper as a "useful foil" for excoriating "a unidimensional ethical scheme" (Bermant, Kelman, & Warwick, 1978, p. 400). So, it is extremely gratifying for me to note that the recent World Population Conference held in Cairo trumpeted as a central and unifying theme the importance of "empowering women" as necessary to the success of any population program.

There continues to be even greater division of opinion among feminists regarding the new reproductive technologies, both about whether and which ones are "good" for women, and about what policies should be created to regulate them. It was quite difficult to get this paper (Tangri & Kahn, 1993) published. Perhaps because the publication is so recent, it is not yet clear to me that it has entered the active forum of discussion on these issues. Yet, I think its contribution lies in the difficult attempt to weigh commonly accepted but competing feminist principles, such as a *woman's right to control her own body* (which emphasizes women's autonomy) and *non-objectification and non-commodification of human beings*, as they apply to these technologies, and especially as they apply to contractual ("surrogate") motherhood. Many of the same arguments appear in feminist discussions of prostitution and pornography.

One of the useful concepts we introduced in this article was the distinction between the ethics *of* these technologies, and the ethics *in* using these technologies. The "ethics of" refers to *whether* these technologies should be used. The "ethics in" refers to *how* they should be used if they are not going to be outlawed (i.e., given the current lack of federal policy forbidding these practices, what precautions, safety measures, and protections for the parties involved should be implemented by State and local governments). Depending on which of these levels (*ethics of; ethics in*) one focusses on, one or the other of several feminist principles appear more relevant.

The paper argues that commercial contracts for producing children (i.e., for a fee) constitute baby-selling and should be illegal. However, consenting responsible adults should be free to create many kinds of families, sharing among themselves the financial and caregiving roles as they see fit, and to which they have both obligations and rights which do not override the rights and obligations of any other members. The prospect of having to maintain ongoing relationships when that is the desire of any member, should slow the impulse to create babies "on demand."

The paper also addresses the ethical responsibilities of psychologists who are called on to evaluate parties contracting for children, or testify on behalf of parties contesting custody of children that result from such contracts. Psychologists are cautioned to respect diversity of parenting styles and not make class-biased comparisons between parties contending for custody (since the contractual mother is usually considerably less well off than the contracting father); to respect mothers' rights to custody of their children in the absence of proven neglect or harm to those children; and to forego income opportunities that require them to violate these or other ethical principles laid out by the American Psychological Association.

Contractual parenting has not been nationally outlawed in this country (as it has in most European countries), and states have varied in their attention to the issue. However, the notoriety of contracts that have failed (as in the Baby M case) and court decisions to uphold in various degrees the rights of contractual mothers, appear to have slowed the traffic in commercial contracts. However, feminists should be alert to the possibility that this activity has simply gone underground, or overseas.

I think there are no parts of my life that have not been affected by feminism, by feminists, and by resistance to feminism. It has certainly been the major force directing my research and teaching. As I turn to tomorrow's questions about women and aging, gender and ethnicity, the questions I ask, the conceptual frameworks behind my questions, and my methods of inquiry will all be influenced by a feminist consciousness, and by a consciousness still being shaped by the experiences of a white woman working in an historically Black university (Tangri, in press).

REFERENCES

Bermant, G., Kelman, H., & Warwick, H. (Eds.). (1978). *The ethics of social intervention.* Washington, DC.: Hemisphere Press.

Germain, A. (1977). On "Women and population studies" and "A feminist perspective on some ethical issues in population programs." *Signs, 2*(4), 924-927.

Gurin, G. (1971). *A study of students in a multiversity.* Final Report, The University of Michigan, Contract No. OE-6-10-034, Office of Education.

Hitchcock, J. L. (1984). *Emotional adaptation to life changes in a post-World War II Cohort of College-Educated Women.* Unpublished doctoral dissertation, Harvard University.

Hulbert, K. D., & Schuster, D. T. (Eds.). (1993). *Women's lives through time. Educated American Women of the twentieth century.* San Francisco: Jossey-Bass.

Jenkins, S. R. (1982). *Person-situation interaction and women's achievement-related motives.* Unpublished doctoral dissertation, Boston University.

Jenkins, S. R. (1987). Need for achievement and women's careers over 14 years: Evidence for occupational structure effects. *Journal of Personality and Social Psychology, 53,* 922-932.

Jenkins, S. R. (1989). Longitudinal prediction of women's career choices: Psychological, behavioral, and social-structural influences. *Journal of Vocational Behavior, 34,* 204-235.

Jenkins, S. R. (in press a). Need for power and women's careers over 14 years: Structural power, job satisfaction, and motive change. *Journal of Personality and Social Psychology.*

Jenkins, S. R. (in press b). Structural power and experienced job satisfaction: The empowerment paradox for women. *Sex Roles.*

Mednick, M., & Tangri, S. (Eds.). (1972). *New Perspectives on Women.* Special Issue of *The Journal of Social Issues, 28*(2).

Ruggiero, J. A., & Weston, L. C. (1988). Work involvement among college-educated women: A methodological extension. *Sex Roles, 19,* 491-507.

Tangri, S. S. (1969). *Role-innovation in occupational choice among college women.* Unpublished doctoral dissertation, The University of Michigan.

Tangri, S. S. (1972). Determinants of occupational role innovation among college women. *Journal of Social Issues, 28*(2), 177-200.

Tangri, S. S. (1974). A feminist perspective on the ethical issues in population programs. *Signs, 1*(4), 895-904; Revised in G. Bermant, H. Kelman, & D. Warwick (Eds.) (1978), *The ethics of social intervention.* Washington, DC: Hemisphere Press (pp. 363-374).

Tangri, S. S. (1977). Reply to Adrienne Germain's Comments on "A Feminist Perspective on Some Ethical Issues in Population Programs" (vol. 1, no. 4). *Signs, 3* (2), 523.

Tangri, S. S. (in press). Living with anomalies. In F. Crosby & K. Wyche (Eds.), *Women's ethnicities: Journeys through Psychology.* Westview Press.

Tangri, S. S., Burt, M. R., & Johnson, L. B. (1982). Sexual harassment at work: Three explanatory models. *The Journal of Social Issues, 38* (4), 33-54.

Tangri, S. S., Burt, M. R., & Johnson, L. B. (1985). Sexual harassment in the U.S. Federal Work Force. In M. Safir, M. T. Mednick, D. Israeli, & J. Bernard (Eds.), *Women's worlds. From the new scholarship.* NY: Praeger (pp. 152-163).

Tangri, S. S., & Hayes, S. M. (in press). Theories of sexual harassment. In W. O'Donohue (Ed.), *Sexual harassment: Theory, Research and Treatment.* Allyn & Bacon.

Tangri, S. S., & Jenkins, S. R. (1986). Stability and change in role innovation and life plans. *Sex Roles, 14,* 647-662.

Tangri, S. S., & Jenkins, S. R. (1993). The Women's Life Paths Study: The Michigan graduates of 1967. In D. T. Schuster & I. D. Hulbert (Eds.), *Women's lives through time: Educated American women of the twentieth century.* San Francisco: Jossey-Bass.

Tangri, S. S., & Kahn, J. (1993). Ethical issues in the new reproductive technologies: Perspectives from feminism and the psychology profession. *Professional Psychology, 24* (3), 271-280.

U. S. Merit Systems Protection Board (USMSPB), (1981). *Sexual harassment in the Federal workforce: Is it a problem?* Washington, DC: U.S. Government Printing Office.

The Transmogrification
of a Feminist Foremother

Lenore E. A. Walker

When I was 30 years old, in 1973, less than one year after I received my doctorate in psychology from Rutgers, my husband served me with divorce papers that accused me of having been transmogrified by the women's movement. Although it would be nice to rewrite history and claim that this marriage ended like thousands of other graduate school failures, in fact, its demise started at its beginning back in 1962 when I was 19 years old, a recent graduate from Hunter College, and was following the nice Jewish girl from the Bronx script of getting a college degree, a husband, and a teacher's license (just as insurance, in case something happened to the husband). Obviously, the divorce was not a shock; in fact, I had tried several times previously to unsuccessfully end the marriage over the years, and had my own attorney preparing papers which served as the counter-suit that eventually prevailed. But, in

Lenore E. A. Walker, EdD, is a licensed psychologist in independent practice with Walker & Associates in Denver, Colorado, Executive Director of the Domestic Violence Institute, and CEO of Endolor Communications. An international lecturer and author who trains at the invitation of governments, private groups and world health organizations, she has done research, clinical intervention, training and expert witness testimony on the impact of abuse on survivors.

Correspondence may be addressed to Lenore E. A. Walker at Walker & Associates, 50 S. Steele Street, Suite 850, Denver, CO 80209.

[Haworth co-indexing entry note]: "The Transmogrification of a Feminist Foremother." Walker, Lenore E. A. Co-published simultaneously in Women & Therapy (The Haworth Press, Inc.) Vol. 17, No. 3/4, 1995, pp. 517-529; and: Feminist Foremothers in Women's Studies, Psychology, and Mental Health (ed: Phyllis Chesler, Esther D. Rothblum, and Ellen Cole) The Haworth Press, Inc., 1995, pp. 517-529; and: Feminist Foremothers in Women's Studies, Psychology, and Mental Health (ed: Phyllis Chesler, Esther D. Rothblum, and Ellen Cole) Harrington Park Press, an imprint of The Haworth Press, Inc., 1995, pp. 517-529. Single or multiple copies of this article are available from The Haworth Document Delivery Service [1-800-342-9678, 9:00 a.m. - 5:00 p.m. (EST)].

517

those days, in New Jersey, divorces were granted and property distributed on the basis of whose fault it was that the marriage failed. What could be better than to blame my feminist activities at the time?

When I finally got a chance to look up the word "transmogrify" in the dictionary, I found that it meant to go in one way and come out another way. What transmogrified you seemed to be a distinct secret, like some mysterious alien forces taking over your mind and maybe, even body. However, my parents said at the time that becoming a feminist was no surprise or mystery. Family stories about my curiosity and independence have been told and retold at the traditional family gatherings. My willingness to explore new places and sense of drama and excitement in the retelling always brought me a crowd of friends willing to find new adventures with me. I remember being about 10 years old and finding a cache of sex manuals in my parent's bedroom. I quickly read them and, recognizing I had newfound knowledge, I began to share them with my friends who promptly crowned me queen of sex education on the block. I probably sealed my fate as a psychologist and teacher then, although I didn't know it at the time.

Graduate school during the late 1960s and early 1970s was an exciting time. I had missed most of the civil rights activism by sitting on the sidelines cheering while rocking my babies to sleep. Although I still worked part-time and finished my master's degree during the ten years between my bachelor's and doctoral degrees, this was certainly more outside activity than most moms took on in those days. Day care was non-existent and I made do with a live-in housekeeper and nursery school to supplement on several mornings a week. Demonstrating in Alabama was not a possibility although my heart and soul were down there fighting for freedom. So, when the women's movement hit New York City and then came to suburban New Jersey, it was no transmogrification to find me leading my contemporaries once again. The accusation only proved my point that my husband never really knew me. In all fairness, perhaps I was very good at adopting the outer shell women were supposed to wear in those days and he wasn't supposed to know what was inside.

Closer to home it was not difficult to fight for women's rights especially with two small children for whom I wanted the world to be better. I quickly joined our local NOW chapter, engaged in a consciousness-raising group which I found more meaningful than years of traditional therapy training, and began making changes in my own already non-traditional lifestyle. We demanded and won the right for women to control their reproductive functions including the right to choose a safe and legal abortion as well as demanding the removal of the stigmatizing concept of one "head-of-household" on the standard government census forms. History tells us about the difficulty of these struggles. In my own family, my son still reminds me that I would not let him play on a little league team because they would not let girls in . . .

On the professional side, I also became an active member of New Jersey Women's Equity Action League (WEAL) which fought for legal rights for women and girls. Insisting on equal access for women and girls to money through credit in our own names, elimination of sex discrimination in the schools and in sports, and equal pay for equal work in the corporations and universities around the country, our chapter worked hard on formulating the rules for implementing the 1972 Education Act that specified such educational changes. Now Supreme Court Justice Ruth Bader Ginsburg was an active member using her Rutger's Law School professorship to help women gain access to their fundamental legal rights. At Rutgers we organized a review of our professor's salaries and demanded both immediate remediation, helping dozens of women professors to be promoted and gain back salaries. Little did I know that I, too, would benefit from our demands for affirmative action when I was hired after graduation to be one of five women professors on the medical school psychiatry faculty of thirty-eight!

My activist work with women and girls in education became a part of my professional responsibilities when I became a director of the educational outreach programs for the community mental health center that was part of our psychiatry department. Negotiating with school superintendents all over the state was a regular part of my work activities to help change structures and provide programs to prevent mental health problems from developing in children. Mental health prevention work was at its heyday in the mid 1970s and adding opportunities for equality for women and girls along with other minorities was the way we were expanding its frontiers. Although I worked with some of these programs in the schools in New York City in the 1960s before I moved to New Jersey, and researched their effectiveness in my doctoral dissertation, coming from the prestigious medical school made their acceptance more legitimate in the schools at that time. It seemed like we were finally going to turn this world around; achieve the goals of civil rights for all people, paying attention to gender as well as all forms of diversity.

Simultaneously, I was working with already identified mentally disturbed children and training other psychologists to identify high-risk children who might benefit from extra programs to prevent even more serious mental health problems from developing. In the early and mid 1970s the issue of physical child abuse and emotional maltreatment and neglect were being highlighted once again. The medical school was dealing with identification of these children and their parents. In case conference after case conference, I sat and listened to the mostly male professionals blame mothers for either inflicting terrible harm or permitting it to be inflicted on their children. It seemed as if the worst sin a woman could commit was to stand by and permit her child to be hurt. Psychoanalytic explanations were rampant in those days (it doesn't seem so different today when a mother does the unspeakable and kills her child) and mothers were blamed for everything bad that happened. Either she didn't pay enough attention to the child (unattached) or she paid too much attention (smothering) to the child. Being in the process of raising two children and having familiarity with lots of moms coupled together with my feminist perspective, I knew that these explanations were simply wrong, as wrong as I believed Freud's attitudes towards women were even before we truly understood how he sold us out for his male collegial affiliation needs. So, I set about trying to figure out what was really going on.

By 1973, a review had appeared in *Ms.* Magazine of Erin Pizzey's book, *Scream Quietly or the Neighbors Will Hear*, that was published in London in 1972. She described the phenomenon of battered women who flocked to her recently-opened shelter for women who needed a place to come and talk to other women. The housing situation in England at that time was difficult; to get new housing, a woman and children might have to wait as long as a year or more on a council list. So, women couldn't leave home easily for the same reason battered women still can't leave home easily, but with the added problems of suitable housing. Pizzey wrote poignantly about the problems of family violence and it captured my mind and heart. Of course, women couldn't protect their children adequately if they, too, were being abused by the same man. And, of course, women were not going to be able to take their equal place in a hostile society, if they were not safe at home either. Perhaps the psychological effects from being battered were responsible for many of the mental health problems in some women, but also served to keep other uppity women in their place because we would know that it could happen to us, too! Rapists are the shock troops that keep women in monogamous relationships, said Susan Brownmiller, while Ann Jones took her analogy one step further and claimed that batterers were the home guard, keeping women in their homes.

The rest of the story seems *beschert,* or like fate just carried it all along. I began to collect stories of women who were battered because when I went to the literature, there were only a few unhelpful articles that still accused women of being masochists, and other explanations that simply discounted women's experiences in a world filled with oppression and discrimination. Lest you think this attitude has been put to rest by compelling data collected over the last twenty years, I would suggest you read the literature carefully; women-blaming shows up in overt terms when society refuses to deal with violence against women and children and in more subtle ways when it is trying to be fair! When the data became so compelling so that no respectable psychologist could refute that our psyches have been molded by men's abusive behavior, they then attack our memories–after all the abuse simply cannot be true, or our defensive behavior by claiming we hit men just as often as they hit us. If this sounds familiar, like what I learned when I first went to the literature to read about woman-abuse, it is the same victim-blaming, "I didn't do it," and "she asked for it" mentality that prompted Freud's own back-tracking at the end of the last century to create his "wish-fulfillment" substitution. However, after twenty years of research, teaching, training, clinical and forensic work with thousands and thousands of battered women, these women do not make up their stories, they do not want to be hurt, and they do not "ask for it" by their behavior, however obnoxious they might act. Rather, every battered woman I have met simply wants the abuse to stop!

Back in those days, at Rutgers, I was fortunate to have a joint appointment on the psychology faculty as well as on the psychiatry faculty in the medical school, so research was encouraged. I went to a faculty meeting and asked my colleagues if any of them had any battered women in their client population whom I could interview for my new research project. Blank stares faced me. Not one to be discouraged, I went on and asked if anyone had a client who had been hit or otherwise hurt by her husband. Now, I got a response. Soon I was interviewing women who told tales of being abused but never telling anyone about it. They tried to tell family who were unhelpful, the police, if called, often sided and joked with the man making the women feel invalidated, physicians weren't interested in knowing where the bruises came from, and their therapists asked them what they did to make the man so angry. Story after story seemed so similar, I thought these women surely must know each other. I traveled to England and met with Erin Pizzey, visited the various shelters there at the time, and came home believing that unless women truly felt physically safe from further abuse, they would not talk about their abuse. However, helping battered women leave abusive relationships did not turn out to be as simple as setting up a shelter in their community. Rather, we have learned in these past twenty years, that leaving does not stop the violence. The abuse may escalate to life-threatening proportions after the woman and children leave. Stalking, harassing, and continuing the power and control that men who batter women abuse, keep the woman terrified long after she may have physically left the relationship.

Psychotherapy is important for some battered women but most really need support, safety, protection from further abuse, and access to independent living.

As I continued my research, after meeting my second husband, psychologist Mort Flax, and moving to Denver, we focused on working with couples to try to help them stop the abuse. Although we had some limited success when we were co-therapists and each had the man and woman in individual therapy first, the work was long, arduous, and we were only able to slow down the cycle of violence, not stop it. Battered women lose the ability to perceive objectivity and neutrality, a must in good couples therapy. Rather, the woman believes that you are either with her or against her, and if you do not show her some signs of validation and advocacy, then she perceives you as someone who can cause her more harm. Abusive men in couples therapy do not learn to take responsibility for their violent behavior and continue to blame the women for their part of the interaction. From this work as well as other work has come the admonition that couples therapy is an inappropriate first step in the treatment process and offender-specific therapy, usually in groups with other abusive men, seems to have the best results in helping men stop their abusive behavior.

The National Institute of Mental Health funded research project on measuring the psychological effects of battering and the theories occupied much of my time after my second husband's death, from 1978 to 1981 when we finally analyzed the wonderful data that we collected from over 400 self-referred, self-identified battered women. From that project as well as the rest of my work, it became clear to me that the psychological toll of battering on women was a high price for all of us to pay whether or not we were physically or sexually abused ourselves. Certainly most women can identify times of serious psychological abuse where we were terrified we would be further hurt and so we backed down, becoming *good girls* again. Ken Pope's data suggests that over 60% of women therapists can identify with having been abused or sexually harassed and if we broaden the definitions, most of us have been there even if it is the fear of a real potential for abuse that keeps us from going out to a movie at night or limits our ambition because we don't want to deal with all the hassles. So, I decided, along with a number of others, some of whom have also told their stories in these tales from our foremothers collection, to form the *Feminist Therapy Institute*, to provide a supportive professional home for those of us who needed to find like-minded souls doing the same kind of trail-blazing work in therapy. I also helped put together a feminist therapy peer support group in Denver that has met once a month since 1981. Without these friendships I do not believe I could have continued this difficult but very rewarding work.

When I first named the *Battered Woman Syndrome* in 1976, I simply substituted "woman" for "child" in the well-accepted *Battered Child Syndrome* that had led me to this research. Remembering the earlier studies of Martin Seligman and his dogs who developed learned helplessness from exposure to non-escapable random and variable aversive stimulation, I hypothesized that battered women may also have lost their ability to predict that what they did would protect themselves from further harm if they perceived the abuse as non-escapable, random and variable punishment. I liked this theory because it explained how women could function so well in one setting and be so ineffective at home in stopping the violence. It also helped explain why women didn't leave; they developed coping strategies that helped them minimize the pain and danger from the abuse at the cost of escape skills. And, the cycle of violence that came through in the women's stories provided the reinforcement for this learning theory model. These men were not always abusive. Rather, they behaved in a three-phase cycle that began with tension-building and moved into the second phase of the acute battering incident, followed by the reinforcer, the kind, loving-contrition. Later research into the third phase found that sometimes the loving behavior dropped out and the absence of tension became reinforcing and in other cases, the dangerous perception of continuous potential for violence was always present providing a situation that could result in homicide, suicide, or serious harm to anyone in that home.

Today, we know much more about the Battered Woman Syndrome (BWS). The psychological research has placed it as a subcategory of Post Traumatic Stress Disorder (PTSD). We know that many battered women develop psychological symptoms as coping strategies that my earlier work measured as learned helplessness strategies. While the high arousal and high avoidance and numbing behaviors may be adaptive in surviving abusive relationships, they are not useful once the woman has escaped. For some women, together with the memory and other cognitive changes, psychotherapy is a necessity to help them heal and get on with their lives. Despite the claims of a few cognitive psychologists who do not believe the overwhelming clinical data from abuse victims, we therapists know that the abuse needs to be talked about, the frightening emotions dealt with in a safe place, and then, integrated into the woman's life experience. It is not feminism that puts these ideas in our client's minds; it is the abuse from men that harms them. Much like my first husband thought I was being transmogrified when he was unable to see that I was only working towards my potential, so, too, does a disbelieving public want to believe that women are responsible for their own fates. Alan Dershowitz's newest claims of all this evidence simply being an *abuse excuse* parallels the minds of many who have not been able to accept the negative underside of male-female relationships.

Several years after I began my research and clinical work with battered women, I gave my first expert witness testimony in a murder trial of a woman who had killed her husband in what she, I and her lawyer believed was self-defense. So did the jury, acquitting her after a short deliberation. How I got to become a forensic psychologist was simply following another opportunity on an uncharted life journey. I was giving a speech in Seattle with over 500 people in the audience including those from the press. Suddenly a question came from a woman in the group who insisted that most of my solutions to the problem of woman abuse were long-term societal change. Many women were being killed every day by unstopped abuse and she thought I should do something about it immediately. Among other alternatives, I suggested that if a battered woman was in danger of being killed by her abusive partner, she should have the right to kill him in self-defense and I would help provide such a defense for her. Obviously, I had been living in the west too long by then! I forgot that the media wire service reporters were listening and the next morning the news headline screamed, "Noted Psychologist Will Defend Women Who Kill Abusive Husbands." By the time I got home to Denver I had my first case in Billings, Montana where the people did believe in old fashioned western self-defense! Although I did confess to Timer Moses, the attorney who called, that I had only been in a courtroom twice before, once to answer a traffic ticket and once for my divorce (I didn't tell him about the transmogrification claims), he assured me that if I could teach him everything I knew about the psychology of battered women he would teach me how to testify as an expert witness in a legal proceeding. It was a bargain I have never regretted!

The rest is history. I have now testified in approximately 350 cases where a battered woman has killed her husband in what she claims is self-defense. It was never intended to be used as another form of mental illness for a diminished capacity or insanity defense (although in some cases the battering may well have created a psychotic state of mind for the woman). Rather it was seen as a way to explain and justify behavior that appeared to be in direct contradiction to our male images of self-defense, since most women killed during a moment of quiet, when he was sleeping after a beating leaving her with threats and intrusive memories of more to come, or before he started, anticipating the danger that lay ahead from the memories of past beatings. Legal decisions and legislation all over the country now permit testimony on BWS (which they define as including the dynamics of a battering relationship as well as the psychological effects) but the battle over admissibility was fierce.

Unlike expert testimony in child sexual abuse cases, which was given by many different experts with both good and not-so-good data, BWS testimony has mostly been limited to a half dozen psychologists during those five or six years when admissibility issues were being fought. Lawyers like to say that bad cases make bad law, a truism that I, too, have found. However, today the field is well enough established so that we can continue to push-the-edges and adapt BWS to other cases where a trauma victim attempts to use force to defend him or herself. The now famous case of the Menendez brothers in Los Angeles which highlighted the plight of abused children who kill one or both parents; Lorena Bobbitt who cut off the offending penis rather than kill the entire man; mothers who fail to protect their children from sexual abuse or murder; women who commit property crimes upon duress from the batterer who threatens more abuse if she does not bring him the money; these cases and others all use components of a BWS defense. And versions of the BWS and PTSD are used to help women win financial compensation for the harm that exposure to abuse and hostile work atmospheres have caused them.

Applying psychology to help resolve legal issues has been an interesting and exciting part of my career. It felt like a merger of those values and actions I had begun and fine-tuned all my life. The courtroom is a great classroom, especially for those with a great sense of drama in the retelling of knowledge that everyone wants to hear about, just like on the streets of the southwest Bronx where I first started sharing sex information with my wannabe friends. It provides an opportunity to blend psychological truth and science together with legal advocacy that then gets media attention to deliver the message to the entire community and sometimes beyond. Although my feminist perspective used to get laughed at by opposing attorneys, the mood of the country makes that a foolish tactic for them to take anymore as it only alienates most of the women and some of the men on the jury. Rather, the subject of domestic violence is taken very seriously, testimony of psychologists who use a combination of scientific research and clinical wisdom are respected, and the question remains for the jury to resolve if that particular person really was acting on a reasonable perception of imminent (not immediate) harm.

In conclusion, even if my then husband was right, I wasn't totally transmogrified by the women's movement. As a good girl, I listened faithfully to my own professor's advice, particularly Virginia Staudt-Sexton and Jack Bardon, who told us that good scientist-practitioners or practitioner-scientists write and publish what they know. So, by 1979 my first book, *The Battered Woman*, was published and the reference list gives a highlight of some of the other books and articles that followed and will give you further information about my work. It's probably no accident that my daughter is studying for her Ph.D. in psychology and my son is now an attorney. Our lives were organized both by choice and by necessity around mom's work. We are in the mid 1990s now and high technology goes beyond publishing books. Television talk shows, high publicity forensic cases, media interviews, volunteer committee work for APA and other psychology organizations, and now, videos for home viewing, all help disseminate the psychological knowledge about battered women and their families. My own plans for the future include continuing to develop my new publishing company, Endolor Communications, which creates materials for training as well as further internationalizing the Domestic Violence Institute so that the feminist and trauma-based models of *Survivor*

Therapy can be used in clinical, forensic and other community applications to help stop domestic violence in my lifetime.

SELECTED BIBLIOGRAPHY

Walker, L.E.A. (1979). *The battered woman.* New York: Harper & Row.

Walker, L.E.A. (1984). *Battered woman syndrome.* New York: Springer.

Walker, L.E.A. (1984). *Women and mental health policy.* Beverly Hills: Sage.

Walker, L.E.A. (1985). Feminist therapy with victims/survivors of interpersonal violence. In L. B. Rosewater & L. E. Walker (Eds.) (1985). *Handbook on feminist therapy: Psychotherapy for women* (203-215). New York: Springer.

Walker, L.E.A. (1987). Inadequacies of the Masochistic Personality Disorder diagnosis for women. *Journal of Personality Disorders, 1,* 183-185.

Walker, L.E.A. (Ed.). (1988). *Handbook on sexual abuse of children.* New York: Springer.

Walker, L.E.A. (1989). *Terrifying Love: Why battered women kill and how society responds.* New York: Harper/Collins.

Walker, L.E.A. (1989). Psychology and violence against women. *American Psychologist, 44,* 695-702.

Walker, L.E.A. (1989). When the battered woman becomes the defendant. In E. Viano (Ed.). *Crime and its victims: International research and public policy.* Proceedings of the Fourth International Institute on Victimology, NATO Advanced Research Workshop, Il Ciocco, Tuscany, Italy (pp. 57-70). New York: Hemisphere Publishing.

Walker, L.E.A. (1990). Psychological assessment of sexually abused children for legal evaluation and expert witness testimony. *Professional Psychology: Research and Practice, 21*(5), 344-353.

Walker, L.E.A. (1991). Post-Traumatic Stress Disorder in women: Diagnosis and treatment of Battered Woman Syndrome. *Psychotherapy, 28* (1), 21-29.

Walker, L.E.A. (1992). Battered woman syndrome and self defense. *Notre Dame Journal of Law, Ethics, and Public Policy, 6,* 321-334.

Walker, L.E.A. (1993). *Survivor Therapy: Clinical assessment and intervention workbook.* Denver, CO: Endolor Communications.

Walker, L.E.A. (1994). *Abused women and Survivor Therapy: A practical guide for the psychotherapist.* Washington, D.C.: American Psychological Association.

Walker, L.E.A. (1994). *Survivor Therapy.* Video Series on Assessment and treatment in psychotherapy. New York: Newbridge Communications.

Walker, L.E.A. (1994). Are personality disorders gender biased? Yes. In S. A. Kirk & S. D. Einbinder (Eds.) *Controversial Issues in Mental Health* (pp. 21-30). Boston: Allyn & Bacon.

Walker, L.E.A., & Browne, A. (1985). Gender and victimization by intimates. *Journal of Personality, 53,* 179-195.

Walker, L.E.A., & Corriere, S. (1991). Domestic violence: International perspectives on social change. In E. Viano (Ed.) *Victims' rights and legal reforms: International perspectives. Proceedings of the Sixth International Institute on Victimology (1990). Onati Proceedings, #9* (135-150). Onati, Spain: University of Onati Institute on Sociology and the Law.

Walker, L.E.A., & Dutton-Douglas, M.A. (1988). Future directions: Development, application and training of feminist therapists. In M.A. Dutton & L.E.A. Walker (Eds.) *Feminist psychotherapies: Integration of therapeutic and feminist systems* (pp. 276-300). Norwood, NJ: Ablex.

Walker, L.E.A., & Edwall, G.E. (1987). Domestic violence and determination of custody and visitation. Chapter in D.J. Sonkin (Ed.) *Domestic violence on trial* (pp. 127-152). New York: Springer.

Walker, L.E.A., & Levant, R. (1993). Gender Dialogue. *The Independent Practitioner, 13.*

Walker, L.E.A., & Sonkin, D.J. (in press). *Empowerment for Victims and Stabilization Programs for Domestic Violence Perpetrators.* Denver, CO: Endolor Communications.

An Unlikely Radical

Elizabeth Friar Williams

I was born in 1931, in Buffalo, the first child and only daughter in an upper-middle-class assimilated Jewish family unlikely to produce any revolutionaries. My father's ancestors came from Holland in 1848. A legal and classical language scholar, he was the youngest child of a successful tobacco plantation owner and wholesaler, who became a banker and an influence in Buffalo "society." My father was a very handsome man, mild-mannered, and intellectual. He remained a distant figure to all three children, never taking us anywhere or playing with us. He really was trained by his longtime Scottish nanny to be a Jesuit priest, and that's exactly what he was like: intellectual, repressed, gentle, and not quite of the earthly world.

My mother's background was, if anything, even more idiosyn-

Elizabeth Friar Williams practiced feminist therapy in New York City from 1969 to 1986, when she moved to San Francisco. She was Spokesperson for the Association for Women in Psychology from 1991-1994 and is a member of the Feminist Therapy Institute and APA, Div. 35. Among the courses she has taught to undergraduate and graduate psychology and education students since 1962 was, most recently, Child and Adolescent Psychotherapy from a Feminist Perspective at New College of San Francisco. A longtime freelance writer and editor, she leads workshops for clinicians and educators on how to write for the general public and is a partner in a self-publishing firm.

Correspondence may be addressed to Elizabeth Friar Williams at 204 22nd Avenue, San Francisco, CA 94121.

[Haworth co-indexing entry note]: "An Unlikely Radical." Williams, Elizabeth Friar. Co-published simultaneously in *Women & Therapy* (The Haworth Press, Inc.) Vol. 17, No. 3/4, 1995, pp. 531-541; and: *Feminist Foremothers in Women's Studies, Psychology, and Mental Health* (ed: Phyllis Chesler, Esther D. Rothblum, and Ellen Cole) The Haworth Press, Inc., 1995, pp. 531-541; and: *Feminist Foremothers in Women's Studies, Psychology, and Mental Health* (ed: Phyllis Chesler, Esther D. Rothblum, and Ellen Cole) Harrington Park Press, an imprint of The Haworth Press, Inc., 1995, pp. 531-541. Single or multiple copies of this article are available from The Haworth Document Delivery Service [1-800-342-9678, 9:00 a.m. - 5:00 p.m. (EST)].

cratic. She was an attorney, the only woman in her Stanford Law School class of 1926 and the only woman to take the bar exam that year in California. She might have been a positive role-model for me, but she was a love-starved child, having lost her father to pneumonia in 1905, when she was 2. Her mother, whose ancestors were Hungarian and German Jews, was an abusive, paranoid, critical person who had a hard life as a young widow. She earned her living as a lace dealer, traveling by boat to buy laces in Belgium several times a year. She took my mother with her, forcing her to entertain the passengers by showing off her skills as a child-prodigy at the piano even though my mother suffered severely from sea-sickness. My mother never went to elementary school, but was tutored in Europe during her mother's visits there. Nonetheless, she graduated with honors from a girls' Catholic high school at fifteen, and, from Mills College in Oakland with a Phi Beta Kappa key, at 17.

My grandmother re-married, in San Francisco, when my mother was 14 and had a second daughter 17 years younger than my mother. As a parent, herself, my mother's particular problems took the form of intense competition with me (as a stand-in for her sister, by whom she felt very threatened), hyper-vigilance, complete emotional unavailability, criticality, and an inability to empathize. She lied to get what she wanted from everyone, including her children, a characteristic she learned from her own manipulative and psychopathic mother.

Because of my mother's intelligence, assertiveness, and a dogmatism that brooked no rational discussion, it was impossible for me, as a child, to contradict her, or assert my rights. I was afraid of her anger and her lack of integrity, and disappointed that my father, who was also probably afraid of her, was unable or uninterested in helping out with the emotional abuse and injustice that I suffered from her.

At 18, before my sophomore year at Vassar, I became pregnant by a man who wanted to marry me and rather than have an illegal abortion, which frightened me (but which my mother encouraged in order to hide my early sexual activity) I married him and lived with him in Buffalo for a couple of years. While having the baby set me apart totally from the other late adolescent girls in my social group, it was a healthy experience for me. My son was the person who made me feel most loved and integrated. This is hard to explain, but from that time on I felt like an adequate personality, competent enough to face whatever difficulties life had in store for me, which turned out to be a lot.

When my son was about two, I left that marriage and moved back to my parents' house with my son. I lived with them so that I could attend the local university as a day student. My parents were glad to pay the minimal tuition because they were terrified (as they frequently reminded me) that I would be their dependent for the rest of their lives. There were many painful scenes relevant to that fear in my early adulthood. One, particularly unforgettable, took place at Yale the day of the graduation of one of my brothers. My young son, then 5, and my parents and I were walking on the campus–I had already moved to New York–when my father turned to me and viciously, without provocation, said, "Don't you ever come back to Buffalo to disgrace us or try to get anything from us. If you do I'll have you put in an insane asylum." Since my parents were both lawyers who knew many judges in Buffalo, I thought that legal commitment was entirely possible. But I never would have gone home to them again, anyway, and was mystified at my father's suggestion that I might and stunned by his uncharacteristic loss of temper. I was also disturbed at the emotional impotence his words implied. Was my father that frightened of me, and so unable to deal with the problems I apparently presented to him? I was only 24 years old, with virtually no power in the family (or anywhere else, heaven knows), while my parents were respected and influential professionals. Apparently my existence posed a formidable threat to them.

That New Haven scene was one which was replicated in varying degrees in many families of girls of my own and earlier generations, as we know from the tragic stories told to us by feminist historians and biographers. The brothers were graduating from a prestigious school, the sexually active and outspoken "bad" daughter is a disgrace to the family and has to be hidden or lied about and is controlled by the threat, or in more than a few families, the actuality, of commitment to a psychiatric facility.

The fear of being controlled by powerful forces and feeling impotent to influence them on my own behalf was surely a consistent theme in my early life and motivated me to seek power through educating myself and then educating others through teaching and writing. So it is natural that feminism (and Chesler's book, *Women and Madness*) would appeal to me and that I would enlist my skills on behalf of other women who may have also grown up feeling powerless against hostile and defaming authority figures and a destructive social climate.

I stayed away from Buffalo, of course, and also tried as hard as I could to support myself and my son in New York. His father was an actor with virtually no income and we received nothing from him at all. I sold hats in a department store and attended City College at night in a Master's program. In those days City was the only place where you could work on a graduate degree at night. Tuition was $25. per credit which my parents agreed to supply, as insurance against my "dependency." At the department store I worked my way up to the advertising department, which was fun until I got fired for doing my homework on the office typewriter. I was denied unemployment insurance because the store claimed they offered me my old job back selling hats, therefore weren't really firing me. I declined the offer.

In those days (the mid-50s) there were no single-mother support groups, no parents-without-partners, no day-care centers, or women's groups of any kind. As it is now, private therapy was exorbitant. There were no support services at all for women who were not in a family network or married. A young woman alone with a child was in a very precarious social, economic, and psychological situation. That was the situation in which I found myself at 26.

When I was fired I lost our tiny apartment and I had to send my adored little son, then six years old, back to Buffalo, to his father's sister's family to live for a year. For a few months I couldn't find a job and had to live in a succession of rented single rooms in other people's apartments and then, ultimately, with my crazy, abusive grandmother (who also lived in New York). I didn't want my child to be exposed to her and of course didn't want him to be with my parents, but his father's sister and her husband were kind people with young children. This was the most crucial decision in my life. I knew that if I didn't stay in New York and complete the psychological separation from my parents, I would be destroyed and I knew my son's well-being, also, ultimately depended on my being an intact personality. So I did what was necessary, separating from him with all the terrible grief for both of us that meant. As a result of remaining in New York on my own—and in graduate school—I grew up as a relatively healthy adult, individuated from my destructive parents. Eighteen months after my son went away, I again found a stable job and an apartment and could have him back with me. We managed well enough after that. Today he is a healthy and loving man, happily married for many years and a wonderful father to two girls. I think he has some residue of that experience, shown occasionally in a too-angry exchange with me or in a heightened sensitivity to separation that seems to me to echo his grief, too, when he was just a little boy, but that may be only my fantasy and my own residue of guilt.

The self-esteem I derived from that early and successful struggle to survive my parents' and particularly, my mother's, virulent antagonism formed the core of what I believe is a basically optimistic and stable personality. Life certainly presented me with subsequent difficulties but that early crucible toughened me and gave me confidence in my inner resources. Because I fully experienced the grief of the separation from my son and the absolute painfulness of the circumstances in which I had to live for awhile, I have never been particularly sympathetic to magical solutions as "psychotherapy" or to religion. No matter how much I prayed for some kind of solace during those early years in New York, none arrived. It seemed to me I was doomed to feel everything.

I told myself that it was a virtue not to avoid the awful emotional reality, but to work through it and come out a wiser and more competent person. I believe that I did that and am a better therapist and person because of it. Obviously, today I am not very sympathetic towards therapies that I consider superficial although I can understand that people need support wherever they find it. But to me support is not work and I believe with the psychoanalysts that "working through" painful feelings is essential to good therapy—even if it is feminist therapy, not psychoanalysis.

My most successful therapy, from 1969 to the mid-70s, was with Dan Rosenblatt, my Gestalt therapist and ultimately supervisor. He is a gay man, as were many of my Gestalt colleagues from whom I learned a good deal about liberation from traditional social roles. Gestalt training in general taught me to challenge traditional therapy models, too, and certainly gave me permission to be my own model which it turned out I had to be as a feminist therapist.

I've been a feminist psychotherapist since 1969. From 1961 until 1967 I taught Developmental Psychology at Queens College where I met my second husband, a young sociologist. When my second child was born in 1967 I wanted to work at home to be able to care for her, or at least supervise her early care, so, somewhat reluctantly because I preferred academic psychology, I became a clinician. I grew to like clinical work much more than I ever thought I would and that is directly the result of the interesting clients I had at that time, the beginning of the feminist therapy movement, and the fascination of the feminist struggle in which I soon became engaged.

My psychotherapy training was with the New York Gestalt Institute. Feminist therapy came a couple of years later. A devastating personal experience in late 1968 focused my attention on feminism: my second husband, 7 years younger than I, and the father of our year-old daughter, admitted, after many denials, that he'd been having an affair with one of his sociology students, 23 years old, and that he intended to marry her. There was, he advised me, nothing I could do to affect this scenario: he would not go to couples' counseling; he prevented me from any input at all into the outcome of our marriage. He did exactly what he said he would do. The helplessness I felt, yet again in my life, as well as the intense rage, motivated me to seek power, as always, through understanding. So, as always, when distressed, I read. The writing that made the most sense to me explained my situation and feelings in feminist terms. That was when I was particularly influenced by Phyllis Chesler's 1970 article in the journal *Radical Therapy* which she later incorporated into three chapters of *Women and Madness* (1972).

Along with other female therapists I was beginning to read about the need for a psychotherapy that would be more sensitive to the ways women were socialized that predisposed them to low self-esteem and depression. Chesler and others were pointing out also that women were ill-treated by the psychotherapy establishment in terms of inadequate and biased theories and clinical practice that took as its goals bringing women into line as submissive wives and self-sacrificing mothers.

I didn't know where one could find training in feminist therapy or even where one could find other therapists who practiced such a therapy, so like other early feminist therapists, at first I simply trained myself. I called myself a "feminist therapist" and put a card on the bulletin board of the Women's Center in West 23rd Street proclaiming that I did "feminist therapy." I don't know whether I had even heard the term before.

This was in 1969, the same year that the Association for Women in Psychology was founded. I charged anywhere from $4-$15 dollars a session. At some point soon thereafter I found other female therapists who were trying to create and practice a feminist therapy and we joined together to discuss and analyze the feminist issues in our clients' situations, and learned feminist therapy with other female therapists in a small peer group that we grandly called the New York Association of Feminist Therapists. The others in the group at the time I joined, in 1971, were: Annette Hollander, Carol Gordon, Betsy Aigen, Barbara Suter, and Dale Bernstein.

For me, the most stimulating aspect of our bi-weekly meetings was looking at how our own socialization as women affected our therapy work—our counter-transferences, as the analysts would say, and some of the business issues, such as how and what we charged.

I had a lot of faith in feminist therapy and thought it was "the answer." I felt everyone should know about it. I still feel that way. I gave a paper in 1973 at the American Psychological Association's annual convention in Montreal in what must have been one of the first symposia devoted to feminist therapy. The interest in feminist therapy at the convention inspired me to think about writing a book for the general public showing how socialization as "girls" affected women's emotional lives in often significantly negative ways.

I, myself, was always so empowered by books that I thought others would be, too. At that time I was particularly driven to reach the general public rather than professional readers but I have changed my mind somewhat about that, particularly since there are many mental health professionals who are still not familiar with feminist therapy or who may not appreciate its value. I had completed all the work and exams for my PhD at NYU and wanted them to take my book manuscript as a dissertation. They refused, and I never did write a traditional dissertation since I thought that would have no social influence at all.

Notes of a Feminist Therapist was published in hardcover in 1976 and in paperback in 1977. As the first book on feminist therapy for the general public it became a classic. It was also read widely by female therapists who were looking for support to do their own brand of feminist therapy. It also kept me in practice for many years. Well over half my practice for 10 years came to me through the book. These were unusually interesting clients who were trying to raise their consciousnesses about feminism and trying to change their relationships accordingly. Many of them had been at one time, or were, simultaneously in consciousness-raising groups. About three-fourths of my practice were women, mostly white, mostly straight, and the rest were men, most of them sent by the women in their lives. One of the shortcomings of my book is that it had relatively little to say about lesbians and nothing at all about people of color. Today both the Feminist Therapy Institute and the Association for Women in Psychology have committed themselves to making their organizations and, consequently, the therapists in them, more sophisticated about the issues of women of color and of all sexual orientations and ages and more aware of their own biases.

My chief supports for practicing and writing about feminist therapy in those early days were, of course, the women in my feminist therapy peer group but also the four men in my Gestalt practicum: Jerry Croghan, Don Resnick, Marty Seif, and for the years he remained with us, our supervisor, Dan Rosenblatt.

Another important influence in my intellectual as well as personal life since 1970 was, and still is, my lover, a distinguished social psychologist, whose work concerns social justice–particularly significant to me, as a victim of my mother's injustice. The Oedipus complex lives–even in feminists!

At 55 years old, in 1986, I moved to San Francisco where both my mother and one brother lived. My mother, brought up in the Bay Area, settled here again after my father's death in Buffalo in 1975. In 1986 my daughter had been away at college for a year. An environmentalist and outdoorswoman, she showed no interest in settling in the East after college. New York, much as it had given me in my early adulthood, became unlivable to me in the yuppie years of the 80s; too expensive and too ugly, dirty, and violent. Too inhumane, I thought, in which to grow older.

So I rescued myself for (at least) the second time in my life and moved to California. My children are, in spite of my divorces from their fathers, happy in their work and love-lives. My son, born in 1950, is a longtime radio journalist, and a winner of many journalistic honors.

My daughter, 17 years younger than her half-brother, is a very gifted writer of both fiction and non-fiction. She lives with her husband in Western Colorado. A kind and happy young woman, she is exactly the age now as I was when I was barely surviving in New York, the sole support of myself and my little boy, beginning my difficult struggle toward emotional maturity and autonomy. My daughter and I have a close and loving relationship which is all the more poignant to me because as a young person I never had anything like that with my own mother, something I still think about with regret.

There are at least a couple of miracles in my life: my relationship with my lover has survived for 24 years (in contrast to my short-lived marriages) in spite of the geographical distance now between us. Even more startling, perhaps, my mother and I were on very good terms by the time she died, in 1991, at 88. She lived long enough for us to resolve some of our problems so that my memories of her will not be only negative. She was very receptive to my moving to San Francisco and was helpful to me here. (Of course, she understood how important it was to have a daughter nearby as she approached her final years.) Her personality problems were such that she had no intimate friends and several of her longtime acquaintances had died or moved away. So great was her need that she was almost able to convince herself that she liked me. I miss her very much and am glad that, while I still didn't know her very well, I had more of a "real" mother in my late middle age than I had ever known. And it wasn't too late.

I've never really had a psychotherapy practice in California, which is all right with me. I much prefer the free-lance writing I do, mostly on issues relating to women's mental health. I consider myself an independent scholar in the old and best sense of the word–unaffiliated academically, thus free to inquire into and write about any topic that interests me, on my own time-clock.

Since 1969, feminist therapy has gone in many directions. Pleasing to me is the new emphasis on understanding and working with women from all backgrounds; less pleasing is the spiritual dimension pasted on therapy which is so antagonistic to my own way of thinking, although I can understand why people like it and even believe they need it.

Psychotherapy as a profession is under pressure now and may never again be as much fun for practitioners as it was in the 1960s when all kinds of radical new theories were sprouting, and when private practices were less regulated by insurers and employers. Today, it's almost impossible to make a living as a therapist only in private practice, so many clinicians have simply lost control of a large portion of their professional lives. I can't imagine a more wonderful work-life than I had, with my office in my home, my lover coming over almost every day for lunch and other pleasures, and marvelous, sophisticated clients who were trying to sort out their identities and relationships in the new feminist climate.

Moreover, therapists so fear litigation that they are inhibited from trying out new clinical techniques with clients. This will hurt feminist psychotherapy, as it will other modalities. But it will also create bored and "burnt out" therapists and lead to resentment of, rather than pleasure in, clients.

Fear of litigation and a kind of pseudo-"professionalism" also make it now impossible for therapists to relate informally to clients. Instead of being able to be friends with clients whom one likes, therapists now, even feminist therapists, think they should affect an authoritarian and impersonal style, which may actually not be in their natures at all, but keeps them "respectable" and beyond lawsuits (or so they believe!). This caution and formality between client and therapist is not at all what we envisioned for feminist therapy. I was glad to be a therapist when I was and I'm glad not to be now.

SELECTED BIBLIOGRAPHY

Books

Voices of Feminist Therapy. Gordon and Breach. Jersey City, N.J. 1995.
Breaking Up and Starting Over. Macmillan. New York, N.Y. 1984.
Notes of a Feminist Therapist. Praeger Publishers. New York, N.Y. 1976. Dell
Publishers. New York, N.Y. 1977.

Articles

"Help me, please. My husband wants a divorce." Family. August, 1989. 32.
"Writing about psychology for the general reader." In Evans, G. (Ed). *The Complete Guide to Writing Non-fiction.* Harper and Row. New York, N.Y. 1988.
355-60.
"How to survive his depression." *Cosmopolitan.* July, 1980. 205.
"When dieting may not be good for you." McCall's. 1978. 119.
"A new therapy for women." New Woman. 1977.

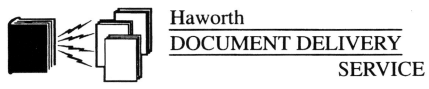

Haworth
DOCUMENT DELIVERY
SERVICE

This valuable service provides a single-article order form for any article from a Haworth journal.

- *Time Saving:* No running around from library to library to find a specific article.
- *Cost Effective:* All costs are kept down to a minimum.
- *Fast Delivery:* Choose from several options, including same-day FAX.
- *No Copyright Hassles:* You will be supplied by the original publisher.
- *Easy Payment:* Choose from several easy payment methods.

Open Accounts Welcome for . . .
- Library Interlibrary Loan Departments
- Library Network/Consortia Wishing to Provide Single-Article Services
- Indexing/Abstracting Services with Single Article Provision Services
- Document Provision Brokers and Freelance Information Service Providers

---

MAIL or *FAX* THIS ENTIRE ORDER FORM TO:

Haworth Document Delivery Service
The Haworth Press, Inc.
10 Alice Street
Binghamton, NY 13904-1580

or FAX: 1-800-895-0582
or CALL: 1-800-342-9678
9am-5pm EST

PLEASE SEND ME PHOTOCOPIES OF THE FOLLOWING SINGLE ARTICLES:

1) Journal Title: _____
   Vol/Issue/Year:_____Starting & Ending Pages:_____
   Article Title:_____
   _____

2) Journal Title: _____
   Vol/Issue/Year:_____Starting & Ending Pages:_____
   Article Title:_____
   _____

3) Journal Title: _____
   Vol/Issue/Year:_____Starting & Ending Pages:_____
   Article Title:_____
   _____

4) Journal Title: _____
   Vol/Issue/Year:_____Starting & Ending Pages:_____
   Article Title:_____
   _____

(See other side for Costs and Payment Information)

COSTS: Please figure your cost to order quality copies of an article.

1. Set-up charge per article: $8.00
   ($8.00 × number of separate articles)   _____

2. Photocopying charge for each article:

   1-10 pages: $1.00   _____

   11-19 pages: $3.00   _____

   20-29 pages: $5.00   _____

   30+ pages: $2.00/10 pages   _____

3. Flexicover (optional): $2.00/article   _____

4. Postage & Handling: US: $1.00 for the first article/
   $.50 each additional article   _____

   Federal Express: $25.00   _____

   Outside US: $2.00 for first article/
   $.50 each additional article   _____

5. Same-day FAX service: $.35 per page   _____

GRAND TOTAL: _____

METHOD OF PAYMENT: (please check one)

❑ Check enclosed   ❑ Please ship and bill. PO # _____
(sorry we can ship and bill to bookstores only! All others must pre-pay)

❑ Charge to my credit card: ❑ Visa; ❑ MasterCard; ❑ Discover;
❑ American Express;

Account Number: _____ Expiration date: _____

Signature: ✗ _____

Name: _____ Institution: _____

Address: _____

_____

City: _____ State: _____ Zip: _____

Phone Number: _____ FAX Number: _____

MAIL or *FAX* THIS ENTIRE ORDER FORM TO:

Haworth Document Delivery Service
The Haworth Press, Inc.
10 Alice Street
Binghamton, NY 13904-1580

or FAX: 1-800-895-0582
or CALL: 1-800-342-9678
9am-5pm EST)